14th International Symposium on System Synthesis

ISSS

MONTRÉAL, CANADA • SEPTEMBER 30 - OCTOBER 3, 2001

Sponsored by
IEEE Computer Society Technical Committee on Design Automation
ACM SIGDA

acm PRESS · sigda · IEEE COMPUTER SOCIETY · IEEE

The Association for Computing Machinery
1515 Broadway
New York, New York 10036

Notice to Past Authors of ACM-Published Articles

ACM intends to create a complete electronic archive of all articles and/or other material previously published by ACM. If you have written a work that has been previously published by ACM in any journal or conference proceedings prior to 1978, or any SIG Newsletter at any time, and you do NOT want this work to appear in the ACM Digital Library, please inform permissions@acm.org, stating the title of the work, the author(s), and where and when published.

ACM ISBN: 1-58113-418-5 **IEEE Catalog No:** 01EX526

Additional copies may be ordered prepaid from:

ACM Order Department
PO Box 11405
New York, NY 10286-1405

Phone: 1-800-342-6626
(US and Canada)
+1-212-626-0500
(all other countries)
Fax: +1-212-944-1318
E-mail: acmhelp@acm.org

ACM Order Number 481010
Printed in the USA

FOREWORD

On behalf of the *ISSS 2001* Steering and Technical Program committees, I would like to welcome you to Montreal and to The International Symposium on System Synthesis (ISSS). ISSS is a major international forum presenting emerging techniques for the system-level design and synthesis of computing systems. Having begun as the International Workshop on High-Level Synthesis in the mid-80's, it attracts leading design automation professionals from around the world.

ISSS 2001 is the 14th in this very successful series of symposia. This year, in addition to regular presentations, the Symposium includes invited talks by leading industrial and academic experts covering emerging network processor technologies, new design paradigms and perspectives in System-on-a-Chip as well as two discussion panels. To encourage discussion among the Symposium participants, each technical session will consist of oral presentations followed by a poster session where the authors of presented papers will answer any further questions and provide additional details of their works. This year technical sessions cover the following topics:

1. System-Level Synthesis
2. Hardware-Software Co-Design
3. Programmable (Multi-) Processor-Based Design and Synthesis
4. System Design Experience and Methodologies
5. Embedded and Real-Time System Software
6. High-Level and Architectural Synthesis
7. Co-design of Distributed and Multiprocessor Architectures
8. Synthesis for Low Power, Testability and Verifiability in the above areas.

The technical program for *ISSS 2001* has been selected by a program committee, which includes experts from industry and academia from 12 different countries. 67 submitted papers, originating from 22 different countries underwent a very strict reviewing process. Each paper has been assigned to 5 reviewers and the response from the reviewers was very high, on the average each paper received 4.63 reviews. I would like to thank all the members of the program committee and the other reviewers for their excellent work. After multiple rounds of e-mail discussion, 24 submitted papers have been selected for regular presentations. Due to the very high quality of the submitted papers and the pertinence of the problems addressed, 16 additional papers have been accepted for short presentations.

This year the Proceedings of the Symposium have been published by ACM. For 2001, the proceedings from *ISSS 2001* will be included on the SIGDA Compendium CDROM. ACM-SIGDA made the CDROMs containing the proceedings of *ISSS 2001* available at the symposium. They subsidized the cost of productions of the CD-ROMs as a benefit to the professional community. They will also post the proceedings on their website along with other notorious conferences. I would like to thank them for the visibility they provide to ISSS.

I would like to express my sincere appreciation to the steering and technical program committees for their dedication and excellent contribution. A Special thanks to Prof. Román Hermida, the General Chair for his continuous support.

I wish you a very productive symposium, and invite you to participate actively to this edition as well as to the next edition which be held in Kyoto, Japan, Oct. 2-4, 2002. Please check for up-to-date information on the ISSS web address http://www.isss-symposium.com.

El Mostapha Aboulhamid
Program Chair
ISSS 2001

Table of Contents

Wednesday, October 3, 2001

8:45-10:25 • Session 9: IP Design and Reuse

Chair: J. Madsen *(Technical University of Denmark)*

11:00 -12:20 • Session 10: Formal Aspects and Distributed Systems

Chair: M. Jacome *(University of Texas, Austin)*

ISSS 2001 Conference Organization

Steering Committee

General Chair: Roman Hermida, *Complutense Universidad*, Madrid, Spain

Program Chair: El Mostapha Aboulhamid, *Université de Montréal,* Québec, Canada

Past Chair: Fadi Kurdahi, *University of California,* Irvine, CA, USA

Publications Chair: Mohamad Sawan, *École Polytechnique de Montréal,* Montréal, Québec, Canada

Local Arrangements Chair: Asim Al-Khalili, *Concordia University,* Montreal, Québec, Canada

Finance Chair: Guy Bois, *École Polytechnique de Montréal,* Montréal, Québec, Canada

Panels, Special sessions Chair: Eduard Cerny, *Nortel Networks Billerica,* MA, USA

Publicity Chair: Yvon Savaria, *École Polytechnique de Montréal,* Montréal, Québec, Canada

Asian Liaison: Yukihiro Nakamura, *Kyoto University,* Kyoto, Japan

Technical Program Committee

Raul Camposano, *Synopsys,* USA
Nikil Dutt, *University of California at Irvine,* USA
Petru Eles, *Linkoping University,* Sweden
Rolf Ernst, *Tech. U. Braunschweig,* Germany
Milagros Fernandez, *Universidad Complutense de Madrid,* Spain
Masahiro Fujita, *University of Tokyo,* Japan
Daniel Gajski, *University of California at Irvine,* USA
Catherine Gebotys, *University of Waterloo,* Canada
Soonhoi Ha, *Seoul National University,* Korea
Margarida Jacome, *University of Texas at Austin*, USA
Ahmed A. Jerraya, *TIMA,* France
Steve Y.L. Lin, *Tsing Hua University,* Taiwan
Juan C. Lopez, *Universidad de Castilla-La Mancha,* Spain
Jan Madsen, *Tech. University,* Denmark
Lev Markov, *Mentor Graphics*, USA
Peter Marwedel, University of Dortmund, Germany
Anne Mignotte, *INSA-Lyon,* France
Walid Najjar, *University of California at Riverside,* USA
Sanjiv Narayan, *Cadence Design Systems,* India
Alice Parker, *University of Southern California,* USA
Preeti Panda, *Synopsys,* USA
B. Ramakrishna (Bob) Rau, *HP Labs,* USA
Wolfgang Rosenstiel, *University of Tubingen/FZI,* Germany
Donatella Sciuto, *Politecnico di Milano,* Italy
Frank Vahid, *University of California at Riverside*, USA
Diederik Verkest, *IMEC,* Belgium
Albert van der Werf, *Philips Research,* The Netherlands
Robert Walker, *Kent State University,* USA
Wayne Wolf, *Princeton University*, USA
Allen Wu, *Tsing Hua University,* Taiwan
Hiroto Yasuura, *Kyushu University,* Japan

ISSS'01 SPONSORS

ISSS'01 gratefully acknowledges:

IEEE COMPUTER SOCIETY

www.ieee.org

sig da — special interest group on design automation — acm

www.acm.org/sigda

With support from

Canadian Microelectronics Corporation
Société canadienne de micro-électronique

Canadian Microelectronics Corporation

GRIAO

Regroupement Stratégique en micro-électronique du Québec

ST

STMicroelectronics

Recherche, Science et Technologie
Québec

Université de Montréal

Faculté des Arts et des Sciences

A Scalable and Flexible Data Synchronization Scheme for Embedded HW-SW Shared-Memory Systems

Om Prakash Gangwal André Nieuwland Paul Lippens[†]

Embedded Systems Architectures on Silicon
Philips Research Laboratories, The Netherlands
o.p.gangwal@philips.com, andre.nieuwland@philips.com

ABSTRACT

This paper describes the implementation of a data-synchronization scheme that can be used in the functional description and hardware realization of algorithms for heterogeneous multi-processor architectures. In this scheme, synchronization primitives are chosen such that they can be implemented efficiently in both hardware and software on distributed shared memory architectures, without the need for atomic semaphore instructions. The proposed solution is flexible as the configuration of the data synchronization is programmable even after a hardware realization. It is also scalable since it can be implemented without the need for central resources. We show with experiments that distributed implementations are needed for scalable and high performance systems-on-a-chip.

1. INTRODUCTION

Signal-processing functions determine the performance requirements for many products based on standards like MPEG-x, DVB, DAB, and UMTS. This calls for efficient implementations of the signal processing components of these products. However, because of evolving standards and changing market requirements, the implementation requires flexibility and scalability as well. A macro-pipeline setup is a natural way to model these applications, since streams of data are processed; in this setup the functions (tasks) are the stages and there are buffers between the stages to form the pipeline. This is a way to exploit task-level parallelism (TLP), because all stages can operate in parallel.

In a Multiple Instruction Multiple Data (MIMD) composition each processor can have its own function on its own data. In this way it is possible to optimize processors to their function. This leads to more efficient solutions both in power and area. For example, for a demanding application, a RISC-CPU, a VLIW, a DSP, an ASIP, and dedicated hardware units can be composed into a single architecture as shown in Figure 1. To fully exploit the available processing power, we need an efficient yet scalable and flexible way of data communication.

[†]Paul Lippens is currently working with Magma design automation.

ISSS'01, October 1-3, 2001, Montréal, Québec, Canada.

In [1, 2, 3, 4], inter-task data transportation and synchronization are combined in a single action (e.g. *read/receive/write/send* operations). A survey on communication in HW-SW embedded systems can be found in [5]. Our proposal is significantly different from previous art, as we advocate the separation of data transportation and synchronization. This provides the flexibility to perform data transportation at a different granularity than synchronization. This separation is especially advantageous in shared memory architectures since only synchronization primitives are needed and no copying of data is required.

In homogeneous shared-memory multi-processor architectures, plenty of algorithms for scalable synchronization exist (see [9]). In this domain, one resource is shared by multiple tasks. This problem is solved either by *spin-lock* or *barrier algorithms* (see [9]), which require special instructions (e.g. `test_and_set`, `swap_with_memory`) or atomic read-modify-write operations.

In standard synchronization algorithms, the same resource may be claimed multiple times by a specific task before it is claimed by another task. With data communication, storage for data elements is claimed by the two tasks in an alternating fashion: First the storage will be claimed for writing by one task, and thereafter by another task for reading. Note that when buffering is available, one task can claim the next storage for data elements before the other task has read the data elements (stored recently). However, one task can not claim the same storage for data elements, which it has filled, until the other task has read that data. As we show in this paper, we can implement this form of synchronization without any special instructions such as atomic read-modify-write. Furthermore, we provide an efficient and flexible implementation of these primitives to support the mapping of signal processing applications onto heterogeneous multi-processor architectures.

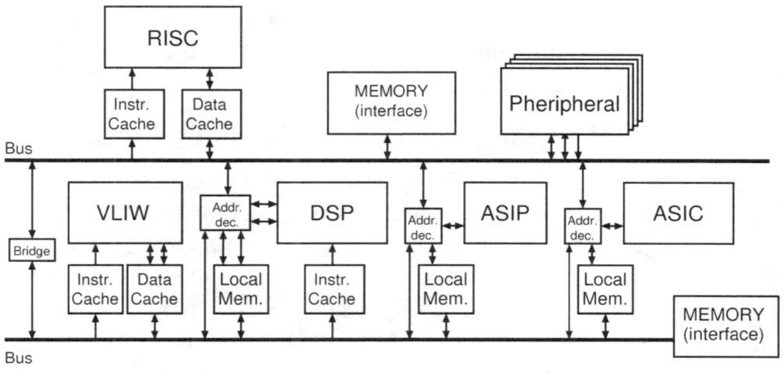

Figure 1: A MIMD architecture

The rest of this paper is organized as follows. In Section 2, we present our target architecture. In Section 3, we introduce the synchronization protocol that is used to specify the signal processing functionality. Section 4 describes the implementation of the protocol on a distributed shared-memory architecture. In Section 5, we present experimental results, followed by conclusions in Section 6.

2. TARGET ARCHITECTURE

In an MIMD setup, the communication infrastructure is as important as the individual components for the overall performance of the system. Moreover, while the choice of processing components depends on the application, the same infrastructure can be used for several applications as long as this infrastructure is scalable.

A common approach to realize MIMD architectures with a macro-pipeline setup is to attach a number of (co-)processors to the main processor using some communication network. The main processor controls the co-processors, and the co-processors implement the functionality of the tasks. We call this kind of architecture a *co-processor* architecture. In order to control the co-processors, the main processor either polls (i.e. repeatedly reads) the status of the co-processors or the co-processors themselves notify (interrupt) the main processor when their task is finished. In order not to overload the main processor, the interrupt rate should be low. Similarly, the time spent in polling should be low. This can be accomplished using (very) large grain synchronization. For example, in a video context, synchronizing on a field or a frame basis.

Large grain synchronization requires large buffers to store the data to be communicated, which due to their size have to reside in off-chip memory. Off-chip memory bandwidth is expensive and power consuming and is already a major bottleneck in systems. This bottleneck can be subsided if the data remains on chip. Since the amount of on-chip memory is limited and quite often already dominant in cost (area), we should look for ways to decrease the on-chip buffer size. One way to accomplish this is to reduce the synchronization grain size. However, in a co-processor architecture, this would lead to unacceptable high interrupt rates for the main processor.

Therefore, we propose a different approach where the (co-)processors are autonomous with respect to synchronization and do not require service from a main processor. We call this kind of architecture a *multi-processor* architecture. With this approach, we can go to a smaller grain of synchronization, which allows smaller buffer sizes, and therefore, enables on-chip communication. When we use multi-processor architectures for the example discussed above, we can synchronize on a line or block basis instead of synchronizing on a frame or field basis.

Multi-processor architectures are better scalable than co-processor architectures. Synchronization in a multi-processor architecture is challenging since all tasks are autonomously scheduled. In this paper, we define and implement a data synchronization protocol for multi-processor architectures. However, the same protocol can be used in co-processor architectures.

3. SYNCHRONIZATION PROTOCOL

Our application specification is based on Kahn process networks [6]. In this model, the overall application is decomposed in a number of parallel processes communicating via *point-to-point unidirectional unbounded channels* with first-in-first-out (FIFO) behavior. In this paper, we refer to these processes as tasks. In this model, when a task wants to read from a channel, and there is no data available, the task will block. However, write actions are non-blocking.

In our model, *FIFOs* are *bounded* since we are addressing efficient implementation of applications and not only the specification. This means that a task will also block when it wants to write to a channel if the associated FIFO is full.

We clearly separate synchronization from data transportation since in a shared memory architecture no copying of data is required. In this context, data transportation is the set of activities required to transport the *data* from one task to another via a (buffered) channel. Synchronization is the set of activities required to *query/claim/release* some amount of the data on a channel. The synchronization takes place on a per *token* basis. While a token is the unit of synchronization, the amount of data associated with a token can vary. However, the size of a token for each channel is set at system configuration.

For efficiency reasons, all communication buffer memory is allocated at setup and is reused during operation. This implies the reuse of physical channel buffers during operation. Therefore, we need primitives to *claim* and *release* buffer memory space. Since we communicate tokens, these primitives operate on a per token basis.

At the data producing side, we want to claim empty token buffers (`claim_space`) and release full token buffers (`release_data`). At the consuming side we want to claim filled token buffers (`claim_data`) and release empty ones (`release_space`). Claiming a token buffer is blocking, i.e. when no buffer is available the task blocks. Releasing is non-blocking.

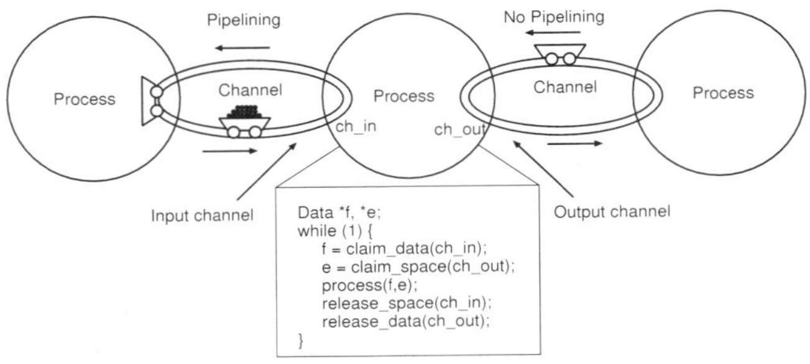

Figure 2: The four synchronization primitives

Figure 2 illustrates the use of the four primitives. The buffers are visualized as train wagons and channels as rail roads. The middle task first has to acquire a full wagon at its input channel and an empty wagon at its output channel. After the processing, the emptied wagon is pushed back on the input channel and the filled one on the output channel. The initial number of wagons on the railroad determines how strongly the tasks are coupled. Only one wagon means that the tasks have to be executed alternately, whereas more than one wagon allows pipelining (parallel execution) of the tasks.

In our implementation, it is allowed to claim (reserve) a number of tokens and process them out of order before releasing them in order. This means that multiple `claim` primitives can be called before the corresponding tokens are released by `release` calls. Note that in that case the number of buffers on the channel should be greater or equal to the number of consecutive `claim` calls, otherwise deadlock occurs.

A non-blocking version of `claim_data/space` primitives called `query_data/space` is also defined to query the availability of data/space. That information can be used by a task to perform some other work until the data/space becomes available, or in a multi-tasking environment where a task itself could indicate the readiness for task switching to an operating system or to a task scheduler.

This synchronization protocol can be extended to exchange tokens between more than two tasks as shown in [7].

4. IMPLEMENTATIONS OF THE PROTOCOL

The protocol is defined and implemented such that it is transparent to the tasks i.e. a task does not have to know whether the task it is communicating with is implemented in hardware or software.

We describe the implementation of channel FIFO buffers that are flexible enough to facilitate implementations of the protocol in hardware and software, in Section 4.1. In Section 4.2, a generic implementation of synchronization primitives is explained. In Section *4.2.1*, we explain optimizations for the software implementation. Optimizations for the hardware implementation are explained in Section *4.2.2*.

4.1 Implementation of channel FIFO buffers

We allocate space in shared memory and control that space in a FIFO manner to implement a channel buffer. This gives us the flexibility to tune the channel buffer and token sizes for an application even after we made a hardware realization. Furthermore, one can change the number of channel buffers and their logical interconnection structure in order to map different applications on the same hardware. In order to provide FIFO behavior of a buffer, some administrative information has to be maintained. The administrative information contains some static and dynamic values. The static values are those values that are written only once when the system is configured. The dynamic values are those values that are modified while the system is running. Examples of static values are the size of a token, a base address of the allocated memory, the maximum number of tokens in a FIFO (*maxtokens*) etc. The dynamic values are a read counter (*readc*), a write counter (*writec*) and the number of filled or empty tokens (*ftokens/etokens*). Two of the dynamic values are necessary and sufficient to control the allocated space in a FIFO manner. Thus, we have the following minimum pairs:

1. *readc* and *ftokens/etokens*.
2. *writec* and *etokens/ftokens*.
3. *readc* and *writec*.

Options 1 and 2 introduce a consistency problem. After producing data, the producing task would increment *ftokens*. The data consuming task is supposed to decrement the same variable after consuming data. For example, when the initial value of *ftokens* is 4, a producing task increments *ftokens*' value from 4 to 5 (after producing data) and simultaneously the consuming task connected to the same channel decrements the same *ftokens*' value from 4 to 3 (after consuming data), which results in a wrong value of *ftokens* (i.e. either 5 or 3) where the correct value after these operations should be 4. Since two concurrent tasks modify the same variable, access to that variable needs to be protected either by means of an atomic read-modify-write, or by guarding through semaphores.

In addition to the consistency problem with the token field in options 1 and 2, there is another consistency problem related to the calculation of the third dynamic value (*readc*, or *writec*). For example, in option 1, when *readc* is 13 and *ftokens* is 4, the derived value of *writec* is 17 (i.e. 13 + 4). After consuming one token the consumer task decrements *ftokens*' value atomically to 3. At this moment, the derived value of *writec* (16, i.e. 13 + 3) is wrong since the value of *readc* is not yet incremented to make the value of *writec* correct (i.e. 17). Therefore *readc* and *ftokens* have to be updated by a consumer task as an atomic unit to derive the correct value of *writec*.

In option 3, a task increments only its own counter i.e. a producing task increments *writec* and a consuming task *readc*. Because *etokens/ftokens* are derived from these values, a producer (consumer) task never sees more empty (full) tokens than available at any time. The *ftokens/etokens* field can always be derived from the counter values. The counters are initialized to zero and count modulo the *maxtokens* value. To solve the ambiguity problem (whether FIFO is full or empty) that arises whenever *writec* and *readc* are equal, we extend both values with an extra bit (*wrap flag*). The wrap flag is initialized to zero, and toggled when the corresponding counter reaches the *maxtokens* value. If the counters are equal and the wrap flags are different then the FIFO is full, otherwise (with identical wrap flags) the FIFO is empty. The wrap flag increases the range of the counters to twice the size of the maximum number of tokens in the FIFO, akin the sliding window protocol for data communication [8]. We choose option 3 since with this option no consistency problem arises

4.2 Implementations of the primitives

When a `claim_data` call is executed and a full token is available in the FIFO, a pointer to the token is returned. The token pointer is calculated from the `readc` value and some static values. Similar actions are performed for a `claim_space` call. When the `release_space` (`release_data`) primitive is called the *readc* (*writec*) counter is incremented.

To facilitate consecutive `claim_data/space` calls, a separate reservation counter (i.e. *readrsvc* corresponding to *readc* and *writersvc* corresponding to *writec*) is implemented. The reservation counters *readrsvc* and *writersvc* behave in the same manner as the *readc* or *writec*. However, they move ahead of them. The reservation counter value is private for each task. With the addition of the reservation scheme, a consuming (producing) task would perform comparisons of the *readrsvc (writersvc)* and *writec(readc)* on a `claim_data` (`claim_space`) call. When the call becomes successful, the token pointer corresponding to the reservation counter *readrsvc (writersvc)* is calculated and the *readrsvc* (*writersvc*) is incremented. However, the reservation scheme does not change the actions required for `release_space` (`release_data`) call. Figure 3 shows a snapshot of a FIFO where two tokens are reserved for reading (writing) while four tokens are available for reading (writing). The figure also shows values of *readc, readrsvc, writec* and *writersvc* with associated wrap flag. Random accesses are permitted within the reserved tokens.

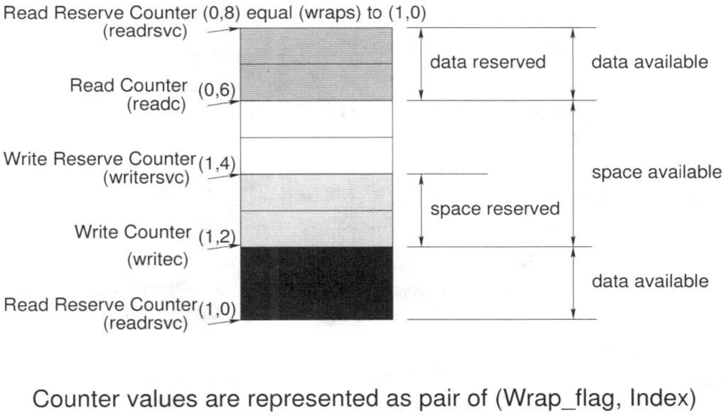

Figure 3: A snapshot of a FIFO with the reservation scheme

In principle, a blocked task polls on the counter value until its synchronization call becomes successful. This *polling-based synchronization* scheme is useful, if the counter value is updated around the same time when a task starts polling. However, polling is not always efficient since it increases bus load and power consumption.

Alternatively, a blocked task can be notified (e.g. by sending a signal) that the status of the FIFO has been changed. We call this scheme *interrupt-based synchronization*. One should choose between polling-based and interrupt-based synchronization depending on the expected wait time, with respect to the time required to serve the wake-up signal.

The signaling should fulfill two requirements. First of all, the signal should not arrive before the data has reached its destination, to prevent the activated task from reading old data. Secondly, the signaling scheme should be scalable since the whole system should be scalable. We implemented the signaling in a memory mapped fashion since it is scalable, and eliminates the need for a dedicated interrupt network. As long as no re-ordering of data is done in the interconnection network, the memory mapped signals will follow the data and will not arrive too early.

4.2.1 *Optimizations in the software implementation*

With an *interrupt-based synchronization*, a task sends a signal at every *release* synchronization call. Whenever an interrupt signal is received in a generic processor, an interrupt service routine (ISR) is called. However, a task does not need these signals (hence no need to execute ISR) if it is *not* blocked. We reduced the number of interrupts seen by the processor by introducing a signal controller (see Figure 4). The signal controller has a mask register to mask the signal register (i.e. used to store signals written by tasks) during normal operation and enables the signal register only when the task is blocked. The signal controller is memory-mapped and instantiated for each generic processor in the architecture.

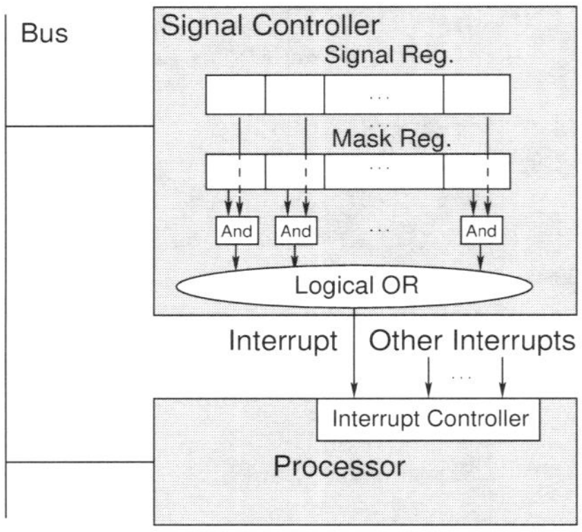

Figure 4: A Signal Controller for a processor

4.2.2 *Optimizations in the hardware implementation*

The hardware implementation of the channel synchronization protocol is called a *channel controller*. Channel controllers are instantiated per channel in a synchronization shell that is attached to an application specific component (see Figure 5). The channel controller is implemented with a generic bus interface to facilitate reuse with any particular bus by adding a *bus adapter*. The synchronization shell has a *signal register* that is used for receiving signals in the interrupt-based synchronization scheme. This signal register is instantiated only once per device. All registers in the synchronization shell are memory-mapped.

Only one channel controller is implemented in hardware, the mode (i.e. input or output) of a channel controller is set at the system configuration. This controller is instantiated for each channel.

In order to reduce the number of system bus accesses, some administrative information values are copied in the channel controller.

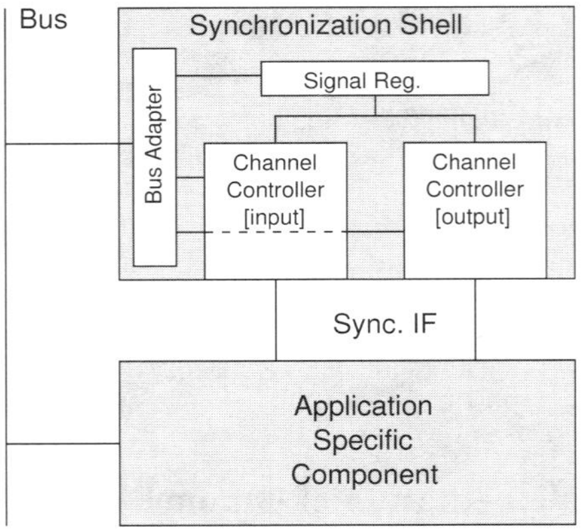

Figure 5: A Synchronization Shell for an Application Specific Component

The copied information also helps to reduce the delay in servicing synchronization calls.

In our implementation, when a coprocessor needs a token address (i.e. by a `claim_data/space` call), the token address can be made available in next clock cycle of the synchronization request. If more tokens are available then they can also be delivered every clock cycle, one by one. In this implementation, `release_space/data` calls also take just one clock cycle for the task. The `release_space/data` primitives are carried out by the channel controller. A channel controller running at 100 MHz is implemented in 0.09 mm^2 for 0.18 micron CMOS technology.

5. RESULTS

We have extended our simulation models [10] to include all previously described implementations of the synchronization primitives. The effect of software and hardware optimizations are presented as well.

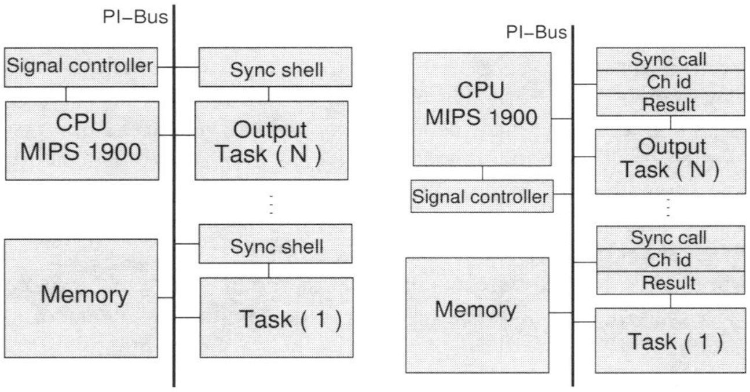

(a) Multi-processor (b) Co-processor

Figure 6: Architecture used for experiments

We built a multi-processor architecture (see Figure 6 a), in which all tasks are mapped onto hardware modules and synchronization is performed by the synchronization shells attached to the hardware modules. On encountering a synchronization call, the task reads the value of a token pointer if a token is available, otherwise it waits. A CPU (i.e. a low-power, low-cost MIPS running pSOS) is used to configure the communication channels between the tasks. After configuration, the CPU goes idle.

We used the same set-up to simulate the classical co-processor architecture. For this purpose, we modified the synchronization shells such that the synchronization can be performed by the CPU (see Figure 6 b). Therefore, we added some (memory mapped) registers to the shells to hold the cause for a service request (*sync-call*), the channel-id for which the request was issued (*ch-id*), and a result register (*result*) to store the value returned by the CPU after completing the service request (*sync-call*).

On encountering a synchronization call, a task fills desired synchronization action, channel-index and a zero value in the *sync-call*, *ch-id* and *result* registers respectively. Subsequently, it sends an interrupt to the CPU. The interrupt can be sent directly to the CPU using traditional methods, e.g. daisy-chain, (i.e. *co-processor non-optimized case*) or by writing the task index of the task to the signal register in the signal controller, which is attached to the CPU (i.e. *co-processor optimized case*). The task polls the *result* register for a non-zero value. The task uses this value as a pointer to the requested token when the value of the *result* register is non-zero. On receiving an interrupt, the CPU invokes an ISR which identifies the source of the interrupt. Thereafter, the ISR reads the values of the *sync-call* and *ch-id* registers from the synchronization shell requesting service. Based on these values, the proper synchronization call is executed for that task. If the synchronization call does not pass, due to the fullness or emptiness of the FIFO buffer, the ISR saves the request until the FIFO buffer is updated by the connected task (producer or consumer). As soon as the FIFO buffer is updated, the saved synchronization call is invoked and the result is written in the result register of the pending task.

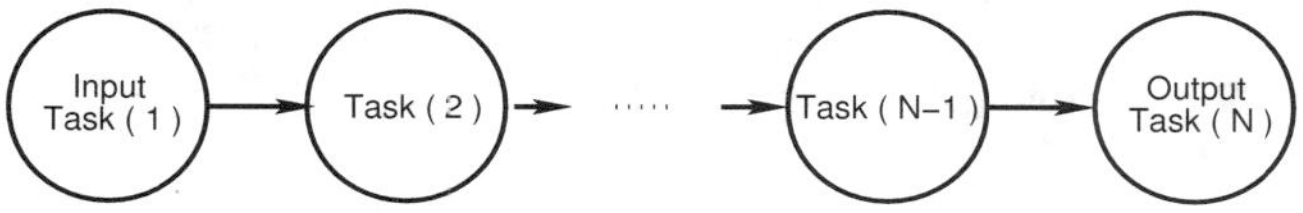

Figure 7: Application used in experiments

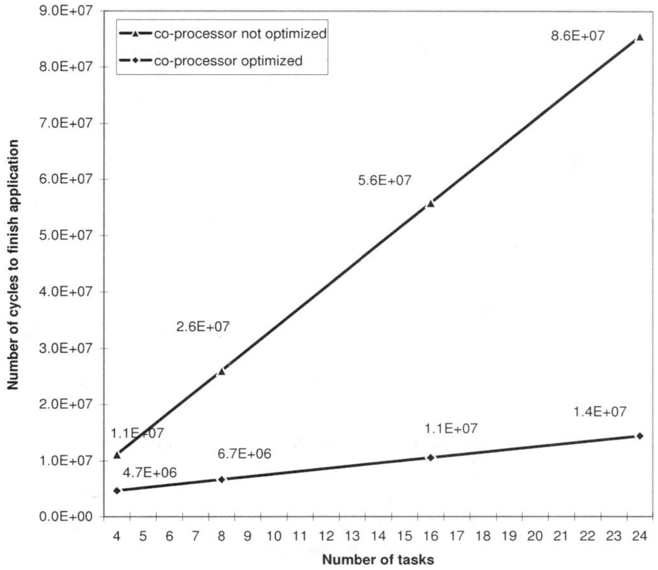

Figure 8: Total time to finish application (using 1000 tokens) in co-processor architectures

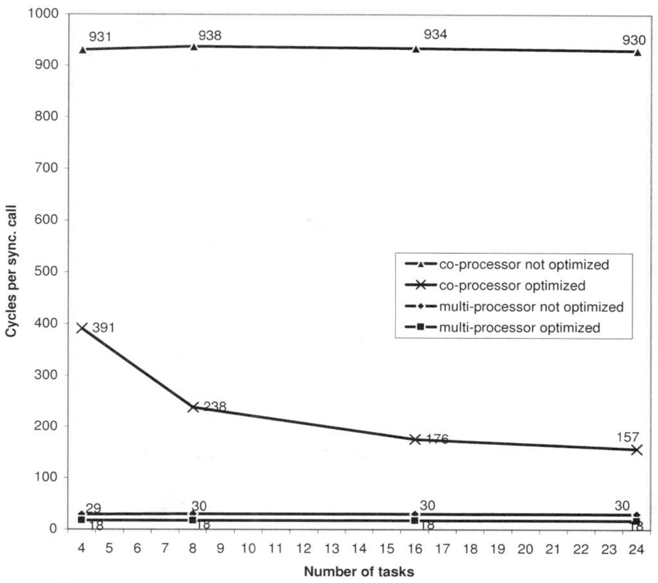

Figure 9: Time per synchronization call

In our experiments, all tasks are only performing synchronization to facilitate the analysis of synchronization performance. No buffer data is accessed. All tasks are connected in a chain in which every task is passing tokens to the next task (see Figure 7). A fixed number of tokens, i.e. 1000, are introduced in the system and the simulation is performed until they reach the last task in the chain. Each task is mapped onto a separate hardware module, which posts a new synchronization call one clock cycle after completion of the previous call. We varied the number of tasks from 4 to 24 in steps of 4, for both the classical co-processor communication scheme as for the proposed multi-processor architecture scheme.

The experimental results for the total execution time for the application is shown in Figures 8, 10 and the average time per synchronization call is shown in Figure 9.

Figure 8 presents the total execution time on the co-processor architecture for this application, as a function of the number of (hardware) tasks. As can be concluded from this figure, the optimized co-processor architecture (using our signal controller) requires significantly less cycles (upto a factor of 6 less) than the non-optimized (traditional interrupt scheme) one. In all variants of the co-processor architecture, the CPU is fully loaded by serving interrupts generated by all tasks since all tasks are performing synchronization at high rates.

As can be seen in figure 9, the average time to execute a synchronization call for the traditional interrupt scheme is nearly constant over the number of tasks. This time can be reduced significantly when our signal controller is used (optimized co-processor curve). Because now, synchronization requests of multiple tasks are serviced within a single ISR execution. Hence, the ISR overhead is divided among all synchronization calls being serviced.

Due to the large synchronization delay for the co-processor, fine grain synchronization, which is needed to reduce on-chip buffering, is hardly possible.

As can be seen from the same figure (Figure 9), the non-optimized multi-processor architecture is a factor of 5 to 13 faster than the optimized co-processor architecture with respect to the number of cycles per synchronization call. The optimized multi-processor architecture is 8 to 21 times faster than the optimized co-processor

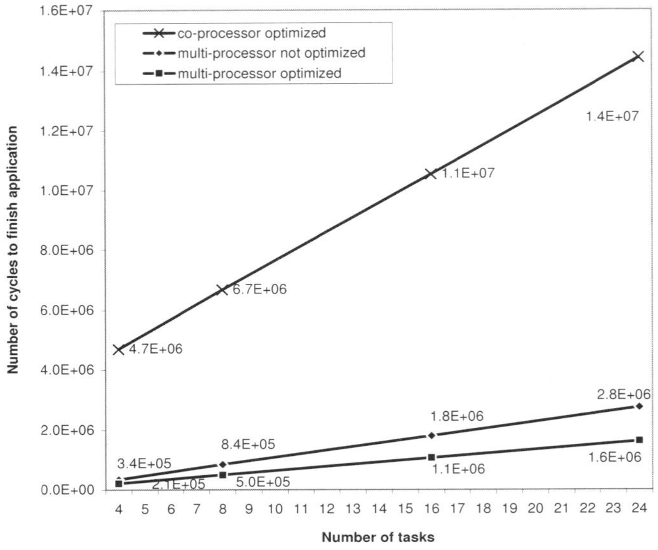

Figure 10: Total time to finish application (using 1000 tokens) in the multi- and optimized co-processor architectures

architecture. Due to the lower synchronization delay, less memory needs to be allocated for communication buffers.

To support the flexible part of an application, tasks could be mapped as software running on the CPU. With the co-processor architecture, these software tasks can not be executed until all interrupts are served. This means that the software tasks are only executed when hardware tasks (which may be communicating to software tasks) are silent, e.g. after filling the FIFO buffer. As a result, the system performance is reduced since all tasks do not execute really in parallel, that is, the software tasks are not running in parallel with the hardware modules because the CPU is (fully) loaded with the synchronization of the hardware modules.

A solution to improve the performance of this co-processor system is to map the centralized synchronizer onto a separate programmable processor or on dedicated hardware. However, the worst case dynamic delay for a synchronization call, which is the waiting time to get its turn on the centralized synchronizer, can be as high as $((number\_of\_tasks - 1) * time\_per\_sync\_call)$.

Hence, the system performance can be affected by these delays for a single synchronization call. Moreover, these larger synchronization times result in larger grain-size communication, hence increased buffer space, which is just what we try to minimize.

In all variants of the multi-processor architecture, the CPU is free to execute (signal processing) tasks since the synchronization is executed in a distributed and autonomous manner. In this case the software tasks synchronize (through software routines) only with the hardware (or software) tasks it is actually communicating with. The hardware tasks use the same shells for communicating with the software as they would use for communicating with each-other. Neither software nor hardware tasks need intervention of a 'third party', nor are they disturbed by synchronization of others. Therefore, the synchronization delays are quite low.

Figure 10 shows the run-time of the synchronization application, for the optimized co-processor architecture and the (non-) optimized multi-processor architectures. From this figure, we can conclude that high performance systems need to be implemented using multi-processor architectures.

6. CONCLUSIONS

In this paper, we have presented an efficient, scalable, and flexible data synchronization protocol for mapping signal processing functions onto heterogeneous distributed shared memory multiprocessor architectures. We assume that the functionality is expressed as a set of parallel tasks communicating through FIFO channels. Both hardware and software implementations of the protocol are explained. The protocol is transparent to the tasks, i.e. a task does not know about the protocol implementation and the implementation of the other tasks. This allows us to easily migrate functionality from hardware to software or from one processor to another. By experiments we have shown that the distributed implementation of this protocol is 8 to 21 times faster than an optimized centralized implementation. Hence it enables the high synchronization rates required to reduce on-chip buffering. Moreover, the area overhead of the distributed implementation is limited (i.e. 0.09 mm^2 per channel controller for 0.18 micron CMOS technology).

7. ACKNOWLEDGMENTS

We would like to thank Albert van der Werf for encouraging this work. We are grateful to Pieter van der Wolf, Wido Kruijtzer and Erwin de Kock for providing critical and stimulating feedback to improve this article.

8. REFERENCES

[1] S. Vercauteren, B. Lin, et al. "Constructing application-specific heterogeneous embedded architectures from custom HW/SW applications," in *Proc. of DAC*, 1996.

[2] D. Verkest, K. Van Rompaey, et al. "CoWare - A Design Environment for Heterogeneous Hardware/Software Systems", Design Automations for Embedded Systems, 1(4), 357-386, 1996.

[3] E.A. de Kock, G. Essink, et al. "YAPI: Application modeling for signal processing systems" in *Proc. of DAC*, 2000, pp. 402–405.

[4] R. Ernst, et al. "Hardware-Software Cosynthesis for Microcontrollers", in *Proc. of IEE ED&RC*, December 1993.

[5] Mattias O'Nils, "Communication within HW/SW Embedded Systems", *ESDLab, Department of Electronics, Royal Institute of Technology, Sweden*, report no. TRITA-ESD-1997-08, ESDlab, KTH-Electrum, Electrum 229, S-16440 Kista, Sweden, 1997.

[6] G. Kahn, "The semantics of a simple language for parallel programming" in *Information Processing*, J.L. Rosenfeld, 1974

[7] J. Kang, A. van der Werf, P. Lippens, "Mapping Array communication on to the FIFO Communication-Towards an Implementation" in *Proc.of International Symposium on System Synthesis*, 2000, pp. 207–213.

[8] Tanenbaum, A. S., *Computer Networks*, Prentice/Hall International, Inc., The Netherlands, 1981.

[9] J.M. Mellor-Crummey and M.L. Scott, "Algorithms for Scalable Synchronization on Shared-Memory Multiprocessors," in *ACM Trans. on Computers Systems*, vol. 9, Feb. 1991, pp. 21-65.

[10] A.K. Nieuwland, P.E.R. Lippens "A heterogeneous HW-SW architecture for hand-held multi-media terminals", in *Proc. of IEEE Workshop on Signal Processing Systems*, 1998, pp. 113–122.

Exploiting Scratch-Pad Memory Using Presburger Formulas *

Mahmut Kandemir
Microsystems Design Lab
Pennsylvania State University
University Park, PA 16802
kandemir@cse.psu.edu

Ismail Kadayif
Microsystems Design Lab
Pennsylvania State University
University Park, PA 16802
kadayif@cse.psu.edu

Ugur Sezer
ECE Department
University of Wisconsin
Madison, WI 53706
sezer@ece.wisc.edu

ABSTRACT

Effective utilization of on-chip storage space is important from both performance (execution cycles) and memory system energy consumptions perspectives. While on-chip cache memories have been widely used in the past, several factors, including lack of data access time predictability and limited effectiveness of compiler optimizations, indicate that they may not be the best candidate for portable/embedded devices. This paper presents a compiler-directed on-chip scratch-pad memory (software-managed on-chip memory) management strategy for data accesses. Our strategy is oriented towards minimizing the number of data transfers between off-chip memory and the scratch-pad memory, thereby exploiting reuse for the data residing in the scratch-pad memory. We report experimental data from our implementation showing the usefulness of our technique.

Keywords

Software Compilation, Scratch-Pad Memories, Data Locality, Presburger Formulas, Array-Dominated Codes.

1. INTRODUCTION AND MOTIVATION

Poor memory behavior is one of the major performance bottlenecks for many applications from high-performance and embedded computing domains. On-chip cache memories help to alleviate this bottleneck to some extent, but very few applications take full advantage of cache memories due to suboptimal data access behavior. In addition to performance, the limits imposed by power consumption are also becoming an important issue in most areas of computing. Portable, battery-operated devices are, by their nature, energy-sensitive; and even in desktop computing, power consumption is a problem due to packaging costs and cooling requirements. Off-chip data accesses are known to be a major energy consumer in many array-dominated image and video processing applications [3]. Therefore, effective exploitation of on-chip storage units (e.g., caches and software-controlled memories) is extremely important from both energy and performance perspectives.

In embedded computing domain, working with cache memories presents several problems. First, since caches introduce variable data access times, predicting execution time (which might be of utmost importance in a real-time constrained environment) becomes very difficult. Although it might be possible to determine the worst-case execution time, this might be far from optimal, and any decision about system/application behavior based on this would be overly pessimistic. Second, a lack of execution time predictability also adversely affects the compiler's ability to optimize the code. Third, many embedded codes from image and video processing domains have very regular data access behavior for which the runtime fine-grain (block-level) data placement/replacement provided by caches may not be the most suitable strategy. Consequently, software-managed on-chip memories, called *scratch-pad memories* (SPM) in this paper, might be better alternatives for exploiting locality. Note that effective exploitation of an SPM can improve program performance (by reducing effective data access time) and reduce energy consumption as on-chip memories consume less per access energy than off-chip DRAMs [3, 7].

In this paper, we present a *compiler-directed* on-chip SPM management strategy for data accesses. Our strategy is oriented towards *minimizing* the number of data transfers between off-chip memory and on-chip SPM, thereby exploiting reuse for the data residing in the SPM. It achieves this by determining the maximal set of loop iterations (possibly coming from different nests in the code) that reuse the elements in the SPM. This program-wide optimization technique employs a polyhedral tool that works with Presburger formulas to enumerate these loop iterations taking into account data dependences.

The remainder of this paper is organized as follows. Section 2 gives background information on Presburger formulas and introduces our target architecture. Section 3 discusses our data decomposition strategy and presents our optimization algorithms. Section 4 reports our experimental results. Finally, Section 5 concludes the paper.

*This work is supported in part by the NSF Career Award 0093082.

ISSS'01, October 1-3, 2001, Montréal, Québec, Canada.

2. BASICS

2.1 Presburger Formulas

Presburger formulas are formulas that contain affine constraints, the usual logical connectives (i.e., 'and', 'or', and 'not' connectives), and $\forall$ (universal) and $\exists$ (existential) quantifiers. Note that many concepts associated with nested loops and array accesses can be expressed using Presburger formulas. For example, the set of iterations executed by a loop nest can be described as $\{(i_1, ..., i_m) : L_1 \leq i_1 \leq U_1$ and ... and $L_m \leq i_m \leq U_m\}$, where L_j and U_j are the affine lower and upper bounds, respectively, for loop index i_j. Similarly, a given array space can be described using similar sets. We can use Presburger formulas for expressing more complex relationships as well. For example, consider a two-level nested loop (with loop indices i_1 and i_2) and a reference $X[2i_1 + 1][i_2 + i_1 - 1]$ to a two-dimensional array X. The *even-numbered* loop iterations (e.g., (2,4), (8,10), etc.) that access array elements in the region $[a..b][c..d]$ can be expressed as:

$$\begin{aligned}\{(i_1, i_2) \quad : \quad & L_1 \leq i_1 \leq U_1 \text{ and } L_2 \leq i_2 \leq U_2 \text{ and} \\ & a \leq 2i_1 + 1 \leq b \text{ and } c \leq i_2 + i_1 - 1 \leq d \text{ and} \\ & \exists k_1, k_2 \text{ such that } i_1 = 2k_1 \text{ and } i_2 = 2k_2\}.\end{aligned}$$

In the most general case, verifying a Presburger formula is provably exponential, so it is a very hard problem. The Omega library [5] is a framework for simplifying and verifying Presburger formulas and is employed in our optimization framework. The library also helps us enumerate the elements that satisfy multiple conditions written as Presburger formulas. In our framework, we use the library to enumerate the iterations that access data elements currently residing in the SPM. For example, assuming that the array region $[a..b][c..d]$ mentioned above resides in the SPM, enumerating the elements in the set shown above gives us the iterations to be executed to make sure that only the data in the SPM are accessed.

2.2 Architecture Model

We assume a memory architecture that contains an on-chip cache, an on-chip scratch-pad memory (SPM), and an off-chip main memory (see Figure 1). It is assumed that on-chip cache and SPM have similar access times (e.g., 2-3 cycles) which are much lower than the main memory access time (around 100 cycles). The address space is divided between SPM and off-chip RAM; the latter is, optionally, accessed through the on-chip cache. It is also possible to explicitly copy (transfer) data from off-chip DRAM to SPM, or vice versa. These explicit data copies incur an overhead (from both energy consumption and performance viewpoints), therefore, the number of copies should be minimized. This can be achieved by reusing the data in the SPM as much as possible, and this paper proposes a strategy to do this. A higher level strategy (e.g., [7]) can be used to decide whether the cache or the SPM should be used for a given piece of data. For example, if two data arrays are expected to cause excessive conflict misses in cache, one of them might be placed in the SPM. This paper does not address the issue of data partitioning between cache and SPM; consequently, we do not discuss cache in the rest of the paper.

In this work, we focus on array-dominated codes frequently used in image and video processing applications. To generate code for our memory architecture, in addition to the conventional optimization steps, the compiler has to schedule explicit data copies between the off-chip memory and the SPM. To accomplish this effectively, it needs to take into account the access pattern of the application, the number and size of the arrays manipulated, the intra- and inter-nest data reuse, and the SPM capacity (size). Note that the SPM space should be divided suitably among the sections of competing arrays. Thus, during the course of execution, a number of (array) sections belonging to a number of different arrays are brought into the SPM, the new values for these array sections (regions) are computed, and the sections are stored back into appropriate locations in off-chip DRAM, if necessary.

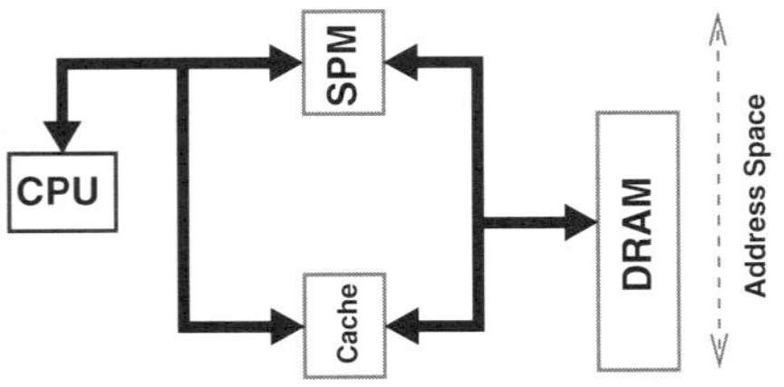

Figure 1: Architecture model.

3. ACCESS PATTERN OPTIMIZATION

Our objective in this paper is to minimize the data transfers between off-chip main memory and on-chip scratch-pad memory (SPM). The idea behind our approach is to reuse the data currently residing in SPM as much as possible. While this can be achieved using several alternate techniques, in this work, we employ a program-wide access pattern re-structuring (optimization) technique based on Presburger formulas.

A program-wide access pattern optimization technique is the one that modifies the access pattern of a given code (e.g., procedure) taking into account the entire computation in the code. Note that this is in contrast with the majority of the techniques from high-performance computing domain that focus on a single loop nest (or, at most, on a couple of loop nests as in the case of loop fusion) at a time. By considering the entire (procedure-wide) access pattern before applying optimizations, our approach has a better chance for making the most suitable optimization decisions. This is particularly important for capacity-constrained resources in embedded systems such as on-chip scratch-pad memories and on-chip caches where effective management of data flow is a must.

3.1 Overview and Definitions

Our strategy for on-chip SPM management has two major components: (1) Selecting the sections of arrays that will be fetched into the SPM (these array sections are collectively called *residence set*), and (2) Re-structuring the code such that, given a residence set, the current computation only uses the data elements in this set (this characteristic is called *residence set reuse*, and the set of loop iterations that access only a single residence set is referred to as *locality set*). The objective here is to increase the sizes of the locality sets. Note that this objective is oriented towards reducing the number of transfers between SPM and off-chip memory. It should also be noted that since we focus on improving the behavior of an entire code, a locality set may (in general) contain iterations from *different loop nests*. Below we explain in detail how we address both these problems. Before this, however, let us make the following definitions:

Iteration Space and Iteration Vector: Given a loop nest which contains m loops (I_1, I_2, ..., I_m, from outermost to innermost), the iteration space is described as the set $\mathcal{I} = \{(I_1, I_2, ..., I_m) : L_1 \leq I_1 \leq U_1, ..., L_m \leq I_m \leq U_m\}$. The vector $(I_1, I_2, ..., I_m)$ is referred to as iteration vector and is written as $\vec{I}$.

Let $f(.)$ and $g(.)$ be two integer (subscript) functions defined on the set $\mathcal{I}$. Consider two statements S_i and S_j, and let $S_i(\vec{I})$ and $S_j(\vec{I})$ refer to the executions of these statements with the iteration vector $\vec{I}$.

Dependence Vector: Statement $S_i(\vec{I})$ is dependent on statement $S_j(\vec{J})$ iff statement S_i contains an array reference $X[f(\vec{I})]$ and statement $S_j(\vec{J})$ contains an array reference $X[g(\vec{J})]$ such that $f(\vec{I}) = g(\vec{J})$ (where $\vec{J} \leq \vec{I}$). In this case, we also say that iteration vector $\vec{I}$ is dependent on iteration vector $\vec{J}$, and the difference vector $\vec{d} = \vec{I} - \vec{J}$ is called data dependence vector. Note that this definition of data dependence includes flow, anti, output, and input dependences. In this paper, we are only interested in dependence vectors where all entries are constant (iteration-independent) since these are the most common form found in embedded image and video processing applications [3].

Reflection Vector: The vector $\vec{r} = f(\vec{I}) - g(\vec{J})$ is called the reflection vector iff $\vec{I}$ is dependent on $\vec{J}$. A reflection vector $\vec{r}$ is said to be *induced* by a dependence vector $\vec{d}$ iff $\vec{r} = f(\vec{I}) - g(\vec{J})$ and $\vec{d} = \vec{I} - \vec{J}$. Note that a reflection vector is, in a sense, the reflection of a data dependence vector on *data (array) space*. In a given loop nest and an array accessed within it, we can have multiple reflection vectors which, collectively, define a reflection matrix $R = [\vec{r_1}; \vec{r_2}; ...; \vec{r_s}]$, where $\vec{r_i}$ is the ith reflection vector. In this paper, we consider only lexicographically positive reflection vectors. This is not a severe restriction since, using data space transformations, a given reflection vector can be made lexicographically positive.

Reflection Graph: The reflection graph is a directed-graph where each node represents an array element, and there is an edge between two nodes $\vec{a}$ and $\vec{b}$ iff $\vec{a} - \vec{b}$ or $\vec{b} - \vec{a}$ is a reflection vector. Note that this graph is the correspondent of the iteration space graph used in data dependence analysis.

Combined Reflection Graph: The definition of a reflection graph is with respect to a single nest (and a single array). For a given array, we define a combined reflection graph as a graph obtained by superimposing the reflection graphs originating from individual nests.

3.2 Single Array Case

Let us first focus on a simple case where a *single* array is accessed in multiple loop nests. The results obtained here will later be extended to handle the multiple array case. Our strategy for the single array case starts by dividing (decomposing) the array into portions (called *slabs*), each of which is as large as possible but not larger than the capacity of the SPM (i.e., each slab fits in the SPM). Then, each slab is visited in turn and brought into the SPM. Once a slab is in the SPM, all the iterations that use the elements in this slab (i.e., the locality set) are executed. Note that in this single array case, a slab is also the entire residence set. A limited form of this style of computation (that is, dividing an array into logical chunks and executing iterations that access each chunk successively) has been explored by the previous cache memory-based research in the context of imperfectly-nested loops in linear algebra codes [6].

Even in this simple case of a single array, there are several important issues that need to be addressed. Let us assume for now that we have only a single nest. First, the compiler needs to decide the shape of the slab. Given a fixed SPM capacity, we can select slabs of the same size with different shapes. There are two important problems here that we need to solve: First, the slab selected should satisfy all data dependences so that executing all loop iterations that touch a given slab should be legal (permissible from the program's semantics point of view). Second, the slab selected should minimize the extra (buffer) memory requirements. These requirements are due to the fact that, in going from one slab to another, a number of elements may need to be maintained in a buffer area (e.g., in a part of the SPM). Our compiler uses the reflection graph concept defined above to select suitable slab shapes. As an example, consider the reflection graph segment given in Figure 2(a) and the (square) slabs shown on it. We see that this slab shape is illegal as, given two neighboring slabs (as shown in the figure), there are reflection vectors going in both directions (from one slab to another and vice versa), which means that it is not possible to process the elements in a given slab (completely) when it is in the SPM. The slabs shown in Figure 2(b) which contain the same number of array elements as those in Figure 2(a) are, on the other hand, legal. Let us now compare these slabs with those shown in Figure 2(c), which are also legal. In deciding between these two alternatives, the compiler needs to take the extra memory requirements into account. In Figure 2(b), the two neighboring slabs shown have three arrows shared between them, meaning that we need a buffer of three elements, whereas the corresponding figure between the slabs in Figure 2(c) is nine. Consequently, the slab shape shown in Figure 2(b) is a better alternative for this example than the one in Figure 2(c). We can define these concepts formally as follows:

Legality: Let $R = [\vec{r_1}; \vec{r_2}; ...; \vec{r_s}]$ be a reflection matrix. Each slab boundary can be defined by a vector perpendicular to it. In k-dimensions, any k vectors $\vec{h_1}$, $\vec{h_2}$, ...,$\vec{h_k}$ define legal slabs if $\vec{h_i}\vec{r_j} \geq 0$ $(1 \leq i \leq k)$, for all $\vec{r_j}$ $(1 \leq j \leq s)$. Here, $\vec{h_i}$ is the vector perpendicular to the ith boundary of the slab. We state this legality condition in matrix form as $HR \geq \vec{0}$, where $H = [\vec{h_1}, \vec{h_2}, ...\vec{h_k}]^T$ is a matrix, whose row i is the vector $\vec{h_i}$ and $\vec{0}$ is a zero vector. The proof for this legality constraint is similar to the proof of legality of iteration space tiles, and is omitted due to lack of space.

Minimizing Buffer Requirements: The buffer requirements of a given slab is proportional to it's communication volume; that is, the number of out-going (or in-going) arrows. In our context, this volume can be minimized by minimizing the sum of the absolute values of all the entries in HR. This is because a nonzero entry r'_{ij} in $R' = HR$ indicates that the jth reflection vector pokes the ith slab boundary.

We can also define a *slab matrix* $P = [\vec{p_1}, \vec{p_2}, ..., \vec{p_k}]$, where the vector $\vec{p_i}$ is the vector that defines the ith tile boundary. Since the ith column of P is orthogonal to the ith row of H, it is easy to show that $P = H^{-1}$.

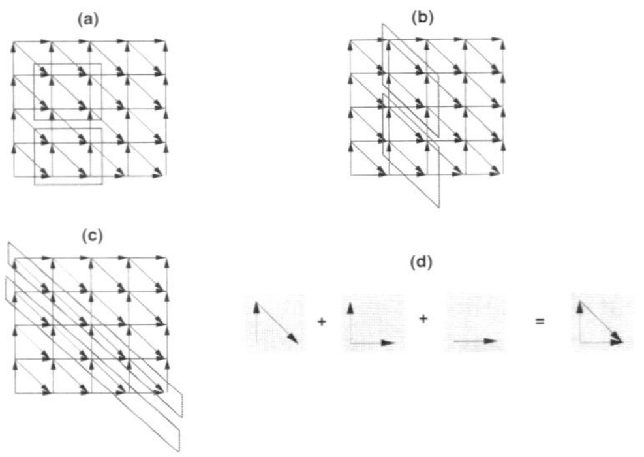

Figure 2: (a), (b), (c) Different slab shapes on an example reflection graph segment. (d) An example combined R.

The question then is to determine a legal H matrix (or equivalently a P matrix) such that the sum of the absolute values of the entries in HR is minimum. For example, if

$$R = \begin{bmatrix} 1 \\ 1 \end{bmatrix} \text{ and } H = \begin{bmatrix} h_{11} & h_{12} \\ h_{21} & h_{22} \end{bmatrix}$$

$$\text{we have } R' = HR = \begin{bmatrix} h_{11} + h_{12} \\ h_{21} + h_{22} \end{bmatrix}.$$

Thus, we want to minimize $|h_{11} + h_{12}| + |h_{21} + h_{22}|$. Also, the H matrix should be invertible. A solution in this case is $h_{11} = 1, h_{12} = 0, h_{21} = -1$, and $h_{22} = 1$, which gives

$$H = \begin{bmatrix} 1 & 0 \\ -1 & 1 \end{bmatrix} \Rightarrow P = H^{-1} = \begin{bmatrix} 1 & 0 \\ 1 & 1 \end{bmatrix}.$$

Note that in this case $|h_{11} + h_{12}| + |h_{21} + h_{22}| = 1$. While it is difficult, in general, to determine an H matrix automatically (as this process involves a non-linear constraint of non-zero determinant), we can reduce the search space by fixing the shape of H at a specific form (with non-zero determinant). One alternative is a lower-triangular integer matrix with unit diagonal entries. For example, for a three-dimensional array, one can use the matrix

$$H = \begin{bmatrix} 1 & 0 & 0 \\ a & 1 & 0 \\ b & c & 1 \end{bmatrix}.$$

The legality condition can be satisfied by selecting sufficiently large values for a, b, and c. For our current example,

$$H = \begin{bmatrix} 1 & 0 \\ a & 1 \end{bmatrix} \Rightarrow R' = HR = \begin{bmatrix} 1 \\ a+1 \end{bmatrix}.$$

The matrix R' should have entries whose sum (of absolute values) is minimum; that is, we need to minimize $|a+1| + 1$ while making sure that $a + 1 \geq 0$ (as all entries in HR need to be non-negative). It is easy to see that $a = -1$ is the value that minimizes $|a+1| + 1$. Note that the fact that we focus only on integer entries and that the determinant of H is 1 guarantees that both H and P are integer matrices.

In the example reflection graph given in Figure 2, we have

$$R = \begin{bmatrix} 1 & 0 & 1 \\ 0 & 1 & -1 \end{bmatrix}.$$

If we use the slab shapes in Figure 2(a), we have

$$R' = HR = \begin{bmatrix} 1 & 0 \\ 0 & 1 \end{bmatrix} \begin{bmatrix} 1 & 0 & 1 \\ 0 & 1 & -1 \end{bmatrix} = \begin{bmatrix} 1 & 0 & 1 \\ 0 & 1 & -1 \end{bmatrix}.$$

Since R' contains a negative value, these tile shapes are not legal. Our approach, on the other hand, selects an H matrix

$$H = \begin{bmatrix} 1 & 0 \\ 1 & 1 \end{bmatrix} \text{ which gives } HR = \begin{bmatrix} 1 & 0 & 1 \\ 1 & 1 & 0 \end{bmatrix}.$$

Note that in this case, $P = H^{-1}$ gives the slab shapes shown in Figure 2(b). Note also that once a slab shape has been determined, the size of the slab can be increased (to a point where the entire SPM space is filled up) by *scaling* its boundaries.

Let us define a slab of array X defined by $P = [\vec{p_1}, \vec{p_2}, ..., \vec{p_k}]$ using Presburger formulas as:

$$B_X(\vec{o}) = \{\vec{x} : \vec{x} = \vec{o} + \sum_{1 \leq i \leq k} x_i \vec{p_i} \text{ and } 0 \leq x_i \leq C_i - 1\}.$$

Here, each slab boundary $\vec{p_i}$ is assumed to be scaled to contain C_i elements (to fill up the SPM space). Note that the set $B_X(\vec{o})$ contains all the elements in the slab whose origin is $\vec{o}$. Given such a $B_X(\vec{o})$, the locality set of a given nest $nest_i$ with respect to this slab can be defined as

$$L_{X,nest_i} = \{\vec{I} : \forall f, f(\vec{I}) \in B_X(\vec{o})\}.$$

In this definition, f is a subscript function to array X referenced in one of the statements in nest $nest_i$. It should be noted that this set excludes an iteration if this iteration accesses (using one of the references in the nest) an array element which is not in $B_X(\vec{o})$. Once a legal slab shape has been determined, the slabs with different origin values can be processed one by one (i.e., can be brought into the SPM, operated on, and stored back in the off-chip memory) observing the dependences between the slabs.

Now, given a series of nests $nest_1$, $nest_2$, ..., $nest_l$ that access a single array, we can generate a code that utilizes the on-chip SPM effectively, as shown on the left portion of Figure 3. In this case, each nest is visited in turn, and (for each nest) a legal slab shape is determined. Then, the innermost 'for loop' iterates over the slabs (with different origins), and after bringing the slab into the SPM (this explicit copy activity is omitted from the code for the sake of clarity), it executes its locality set. This process is repeated for all nests in the code. Note that under this scheme, for a given loop nest, each slab is brought into SPM only once (under our assumption of lexicographically positive reflection vectors). Note also that this approach is similar to the data shackling strategy proposed by Kodukula et al. [6] with one important difference: the data shackling strategy does not determine dependence-free slab shapes automatically; instead, a reliance is placed upon the observation that, in linear algebra codes, the majority of nested loops are dependence free, so a simple square-shaped slab strategy should work fine. Many codes from embedded image and video processing domain, however, exhibit more complex dependences. While the algorithm on the left portion of Figure 3 can generate good results for some cases, it does not take advantage of the fact that iterations from *different nests* can be mixed as long as data dependences allow this. In other words, the locality set concept here is limited to the iterations of a single nest only. The right portion of Figure 3 gives an alternative code

```
for each nest_i do
  compute R
  determine a legal H
  for each slab B_X(σ) do
    execute locality set L_{X,nest_i}
  endfor
endfor
```

```
𝓘=∪ all iteration sets
compute a combined R
determine a legal H
while 𝓘 is not empty do
  for each slab B_X(σ) do
    execute locality set L_X
    𝓘 = 𝓘 − L_X
  endfor
endwhile
```

Figure 3: Optimization algorithms for single array case.

generation strategy. In this strategy, first, all iteration sets (from all nests) are combined into a single set $\mathcal{I}$ (the symbol $\cup$ denotes set combination). Using the combined reflection graph, a combined R and an appropriate H are determined (see Figure 2(d) for an example combined R obtained from three nests). Then, using this H, each slab is visited (within the 'for loop') and all iterations (possibly coming from different nests) that use the elements in the current slab are executed (without violating any data dependence). In the algorithm, L_X refers to this combined locality set. Note that the 'while loop' in this algorithm is necessary in cases where a slab (or a group of slabs) need to be re-visited (as a result of data dependences between iterations from different nests). In other words, each slab might be visited more than once. Note also that in each execution of the 'while loop', L_X contains only the iterations that could not be executed so far (in previous executions of the 'while loop') due to data dependences.

3.3 Multiple Array Case

Let us now consider the most general case where each nest accesses a subset of the arrays declared in the program. An algorithm for handling this case is an extension of the approach described for the single array case. The algorithm sketched on the left portion of Figure 4 visits nests one by one, and optimizes each nest in isolation. For each nest, it first selects a *dominant array*, and determines a legal slab shape for the dominant array. Then, the locality set is computed and executed. Note that the iterations determined based on the dominant array will also impose slab shapes for other arrays in the nest. All these slabs (potentially originating from different arrays) collectively constitute a residence set. If there are any left-over iterations (i.e., the iterations that do not access the dominant array), these iterations are executed, possibly, considering the second dominant array, and so on. The 'for j' loop in the figure fullfils this functionality. A (potentially) better approach is given on the right portion of Figure 4. Here, first, all iteration sets (from different nests) are combined into a single set $\mathcal{I}$. Then, all the arrays declared in the program are evaluated, and are ordered according to an importance criterion. After that, a slab shape is selected for the most dominant (most important) array. Then, all the iterations (possibly coming from different nests) that access the slabs (the slabs of the most dominant array are traversed one by one) are executed. Note that a given slab from the most dominant array imposes different slabs for other arrays in each nest (This step is omitted from the figure for the sake of clarity). Then, we move to the second dominant array, and repeat the same procedure considering only the iterations that have not been executed so far and so on.

```
for each nest_i do
  𝓘_i=iteration set of nest_i
  determine an order for
  arrays as X_1, X_2, ..., X_{v_i}
  for j = 1,2,...,v_i do
    while 𝓘_i is not empty do
      compute R for X_j
      determine a legal H
      calculate locality set L_{X_j}
      find Hs for other arrays
      execute locality set L_{X_j}
      𝓘_i = 𝓘_i − L_{X_j}
    endwhile
  endfor
endfor
```

```
𝓘=∪ all iteration sets
  determine an order for
  arrays as X_1, X_2, ..., X_v
  while 𝓘 is not empty do
    for j = 1,2,...,v do
      compute a combined R
        for X_j
      determine a legal H
      execute locality set L_{X_j}
      𝓘 = 𝓘 − L_{X_j}
    endfor
  endwhile
```

Figure 4: Optimization algorithms for multiple array case.

4. EXPERIMENTAL RESULTS

We performed experiments with four array-dominated codes: *fft*: a two-dimensional Fast Fourier Transform code; *flt*: an array-based filtering routine; *est*: a motion estimation code that uses the full-search approach; and *tomcatv*: an array dominated code from the Spec benchmark suite. The input sizes for these codes are 86KB, 91KB, 70KB, and 258KB, respectively.

We experimented with three different versions of each code:

- *s-opt:* This is a static, SPM-based approach where the compiler determines the most frequently used data elements (considering the entire code) and keeps them in the SPM throughout the execution.
- *cache:* This version uses a conventional cache memory (of the same size) instead of the SPM.
- *d-opt* This is the dynamic, SPM-based approach presented in this paper (the algorithm on the right part of Figure 4).

Both *s-opt* and *d-opt* have been implemented within the SUIF experimental compiler [1] using the Omega library [5] (to enumerate the Presburger formulas). In experiments with the *cache* version, we hand-applied loop permutation and tiling to increase data locality as much as possible. After experimenting with several tile sizes, for each code and cache size, we selected the best tile sizes from energy and performance perspectives. Note that when we make a quantitative comparison between these three versions, we always fix the on-chip storage space (whether it is SPM or cache) at a specific value (for all three versions).

We evaluated our approach and compared it to *s-opt* and *cache* versions using two different metrics: (i) the number of references to the off-chip memory, and (ii) the energy-delay product. Here, 'delay' means 'total memory access time' (for data references), and 'energy' means 'total memory system (on-chip + off-chip) energy' (due to data references). In experiments with the *cache* version, the number of memory references and number of hits/misses are obtained using the Shade simulator environment [4]. Shade is an instruction-set simulator and custom trace generator. To compute the cache access times for different configurations, we used the CACTI timing model [8]. Using cache access times, the number of dynamic instructions, and a miss penalty of 100 cycles/miss, we calculated the total execution time. In experiments that involve the SPM, we used (as access time) the access time of a direct-mapped cache of the same size.

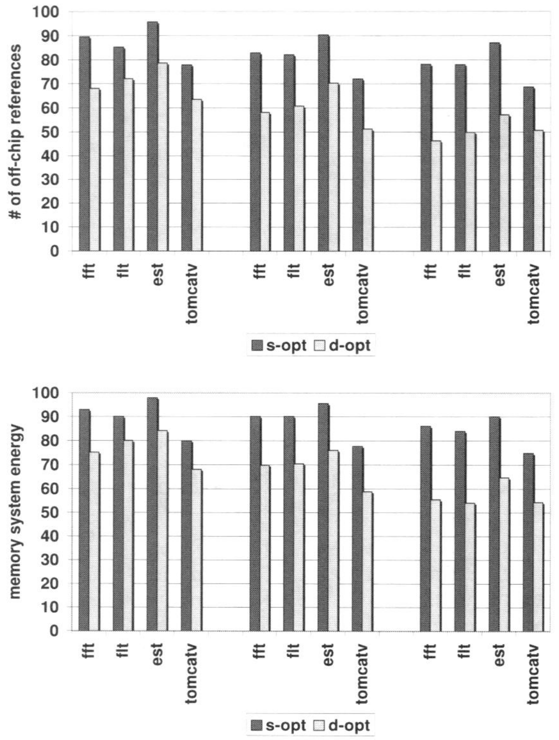

Figure 5: Top: Normalized number of off-chip references. Bottom: Normalized energy-delay product. The three groups of bars correspond to, from left to right, 8KB, 4KB, and 2KB on-chip storage capacities.

Note that this is a conservative approach as, in reality, we can expect the access time of a cache to be higher than that of the same-sized SPM (due to tag comparison). The energy values for the cache configurations, on the other hand, have been calculated based on 0.8 micron technology.

The top portion of Figure 5 shows the number of off-chip memory references for the *s-opt* and *d-opt* versions *normalized* with respect the corresponding values for the *cache* version. The three groups of bars in this figure correspond to, from left to right, 8KB, 4KB, and 2KB on-chip storage capacities. Due to lack of space, each bar in this figure corresponds to an averaged value of direct-mapped, two-way, and four-way associative caches (of the same capacity). We see from these numbers that *s-opt* and *d-opt* reduces the number of off-chip references by 17.6% and 39.4%, respectively, indicating the usefulness of dynamic SPM management. The bottom portion of Figure 5 gives the energy-delay product for the same codes and versions, *normalized* with respect to the energy-delay product of the *cache* version. It can be observed that *s-opt* and *d-opt* improve the energy-delay product by 12.5% and 32.4%, respectively. We can conclude from these numbers that the effectiveness of our dynamic approach increases with smaller on-chip storage capacities, which is good when one considers the fact that dataset sizes keep getting bigger and bigger. We also observe that fixing the contents of the SPM throughout the entire execution (as with the *s-opt* version) is not a very good idea due to dynamic changes in the working set of codes.

	8KB	4KB	2KB		8KB	4KB	2KB
fft	7.9%	9.5%	12.2%	*est*	9.4%	10.8%	11.4%
flt	10.3%	10.4%	10.4%	*tomcatv*	8.6%	9.7%	11.1%

Figure 6: Energy-delay product comparisons of the two algorithms in Figure 4.

To see the difference between the two algorithms in Figure 4, we performed another set of experiments. Figure 6 shows the difference in energy-delay products between these two algorithms (i.e., how much the algorithm on the right is better, on the average, than the one on the left). As before, all values are averages over three different set associativities. We can see from these numbers that considering iterations from different nests (instead of focusing on a single nest at a time) brings a 10.1% improvement on the average.

5. CONCLUSIONS

Optimizations aimed at improving the efficiency of on-chip memories are extremely important. In this paper, we propose a compiler-controlled dynamic on-chip scratch-pad memory (SPM) management framework. Our framework represents the portions of the arrays in the SPM and the sets of iterations that manipulate them using Presburger sets, and uses a polyhedral tool to enumerate these sets. Experimental results using four complete programs illustrate the benefits of this technique. Our current work along this direction includes dynamic management of multiple on-chip SPMs.

6. REFERENCES

[1] S. P. Amarasinghe, J. M. Anderson, M. S. Lam, and C. W. Tseng. The SUIF compiler for scalable parallel machines. In Proc. *the Seventh SIAM Conference on Parallel Processing for Scientific Computing,* February, 1995.

[2] L. Benini, A. Macii, E. Macii, and M. Poncino. Increasing energy efficiency of embedded systems by application-specific memory hierarchy generation. *IEEE Design & Test of Computers,* pages 74–85, April, 2000.

[3] F. Catthoor, S. Wuytack, E. D. Greef, F. Balasa, L. Nachtergaele, and A. Vandecappelle. Custom memory management methodology – exploration of memory organization for embedded multimedia system design. *Kluwer Academic Publishers,* June, 1998.

[4] B. Cmelik and D. Keppel. Shade: a fast instruction-set simulator for execution profiling. In Proc. *the 1994 ACM SIGMETRICS Conference on the Measurement and Modeling of Computer Systems,* May 1994, pp. 128–137.

[5] W. Kelly, V. Maslov, W. Pugh, E. Rosser, T. Shpeisman, and David Wonnacott. The Omega Library interface guide. Technical Report CS-TR-3445, CS Dept., University of Maryland, College Park, March 1995.

[6] I. Kodukula, N. Ahmed, and K. Pingali. Data-centric multi-level blocking. In *Proc. SIGPLAN Conf. Prog. Language Design and Implementation,* June 1997.

[7] P. R. Panda, N. D. Dutt, and A. Nicolau. Efficient utilization of scratch-pad-memory in embedded processor applications. In Proc. *European Design and Test Conference (ED&TC'97),* Paris, March 1997.

[8] S. Wilton and N. P. Jouppi. CACTI: an enhanced cycle access and cycle time model. *IEEE Journal of Solid-State Circuits,* pp. 677–687, 1996.

System-level Interconnect Architecture Exploration for Custom Memory Organizations

Tycho van Meeuwen
Arnout Vandecappelle
IMEC vzw
Kapeldreef 75
3001 Leuven
Belgium
vmeeuwen@imec.be
vdcappel@imec.be

Allert van Zelst
currently with
Agere Systems
Zadelstede 1–10
3431 JZ Nieuwegein
The Netherlands
zelst@agere.com

Francky Catthoor†
Diederik Verkest
IMEC vzw
Kapeldreef 75
3001 Leuven
Belgium
†Also professor at
Katholieke Univ. Leuven
catthoor@imec.be
verkest@imec.be

ABSTRACT

For data dominated applications, power consumption and memory bandwidth bottlenecks can be significantly alleviated with a custom memory organization. However, this potentially entails complex memory interconnections and a large routing overhead. This is undesirable for area cost, power consumption, and layout design complexity. By exploiting time-multiplexing opportunities over the long memory buses, this overhead can be significantly reduced. This paper proposes a system-level methodology for automated exploration of the interconnect architecture, which finds the optimal trade-off points for memory bus time-multiplexing. Experiments performed on real-life applications using our prototype tool show that even for very distributed memory organizations, the interconnect complexity can be significantly reduced to a cost-efficient, manageable level.

1. INTRODUCTION AND RELATED WORK

For data intensive applications (e.g. multimedia), a very large part of the power consumption is due to the storage and transfer of data, and the memory bandwidth is a bottleneck for performance. These bottlenecks can be removed with a more customized, distributed and hierarchical memory architecture [2]. However, this implies that there are complex interconnections between the memories and the processing units. In current design practice, typically two options are considered: allocating a separate bus for every memory-port-to-data-path connection, or routing all transfers over a single high-speed bus.

An interconnect architecture with one bus for every memory port creates a big area overhead and potential bottlenecks during the physical design. First, for interconnections with off-chip memories, this requires many I/O pins on the chip. Second, on-chip global interconnections are either routed in extra non-active routing area or in the extra top metal layers, which contribute directly to the production cost. Finally, the size of the place and route problem increases tremendously and the delay constraints become very hard to satisfy.

To avoid the overhead of many buses, it is possible to allocate one shared bus for different memories instead, but this may come at a cost in power consumption and does not solve the physical design complexity. First, this bus must run at a higher frequency to still provide the required memory bandwidth. This may result in an increased power consumption, and also makes the delay constraints for place and route more stringent. Moreover, extra logic is required to select the correct memory, to arbitrate the bus access, and to synchronize the bus with the memories. Finally, the overall bus length may increase because detours and tap lines to all memory ports have to be foreseen; this results in a higher power consumption, and still a complex place and route problem.

Our goal is to find a cost-efficient middle way between the full interconnect solution and a single global bus, by time-multiplexing the data transfers over a number of shared buses. To reduce the amount of required multiplexer and control overhead, and to reduce the length of each bus and the complexity of routing it, we minimize the number of buses each memory is connected to and vice versa. In addition, we make sure the real time constraints are met without requiring higher clock speeds or arbitration logic. A system-level bandwidth optimization step [17] precedes our bus sharing exploration and provides it with information on conflicting transfers, which is taken as a constraint on which interconnections may be shared over one bus.

After discussing the related work, this paper presents a model of the freedom which exists at the system level for time-multiplexing the memory interconnections (section 2). This model allows systematic and automated exploration of the search space, to trade off the number of buses against the overhead from the bus selection logic. We have implemented this technique in a fully automated prototype tool to support the designer in this complex and relevant design issue. Experiments on real-life applications (section 3) show that the interconnection overhead introduced by a distributed memory architecture can be significantly reduced, with minimal additional multiplexing overhead.

The work presented in this paper fits in the context of background memory management. One of the approaches is based on

ISSS'01, October 1-3, 2001, Montréal, Québec, Canada.

the data stream model of PHIDEO [7], which has recently been extended with a technique for allocating bandwidth [15]. A second approach is the array-variable clustering method [9], where the allocation of memory modules is done prior to scheduling, taking into account the possible bounds within which data will be accessed. Finally, the data transfer and storage exploration script of IMEC [2] provides a global methodology to design a custom background memory architecture, based on a partial ordering of memory accesses. Although all of these methods propose customized memory organizations, they currently largely ignore the associated problems in the global memory interconnections.

The problem of interconnections also occurs in the data paths, and this is tackled in the data transfer binding step performed during data path synthesis [1, 5, 13]. It consists of constructing the communication paths, including buses, tristate buffers and multiplexers, between functional units and register files (foreground memory). This step is either performed after scheduling and allocation, or they can be combined to globally optimize the number of registers and interconnection netlist [10]. However, the problem of the global memory interconnections can not effectively be solved at this level. First, the detailed data path scheduler is not sufficiently aware of the importance of the global buses, and may therefore create more conflicts between the data transfers than is strictly necessary to meet the real time constraints. The time-multiplexing exploration of the memory buses should therefore be performed *before* behavioral scheduling. Second, the data path synthesis makes no distinction between the local buses to register files and the global buses to background memory. However, for the global buses, the time-multiplexing overhead is almost negligible compared to the gain of sharing two buses.

The techniques which are proposed for optimizing the interconnections in the data path can not be simply reused for time-multiplexing the memory buses at the system level. For one, since this should be performed before behavioral synthesis, no detailed scheduling information is available, nor can it be assumed that everything runs at the same clock speed. System-level information about the data transfer conflicts should be used instead. Second, the data path techniques do not take into account that the memory architecture is structured as a hierarchy, with data being copied from layer to layer. Third, these techniques do not exploit the freedom for choosing which port to use for each access to a multiport memory. Fourth, they assume a simple, linear bus structure, while for the global buses there is more freedom. For example, buses can temporary be connected by inserting a switch between them [4, 6]. Fifth, they do not sufficiently exploit the different bitwidths of the signals traveling over the shared bus. Finally, they do not support the possibility to alternate between two or more different buses for the same memory-port-to-data-path connection. Therefore, we propose a new approach for interconnect optimization for customized background memory organizations.

Global interconnections receive special attention in the field of new design flows targeted at the problems emerging from the deep submicron challenge [14]. Also in the synthesis of the communication channels between concurrent processor blocks, opportunities for time-multiplexing the interconnections are encountered [3], although not many approaches have been proposed to exploit these opportunities. These approaches usually suffer from the same drawbacks as the data path synthesis approaches, as mentioned in the previous paragraph. The approach proposed in this paper could be used to optimize the global wires between any set of blocks with mutual data transfers, but this possibility has not been worked out in this paper.

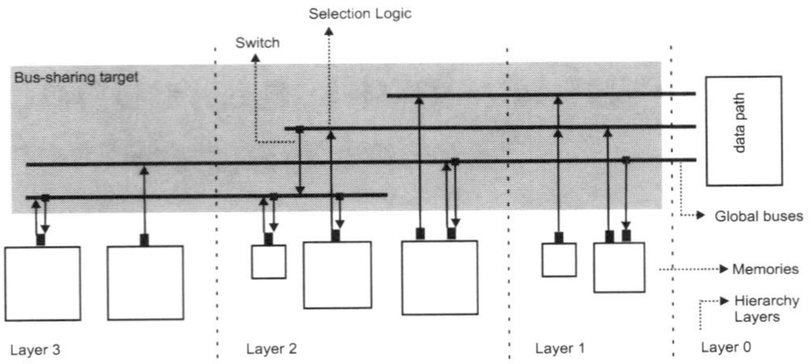

Figure 1: Target architecture for bus sharing. To reduce the number of global buses, selection logic is needed. Our approach maximally exploits the existing memory hierarchy layering by inserting switches.

2. BUS SHARING METHODOLOGY

To reduce the complexity of the memory interconnections, they can be time-multiplexed; this decision is called *bus sharing*. The bus sharing step explores alternatives fitting on an abstract architectural template. Its goal is to find a cost-efficient interconnection architecture, which still provides enough memory bandwidth to meet the real time constraints. Our approach consists of three steps. In the first step, transfer-to-bus assignment (section 2.1), the application's transfers are assigned to shared buses, taking into account parallelism required for real time operation. The second step is the transfer-to-port assignment (section 2.2), where for each access to a multiport memory we determine which port is going to be used. Finally, the third step consists of instantiating the abstract labeling representations into a netlist of interconnections and multiplexing logic (section 2.3). The cost of its implementation is estimated, steering the exploration of the first two steps.

Figure 1 shows our target architecture for bus sharing. Since we work at the system level, an abstraction is made of many details. The global buses which connect memories with each other and to the data path are accessed via bus selection logic. The memories are distributed over several memory hierarchy layers. For transfers which cross more than one memory hierarchy layer boundary (multiboundary transfers), either one long global bus can be used or it can be routed over several buses. The latter is possible with the aid of a *switch*, which can either connect the two buses or isolate them from each other.

2.1 Transfer-to-bus assignment

The time-multiplexing freedom of the memory buses is limited by the parallelism required to achieve real time operation. We explore the available freedom with a model of the real-time constraints, the Transfer Conflict Graph (TCG), which contains the *conflicts* (hyperedges) between the application's memory *transfers* (nodes). Figure 2(b) shows an example of a TCG, for the memory architecture and global transfers shown in figure 2(a).

A *transfer* T_p is defined by its *source* and *sink* resource (memory or data path). All data movements ever occurring from one particular resource to another are considered as one single transfer. Only a distinction in the direction is made. A transfer is represented by a node in the TCG, with a number corresponding to the transfer number in figure 2(a).

A *conflict* occurs when a number of transfers take place in parallel. Conflicts are derived from the analysis of the memory bandwidth requirements, which we assume to take place at an earlier stage. We use our storage bandwidth optimization approach [17],

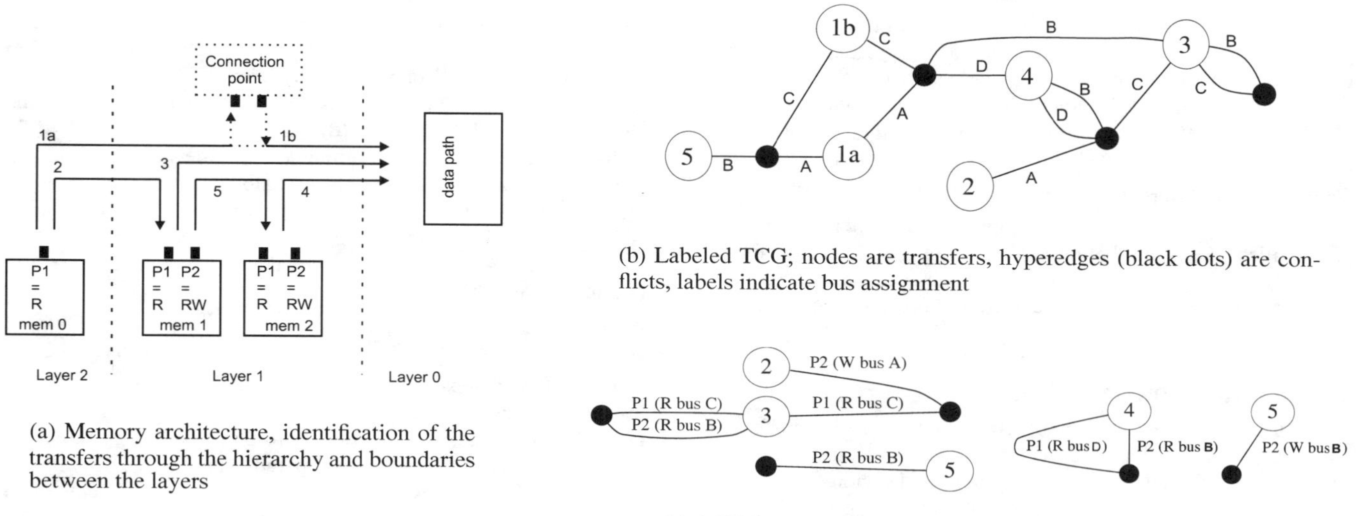

(a) Memory architecture, identification of the transfers through the hierarchy and boundaries between the layers

(b) Labeled TCG; nodes are transfers, hyperedges (black dots) are conflicts, labels indicate bus assignment

(c) ACG for mem 1

(d) ACG for mem 2

Figure 2: Red-thread example of bus sharing methodology

but any other system-level technique which arrives at conflicts between data transfers can be used as well, e.g. the PHIDEO scheduler [15] or the scheduler from the University of Arizona [12]. All these techniques order the data transfers from the memories in time, so that the overlap between transfers is minimized. The storage bandwidth optimization approach we use is driven by a cost per conflict (one conflict may comprise several overlaps between two transfers) and takes into account the conflict probabilities, which makes it ideally suited for system-level interconnect architecture exploration. No full ordering is imposed, which is crucial at the system level to remove the global buses.

A conflict is represented by a hyperedge in the TCG (a black dot and its connected edges in figure 2(b)). A hyperedge E is defined as a set of transfers where there is some point in time that all $T_p \in E$ overlap each other.

With the aid of a switch, a transfer may be routed over several buses when it crosses several memory hierarchy layers. Therefore, multiboundary transfers are split up in single-boundary parts terminating at a *connection point*, which models a potential switch between buses. A transfer T_p is split up in single-boundary transfers $T_{p,a}$ as follows:

$$\text{source}(T_{p,a}) = \begin{cases} \text{source}(T_p) & \text{for } a = 1, \\ C_{p,a-1} = \text{sink}(T_{p,a-1}) & \text{for } a > 1. \end{cases}$$

$$\text{sink}(T_{p,a}) = \begin{cases} C_{p,a} = \text{source}(T_{p,a+1}) & \text{for } a < d(T_p), \\ \text{sink}(T_p) & \text{for } a = d(T_p). \end{cases}$$

where $d(T_p) = |\text{layer}(\text{source}(T_p)) - \text{layer}(\text{sink}(T_p))|$ is the number of layers crossed by the transfer, and $C_{p,a}$ represents a connection point for transfer T_p on the a'th layer. In figure 2(b), transfer 1 is such a split transfer. All conflicts of the original transfer are valid for each of its parts. Therefore, original edge $E = \{T_p, T_q, \dots\}$ must be extended to $E_s = \{T_{p,1}, T_{p,2}, \dots, T_{q,1}, \dots\}$.

With the TCG model, any transfer-to-bus assignment decision can be represented by labeling every hyperedge endpoint of the TCG with the bus which will be used for its adjacent transfer: $\lambda(E_s, T_{p,a}) \in \mathcal{B}$, where $\mathcal{B}$ is the set of available buses; transfers also need a label at points in time when they are not in conflict: $\lambda(0, T_{p,a}) \in \mathcal{B}$. A labeling is valid only if all endpoints of a hyperedge have a different label: $\forall E_s : \forall T_{p,a}, T_{q,b} \in E_s : \lambda(E_s, T_{p,a}) \neq \lambda(E_s, T_{q,b}) \vee p = q$. The nodes $T_{p,1}, T_{p,2}, \dots$ comprising a multiboundary transfer, however, are allowed to be labeled with the same bus. Indeed, even though they always belong to the same hyperedges, it is possible to route these transfers over a single global bus. Thus, the labeling $\lambda(E_s, T_{p,a}) = \lambda(E_s, T_{q,b})$ is allowed by the above labeling constraint if $p = q$.

The minimum number of buses in $\mathcal{B}$ within one layer is equal to the hyperedge of the largest degree (within that layer). Indeed, all hyperedge endpoints within one layer have to be labeled differently, but otherwise the same labels may be reused without constraint. Globally, the hyperedge of the largest degree within one layer is a lower bound for the number of buses.

Labeling the TCG allows a formal exploration of the transfer-to-bus assignment possibilities. Several labeling solutions with the same number of buses are possible for a single TCG. These can be evaluated by constructing the resulting interconnection netlists and then estimating and comparing their cost (see section 2.3).

2.2 Transfer-to-port assignment

The transfer-to-bus assignment determines to which buses each memory should be connected, but this does not necessarily imply that all ports of a multiport memory must be connected to all of these. The transfer-to-port assignment step exploits this, within the constraints of the conflicts between transfers and the different types of ports (read, write, read/write). The conflict information is represented by an *Access Conflict Graph (ACG)*, which contains the *conflicts* (edges) between the application's memory *accesses* (nodes). For each multiport memory, an ACG is constructed and subsequently labeled. Figure 2(c) shows the ACG for the multiport memory mem 1 and figure 2(d) for mem 2.

Accesses are derived from transfers: each transfer T_p defines two accesses, a read access A_p^r at its source, a write access A_p^w at its sink. In figure 2(c) and 2(d), these are indicated with the numbers of the corresponding transfer. The ACG contains hyperedges for conflicting accesses, which are taken over from the TCG: $E'_M = \{A_p^r | \text{source}(T_p) = M \wedge T_p \in E\} \cup \{A_p^w | \text{sink}(T_p) = M \wedge T_p \in E\}$. The bus labels at the edge ends are taken over as well.

With the ACG model, any port assignment decision can be represented by labeling every hyperedge endpoint of the ACG with the port which will be used for its adjacent access: $\pi(E'_M, A^r_p) \in \mathcal{P}^r_M$, where $\mathcal{P}^r_M$ is the set of available read and read/write ports on memory M; accesses also need a label at points in time when they are not in conflict: $\pi(0, A^r_p) \in \mathcal{P}^r_M$. Similarly for write and read/write ports: $\pi(E'_M, A^w_p) \in \mathcal{P}^w_M$. A labeling is valid only if all endpoints of a hyperedge have a different label: $\forall E'_M : \forall A^x_p, A^y_q \in E'_M : \pi(E'_M, A^x_p) \neq \pi(E'_M, A^y_q)$. This allows a formal exploration of the port assignment possibilities. Several labeling solutions are possible for a single ACG. To select the best possibility, they are passed to the netlist construction (together with the labeled TCG), were a cost analysis will be made.

2.3 Netlist construction

The labeled TCG is an abstract representation of the transfer-to-bus assignment decisions and the labeled ACGs are abstract representations of the transfer-to-port assignment decisions. However, the goal of these assignments was to make sure the bus architecture meets the real time constraints. Therefore, the labeled TCG and ACGs have to be translated to a list of connections between memory ports and buses. Based on this interconnection netlist, also the cost-efficiency of the bus architecture is evaluated.

The interconnection netlist is constructed by the following four steps. First, a bus is created for every label used in the TCG. Second, switches are introduced for every pair of buses for which there exists a pair of hyperedge endpoints that are labeled with those buses, that originate from the same endpoint before transfer splitting, and that are adjacent to transfers with the same connection point as destination. Thus, the set of switches is $\mathcal{S} = \{(A,B) \in \mathcal{B}^2 | A \neq B \wedge \exists E, T_p, a : A = \lambda(E_s, T_{p,a}) \wedge B = \lambda(E_s, T_{p,a+1})\}$. Third, for every memory port, the buses it connects to are determined by combining all the labels on the edge endpoints of the transfers and accesses from or to that memory. This is done for the two directions separately. The set of port-to-bus connections for memory M is $\mathcal{C}^r_M = \{(P,A) \in \mathcal{P}^r_M \times \mathcal{B} | \exists E, T_p : \text{source}(T_p) = M \wedge \lambda(E_s, T_{p,1}) = A \wedge \pi(E'_M, A^r_p) = P\}$. The set of bus-to-port connections for memory M is $\mathcal{C}^w_M = \{(P,A) \in \mathcal{P}^w_M \times \mathcal{B} | \exists E, T_p : \text{sink}(T_p) = M \wedge \lambda(E_s, T_{p,d(T_p)}) = A \wedge \pi(E'_M, A^w_p) = P\}$. Selection logic is introduced here. It can take the form of tristate buffers, (de)multiplexers, crossbar switches, etc. The subsequent data path synthesis stage should choose the implementation of this selection logic and its control circuitry. The final step removes redundant connections due to switches. Although a switch is introduced for multiboundary transfers, also other transfers can make use of them if this saves connection logic. This occurs when a memory is connected to both buses connected by the switch. In this case, one of the connections can be removed.

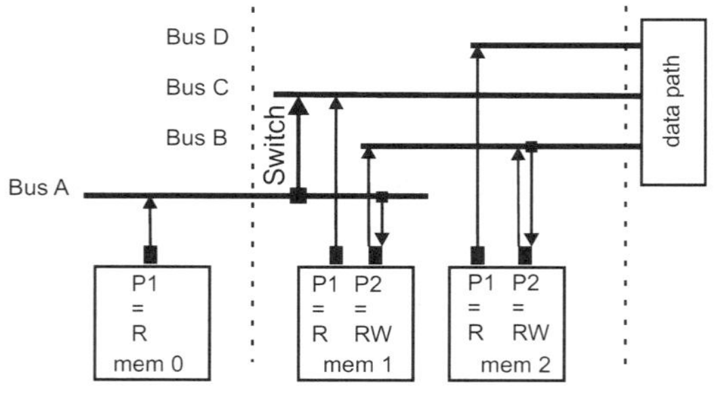

Figure 3: Netlist with four buses and a switch, corresponding to labeled TCG and ACGs of figure 2

Figure 3 shows the resulting netlist for the labeled TCG of figure 2(b). First, global buses A, B, C and D are created. Second, a switch is introduced because transfer 1a and transfer 1b are labeled with bus A and bus C in the same hyperedge. Third, connections are made between the memory ports and the buses according to the labels in figure 2(b), 2(c) and 2(d).

To distinguish different assignments a high-level cost estimation is used. The complexity of the selection logic is estimated based on bitwidth and direction of the connections between buses and ports and of the switches. Area and power estimations are based on the amount of memories a bus connects, the widest transfer a bus has to transport and the toggle activity of bits passing a bus.

3. REAL-LIFE APPLICATION RESULTS

The different steps in the bus sharing methodology as described in section 2 are implemented in a tool to automate the process. Possible transfer-to-bus and transfer-to-port assignment possibilities are explored and they are compared using the cost estimation functions. The complexity of finding the optimal bus architecture is very high. Therefore, we have developed heuristics to reduce the search space. They are based on the branch-and-bound approach, but where the bound is a preliminary estimate of the global cost based on a partial solution. The details fall outside the scope of this paper however. Note that the minimum amount of buses (cfr. the end of section 2.1) is always found, only the number of bus-to-port connections may be suboptimal.

We have applied the bus sharing tool on several small examples and also on two applications of industrial relevance. One is from the multimedia domain, the Binary Tree Predictive Coding (BTPC) encoder (section 3.1), the other from the telecommunication domain, the Digital Audio Broadcasting (DAB) receiver (section 3.2).

3.1 Binary Tree Predictive Coding (BTPC)

Binary Tree Predictive Coding (BTPC) [11] is a lossless or lossy image compression algorithm based on multiresolution. The application consists of a number of nested loops. In a preceding stage, the memory bandwidth requirements were analyzed and a custom memory architecture was derived [16]. The result of the bandwidth requirement analysis is a set of conflicts between the data transfers. These conflicts are then used as a restriction on the freedom for the custom memory architecture. Finally, the memory architecture shown in figure 4(a) was developed. It contains a large off-chip memory, two dual-port memories for the arrays which are accessed very frequently, and two further on-chip (read-only) memories for the other arrays, to minimize power consumption. The memory hierarchy contains layers, with copies from the off-chip memory to two of the on-chip local memories.

Without time-multiplexing of the memory buses, seven buses would be required for this application: one for every port in the memory architecture. Also, one port of memories mem 1 and mem 2 would be connected to the global bus to mem off, to allow the memory-to-memory copies. Such an architecture requires 60 global wires for the data bits, and 2 additional control lines for selecting which memory accesses the global bus to mem off. A total of 48 tristate buffers would be required to connect the memories with the bidirectional buses. In an ad hoc approach to time-multiplex some of these buses, one would be able to share some buses, taking into account the real time constrains. One could eventually arrive to a similar solution as the one found by our approach, but only after many lengthy iterations through high-level synthesis.

Based on the partial ordering from the storage bandwidth optimization stage, a TCG is constructed for the BTPC, as shown in figure 4(b). Based on this TCG, transfer-to-bus assignment alter-

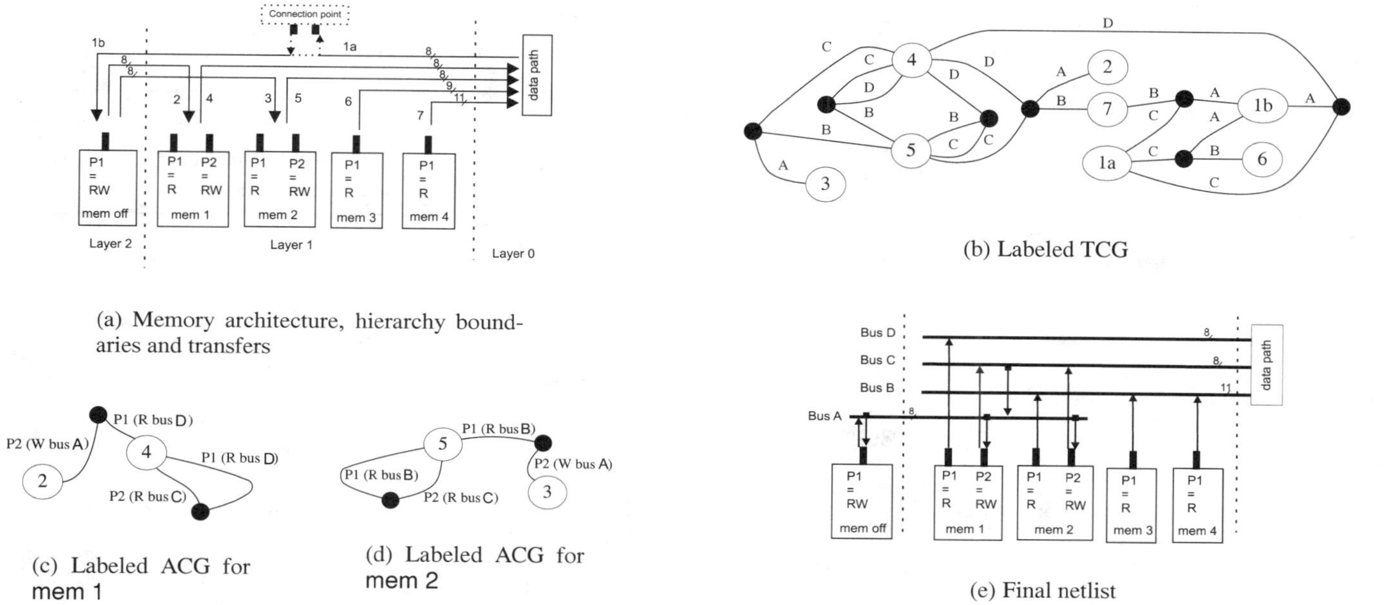

(a) Memory architecture, hierarchy boundaries and transfers

(b) Labeled TCG

(c) Labeled ACG for mem 1

(d) Labeled ACG for mem 2

(e) Final netlist

Figure 4: Bus sharing for the BTPC application

natives are explored by labeling the graph. Now, the real time constraints will surely be met, because no two transfers are assigned to the same bus when they are in conflict. Then the transfer-to-port assignment alternatives are explored. Finally, the tool has found the labeling indicated in the TCG (figure 4(b)) and ACGs (figures 4(c) and 4(d)) to lead to the lowest cost.

The netlist resulting from the labeled TCG is shown in figure 4(e). The number of global buses is reduced from the original seven to only one on the first layer boundary and three on the second layer boundary. A switch is required for this, to allow transfers 2, 4, 5 and 7 to go in parallel while also creating a path for transfer 1. Now, only 35 data wires in total are present in the memory interconnect architecture, and one extra control wire is needed to steer the switch. This means an overall reduction of more than 40% in the number of global wires. In addition, bus A is much shorter than the original bus needed to connect mem off to the data path, so the total wirelength decreased even more. Bus B is a shared bus, but only unidirectional access from the memories to the data path is needed. Bus D is not a shared bus, but simply a unidirectional point-to-point connection.

The penalty of time-multiplexing the global buses is the introduction of extra logic to select which bus to use for every access. We evaluate this penalty by counting the number of tristate buffers required to connect memory ports to buses. The shared bus architecture requires 92 tristate buffers (including what is required for the switch), compared to the original 48, or an overhead of almost a factor of 2. This area overhead from tiny tristate buffers is however completely compensated by the huge savings from sharing the buses.

3.2 Digital Audio Broadcasting (DAB)

A second application for our bus sharing experiments is a receiver for Digital Audio Broadcasting [8]. It decodes raw antenna data into a bitstream. The architecture can be split in three parts: a demodulator (including input processing and a high speed FFT processor), a deinterleaver, and a Viterbi decoder. To achieve real time operation and a power-efficient data storage, an optimized distributed memory architecture was derived for this application. Eight memories are needed to minimize power consumption and to meet the memory bandwidth requirements. There is no hierarchy in this application, each memory is simply connected to the datapath. Six memories have read and write transfers, the last two are read-only.

Such a heavily distributed memory architecture exposes many opportunities for sharing the memory buses. The TCG that comes out of the partial ordering step is shown in figure 5(a). Indeed, although there are many conflicts in this graph, the maximum hyperedge is only of degree 3. Therefore, the number of buses can be reduced to three. The bus sharing tool labeled the TCG, resulting in the netlist shown in figure 5(b). Note that the memory architecture for the DAB contains no multiport memories, so no ACGs need to be labeled.

Applying the bus sharing approach yields a reduction in the number of global data wires from 172 lines to only 96 lines. An additional overhead of 3 control wires is needed. This means an overall reduction in the number of global wires of about 40%. To achieve this, the original amount of 280 tristate buffers have increased to 424 (50% overhead).

4. CONCLUSIONS

Hierarchical, distributed memory organizations provide parallelism in the data transfers and drastic reductions in the power consumption. However, their interconnection architecture may incur a large overhead if not carefully designed. Therefore, we exploit the opportunities which exist at the system level to time-multiplex the data transfers over the memory buses. In this paper, we propose a system level technique to optimize the connectivity between memory ports and global buses. It supports multiport memories, switches in the interconnect architecture, and memory-to-memory copies. It is based on system-level constraints on the memory bandwidth, not on detailed scheduling of foreground operations. The effectiveness of our prototype tool is demonstrated on two real-life data intensive applications for which a custom memory organiza-

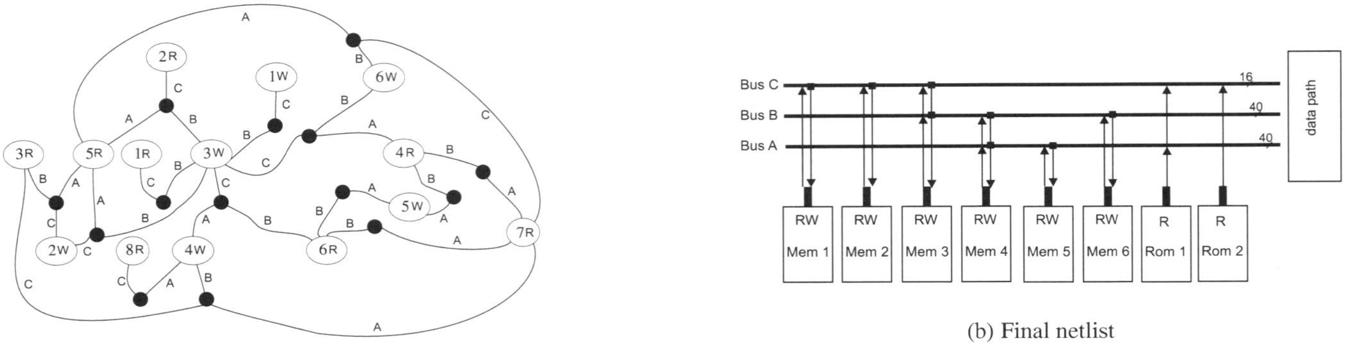

(b) Final netlist

(a) Labeled TCG

Figure 5: Bus sharing for the DAB application

tion was designed. More than one third is gained in terms of number of global wires, including control wires. Although the tool's run-time is already reasonable, with improved heuristics the approach can be applied to even larger designs.

Our approach can be extended to also support the global interconnections between other blocks in the system, for example communicating processor cores. Also it can be applied in a context of a predefined platform with a reconfigurable interconnect architecture. Our future focus lies in these directions.

5. REFERENCES

[1] M. Balakrishnan, A. K. Majumdar, D. K. Banerji, J. G. Linders, and J. C. Majithia. Allocation of multiport memories in data path synthesis. *IEEE Trans. on Comp. Aided Design*, CAD-7(4):536–540, Apr. 1988.

[2] F. Catthoor, S. Wuytack, E. De Greef, F. Balasa, L. Nachtergaele, and A. Vandecappelle. *Custom Memory Management Methodology, Exploration of memory organization for embedded multimedia system design*. Kluwer Academic Publ., Boston, MA, 1998.

[3] D. Filo, D. Ku, C. Coelho Jr., and G. De Micheli. Interface optimization for concurrent systems under timing constraints. *IEEE Trans. on VLSI Systems*, 1(3):268–281, Sept. 1993.

[4] C.-T. Hsieh and M. Pedram. Architectural power optimization by bus splitting. In *3rd ACM/IEEE Design and Test in Europe Conf.*, pages 612–616, Paris, France, Mar. 2000.

[5] Y.-M. Jiang, T.-F. Lee, T. Hwang, and Y.-L. Lin. Performance-driven interconnection optimization for microarchitecture synthesis. *IEEE Trans. on Comp. Aided Design*, 13(2):137–149, 1994.

[6] W. Koh, A. Yeung, P. Hoang, and J. M. Rabaey. A configurable multiprocessor system for DSP behavioral simulation. In *Proc. IEEE Int. Symp. on Circuits and Systems*, pages 1403–1406, New York, NY, 1989.

[7] P. Lippens, J. van Meerbergen, W. Verhaegh, and A. van der Werf. Allocation of multiport memories for hierarchical data streams. In *Proc. IEEE Int. Conf. Comp. Aided Design*, Santa Clara, CA, Nov. 1993.

[8] P. Lippens, W. Baetens, E. Brockmeyer, N. Busa, F. Catthoor, J. Huisken, and R. Peset-Llopis. Power optimisation and analysis of a Digital Audio Broadcast (DAB) reciever. In *3rd Intnl. Wsh. of the Europ. Low Power Initiative for Elec. System Design*, pages 265–298, Rapallo, Italy, July 2000.

[9] L. Ramachandran, D. D. Gajski, and V. Chaiyakul. An algorithm for array variable clustering. In *Proc. 5th ACM/IEEE Europ. Design and Test Conf.*, pages 262–266, Paris, France, Feb. 1994.

[10] C. P. Ravikumar, R. Aggarwal, and C. Sharma. A graph-theoretic approach for register file based synthesis. In *Proc. 10th Int. Conf. on VLSI Design*, pages 118–123, 1997.

[11] J. Robinson. Efficient general-purpose image compression with binary tree predictive coding. *IEEE Trans. on Image Processing*, 6(4):601–608, Apr. 1997.

[12] W.-T. Shiue, S. Tadas, and C. Chakrabarti. Low power multi-module, multi-port memory design for embeddes systems. In *Proc. IEEE Wsh. on Signal Processing Systems (SIPS)*, pages 529–538, Lafayette, LA, Oct. 2000. IEEE Press.

[13] L. Stok. Data path synthesis. *Integration, the VLSI journal*, 18:1–71, June 1994.

[14] D. Sylvester and K. Keutzer. Getting to the bottom of deep submicron. In *Proc. IEEE Int. Conf. Comp. Aided Design*, pages 203–211, San Jose, CA, Nov. 1998.

[15] A. Timmer, F. Harmsze, J. Leijten, M. Strik, and J. van Meerbergen. Guaranteeing on- and off-chip communication in embedded systems. In *Proc. IEEE CS Annual Workshop on VLSI*, pages 93–98, Orlando, FL, Apr. 1999.

[16] A. Vandecappelle, M. Miranda, E. Brockmeyer, D. Verkest, and F. Catthoor. Global multimedia system design exploration using accurate memory organization feedback. In *Proc. 36th ACM/IEEE Design Automation Conf.*, pages 327–332, New Orleans, jun 1999.

[17] S. Wuytack, F. Catthoor, G. de Jong, and H. De Man. Minimizing the required memory bandwidth in VLSI system realizations. *IEEE Trans. on VLSI Systems*, 7(4):433–441, Dec. 1999.

An Optimal Memory Allocation for Application-Specific Multiprocessor System-on-Chip

Samy Meftali Ferid Gharsalli Frederic Rousseau Ahmed A. Jerraya

TIMA laboratory, 46 av. Felix Viallet 38031 Grenoble cedex (France)
Tel : (00 33) 4 76 57 46 41
{samy.meftali, ferid.gharsalli, frederic.rousseau, ahmed.jerraya}@imag.fr

ABSTRACT

In this paper, we present a novel and systematic approach for the design of shared memory architectures in the case of application-specific multiprocessor system-on-chip. This paper focuses on a memory allocation step which is based on an integer linear programming model. It permits to obtain an optimal distributed shared memory architecture minimizing the global cost to access the shared data in the application, and the memory cost. Our approach allows automatic generation of an architecture-level specification of the application. The effectiveness of this approach is illustrated by a packet routing switch example.

General Terms

Design.

Keywords

Multiprocessor SoC, shared memory, abstraction levels, memory allocation, integer linear programming, code transformation.

1. INTRODUCTION

The design of modern digital systems is influenced by technological and market trends, including the ability to produce ever more complex chips (capacity of embedding DRAMs with logic on the same chip, SoC with 200 million gates...) but with increasingly shorter time-to-market.

Time-to-market considerations have driven the need for automation in the embedded systems-on-chip (SoC) design industry. Although a completely manual approach relying on an expert designer's intuition helps reduce chip area and improve performances and power metrics, The time spent by a human designer to optimize the complex chips designed today is prohibitively high, and the manual approach becomes impractical. This is why, most application-specific systems rely on the use of Computer Aided Design (CAD) tools that generate the electronic circuitry from a high-level description of the SoC [15].

In embedded systems the memory architecture can be chosen more or less freely, it is only constrained by the application requirements. Different choices can lead to solutions with a very different cost, which means that it is important to make the right choice. For this reason, the allocation of the memory blocs a major steps in the SoC design flow.

The goal of the memory allocation and assignment is to make use of the memory architecture freedom to minimize the cost related to background memory storage and transfers.

Many applications in fields such as multi-media (audio and video) and image processing handle bulky and strongly dependent data. They consequently require the integration of a great number of memories of various types (local private, local distributed and on-chip global shared memory). Moreover, up to 70% of the chip area is dedicated to memory. Unfortunately, nowadays, there is not a complete and automatic method allowing designers to integrate all these memory types (particularly the shared memory) in the SoC from a high abstraction level.

Our objective is to provide designers with a global and fast method as well as tools to design these systems in order to meet the time-to-market constraints. We use a generic memory architecture and in this paper we focus on the memory allocation problem. We propose an optimal approach to resolve this problem minimizing the memory architecture area and the global time of accesses to the shared data of the application. Actually, multiprocessor SoCs integrate more and more elements, and the description of such systems at the architecture level can reach 200K lines of code (SystemC, C, VHDL). Therefore, we propose in our memory design flow a stage of automatic application-code transformation taking into account the chosen memory architecture, which is very beneficial to the designers from the time-to-market point of view.

This paper is organized as follows: in Section 2, we give a review of several previous works on memory architecture system design. In Section 3, we present our multiprocessor system design methodology and our memory design flow. Section 4 describes the allocation of data in memory and code transformations required when a shared memory is added. Allocation and code transformations are detailed on an application in Section 5. We conclude this paper in Section 6.

2. PREVIOUS WORK AND CONTRIBUTION

We have found a lot of works concerning memory integration and optimization in the field of single or multiprocessor system design. Some of them deal with memory allocation.

In this work we only deal with SoC. These are different from classic general purpose architectures [6] because they target a specific application. Which makes the memory architecture and the communication network specific to the application and then simpler. For instance in most of these applications data regularity is quite trivial or non existing and thus no sophisticated data cache is required.

Since 1989, IMEC has worked on the DTSE (Data Transfer and Storage Exploration) methodology [4, 5, 7]. This approach concerns real-time data-flow applications such as multimedia ones. The main goal is to optimize area and power consumption, by trying to find the best memory architecture. Starting from a specific graph representing data access conflicts, they produce memory allocation (number of memories, type of each memory), data memory assignment and connections). Depending on the memory type, some code transformations must be made. This approach seems efficient for single processor architectures with specific hardware parts. It uses the knowledge of low level characteristics of memories. Memory design is performed at the end of system design flow.

In Princeton, they published a hardware/software synthesis algorithm [12, 13] to optimize cache hierarchy size for periodic real time systems. The target architecture being multiprocessor, this algorithm synthesizes tasks on processors, and tries to optimize cache size. A lot of other works focus on cache optimization [15, 18] for a given application.

In the last few years, we saw a lot of research groups working on the definition of systems with distributed shared memories [16], different methods which permit to implement the DSM concepts [2][11] and some solutions for consistency problem [1]. These works have a major importance because they treat all the aspects related to the distributed. shared memories. Unfortunately, they do not treat the automatic integration of these memory architectures in multiprocessor system-on-chip design flow. Still, the distributed shared memories were not yet integrated in automatic tools.

The contribution of our work is a full systematic approach allowing an optimal distributed shared memory allocation for application-specific SoCs, and automatic architecture-level application-code generation.

3. INTEGRATING SHARED MEMORY INTO THE SOC MULTIPROCESSOR DESIGN FLOW

The methodology and tools we developed to design multiprocessor SoCs are described in [3, 14]. System design starts with the system specification of a given application with system level communication (written in SystemC for example) and an abstract multiprocessor architecture (Figure 1).

Processors and communication components are allocated, and system behavior and communication (ports and channels) are mapped/scheduled on processors and communication components of the architecture template (by the designer). After the allocation/mapping /scheduling step, we obtain a system specification at the architecture-level.

For each processor, the software code (Operating System and application code of tasks) is generated [8]. Interfaces between processors and the communication network are also generated [14]. We obtain the micro-architecture of the system, as shown in Figure 1.

The choice of the processor was based on availability (only ARM7 and MC68K processors), and the communication network is a point-to-point network. Designers can modify some parameters such as the number of CPUs, the memory size and I/O ports for each processor, the interconnection between processors, the communication protocols and the external connections (peripherals).

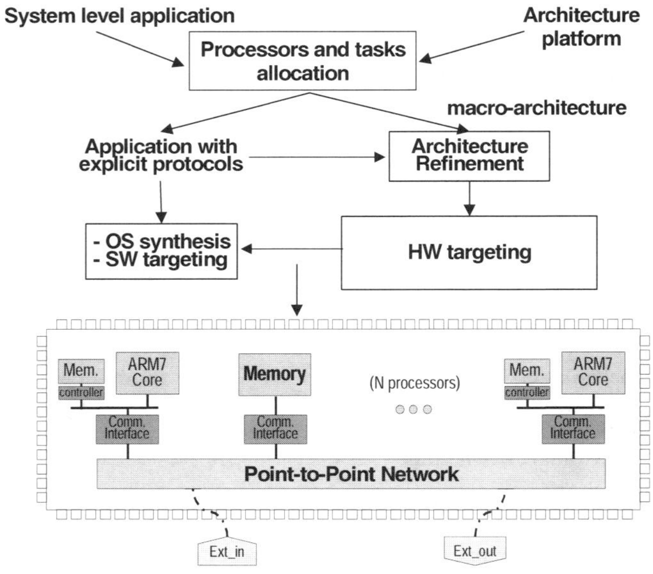

Figure 1. Our design flow

3.2. How to integrate shared memory

Typical applications using shared memory are signal, data, and image processing, multimedia, and all distributed applications dealing with a large amount of data.

In the design methodology presented before, each processor is connected to the communication network by an interface. In such a system, processors have their own local memory and to share data, processors need to send data to the others via interfaces. Our idea is to allow designers to insert shared memory in the platform architecture (Figure 1) as an IP. This means that an interface is introduced between the communication network and the memory. This interface is both a protocol adapter and a memory controller.

If we introduce shared memory, the application code requires some transformations. For example, suppose that a variable A is assigned to the shared memory, the instruction B = A in the original application code is transformed into B = readmem(Mem_name, @A, size_of(A)). Actually, we assume that the application designer takes charge of the consistency problems by the synchronization at the system-level.

3.3. Memory design flow description

Our memory design flow is presented in. Starting from a system level specification and an architecture model, we suppose that processors and tasks allocation is done by the designer. The first step is to decide if the application needs a shared memory. It is the memory allocation step.

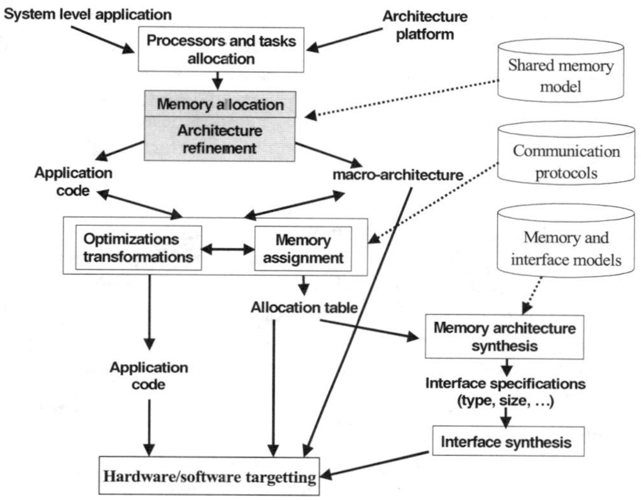

Figure 2. Our memory design flow

The architecture refinement is performed to insert this shared memory. We obtain an architecture with interconnected processors, IPs and memories. The application code may be transformed if necessary. This memory allocation is described in section 4.

The next step is memory assignment. We have to decide the best address for each data in the shared memory. For data in local memory, we let compilers do this work. We have two main objectives: reducing memory size and improving performances using fast memory accesses such as burst mode in SDRAM. This assignment is done simultaneously with the application code transformations and optimizations to take into account memory characteristics. The output of this assignment step is a new application code and an allocation table in which each variable is assigned to one memory (and one address for each variable in the shared memory).

Memory synthesis consists of using existing memory blocs from a library. Then, we could define the interface specification to generate the interface between memory and communication network.

Hardware/software targeting consists of the generation of interfaces from processors and communication network, and software generation (operating system and adapted application code) [8].

4. MEMORY ALLOCATION STEP

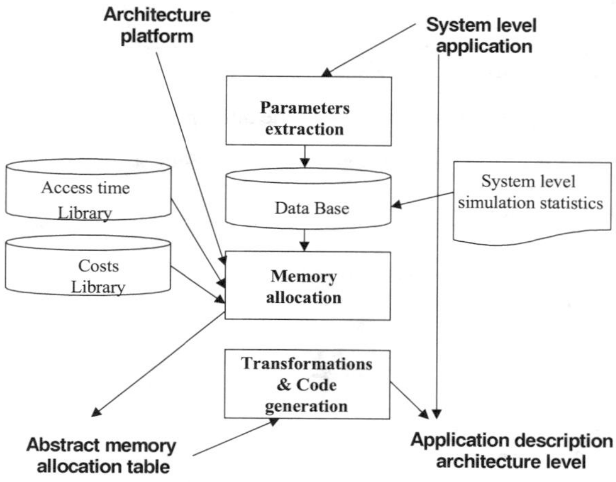

Figure 3. Memory allocation and code generation flow

Our memory allocation flow (Figure 3) takes as input a system level specification of the application (after processor allocation), a generic architecture model and libraries containing the estimated access time of each processor to memories and memory costs. This flow is mainly composed of three parts. The first consists in extracting parameters from the application code. The second carries out the memory allocation using an integer linear program (generated automatically). The third reads/writes primitives of the shared data in the application code (taking into account the memory allocation results), and generates an architecture-level description of the application. These three parts will be detailed in this section.

4.1. Parameter extraction

This stage consists in extracting from the system level description of the application some information about the handled data, such as their names, sizes (types) and the use of the communication channels (for each communication channel connecting two processors, we determine the variables exchanged through this channel).

4.2. Allocation

Using the parameters extracted in the previous step and the results of the system-level simulation of the application, we generate automatically an integer linear program. This program gives an exact solution for the memory blocs allocation minimizing the memory cost and the global time to access the shared data in the application as follows.

The objective function "F" consists in minimizing the total access time (reading and writing) of the processors accessing the shared data ((1), (2))+ Costs due to the memories sizes and to their integration in the system ((3)).

"F" has to be minimized subject to the following constraints:

The sum of data sizes assigned to the memory k has to be smaller or equal to the size of the memory k. This constraint allows us to compute the memory sizes (4).

If the memory k is not included in the architecture, its size must be equal to zero (5).

If the memory k is included in the architecture, its size must be bigger than zero (6).

Each variable must be assigned to one and only one memory (7).

The variables X_{kj} & Y_k are binary; TM_k are integer.

Thus, we obtain:

$$(1) \quad \text{Min } F = \sum_{i=1}^{p} \sum_{j=1}^{v} nb\_read(i,j) \sum_{k=1}^{m} T\_read(i,k) X_{kj} +$$

$$(2) \quad \sum_{i=1}^{p} \sum_{j=1}^{v} nb\_write(i,j) \sum_{k=1}^{m} T\_write(i,k) X_{kj} +$$

$$(3) \quad \sum_{k=1}^{m} CBM_k TM_k + \sum_{k=1}^{m} CUM_k Y_k$$

Subject to:

$$(4) \quad \sum_{j=1}^{v} Taille\_var(j) X_{jk} \le TM_k \qquad k = 1,..,m$$

$$(5) \quad TM_k \le AY_k \qquad k = 1,..,m \qquad A >>> 0$$

$$(6) \quad TM_k \ge AY_k - A + 1 \qquad k = 1,..,m$$

$$(7) \quad \sum_{k \in S_j} X_{kj} = 1 \qquad j = 1,..,v$$

$$(8) \quad X_{jk} \in \{0,1\} \qquad j = 1,..,v \quad \text{et} \quad k = 1,..,m$$

$$(9) \quad Y_k \in \{0,1\} \quad \text{and} \quad TM_k \in N \qquad k = 1,..,m$$

- P = number of processors; V = number of variables

- M = number of memories (<= P+1); TM_k = size of the memory k

- S_j = set of indexes of memories associated with processors using the data j, plus the index of the shared memory

- X_{jk} = 1 if and only if the variable j is assigned to the memory k

- Y_k = 1 if and only if the memory k is integrated to the architecture

- Nb_read(i,j) (resp. Nb_write(i,j)) = the number of processor i's read (resp. write) accesses to the variable j (obtained by a system level simulation)

- T_read(i,k) (resp. T_write(i,k)) = estimated read (resp. write) access time of the processor i to the memory k

- Taille_var(j) = size of the variable j

- CBM_k (resp. CUM_k) is the cost due to the memory k's size (resp. average cost of the integration of the memory k in the architecture).

Model complexity

For a problem instence we obtain:

- at least $[(P + 1).V]^a + [P + 1]^b + [P + 1]^c = (P + 1)(V + 2)$ variables.

With:

a = number of X_{jk} variables,

b = number of Y_k variables,

c = number of TM_k variables.

- NB_constraintes = (P + 1) + (P + 1) + (P + 1) + V constraintes

Note that in the computation of the number of variables we supposed that each one of the V shared data is used by all the processors, this is still very theorical. In real applications that we know the NB_Variables tends generally to (P + 1) (V + 2)/2.

4.3. Code transformation

This third module avoids the boring and error prone task of analyzing all the application description files in order to insert the shared memory module, and to carry out the necessary code modifications. Indeed, it rewrites the application description at the architecture level and adds a new module which is the shared memory and its controller. All the read and write operations on the shared data are changed by explicit read/write primitives on the shared memory.

4.4. Libraries

The flexibility of any tool is defined by the set of parameters (inputs) that one can modify more or less easily. Thus, our tool takes certain parameters, such as processor types and their memory access models, provided in the form of libraries in order to make it easy to modify them. To add a new type of processor, it is enough to have an estimation of its access times with different memory types. The contents of the libraries are described below.

-Library of access time: it contains access time to different memory types (local private, local distributed, global shared) for each type of processor (currently MC68k and ARM7). These access times can be both at a functional level or at RT level (taking into account the specificity of our operating system and interfaces), offering to the designer a great memory architecture exploration space. These access time depend mainly on processor connetions to the communication network [14] and the processor specific operating system [8]. To integrate another processor to the library, we have only to estimate its read/write operations times to memories.

-Memories library: it defines the designer restrictions on the memory types which we would or not include in the architecture (local distributed and global shared memory). This library contains also the average cost of the integration of each type of memory in the architecture (Figure 1) as well as the average cost according to the memory size. We take the memory size cost as the average SDRAM price /size. The cost of the memory integration into the architecture is just based on the performances estimations of the RT level designer. The precision of these cost estimations does not at all affect the model performances, because they are only used to allow the model to choose between different memory types and not to give the real cost of the memory architecture.

5. APPLICATION

In order to illustrate the efficiency of the proposed memory allocation and code generation method, we detail in this section the flow steps on a packet routing switch [10].

It constitutes a powerful solution for large-frame or cell-switching systems. The version we present here consists of two input controllers and two output controllers. Each of the controllers handles one communication channel. The communication links between input and output controllers are configured by an external signal to be direct or switched. Figure 4 shows the block diagram of the packet routing switch.

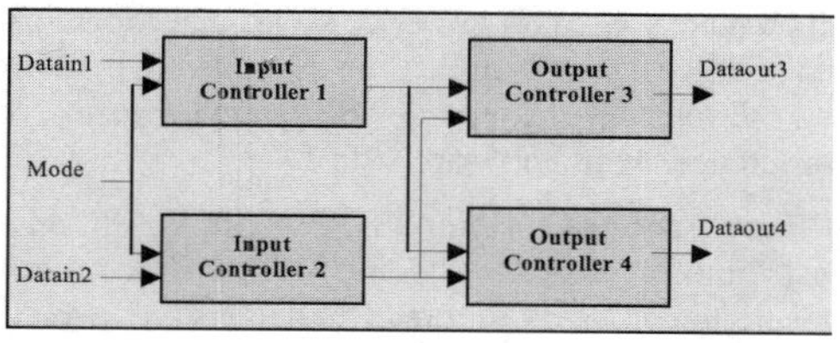

Figure 4. Block diagram of the packet routing switch

5.1. Communication between processors

At the system level, the data exchange between the processors is made in a direct way. Indeed on the external signal (mode = 1), the controller Ctrl1 (Figure 4) sends the data "X" directly to the controller Ctrl3. The latter, receives directly the data "X" on the channel which connects it to Ctrl1. This application was described in SystemC (version 0.9).

```
//Implementation of Ctrl1//

void ctrl1 ::entry()
 {
       ...
if( ordre.read()==true)
{
dataCtrl1_C3C4.write(x);
signalCtrl1_C3.write(true);
```

```
/Implementation of   Ctrl 3 //

void ctrl3 ::entry()
 {
       ...
if (sig_Ctrl1_C3.read()==true)
{
 y = dataCtrl1_C3C4.read()     ;
 output3.write(y)  ;
```

Figure 5. Communication between Ctrl1 and Ctrl3

5.2. Parameters extraction

Size	Name	Processors
100*int	data1	Ctrl1, Ctrl3, Ctrl4
100*int	data2	Ctrl2, Ctrl3, Ctrl4

Figure 6. Information extracted from the system level description

This information (Figure 6) is extracted primarily from the system-level application-code. In this example, data1 used by processors Ctrl1, Ctrl3 and Ctrl4 (resp. data2 data1 used by processors Ctrl2, Ctrl3 and Ctrl4) corresponds to the instantiation of the signal dataCtrl1_C3C4 (resp. dataCtrl2_C3C4).

5.3. Linear program resolution

We associate one boolean variable for each pair (shared signal - memory or shared variable - memory) Actually, data1 is used by Ctrl1, Ctrl3 and Ctrl4, so the X1i variables, where i={1,3,4} correspond to the local distributed memories of respectively Ctrl1, Ctrl3 and Ctrl4 and X15 to the global shared memory. In the same way, we define the variables which correspond to the signal data2.

So, for 4 local distributed memories, one global memory and 2 shared data we obtain 9 boolean variables and 3 integer ones.

5.4. Application code generation

This stage modifies the application code by taking into account the linear program results. These modifications are primarily related to the processors accesses to shared memory (Figure 7). Indeed, processor Ctrl1 writes the data " X " in the global shared memory and processor Ctrl3 reads the data from the shared memory.

```
//Implementation of Ctrl1//

void ctrl1 ::entry()
 {
       ...
if( ordre.read()==true)
{
dataCtrl1_mem.write(x);
signalCtrl1_C3.write(true);
       ...
```

```
/Implementation of Ctrl 3 //

void ctrl3 ::entry()
 {
       ...
if (sig_Ctrl1_C3.read()==true)
 {
y = sig_mem3_out.read()
output3.write(y)     ;
       ...
```

Figure 7. Communication between Ctrl1 and Ctrl2 using a global shared memory.

At this step a shared memory module is generated and automatically integrated into the application description (Figure 8).

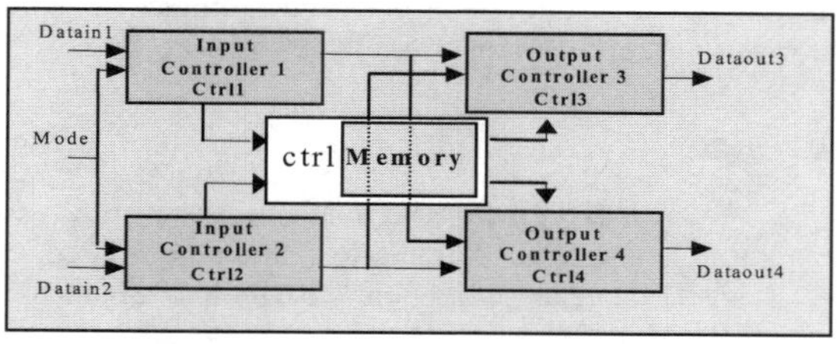

Figure 8. Packet routing switch description at architecture level.

5.5. Analysis

This application was described at the functional level mainly in 4 interface files and 4 implementation files. Automatic refinement adds to the specification 4 files (2 interfaces and 2 implementations) corresponding to the memory body and to the memory's controller (200 lines at the functional level). The interfaces of the 4 processors were modified automatically in order to connect them to the global shared memory, and all the accesses to the data stocked in this memory were modified (Figure 8). Then, we obtained the application code at the architecture-level with a shared memory architecture in a complete automatic way.

The modeling of the memory allocation problem by an integer linear programming approach presents some major advantages as:

- it is an exact method, which contrary to the heuristic based methods, gives an optimal solution,

- it is a very generic model which allows the integration of all the memory types (local private, local distributed and global shared memories) in the architecture,

- it resolves two problems: allocation of the memory blocs, and the data assignation into these blocs,

- there are many available tools which permit the resolution of such a model.

Since some variables in our model are boolean, the resolution step can be slow depending on the number of such variables. So, for the applications integrating lot of processors, we recommend the use of stochastic methods instead of the linear model.

Our future works will consist of the development of algorithms allowing the optimization of the variables placement in a given memory and the automatic interface generation. These algorithms will have to take into account the physical characteristics of the memories and the access modes.

6. CONCLUSION

In this paper, we presented an automatic application-specific shared memory architecture design flow, starting from a parallel system-level description of a given application. We use an exact method to resolve the memory allocation problem for the fixed criteria (total access time to the shared data and the cost of the memory architecture). The proposed methodology permits a systematic generation of generic memory architecture for multiprocessor embedded SoC, from a high abstraction level distributed specification of the application. We use the results of our linear model resolution to carry out automatically the code transformations corresponding to this new architecture.

References

[1] S.V Adve, V.S Pai, P. Ranganathan, "Recent Advances in Memory Consistency Models for Hardware Shared Memory Systems", Special issue on distributed Shared-Memory Systems, Mars 1999.

[2] C. Amza, A. Cox, S. Dwarkadas, L. Jin & al, "Adaptive Protocols for Software Distributed Shared Memory", Special issue on distributed Shared-Memory Systems, Mars 1999.

[3] A. Baghdadi, D. Lyonnard, N-E. Zergainoh, A.A. Jerraya, "An Efficient Architecture Model for Systematic Design of Application-Specific Multiprocessor SoC", Proc. of DATE 2001, Mar 2001.

[4] F. Cathoor & al, Custom Memory Management Methodology, Kluwer Academic Publishers, 1998.

[5] F. Cathoor, S. Wuytack & al, "System level transformations for low power data transfer and storage", in paper collection "low power CMOS design », IEEE Press, pp.609-618, 1998.

[6] D. Culler, J.P. Singh, A. Gupta, "Parallel computer architecture :A Hardware/Software approach", Maurgan Kauffman publishers, August 1998.

[7] K. Danckaert, F. Cathoor & al, "System-level memory optimization for hardware-software co-design", Proc. of Workshop on hardware/software co-design, Braunschweig, Germany, pp.55-59, March 1997.

[8] L. Gauthier, S. Yoo, A.A. Jerraya, "Automatic Generation and Targeting of Application Specific Operating Systems and Embedded Systems Software", Proc. of DATE conference, Munich, March 2001.

[9] J. Hennessy, M. Heinrich, A. Gupta, "Cache-Coherent Distributed Shared Memory : Perspectives on Its Development and Future Challenges", Special issue on distributed Shared-Memory Systems, March 1999.

[10] IBM, Inc. "28.4G Packet Rooting Switch", Networking Technology Data sheets, http://www.chips.ibm.com/techlib/products/commun/datasheets.html.

[11] H.F. Leung, H.F. Ting, "An Optimal Algorithm for Global Termination Detection in Shared-Memory Asynchronous Multiprocessor Systems", IEEE Transactions on parallel and distributed systems, May 1997.

[12] Y. Li, W. Wolf, "Allocation of Multirate Systems on Multiprocessors with Memory Hierarchy Modeling and Optimization", Proc. of CODES/CASHE '97, Braunschweig, Germany, March, 1997.

[13] Y. Li, W. Wolf, "Hardware/Software Co-Synthesis with Memory Hierarchies", IEEE transaction on computer-aided design of integrated circuit and Systems, October 1999.

[14] D. Lyonnard, S. Yoo, A. Baghdadi, A.A. Jerraya, "Automatic Generation of Application-Specific Architectures for Heterogeneous Multiprocessor System-on-Chip", Proc. of DAC 2001, June 2001, Las Vegas, Nevada, USA.

[15] P. R. Panda, N. Dutt, A. Nicolau, Memory Issues in Embedded Systems-on-chip : Optimization and exploration, Kluwer Academic Publishers, 1999.

[16] J. Protic, M. Tomasevic, V. Milutinovic, "Distributed Shared Memory : Concepts and Systems", IEEE Parallel & Distributed Technology; Summer 1996.

[17] SystemC « user's manual », http://www.systemc.org.

[18] S. Wuytack, J.P. Diguet & al, "Formalized methodology for data reuse exploration for low-power hierarchical memory mapping", IEEE Trans, on VLSI Systems, Vol6, 1998.

APEX: Access Pattern based Memory Architecture Exploration*

Peter Grun
pgrun@cecs.uci.edu

Nikil Dutt
dutt@cecs.uci.edu

Alex Nicolau
nicolau@cecs.uci.edu

Center for Embedded Computer Systems
University of California, Irvine, CA 92697-3425, USA

ABSTRACT

Memory accesses represent a major bottleneck in embedded systems power and performance. Traditionally, designers tried to alleviate this problem by relying on a simple cache hierarchy, or a limited use of special purpose memory modules such as stream buffers. Although real-life applications contain a large number of memory references to a diverse set of data structures, a significant percentage of all memory accesses in the application are generated from a few memory instructions that exhibit predictable, well-known access patterns; this creates an opportunity for memory customization, targeting the needs of these access patterns. We present APEX, an approach that extracts, analyzes and clusters the most active access patterns in the application, and aggressively customizes the memory architecture to match the needs of the application, exploring a wide range of cost, performance and power designs. We use a heuristic to prune the design space, guiding the exploration towards the best cost/gain ratios. We present experiments on a set of large real-life benchmarks, showing significant performance improvements for varied cost and power characteristics, allowing the designer to best target the system goals.

1. INTRODUCTION

In programmable embedded systems, memory represents a major performance and power bottleneck [16]. Traditionally, designers have attempted to improve memory behavior by exploring different cache configurations, with limited use of more special purpose memory modules such as stream buffers [9]. However, while real-life applications contain a large number of memory references to a diverse set of data structures, a significant percentage of all memory accesses in the application are generated from a few instructions in the code. For instance, in Vocoder, a GSM voice coding application with 15K lines of code, 62% of all memory accesses are generated by only 15 instructions. Furthermore, these instructions often exhibit well-known, predictable access patterns. This presents a tremendous opportunity to customize the memory architecture to match the needs of the predominant access patterns in the application, and significantly improve the memory system behavior. .

In the context of disk file systems [14, 15] there have been many approaches to employ the file access pattern to customize the file system to best match the access characteristic of the application. Likewise, many approaches have proposed customizing the processor through special purpose instructions and special functional units to target the predominant computations in embedded applications (such as MAC, FFT, etc.). However, to our knowledge none of the previous approaches have attempted to analyze the memory access patterns information in the application, and use it to aggressively customize the memory architecture. We present here such an approach, where we extract, analyze and cluster the most active memory access patterns in the application, and customize the memory architecture by mixing-and-matching custom memory modules from a library, to explore a wide range of cost, performance and power designs. We use a heuristic to prune the design space of such memory customizations, and guide the search towards the designs with best cost/gain ratios, exploring a space well beyond the one traditionally considered, allowing the designer to efficiently target the system goals.

In Section 2 we present the related work in the area of memory subsystem optimizations. In Section 3 we present the flow of our approach. In Section 4 we use a large real-life example to illustrate our approach and in Section 5 we present an outline of our Access Pattern based Memory Exploration (APEX) approach. In Section 6 we present a set of experiments that demonstrate the customization of the memory architecture for a set of large multimedia and scientific applications, and present exploration results showing the wide range of performance, power and cost tradeoffs obtained.

2. RELATED WORK

There has been related work in four main domains: (I) Disk file systems and databases, (II) High-level synthesis, (III) Computer Architecture, and (IV) Programmable embedded systems.

(I) In the domain of file systems and databases, there have been several approaches to use the file access patterns to improve the file system behavior. Parsons et al. [14] present an approach allowing the application programmer to specify

*This work was partially supported by grants from NSF (MIP-9708067), DARPA (F33615-00-C-1632) and a Motorola fellowship.

ISSS'01, October 1-3, 2001, Montréal, Québec, Canada.

the file I/O parallel behavior using a set of templates which can be composed to form more complex access patterns. Patterson et al. [15] advocate the use of hints describing the access pattern (currently supporting sequential accesses and an explicit list of accesses) to select particular prefetching and caching policies in the file system.

(II) In the domain of High-Level Synthesis, custom synthesis of the memory architecture has been addressed for design of embedded ASICs. Catthoor et al. [2] address memory allocation, packing the data structures according to their size and bitwidth into memory modules from a library, to minimize the memory cost, and optimize port sharing. Wuytack et al. [22] present an approach to manage the memory bandwidth by increasing memory port utilization, through memory mapping and code reordering optimizations. Bakshi et al. [1] present a memory exploration approach, combining memory modules using different connectivity and port configurations for pipelined DSP systems. We complement this work by extracting and analyzing the prevailing accesses in the application in terms of access patterns, their relationships, similarities and interferences, and customize the memory architecture using memory modules from a library to generate a wide range of cost/performance/power tradeoffs in the context of programmable embedded systems.

(III) In the domain of Computer Architecture, [9], [12] propose the use of hardware stream buffers to enhance the memory system performance. Reconfigurable cache architectures have been proposed recently [20] to improve the cache behavior for general purpose processors, targeting a large set of applications. However, the extra control needed for adaptability and dynamic prediction of the access patterns while acceptable in general purpose computing where performance is the main target may result in a power overhead which is prohibitive in embedded systems, that are typically power constrained. Instead of using such dynamic prediction mechanisms, we statically target the local memory architecture to the data access patterns.

On a related front, Hummel et al. [8] address the problem of memory disambiguation in the presence of dynamic data structures to improve the parallelization opportunities. Instead of using this information for memory disambiguation, we use a similar type of closed form description generated by standard compiler analysis to represent the access patterns, and guide the memory architecture customization.

(IV) In the domain of programmable embedded systems, Kulkarni et al. [10], Panda et al. [13] have addressed customization of the memory architecture targeting different cache configurations, or alternatively using on-chip scratch pad SRAMs to store data with poor cache behavior. [5] presents an approach that customizes the cache architecture to match the locality needs of the access patterns in the application. However, this work only targets the cache architecture, and does not attempt to use custom memory modules to target the different access patterns.

The work we present differs significantly from all the related work in that we aggressively analyze, cluster and map memory access patterns to customized memory architectures; this allows the designer to trade-off performance and power against cost of the memory system.

3. OUR APPROACH

Figure 1 presents the flow of our Access Pattern based Memory Exploration (APEX) approach. We start by extracting the most active access patterns from the input C application; we then analyze and cluster these access patterns according to similarities and interference, and customize the memory architecture by allocating a set of memory modules from a Memory Modules IP Library. We explore the space of these memory customizations by using a heuristic to intelligently guide the search towards the most promising cost/performance memory architecture tradeoffs. We prune the design space by using a fast time-sampling simulation to rule-out the non-interesting parts of the design space, and then fully simulate and determine the power consumption only for the selected memory architectures. After narrowing down the search to the most promising cost/performance designs, we allow the designer to best match the power requirements of the system, by providing full cost/performance/power characteristics for the selected designs.

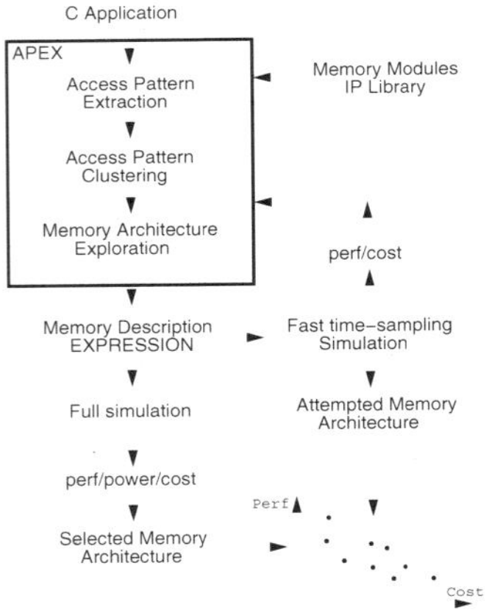

Figure 1: The flow of our Access Pattern based Memory Exploration Approach (APEX).

The basic idea is to target specifically the needs of the most active memory access patterns in the application, and customize a memory architecture, exploring a wide range of designs, that exhibit varied cost, performance, and power characteristics.

Figure 2 presents the memory architecture template. The memory access requests from the processor are routed to one of the memory modules 0 through n or to the cache, based on the address. The custom memory modules can read the data directly from the DRAM, or alternatively can go through the cache which is already present in the architecture, allowing access patterns which exhibit locality to make use of the locality properties of the cache. The custom memory modules implement different types of access patterns, such as stream accesses, linked-list accesses, or a simple SRAM to store hard-to-predict or random accesses. We use custom memory modules to target the most active access patterns in the application, while the remaining, less frequent access patterns are serviced by the on-chip cache.

4. ILLUSTRATIVE EXAMPLE

We use the *compress* benchmark (from SPEC95) to illustrate the performance, power and cost trade-offs generated

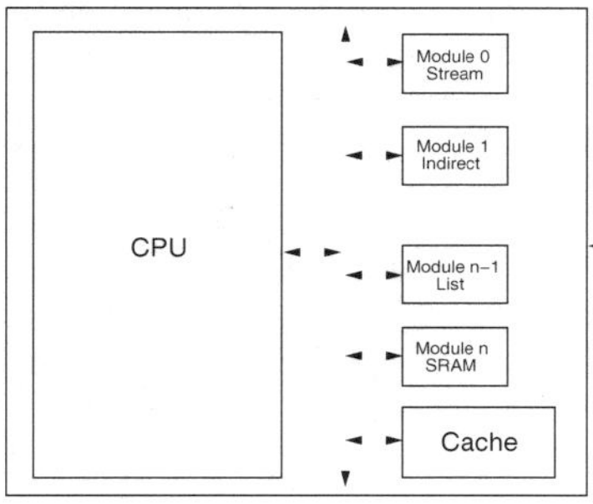

Figure 2: Memory architecture template.

```
while ( ... )
  ...
  ... = htab[code];
  code = codetab[code];
  ...
while ( ... )
  ...
  ... = rmask[r_off]
  ...

Access patterns:
    ap1 = htab[ap2]
    ap2 = codetabl[ap2]
    ap3 = rmask[unknown]
```

Figure 3: Example access patterns.

by our approach. The benchmark contains a varied set of access patterns, presenting interesting opportunities for customizing the memory architecture. We start by profiling the application, to determine the most active basic blocks and memory references. In the *compress* benchmark, 40% of all memory accesses are generated by only 19 instructions. Indeed, this is a typical situation: in many large real-life applications, a significant percentage of the memory accesses are generated from a few instructions in the code.

By traversing the most active basic blocks, we extract the most active access patterns from the application. Figure 3 shows an excerpt of code from *compress*, containing references to 3 arrays: htab, codetab, and rmask. htab is a hashing table represented as an array of 69001 unsigned longs (we assume that both longs and ints are stored on 32 bits), codetab is an array of 69001 shorts, and rmask is an array of 9 characters. The sequence of accesses to htab, codetab, and rmask represent access patterns ap1, ap2 and ap3 respectively. The hashing table htab is traversed using the array codetab as an indirect index, and the sequence of accesses to the array codetab is generated by a self-indirection, by using the values read from the array itself as the next index. The sequence in which the array rmask is traversed is difficult to predict, due to a complex index expression computed across multiple functions. Therefore we consider the order of accesses as unknown. However, rmask represents a small table of coefficients, accessed very often.

Compress contains many other memory references exhibiting different types of access patters such as streams with positive or negative stride. We extract the most active access patterns in the application, and cluster them according to similarity and interference. Since all the access patterns in a cluster will be treated together, we group together the access patterns which are compatible (for instance access patterns which are similar and do not interfere) in the hope that all the access patterns in a cluster can be mapped to one custom memory module.

Next, for each such access pattern cluster we allocate a custom memory module from the memory modules library. We use a library of parameterizable memory modules containing both generic structures such as caches and on-chip SRAMs, as well as a set of parameterizable custom memory modules developed for specific types of access patterns such as streams with positive, negative, or non-unit strides, indirect accesses, self-indirect accesses, linked-list accesses. Although these custom memory modules themselves are not the contribution of the paper (we simply use them as input to our memory architecture exploration algorithm), we briefly describe one such module for illustration purposes. The custom memory modules are based on approaches proposed in the general purpose computing domain [3, 9, 18], with the modification that the dynamic prediction mechanisms are replaced with the static compile-time analysis of the access patterns, and the prefetched data is stored in special purpose FIFOs.

For instance, for the example access pattern ap2 from *compress*, we use a custom memory module implementing self-indirect access pattern, while for the access pattern ap3, due to the small size of the array rmask, we use a small on-chip SRAM [13]. Figure 4 presents an outline of the self-indirect custom memory module architecture used for the access pattern ap2, where the value read from the array is used as the index for the next access to the array. The base register stores the base address of the array, the index register stores the previous value which will be used as an index in the next access, and the small FIFO stores the stream of values read from the next memory level, along with the address tag used for write coherency. When the CPU sends a read request, the data is provided from the FIFO. The empty spot in the FIFO initiates a fetch from the next level memory to bring in the next data element. The adder computes the address for the next data element based on the base address and the previous data value. We assume that the base register is initialized to the base of the codetab array and the index register to the initial index through a memory mapped control register model (a store to the address corresponding to the base register writes the base address value into the register).

The custom memory modules from the library can be combined together, based on the relationships between the access patterns. For instance, the access pattern ap1 uses the access pattern ap2 as an index for the references. In such a case we use the self-indirection memory module implementing ap2 in conjunction with a simple indirection memory module, which computes the sequence of addresses by adding the base address of the array htab with the values produced by ap2, and generate ap1=htab[ap2].

After selecting a set of custom memory modules from the library, we map the access pattern clusters to memory modules. Starting from the traditional memory architecture, containing a small cache, we incrementally customize access pattern clusters, to significantly improve the memory behavior. Many such memory module allocations and mappings are possible. Exploring the full space of such designs would be prohibitively expensive. In order to provide the designer with a spectrum of such design points without the time penalty of investigating the full space, we use a heuris-

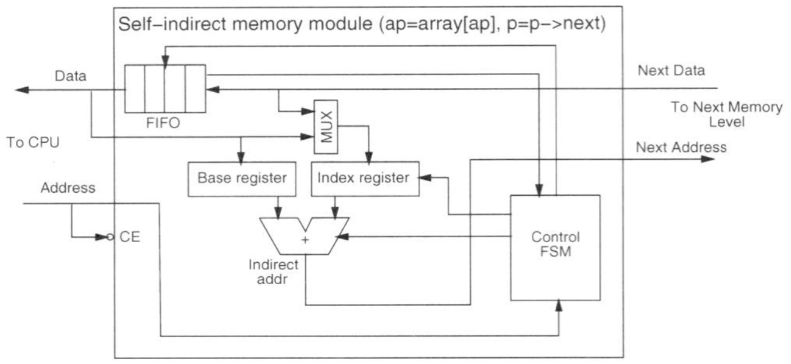

Figure 4: Self-indirect custom memory module.

```
Procedure GenerateAccessPatternClusters
Input: Application in C and Access Pattern Assertions
Output: Access Pattern Clusters
begin
  1. Extract Access Patterns from application
  2. Build Access Pattern Graph APG(AP,Arcs)
  3. Build Access Pattern Compatibility Graph
         APCG(AP,CompatibilityArcs)
  4. Choose Cliques Of Compatibility Arcs to form
         Access Pattern Clusters
end
```

Figure 5: Access Pattern Clustering algorithm.

tic to select the most promising memory architectures, providing the best cost/performance/power tradeoffs.

For the *compress* benchmark we explore the design space choosing a set of 5 memory architectures which provide advantageous cost/performance tradeoffs. The overall miss rate of the memory system is reduced by 39%, generating a significant performance improvement for varied cost and power characteristics (we present the details of the exploration in Section 6). In this manner we can customize the memory architecture by extracting and analyzing the access patterns in the application, thus substantially improving the memory system behavior, and allowing the designer to trade off the different goals of the system.

5. THE ACCESS PATTERN BASED MEMORY EXPLORATION (APEX) APPROACH

Our Access Pattern based Memory Exploration (APEX) approach is a heuristic method to extract, analyze, and cluster the most active access patterns in the application, and customize the memory architecture, explore the design space to tradeoff the different goals of the system. It contains two phases: (I) Access pattern clustering and (II) Exploration of custom memory configurations.

5.1 Access Pattern Clustering

In the first phase of our approach, we extract the access patterns from the application, analyze and group them into access pattern clusters, according to their relationships, similarities and interferences. Figure 5 presents an outline of the access pattern extraction and clustering algorithm. The access pattern clustering algorithm contains 4 steps.

(1) We extract the most active access patterns from the input application. We consider three types of access patterns: (a) Access patterns which can be determined automatically by analyzing the application code, (b) Access patterns about which the user has prior knowledge, and (c) Access patterns that are difficult to determine, or are input-dependent.

(a) Often access patterns can be determined at compile time, using traditional compiler analysis. Especially in DSP and embedded systems, the access patterns tend to be more regular, and predictable at compile time (e.g., in video, image and voice compression).

First, we use profiling to determine the most active basic blocks in the application. For each memory reference in these basic blocks we traverse the use-def chains to construct the address expression, until we reach statically known variables, constants, loop indexes, or other access patterns. This closed form formula represents the access pattern of the memory reference. If all the elements in this expression are statically predictable, and the loop indexes have known bounds, the access pattern represented by this formula is predictable.

(b) In the case of well-known data structures (e.g., hashing tables, linked lists, etc.), or well-understood high-level concepts (such as the traversal algorithms in well-known DSP functions), the programmer has prior knowledge on the data structures and the access patterns. By providing this information in the form of assertions, he can give hints on the predominant accesses in the application. Especially when the memory references depend on variables which traverse multiple functions, indirections, and aliasing, and determining the access pattern automatically is difficult, allowing the user to input such readily available information, significantly improves the memory architecture customization opportunities.

(c) In the case of memory references that are complex and difficult to predict, or depend on input data, we treat them as random access patterns. While for such references it is often impossible to fully understand the access pattern, it may be useful to use generic memory modules such as caches or on-chip scratch pad memories, to exploit the locality trends exhibited. A detailed description of the access pattern clustering algorithm is presented in [6].

(2) In the second step of the Access Pattern Clustering algorithm we build the Access Pattern Graph (APG), containing as vertices the most active access patterns from the application. The arcs in the APG represent properties such as similarity, interference, whether two access patterns refer to the same data structure, or whether an access pattern uses another access pattern as an index for indirect addressing, or pointer computation.

(3) Based on the APG, we build the Access Pattern Compatibility Graph (APCG), which has the same vertices as the APG (the access patterns), but the arcs represent compatibility between access patterns. We say two access patterns are *compatible*, if they can belong to the same access pattern cluster. For instance, access patterns that are similar (e.g., both have stream-like behavior), but which have little interference (are accessed in different loops) may share the same custom memory module, and it makes sense to place them in the same cluster. The meaning of the access pattern clusters is that all the access patterns in a cluster will be allocated to one memory module.

(4) In the last step of the Access Pattern Clustering algorithm, we find the cliques of fully connected subgraphs in the APCG compatibility graph. Each such clique represents an access pattern cluster, where all the access patterns

```
Procedure Exploration
Input: Access Pattern Clusters, and the Memory Modules Library
Output: The Memory Architecture design points w/ best cost/perf ratios
begin
  Initialize the memory architecture to contain the initial_cache
  While cost of memory architecture < cost_constraint do
    While cost of memory architecture < cost_constraint and
      more allocations and mappings possible do
      For all access pattern clusters sharing a memory module
        Allocate a memory module and map the cluster to it
        Estimate cost of new memory architecture
        If (cost of new memory architecture > cost_constraint) continue
        Estimate performance of new memory architecture (time-sampling)
        Save current memory architecture alternative
        Undo memory module allocation and mapping
      end
      Choose the memory architecture with best cost/performance
      Perform full simulation of new design point
    end
    Double the cache size
  end
end
```

Figure 6: Exploration algorithm.

are compatible, according to the compatibility criteria determined from the previous step (for a complete description of the compatibility criteria, please refer to [6]). Each such access pattern cluster will be mapped in the following phase to a memory module from the library.

5.2 Exploring Custom Memory Configurations

In the second phase of the APEX approach, we explore the custom memory module implementations and access pattern cluster mappings, using a heuristic to find the most promising design points.

Figure 6 presents an outline of our exploration heuristic. We first initialize the memory architecture to contain a small traditional cache, representing the starting point of our exploration.

For each design point, the number of alternative customizations available is large, and fully exploring them is prohibitively expensive. For instance, each access pattern cluster can be mapped to custom memory modules from the library, or to the traditional cache, each such configuration generating a different cost/ performance/power tradeoff. In order to prune the design space, at each exploration step we first estimate the incremental cost and gain obtained by the further possible customization alternatives, then choose the alternative leading to the best cost/gain ratio for further exploration. Once a customization alternative has been chosen, we consider it the current architecture, and perform full simulation for the new design point. We then continue the exploration, by evaluating the further possible customization opportunities, starting from this new design point.

We tuned our exploration heuristic to prune out the design points with poor cost/ performance characteristics, guiding the search towards points on the lower bound of the cost/performance design space.

For performance estimation purposes we use a time-sampling technique, which significantly speeds the simulation process. While this may not be highly accurate compared to full simulation, the fidelity is sufficient to make good incremental decisions guiding the search through the design space. To verify that our heuristic guides the search towards the pareto curve of the design space, we compare the exploration results with a full simulation of all the allocation and access pattern mapping alternatives for a large example. Indeed, as shown in Section 6, our algorithm finds the best cost/performance points in the design space, without requiring full simulation of the design space. For more details on our APEX algorithm, please refer to [6].

6. EXPERIMENTS

We performed a set of experiments on a number of large multimedia and scientific applications to show the performance, cost and power tradeoffs generated by our approach.

6.1 Experimental Setup

We simulated the design alternatives using our simulator based on the SIMPRESS [11] memory model, and SHADE [4]. We assumed a processor based on the SUN SPARC [1], and we compiled the applications using gcc. We estimated the cost of the memory architectures (we assume the cost in equivalent basic gates) using figures generated by the Synopsys Design Compiler [19], and an SRAM cost estimation technique from [2].

We computed the average memory power consumption of each design point, using cache power figures from CACTI [17]. For the main memory power consumption there is a lot of variation between the figures considered by different researchers [2, 7, 21], depending on the main memory type, technology, and bus architecture. The ratio between the energy consumed by on-chip cache accesses and off-chip DRAM accesses varies between one and two orders of magnitude [7]. In order to keep our technique independent of such technology figures, we allow the designer to input the ratio R as:

$R = E\_main\_memory\_access / E\_cache\_access$

where E_cache_access is the energy for one cache access, and E_main_memory_access is the energy to bring in a full cache line. In our following power computations we assume a ratio R of 50, relative to the power consumption of an 8k 2-way set associative cache with line size of 16 bytes.

The use of multiple memory modules in parallel to service memory access requests from the CPU requires using multiplexers to route the data from these multiple sources. These multiplexers may increase the access time of the memory system, and if this is on the critical path of the clock cycle, it may lead to the increase of the clock cycle. We use access times from CACTI [17] to compute the access time increases, and verify that the clock cycle is not affected.

Different cache configurations can be coupled with the memory modules explored, probing different areas of the design space. We present here our technique starting from an instance of such a cache configuration. A more detailed study for different cache configurations can be found in [6].

6.2 Results

Figure 7 presents the memory design space exploration of the access pattern customizations for the compress application. The compress benchmark exhibits a large variety of access patterns providing many customization opportunities. The x axis represents the cost (in number of basic

[1]The choice of SPARC was based on the availability of SHADE and a profiling engine; however our approach is clearly applicable to any other (embedded) processor as well

gates), and the y axis represents the overall miss ratio (the miss ratio of the custom memory modules represents the number of accesses where the data is not ready when it is needed by the CPU, divided by the total number of accesses to that module).

The design points marked with a circle represent the memory architectures chosen during the exploration as promising alternatives, and fully simulated for accurate results. The design points marked only with an X represent the exploration attempts evaluated through fast time-sampling simulation, from which the best cost/gain tradeoff is chosen at each exploration step. For each such design we perform full simulation to determine accurate cost/performance/power figures.

The design point labeled 1 represents the initial memory architecture, containing an 8k 2-way associative cache. Our exploration algorithm evaluates the first set of customization alternatives, by trying to choose the best access pattern cluster to map to a custom memory module. The best performance gain for the incremental cost is generated by customizing the access pattern cluster containing a reference to the hashing table htab, which uses as an index in the array the access pattern reading the codetab array (the access pattern is htab[codetab[i]]). This new architecture is selected as the next design point in the exploration, labeled 2. After fully simulating the new memory architecture, we continue the exploration by evaluating the further possible customization opportunities, and selecting the best cost/performance ratio. In this way, we explore the memory architectures with most promising cost/performance tradeoffs, towards the lower bound of the design space.

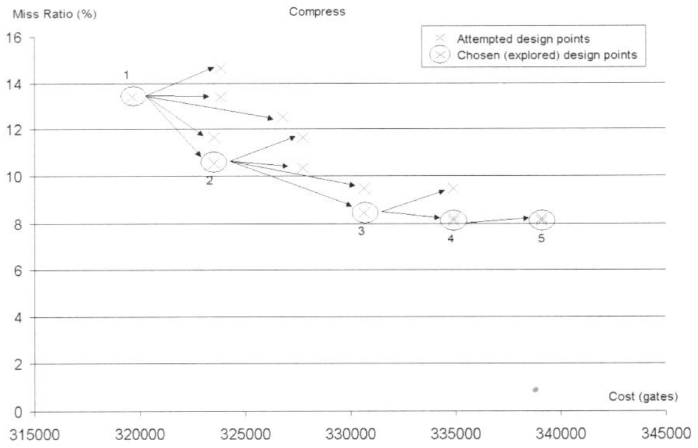

Figure 7: Miss ratio versus cost trade-off in Memory Design Space Exploration for Compress (SPEC95)

The miss ratio of the compress application varies between 13.42% for the initial cache-only architecture (for a cost of 319,634 gates), and 8.10% for a memory architecture where 3 access pattern clusters have been mapped to custom memory modules (for a cost of 334,864 gates). Based on a cost constraint (or alternatively on a performance requirement), the designer can choose the memory architecture which best matches the goals of the system.

In order to validate our space walking heuristic, and confirm that the chosen design points follow the pareto-curve-like trajectory in the design space, we compared the design points generated by our approach to the full simulation of the design space considering all the memory module allocations and access pattern cluster mappings for the compress example benchmark. Figure 8 shows the design space in terms of the estimated memory design cost (in number of basic gates), and the overall miss rate of the application. The design points marked with an X represent the points explored by our heuristic. The points marked by a black dot, represent a full simulation of all allocation and mapping alternatives. The points on the lower bound of the design space are the most promising, exhibiting the best cost/performance tradeoffs. Our algorithm guides the search towards these design points, pruning the non-interesting points in the design space. Our exploration heuristic successfully finds the most promising designs, without fully simulating the whole design space: each fully simulated design on the lower bound (marked by a black dot) is covered by an explored design (marked by an X) [2]. This provides the designer the opportunity to choose the best cost/performance trade-off, without the expense of investigating the whole space.

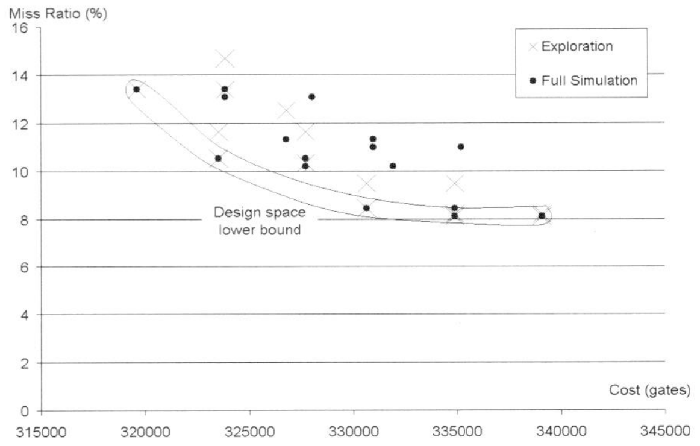

Figure 8: Exploration heuristic compared to simulation of all access pattern cluster mapping combinations for Compress

Table 1 presents the performance, cost and power results for a set of large, real-life benchmarks from the multimedia and scientific domains. The first column shows the application, and the second column represents the memory architectures explored for each such benchmark. The third column represents the cost of the memory architecture (in number of basic gates), the fourth column represents the miss ratio for each such design point, the fifth column shows the average memory latency (in cycles), and the last column presents the average memory power consumption, normalized to the initial cache-only architecture (represented by the first design point for each benchmark).

In Table 1 we present only the memory architectures with best cost/performance characteristics, chosen during the exploration. The miss ratio shown in the fourth column represents the number of memory accesses when the data is not yet available in the cache or the custom memory modules when required by the CPU. The average memory latency shown in fifth column represents the average number of cycles the CPU has to wait for an access to the memory system. Due to the increased hit ratio, and to the fact that the custom memory modules require less latency to access the small FIFO containing the data than the latency required by the

[2]Not all exploration points (X) are covered by a full simulation point (black dot), since some of the exploration points represent estimations only

large cache tag, data array and cache control, the average memory latency varies significantly during the exploration.

By customizing the memory architecture based on the access patterns in the application, the memory system performance is significantly improved. For instance, for the compress benchmark, the miss ratio is decreased from 13.4% to 8.10%, representing a 39% miss ratio reduction for a relatively small cost increase. However, this comes at the cost of an increased memory power consumption by a factor between 1.1 and 1.4 mainly due to the increased main memory bandwidth generated by the custom memory modules implementing the access pattern clusters in the application. However, by exploring a varied set of design points, the designer can tradeoff the cost, power and performance of the system, to best meet the design goals.

Benchmark	Design Point	Cost (gates)	Miss ratio (%)	Mem Latency (cycles)	Mem. Power (normalized)
Compress	1	319634	13.4200	28.56	1
	2	323521	10.5400	22.58	1.18
	3	330657	8.4500	18.42	1.36
	4	334864	8.1000	17.40	1.41
	5	339071	8.1000	17.35	1.41
li	1	319634	6.9800	15.82	1
	2	323841	4.6700	11.21	1.23
	3	332302	4.6200	11.01	1.24
	4	340763	4.6200	10.96	1.24
vocoder	1	40295	1.4600	4.90	1
	2	44502	1.3600	4.45	1.01
	3	48709	1.2600	4.16	1.02
	4	53765	1.2600	4.09	1.03
	5	80201	0.8100	3.61	0.68
	6	84408	0.7600	3.26	0.70
	7	88615	0.7400	3.13	0.70
	8	93671	0.7400	3.07	0.70

Table 1: Exploration results for our Access Pattern based Memory Customization algorithm.

Vocoder is a multmedia benchmark exhibiting mainly stream-like regular access patterns, which behave well with small cache sizes. Since the initial cache of 1k has a small cost of 40,295 gates, there was enough space to double the cache size. The design points 1 through 4 represent the memory architectures containing the 1k cache, while the design points 5 through 8 represent the memory architectures containing the 2k cache. As expected, the performance increases significantly when increasing the cost of the memory architecture. However, a surprising result is that the power consumption of the memory system decreases when using the larger cache: even though the power consumed by the larger cache accesses increases, the main memory bandwidth decrease due to a lower miss ratio results in a significantly lower main memory power, which translates into a lower memory system power. Clearly, this type of results are difficult to determine by analysis alone, and require a systematic exploration approach to allow the designer to best trade off the different goals of the system.

The wide range of cost, performance, and power tradeoffs obtained are due to the aggressive use of the memory access pattern information, and customization of the memory architecture beyond the traditional cache architecture.

7. SUMMARY

We presented an approach where by analyzing the access patterns in the application we gain valuable insight on the access and storage needs of the input application, and customize the memory architecture to better match these requirements, generating significant performance improvements for varied memory cost and power.

Traditionally, designers have attempted to alleviate the memory bottleneck by exploring different cache configurations, with limited use of more special purpose memory modules such as stream buffers [9]. However, while real-life applications contain a large number of memory references to a diverse set of data structures, a significant percentage of all memory accesses in the application are generated from a few instructions, which often exhibit well-known, predictable access patterns. This presents a tremendous opportunity to customize the memory architecture to match the needs of the predominant access patterns in the application, and significantly improve the memory system behavior. We presented here such an approach called APEX that extracts, analyzes and clusters the most active access patterns in the application, and customizes the memory architecture to explore a wide range of cost, performance and power designs. We generate significant performance improvements for incremental costs, and explore a design space beyond the one traditionally considered, allowing the designer to efficiently target the system goals. By intelligently exploring the design space, we guide the search towards the memory architectures with the best cost/performance characteristics, and avoid the expensive full simulation of the design space.

We presented a set of experiments on large multimedia and scientific examples, where we explored a wide range of cost, performance and power tradeoffs, by customizing the memory architecture to fit the needs of the access patterns in the applications. Our exploration heuristic found the most promising cost/gain designs compared to the full simulation of the design space considering all the memory module allocations and access pattern cluster mappings, without the time penalty of investigating the full design space.

In this work we assumed a simple connectivity model between the memory modules and the CPU. In our future work we plan to explore the connectivity space, by using specific on-chip and off-chip busses and connections from a bus IP library.

8. ACKNOWLEDGMENTS

We would like to acknowledge and thank Ashok Halambi, Prabhat Mishra, Srikanth Srinivasan, Partha Biswas, Aviral Shrivastava, Radu Cornea and Nick Savoiu for their contributions to the EXPRESS/ EXPRESSION project.

9. REFERENCES

[1] S. Bakshi and D. Gajski. A memory selection algorithm for high-performance pipelines. In *EURO-DAC*, 1995.

[2] F. Catthoor, S. Wuytack, E. De Greef, F. Balasa, L. Nachtergaele, and A. Vandecappelle. *Custom Memory Management Methodology*. Kluwer, 1998.

[3] Tzi cker Chiueh. Sunder: A programmable hardware prefetch architecture for numerical loops. In *Conference on High Performance Networking and Computing*, 1994.

[4] R. Cmelik and D. Keppel. Shade: A fast instruction set simulator for execution profiling. Technical report, SUN MICROSYSTEMS, 1993.

[5] P. Grun, N. Dutt, and A. Nicolau. Access pattern based local memory customization for low power embedded systems. In *DATE*, 2001.

[6] P. Grun, N. Dutt, and A. Nicolau. Exploring memory architecture through access pattern analysis and clustering. Technical report, University of California, Irvine, 2001.

[7] P. Hicks, M. Walnock, and R.M. Owens. Analysis of power consumption in memory hierarchies. In *ISPLED*, 1997.

[8] J. Hummel, L Hendren, and A Nicolau. A language for conveying the aliasing properties of dynamic, pointer-based data structures. In *Proceedings of the 8th International Parallel Processing Symposium*, 1994.

[9] N. Jouppi. Improving direct-mapped cache performance by the addition of a small fully-associative cache and prefetch buffers. In *ISCA*, 1990.

[10] C. Kulkarni. *Cache optimization for Multimedia Applications*. PhD thesis, IMEC, 2001.

[11] P. Mishra, P. Grun, N. Dutt, and A. Nicolau. Processor-memory co-explotation driven by a memory-aware architecture description language. In *International Conference on VLSI Design*, Bangalore, India, 2001.

[12] S. Palacharla and R. Kessler. Evaluating stream buffers as a secondary cache replacement. In *ISCA*, 1994.

[13] P. Panda, N. Dutt, and N. Nicolau. *Memory Issues in Embedded Systems-on-Chip*. Kluwer, 1999.

[14] I. Parsons, R. Unrau, J. Schaeffer, and D. Szafron. Pi/ot: Parallel i/o templates. In *Parallel Computing, Vol. 23, No. 4-5, pp. 543-570, May 1997.*

[15] R. Patterson, G. Gibson, E. Ginting, D. Stodolsky, and J. Zelenka. Informed prefeching and caching. In *SIGOPS*, 1995.

[16] S. Przybylski. Sorting out the new DRAMs. In *Hot Chips Tutorial*, Stanford, CA, 1997.

[17] G. Reinman and N. Jouppi. An integrated cache timing and power model. In *Summer Internship Report, COMPAQ Western Research Lab, Palo-Alto*, 1999.

[18] A. Roth, A. Moshovos, and G. Sohi. Dependence based prefetching for linked data structures. In *ASPLOS*, 1998.

[19] Synopsys Design Compiler. *www.synopsys.com.*

[20] A. Veidenbaum, W. Tang, R. Gupta, A. Nicolau, and X. Ji. Adapting cache line size to application behavior. In *ICS*, 1999.

[21] N. Vijaykrishnan, M. Kandemir, M. J. Irwin, H. S. Kim, and W. Ye. Energy-driven integrated hardware-software optimizations using simplepower. In *ISCA*, 2000.

[22] S. Wuytack, F. Catthoor, G. de Jong, B. Lin, and H. De Man. Flow graph balancing for minimizing the required memory bandwith. In *ISSS*, La Jolla, CA, 1996.

Powering Networks on Chips

Energy-efficient and reliable interconnect design for SoCs

Luca Benini
DEIS Università di Bologna
Bologna, Italy 40136
lbenini@deis.unibo.it

Giovanni De Micheli
CSL Stanford University
Stanford, CA 94305
nanni@stanford.edu

ABSTRACT

We consider *systems on chips* (SoCs) that will be designed and produced in five to ten years from today, with gate lengths in the range 50-100nm. We address the distinguishing features of a design methodology that aims at achieving reliable designs under the limitations of the interconnect technology. Specifically, we consider energy consumption reduction, under guaranteed *quality of service* (QoS), as a main objective in system design.

Keywords

Systems on Chips, low-energy design, networks

1. INTRODUCTION

Systems on chip (SoCs) will be soon designed and fabricated in technologies with gate lengths in the range 50-100nm. Several challenges arise from the complexity of designing billion-transistor chips. Thus current design tools and methods will require evolutionary and revolutionary changes. We believe that such changes will be driven by the following factors:

- Systems on chip will be designed using pre-existing components, such as processors, controllers and memory arrays. Design methodologies will support component re-use in a plug-and-play fashion.
- SoCs will have to provide a functionally-correct, reliable operation of the interacting components. The physical interconnections on chip will be a limiting factor for performance and energy consumption.
- The overall design goal (for most SoCs) will be to satisfy some *quality of service* (QoS) metric with the least energy consumption. Most QoS metrics encompass performance and reliability measures.

In this paper, we address a methodology for the design of energy-efficient communication for SOCs.

ISSS'01, October 1-3, 2001, Montréal, Québec, Canada.

2. TECHNOLOGY TRENDS

The *international technology roadmap for semiconductors* (ITRS) [22] projects that we will be designing multi-billion transistor chips by the end of this decade, with feature sizes around $50nm$ and clock frequencies around $10Ghz$. Delays on wires will dominate: global wires spanning a significant fraction of the chip size will carry signals whose propagation delay will exceed the clock period. Moreover, synchronization of chips with a single clock source and negligible skew will be extremely hard or impossible. The most likely synchronization paradigm for future chips is *globally-asynchronous locally-synchronous* (GALS), with many different clocks. Global wires will span multiple clock domains, and synchronization failures in communicating between different clock domains will be rare but unavoidable events [8].

SoC design will be guided by the principle of consuming the least possible power. This requirement matches the need of using SoCs in portable battery-powered electronic devices and of curtailing thermal dissipation which can make chip operation infeasible or impractical. Energy considerations will impose small logic swings and power supplies, most likely below 1 Volt. Electrical noise due to *cross-talk*, *electro-magnetic interference* (EMI) and radiation-induced charge injection (*soft errors*) will be likely to produce *data upsets*. Thus, the mere transmission of digital values on wires will be *inherently unreliable*.

As a result, the distinguishing challenge for SoC design will be to provide adequate *quality of service* (QoS), with a limited energy budget under strong limitations of the technology. QoS requirements include, but are not limited to, performance and reliability. High performance is demanded by the increasingly complex software applications required to run even on small portable appliances (e.g., multi-media on cell phones). Reliability is mandated by the increasing reliance of consumers on electronic communication and control systems in every day's life.

We propose to use network design technology to analyze and design SoCs. In other words, we view a SoC as a *micro-network* of components. We postulate that SoC interconnect design can be done using the *micro-network stack* paradigm, which is an adaptation of the protocol stack [15] (Figure 1). Thus the electrical, logic, and functional properties of the interconnection scheme can be abstracted.

SoCs differ from wide-area networks because of local proximity and because they exhibit much less non-determinism. Local, high-performance networks (such as those developed for large-scale multiprocessors), have similar requirements and constraints. A few distinctive characteristics are unique

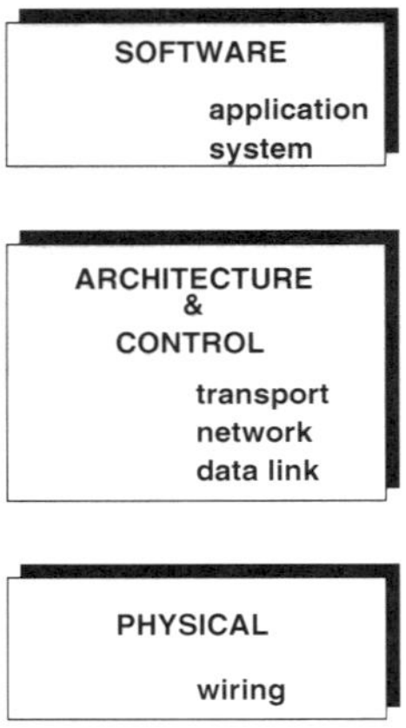

Figure 1: Micro-network stack

of SoC networks, namely, **energy constraints** and **design-time specialization.** This papers addresses specifically the former problem.

The SIA roadmap projects that power consumption can marginally scale up while moving from $100nm$ to $50nm$ technology. At the same time, projected clock frequency and number of devices on-chip are increased significantly. These trends translate directly into much tighter power budgets for all system components. Voltage scaling, as predicted by the roadmap, is helpful in reducing power. Nevertheless, voltage scaling alone will not suffice, and specific design choices for low-energy energy consumption will be required.

Whereas computation and storage energy greatly benefits from device scaling (smaller gates, smaller memory cells), the energy for global communication does not scale down. On the contrary, projections based on current delay optimization techniques for global wires [13, 14, 11] show that global communication on chip will require increasingly higher energy consumption. Hence, communication-energy minimization will be a growing concern in future technologies. Furthermore, network traffic control and monitoring can help in better managing the power consumed by networked computational resources. For instance, clock speed and voltage of end nodes can be varied according to available network bandwidth. The emphasis on energy minimization creates a sleuth of novel challenges that have not been addressed by traditional high-performance network designers.

Design-time specialization is another facet of the SoC network design. Whereas macroscopic networks emphasize general-purpose communication and modularity, in SoCs networks these constraints are less restrictive. The communication network fabric is designed on silicon from scratch. Standardization is needed only for specifying an abstract network interface for the end nodes, but the network architecture itself can be tailored to the application, or class of applications, targeted by the SoC design. Hence, we envision a vertical design flow where every layer of the micro-network stack is specialized and optimized for the target application domain. From a design stand-point the network reconfigurability will be key in providing plug-and-play use of components, since they will interact with the others through (reconfigurable) protocols.

3. A LAYERED DESIGN METHODOLOGY

We consider now on-chip communication and its abstraction as a micro-network. We analyze the various levels of the micro-network stack bottom-up.

3.1 Physical layer

Global wires are the physical implementation of the communication channels. Physical layer signaling techniques for lossy transmission lines have been studied for a long time by high-speed board designers and microwave engineers [2, 8].

Traditional rail-to-rail voltage signaling with capacitive termination, as used today for on-chip communication, is definitely not well-suited for high-speed, low-energy communication on future global interconnect [8]. Reduced swing, current-mode transmission, as used in some processor-memory systems, can significantly reduce communication power dissipation while preserving speed of data communication.

Nevertheless, as the technology trends lead us to use smaller voltage swings and capacitances, the upset probabilities will rise. Thus the trend toward faster and lower-power communication may decrease reliability as an unfortunate side effect. Reliability bounds as voltages scale can be derived from theoretical (entropic) considerations [5] and can be measured also by experiments on real circuits.

We conjecture that a paradigm shift is needed to address the aforementioned challenges. Current design styles consider wiring-related effects as undesirable parasitics, and try to reduce or cancel them by specific and detailed physical design techniques. It is important to realize that a well-balanced design should not over-design wires so that their behavior approaches an ideal one, because the corresponding cost in performance, energy-efficiency and modularity may be too high. Physical layer design should find a compromise between competing quality metrics and provide a clean and complete abstraction of channel characteristics to micro-network layers above.

3.2 Data link, network and transport layers

Due to the limitations at the physical level and to the high bandwidth requirement, we conjecture that SoC design will use network architectures similar to those used for multi-processors. Whereas *shared medium* (e.g., bus-based) communication dominates in today's chip designs, scalability reasons make us conjecture that more general network topologies will be used in the future. In this perspective, micro-network design entails the specification of *network architectures* and *control protocols* [9]. The architecture specifies the topology and physical organization of the interconnection network, while the protocols specify how to use network resources during system operation.

The *data-link layer* abstracts the physical layer as an unreliable digital link, where the probability of bit upsets is non null (and increasing as technology scales down). Furthermore, reliability can be traded off for energy [5]. The main purpose of data-link protocols is to increase the reliability of the link up to a minimum required level, under the assumption that the physical layer by itself is not sufficiently reliable.

An additional source of errors is contention in shared-medium networks. Contention resolution is fundamentally a non-deterministic process, because it requires synchronization of a distributed system, and for this reason it can be seen as an additional noise source. In general, non determinism can be virtually eliminated at the price of some performance penalty. For instance, centralized bus arbitration in a synchronous bus eliminates contention-induced errors, at the price of a substantial performance penalty caused by the slow bus clock and by bus request/release cycles.

Future high-performance shared-medium on-chip micro-networks may evolve in the same direction as high-speed local area networks, where contention for a shared communication channel can cause errors, because two or more transmitters are allowed to concurrently send data on a shared medium. In this case, provisions must be made for dealing with contention-induced errors.

An effective way to deal with errors in communication is to *packetize* data. If data is sent on an unreliable channel in packets, error containment and recovery is easier, because the effect of errors is contained by packet boundaries, and error recovery can be carried out on a packet-by-packet basis. At the data link layer, error correction can be achieved by using standard *error correcting codes* (ECC) that add redundancy to the transferred information. Error correction can be complemented by several packet-based error detection and recovery protocols. Several parameters in these protocols (e.g., packet size, number of outstanding packets, etc.) can be adjusted depending on the goal to achieve maximum performance at a specified residual error probability and/or within given energy consumption bounds.

At the *network layer*, packetized data transmission can be customized by the choice of switching and routing algorithms. The former, (e.g., *circuit, packet*, and *cut-through* switching), establish the type of connection while the latter determine the path followed by a message through the network to its final destination. Switching and routing for on-chip micro-networks affect heavily performance and energy consumption. We conjecture that future approaches will emphasize speed and decentralization of routing decisions. Robustness and fault tolerance will also be highly desirable.

At the *transport layer*, algorithms deal with the decomposition of messages into packets at the source and their assembly at destination. Packetization granularity is a critical design decision, because the behavior of most network control algorithms is very sensitive to packet size. Packet size can be application-specific in SoCs, as opposed to general networks. In general, flow control and negotiation can be based on either deterministic or statistical procedures. Deterministic approaches ensure that traffic meets specifications, and provide hard bounds on delays or message losses. The main disadvantage of deterministic techniques is that they are based on worst cases, and they generally lead to significant under-utilization of network resources. Statistical techniques are more efficient in terms of utilization, but they cannot provide worst case guarantees. Similarly, from an energy viewpoint, we expect deterministic schemes to be more inefficient than statistical schemes, because of their implicit worst-case assumptions.

3.3 Software layers

Software layers comprise system and application software. We limit our considerations to system software, which includes processing element and network operating systems. The system software provides us with an abstraction of the underlying hardware platform. In a nutshell, we can view the system as a queueing network of components. Each component models a computational or storage unit, while the queueing network abstracts the micro-network. Moreover, we can assume that:

- Each component can operate at various service levels, providing corresponding performance and energy consumption levels. This abstracts the physical implementation of components with adjustable voltage and/or frequency levels, as well as with the ability to disable their functions in full or in part.
- The information flow between the various units can be controlled by the system software to provide the appropriate quality of service. This entails controlling the routing of the information, the local buffering into storage arrays and the rate of the information flow.

The system software must support *dynamic power management* (DPM) of its components as well as *dynamic information-flow management.* DPM is currently applied within system design. We consider dynamic voltage/frequency scaling as a form of power management, because its limiting cases, i.e., powering off or stopping the clock, are the most common realizations of DPM.

Dynamic power management entails selecting the appropriate component state to service a workload with the minimum energy consumption. DPM *policies* are the control algorithms for state transitions [3]. Note that transitions among states have a finite delay penalty, even when changing the operation frequency. Thus, the computation of policies that maximize performance under energy constraints, or solving the dual problem, may be computationally complex [3, 4].

Dynamic information-flow management relates to configuring the network and the bandwidth of the local interconnection to satisfy the information flow requirements. This problem is tightly related to DPM, and can be seen as an application of DPM to the micro-network instead of to a component. Again, policies implemented at the system software layer request either specific protocols or parameters at the lower layers to achieve the appropriate information flow, using the least amount of resources and energy.

4. ENERGY-EFFICIENT DESIGN: TECHNIQUES AND EXAMPLES

In this section we delve in a few specific instances of energy-efficient micronetwork design problems. In most cases, we also outline specific solutions that have been proposed in the literature, even though it should be clear that many design issues are open and significant progress in this area is expected in the near future.

4.1 Physical layer

At the physical layer, low-swing signaling is actively investigated to reduce communication energy on global interconnects [20]. In the case of a simple CMOS driver, low-swing signaling is achieved by lowering the driver's supply voltage V_{dd}. This implies a quadratic dynamic power reduction (because $P_{dyn} = KV_{dd}^2$). Unfortunately, swing reduction at the transmitter complicates the receiver's design. Increased sensitivity and noise immunity are required to guarantee reliable data reception. Differential receivers have superior sensitivity and robustness, but they require doubling the bus width. To reduce the overhead, pseudo-differential schemes have been proposed, where a *reference* signal is shared among several bus lines and receivers, and incoming data is compared against the reference in each receiver. Pseudo-differential signaling reduces the number of signal transitions, but it has reduced noise margins with respect to fully differential signaling. Thus, reduced switching activity is counterbalanced by higher swings and determining the minimum-energy solution requires careful circuit-level analysis.

Another key physical-layer issue is synchronization. Traditional on-chip communication has been based on the synchronous assumption, which implies the presence of global synchronization signals (*i.e.*, clocks) that define data sampling instants throughout the chip. Unfortunately, clocks are extremely energy-inefficient, and it is a well-known fact that they are responsible for a significant fraction of the power budget in digital integrated systems. Thus, postulating global synchronization when designing on-chip micronetworks is not an optimal choice from the energy viewpoint. Alternative on-chip synchronization protocols that do not require the presence of a global clock have been proposed in the past [21, 23] but their effectiveness has not been studied in detail from the energy viewpoint.

4.2 Data-link layer

At the data-link layer, a key challenge is to achieve the specified communication reliability level with minimum energy expense. Several error recovery mechanisms developed for macroscopic networks can be deployed in on-chip micronetworks, but their energy efficiency should be carefully assessed in this context. As a practical example, consider two alternative reliability-enhancement techniques: *error-correcting codes* and *error-detecting codes with retransmission*. Both approaches are based on transmitting redundant information over the data link, but error-correction is generally more demanding than error detection in terms of redundancy and decoding complexity. Hence, we can expect error-correcting transmission to be more power-hungry in the error-free case. However, when an error arises, error detecting schemes require retransmission of the corrupted data. Depending on the network architecture, retransmission can be very costly in terms of energy (and performance).

Clearly, the tradeoff between the increased cost of error correction and the energy penalty of retransmission should be carefully explored when designing energy-efficient micronetworks [5]. Either scheme may be optimal, depending on system constraints and on physical channel characteristics. Automatic design space exploration could be very beneficial in this area.

In case of shared-medium network links (such as busses), the media-access-control function of the data link layer is also critical for energy efficiency. Currently, centralized time-division multiplexing schemes (also called centralized arbitration) are widely adopted [1, 7, 17]. In these schemes, a single arbiter circuit decides which transmitter accesses to the bus for every time slot. Unfortunately, the poor scalability of centralized arbitration indicates that this approach is likely to be energy-inefficient as micronetwork complexity scales up. In fact, the energy cost of communicating with the arbiter, and hardware complexity of the arbiter itself scale up more than linearly with the number of bus masters

Distributed arbitration schemes as well as alternative multiplexing approaches, such as code division multiplexing, have been extensively adopted in shared-medium macroscopic network, and are actively investigated for on-chip communication [18]. However, research in this area just burgeoning, and significant work is needed to develop energy-aware media-access-control for future micronetworks.

4.3 Network layer

Network architecture heavily influences communication energy. As hinted in the previous section, shared-medium networks (busses) are currently the most common choice, but it is intuitively clear that busses are not energy-efficient as network size scales up [10]. In bus-based communication, data is always broadcasted from one transmitter to all possible receivers, while in most cases messages are destined to only one receiver, or a small group. Bus contention, with the related arbitration overhead further contributes to the energy overhead.

Preliminary studies on energy-efficient on-chip communication indicate that hierarchical and heterogeneous architectures are much more energy-efficient than busses [12, 21]. In their work, Zhang *et al.* [21] develop a *hierarchical generalized mesh* where network nodes which high communication bandwidth requirement are clustered and connected through a programmable generalized mesh consisting of several short communication channels joined by programmable switches. Clusters are then connected through a generalized mesh of global long communication channel. Clearly such architecture is heterogeneous because the energy cost of intra-cluster communication is much smaller than that of inter-cluster communication. While the work of Zhang *et al.* demonstrates that power can be saved by optimizing network architecture, many network design issues are still open, and we need tools and algorithms to explore the design space and to tailor network architecture to specific applications or classes of applications.

Network architecture is only one facet of network layer design, the other major facet being network control. A critical issue in this area is the choice of a switching scheme for indirect network architectures. From the energy viewpoint, the tradeoff is between the cost of setting up a circuit-switched connection once for all, and the overhead of switching packets throughout the entire communication time on a packet-based connection. In the former case the network control overhead is "lumped" and incurred once, while in the latter case, it is distributed over many small contributions, one for each packet. When communication flow between network nodes is extremely persistent and stationary, circuit-switched schemes are likely to be preferable, while packet switched schemes should be more energy-efficient for irregular and non-stationary communication patterns. Needless to say, circuit switching and packet switching are just two extremes of a spectrum, with many hybrid solutions in between [15].

4.4 Transport layer

Above the network layer, the communication abstraction is an end-to-end connection. The transport layer is concerned with optimizing the usage of network resources and providing a requested quality of service. Clearly, energy can be seen as a network resource or a component in a quality-of-service metric. An example of transport-layer design issue is the choice between connection-oriented and connectionless protocols. Energy efficiency can be heavily impacted by this decision. In fact, connection-oriented protocols can be energy inefficient under heavy traffic conditions because they tend to increase the number of re-transmissions. On the other hand, out-of-order delivery of data may imply additional work at the receiver, which causes additional energy consumption. Thus, communication energy should be balanced against computation energy at destination nodes.

Another transport-layer task with far-reaching implications on energy is flow control. When many transmitter compete for limited communication resources, the network becomes congested and the cost per transmitted bit increases, because of increased contention and contention resolution overhead. Flow control can mitigate the effect of congestion by regulating the amount of data that enters the network, at the price of some throughput penalty. Energy reduction by flow control has been extensively studied for wireless networks [15, 16], but it is an unexplored research area for on-chip micronetworks.

4.5 Application and system layer

End-nodes (processing elements) in SoC micronetworks will most likely be power-manageable, and one of the key tasks of the system software will be to control their power states. We can envision two alternative approaches to the power management problem, namely *node-centric* and *network-centric*. In the former case, system software running on a power-manageable component determines its state transitions, based on the system state and on its workload. Thus, the system software of the component has a local DPM policy and controls the underlying hardware through appropriate system calls. In the latter case, components send messages to neighbors to request state changes. Such requests originate and are serviced at the system software levels. For example, an image processor can be required to raise its service levels before receiving a stream of data. In this case, the system software supports policies that accept requests from other components and perform transitions according to such requests. At the same time, the policies can originate requests for other components. We conjecture that system-level power management for future SoCs will gradually evolve from a node-centric toward a network-centric view.

Application software development for SoCs should achieve two major goals. First, preserve portability and generality of the applications across different platforms. Second, provide some intelligence to leverage the distributed nature of the underlying platform for reducing its energy consumption. These two objectives are apparently conflicting. A possible strategy to satisfy both goals is to provide power-aware *application programming interfaces* (APIs) that let applications dialogue with system software. Thus, applications may acquire information from the system software about the specific platform. At the same time, applications can request the system software to set the hardware in specific power states to provide adequate quality of service with minimal power. System software can serve or deny requests from applications, according to the state of other running processes. The design of energy-aware APIs is an open and promising research area.

5. CONCLUSIONS

The challenges of designing SoCs in 50-100nm technologies available in the second part of this decade include coping with design complexity, providing reliable, high-performance operation and minimizing energy consumption. Starting from the observation that interconnect technology will be the limiting factor for achieving the operational goals, we envisioned a communication-centric view of design. We focused on energy efficiency issues in designing the communication infrastructure for future SoCs. We described several open problems at various layers of the communication stack, and we outlined basic strategies to effectively tackle the energy efficiency challenge for on-chip communication networks.

6. REFERENCES

[1] P. Aldworth, "System-on-a-Chip Bus Architecture for Embedded Applications," *IEEE International Conference on Computer Design*, pp. 297-298, 1999.

[2] H. Bakoglu, *Circuits, Interconnections, and Packaging for VLSI*, Addison-Wesley, 1990.

[3] L. Benini, A. Bogliolo, G. De Micheli, "A Survey of Design Techniques for System-Level Dynamic Power Management," *IEEE Transactions on Very Large-Scale Integration Systems*, vol. 8, no. 3, pp. 299-316, June 2000.

[4] L. Benini, G. De Micheli, "System-Level Power Optimization: Techniques and Tools," *ACM Transactions on Design Automation of Electronic Systems*, vol. 5, no. 2, pp. 115-192, April 2000.

[5] R. Hegde, N. Shanbhag, "Toward achieving energy efficiency in presence of deep submicron noise," *IEEE Transactions on VLSI Systems*, pp. 379–391, vol. 8, no. 4, August 2000.

[6] D. Bertsekas, R. Gallager, *Data Networks*. Prentice Hall, 1991.

[7] B. Cordan, "An efficient bus architecture for system-on-chip design," *IEEE Custom Integrated Circuits Conference*, pp. 623–626, 1999.

[8] W. Dally and J. Poulton, *Digital Systems Engineering*, Cambridge University Press, 1998.

[9] J. Duato, S. Yalamanchili, L. Ni, *Interconnection Networks: an Engineering Approach*. IEEE Computer Society Press, 1997.

[10] P. Guerrier, A. Grenier, "A generic architecture for on-chip packet-switched interconnections," *Design Automation and Test in Europe Conference*, pp. 250–256, 2000.

[11] R. Ho, K. Mai, M. Horowitz, "The Future of wires," *Proceedings of the IEEE*, January 2001.

[12] C. Patel, S. Chai, S. Yalamanchili, D. Shimmel, "Power constrained design of multiprocessor interconnection networks," *IEEE International Conference on Computer Design*, pp. 408-416, 1997.

[13] D.Sylvester and K.Keutzer, "A Global Wiring Paradigm for Deep Submicron Design," *IEEE Transactions on CAD/ICAS*, Vol.19, No. 2, pp. 242-252, February 2000.

[14] T. Theis, "The future of Interconnection Technology," *IBM Journal of Research and Development*, Vol. 44, No. 3, May 2000, pp. 379-390.

[15] J. Walrand, P. Varaiya, *High-Performance Communication Networks*. Morgan Kaufman, 2000.

[16] I. Papadimitriou, M. Paterakis, "Energy-conserving access protocols for transmitting data in unicast and broadcast mode," *International Symposium on Personal, Indoor and Mobile Radio Communication*, pp. 416–420, 2000.

[17] S. Winegarden, "A bus architecture centric configurable processor system," *IEEE Custom Integrated Circuits Conference*, pp. 627–630, 1999.

[18] R. Yoshimura, T. Koat, S. Hatanaka, T. Matsuoka, K. Taniguchi, "DS-CDMA wired bus with simple interconnection topology for parallel processing system LSIs," *IEEE Solid-State Circuits Conference*, pp. 371-371, Jan. 2000.

[19] H. Zhang, V. Prabhu, V. George, M. Wan, M. Benes, A. Abnous, J. Rabaey, "A 1-V Heterogeneous Reconfigurable DSP IC for Wireless Baseband Digital Signal Processing," *IEEE Journal of Solid-State Circuits*, vol. 35, no. 11, pp. 1697–1704, Nov. 2000.

[20] H. Zhang, V. George, J. Rabaey, "Low-swing on-chip signaling techniques: effectiveness and robustness," *IEEE Transactions on VLSI Systems*, vol. 8, no. 3, pp. 264-272, June 2000.

[21] H. Zhang, M. Wan, V. George, J. Rabaey, "Interconnect architecture exploration for low-energy configurable single-chip DSPs," *IEEE Computer Society Workshop on VLSI*, pp. 2-8, 1999.

[22] International Technology Roadmap for Semiconductors *http://public.itrs.net/*

[23] W. Bainbridge, S. Furber, "Delay insensitive system-on-chip interconnect using 1-of-4 data encoding," *IEEE International Symposium on Asynchronous Circuits and Systems*, pp. 118-126, 2001.

Retargetable Static Timing Analysis for Embedded Software

Kaiyu Chen
Department of Electrical Engineering
Princeton University
Princeton, NJ 08544
Kchen@ee.princeton.edu

Sharad Malik
Department of Electrical Engineering
Princeton University
Princeton, NJ 08544
Sharad@ee.princeton.edu

David I. August
Department of Computer Science
Princeton University
Princeton, NJ 08544
August@cs.princeton.edu

ABSTRACT

This paper presents a novel approach for retargetable static software timing analysis. Specifically, we target the problem of determining bounds on the execution time of a program on modern processors, *and solve this problem in a retargetable software development environment*. Another contribution of this paper is the modeling of important features in contemporary architectures, such as branch prediction, predication, and instruction pre-fetching, which have great impact on system performance, and have been rarely handled thus far. These ideas allow to build a timing analysis tool that is efficient, accurate, modular and retargetable. We present preliminary results for sample embedded programs to demonstrate the applicability of the proposed approach.

1. INTRODUCTION

Static timing analysis is essential in real-time systems development, where the schedulability analysis [1] of programs with hard real-time constraints depends on the estimated extreme case performance. It is also useful in verification of timing critical systems, hardware/software co-design of embedded systems, and early design space exploration.

Because of its importance, many researchers have studied the problem and proposed various solutions. However, two problems remain largely unresolved. First, many analysis techniques are highly architecture specific, which makes them expensive to migrate to other architectures. Second, many advanced features in modern processors are still difficult to model. Since they have great impact on system performance, it is overly pessimistic to simply ignore their presence.

In this paper we describe a general approach for solving these problems. We address the first difficulty by integrating a machine independent timing analysis scheme with our programmable platform-based software development infrastructure (called MESCAL) [2], which allows automatic retargetability by using a unified machine description language. We address the second one by modeling the effects of several, hitherto largely ignored, important features in modern processors.

To be suitable for static timing analysis, the program must be statically predictable, e.g. it cannot have infinite loops or dynamic function calls. In general, the analysis is performed at task-level, in which we do not consider the effects of preemption or interrupts.

This paper is organized as follows. In Section 2 we survey related work. Section 3 provides a review of a powerful integer linear programming (ILP) based software performance bounding technique, which forms the foundation of our tool. We present our retargetable design methodology in Section 4. In Section 5, we describe how to extend the analysis scheme to model the effects of branch prediction, predication, and instruction pre-fetching. Some preliminary experimental results are presented in Section 6 to demonstrate the applicability of the proposed approach. We conclude our work in section 7.

2. RELATED WORK

Early work in the field of timing analysis relies on measuring the program runtimes on the target machine [3]. However, this is known to be unsafe and inaccurate, since it is often impossible to identify the worst-case scenario. Most recent researches focus on analytical methods, in which the analysis is based on information collected before or at compile time.

In order to get fairly accurate estimation results, both program flow and system resource utilization must be analyzed. Since the number of feasible program execution paths can be exponential, explicit [8] and implicit [10] path enumeration techniques are proposed to identify the worst-case program execution sequence efficiently. Micro-architecture affects program execution time by changing instruction timing and program flow. Commonly used mechanisms in modern processors for the purpose of boosting system performance often introduce uncertainty about dynamic program behavior. In particular, the effects of pipelines [4] and caches [5, 6] have been studied extensively. However, most of these approaches only handle some aspect of the problem.

More recently, there have been researches trying to integrate multiple efforts. In [7] the author proposes an integrated path and timing analysis method based on cycle-level symbolic execution. The work in [8] focus on straight line-code and covers aspects on the assembly instruction level as well as on the programming

ISSS'01, October 1-3, 2001, Montréal, Québec, Canada.

language level. The authors in [9] present a prototype for worst-case execution time (WCET) analysis system, which is similar to ours, but in their work the level of retargetability is unclear. In general, due to the dependency on built-in-house development tools (e.g. simulator/compiler) or target specific data schema, the portability of most existing works are rather limited.

To our knowledge, there has been little work on modeling of predication and software instruction pre-fetching for timing estimation. The effect of branch prediction is studied in [11]. However, it's based on branch target buffer modeling by considering *all* possible program execution paths.

3. INTEGER LINEAR PROGRAMMING (ILP) BASED TIMING ANALYSIS SCHEME

In this section we briefly review the ILP based bounding technique used in Cinderella [10], which is adapted as the core analysis scheme in our work. Cinderella is a timing analysis tool for simple embedded processors. It consists of two components for solving the WCET problem: program flow analysis and micro-architecture modeling.

Program flow analysis characterizes the program flow by two types of linear constraints, namely *structural constraints* and *functionality constraints*. The construction of these constraints is illustrated in Figure 1, where the label on the node/edge denotes its execution/flow count.

```
/* k >= 0 */
s = k;
while (k < 10) {
    if (ok)
        j++;
    else {
        j = 0;
        ok = true;
    }
    k++;
}
r = j;
```

(a) Code

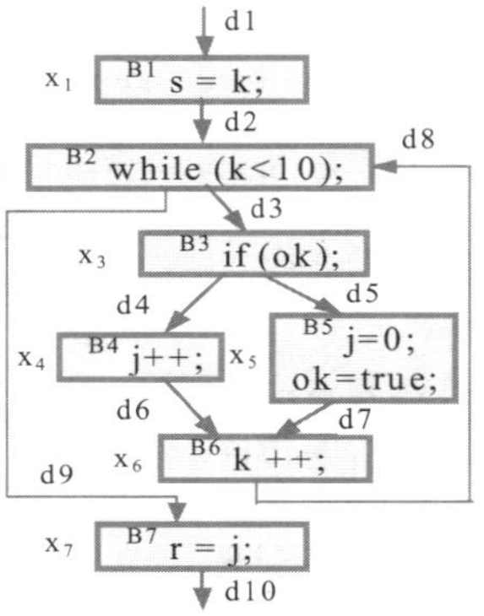

(b) Control flow graph

Figure 1. Code segment example and its CFG.

Structural constraints can be automatically derived from the Control Flow Graph (CFG) based on the flow constraints at each node, i.e. the basic block execution count is equal to the number of times that the controls enters the node (inflow), and is also equal to the number of times that the control exists the node (outflow). For example: $x_1=d_1=d_2$. *Functionality constraints* can be derived by performing data flow analysis, or more effectively specified by the user. They provide two types of logical flow information. The first type gives loop bounds in the program. For example, we can see in the code fragment above that the loop body will be executed between 0 and 10 times each time the loop entered, this information can be specified as: $0x_1 \leq x_3 \leq 10x_1$. The second type specifies other path information that may help tighten the analysis results. For example, due to the correlation between basic blocks B_4 and B_5, the *else* statement can be executed at most once inside the loop, this information can be specified as: $x_5 \leq 1x_1$.

If we assume that the execution time of a basic block B_i of the program is a constant c_i (e.g. each instruction has fixed timing), let x_i be the execution count, then the total execution time of the program can be expressed as $\boldsymbol{\sum c_i x_i}$. Since all the constraints on x_i are expressed as integer linear formulas, we can solve the WCET problem by maximizing the cost function of total execution time under the constraints derived above using ILP techniques.

Nevertheless, in modern architectures instruction timing may vary depending on factors such as operand value and machine state. Micro-architecture modeling is used to account for these effects on dynamic program behavior. For example, a simulator can be used to obtain the cost coefficient of a basic block by modeling pipeline interaction within a known sequence of instructions. Cache behavior is hard to model because it depends potentially on a long trace in history. To tackle this problem Cinderella uses a refined solution based on the same ILP technique. The analysis for a direct mapped Icache is illustrated as follows:

Define an l-block as a contiguous sequence of instructions within the same basic block that are mapped to the same set in the Icache, and thus have identical hit/miss behavior. Denote an l-block inside a basic block as Bi.j. It is associated with two variables $x_{i.j}^{hit}$ and $x_{i.j}^{miss}$, which represent its hit and miss counts. Let $c_{i.j}^{hit}$ and $c_{i.j}^{miss}$ represent the hit and miss execution time of Bi.j respectively, then the new cost function for total execution time can be expressed as: $\boldsymbol{\sum_i \sum_j (c_{i.j}^{hit} x_{i.j}^{hit} + c_{i.j}^{miss} x_{i.j}^{miss})}$. Since the total execution count of Bi.j is equal to that of the basic block containing it, we have: $x_i = x_{i.j}^{hit} + x_{i.j}^{miss}$.

For any two l-blocks mapped to the same cache set, they *conflict* with each other if their address tags are different. Otherwise they are said to be *non-conflicting*. If there are less than one conflicting l-blocks mapped to a cache set, *the sum of their miss counts must be at most 1*. For each cache set containing two or more conflicting l-blocks, a *cache conflict graph (CCG)* is constructed. It contains a start node 's' (representing the start of the program), an end node 'e' (representing the end of the program), and a node '$B_{k.l}$' for every l-block $B_{k.l}$ mapped to the same cache set. There is a directed edge drawn from node $B_{k.l}$ to $B_{m.n}$, if there exists a path in the CFG from basic block B_k to basic block B_m without passing through any other l-blocks of the same cache set. We assign a new variable p(k.l, m.n) to count the number of times that control pass the edge. Then we can derive a new set of linear constraints from the CCG as follows.

Similar to the CFG analysis, for each node $B_{i.j}$ the sum of inflow must be equal to its execution count and the sum of the outflow. Therefore, we have: $x_i = \sum_{u.v} p(u.v,\ i.j) = \sum_{u.v} p(i.j,\ u.v)$, where "u.v" denotes some other node $B_{u.v}$ that is connected with $B_{i.j}$. In particular, for the start node 's', *the sum of outflow is equal to the number of times the program segment is executed.* Note that the constraints link the new variables to those we used in CFG analysis, therefore allow the effect of all parts to be considered in a global way. Besides, according to the definition of the CCG, the number of the cache hits can be determined by: $p(i.j,\ i.j) \leq x_{i.j}^{hit} \leq p(s,\ i.j) + p(i.j, i.j)$. These constraints, together with the structural constraints and functionality constraints, are used to solve the ILP problem for the new cost function. The same technique can be extended to model set associative caches and data caches. More details can be found in [10].

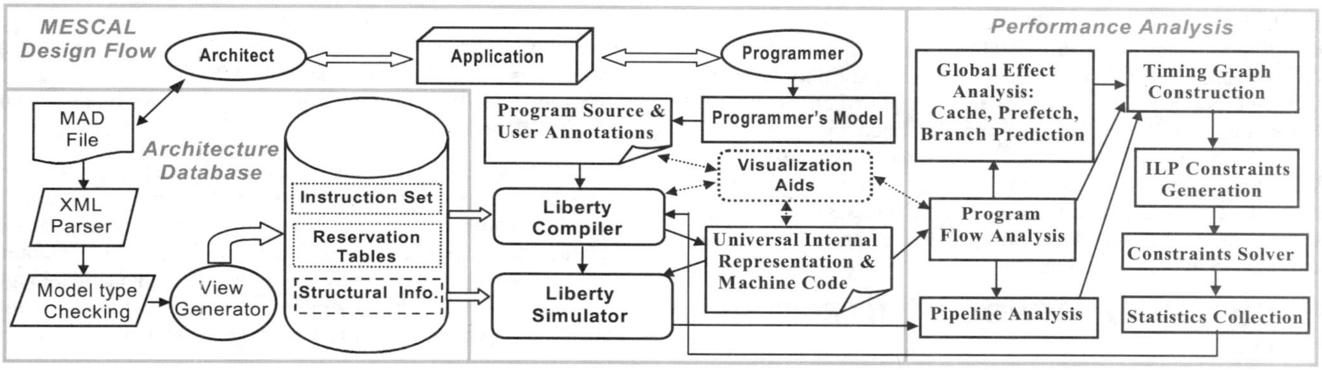

Figure 2. System overview.

4. DESIGN METHODOLOGY

As previously mentioned, both program flow and micro-architecture need to be modeled for accurate timing analysis. In general both depend heavily on target specific information, which varies a lot for different machines. For example, in program flow analysis we need to understand the instruction set architecture, while in micro-architecture modeling we need to know the system resource utilization and their effects on program's dynamic behavior. Traditionally, such information is hard-coded into the development tools, which makes it hard to retarget to different architectures. In this paper we show how we can reduce the overall design efforts and complexity of the problem, through the adoption of an approach that minimizes the overhead in doing so. Figure 2 gives the overview of our approach.

4.1 MESCAL Software Design Environment

The goal of MESCAL [2] project is to provide a programmer's model and software development environment that allows for efficient implementation of an interesting set of applications onto a family of fully-programmable architectures/micro-architectures. As depicted in Figure 2, software development tools involve the compiler, simulator, performance analyzer, debugger, and visualization aids. Despite their functionality division, they are closely related and often share common information about target platform. For example, both the compiler and the simulator need to know the information contained in the reservation table for a VLIW processor. These common dependencies motivate us to use a unified architecture description to drive the whole development system.

There have been a lot of research efforts in the area of machine description, such as MDES used in IMPACT compiler [12]. Our approach is different from traditional ones in that MESCAL Architecture Description (MAD) aims to provide both simulator view and compiler view for the target processor. MAD is a mixed level description that has combined instruction semantics and structural specification, which provides the flexibility to express the variety of architectural features found in modern processors. It is written using XML as syntax. We chose XML because of its flexibility and its popularity in public domain. Currently the description consists of five sections: The **Declaration section** specifies abstract machine parameters. For example: whether interlocking is supported or not, in-order or out-of-order instruction issue, etc. The **Unit section** describes pipeline stages and special function units, such as register files, memory, branch predictor, etc. The **Operand section** corresponds to the layer between the storage units and the operation, where different addressing modes are enumerated. The type of operand can be immediate, register, or composite. The **Operation section** has two elements. *Operation* specifies the attributes of individual instructions, such as instruction format, encoding, and behavior. *Opergroup* groups instruction into instruction sets for the convenience of later reference. The **Connection section** defines two types of connection: *pipe* and *link*. The former specifies the pipeline flow in the architecture and the latter specifies the data flow.

4.2 Implementation Strategy

As described in section 3, our core analysis scheme is machine independent and based on ILP model. However, in Cinderella's case the user still needs to develop a handcrafted backend support (including disassembler and simulator) for each different target processor, which is difficult and inefficient for complicated architectures. In our implementation, the program flow analysis is performed on the compiler universal intermediate representation of the program [16]. In this way we can have a unified interface and processing mechanism for the compiled "program", while the differences between architectures are captured by the machine description and handled by the front end of compiler.

Other information required by flow analysis can be derived from the architecture description. For example, to build the program's flow control graph we need to identify the instructions that may change program flow. We can build a table from the architecture description files to store this kind of ISA information (i.e., the mapping between instructions and their types - conditional jump, function call, return, etc.). The data structures for such records are machine independent and manipulated by the core analysis algorithm. Note that although some information is not explicitly presented in the architecture description, it can be inferred from the associated attributes (e.g. function call has a special register PC as its arguments).

As integrated in the same framework, the tools can benefit from each other. The compiler may provide other useful information, such as the profiling results, to assist the analysis. With the help of visualization aids, the user can add annotation and additional constraints to help tighten the estimation results [10], which can be then used as feedback to help tune the design performance.

The modeling of the micro-architecture consists of two parts. The first models the timing of program's execution in a restricted scope. The simulator can be used for this purpose. It accurately models the effect of the pipeline and gives the cost coefficients of basic blocks. The overhead of crafting a simulator from scratch can be avoided as the simulator is automatically built from the machine description. The second one is the global effect analysis. One example is the cache modeling described in section 3, in which the required information, such as the cache size and set associativity, can also be automatically extracted from the architecture description. Hence the core analysis module is kept machine independent and the analysis framework can be easily retargeted to new architectures.

5. ADVANCED MICRO-ARCHITECTURE MODELING

Similar to cache, there are other features in modern processors that affect program's execution in a global way, such as branch prediction, predication, and instruction pre-fetching. These features dramatically reduce the program execution time and an inability to model them will result in a severely pessimistic analysis. In this section we demonstrate how to extend the analysis scheme to model their effects on program timing.

5.1 Branch Prediction Analysis

To reduce the penalty caused by control hazards in pipeline processors, it is common to predict the outcome of a branch without interrupting the instruction flow. In modern processors, both *static* and *dynamic* branch prediction schemes are employed. The analysis for commonly used static prediction schemes can easily fit into our ILP based solution. The dynamic schemes are much harder to model statically, due to the fact that the prediction results are based on program behavior at runtime. Existing methods rely on static simulation techniques, such as BTB modeling used in [11], to identify worst case branching cost and then combine it with high-level analysis for WCET estimation.

Three commonly used static prediction schemes are: *predict-taken*, *predict-untaken*, and *delayed-branch-with-canceling* [13]. It is the compiler's responsibility to determine the predicted outcome and schedule code appropriately. In many cases the decision is based on examination of program flow behavior. This makes it suitable for static timing analysis. An example is shown in Figure 3.

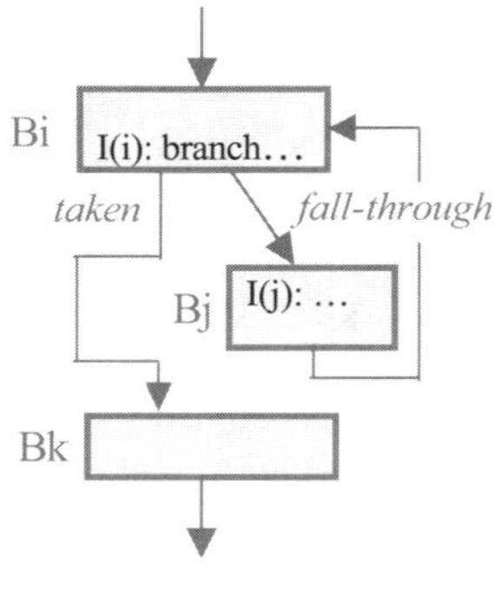

Figure 3. Control flow example.

Suppose instruction I(i) inside the loop is predicted as not taken, which is the case in most execution times. At runtime, the processor will check the result after the branch is resolved. If it is the same as predicted, then no penalty is involved. Otherwise, the instruction I[j] scheduled after the branch instruction is turned into a no-op and the program will continue to execute in the correct direction. To model this effect, we can count the execution time of I[j] into that of the basic block B_i. Then its corresponding term $c_i x_i$ in the original cost function of the program's total execution time would be replaced by: $(c_i^{miss\text{-}predict} x_i^{miss\text{-}predict} + c_i^{correct\text{-}predict} x_i^{correct\text{-}predict})$, where $x_i = x_i^{miss\text{-}predict} + x_i^{correct\text{-}predict}$. Suppose the shown program fragment is executed only once, then there would be only one miss-prediction, which corresponds to: $x_i^{miss\text{-}predict} = 1$. These constraints link the new variables with those we used in program flow analysis and cache analysis, and are sufficient to bound the observed case. We can model similar cases and other schemes using the same approach.

Nevertheless, there are other cases where the branch does not come from loops, and where the compiler depends on profiled information to predict the outcome. In these cases, we can still represent the variances in execution time by linear constraints. The worst-case scenario may be assumed to have the longest execution path (e.g. always predicted wrong), or we can rely on data flow analysis and user annotation for the bounds.

5.2 Predication Analysis

Modern compilers use a more aggressive optimization technique to transform the control flow into predication, and thus eliminate inefficiencies in handling branch instructions. In this approach, most instructions can be tagged with some guarding predicate, a special 1-bit register. The execution of the instruction may be nullified at runtime if the predicate value is FALSE (0). As a result the instruction latency may vary depending on the results of the predicate define instructions. To model this optimization effect, we can partition the instructions within a basic block into smaller groups based on their predicates. Thus the total execution time would be the sum of cost terms of each group of instructions, which is the product of its normal execution time and count plus the product of its nullified execution time and count. In the worst case we may have one cost term for each instruction. An example using IA-64 architecture [14] is shown in figure 4. The default semantics of "cmp.eq" is to set p1 and p2 to complementary values depending on the comparison results. Therefore we can derive that instruction B and instruction D are mutually exclusive and cannot be executed normally at the same time. The dependence among the predicates (e.g. dominance, mutual exclusion, exhaustion, etc.) can be derived from a BDD package [15] generated when the compiler performs the optimization, or provided by user annotations.

```
      cmp.eq  p1, p2 = r5,r4 ;: // cycle 0: instr A
(p1)  ld8     r1 = [r3] ;:      // cycle 1: instr B
      add     r3 = r1, r2 ;:    // cycle ?: instr C
(p2)  ld8     r4 = [r6] ;:      // cycle ?: instr D
      add     r6 = r4, r5 ;:    // cycle ?: instr E
```

(a) Basic block Xi

$$
\begin{aligned}
Xi &= X_{iA} = X_{iC} = X_{iE} && \text{//execution count equation} \\
&= X_{iB}^{N} + X_{iB}^{n} && \text{//'N' denotes normal case} \\
&= X_{iD}^{N} + X_{iD}^{n} && \text{//'n' denotes nullified case} \\
X_{iB}^{N} &= X_{iD}^{n} \quad (X_{iB}^{n} = X_{iD}^{N})
\end{aligned}
$$

(b) Linear constraints for execution counts

$$
\begin{aligned}
\text{Total\_execution\_time} = {} & X_{iA} C_{iA} + X_{iC} C_{iC} + X_{iE} C_{iE} \\
& + X_{iB}^{N} C_{iB}^{N} + X_{iB}^{n} C_{iB}^{n} \\
& + X_{iD}^{N} C_{iD}^{N} + X_{iD}^{n} C_{iD}^{n}
\end{aligned}
$$

(c) Modified cost function

Figure 4. Predication modeling example.

5.3 Instruction Pre-fetching Analysis

Instruction pre-fetching [17] is another important scheme to hide the relatively slow speed of memory system. In software controlled methods, since pre-fetching instructions can change the state of cache, their effects must be modeled in the cache analysis. Based on the observation that, in the case of pre-fetching, the program flow is still characterized by the execution of the pre-fetching l-block, while the cache content is determined by the pre-fetched data, we can modify our cache analysis scheme described earlier to factor in the effect of pre-fetching instructions.

An example using a directed mapped Icache is shown in Figure 5, in which $B_{5.3}$ and $B_{6.1}$ are non-conflicting l-blocks. They both conflict with $B_{4.1}$, which is pre-fetched by $B_{1.1}$. The modified cache conflict graph CCG' that corresponds the cache set they are mapped to is constructed as follows: first we add in the l-block that contains instructions pre-fetching to the same cache set, in this case $B_{1.1}$. The 'pre-fetch' nodes are distinguished from the normal nodes by attached attributes. The edges for the newly added nodes are drawn in the same way as for constructing the CCG. We can then determine if an edge represents a transition that results in a cache miss (denoted as 'C' in the graph, otherwise denoted as 'N') by looking at the cache content of the nodes it connects. Note that for a 'pre-fetch' node, we need to consider its pre-fetched data when we decide the hit/miss property of its connected edge. For example, since $B_{1.1}$ pre-fetches $B_{4.1}$, and $B_{4.1}$ conflict with $B_{5.3}$, the edge from $B_{1.1}$ to $B_{4.1}$ is counted as a hit, while the edge from $B_{1.1}$ to $B_{5.3}$ is counted as miss. Therefore, we can generate the constraints for bounding cache hits of the l-blocks, e.g., $x_{4.1}^{hit} = p(4.1,4.1) + p(1.1,4.1)$. Other types of constraints can be generated as we have described for the CCG, with the modification that when generating the flow related constraints, we need to count the execution of the pre-fetching l-block associated with a 'pre-fetch' node. For example, the constraints for node $B_{1.1}$ would be: $p(s,1.1) = p(1.1,e) + p(1.1,4.1) + p(1.1,5.3) = x_1$. Similarly we can extend the scheme to model other cases and set associative caches, which have been omitted for sake of brevity.

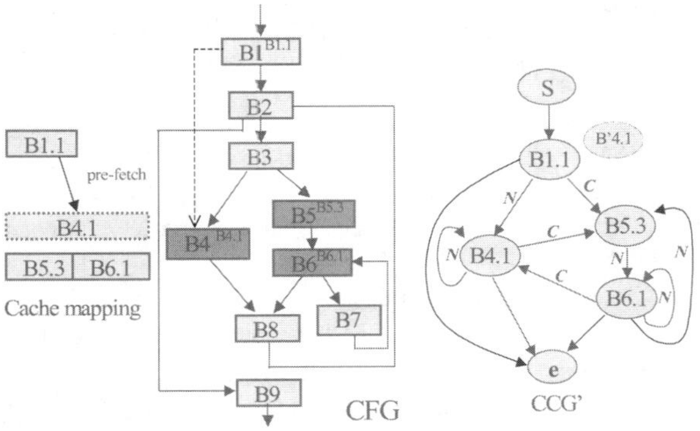

Figure 5. Example of cache analysis with pre-fetching.

6. EXPERIMENTAL RESULTS

As an initial proof-of-concept experiment to verify the applicability of our approach, we have incorporated and tested the core analysis scheme as described in section 3 within the Liberty compiler infrastructure [16]. The target architectures we experiment with belong to the IMPACT EPIC [12] class, which allows effective exploitation of instruction-level parallelism and has configurable aspects such as memory characteristics, register file sizes, number of functional units, and specialized functional units. The architecture configuration from which we obtained the test data are IMPACT EPIC-8G-1BL [12], which is an 8-issue 1-branch-slot VLIW processor that supports general speculation, and EPIC-1G-1BL, which is an 1-issue processor. Table 1 gives a brief description of the programs we tested. The CPU time is measured on a server running Linux with Pentium III 800Mhz CPU and 2 Gig memory.

Table 1. Description of tested programs.

Program Name	Description
Jfdctint	JPEG slow-but-accurate implementation of DCT
Stats	Calculate the sum, mean and variance of two arrays
FFT	1024-point Fast Fourier Transform
Matcnt	Summation of 2 100*100 matrices
Sort	Sort an array using BubbleSort

Table 2 shows the flow analysis results. The cost coefficients of the basic blocks are derived from the instruction scheduling information, which is feasible as the compiler has fully knowledge of pipeline resource usage for VLIW processors. The estimation results are compared with the those obtained from compiler profiling, in which we have to manually set the worst case scenario input data, therefore may not get the *exact* actual bound. The unit of the data listed for WCET is 'cycle'. The last column shows the ILP solver (lp_solve) runtime in 'second'.

Table 2. Experimental results of flow analysis.

(a) Using configuration EPIC-1G-1BL

Program	Estimated WCET	Profiled WCET	Time
Jfdctint	1471	1471	0.00
Stats	151202	151202	0.03
FFT	198272	198272	0.03
Matcnt	491063	481063	0.01
Sort	2626261	2626261	0.02

(b) Using configuration EPIC-8G-1BL

Program	Estimated WCET	Profiled WCET	Time
Jfdctint	1434	1434	0.00
Stats	126113	126113	0.03
FFT	195708	195708	0.03
Matcnt	380620	380620	0.01
Sort	1625752	1625752	0.02

Table 3 shows the Icache analysis results. Comparisons are presented with the results obtained from the Dinero IV cache simulator. The input to Dinero IV is the program's execution trace generated by Liberty emulator. Note that to verify the cache analysis accuracy, we explicitly set the basic block execution counts so that they match the execution trace. The units of the data shown are 'total_access_count / total_miss_count'.

We can see that the estimated results are very close to those given by other standard tools. As analyzed in [10] the ILP technique is efficient compared with other methods. In general, the problem size will grow with the number of variables (corresponding to vertices and edges in the constructed timing graphs), program structure complexity (represented by the generated linear constraints), and architecture configuration (e.g. cache associativity). Furthermore, as indicated in table 3-c, the overhead of static analysis can be much lower than simulation based scheme, especially for programs with long execution trace but unsophisticated structures.

Table 3. Experimental results of cache analysis.

(a) Cache configuration: Size = 512; Line Size = 32; Assoc. = 1

Program Name	Cache Analysis	Dinero IV
Jfdctint	1583 / 38	1583 / 38
Stats	209394 / 2072	209394 / 2072
FFT	167068 / 1023	167068 / 1023
Matcnt	721196 / 39	721196 / 39
Sort	4996587 / 20	4996587 / 20

(b)Cache configuration: Size = 512; Line Size = 16; Assoc. = 2

Program Name	Cache Analysis	Dinero IV
Jfdctint	1583 / 73	1583 / 73
Stats	209394 / 145	209394 / 145
FFT	167068 / 60	167068 / 60
Matcnt	721196 / 76	721196 / 76
Sort	4996587 / 37	4996587 / 37

(c) Measured runtime in experiment (a)

Program Name	Cache Analysis	Dinero IV
Jfdctint	0.06	0.02
Stats	0.19	0.38
FFT	0.08	0.28
Matcnt	0.09	1.19
Sort	0.03	8.25

7. CONCLUSION

In this paper we have described an approach for retargetable static software timing analysis. We propose to integrate a machine independent timing analysis scheme with our programmable platform-based software development environment.

The advantages of this approach are twofold. First, by separating machine dependent and independent parts, and carefully designing the interface, we can make the timing analysis tool retargetable and modular. Second, due to the close interaction, the modules in the infrastructure can benefit from each other. Compared with other methods, in our approach significant design efforts can be leveraged among the modules in the same development infrastructure, including the highly optimizing compiler and automatically built simulator. The core analysis scheme can handle both software/hardware aspects in a uniform ILP framework and remains primarily unchanged. Furthermore, as we have demonstrated, the core analysis scheme can be easily extended to model several of the most important features in contemporary architectures, and thus produce tighter bounds.

8. ACKNOWLEDGEMENT

The authors would like to acknowledge the support from GSRC, and suggestions from all colleagues, in particular Yau-Tsun Steven Li. This work is partly sponsored by Hangseng Overseas Scholarship.

9. REFERENCES

[1] J. Stankovic, M. Spuri, M. Di Natale, and G. Buttazzo. "Implications of classical scheduling results for real-time scheduling". *IEEE Computer,* pages 16--25, June 1995.

[2] K. Keutzer, S. Malik, A. R. Newton, J. Rabaey and A. Sangiovanni-Vincentelli. "System Level Design: Orthogonolization of Concerns and Platform-Based Design". *IEEE Transactions on Computer-Aided Design of Integrated Circuits and Systems*, 19(12), December 2000.

[3] P. Gopinath and R. Gupta. "Applying compiler techniques to scheduling in Real-time systems". In *Proceedings of 1990 IEEE Real-Time Systems Symposium*, pages 247--256, 1990.

[4] S. Lim, Y. H. Bae, G. Tae Jang, B. Rhee, S. Lyul Min, C. Y. Park, H. Shin, K. Park, S. Moon, C. S. Kim, "An Accurate Worst Case Timing Analysis Technique for RISC Processors," In *Proceedings of the 15th Real-Time Systems Symposium*, 1994.

[5] R. T. White, F. Mueller, C. A. Healy, D. B. Whalley, and M. G. Harmon, "Timing Analysis for Data Caches and Set-Associative Caches". In *Proceedings of the IEEE Real-Time Technology and Applications Symposium*, Montreal, Canada, pp. 192—202, June 1997.

[6] F. Mueller. "Timing predictions for multi-level caches". In *ACM SIGPLAN Workshop on Language, Compiler, and Tool Support for Real-Time Systems*, pages 29--36, 1997.

[7] T. Lundqvist and P. Stenstrom. "An integrated path and timing analysis method based on cyclelevel symbolic execution". *Journal of Real-Time Systems*, November 1999.

[8] F. Stappert and P. Altenbernd. "Complete Worst-Case Execution Time Analysis of Straight-line Hard Real-Time Programs." *Journal of Systems Architecture*, 46(4), 2000.

[9] J. Engblom, A. Ermedahl, M. Sjodin, J. Gustafsson, and H. Hansson, "Worst-Case Execution-Time Analysis for Embedded Real-Time Systems". *Unpublished technique report*, Department of Computer Systems, Uppsala University, Sweden, 2000.

[10] Y. S. Li, S. Malik and A. Wolfe, "Cache Modeling for Real-Time Software: Beyond Direct Mapped Instruction Caches". In *Proceedings of the IEEE Real-Time Systems Symposium*, December 1996.

[11] A. Colin and I. Puaut. "Worst case execution time analysis for a processor with branch prediction". In *Real-Time Systems*, 18(2-3): 249--274, May 2000.

[12] "The IMPACT Research Group", http://www.crhc.uiuc.edu/IMPACT

[13] J. Hennessy, J. L. Hennessy, D. Goldberg, D. A. Patterson. "Computer Architecture : A Quantitative Approach". Morgan Kaufmann Publishers, 1996.

[14] Itanium^{TM} Processor Microarchitecture Reference. *Technical report*, Intel Corp., August 2000. http://developer.intel.com/design/ia-64/

[15] J. W. Sias, D. I. August, and W. W. Hwu. "Accurate and Efficient Predicate Analysis with Binary Decision Diagrams". In *Proceedings of the 33rd International Symposium on Microrchitecture*, December 2000.

[16] "The Liberty Computer Architecture Research Group", http://liberty.cs.princeton.edu

[17] C. Luk and T. Mowry. "Cooperative Prefetching: Compiler and Hardware Support for Effective Instruction Prefetching in Modern Processors". In *Proceedings of 31st International Symposium on Microarchitecture*, pages 182--193, December 1998.

Performance Analysis with Confidence Intervals for Embedded Software Processes

Per Bjuréus
Saab Avionics, Sweden
perb@imit.kth.se

Axel Jantsch
Royal Institute of Technology, Sweden
axel@imit.kth.se

Abstract

The choice of algorithms has a large impact on the performance of embedded real-time systems. Therefore, performance estimation of embedded software is vital in an early design phase. Consequently, high-level estimation techniques have been devised, but the accuracy of the estimations vary a lot depending on the algorithm and its context. We address this problem by proposing an estimation technique that both estimates the performance and computes the expected accuracy. The accuracy is used to provide a confidence interval to the estimated performance. The estimation framework presented in this paper has been crafted to fit with the MASCOT environment, but the underlying techniques can also be applied to other high-level design exploration frameworks.

1. Introduction

Performance estimation of high-level specifications is mostly performed in a back-of-the-envelope fashion based on user experience. This procedure either leads to unpredictable and poor accuracy or involves many experienced engineers participating in time consuming discussions and studies. Hence, estimation tools have been developed, e.g. Cadence VCC [6], the SPI workbench [1], and the Polis Codesign tool from UC Berkeley [2]. Using tools is much faster and a large number of different solutions can be explored in short time. Unfortunately, the accuracy of the estimations varies widely and, even more important, it is largely unknown. This is the problem that we address.

Under the assumption that the system is specified as a collection of concurrent processes that are invoked sporadically, the estimator computes the execution time of invocations and provides a confidence interval. The technique uses an execution trace, generated by simulation, which is hierarchically decomposed. The decomposition exposes the source of uncertainty, and enables the user to focus on profiling and characterization of components and operations that contribute most to the inaccuracy. Hence, the estimation can be gradually improved until a satisfactory level of accuracy has been reached.

Performance analysis and estimation can be divided into static and dynamic techniques. Static techniques [1][4][8] are concerned with the analysis of a specification without simulating or executing the specification. It is often employed for worst-case analysis and is suitable for finding corner cases that are hard to cover with simulation or execution. Dynamic techniques [2][6][7] on the other hand, are concerned with the analysis of run-time behavior, and relies on test vectors and input scenarios. Dynamic techniques are preferred when the system performance is heavily dependent on the input data, and in cases where the average performance is more relevant than worst-case behavior.

Besides classification into static and dynamic approaches, the level of abstraction also characterizes different performance estimation techniques. Low-level estimation [5] considers compiled and optimized machine code and employs detailed models of the processor architecture and memory hierarchy. Low-level estimation can thus accurately account for operating system, pipelining and cache effects. High-level estimation [9][10] on the other hand deals with high-level specifications and employs a very abstract model of the architecture. Both low-level and high-level estimation fulfills important needs in system design; high-level techniques are excellent for early feasibility studies, and low-level techniques yield unprecedented accuracy in a late design phase.

Our method is a high-level, dynamic estimation technique. However, it not only estimates the performance but also the accuracy of the result. In this respect, it is complementary to most other high-level estimation techniques. The main features are the following:

- Performance estimation is performed on an arbitrary *high-level specification*, where the actual code or RTL description is largely unknown. This means that we have little hope of getting high accuracy. Instead, we try to compute the accuracy, and provide information about the origin of potential inaccuracy.
- Our approach is *trace-based*, which means that the simulation needs only be run once in "trace-mode", where all operations are recorded. This decouples the behavioral

specification from the estimation and speeds up the estimation significantly when compared to annotated performance simulation.

- We employ a *hierarchical decomposition* of functions, which gives the developer a quick and dirty first approximation but at the same time allows for detailed profiling and characterization of complex algorithms. This also enables designers to collect and post knowledge and experience into the framework for future use.
- The estimation is based on *statistical models*, which is the key to accuracy analysis.

2. Framework and Workflow

The estimation framework and workflow is compatible with the MASCOT [12] modeling environment. The workflow is based on a separation of the behavioral specification from the architectural model (Figure 1).

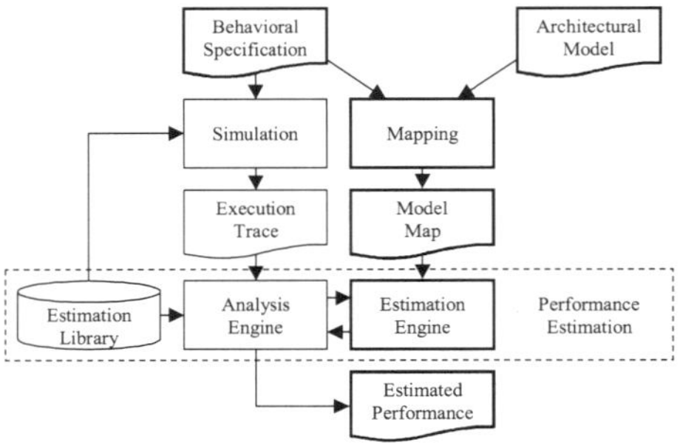

Figure 1. Estimation workflow

The behavioral specification, simulation, and execution trace is discussed below. The architectural model and the mapping is described in section 3.

Although important, we do not address communication in this paper. However, we include communication primitives (e.g. signals, channels, transactions, etc.) in the definitions that follow for completeness.

2.1. Behavioral Specification and Simulation

The behavioral model consists of a set of concurrent communicating processes. A process is able to consume input signals, perform necessary computations and produce output signals. Communication is carried out asynchronously with unbounded FIFO buffers.

Definition 1. A *behavioral specification* is a network of processes represented as a tuple $B=(P, C, S, a)$, where P is a set of processes, $C \in P \times P$ is a set of channels, S is a set of signals, and $a: S \rightarrow C$ is a function mapping signals to channels.

Execution and communication is supposed to be ideal in the sense that it takes zero time. Consequently, time is only advanced by the simulation stimuli or internal timers. This implies that the external stimuli or an internal timer may trigger an arbitrarily long sequence of internal events, which must be completely resolved before the next external event or timer can be processed. During simulation, all process execution and signal communication is recorded in an *execution trace*. It is left to the designer's discretion to ensure that the simulation is realistic.

2.2. Execution Trace

Using an execution trace decouples the behavioral specification from the estimation environment. There are two reasons to do this. First, the specification that we primarily target is heterogeneous, e.g. a mixed Matlab-SDL model, but a homogeneous input to the estimator is preferred since it is easier to process. Second, we envision an estimation framework that can be used with other system specifications, which requires a well defined intermediate format that links the specification and the estimator. Note that this cannot be achieved easily with annotated performance simulation.

There are two atomic elements of the execution trace, the operation and the transaction, as defined below.

Definition 2. An *operation* is a five-tuple: $op=(i, id, pl, ol, r)$, where $i \in \mathbf{N}$ is the instance count, $id \in ID$ is a unique name, $pl=\{p_1,p_2,...,p_n\}$, $n \in \mathbf{N}$ is a parameter list, $ol=\{op_1,op_2,...,op_n\}$, $n \in \mathbf{N}$ is an operation list, and $r \in \mathbf{N}$ is the repeat count.

The operation list component ol allows us to build hierarchical operations of arbitrary depth. The instance count, i determines the number of instances of the operation that can be performed in parallel, and the repeat count r establishes the number of times the operation must be performed in sequence. This allows a crude estimation of parallelism for devices where operations may be performed concurrently, e.g. in SIMD architectures. For sequential processing, such as software executed on an instruction set processor (ISP), the two numbers i and r, are simply multiplied to give the total count of the operation.

Definition 3. A *transaction* is a pair: $tr=(n, w)$, where $n \in \mathbf{N}$ is the number of data tokens transmitted, and $w \in \mathbf{N}$ is the bit width of each token.

Definition 4. An *execution trace* is a list of invocations: $et=\{I_1, I_2, \ldots, I_n\}$, $n \in \mathbf{N}$. An invocation is a tuple $I_k=(t_k, id, sl, el)$, where $t_k \in \mathbf{R}$ is a time-stamp, $id \in P \cup S$ uniquely identifies a process or signal, $sl=\{s_1, s_2, \ldots, s_n\}$, $n \in \mathbf{N}$, $s_k \in S$ is a list of triggering signals, and

$$el = \begin{cases} \{op_s, op_2, \ldots, op_n\} & \text{if } id \in P \\ \{tr_s, tr_2, \ldots, tr_n\} & \text{if } id \in S \end{cases}$$

is either a list of operations or a list of transactions.

The time stamps of the invocations are non-decreasing, i.e. $t_k \le t_{k+1}$. Since an external event or internal timer can trigger a sequence of invocations with the same time stamp, the list of triggering signals is used to resolve data dependencies.

In MASCOT, we generate execution traces both from SDL and from Matlab. The SDL simulator allows us to generate an execution trace simply by switching on the logging function. In Matlab, we have devised a technique to generate an execution trace that relies on object-orientation and overloading of operations with the ability to write the trace to a file. After simulation, the generated files are merged and filtered to create the execution trace.

3. Architectural Model

The architectural model consists of a set of connected processing and communication units.

Definition 5. An architectural model is a triple $am=(X, T, E)$, where X is a set of processing (execution) units, T is a set of communication (transmission) units, and $E \subseteq X\times X \cup T\times T \cup X\times T \cup T\times X$ is a set of directed edges connecting the units.

A processing unit is modeled as an abstract machine characterized by a *virtual instruction* set. The abstract machine cannot perform any computation, but only models the performance of the unit.

Definition 6. A *processing unit* is a triple $x=(V, W, \Delta)$, where V is a virtual instruction set, W is an extended instruction set, and Δ is a set of instruction profiles. An instruction profile $\delta\in\Delta$ is a function $\delta: V\cup W \rightarrow \mathbf{R}\times\mathbf{R}$ such that $\delta(op)=(\mu, \sigma^2)$, where $op\in V\cup W$, and $\mu\in\mathbf{R}$ and $\sigma^2\in\mathbf{R}$ associates virtual instructions with a mean execution time and variance.

Selection of a virtual instruction set is a delicate task, where the goal is to select instructions that are abstract enough to support a large variety of processing units, but specific enough to differentiate between distinct types of instructions. A complete treatment of the selection of a virtual instruction set is not within the scope of this paper. The selection of a proper profile $\delta\in\Delta$ for estimation can be done manually or automatically e.g. with signatures and discriminating functions [3].

3.1. Processor Characterization

Processor characterization can be performed analytically or empirically. The analytical approach is based on datasheet analysis [3] and it does not require any compilation or execution. Although a range of execution times can be derived with datasheet analysis, it is hard to capture the statistical distribution of virtual instruction execution times that reflect compiler optimizations and program context. The empirical approach on the other hand is based on benchmarks [11] that are compiled and analyzed. This approach readily captures the statistical distribution but requires representative benchmark suites.

The virtual instruction set models the operations of generic processors, but sometimes we must also be able to capture processor specific features. One example is the MAC operation of a DSP processor that comprises a MUL and an ADD instruction. A similar situation may arise when the user has access to the execution time of a specific function, e.g. as provided by the processor manufacturer. In both cases, the user needs to add an interpretation of the operation to the estimator. There are two ways to handle this. Either the operation is added to the extended instruction set, W of the processor, or the operation is modeled as a macro that is posted in the Estimation Library. The former is less general but more accurate than the latter. To utilize extended operations in estimation, the behavioral specification is annotated with extra trace calls. Note that adding an extended instruction to one processor model does not require changes in other processor models. Note also that introducing extra trace calls in the behavioral specification does not change the behavior.

3.2. Mapping

The behavioral model is mapped to the architectural model through a pair of mapping functions:

Definition 7. A *model map* is a pair $mm = (pm, sm)$, where $pm:P\rightarrow X$ maps processes to process units, and $sm:S\rightarrow T$ maps signals to communication units.

4. Performance Estimation

The estimation workflow in Figure 1 shows that the performance estimator in the dashed box has been divided into three parts: The estimation engine, the analysis engine, and the Estimation Library containing trace macros. The division between estimation engine and analysis engine allows us to plug in different estimation engines without changing the analysis engine. The estimation engine dictates what we estimate and can be tailored to a particular architectural component. Several engines can be used in the same estimation session. The Estimation Library, containing trace macros, unburdens the execution trace, increases the accuracy, and simplifies instruction identification. The framework and performance estimator has been implemented in the *EstiMate* tool.

4.1. Estimation Procedure

EstiMate implements data structures for the framework and orchestrates the analysis and estimation engines. During estimation the following procedure is exercised:

1. The analysis engine reads the execution trace, and for each invocation in the trace performs steps 2 through 9 below.

2. The analysis engine uses the model map to figure out which processor the invoked process runs on, and the proper estimation engine is called.
3. The estimation engine traverses the invocation operation list, and for each operation performs steps 4 through 8 below.
4. If the operation encountered is found in $V \cup W$ of the processor model, the mean and variance for the operation is recorded.
5. If the operation is not found, but it does contain an operation list, the operation list is expanded and step 4 is repeated for each sub-operation.
6. If the operation is not found, and cannot be expanded, the estimation engine queries the analysis engine for an estimation library equivalent.
7. If the analysis engine receives a library query, it performs a lookup, and expands the operation with the equivalent operation list. Back to 4.
8. When the entire invocation has been traversed, the invocation, annotated with execution time mean and variance, is returned.
9. The analysis engine computes the overall execution time for the invocation, and continues from step 1 until all invocations have been read.

4.2. Probabilistic Analysis

The probabilistic analysis takes place when the analysis engine has traversed the execution trace according to the algorithm in section 4.1. The theorems in the following paragraphs are fetched from [14], but can be found in any standard book on probability theory and statistics.

To estimate the execution time of an invocation, we may treat each operation in the execution trace as a stochastic variable, denoted ξ_k^{op}, where $op \in V \cup W$ identifies the instruction, and $1 \leq k \leq n_{op}$, where $n_{op} \in \mathbf{N}$ is the total number of times that the operation op is executed in the invocation. The total execution time of the invocation will thus be a stochastic variable t:

$$t = \sum_{\forall op} \sum_{k=1}^{n_{op}} \xi_k^{op} \tag{1}$$

Consider the inner summation, where the execution times of individual operations are added:

$$t_{op} = \sum_{k=1}^{n_{op}} \xi_k^{op} = \xi_1^{op} + \xi_2^{op} + \ldots + \xi_{n_{op}}^{op} \tag{2}$$

Theorem 1. *Applied central limit theorem.* Let the mean $E[\xi_k^{op}] = \mu_{op}$ and the variance $Var[\xi_k^{op}] = \sigma_{op}^2$. If n_{op} is large and the stochastic variables ξ_1^{op}, ξ_2^{op}, ... are independent, the sum of the stochastic variables, t_{op} is approximately normal distributed:

$$t_{op} \text{ is } N(n_{op}\mu_{op}, \sigma_{op}\sqrt{n_{op}}) \quad \blacksquare$$

Where $N(\mu, \sigma)$ denotes a normal distribution with mean μ and standard deviation σ. Now, combining the outer summation of (1) (where the sums of execution times for different operations are added) with (2) yields:

$$t = \sum_{\forall op} t_{op} \tag{3}$$

Remembering that each t_{op} is normal distributed, and assuming that the stochastic variables t_{op} are independent, we apply the addition theorem for normal distribution:

Theorem 2. *Normal distribution addition theorem.* If ξ_1 is $N(\mu_1, \sigma_1)$, and ξ_2 is $N(\mu_2, \sigma_2)$, then:

$$\xi_1 + \xi_2 \text{ is } N(\mu_1 + \mu_2, \sqrt{\sigma_1^2 + \sigma_2^2}) \quad \blacksquare$$

This yields the distribution for the total execution time:

$$t \text{ is } N(\sum_{\forall op} n_{op}\mu_{op}, \sqrt{\sum_{\forall op} n_{op}\sigma_{op}^2}) \tag{4}$$

Note that we have made two rather strong assumptions, first we have assumed that n_{op} is large, and second that operation execution times are independent. We address these issues in the following paragraphs.

When n_{op} is not large, the stochastic variable t_{op} will not be normal distributed. However, as long as the execution times of different operations are independent, we can use the addition theorem for stochastic variables:

Theorem 3. *Addition Theorem.* Let ξ and η be two independent stochastic variables, then $E[\xi+\eta] = E[\xi]+E[\eta]$, and $Var[\xi+\eta] = Var[\xi]+Var[\eta]$. ■

Since the stochastic variables ξ and η are not normal distributed, the sum will not be normal distributed either. When determining a confidence interval for an arbitrary distribution with known mean and variance, we have to resort to a more conservative method, which is based on Chebyshev's inequality:

Theorem 4. *Chebyshev's inequality.* If ξ is a stochastic variable with $\mu = E[\xi]$ and $\sigma^2 = Var[\xi]$, then

$$P(|\xi - \mu| \geq k\sigma) \leq \frac{1}{k^2}, \quad k > 0 \quad \blacksquare$$

If the execution times of different operations in the execution trace are not independent, we are not allowed to add the variance according to the addition theorem. Consider an execution trace where the same operation is executed several times, either due to the instance and repeat counts, or because it is located inside a loop. That instance of an operation will not likely change its execution time between different executions. The variance must be computed according to the following theorem:

Theorem 5. *Real factor*. If ξ is a stochastic variable, and a is a real number then $Var[a\xi] = a^2 Var[\xi]$. ■

5. Experiments

We have carried out two experiments to investigate the applicability of the proposed framework and method. The behavioral specifications used were the *test1* program from [10], and an image rotation program *imrotate*. Both programs were translated both to Matlab and to C code.

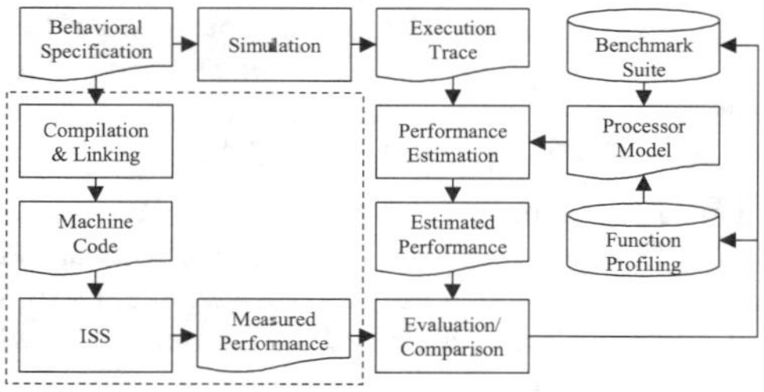

Figure 2. SW Estimation experimental setup

The experimental setup is shown in Figure 2. The Matlab code was simulated, generating an execution trace, which was fed to *EstiMate* along with a processor model. The C code was compiled for an ARM7TDMI processor, and executed with an instruction set simulator (ISS). The estimation engine returned an execution time interval with a confidence degree, which was compared with the measured performance from the ISS.

The ARM7TDMI processor was modeled with a virtual instruction set shown in Table 1.

Table 1. ARM7TDMI Virtual Instruction Set

Instruction	μ	σ^2
ADD	1.500000	0.500000
LOOP	5.000000	0.500000
LE	5.500000	0.500000
FLOOR	1.000000	0.100000
MUL	1.500000	1.000000
SUB	1.500000	0.500000
GT	5.500000	1.000000
DIV	1.500000	1.000000
subsref	2.000000	0.200000

The model was derived empirically using a small set of the program itself as benchmark. All operations in the *test1* program are integer operations, explaining the short execution time and low variance.

We ran the experiment 16 times, varying the number of loop iterations of the four loops of the program (L1-L4). The confidence degree was set to 95% and the estimator computed a two-sided confidence interval based on a normal distribution. The result is shown in Figure 3, where the vertical bars represent the estimated interval, and the diamond shows the measured execution time.

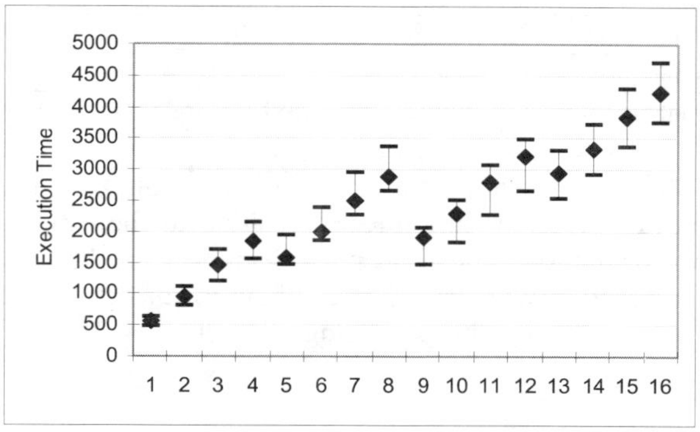

Figure 3. Outcome of test1 experiment

For the second example (image rotation), we had to derive a different processor profile to be able to estimate floating-point emulation. The Virtual Instruction set was enlarged to contain 16 different virtual instructions. An additional 3 instructions were modeled using the Extended Instruction set and 11 instruction were added as trace macros to the Estimation Library to model special Matlab functions. In the image rotation program, the number of independently executing operations was relatively small, and therefore a confidence interval based on Chebyshev's inequality was selected. The measured execution time was well within the estimated interval. Figure 4 shows a screenshot from the execution time analysis in *EstiMate*.

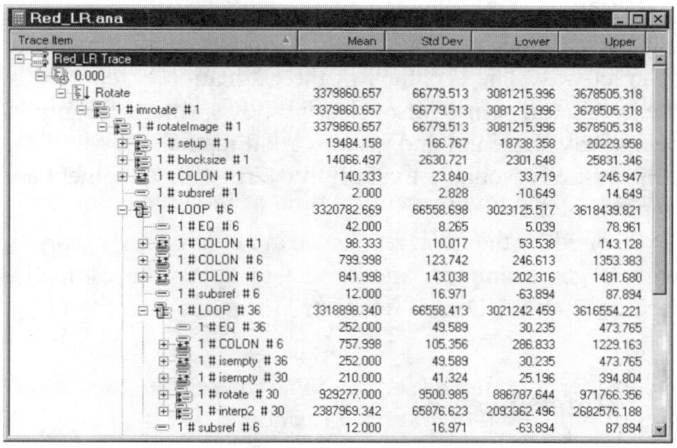

Figure 4. Execution time analysis of imrotate

We observed that the relative accuracy of the estimation increases when the number of independent variables decreases, see Table 2. At the same time, we observe a larger relative error in the estimated execution time, which is what we should expect.

Table 2. Relative error and estimated accuracy

Segment	Measure	Estimate	Error	Accuracy
imrotate	3220928	3379861	4,9%	±8,4%
• blocksize	20552	14066	-31,6%	±83,6%
•• initbounds	1295	1215	-6,1%	±29,6%
•• init_rows	152	133	-12,3%	±69,2%
•• init_image	17402	7882	-54,7%	±149,1%

The accuracy in the table above is computed as the estimated execution time interval relative to the estimated mean execution time. The code segments are hierarchically ordered, with the number of operations in the segments decreasing with increasing hierarchal level.

6. Conclusion

We have presented a novel technique for dealing with accuracy in high-level performance estimation. The technique resides in a formally defined design exploration framework, which provides a stable environment for tools and methods. A performance estimation tool has been developed called *EstiMate*. The results reported in this paper demonstrates the workflow, and shows that the technique can successfully be used, encouraging further development.

It is important to remember what one is actually estimating, especially when dealing with high-level specifications as we do. There are innumerous possible implementations of the algorithms we estimate, some clever and some not. The estimated execution time that our estimator delivers corresponds to *one possible* implementation of the specification. To increase the awareness of what is being estimated, the trace macro library plays an important role giving the designer an opportunity to model algorithms in an abstract way. The accuracy of the estimation is reported by the estimator, which also clearly shows where the bottlenecks may show up, and gives a good idea about what constraints are reasonable to apply for further development and implementation.

Inspired by the good results we are continuously working with larger examples, and expect to apply the estimation technique on the Digital Receiver [13] in the near future.

7. References

[1] Marek Jersak, Dirk Ziegenbein, Fabian Wolf, Kai Richter, Rolf Ernst, "Embedded System Design using the SPI Workbench", *Proceedings of the 3rd International Forum on Design Languages*, Tübingen, Germany, September 2000.

[2] Felice Balarin, Massimiliano Chiodo, Paolo Giusto, Harry Hsieh, Attila Jurecska, Luciano Lavagno, Claudio Passerone, Alberto Sangiovanni-Vincentelli, Ellen Sentovich, Key Suzuki, Bassam Tabbara, *Hardware-Software Co-Design of Embedded Systems: The Polis Approach*, Kluwer Academic Press, 1997.

[3] Paolo Giusto, Grant Martin, Ed Harcourt, "Reliable Estimation of Execution Time of Embedded Software", *Proceedings of the Design, Automation, and Test in Europe (DATE) Conference 2001*, Munich, March 2001.

[4] Luca P. Carloni, Alberto L. Sangiovanni-Vincentelli, "Performance Analysis and Optimization of Latency Insensitive Systems", *Proceedings of the 37th annual Design Automation Conference (DAC)*, Los Angeles, 5-9 June 2000, pp. 361-367.

[5] Mihai T. Lazarescu, Jwahar R. Bammi, Edwin Harcourt, Luciano Lavagno, Marcello Lajolo, "Compilation-based Software Performance Estimation for System Level Design", *Proceedings of the IEEE International High-Level Design Validation and Test Workshop*, Berkeley, CA, USA, 8-10 November 2000, pp. 167-172.

[6] Jwahar R. Bammi, Edwin Harcourt, Wido Kruijtzer, Luciano Lavagno, Mihai T. Lazarescu, "Software Performance Estimation Strategies in a System-Level Design Tool", *Proceedings of the Eighth International Workshop on Hardware/Software Codesign. CODES 2000,* San Diego, CA, USA, 3-5 May 2000, pp. 82-86.

[7] Jie Liu, Marcello Lajolo, Alberto Sangiovanni-Vincentelli, "Software Timing Analysis Using HW/SW Cosimulation and Instruction Set Simulator", *Proceedings of the Sixth International Workshop on Hardware/Software Codesign. (CODES /CASHE'98)*, Seattle, WA, 15-18 March 1998, pp. 65-69.

[8] Maher Rahmouni, Ahmed A. Jerraya, "Formulation and Evaluation Of Scheduling Techniques For Control Flow Graphs", *Proceedings of EURO-DAC European Design Automation Conference*, Brighton, UK, 18-22 September 1995, pp. 386-391

[9] Subhrajit Bhattacharya, Sujit Dey, Franc Brglez, "Performance Analysis and Optimization of Schedules for Conditional and Loop-Intensive Specifications", *Proceedings of 31st ACM/IEE Design Automation Conference*, San Diego, CA, USA, 6-10 June 1994, pp. 491-496.

[10] Kamal S. Khouri, Niraj K. Jha, "Clock Selection for Performance Estimation of Control-Flow Intensive Behaviors", *IEEE Transactions on Computer-Aided Design of Integrated Circuits and Systems, Vol. 20, No. 1*, January 2001, pp. 158-165.

[11] Umesh Krishnaswamy, Isaac D. Scherson, "A Framework for Computer Performance Evaluation Using Benchmark Sets", *IEEE Transactions on Computers, Vol. 49, No. 12*, December 2000, pp. 1325-1338.

[12] Per Bjuréus, Axel Jantsch, "MASCOT: A Specification and Cosimulation Method Integrating Data and Control Flow", *Proceedings of the Design, Automation & Test in Europe Conference (DATE)*, Paris, France, March 2000.

[13] Per Bjuréus, Fredrik Hoffman, "Modeling a Digital Receiver with MASCOT", *Proceedings of the Designer's Forum at Design, Automation & Test in Europe Conference (DATE)*, Munich, Germany, March 2001.

[14] Lennart Råde, Mats Rudemo, *Sannolikhetslära och Statistik*, Biblioteksförlaget, Stockholm, 1984.

On-Line Fault Detection in a Hardware/Software Co-Design Environment: System Partitioning

C. Bolchini
Politecnico di Milano
P.zza L. da Vinci, 32
20133 Milano - Italy
+39-02-23993619
bolchini@elet.polimi.it

L. Pomante
Politecnico di Milano
P.zza L. da Vinci, 32
20133 Milano - Italy
+39-02-23993636
pomante@elet.polimi.it

F. Salice
Politecnico di Milano
P.zza L. da Vinci, 32
20133 Milano - Italy
+39-02-23993636
salice@elet.polimi.it

D. Sciuto
Politecnico di Milano
P.zza L. da Vinci, 32
20133 Milano - Italy
+39-02-23993662
sciuto@elet.polimi.it

ABSTRACT

System reliability aspects are receiving a lot of attention in the design of systems for critical application fields. Often these issues are approached at low abstraction levels, toward the end of the design process, introducing significant overheads. By introducing fault detection requirements at system level, when a Hardware/Software Co-Design process is to be carried out, it is possible to evaluate the overheads and benefits of different solutions. The traditional partitioning phase has been modified in order to take into account the reliability issues, for selecting among the several identified reliable solutions the one that best responds to the user's requirements. The paper presents the partitioning for a Co-Design flow aimed at providing fault detection properties to the final system, selecting the hardware tasks and the software tasks for implementing both the system functionality and the checking capabilities.

Categories and Subject Descriptors

B.6.2 [**Performance and Reliability**]: Reliability, Testing, and Fault-Tolerance.

General Terms

Design. Reliability.

Keywords

Concurrent fault detection, hw/sw co-design, system partitioning.

1. INTRODUCTION

The adoption of Hardware/Software Co-Design methodologies allows the designer to explore the system space for identifying the most promising solution according to the given goals and constraints. By acting at system level the user can take into account, early in the design process, several issues, such as time constraints, area, power consumption, testability, leading to the selection of one solution rather than another, coping with the increasing complexity of the systems to be implemented. In fact, if these aspects are taken into account after system design, when choices have been made, often the impact is quite relevant, allowing a limited manipulation of the system in order to fulfill the additional quality requirements. The reliability co-design project aims at introducing fault detection properties in the specification at system level, so that the subsequent binding of functionalities to either hardware or software may be driven also by reliability issues. The achievement of this reliability co-design goal consists of three main aspects: system specification, design methodologies and hw/sw system partitioning. System specification must allow the user to select and identify those parts of the system (or its entireness) that are particularly important and for which fault detection requirements need to be enforced. A set of design methodologies is necessary to implement the desired detection capabilities, either in hardware or in software. The techniques provide the set of solutions constituting the design space, to be explored by means of metrics (or a cost function) guiding the system partitioning process performing the binding between nominal and fault detection tasks and the hardware and software.

The goal of this paper is to present the hw/sw system partitioning which takes into account also the aspects related to the desired fault detection capabilities. This step is one of the most significant, since it is responsible for the identification of a feasible solution meeting all user's objectives and constraints.

The paper is organized as follows. Section 2 introduces the reliability co-design project, briefly presenting all the aspects of the entire environment. The next section then presents the proposed hw/sw partitioning. Metrics and optimizations are exploited in section 4 explaining the guiding lines for the selection of the solution. Conclusions and future work are presented in the last section.

2. THE RELIABILITY CO-DESIGN FLOW

This section presents the fundamental elements of a traditional hw/sw co-design flow, modified according to the need to cope with fault detection requirements to provide a reliable final system.

2.1 System specification

The first element that needs to be exploited in order to support fault detection issues in a hw/sw co-design environment is the specification language. The user must be able to specify which parts (sections) of the system require an integrity checking; eventually the entire system can be identified as a special case, where all sections need to be checked for fault detection.

Two languages have been considered for the purpose, Occam II [1] and SystemC [2]. The former is at the basis of the TOSCA Co-Design environment, used to carry out our studies [3]. The latter is becoming increasingly a popular system level specification language; since we aim at integrating the proposed approach in a real design flow, the language must be supported. There is no better language, the first one allowed us to experiment the proposed co-design flow, the enhancement of SystemC, on the other hand, provided the feasibility of the approach in industrial design flows.

2.2 System architecture and fault model

The reference architectural model under consideration is the one showed in Figure 1. It consists of the basic processor block (either general purpose or DSP), which executes software processes, main memory and a set of co-processors (ASIC or FPGA) implementing hardware functionalities if required. Communication between modules uses the available bus or the memory. Communications between co-processors are carried out by means of dedicated channels.

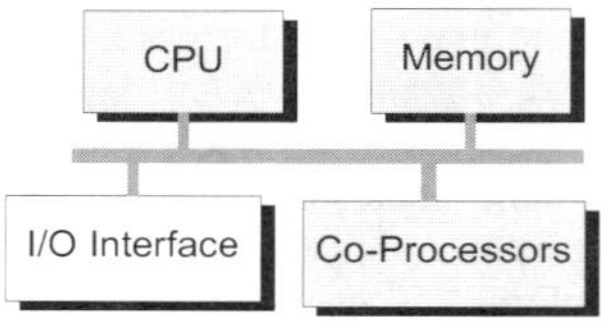

Figure 1. The reference basic architecture.

The adopted fault model is represented by the *single functional failure*, where any number of physical faults causes a functional module to perform incorrectly. The considered faults affect the hardware structure of the system, mining the behavior of the software too, but no software failures are considered in this work. The modules that may fail are, thus, the main processor, one of the co-processors, the main memory, the system bus or the dedicated channels for hardware-hardware module communication. Such a single failure model is based on a commonly adopted hypothesis: module failure is detected before another module fails [4] [5].

2.3 On-Line Testing Hw/Sw Design Methodologies and metrics

The reliability project has investigated design methodologies for guaranteeing fault detection capabilities based on the adoption of redundancy strategies. Temporal, architectural, and information redundancy methodologies are usually adopted, preferring the latter two approaches since they provide a better coverage and a prompt detection of failures. These aspects are significant especially when working in a critical applications environment.

A suite of methodologies has been selected as a viable solution to provide the desired reliability, evaluating benefits and costs for each one of them.

The methodologies that have been analyzed and developed are classified first on the basis of the functionality to be performed and controlled (application execution, communication), then on the partitions (HW or SW) and finally on the Concurrent Error Detection (CED) techniques adopted for guaranteeing the reliability properties. The next section details the aspects related to the application execution, whereas communications will be dealt later.

2.3.1 Reliable data processing

The design approach considers as the basic element any functionality (or part of it) that the system must provide; with the term *nominal* we will denote the original functional system elements. The term *checking* will be used to identify the redundant elements designed to provide fault detection capabilities. The *checker* is the functional element for comparing the elaboration of the nominal and checking elements in order to detect a mismatching behavior due to failures.

Each one of these three elements (nominal, checking and checker) can be independently implemented in hardware or in software.

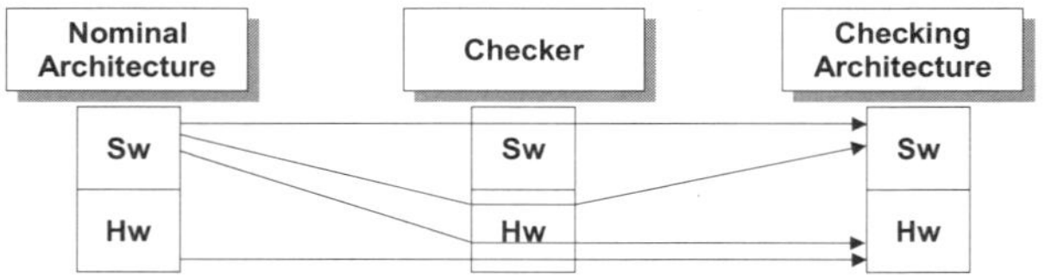

Figure 2. Significant combinations of the hardware-software system parts.

A preliminary analysis of the alternatives led to discarding half of them, due to their intrinsic inefficiency. Consider, as an example, the discarded solution with the nominal architecture implemented in hardware – usually to meet timing constraints – and controlled by a checking section. The checking architecture will not perform as fast as the nominal one thus providing an inefficient detection capability, either slowing the original architecture or detecting faults with a high latency or at high costs for storing data between the two implementations. Similar considerations can be drawn for the other discarded solutions; our effort has been devoted to the most promising solutions, reported in Figure 2. In the following, we briefly report the results of the CED techniques that can be adopted.

Nominal SW, checker SW, and checking SW

This class of solutions is based on software implementations of concurrent error detection capabilities for critical sections that are also implemented in software. This implies that the code dedicated to error detection tasks (both checking and checker) is executed either by the system processor or by a dedicated one.

It is possible to identify several approaches, differing on the adopted CED technique, that represent a trade-off between costs and effectiveness. The most promising ones are: *Self-Checking Sw* [6][7][8], *Assertions* [9][10], *Dual-Processor* [11], and *VLIW* [11][12].

Nominal SW, checker HW, and checking SW

This class of solutions adopts a mixed hw/sw approach to implement concurrent error detection capabilities for critical sections that are allocated in software. In more detail the checking functionality is implemented in software while the checker is hardware. Three different CED techniques have been identified and analyzed: *Interface for Functional Redundancy Check* [13], *DMA Checker* [11], and *VLIW with Hw checker* [11].

Nominal SW, checker HW, and checking HW

This class of solutions is based on hardware implementations of concurrent error detection capabilities for critical sections implemented in software. The best solution identified is based on a *Dynamically configurable checker* [11].

Nominal HW, checker HW, and checking HW

This class of solutions represents the classical approach in the field of the design of reliable devices. It is based on hardware implementation of CED capabilities for modules that are also implemented in hardware. Among several techniques, we selected the following ones: *Duplication* [11], *TSC scheduling* [14], and *TSC devices* [5][15].

2.3.2 Methodologies analysis

All methodologies have been analyzed ([11]) by adopting a reference schema, in order to give prominence to main design issues and to evaluate benefits and costs of each one of them. Such schema is composed by the following set of key concepts:

- selection of number and type of processing elements;
- detection of the need for a special architecture (important in partitioning step);
- analysis of synchronization issues between processing elements;
- analysis for possible physical and logical resource sharing;
- detection of modification needs of the original specification;
- selection of the execution policies for each processing element;
- allocation of the checker memory space;
- selection of the checking policies;
- analysis of the checker structure and complexity;
- selection of a mechanism to enable the checker to raise exceptions to report error detection.

Given the qualitative description of the main design issues, a quantitative analysis of benefits and costs has been performed focusing on a set of significant parameters constituting the basic elements needed to build metrics useful to compare the quality of different solutions, metrics that play a relevant role in the partitioning step.

More precisely, the parameters considered are defined in the following.

Definition 1

Let us define the *Efficiency* of a given methodology as its characterization relatively to three factors:

- *detection latency* is the time between the instant a fault causes an error and the instant the error is detected;
- *coverage* is the percentage of functional faults that is possible to detect with respect to the complete fault set;
- *performance degradation* relates to the overhead (i.e., additional execution time) caused by fault detection tasks with respect to the original system.

Definition 2

Let define the *Cost* of a given solution as the overhead with respect to the original system. There are two main factors:

- *material cost* represents the cost of the physical components added to the original architecture;
- *design cost* represents the effort needed to design and implement a given solution.

2.3.3 Reliable communications

Data processing and communications are the two elements constituting the general system. More precisely, it is necessary to guarantee that any fault on communication lines is detected. Either hardware redundancy (lines duplication) or information redundancy (data encoding) can be adopted, independently of the communication channels being used. The checking functionality can be implemented in hardware or software. We explored the different possibilities (communications between procedures implemented in hardware, or between different kinds of procedures, hw/sw, sw/sw, etc.) analyzing costs and benefits to find out that the best cost-effectiveness is obtained by keeping encoded data in memory, letting the CPU work only with not encoded data, while pairs of hardware sections communicates by means of dedicated lines (duplicated, encoded, or a combination of both) [11].

3. Hw/sw system partitioning

Once the system is specified, the critical sections are identified and accordingly tagged, and given the set of possible design solutions, the partitioning step selects the implementation of each task, either hardware or software. The achieved solution is checked against the designer's constraints and if they are met the solution is accepted, otherwise a backtrack is performed and another allocation solution is pursued.

This process is extremely complex and time consuming, due to the large number of possible alternatives and to the fact that, although heuristics and tuned estimation functions have been defined, it is the final co-simulation of the suggested system implementation that confirms it to be a solution or not.

Given these premises, the reliability aspects add a significant number of parameters to the partitioning step for the selection of the final implementation, making this task too complex. In order to cope with the complexity of the partitioning step when reliability goals are also included, a two-level approach is here proposed. A first partitioning is performed which takes into account only the classical aspects and cost functions, meeting the usually stringent time constraints [16][17][18][19]. Given the first assessed solution, a second-level partitioning considers the additional reliability constraints, analyzes the possible approaches, within the set of defined methodologies, which fulfill them and provides the solution that has the best tradeoff (if it exists). Figure 3 presents this two-level partitioning where a transparent background identifies the classical elements of a co-design flow, whereas the shaded areas point out the elements related to the reliability goals. As it can be seen, if no reliability requirements are specified the process skips the second phase of the partitioning and proceeds with the hw/sw synthesis of the hardware sections, the software and the communication channels. Yet, from the outside, the partitioning is seen as a unique process, providing a solution, eventually with hardware, software and communication sections for reliability if required. It is worth noting that before providing the solution to be synthesized, when existing, eventually an additional iteration can be performed to better distribute hw/sw sections when the final architecture is peculiar. This means that, if the final reliable implementation of the reliable systems imposed the introduction of a second processor, it is worth re-executing the first level partitioning, assuming a two-processors architecture, thus exploiting this elaboration power for the allocation of the nominal sections, as well. Let us consider, for instance, the case where a dual processor solution is the reliable acceptable solution; the first partitioning could benefit from the early knowledge of the final architecture, thus a new scheduling for optimizing the exploit of the resources is carried out.

Furthermore, it may happen that given the first classical solution there is no possible allocation of critical sections fulfilling all reliability constraints; the first level partitioning thus needs to be repeated. If no solution exists fulfilling both classical and reliability constraints a solution does not exists and constraints need to be relaxed.

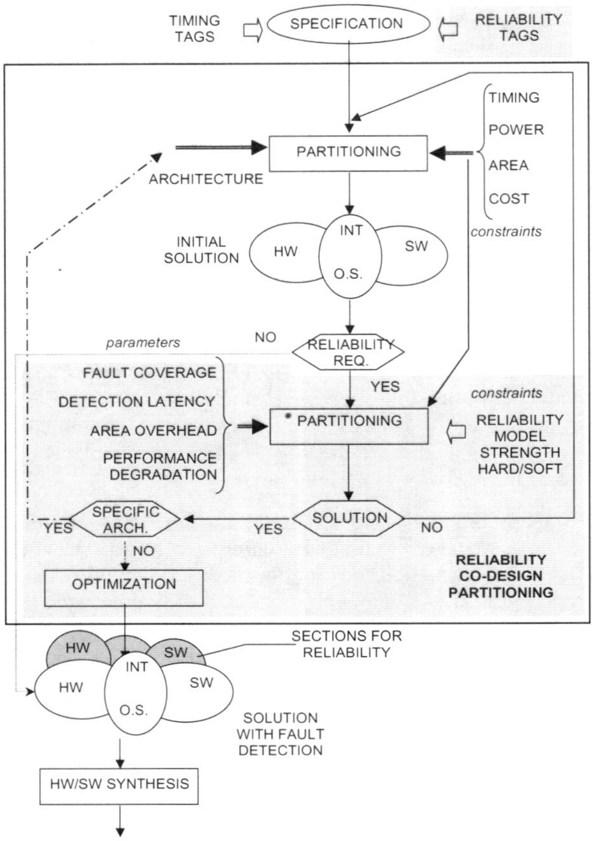

Figure 3. The enhancement of a classical co-design partitioning to introduce reliability properties.

The second-level partitioning, aimed at providing an acceptable allocation of hardware and software sections to the necessary tasks, must fulfill the initial, classical constraints considered by the first-level partitioning and has to meet the reliability constraints. These reliability constraints, explicitly stated in the system specification, refer to the strength of reliability required by each section: it may be *hard* or *soft*. A *hard reliability* requirement imposes that 100% fault coverage must be guaranteed for the section under consideration. A *soft reliability* requirement relaxes the constraint, to specify that any fault coverage is acceptable. This strength of the reliability enforcement is the main constraints guiding the second-level partitioning; the parameters considered in the cost function for selecting among the available CED methodologies are the following ones:

- Fault coverage – either a 100% or a partial coverage dependent on the CED methodology and the specific functionality;
- Detection latency – either 0 or a latency;
- Area overhead – as additional hardware resources and as additional software resource (code, memory space ...);
- Performance degradation – either 0 or a latency dependent on the CED methodology and the specific functionality.

It is worth noting that all these parameters are rather qualitative than quantitative, influenced by the functionality of the specific section and its implementation solution. The next sections introduces the metrics and optimizations we defined for the second-level partitioning, presenting also a comparative analysis of the possible approaches, guiding the process.

4. Metrics and optimizations

The step after the extraction of an admissible solution from the first partitioning step consists in adapting the system, in terms of hardware and software, in order to meet the reliability constraints. The identification of the methodology to be applied to the partitioned system requires the enforcement of a suitable cost function or the application of a specific criterion. Independently of the implemented mechanism, the key element of the decisional process is constituted by the set of directives defined on the task (latency, area, performance degradation and constraint strength); thus, each task is associated with the reliability methodology that best fits the designer's expectations. However, the set of solutions locally identified does not typically represent the solution of the problem in the whole. In fact, the reliability methodologies locally identified are seldom uniform and not overlapped. For instance, consider a simple two tasks system where a task is associated with the assertion method (weak reliability constraint) while the other is associated with *IFRC* (strong reliability requirement), the first method is overlapped by the second one so that the first task is checked twice. Furthermore, the first method is covered by second one, making the application of assertions a useless cost overhead.

The partitioning problem consists of both (i) defining a criterion for the identification of the relation between the constrained task and the most suitable CED method and (ii) optimizing the result produced by the assignment criteria with respect to the global solution. It is worth noting that the optimization task has to be applied concurrently with the method identification since the effects of dominance reduce the solution space.

4.1 Reliability model identification

The criterion for the identification of the most suitable CED method uses the set of requirements and constraints that have been applied to the system specification. The considered parameters, as reported in a previous section, are fault coverage, detection latency, area overhead and, performance degradation. All these parameters identify a fuzzy description of the system components properties for CED characterizations, with the exclusion of a point of discontinuity for some of them. In particular, for all of them it is possible to identify a correct evaluation of the parameter (e.g., 0 performance degradation) – **hard** – or a qualitative estimation (*minimum*, *medium* or *maximum*) – **soft** –. It is worth noting that a *fuzzy* tag (i.e. *min*, *med* and *max*) represents a system requirement (soft constraint) that is a design directive of the required effort for the identification of anomalies during the operational time of the device. This situation occurs every time the system section is considered either marginally critical or the designer intends to reduce the reliability impact on the device. Conversely, a *crisp* tag (100% fault coverage, 0 detection latency, ...) represents a hard system constraint that has to be enforced at any cost.

Note that, for soft requirements, a *maximum* requirement includes methodologies belonging to the *medium* or *minimum* partitions; and a *medium* requirement includes *minimum*.

By taking into account the above expressed issues and considering the intrinsic properties of the methodologies that can be applied, it is reasonable to observe that crisp tags force a partition on the methodologies set. Furthermore, since the applicability of a methodology to a specific task depends on its hardware/software characteristic, a further partition is induced. In particular, 100% fault coverage induces the partitions π_{hard_fc} and π_{soft_fc}, 0 detection latency induces the partitions π_{hard_dl} and π_{soft_dl} while, 0 performance degradation induces the partition π_{hard_pd}; π_{soft_pd}. In turn, such partitions are subdivided in relation with hardware and software aspects. For the sake of clearness, the following identifiers will be used:

- `IFRC`= Interface for Functional Redundancy Check;
- `DP` = Dual-Processor;
- `DMAC` = DMA Checker;
- `DCC` = Dynamically Configurable Checker;
- `VLIWH` = VLIW with Hardware checker;
- `VLIWS` = VLIW with Software checker;
- `A` = Assertions;
- `SCS` = Self-Checking Software;
- `TSCS` = Totally Self-Checking Scheduling;
- `TSCD` = Totally Self-Checking Devices;
- `D` = Duplication;
- `QSC` = Quasi Self-Checking.

By analyzing the properties of the methodologies, the following partitions are identified:

πsw_{fc}={πsw_{hard_fc}; πsw_{soft_fc}}={{IFRC, DP, DMAC, DCC, VLIWH, VLIWS};{A, SCS}}

πhw_{fc}={πhw_{hard_fc}; πhw_{soft_fc}}={{TSCS, TSCD, D};{QSC}}

πsw_{dl}={πsw_{hard_dl}; πsw_{soft_dl}}={{IFRC, VLIWH, VLIWS};{DP, DMAC, DCC, A, SCS}}

πhw_{dl}={πhw_{hard_dl}; πhw_{soft_dl}}={{D, TSCD};{TSCS, QSC}}

πsw_{pd}={πsw_{hard_pd};π sw_{soft_pd}}={{IFRC, VLIWH};{DMAC, DP, DCC, VLIWS, A, SCS}}

πhw_{pd}={πhw_{hard_pd}; πhw_{soft_pd}}={{D, TSCD};{{TSCS, QSC}}}

The second level partitioning takes into account the *hard* parameters first for selecting suitable CED techniques, and uses the *soft* parameters for selecting among them. More precisely, for each critical task, on the basis of its allocation in hardware or in software, the π partitions fulfilling the *hard/soft* requirements are selected and the intersections of their subsets (the CED techniques) provides the set of suitable techniques. Do note that, for *hard* requirements, π_{hard} needs to be selected, whereas for *soft* requirements, both π_{hard} and π_{soft} partitions are considered. Do note that for *soft* requirements, the user must give a priority to indicate the order for considering not stringent constraints in the selection among the CED methodologies. Clearly, the importance of performance degradation when compared to other *soft* requirements is more important, since it is related to the timing constraints allowing the acceptance or rejection of a solution.

Furthermore, *hard* requirements are fully met by all methodologies in the π_{hard} so all methodologies belonging to the partition are selected. On the other hand, *soft* requirements cover a spectrum of possibilities with respect to the solutions: more precisely, methodologies belonging to the π_{soft} can achieve a either a medium or high degradation. A first screening of the methodologies in the π_{soft} partition can reject some solutions on the basis of the specified *soft* requirement (*medium*, *minimum*, *maximum*).

The following Table 1 shows a characterization of the CED methodologies with respect to the parameters taken into consideration; fault coverage is not included since it is either 100% or a lower percentage that can be estimated and compared only on the implemented application.

As an example, consider a task allocated in hardware, with the following reliability parameters: fault coverage – *hard*, detection latency – *soft* (medium), performance degradation – *soft* (minimum).

The first parameter leads to the forced selection of the following partitions: π_{hard_fc}, πhw_{dl}, πhw_{pd}. The intersection of these partitions produces the following set of suitable CED methodologies: {TSCS, TSCD, D}. Within this set, a possible solution is selected on the basis of the *soft* parameters, identifying the methodology that provides (among those) at the most a medium detection latency and a minimum performance degradation. In our case, three possible solutions are found. The partitioning thus proceeds with the next critical task and moves toward the end of this local CED "allocation" analysis. At the end, all tasks are associated with a set of admissible CED implementations. The global solution determining for each task the CED technique actually adopted is pursued by means of a process of solution extraction and simulation, to verify that the constraints of the first partitioning are still met. The algorithms adopted in this phase are the classical ones, simulated annealing, tabu search, genetic algorithms [17][20]. This process takes into account the fact that there are techniques with a global effect (such as `IFRC`, `DP`) which prevail over those with a local impact (`A`, `SCS`). As an optimization policy, the final solution does not include overlapped methods in order to achieve a significant efficiency.

5. Conclusions and future research trends

The authors presented the partitioning step of a hw/sw co-design flow, enhanced to take into account user's requirements related to fault detection properties. The traditional system partitioning metrics have been modified to consider also the elements characterizing fault detection enforcement, i.e. checking and checker policies and structures, detection latency, performance degradation, fault coverage and area overhead.

The result is a co-design environment supporting the designer in the realization of a final system with on-line testing properties. Future research will focus on fault tolerance properties, for designing a system able to continue to perform correctly even if faults have occurred.

Table 1. A qualitative comparison analysis of the CED methodologies taken into consideration with respect to detection latency, performance degradation and area overhead.

Hard Constraints sw	Minimum	Medium	Maximum
πsw_{hard_dl}	VLIWS, VLIWH, IFRC	DCC, DP, DMAC	DP, DMAC
πsw_{hard_pd}	IFRC, DP, DMAC	VLIWS, VLIWH, DCC	VLIWS, VLIWH, DCC
πsw_{hard_area}	IFRC, DP, DMAC	VLIWS, VLIWH, DP, DCC	DCC, VLIWS
Soft Constraints sw			
πsw_{soft_dl}	A	SCS	SCS
πsw_{soft_pd}		A, SCS	A, SCS
πsw_{soft_area}		A, SCS	A, SCS
Hard Constraints hw			
πhw_{hard_dl}	TSCD, TSCS, D	TSCS	TSCS
πhw_{hard_pd}	TSCD, TSCS, D	TSCS	TSCS
πhw_{hard_area}	TSCD, TSCS	TSCS	D
Soft Constraints hw			
πhw_{soft_dl}		QSC	QSC
πhw_{soft_pd}	QSC	QSC	QSC
πhw_{soft_area}	QSC	QSC	

6. References

[1] SGS-Thompson Microelectronics Limited, OCCAM 2.1 Reference Manual, May 1995.

[2] Synopsys Inc., CoWare Inc., Frontier Design Inc. SystemC v.1.1 User's Guide.

[3] C. Brandolese, A. Allara, W. Fornaciari, F. Salice, and D. Sciuto. "System-Level Performance Estimation Strategy for SW and HW". ICCD 98, Austin, Texas, USA, Oct. 1998.

[4] D. P. Siewiorek, R. S. Swarz, *The Theory and Practice of Reliable System Design*, Digital Press, 1982.

[5] D. K. Pradhan, editor. *Fault Tolerant computing, Theory and Techniques*, Vol. 1, Prentice Hall, Englewood Cliffs, NJ, U.S.A., 1986.

[6] M. Blum, and H. Wasserman. "Reflections on the Pentium division bug". IEEE Trans. on Computers, Vol. 45, Issue 4, April 1996, pp. 385 –393.

[7] D.C. Shreve, D.J. Mellema, C.B. Boettcher. "Real-time checkers: built-in-test for mission-critical software". Digital Avionics Systems Conference, 1997, 16th DASC, AIAA/IEEE, Vol. 1, pp. 1.4 -1-8.

[8] H. Wasserman, and M. Blum, "Software reliability via run-time result checking," Journal of the ACM, 44(6): 826-849, November 1997.

[9] Z. Alkhalifa, V. S. S. Nair, J. A. Abraham, "Design and evaluation of system-level checks for on-line control flow error detection," IEEE Trans. Parallel and Distributed System, vol. 10, no. 6, June 1999, pp. 627-641.

[10] G.A. Kanawati, V.S.S. Nair, N. Krishnamurthy, and J.A. Abraham. "Evaluation of integrated system-level checks for on-line error detection". Proceedings of IEEE International Computer Performance and Dependability Symposium, 1996, pp. 292 –301.

[11] L. Pomante, "System Level Concurrent Error Detection," Technical report RT-00003. Cefriel-Politecnico di Milano.

[12] F. Rashid, K. K. Saluja, P. Ramanathan, "Fault tolerance through re-execution in multiscalar architecture", Proc. Int. Conference on Dependable Systems and Networks (DNS 2000), 482-491, 2000.

[13] C. Bolchini, F. Salice, D. Sciuto, "Designing Reliable Embedded Systems Based on 32 bit Microprocessors," to appear Proc. 7th IEEE International On-Line Testing Workshop, July 2001.

[14] Chan Wah, A. Orailoglu, "High-level synthesis of gracefully degradable ASICs, " Proc. European Design and Test Conference, 1996. (ED&TC'96), pp. 50 –54, 1996.

[15] J.E. Smith. "A theory of Self-Checking System Design". IEEE Trans. on Computers, September 1983, Vol. C-32, No. 9, pp. 831-844.

[16] P.Eles, Z. Peng, K. Kuchcinski, A. Doboli, "Performance Guided System Level Hardware/Software Partitioning with Iterative Improvement Heuristics", Res. Rep. LiTH-IDA-R-95-26, Dep. of Comp. Inf. Science, Linköping Univ., 1995.

[17] A. Kalavade, E.A. Lee, "A Global Criticality/Local Phase Driven Algorithm for the Constrained Hardware/Software Partitioning Problem", Proc. of Third International Workshop on Hardware/Software Codesign, 1994, 42-48.

[18] B.W. Kernighan, S. Lin, *An Efficient Heuristic Procedure for Partitioning Graphs*, Bell Systems Tech. J. vol. 49, no. 2, 1970, 291-307.

[19] R. Niemann, P. Marwedel, "Hardware/Software Partitioning using Integer Programming", Proc. of Electronic Design & Test Conference (ED&TC'96), 1996, pp. 473-479.

[20] M. Mitchell , *An Introduction to Genetic Algorithms*, M.I.T. Press, 1996.

Using Static Scheduling Techniques for the Retargeting of High Speed, Compiled Simulators for Embedded Processors from an Abstract Machine Description

Gunnar Braun, Andreas Hoffmann, Achim Nohl, Heinrich Meyr
Aachen University of Technology (RWTH)
Institute for Integrated Signal Processing Systems
Templergraben 55
52056 Aachen, Germany
braun[hoffmann,nohl,meyr]@iss.rwth-aachen.de

ABSTRACT

Instruction set simulators are indispensable tools for both the design of programmable architectures and software development. However, due to a constantly increasing processor complexity and the frequent demand for cycle-accurate models, such simulators have become defectively slow. The principle of *compiled simulation* addresses this shortcoming. Compiled simulators make use of a priori knowlegde to accelerate simulation, with the highest efficieny achieved by employing static scheduling techniques.

In the past, such statically scheduled simulators have only been implemented for specific DSP architectures. The approach presented here discusses the application of static scheduling techniques to retargetable simulation tools based on the processor description language LISA. Principles and implementation issues are discussed in this paper, and results are presented for two selected processor architectures.

Categories and Subject Descriptors

I.6.3 [**Simulation and Modeling**]: Simulation Support Systems; I.6.3 [**Simulation and Modeling**]: Model Validation and Analysis; D.3.2 [**Programming Languages**]: Design Languages—*LISA*; C.0 [**General**]: Modeling of Computer Architecture

General Terms

Design, Languages, Performance

Keywords

Compiled simulation, static scheduling, retargetable simulation, instruction set architectures

1. INTRODUCTION

Architectural simulators are essential tools for both the design of programmable architectures and software development. As particularly processor architectures targeting the market of digital communications have become increasingly complex, so have the simulators. While this complexity has significantly improved the performance of the processors, it has had the opposite effect on simulator speed. Simulators based on complex processor models run slowly, which impairs their usefulness in evaluating architecture implementations or developing software.

Compiled simulators for programmable architectures have been proven to outperform the commonly used interpretive simulators by roughly two orders in magnitude in speed without any loss in accuracy [10]. The principle of compiled simulation takes advantage from a priori knowlegde and moves frequent operations from simulation run-time to compile-time in order to provide the highest possible simulation speed. Between fully compiled and fully interpretive simulation different levels of compiled simulation can be distguished, ranging from the mere compile-time instruction decoding up to compile-time scheduling for pipelined processor models (*static* scheduling). Such simulators have been realized for specific processor architectures [10].

However, compiled simulators for programmable architectures are complex pieces of software that are difficult to write, debug, and validate. These efforts have been signicantly reduced by retargeting such simulators from machine descriptions using the processor description language LISA [9]. Compiled instruction set simulators generated from LISA descriptions incorporate a *dynamic scheduler*, that means, the task of selecting operations from overlapping instructions in the pipeline is performed at run-time of the simulation.

This paper explores the application of static scheduling techniques to retargetable processor simulation based on processor descriptions in LISA. We present two different approaches for processor models on different levels of abstraction. For instruction-accurate architecture descriptions lacking the model of instruction pipelines, we introduce the technique of *instruction-based code translation*, while the technique of *static operation scheduling* is proposed for cycle-accurate models with pipelines.

2. RELATED WORK

Hardware description languages (HDL) like VHDL, Verilog and recently SystemC are widely used to model and simulate processors, but mainly with the goal of developing hardware. Thus, these languages are generally not well-suited for instruction set simulation, since they cover hardware implementation details unnecessary for performance evaluation and software verification. Information about the processor's instruction set like assembly syntax is even

ISSS'01, October 1-3, 2001, Montréal, Québec, Canada.

completely missing. Moreover, the detailed description of hardware structures has a significant impact on simulation speed, impairing the usefulness of the simulators for architecture exploration and software development [12].

Instruction set or *architecture description languages* (ADL) allow modeling on higher abstraction levels. Several approaches address retargetable compilation and simulation based on such ADLs.

The architecture description language nML [2] was initially developed for retargetable code generation, but it has been employed in other projects for the generation of instruction-accurate interpretive and compiled instruction set simulators [5]. The Sim-nML language is an extension to nML to enable cycle-accurate modeling of pipelined processors [11]. However, due to the simplicity of the underlying instruction sequencer, it is not possible to describe processors with more complex pipeline control mechanisms like the Texas Instruments TMS3205000 or TMS3206000 at the level of cycle-accuracy. These restrictions also apply to ISDL [3], which only supports the development of *cycle-count*-accurate models. Both languages model instruction timing by latency annotation, however, cycle-true modeling of pipelined processors requires a pipeline-accurate behavior description beyond pure semantics.

The language EXPRESSION [4] is used for rapid design space exploration (DSE) and allows the cycle- and bit-true modeling of pipelined processors [7]. Previous publications have shown its suitabilty for modeling real-world architectures like the Motorla DSP 56k or Texas Instruments TMS320C6000, however, no results are available on the performance of the generated simulators.

The RADL ADL [14] is derived from earlier work of LISA and extended to support modeling of multiple pipelines. There are no publications indicating the realization of cycle-accurate simulators, though.

Other approaches to retargetable simulation are the JACOB system [8], FACILE [13] and SimC [1]. Although achieving a reasonably high simulation performance (by employing compiled techniques), retargetability is limited to small classes of architectures.

In summary, none of the above approaches allows the generation of fast, cycle-accurate simulators for pipelined processors suitable for efficient architecture exploration and software verification. The LISA language has been proven to be capable of the retargeting of fast and cycle-accurate instruction set simulators for various real-world DSP and μC architectures [9, 6]. However, larger parts of the information contained in a LISA model description can be utilized already at compile-time, thus further increasing the performance of the generated simulators - as will be shown in the following sections.

3. LISA LANGUAGE

A LISA processor model is a mixed structural/behavioral description of the modeled architecture. The structural part is represented in the definition of the processor resources like registers, buses, memories and pipelines. The description of the processor's instruction set including binary coding, assembly syntax, functional behavior and timing is distributed over a number of *operations*. Each instruction is made up of several operations, some of which provide portions of coding and syntax while others might only contribute to the instruction's behavior. Most of the operations are related to each other concerning coding, syntax, behavior or temporal execution order, thus establishing a tree-like structure for each of these attributes. Within this section, focus is laid on the behavior/activation tree, which is composed of all operations contributing to the behavioral model of the processor.

Example 3 shows an exemplary implementation of a conditional branch instruction, based on a simple four-stage pipeline containing a fetch, decode, execute and writeback stage. For simplicity

```
OPERATION decode IN pipe.dc {
  DECLARE {
    GROUP insn = { add || sub || branch };
  }
  CODING { insn }
  IF (insn == branch) THEN {
    ACTIVATION {
      test_condition,
      stall_fetch
    }
  ACTIVATION { insn }
  }
}

OPERATION branch IN pipe.ex {
  ACTIVATION {
    if (C) {
      update_pc
      ; flush_fetch
    }
  }
}

OPERATION update_pc IN pipe.wb {
  BEHAVIOR USES (OUT PC;) { PC = ... }
}
```

Example 1: Conditional branch instruction

reasons, information about coding and syntax is (partially) omitted in this example. The decode operation defines a group of three alternate operations add, sub and branch. Since all these operations have to provide a coding section, the group can be evaluated to one of these operations upon decoding, and the respective operation can be *activated*.

The activation of an operation leads to the execution of its corresponding behavior code, however, unlike function calls, execution is delayed until the instruction reaches the pipeline stage the operation is assigned to. Pipeline stage assignment is achieved with the keyword `IN` followed by pipeline and stage identifier. Assuming the decoding of a branch instruction, the operations test_condition and stall_fetch are executed immediately in the decode stage (dc), since they are usually not assigned to a particular pipeline stage (not shown). The branch operation, however, is not executed until the occurence of a pipeline shift, moving the execution context of the instruction into the execute stage.

Moreever, the example shows the difference between *compile-time* and *run-time* conditions. While the expression following the capital `IF` can be evaluated upon decoding (operation selection), the if-else construct embedded *into* the activation section must be evaluated during simulator run-time, since it depends on the current state of the processor, i.e. the contents of the condition register C. If the condition evaluates true, the operations flush_fetch and update_pc are scheduled for execution in the following cycle (when the instruction reaches the writeback stage).[1]

Besides the presented mechanisms of pipeline stage assignment and operation activation to control operation precendence and timing, LISA provides reserved operations for controlling the pipeline, including executing and shifting the pipeline as well as stalling and flushing particular stages or even the entire pipeline. This allows the unambigious behavioral description of even complex interlocked or multi-issue pipelines.

4. COMPILED SIMULATION

The objective of compiled simulation is to reduce the simulation time. Considering instruction set simulation, efficient run-time re-

[1] The semicolon inserts an additional delay cycle to ensure that flush_fetch is executed in the following cycle.

duction can be achieved by performing repeatedly executed operations only once *before* the actual simulation is run, thus inserting an additional translation step between application load and simulation. The preprocessing of the application code can be split into three major steps [9].

1. Within the step of *instruction decoding*, instructions, operands and modes are determined for each instruction word found in the executable object file. In compiled simulation, the instruction decoding is only performed once for each instruction, whereas interpretive simulators decode the same instruction multiple times, e.g. if it is part of a loop. This way, the instruction decoding is completely omitted at run-time, thus significantly reducing simulation time.

2. *Operation sequencing* is the process of determining all operations to be executed for the accomplishment of each instruction found in the application program. During this step, the program is translated into a table-like structure indexed by the instruction addresses. The table lines contain pointers to functions representing the behavior code of the respective LISA operations. Although all involved operations are identified during this step, their temporal execution order is still unknown.

3. The determination of the operation timing (scheduling) is performed within the step of *operation instantiation and simulation loop unfolding*. Here, the behavior code of the operations is instantiated by generating the respective function calls for each instruction in the application program, thus unfolding the simulation loop that drives the simulation into the next state.

Besides fully compiled simulation, which incorporates all of the above steps, partial implementations of the compiled principle are possible by performing only some of these steps. Previous publications presented the realization of a retargetable, *dynamically scheduled* simulator [9] implementing compile-time instruction decoding and operation sequencing. Since the operation scheduling is still performed at simulator run-time, this level of compiled simulation is refered to as *dynamic* scheduling.

With regard to the implementation of the conditional branch instruction in example 3, this means that, although the affiliation of the branch operation to the respective instruction has been identified *before* run-time, the operation is not scheduled until the *activating* operation (here: decode) is executed. This run-time scheduling is achieved by employing a generic pipeline model, which is parameterized by the LISA model description. The predefined pipeline operations (execute, shift, flush, stall) as well as the activation code change the state of the pipeline model during run-time of the simulation.

It is obvious that the maintainance of the pipeline model at simulation time is expensive. Execution profiling on the generated simulators for the Texas Instruments TMS320C62xx and TMS320C54x revealed that roughly fifty percent of the simulator's run-time is consumed by the simulation of the pipeline.

The situation could be improved by implementing the step of operation instantiation, consequently superseding the need for simulation of the pipeline. This, in turn, implies *static* scheduling, in other words, the determination of the operation timing due to overlapping instructions in the pipeline taking place at compile-time.

Although there is no pipeline model in instruction-accuate processor models, it will be shown that operation instantiation also gives a significant performance increase for these models. Beyond that, operation instantiation is relatively easy to implement for instruction-accurate models (in contrast to pipelined models).

5. STATIC SCHEDULING

Generally, operation instantiation can be described as the generation of an individual piece of (behavioral) simulator code for each instruction found in the application program. While this is straightforward for instruction-accurate processor models, cycle-true, pipelined models require a more sophisticated approach.

Considering instruction-accurate models, the shortest temporal unit that can be executed is an instruction. That means, the actions to be performed for the execution of an individual instruction are determined by the instruction alone. In the simulation of pipelined models, the granularity is defined by cycles. However, since several instructions might be active at the same time due to overlapping execution, the actions performed during a single cycle are determined by the respective state of the instruction pipeline. That means, instead of instantiating operations for each single instruction of the application program, behavioral code for each occurring *pipeline state* has to be generated. Several of such pipeline states might exist for each instruction, depending on the execution context of the instruction, i.e. the instructions executed in the preceding and following cycles.

5.1 Implementation Overview

As pointed out previously, the principle of compiled simulation relies on an additional translation step taking place before the simulation is run. This step is performed by a so-called *simulation compiler*, which implements the three steps presented in section 4. Obviously, the simulation compiler is a highly architecture-specific tool, which is therefore retargeted from the LISA model description. In the following paragraphs, focus is laid on the steps of operation sequencing and operation instantiation.

Operation Sequencing

Each time after an instruction from the application program has been decoded, the sequence of involved LISA operations is determined by following its path in the *activation tree*. The root of the activation tree is always represented by the (reserved) *main operation*. This particular operation is responsible for initiating further operations, thus pushing the simulation forward during run-time. Naturally, the main operation is not assigned to a pipeline stage.

Starting with the main operation and following the occurring activations for the conditional branch instruction from example 3 leads to the activation chain shown in figure 1. The grey shaded circles represent the LISA operations involved in the execution of the branch instruction, ordered by assigned pipeline stages and activation precedence (intra-instruction precedence). For each instruction in the application program, the corresponding partial graph is determined and stored for later use by the operation scheduler.

Operation Instantiation

The objective of operation instantiation is the determination of all possible pipeline states according to the instructions found in the application program. For purely sequential pipeline flow, i.e. in case that no control hazards occur, the determination of the pipeline states can be achieved simply by overlapping consecutive instructions subject to the structure of the pipeline. In order to store the generated pipeline states, *pipeline state tables* are used, providing an intuitive representation of the instruction flow in the pipeline. Inserting instructions into pipeline state tables is refered to as *scheduling* in the following.

A pipeline state table is a two-dimensional array storing pointers to LISA operations. One dimension represents the location within the application, the other the location within the pipeline, i.e. the stage in which the operation is executed. When a new instruction has to be inserted into the state table, both intra-instruction and

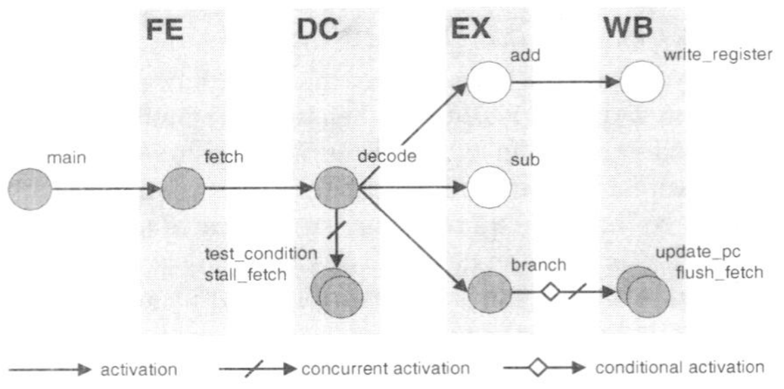

Figure 1: Activation chain of conditional branch

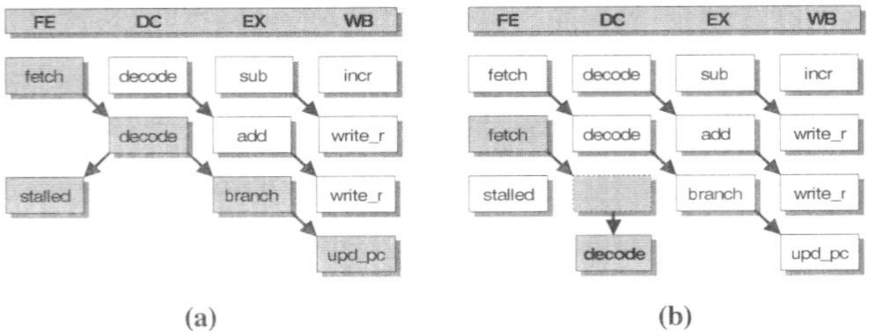

Figure 2: Inserting instructions into pipeline state table

Table 1: Control flow instructions

instruction type	target address known at	no. paths
direct branch	compile-time	1
indirect branch	run-time	1
direct cond. branch	compile-time	2
indirect cond. branch	run-time	2
same as above applies to calls		
return	run-time	1
cond. return	run-time	2
software interrupts	run-time	1

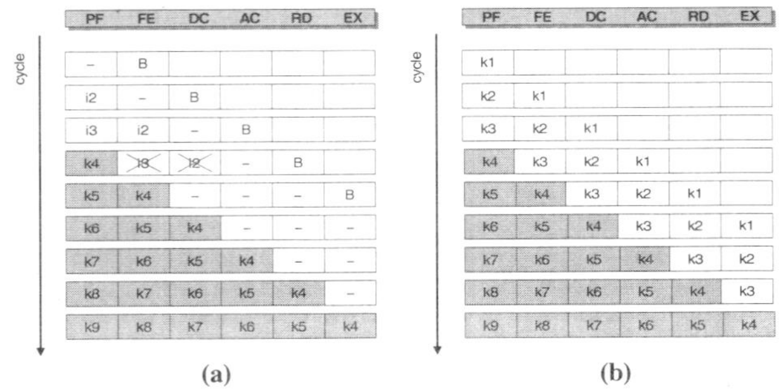

Figure 3: Same instruction within different context

inter-instruction precedence must be considered to determine the table elements, in which the corresponding operations will be entered. Consequently, the actual time an operation is executed at depends on the scheduling of the preceding instruction as well as the scheduling of the operation(s) assigned to the preceding pipeline stage within the current instruction. Futhermore, control hazards causing pipeline stalls and/or flushes influence the scheduling of the instruction following the occurrence of the hazard.

A simplified illustration of the scheduling process is given in figure 2. Figure 2a shows the pipeline state table after a branch instruction has been inserted, composed of the operations fetch, decode, branch and update_pc as well as a stall operation. The table columns represent the pipeline stages, the rows represent consecutive cycles (with earlier cycles in upper rows). The arrows emphasize activation chains.

The scheduling of a new instruction always follows the intra-instruction precedence, that means, fetch is scheduled before decode, decode before branch, and so on. The appropriate array element for fetch is determined by its assigned pipeline stage (FE) and according to inter-instruction precedences. Since the branch instruction follows the add instruction (which has already been scheduled), the fetch operation is inserted below the first operation of add (not shown in the figure 2a). The other operations are inserted according to their precedences.

The stall of pipeline stage FE, which is issued from the decode operation of branch, is processed by tagging the respective table element as stalled. When the next instruction is scheduled, the stall is accounted for by moving the decode operation to the next table row resp. next cycle (see figure 2b). Pipeline flushes are handled in a similar manner: if a selected table element is marked as flushed, the scheduling of the current instruction is abandoned.

Assuming purely sequential instruction flow, the task of establishing a pipeline state table for the entire application program is very straightforward. However, every (sensible) application contains a certain amount of control flow (e.g. loops) interrupting this sequential execution. The occurrence of such control flow instructions makes the scheduling process extremely difficult or even impossible in a few cases.

5.2 Control Flow Instructions

An overview of the most common control flow instructions is given in table 5.2. Generally, all instructions modifying the program counter cause interrupts in the control flow. Furthermore, only instructions providing an immediate target address, that is, branches and calls whose target address is known at compile-time, can be scheduled statically. The scheduling of conditional and unconditional types of these instructions is discussed in the following paragraphs, while a brief discussion on the indirect types is given in section 5.4.

Figure 3a shows an excerpt of a pipeline state table for an *unconditional, direct branch* instruction from the TMS320C54x DSP. Within the fourth cycle shown in the figure, the target address of the branch is put on the program address bus, and scheduling is continued with *k4* and subsequent instructions. The information required in order to perform compile-time scheduling, that is, the target address and the time at which the program counter (resp. program address bus) is written, has been extracted from the LISA model description and is contained in the activation graph. However, if instruction *k4* has already been scheduled in its sequential context shown in figure 3b, the scheduler would perform unrolling of an infinite loop, ever enlarging the pipeline state table. In order to prevent from this behavior, new instructions are only scheduled until a pipeline state is reached, which is no more dependent on the branch instruction. Comparing figures 3a and b, this condition is fulfilled when *k9* enters the pipeline. Thus, the last row of the pipeline state table in figure 3a is replaced by a link to the already exitisting state in figure 3b.

The scheduling of *conditional, direct branches* is more complex, since the condition they depend on cannot be evaluted until the instruction is executed. Therefore, scheduling has to be performed for both eventualities (condition true resp. false), splitting the program into alternative execution paths. The corresponding pipeline states for the C54x are shown in figure 4. The selection of the appropriate block of prescheduled pipeline states is performed by switching among different state tables at simulator run-time. In

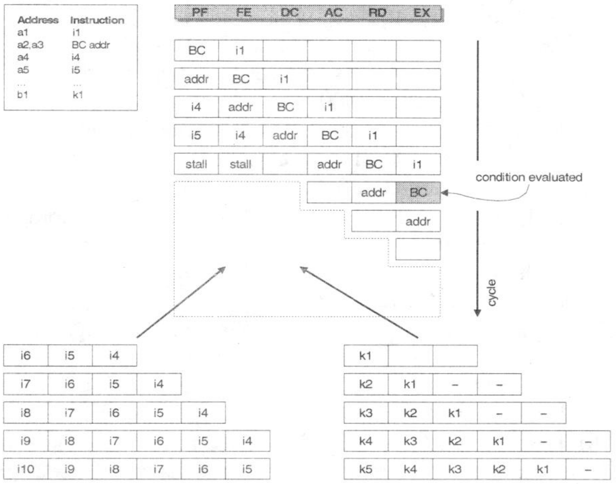

Figure 4: Pipeline behavior for a conditional branch

order to prevent from doubling the entire pipeline state table each time a conditional branch occurs, alternative execution paths are left as soon as an already generated state has been reached. Unless several conditional instructions reside in the pipeline at the same time, these usually have the length of a few rows.

5.3 Simulator Instantiation

After all instructions of the application program have been processed, and thus the entire operation schedule has been established, the simulator code can be instantiated. The simulation compiler backend thereby generates either C code or an operation table with the respective function pointers, both describing alternative representations of the application program. Example 5.3 shows a simplified excerpt of the generated C code for a branch instruction. Cases represent instructions, while a newline starts a new cycle.

```
switch (pc) {
  case 0x1584: fetch(); decode(); sub(); write_registers();
  case 0x1585: fetch(); decode(); test_condition(); add();
  case 0x1586: branch(); write_registers();
               fetch(); update_pc();
               fetch(); decode();
               fetch(); decode(); load(); goto _0x1400_;
}
```

Example 2: Generated simulator code

5.4 Limitations

In general, all instructions setting the program counter to a value which cannot be determined at compile time, e.g. indirect branches, cannot not be scheduled statically. For such instructions (whose target address is not known before run-time), a fallback to dynamic scheduling is inevitable.

Therefore, the performance gain of statically scheduled simulation decreases with the likeliness of occurrence of those unpredictable instructions, since a fallback to dynamic scheduling at run-time is expensive in terms of simulator speed. Fortunately, in many applications, the number of occurring direct branches and calls outweighs the number of the indirect ones. Generally, data flow applications like commonly used in DSP benefit most of the static scheduling.

Another limitation is that compiled simulators do not consider program code changes at run-time, which again aligns the field of application to DSP applications in contrast to operating systems, for instance.

6. CODE TRANSLATION

6.1 Overview

The need for a scheduling mechanism arises from the presence of an instruction pipeline in the LISA model. However, even instruction-accurate processor models without pipeline benefit from the step of operation instantiation. The technique applied here is called *instruction-based code translation*. Due to the absence of instruction overlap, simulator code can be instantiated for each instruction independently, thus simplifying simulator generation to the concatenation of the respective behavioral code specified in the LISA description.

In contrast to direct binary-to-binary translation technqiues [15], the translation of target-specific into host-specific machine code uses C source code as intermediate format. This keeps the simulator portable, and thus independent from the the simulation host.

6.2 Limitations

Since the instruction-based code translation generates program code that linearly increases in size with the number of instructions in the application, the use of this simulation technique is restricted to small and medium sized applications (less than $\approx 10k$ instructions, depending on model complexity). For large applications, the resultant worse cache utilization on the simulation host reduces the performance of the simulator significantly.

7. IMPLEMENTATION RESULTS

In order to evaluate the applicability and efficiency of statically scheduled simulation in a retargetable environment, simulation generators have been implemented which incorporate the presented techniques static scheduling and instruction-based code translation.

Using these generators, compiled simulators have been successfully generated from model descriptions of the Texas Instruments TMS320C54x DSP (cycle-accurate) and the Advanced Risc Machines ARM7 microcontroller core (instruction-accurate). The processor model descriptions are part of previous work and were realized by one designer within eight weeks and two weeks, respectively. As a comparison, the implementation of a custom compiled simulator for the C54x took more than twelve months [10].

Benchmarking results were obtained from both simulators using an 800 MHz Athlon PC running Linux as simulation host. The generated simulator code was compiled with the GNU compiler `gcc`, version 2.95, with optimizations turned on (`-O3`).

Figure 5 shows the simulation performance of the generated and the vendor simulator (Code Composer Studio) for the C54x running an 80-tap FIR filter. It can be seen that the application of static scheduling gives a performance increase of factor two to four compared to dynamically scheduled simulation. Roughly the same performance gain has been reported for the handwritten, compiled simulator for the C54x [10]. Moreover, concerning the simulation compiler backend, the instantiation of the simulator code by generation of C source code is proven to be more efficient than by generation of an operation table (see 5.3), since the table-based simulator runs at about half the speed of the directly instantiated one.

The LISA model of the ARM7 core is substancially simpler than the C54x model, solely as a consequence of the lack of the pipeline. Naturally, simulation performance is with roughly five million simulated instructions per second (for the dynamically scheduled simulator) much higher for the less accurate model. If code translation

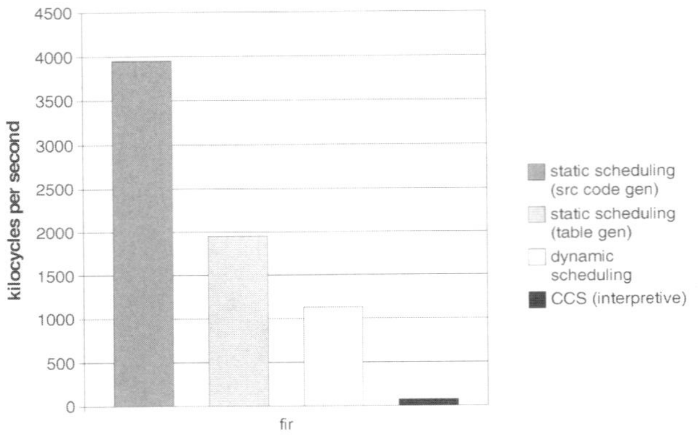

Figure 5: Simulator performance C54x

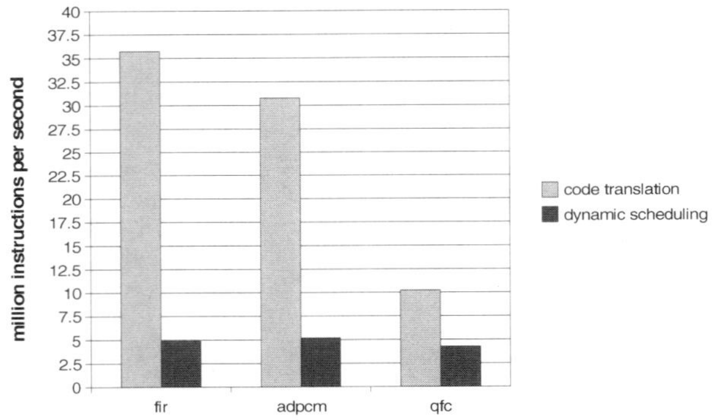

Figure 6: Simulator performance ARM7

is applied, the simulator executes up to 35 million instructions per second (see figure 6).

The figure also reveals a strong dependency between simulation performance and application size, since the implementation of the qfc protocol stack is far more complex (in terms of the number of instructions in the application) than the adpcm codec and the fir filter. This is a direct consequence of the circumstances discussed in section 6.2. The qfc application comprises about 12,000 machine instructions.

8. CONCLUSION AND FUTURE WORK

In this paper, we presented the new approach of applying static scheduling techniques to retargetable processor simulation environments. While in the past only the first two steps of compiled simulation, instruction decoding and operations sequencing, have been applied, this paper explored implementation, benefits and limitations of the third step of operation instantiation and simulation loop unfolding. Performance results for selected processor architectures proved feasibility and value of the presented approach.

Future work will focus on the application of these technqiues to further real-world processor architectures with more complex execuction schemes, e.g. VLIW or multi-issue pipelines.

Beyond retargetable simulation, current research aims at the retargeting of code generators and generation of synthesizable HDL descriptions from LISA architecture models.

9. REFERENCES

[1] F. Engel, J. Nührenberg, and G. Fettweis. A generic tool set for application specific processor architectures. In *Proceedings of the Eighth International Workshop on Hardware/Software Codesign (CODES)*, pages 126–130, San Diego, CA USA, May 2000.

[2] M. Freericks. The nML machine description formalism. Technical Report 1991/15, Technische Universität Berlin, Fachbereich Informatik, Berlin, 1991.

[3] G. Hadjiyiannis, P. Russo, and S. Devadas. A methodology for accurate performance evaluation in architecture exploration. In *Proc. of the ACM/IEEE Design Automation Conference (DAC)*, Jun. 1999.

[4] A. Halambi and P. Grun. EXPRESSION: A language for architecture exploration through compiler/simulator retargetability. In *Proceedings of the European Conference on Design, Automation and Test (DATE)*, Mar. 1999.

[5] M. Hartoog and J. Rowson. Generation of software tools from processor descriptions for hardware/software codesign. In *Proc. of the ACM/IEEE Design Automation Conference (DAC)*, Jun. 1997.

[6] A. Hoffmann, A. Nohl, G. Braun, and H. Meyr. A survey on modeling issues using the machine description language LISA. In *Proceedings of the IEEE International Conference on Acoustics, Speech and Signal Processing (ICASSP)*, Salt Lake City, USA, May 2001.

[7] A. Khare and N. Savoiu. V-SAT: A visual specification and analysis tool for system-on-chip exploration. In *Proceedings of the 25th Euromicro Conference*, Milan, Italy, Sep. 1999.

[8] R. Leupers, J. Elste, and B. Landwehr. Generation of interpretive and compiled instruction set simulators. In *Proceedings of the Asia and South Pacific Design Automation Conference (ASP-DAC)*, Jan. 1999.

[9] S. Pees, A. Hoffmann, and H. Meyr. Retargeting of compiled simulators for digital signal processors using a machine description language. In *Proceedings of the European Conference on Design, Automation and Test (DATE)*, Paris, March 2000.

[10] S. Pees, V. Živojnović, A. Ropers, and H. Meyr. Fast simulation of the TI TMS320C54x DSP. In *Proc. Int. Conf. on Signal Processing Application and Technology (ICSPAT)*, pages 995–999, San Diego, Sep. 1997.

[11] V. Rajesh and R. Moona. Processor modeling for hardware software codesign. In *Proceedings of the International Conference on VLSI Design*, Jan. 1999.

[12] J. Rowson. Hardware/Software co-simulation. In *Proc. of the ACM/IEEE Design Automation Conference (DAC)*, 1994.

[13] E. Schnarr, M. Hill, and J. Larus. Facile: A language and compiler for high-performance processor simulators. In *Proceedings of ACM SIGPLAN Conference on Programming Language Design and Implementation (PLDI)*, Utah, USA, Jun. 2001.

[14] C. Siska. A processor description language supporting retargetable multi-pipeline DSP program development tools. In *Proceedings of the International Symposium on System Synthesis (ISSS)*, Dec. 1998.

[15] R. Sites. Binary translation. *Communications of the ACM*, 36(2):69–81, Feb. 1993.

Design and Simulation of a Pipelined Decompression Architecture for Embedded Systems

Haris Lekatsas
NEC USA

Jörg Henkel
NEC USA

Wayne Wolf
Princeton University

Abstract

In the past, systems utilizing code compression have been shown to be advantageous over traditional systems especially in terms of smaller memory need. However, in order to take full advantage of other design criteria like increasing performance and/or minimizing power consumption, the decompression should take place as close as possible to the CPU. We have designed such a decompression unit that, in spite of the higher bandwidth constraints close to the CPU, does improve performance and minimize power consumption of a whole embedded system. By means of extensive simulations we have designed and eventually sized the various parameters of the decompression engine (#pipelines, #pipeline stages, input/output buffer sizes etc.). As a result, the system's performance is increased by up to 46%. Unlike other approaches we have implemented our engine as a soft IP core such that it can be used directly within a SOC design without any modification on the CPU architecture.

1 Introduction

Code compression has been studied and deployed extensively during the past decade, relying on data compression techniques which have been around almost as long as there exist computers. However, the focus has mainly been on saving expensive memory size since a compressed i.e. smaller program resides in the memory. Typically, instructions are then decompressed on-the-fly and transferred to an instruction cache from where the CPU finally accesses the already decompressed code. Due to the rapidly increasing sizes of SOCs (Systems-On-a-Chip) that can compromise more than 400 millions of transistors on a single chip using 0.07μ [5], memory size is no longer the most important design constraint. Rather, with the emergence of complex mobile hand-held computing/communication/internet devices, performance and power are the driving constraints in embedded system design.

We designed an architecture where the decompression unit is located between the cache and the CPU (see Fig. 1). The advantages are apparent: first, the bandwidth on Bus1 is increased since compressed code is transmitted to the cache rather than larger decompressed code. Say, for example we would have a compression ratio of 50% (compressed code size to uncompressed code size) then the number of instruction-related transactions through Bus1 would just be half[1]. Conversely, we can argue that in the same amount of time twice as many instructions can be transmitted via Bus1. Thus the performance of such a system is increased via a higher bandwidth on Bus1. But also the power consumption on Bus1 decreases due to a decreased number of total (instruction-related) transactions implying less bus transition and thus a smaller power consumption. A similar argument can be held for Bus2 when the decompression unit is close to the CPU i.e. Bus2 also transmits compressed code. The instruction cache reveals additional benefits: the cache can hold twice as many (in our example) instructions. That means that the cache effectively seems larger (i.e. double size in the example). Consequently, time consuming cache misses occur less often thus increasing the performance of such a system. In addition, power consumption also decreases since much less power consuming bus transactions related to cache misses occur.

The flip side of the coin are the increased constraints imposed to a decompression engine that is located between cache and CPU close to the CPU: high-performance CPUs feature a high instruction fetch ratio, thus requiring a high bandwidth on Bus2. On the other side, decompression needs time proposing that a decompression unit could slow down the traffic on Bus1.
This is the problem we are focusing on in this paper. The question is in which way we can design a decompression unit that does not slow down the traffic on Bus1 (compared to an identical system using no code compression) and can even increase performance through the effects discussed before. Our proposed architecture consists of four pipelines, I/O buffers, control logic to minimizes penalties during branches etc. We have simulated this architecture extensively and eventually dimensioned the parameters such that it improves performance without introducing substantial complexity.

This paper is a companion paper to our other work [6]. The focus here is on the pipelined architecture. This paper is structured as follows: Section 2 presents related work in the code compression for embedded systems

[1] This assumes that more than one compressed instructions, i.e. two in the example, are packed into one word that is transmitted though the bus.

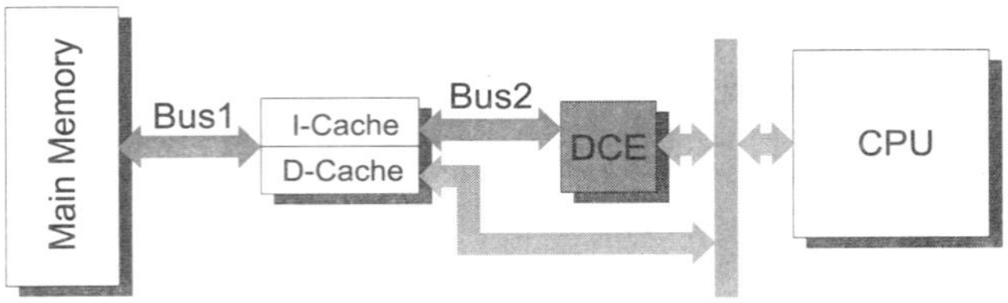

Figure 1: Basic system architecture with De-Compression Engine (DCE)

area. Section 3 describes the architecture that includes a compressed code cache. Section 4 explores the design space in order to locate the best parameters for the cache size in the system and presents experimental results. We conclude in Section 5.

2 Related work

Wolfe et al. [3] were first to apply code compression to an embedded system design. They compressed cache blocks and used Huffman Coding [9] for compression. Dictionary-based code compression [7] approaches have been applied by Lefurgy et al. [4] and by Liao et al. [8] Dictionary-based approaches are easily to decompress since they are look-up tables assigning codes to instructions based on the frequency of their occurrency within a program. Yoshida et al. [2] propose a logarithmic-based compression scheme where they compress 32 bit long instructions to a smaller but fixed bit-size of compressed instructions.
Other research has focused on architectural issues. Industrial approaches to modify the processor architecture to accomplish execution of compressed code have been conducted for the MIPS architecture [11] and for the ARM Thumb architecture [12]. Both of these approaches modify the decoding unit of the particular processor. Wolfe et al. [3] focused on a pre-cache architecture i.e. a stand-alone decompression unit that is located between main memory and cache. Other approaches do not investigate the impact of a cache like Benini et al. [10] and Lefurgy et al. [4].

Our approach is new in the sense that it is the first architecture that is a stand-alone implementation being located between cache and CPU in order to maximize the benefits as discussed in the introduction. Please note that the focus of this paper is on the the design and dimensioning of our decompression unit that is located between cache and CPU. This paper is not about our decompression/compression algorithm (this is described in [6]). Only those aspects of our decompression/compression algorithm are shortly explained here that are relevant for the design of the architecture to implement it.

3 Architecture of the decompression engine

In this section the architecture of our decompression engine is described. As opposed to other approaches using compressed instruction code, our architecture is distinct in that it is:

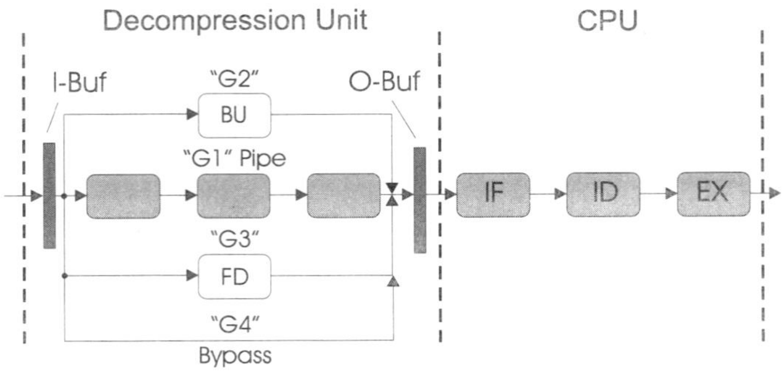

Figure 2: Combined pipeline of decompression engine and CPU

a) located between cache and CPU

b) a stand-alone decompression unit (not integrated into the CPU pipeline and thus can be used in core-based design with relatively small effort

c) it is efficient in all three major design goals, namely increasing performance, decreasing power and reducing area of the whole system.

Note that we only shortly repeat some major characteristics of our compression/decompression here as it is important for the following explanations. For our compression and decompression algorithms, please refer to [6]. Instructions are separated into four groups before compression in order to enhance compressibility and ease the decoding effort (i.e. reduce the complexity of the decompression engine). The four groups consist of instructions with immediates (*Group 1*), branch and call instructions (*Group 2*), instructions without any immediate fields (*Group 3*), and finally instructions that are hard to compress and are left uncompressed. For each instruction group a pipeline has been designed within the decompression engine.

Fig. 2 shows the four pipelines (plus the CPU pipeline stages for later discussion). It shows the pipe for *Group 1*, the pipeline for the *Group 2* (branch unit BU), *Group 3* (fast dictionary FD) and the bypass for uncompressed instructions. The gray-underlayed path represents the critical path i.e. the path with the longest combined number of pipeline stages in both the decompression unit and the CPU. Within the decompression unit the longest path goes through the *G1* pipeline. Also note that the buffers (*I-Buf* and *O-Buf*) do not matter in terms of delay since data from any location within the buffer can directly be accessed (not a FIFO) and write-to and read-from is done as part of the adjacent pipeline stage. Since we have a maximum of three stages and each state is designed to complete in one cycle, in the worst case there will be not be produced a (decompressed) instruction work at any cycle. But note (as we will show later) that all four pipelines can execute at the same time. It might occur that an instruction "$instr_b$" that follows in the program *after* an instruction "$instr_a$" will be decoded faster and thus be earlier available at the exit of the decompression unit since, for example, "$instrc_b$" belongs to *Group 1* and "$instr_a$" belongs to *Group 2*. As a result the decompressed instructions in the output buffer *O-Buf* may be out of order. Though additional complexity is imposed for the design of the DCE (as we

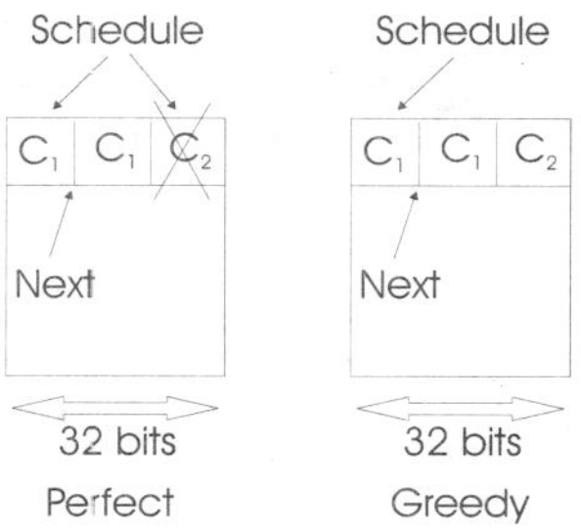

Figure 3: Input buffer strategies

will discuss later), this characteristic with the parallel execution of the various pipelines is a major design feature that enables high throughput and keeps the CPU almost (we discuss exceptions later on) always busy i.e. it prevents stalling. Actually, the CPU is fed with more instructions per cycle as compared to a system not using compression. One effect that helps is the increased bandwidth on *Bus1* and *Bus2* as mentioned in the introduction. Details are discussed in the following sections.

3.1 Input buffer algorithms

In the following we will use the SPARC instruction set. Compressed instructions are fed to the decompression engine through data bus *Bus1* (Fig. 1). In each cycle 32 bits of compressed code are written in the input buffer. As should be clear from the previous section these compressed 32 bits can correspond to anything from a portion of an uncompressed instruction up to multiple uncompressed instructions [2]. During the first stage of the decompression engine's pipeline the tag bits are read and one or more compressed instructions are sent to the appropriate paths. A buffer is needed because in some cases there will not be any whole instruction for the decoder to send to its path, and the 32 bits must be stored until the next cycle when the rest of the instruction will arrive. This case is essentially the uncompressed instructions case (group 4). Another reason for having a buffer is that if the pipeline (where instructions go through multiple times to be decompressed) is full, if more than one instruction from the same group instructions arrive from the cache they must be buffered until there is an empty slot in the pipeline.

Designing the input buffer is tricky; a simple circular buffer would be ideal and can be designed very efficiently in hardware. However, this buffer cannot be circular, because it is possible to have two instructions of the same kind appear in the same cycle. Fig. 3 illustrates this problem: suppose the current bus transaction brings three compressed instructions, two of *Group 1* and one of *Group 2*. A circular buffer would use two pointers: the *read* pointer to point to the next location to be read, and the *write* pointer to point to the location that must be written next. A power-of-two buffer size is helpful because we can avoid unnecessary comparison and make the pointers cycle when they reach the boundaries with a simple AND operation.

[2]Note that uncompressed instructions will be stored in more than 32 bits since the code "101" is appended to them.

	1	2	3	4	5	6	7	8	9
be	G2	IF	ID	EX					
mov	G3	-	IF	ID	EX				
call		G2	-	IF	ID	EX			
nop		G3	-	-	IF	ID	EX		
sethi			G2	-	-	IF	ID	EX	
call				G2	-	-	IF	ID	EX
...	...	...	...	...	...	...	...	...	...

Figure 4: Pipeline stages over time: example where a branch is not taken

Fig. 3 illustrates two different cases and shows what happens when two instructions of the same kind appear in the same cycle. As seen in the Figure when two instructions of the same kind appear followed by another instruction, a gap appears in the input buffer since the second c_1 instruction cannot be scheduled in the current cycle. To avoid increasing the complexity of the input buffer by introducing extra pointers, we propose a greedy algorithm: if a second instruction of the same kind appears in the buffer, no more instructions are scheduled. That means that in Fig. 3 instruction c_2 will not be scheduled in the current cycle since because of the second c_1 it will stop any further scheduling.

3.2 Handling branches

As shown in Fig. 1 the effective pipeline is 6 stages long in the worst case including the *Group 2* pipeline of the DCE plus the three pipeline stages of the CPU. This makes the system especially sensitive in case a *branch* or *call* etc. is not taken. We explain some of the effects and discuss how we resolved the problem of flushing the whole combined pipeline. Remember that performance is key in order to make the DCE useful for an embedded system design as discussed earlier. Also note that our goal is not to modify an already optimized architecture like the CPU. Hence, the only means to guarantee performance constraints is in form of the DCE architecture. Whether a *branch* is taken or not is decided in the *ID* stage of the CPU.

The following code, includes a conditional branch (*be*):

```
12288:  be      0x12298
1228c:  mov     %g1, %o0
12290:  call    atexit
12294:  nop
12298:  sethi   %hi(0x2d400), %o0
1229c:  call    atexit
```

None of the involved instructions uses the longest path through the DCE.[3].

In the case shown in Fig. 4 the branch is taken and only three instructions need to be flushed from the

[3]This is a demonstrative example only and similar discussion can be given for the case where pipe *G1* is used

	1	2	3	4	5	6	7	8	9
be	G2	IF	ID	EX					
mov	G3	-	IF	ID					
call		G2	-	nu					
nop		G3	-	nu					
sethi			G2	IF	ID	EX			
call				G2	IF	ID	EX		
...	...	...	...	...	...	...	...	...	...

Figure 5: Pipeline stages over time: example where a branch is taken

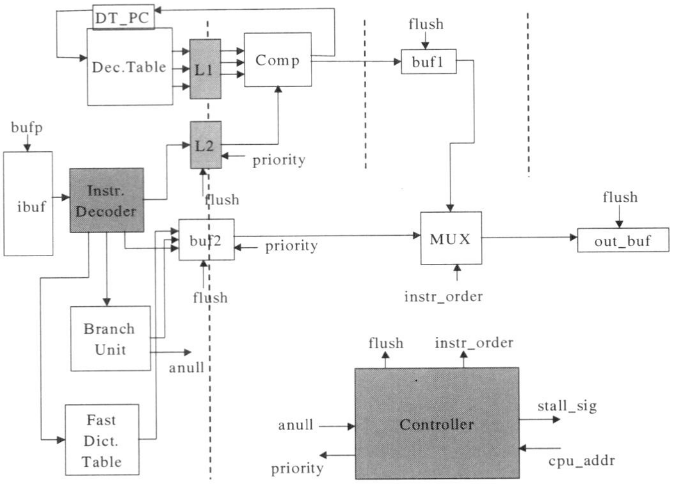

Figure 6: Combined pipeline of decompression engine and CPU

pipelines i.e. *mov, call, nop*. The whole unit consisting of DCE and CPU can host up to eight instructions (i.e. the total number of combined pipeline stages) plus the number of already decompressed instructions (if any) residing in the buffer between DCE and CPU. In fact, we only need three cycles to get the new branch target in the *EX* stage of the CPU. This is because of an architectural feature in the DCE called ITT (Instruction Trace Tagging). The ITT keeps track of any instruction that is in any stage of the DCE. It is a set of 4 bits accompanying each instruction through their way within the DCE. In case a *branch* (or *call, jmp*) that is taken, the CU (Control Unit) of the DCE finds the target (if it is in the DCE) and prevents flushing the *whole* DCE. Rather, it *selectively* flushes only those instructions that will not be used and preserves the others. This can save time as such small branches appear frequently in our benchmark programs. A comparison to the case where the branch is not taken shows that the given sequence needs seven cycles to execute compared to only nine when the branch is taken (Fig. 5. As a result, we have a delay of only two cycles even though we have a very long combined (DCE plus CPU) pipeline.

3.3 The DCE pipeline in detail

As mentioned before, instructions are separated into 4 groups. Instructions in *Group 1* will generally take longer for decompression than instructions in other classes since our compression/decompression algorithm (*SAMC*) will in average decode about 6-8 bits/cycle [6]. This is due to a compromise between performance and complexity of the implementation. Since *Group 1* (i.e. *SAMC*) instructions are the bottleneck we designed our DCE such that subsequent instructions are decompressed in parallel as long as they do not belong to the same group and are thus decompressed in different pipelines.

In each of the 4 groups of instructions the output is written to either *buf1* or *buf2*. (see Figure 6). *Groups 2,3,4* always write 32 bits (one decoded instruction) to their local buffer. Local *buf1* has enough capacity to handle multiple 32 bit instructions. It must have at least a storage capacity of 4 (since 4 is the number of parallel pipelines) such that the highest-throughput case (i.e. each pipeline produces an instruction) can be handled. Among other things, the Controller (see Figure 6) is used to re-order the results in the output buffers so that the processor can collect the decompressed instructions in the right order. This is mandatory because *Group1* instructions take generally longer to decompress (see above), hence instructions are produced out of order. For that reason, each instruction is assigned a set of 4 bits (ITT: Instruction Trace Tagging) a number which is used by the Controller to decide which one should be written to *out_buf*. This is controlled by the *instr_order* signal (see Figure 6).

The Controller is used to send the appropriate signals to the various sub-units carrying out de-compression. Depending on the bits in the input buffer, one of 4 paths is chosen. In case of a branch the *anull* signal is set by the branch unit which may result in flushing. The stall signal is also generated, if the *Group1* pipeline or *buf2* are full. In such cases, the input buffer is not updated with compressed code sent via the bus.

The following pseudo-code illustrates the input buffer's operation:

The function *schedule* directs un-compressed instructions out of the input buffer into the appropriate pipeline. The function delete_from_pipes is responsible for flushing all instructions from the pipelines that have addresses equal to the pc's given as their arguments.

In general, the DCE may stall for the following reasons:

1. The latch storing *SAMC* instructions is full and cannot accept any more words from the input buffer (all stages are busy). If it is full, a stall signal is used to tell the CPU to stop providing addresses, and nothing is written to the input buffer.

2. Buffer 2 which stores the results of cases 2,3 and 4 may be full. A stall signal prevents any more writing and fetching from cache, until an empty slot is available.

3. A branch instruction has altered the flow and some entries need to be flushed. For the SPARC architecture, this is typically the case where an instruction has been inserted in the delay slot and must be flushed due to a change in program flow.

```
for (;;) {
    if (ibuffer_not_full())
        read_from_cache(new_pc);
    if (new_pc ! = pc+4) { // we have a branch
        delete_from_pc_history_table();
        if (new_pc > pc) // forward branch
            delete_from_pipes(pc+8 ... target_pc-4);
        else
            delete_from_pipes(all pc's > pc + 4);
    }
    schedule();
    if (obuffer_not_full())
        write_to_obuffer();
    if (earliest_pc_in_history_table_is_in_obuffer) {
        delete_from_obuffer(earliest_pc); // CPU gets it
        delete_from_history_table(earliest_pc);
    }
}
```

Figure 7: Pseudo code of the Controller Unit

The controller is shown in Figure 2. Its inputs are the address requested by the CPU and the anulling bit from the branch unit. The controller outputs a stall signal for the CPU, a flush signal which contains the priority number for each instruction, and the instruction order signal which tells the MUX which local output buffer result should be used. When an instruction is retrieved from the input buffer a number (priority) is assigned to it, which corresponds to the order required by the processor. This is needed since decompression time is variable, and later instructions may finish before earlier ones.

4 Experimental results

In this section we discuss some of the design issues and present experimental results. The architecture we have used consists of main memory, a cache, a decompression engine and the CPU. Furthermore, the decompression engine is placed as a standalone unit (soft core). This means that all levels of memory hierarchy store compressed code allowing us to benefit from reduced cache misses.

Fig. 8 shows miss ratios on one of our applications for different cache sizes. This Figure shows that code compression can have a big impact on the cache size chosen for a given application. The question is which cache size will give us the best performance while not consuming too much area. In terms of cache miss ratios, a cache size of 1024 seems to be the best choice.

There is no change on the cache design to store compressed code. The cache is a regular cache that can be accessed on word boundaries only. This a compressed instruction will in general be stored on any byte boundary in the cache and can possibly span two cache lines. Therefore, one instruction can cause in the worst case, two cache misses. We take into account this effect in our experiments above.

Fig. 9 shows CPI results for the MPEG application

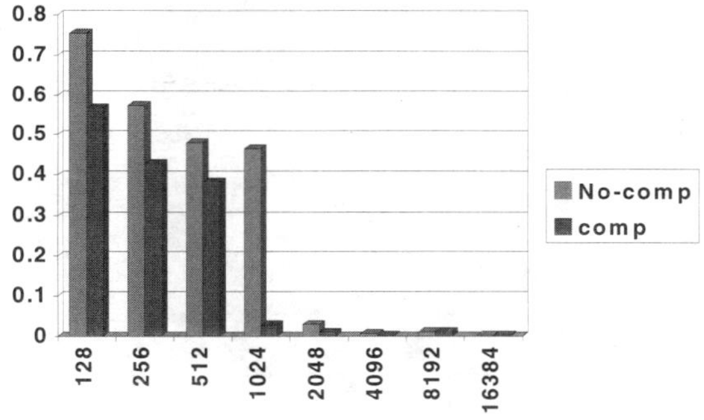

Figure 8: Cache miss ratios for *MPEG*

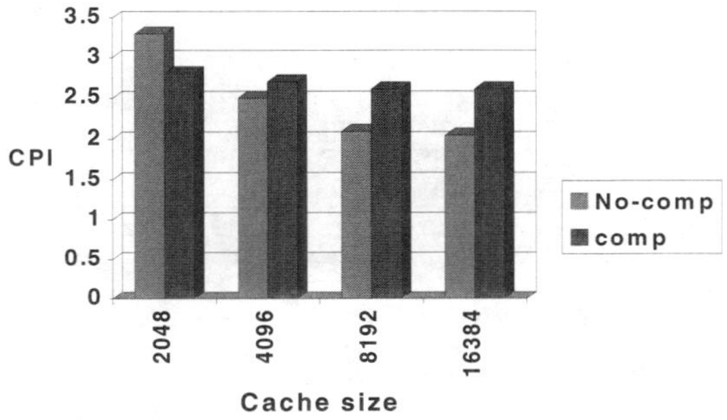

Figure 9: CPI for *MPEG*

for different cache sizes. Clearly, a cache size of 1 or 2K will have an advantage for the compressed architecture as there is a significant difference in cache miss ratios. However, a larger cache will result in a lower cache miss ratio for the non-compressed architecture as well making it a better choice. Since we are designing an embedded system, such cache sizes may not make a sense as a small chip may be a major design goal.

From Figures 9 and 8 it is clear that the best design point to achieve our goals would be a cache size of 2048 bytes[4]. Similar graphs can be compiled for other applications.

Table 2 shows the compression results on diverse applications. **CR** denotes *Compression Ratio* and **G1** denotes Group 1 instructions etc. We use compression ratios, defined as the compressed size over the original instruction segment size. Hence, smaller numbers mean higher compression. Note that the overall compression ratio is not the average of the compression ratio of branches (Group 2), instructions with *immediate* fields (Group 1), and instructions with no *immediate* fields (Group 3), since these groups have different percentages in our applications. In particular, we found that around 53.0% of the instructions belong into

[4] A 1024-cache gives even better results. However, it is not a good design choice for a non-compression architecture

Application	# Scheduled instructions	Compressed I-fetches	G1 usage	G2 usage	G3 usage
i3d	19911	11990	10941	6167	2803
diesel	34368	19743	17661	9283	7424
key	9849864	5894826	6047993	1633457	2168414
smo	1716150	976439	954312	290985	480853
trick	520860	281544	239706	125906	155248

Table 1: Pipeline statistics

Application	G1	G2	G3	Overall CR
i3d	0.53	0.50	0.34	0.53
cpr	0.58	0.53	0.34	0.56
diesel	0.53	0.50	0.34	0.52
key	0.57	0.50	0.34	0.55
mpeg	0.56	0.50	0.34	0.55
smo	0.55	0.53	0.34	0.54
trick	0.58	0.49	0.34	0.54

Table 2: Compression Results

Benchmark	G1 [%]	G2 [%]	G3 [%]	G4 [%]
i3d	53.5	28.8	16.0	0.7
cpr	50.6	32.3	17.0	1.1
diesel	51.0	28.9	20.0	0.1
key	57.7	19.9	21.7	0.7
mpeg	57.9	23.9	17.3	0.9
smo	51.1	26.3	22.2	0.4
trick	48.9	26.9	23.7	0.5

Table 3: Number of instructions in each group

group1, 26.7% into *group 2*, 19.7% into *group3*, and finally 0.6% in the fourth group. Furthermore, the overall compression ratio takes into account the byte alignment of branch targets.

Finally, in Table 1 we show some pipeline statistics for our applications. The number of compressed I-fetches shows the gain over the total number of scheduled instructions. We observe fewer fetches because each instruction fetch now contains on average more than one instruction. Note that the total number of scheduled instructions is equal to the total number of instructions in the trace. The other columns show the total number of cycles each pipeline was busy. As *G1* instructions are the most common, the *G1* pipeline is the most frequently used. Clearly there is some redundancy as for some cycles certain pipes will stay idle.

5 Conclusions

We presented and discussed the design of a pipelined decompression architecture for embedded systems. In addition to a decreased size of the main memory we especially achieve performance gains for the whole embedded system. This is achieved by carefully selecting the cache size and adapting the parameters of the decompression architecture accordingly. It is the first decompression architecture that improves all three major design constaints: performance and power and area. For example, we achieve a aperformance increase of up to 46%. Our decompression architecture is only useful in embedded systems where the software running on the system is known a priori.

References

[1] T.M.Kemp, R.K.Montoye, J.D.Harper, J.D.Palmer and D.J.Auerbach, *A Decompression Core for PowerPC*, IBM Journal of Research and Development, vol. 42(6) pp. 807-812, November 1998.

[2] Y. Yoshida, B.-Y. Song, H. Okuhata and T. Onoye *An Object Code Compression Approach to Embedded Processors*, Proceedings of the International Symposium on Low Power Electronics and Design (ISLPED) pp. 265-268, ACM, August 1997.

[3] A. Wolfe and A. Chanin, *Executing Compressed Programs on an Embedded RISC Architecture*, Proc. 25th Ann. International Symposium on Microarchitecture, pp. 81-91, Portland, OR, December, 1992.

[4] C. Lefurgy, P. Bird, I. Cheng and T. Mudge, *Code Density Using Compression Techniques*, Proc. of the 30th Annual International Symposium on MicroArchitecture, pp. 194-203, December, 1997.

[5] *TI's 0.07 Micron CMOS Technology Ushers In Era of Gigahertz DSP and Analog Performance*, Texas Instruments, Published on the Internet, http://www.ti.com/-sc/docs/news/1998/98079.htm, 1998.

[6] H. Lekatsas, J. Henkel and W. Wolf, *Code Compression for Low Power Embedded System Design*, Submitted for publication, Design Automation Conference 2000.

[7] T.C. Bell, J.G. Cleary and I.H. Witten, *Text Compression*, Prentice Hall, New Jersey, 1990.

[8] S.Y. Liao, S. Devadas and K. Keutzer, *Code Density Optimization for Embedded DSP Processors Using Data Compression Techniques*, Proceedings of the 1995 Chapel Hill Conference on Advanced Research in VLSI, pp. 393-399, 1995.

[9] D.A. Huffman, *A Method for the Construction of Minimum-Redundancy Codes*, Proceedings of the IRE, vol 4D, pp. 1098-1101, September, 1952.

[10] L. Benini, A. Macii, E. Macii and M. Poncino, *Selective Instruction Compression for Memory Energy Reduction in Embedded Systems*, IEEE/ACM Proc. of International Symposium on Low Power Electronics and Design (ISLPED'99), pp. 206-211, 1999.

[11] K.D. Kissell, *MIPS16: High Density MIPS for the Embedded Market*, Silicon Graphics Group, 1997.

[12] Advanced Risc Machines Ltd., *An Introduction to Thumb*, March, 1995.

RTL Semantics and Methodology

Brian Bailey
Mentor Graphics Corp.
Wilsonville, OR 97070
brian_bailey@mentor.com

Dan Gajski
University of California
Irvine, CA 92697
gajski@uci.edu

ABSTRACT

In the past, the EDA industry and designers have struggled with the issues of having multiple languages in use for describing, implementing and verifying their designs, such as Verilog and VHDL. This has led to gross inefficiencies in the industry with tool vendors needing to support multiple languages, which are often dissimilar, and in some cases contradictory, and with users having to deal with incompatible library issues. With the industry embarking on the search for new system level languages we already have several languages based on C or C++ that are emerging and the distinct possibility is arising that we will again be faced with language "wars". In order to prevent this we need to ensure a minimum level of compatibility between them so that it can guaranteed that information could be moved from one language to another without loss of information. It is for this reason that an Accellera working group was formed with the intention of creating a standardized set of semantics that can be shared between all of the language organization. This paper will take a look at the progress made by the group and its results to date.

Categories and Subject Descriptors

D.3.3 [**Programming Languages**]: Language Semantics for the RTL level

General Terms

Standardization, Languages, Theory.

Keywords

Accellera, RTL semantics, FSMD, RTL processor

1. INTRODUCTION

Creating a language is easy. You just need to throw together some syntax and voila, there you have it. However, there are two problems with this. The first issue is: does the language solve a useful task? We will not be addressing this subject in this paper. The second issue is: does everyone who reads your new language know what it is meant to do under all circumstances? If the answer to this is 'yes', then it probably means that you have designed the language based on a well defined semantic foundation. Unfortunately in most cases the answer to this is 'no' and we finish up with languages that are open to interpretation and in some cases unpredictable results. What makes matters worse is that in most cases, the language is designed for one task and used for another, which causes the community to sub-set the language to one suitable for the second task. In these cases it is usually found that the semantics are not clear enough to define the outcome required in the second task which makes tools unpredictable and difficult to obtain consistent results from. Within the EDA community we have seen this happening on too many occasions already and it has cost all parts of the community a lot of time and effort. This paper is intended to relate RTL theory and practice with RTL modeling and synthesis/simulation issues. With a firm foundation it will become possible to start defining the semantics needed in higher level languages. RTL semantics must be based on simple implementable models. Semantics defines what an RTL model means, which in turn is defined by how RTL design is implemented. In this paper we start with a generic RTL building block, called an RTL processor, and then describe how to build the systems out of these RTL processors. This way we can define semantics for RTL modeling, simulation, and synthesis.

ISSS'01, October 1-3, 2001, Montréal, Québec, Canada.

2. RTL PROCESSOR

In order to define the RTL design flow we first define the RTL processor model. Such a model consists of a controller and a datapath. As shown in Figure 1, the model has two types of I/O ports. One type of I/O ports are data ports, which are used by the outside environment to send and receive data to and from the model. The other type of I/O ports are control ports, which are used by the outside environment to receive the information about the status of the model and to send the information about the status of the environment.

The datapath consist of storage units such as registers, register files, and memories, and combinatorial units such as ALUs, multipliers, shifters, and comparators. These units and their input and output ports are connected by buses. The datapath takes the operand from storage units or input ports, performs the computation in the combinatorial units, and returns the results to storage units or output ports during each state, which is usually equal to one clock cycle.

The selection of operands, operations, and the destination of the result are controlled by the control unit by setting proper values of the datapath control signals. The datapath also indicates, through status signals, when a particular value is stored in a particular storage unit or when a particular relation between two data values stored in the datapath is satisfied. The input ports can be connected directly to register or storage units or to any other component in the datapath including the output ports. The output ports could be used for possible connections to other RTL processors through outside buses or directly through point-to-point connection.

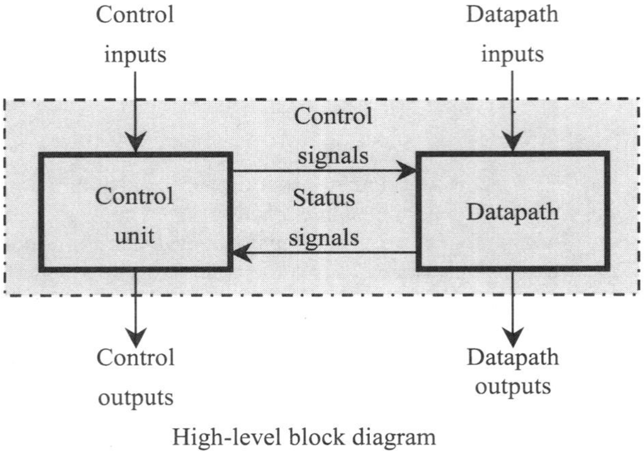

FIGURE 1. **RTL Processor**

Similar to the datapath, a controller has a set of input and a set of output signals. There are two types of input control signals: external signals and status signals. External signals represent the conditions in the external environment on which the model must respond. The *Start* signal in the one's counter example shown in Figure 2, which starts the one's counter, is such an input signal. On the other hand, the status signals represent the state of the datapath. Their value is obtained by comparing values of selected variables stored in the datapath. For example, *Data* = 0 in the one's counter example is such a signal whose value is equal to 1 when the value of Data is equal to 0 and 0 when the value of *Data* is not equal to 0.

There are also two types of output control signals: datapath control signals and external signals. The control signals select the operation for each component in the datapath, while the external signals identify to the environment that the model has reached a certain state or finished a particular computation.

A controller consists of a state register and next-state and output logic. Next-state logic generates the value for the state register in the next clock cycle while output logic generates the value of control and external signals.

Each RTL processor follows this general architecture, although two RTL processors may differ in the number and type of control units and datapaths, the number of components and connections in the datapath, the number of states in the control unit, and the number and type of I/O ports.

An RTL processor may also be pipelined in several different ways:

(a) By inserting latches or registers on control signals and/or status signals, we obtain pipelined control.

(b) The datapath can also be pipelined by inserting latches or registers on selected connections, such as after storage elements, before functional units, and after functional units.

(c) Each function unit can be pipeline by dividing it into several stages and inserting latches between the stages.

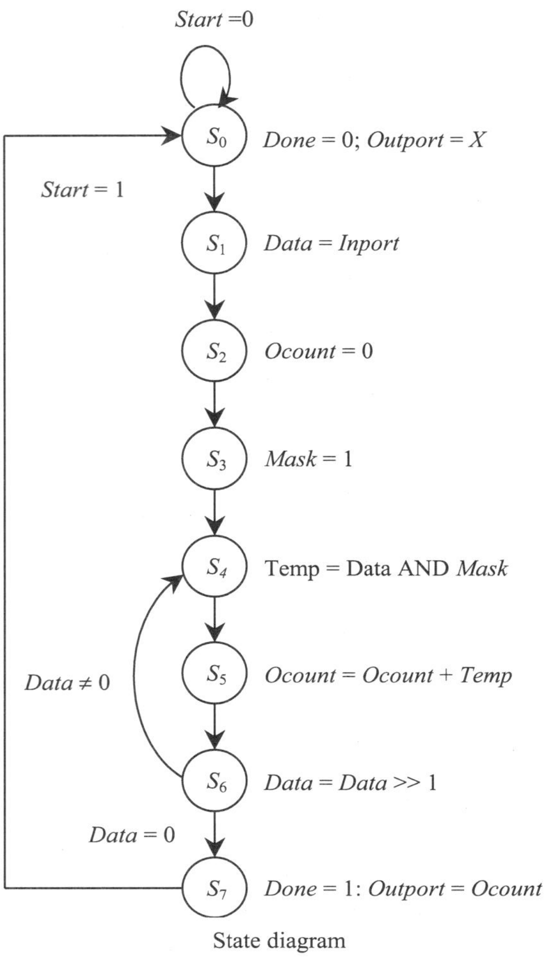

FIGURE 2. **One's counter specification**

3. FSMD DEFINITION

In Section 2, we discussed in general terms the RTL processor model. In this section we discuss how to specify its functionality. We will introduce it on the example of one's counter, which counts the number of 1's in the word presented at the *Inport* as shown in Figure 2.

The one's counter is specified by an FSM, representing the control unit and a set of variable assignments representing register transfers in the datapath. The FSM has eight states and transitions from one state to another under the control of the external signal *Start* and the status signal (*Data* = 0). In each state the FSM assigns values to a set of datapath variables. A variable assignment statement gives an expression to be used for computation of the new variable value. In each state and for each variable assignment associated with that state the datapath evaluates the expression on the right-hand side of the assignment and assigns it to the variable on the left-hand side of the assignment. Generalizing from the one's counter specification, we may say that an FSM model with assignment statements added to each state, called an **FSM with data**, or FSMD, (reference 2) can completely specify the behavior of an arbitrary RTL processor.

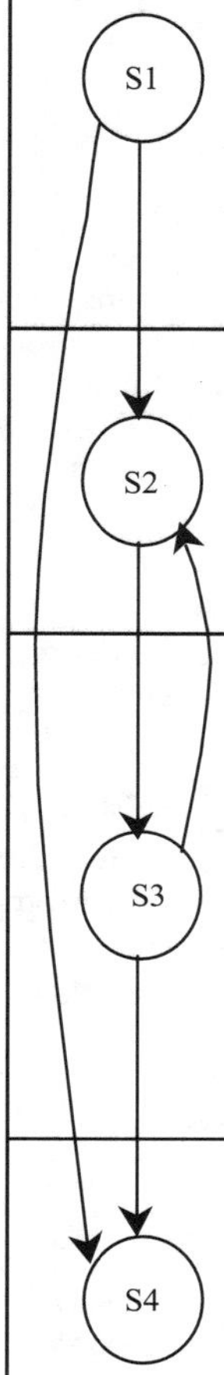

STATE TRANSITIONS	UNMAPPED RTL (STYLE 1)	STORAGE MAPPED RTL (STYLE 2)	FUNCTION MAPPED RTL (STYLE 3)	CONNECTION MAPPED RTL (STYLE 4)	EXPOSED CONTROL RTL (STYLE 5)	STRUCTURAL RTL
	a = d * e b = f+( ) c = . . . f3(a,b,c)	r1 = f* (r1,M(0)) r2 = f+ (. . .) M(0) = . . .	r1 = FU2(*,r1,M(0)) r2 = . . . M(0) = . . .	Bus1 = r1 Bus2 = M(0) Bus3 = FU2(*,Bus1,Bus2) r1 = Bus3 . . .	C1 = 1 C2 = 0 C3 = 1 C4 = 0 C5 = 1 C6 = X C7 = 0 C8 = 0 C9 = 0	
	d = f4 (a,b) e = f5 (c,d,e)	r1 = . . . M(0) = . . .	r1 = . . . M(0) = . . .			
	f = a - b g = f#(. . .) h = . . .	r1 = f-(r1, r2) r2 = . . . M(1) = . . .	r1 = FU1(-,r1,r2) M(1) = r1	Bus1 = r1 Bus2 = r2 Bus3 = FU1 (-,Bus1,Bus2) r1 = Bus3 . . .	C1 = 1 C2 = 1 C3 = 0 C4 = 1 C5 = 0 C6 = 1 C7 = X . . .	
	i = . . . j = . . . k = . . .	M(2) = . . . r2 = . . . r1 = . . .	M(2) = . . . r2 = . . . r1 = . . .			
MAPPINGS	Storage mappings {a,d,f,k} = r1 {b,h,j} = r2 {c,e} = M(0) {g} = M(1) {i} = M(2) . . .	Function mappings {f-, f+} = FU1 {f*, f#} = FU2 {f3,f4,f5} = FU3 . . .	Connection mappings r1_to_FU1L = Bus1 r1_to_FU2L = Bus1 r2_to_FU1R = Bus2 M(0)_to_FU2R = Bus2 FU1_to_r1 = Bus3 FU2_to_r1 = Bus3 . . .	Control mappings r1_to_Bus1 = C1 r2_to_Bus2 = C2 M_to_Bus2 = C3 FU1_to_Bus3 = C4 FU2_to_Bus3 = C5 FU1 = C6 FU2 = C7 M(address) = C8 M(read/write) = C9		

State diagram with different levels and mappings

***FIGURE* 3. An incomplete example**

From our FSMD we see that in each state we compute the next state which depends on some condition from the outside environment or on some status signal computed from values of FSMD variables. The FSMD definition also allows assignment of values to any variable in each state. However, variables and functions in the definition of FSMD may have different interpretations which in turn defines several different styles of RTL semantics.

Figure 3 shows five different RTL styles for a 4-state segment of a FSMD definition and necessary mappings to arrive at that particular style.

Unmapped RTL (Style 1)

In the Unmapped RTL the variables are divided into ports and internal variables, while ports are further divided into control and data ports, where each could be an input, output or input-output port. Unmapped RTL only specifies in each state the change of values for the variables. The order in which assignments are executed is determined by control dependencies, that is, the order written in the description. States, transitions and assignment statements are in no way related to any implementation. The variables do not represent registers or busses and functions or operations do not represent any functional units.

The Unmapped RTL is equivalent to the programming language code with the exception that such code is divided into states, with conditional transition between states added to the code.

For example, we see several assignment statements in each state in Figure 3. All statements assign values to uninterpreted variables. The values are computed by using standard language operators or functions if values require more complex computation. It is assumed that each operator or a function is computed in one clock cycle or less.

Mapped RTL

In the mapped RTL, the uninterpreted variables are mapped into storage units or wires/buses and computing functions or operators are assigned to functional units. Although this mapping can be performed in any order, it is convenient to map variables into storage first, followed by function mapping and then mapping of wires to buses. In this way, we can define three styles of mapped RTL.

Storage-mapped RTL (Style 2)

The variables in Style 1 can be of two types. One type is variables whose value is used in the same state in which that value is assigned. These variables represent wires. The other type is variables whose values are assigned in one state and used in the other state. The states between the value assignment and its last usage define the lifetime of each variable. These variables must be mapped to storage units such as register, register files, and memories. Thus, storage-mapped RTL is a RTL description in which the second type of variables with non-overlapping lifetimes are grouped and assigned to storage units. In other words, a group of internal variables is replaced by a new variable of type storage.

In our example in Figure 3, we grouped variables *a, d, f* and *k* and assigned them to register *r1* while *b*, *h,* and *j* were assigned to register *r2*. Similarly variables *c* and *e* were assigned to memory location *M(0)* while *g* and *i* to memory locations *M(1)* and *M(2)*. This assignment is shown in storage mapping table at the bottom of Style 1 in Figure 3. Note, that in Style 2 we used functional notation for all the operators for uniformity sake.

Function-mapped RTL (Style 3)

In Function-mapped RTL, the operators and/or functions with non-overlapping lifetimes are grouped into functional units, and a control encoding is assigned to each operation in the functional unit. Therefore, in Style 3 we must identify the operation performed by each function unit in each state. Style 3 is the same as Style 2 with functions replaced by multi-operation functional units. Note, that original functions and functions representing functional units use the same syntax.

As we see in Function mapping table in Figure 3, we have three functional units: *FU1* performing addition and subtraction, *FU2* performing multiplication and operation #, and *FU3* performing functions *f3*, *f4*, and *f5*. Thus, in Style 3 in Figure 3 the operators and functions are replaced by functions performed by functional units *FU1*, *FU2*, and *FU3*. If a functional unit needs more than one state to generate result then its input must be the stable through all the states while its output is loaded only in the last state. Functional unit may have several outputs, each of which must be clearly declared when assigning a new value to a variable.

Connection-mapped RTL (Style 4)

Similarly to Style 2, the variables, with non-overlapping life times, that represent wires as well as inputs and outputs to and from storage elements and functional units are grouped and assigned to busses. Syntactically, there is no difference between wires and buses. The only difference is in additional bus drivers that must be inserted in Style 5. Similarly, we can merge (multiplex) ports if they are not used at the same time. We see from the Connection mapping table in Figure 3, that connections from register *r1* to *FU1* and *FU2* are assigned to *Bus1*, connections from register *r2* to *FU1* and memory *M* to *FU2* to *Bus2*, while connections from *FU1* and *FU2* to register *r1* are assigned to *Bus3*. The refinement from Style 3 to Style 4 is similar to compiling a programming language into assembly language. Each assignment statement is decomposed into statements representing transfers from storage elements to functional units, functional units operation, and transfers back from functional units to storage elements. For demonstration purposes, this decomposition is performed only for the first assignment statement in states *S1* and *S3* in Figure 3.

Exposed-control RTL (Style 5)

In Exposed-control RTL, the FSMD model consists of two parts: a netlist of datapath components and a controller that assign a constant to each control variable in each state. The control variables specify the operation of each storage, functional or bus component in the datapath. Control mappings to perform the Style 4 assignments in Figure 3 are shown in the control mapping table. Thus, the transfers and operations are replaced by assignments to control signals for all storage, functional and bus units. The Style 5 column shows the control assignments for two statements given in Style 4. In addition, the partial design corresponding to these two statements is shown in Figure 4.

The datapath netlist consists of declared components (storage, functional and connection) and two types of variable assignments, component ports. The datapath netlist consists of declared components (storage, functional and connection) and two types of variable assignments, component ports to wires or buses, and buses to ports. Note that more than two ports, can be assigned to each bus, but not in the same state. This situation requires that each port has a tristate driver that is allowed to drive the bus when its corresponding control signal is asserted. Similarly, two or more buses can be assigned to the same port requiring insertion of a selector. Such a selector (multiplexer) is controlled by corresponding control signal from the controller.

4. COMMUNICATING FSMDs

As we defined in the previous section, each FSMD is uniquely defined by a set of ports and a description in any of the styles 1-5. The ports are defined by name: type, data, size, and attributes. Type is usually Boolean, bit-vector, integer, floating-point, character or other user defined type.

Attributes may include electrical, mechanical, simulation, test and synthesis requirements or metrics. The two necessary attributes for synthesis are **setup** and **hold** time for the input ports and **delay** time for the output ports. It is not possible to synthesize a design in which an RTL processor is a component without these timing attributes for ports. With such attributes included in the FSMD model we can combine two or more FSMDs into communicating FSMDs. The input ports can be connected to any component inside the datapath and output port can also be driven by any component in the datapath.

In such a structure of communicating FSMDs, any output ports can be connected to any input ports as long as the type, size, and attributes match or connection is unambiguously specified for non-matching ports. Note that the above definition allows a dataport to be connected to a control port and vice versa.

The communicating FSMDs may be driven by the same clock signal or different clock signals. In the first case, the delay time of an output port, the setup time of the input port, and delay of the connecting wires must be less than the clock period in case of

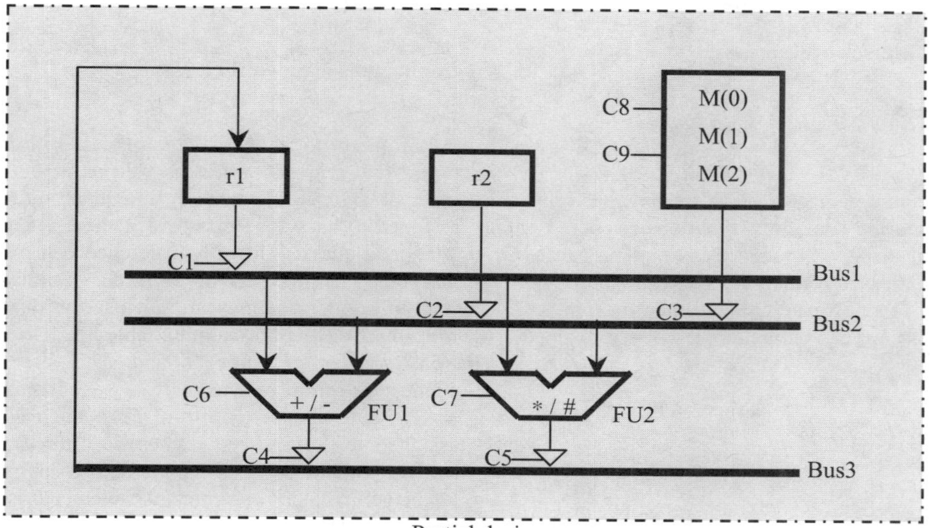

Partial design

***FIGURE* 4. An incomplete example**

state-based FSMDs. Otherwise, the delay for any register to register transfer even through several FSMD, must be less than a clock cycle. In the second case, we must make sure that two FSMDs are synchronized during data exchange if the clocks are not multiples of each other. If they are, then the rules for FSMDs with the same clock apply.

In the case of two FSMDs with different clock signals (or two input-based FSMDs) we can synchronize the data exchange by using protocol with *Ready* and *Ack* signals. Such a protocol, in essence, transforms two input-based FSMDs into two state-based FSMDs for the duration of two states during data exchange, and thus interrupts the feedback loop.

5. Hierarchical FSMDs

The definition of an FSMD in section 3 allows for hierarchical composition of FSMDs. Each FSMD can be a component in another FSMD. In other words, an FSMD may implement an arbitrary functional unit or a storage unit. These component FSMDs may need a fixed number of states to finish. In the case of a *FIFO,* an output may be used only after a fixed number of states. In other cases the component FSMD may be synchronized with the controller by the use of *Start* and *Done* signals. The controller asserts the *Start* signal when the data at the input port is valid and the component FSMD asserts the *Done* signal when it is finished so that the data at its output port can be used. In case the component and composite FSMDs run at different clock cycle then synchronization with *Start* and *Done* signals must be used. Any number of FSMDs can be combined together in serial or parallel way to form larger FSMDs.

6. Conclusions

This paper presented some basic concepts of RTL design and attempted to explain the RTL methodology. It is the purpose of this paper to familiarize readers with the basic concepts explaining the pros and cons behind the devices and to serve as the accompanying document for the more complete specification for the RTL semantics standard. For details see Reference 1.

7. Acknowledgements

The authors would like to thank all the members of the Accellera working group who contributed their time and assistance to improve the quality of this standard.

8. References

[1] Accellera proposed standard http://www.eda.org/alc-cwg

[2] Gajski, Dutt, Wu, Lin; "High-Level Synthesis," Kluwer Academic Publishers,1992

[3] John F. Wakerly; "Digital Design: Proniciples and Practice," Prentice Hall, 2000

[4] Randy H. Katz; "Contemporary Logic Design," Benjamin/Cummings, 1994

[5] Daniel Gajski; "Principles of Digital Design," Prentice Hall, 1997

SystemC - A modeling platform supporting multiple design abstractions

Preeti Ranjan Panda
Synopsys Inc.
700 E. Middlefield Rd.
Mountain View, CA 94043, USA
panda@synopsys.com

ABSTRACT

SystemC is a C++ based modeling platform supporting design abstractions at the register-transfer, behavioral, and system levels. Consisting of a class library and a simulation kernel, the language is an attempt at standardization of a C/C++ design methodology, and is supported by the Open SystemC Initiative (OSCI), a consortium of a wide range of system houses, semiconductor companies, Intellectual property (IP) providers, embedded software developers, and design automation tool vendors. The advantages of SystemC include the establishment of a common design environment consisting of C++ libraries, models and tools, thereby setting up a foundation for hardware-software co-design; the ability to exchange IP easily and efficiently; and the ability to reuse test benches across different levels of modeling abstraction. We outline the features of SystemC that make it an attractive language for design specification, verification, and synthesis at different levels of abstraction, with particular emphasis on the new features included in SystemC 2.0 that support system-level design.

Categories and Subject Descriptors

B.5.2 [**Register-Transfer-Level Implementation**]: Design Aids—*Automatic Synthesis, Hardware description languages, Optimization, Simulation, Verification*; B.6.3 [**Logic Design**]: Design Aids—*Hardware description languages*; B.7.2 [**Integrated Circuits**]: Design Aids—*Simulation, Verification*; C.0 [**General**]: *Hardware/software interfaces, System specification methodology*; C.3 [**Special-purpose and application based systems**]: *Signal processing systems, Real time and embedded systems*; I.6.5 [**Simulation and Modeling**]: Model Development—*Modeling methodologies*

General Terms

Design, Languages, Standardization, Verification, Performance

Keywords

SystemC, C/C++ based design, System level design, Hardware description language

1. INTRODUCTION

The level of abstraction at which hardware is designed has increased significantly with the widespread adoption of Hardware Description Languages (HDLs) as the specification format, or the design entry point, which has led to an enormous increase in productivity over the earlier schematic entry based design methodology. The leap in productivity came about because HDLs such as VHDL and Verilog allowed designers to specify complex functionality at the behavioral and register transfer level (RTL) in a relatively succinct manner compared to the earlier structural-only view. However, after a decade of successful deployment, it appears that the current generation of HDLs are insufficiently equipped to handle the ever-increasing complexity hardware design and system-level design. It is no longer productive for designers to model at the level of individual bits imposed by HDL; more sophisticated data abstraction capabilities are needed. Further, hardware is no longer designed as an independent entity. Hardware modules frequently co-exist on the same chip with processor cores, embedded software, and other complex IP blocks, which forces designers to perform slow and inefficient co-simulations of hardware and software parts when attempting to simulate the entire system together. A cleaner mechanism for handling software and hardware components in the same environment is badly needed.

Several modeling platforms have been proposed in the past years for increasing the level of abstraction and enabling hardware-software co-design. Specification at higher levels of abstraction is possible in environments such as SpecC [4]. A unified and integrated approach to hardware-software co-design is possible if the hardware modeling description is based on the C/C++ languages that are popular in the software community. Hardware-C [6] is an example of such a proposal.

SystemC [7, 5, 8, 3] is an emerging standard modeling platform based on C++ that addresses the issues discussed above, and supports design abstraction at the RTL, behavioral, and system levels. Consisting of a class library and a simulation kernel, the language is an attempt at standardization of a C/C++ design methodology, and is supported by the Open SystemC Initiative (OSCI), a consortium of a wide range of system houses, semiconductor companies, IP providers, embedded software developers, and design automation tool vendors. Apart from the modeling benefits available in C++ such as data abstraction, modularity, and object orientation, the advantages of SystemC include the establishment of a common design environment consisting of C++ libraries, models and tools, thereby setting up a foundation for hardware-software co-design; the ability to exchange IP easily and efficiently; and the ability to reuse test benches across different levels of modeling abstraction.

We discuss the overall SystemC design flow in Section 2; the

SystemC features that enable hardware and system level modeling in Sections 3 and 4; the language architecture in Section 5; and our conclusions in Section 6.

2. THE SYSTEMC DESIGN FLOW

We outline here a typical design flow using the SystemC environment. The flow highlights the most important steps involved in the verification and synthesis/implementation tasks and is not exhaustive. Since the technology is new, several tools and methodologies aimed at providing a more complete design environment are currently under development.

2.1 Simulation with SystemC

Figure 1 illustrates a typical simulation methodology in the SystemC environment. The designer writes the SystemC models at the system level, behavioral level, or RTL level using C/C++ augmented by the SystemC class library. The class library serves two important purposes. First, it provides the implementation of many types of objects that are hardware-specific, such as concurrent and hierarchical modules, ports, and clocks. Second, it contains a lightweight kernel for scheduling the processes. The user's SystemC code can now be compiled and linked together with the class library with any standard C++ compiler (such as GNU's `gcc`), and the resulting executable serves as the simulator of the user's design. The testbench for verifying the correctness of the design is also written in SystemC and compiled along with the design. The executable can be debugged in any familiar C++ debugging environment (such as GNU's `gdb`). Additionally, trace files can also be generated to view the history of selected signals using a standard waveform display tool.

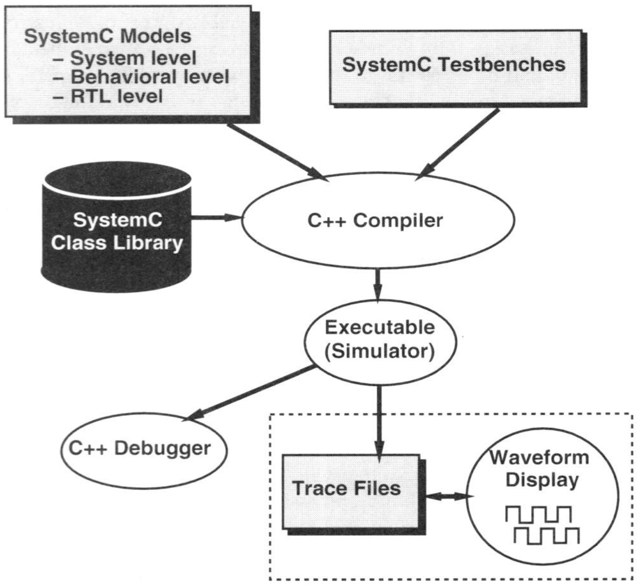

Figure 1: Simulation methodology. SystemC models and test benches are processed by a standard C++ compiler. The generated executable serves as the simulator, and can also be debugged using a standard C++ debugger. History of selected signals can be dumped into a trace file for waveform display. (The figure is adapted from an illustration in [5])

The import of a traditional software development environment into the hardware design and system design scenario entails some powerful advantages. The sophisticated program development infrastructure already in place for C/C++ can be directly utilized for the SystemC verification and debugging tasks. For hardware designers traditionally used to viewing simulation data in the form of waveform displays, the trace file generation facility provides a familiar interface. Conceptually, the most powerful feature is that the hardware, software, and testbench parts of the design can be simulated in one simple and unified simulation environment without the need for clumsy co-simulations of disparate modeling paradigms.

The source code for the latest SystemC class library (currently version 2.0 beta) can be freely downloaded from [1].

2.2 Implementation and Synthesis

The most important feature of the SystemC implementation flow is that the specification is in a common language for both hardware and software parts. In fact, in the system level SystemC model, the two are indistinguishable as the assignment of modules to hardware or software has not yet been made. Thus, trace-offs in the implementation of different parts of the design in hardware or software, can be explored in a seamless fashion, eliminating the need for re-implementing each module in both C and HDL. This also eliminates the need for the system design tools to understand and analyze the syntax and semantics of two disparate modeling environments.

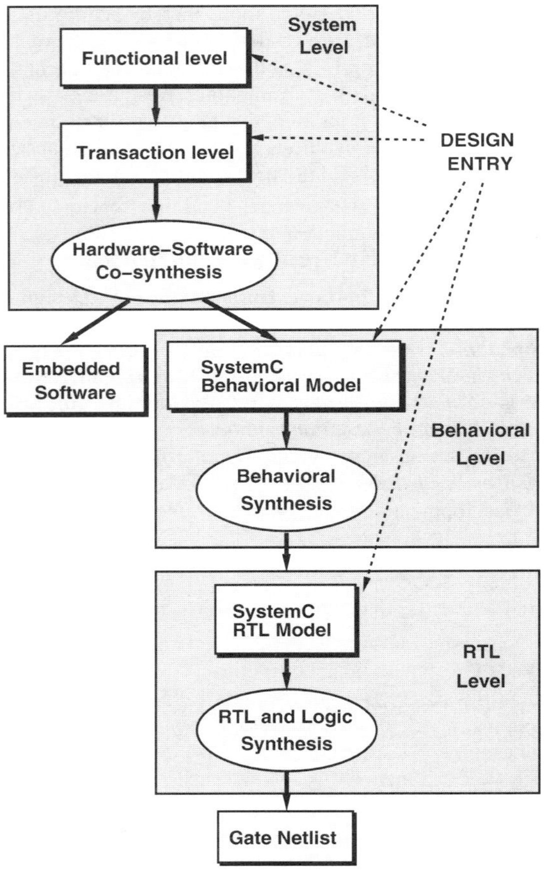

Figure 2: Synthesis/Implementation flow. Design entry could be at the System, Behavioral, or RTL levels. The same test bench could be used to validate models at different levels of abstraction

A typical top-down synthesis/implementation flow is illustrated in Figure 2. The design entry could be at any level of abstraction: system level (which could be an untimed functional model, or a transaction-level model), behavioral level, or RTL level. The transition from a higher level to a lower level of abstraction could be achieved either through automatic synthesis and compilation tools (such as hardware/software partitioning and co-synthesis tools for determining which portion of the design is synthesized into gates and which portion is compiled into embedded software; and behavioral synthesis tools), or through a manual refinement process. Finally, the RTL-level design, whether generated by hand or by previous synthesis steps, is the input to RTL- and logic-synthesis tools familiar to hardware designers; the output is a gate-level netlist.

The specification language remains the same across all levels of synthesis, and the changes in abstraction level involves a refinement into greater detail within the same language and design environment. This allows, for example, the same test bench to be used to verify the design at multiple levels, if carefully designed, resulting in a design environment that is very tightly integrated. Of course, since C++ has many constructs that are unrelated to hardware, appropriate subsets (e.g., a synthesizable RTL style [9]) will have to be used for synthesis.

Model refinement, where we proceed from an abstract specification into a more detailed one, could be in terms of either data or communication. Data refinement involves the fixing of the exact number of bits for each data item, and is typically performed late in the design phase, i.e., in the behavioral and RTL design phases. In contrast, communication refinement typically occurs early in the system design phase. Early models of system designs may employ abstract transactions for communication, which, after verification, need to be replaced by an actual implementation. SystemC provides a powerful communication refinement mechanism where such a refinement can be performed easily by first fixing the interface of the communication channels and then replacing abstract protocols with concrete implementations. Such facilities, which are absent in current HDLs, make SystemC an attractive design language at the system level.

3. HARDWARE MODELING

In order for a language to be acceptable for designing at multiple levels of abstraction, it is important that its expressive power should at least match that of the current hardware description languages familiar to designers. SystemC provides mechanisms to model the typical hardware functionality by means of constructs analogous to HDLs.

3.1 Structure and Hierarchy

Modules

Structural decomposition is one of the fundamental hardware modeling concepts because it helps partition a complex design into smaller entities. In SystemC, structural decomposition is specified with modules, which are the basic building blocks. A SystemC description consists of a set of connected modules, each encapsulating some behavior or functionality. Modules can be hierarchical, containing instances of other modules. The nesting of hierarchy can be arbitrarily deep, which is an important requirement for structural design representation.

Signals and Ports

The simplest means of connecting together different SystemC modules is by using ports and signals. Actually, the interface of modules to the external world can be much more general and sophisticated, and is described in Section 4.2, but the interface at the lowest and most primitive levels matches the typical facilities available in current HDLs. A port has an associated direction which can be input, output, or bidirectional.

Figure 3 illustrates a simple structural design consisting of a module C with hierarchical instantiations of two modules A and B within it (the instantiations being named $A1$ and $B1$ respectively) with the following characteristics:
Module A: input ports $a1$ and $a2$ and output port $a3$
Module B: input ports $b1$ and $b2$ and output port $b3$
Module C: input ports $c1$ and $c2$ and output port $c3$

The ports are connected as shown in Figure 3. The SystemC description of the above structure looks as follows.

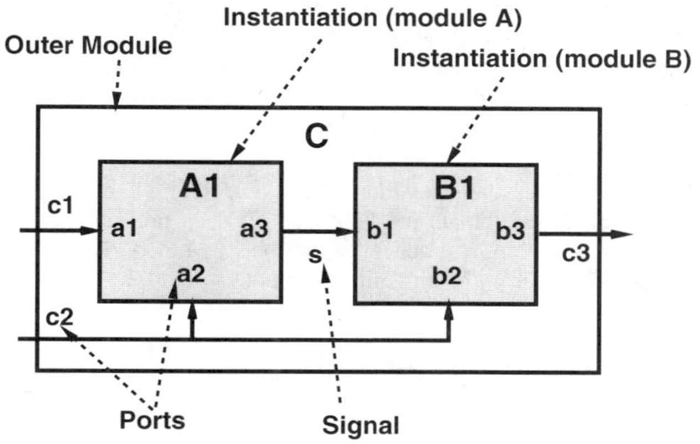

Figure 3: Illustration of modules, ports, signals, and hierarchy. Modules A and B are instantiated within module C. Signal s is used to connect ports of A and B.

```
SC_MODULE (A) { // Module declaration
sc_in<bool> a1; // Port declarations
sc_in<bool> a2;
sc_out<bool> a3;
// rest omitted
};
SC_MODULE (B) {
sc_in<bool> b1;
sc_in<bool> b2;
sc_out<bool> b3;
// rest omitted
};
SC_MODULE (C) {
sc_in<bool> c1;
sc_in<bool> c2;
sc_out<bool> c3;
A *A1;
B *B1;
sc_signal<bool> s; // signal declaration
 SC_CTOR (C) {
   A1 = new A ("A1"); // Module instantiation
   (*A1) (c1, c2, s); // Port mapping
   B1 = new B ("B1");
   (*B1) (s, c2, c3);
 }
};
```

A module is declared with the keyword `SC_MODULE`, and ports are specified with `sc_in`, `sc_out`, and `sc_inout` keywords, with the template parameter <bool> indicating that the type is boolean (single bit). Other data types, including user defined ones, could also be used as port types. The structural hierarchy is specified inside the *constructor* for the module, specified with the keyword SC_CTOR. The pointer declaration and invocation of new for $A1$ and $B1$ establish a module instantiation. The port mapping parameters connect ports $c1$, $c2$, and signal s to three ports of $A1$. Thus, signal s serves as the wire connecting the output port $a3$ of $A1$ to the input port $b1$ of $B1$.

3.2 Functionality and Concurrency: Processes

The functionality of a system is described in processes in SystemC. Analogous to VHDL processes, the SystemC processes are used to represent concurrent behavior - multiple processes within a module represent hardware or software blocks executing in parallel. Processes have an associated sensitivity list - a list of signals that trigger the execution of the process. There are two important types of processes.

Methods

A method process behaves like a function call and can be used to model simple combinational behavior. It does not have its own thread of execution, and hence, cannot be suspended. This characteristic allows for high simulation efficiency.

Threads

A thread process can be used to model sequential behavior. It is associated with its own thread of execution, and can be suspended and re-activated.

A simple example involving method and thread processes is shown below. Functions p and q (whose definitions are omitted) are registered as a method process and a thread process respectively. The sensitivity list is specified using the sensitive keyword and the << operator.

```
SC_MODULE (X) {
sc_in<bool> a, b;
void p(); // Function definition omitted
void q();
 SC_CTOR (X) {
    SC_METHOD (p); sensitive << a;
    SC_THREAD (q); sensitive << a << b;
 }
};
```

3.3 Time and Clocks

Since the concepts of time and clocks are very important in modeling hardware, SystemC provides a mechanism to specify them. A clock with a period of 10 ns can be specified as:

```
sc_clock clk ("clk", 10, SC_NS);
```

The sensitive, sensitive_pos, and sensitive_neg keywords can be used to specify synchronization of a process to a clock.

```
SC_THREAD (x);
sensitive_pos << clk;
```

ensures that process x is activated on the positive edge of clock signal clk.

3.4 Test Benches

Test bench design is an important part of hardware modeling and consumes a significant amount of time. In SystemC, a test bench is specified with an SC_THREAD, just like any other process, and is easily integrated into the overall design. Sophisticated test benches can be built using all the constructs available in C++, in contrast to the relatively primitive capabilities of VHDL and Verilog with respect to, for example, file I/O, data abstraction, and text processing. Since the test bench does not need to be synthesized, there is no need to conform to any synthesizable subset of C++ while writing them.

3.5 Data Types

In addition to the standard C++ data types such as int, bool, char, etc., SystemC provides a rich set of data types which can be used to model hardware-specific concepts. We outline some useful data types here. The complete list of data types is given in [2].

4-state Logic

In addition to the standard bit values '0' and '1', it is useful to provide a mechanism to indicate that the value of a bit is *unknown*. This helps identify initialization or conflict (multiple driver) problems during simulations. Further, there is the need to specify the *high impedance* (or *tristate*) state on signals. With this in mind, SystemC provides sc_logic, a four state logic data type, the states being '0' (low or false), '1' (high or true), 'X' (unknown), and 'Z' (high impedance or tristate).

A logic vector data type, sc_lv, is used to specify data items more than one bit wide that need to be modeled with 4-state logic, e.g., a tristatable data bus. A bus can be tristated as follows:

```
sc_lv<8> data; // 8 bits wide
data = "ZZZZZZZZ"; // set to high impedance
```

SystemC also provides data types to represent resolved logic signals which is useful in modeling wires and buses with multiple drivers.

Bit and Bit Vector

The sc_bit and sc_bv types can be used to model bits and bit vectors for which only two states, '0' and '1' are sufficient, and on which logical operations such as *logical AND, logical OR*, etc are performed. Useful operations for these types include the reduction (and_reduce, or_reduce, and xor_reduce) and part-select (range). For example,

```
sc_bv<100> x,y; // 100-bit vectors
x = x | y; // logical OR
sc_logic r = x.and_reduce(); // AND reduction
sc_bv<50> z = x.range (49,0); // part select
```

Fixed and Arbitrary Precision

The integer data types provided in C++, such as int and unsigned have an implementation dependent bit width. However, the designer may wish to fix the precision of a data item if the range of values it takes is known in advance. SystemC provides two data type families for achieving this: fixed precision and arbitrary precision.

The fixed precision types sc_int and sc_uint can be used to model data that is up to 64 bits wide. These data types are implemented with a 64 bit integer. The usual operations associated with C++ integers can be applied to the fixed precision types, one useful addition being the bit-select operation. For example:

```
sc_int<48> x; // signed, 48 bits wide
sc_uint<40> y; // unsigned, 40 bits wide
x = x * y; // result truncated to 48 bits
sc_logic p = x[3]; // bit select
```

There may be cases where a bit-width larger than 64 bits is needed to model some data, for example, a wide data bus. In such cases, the arbitrary precision types, `sc_bigint` and `sc_biguint` provided by SystemC can be utilized. For example,

```
sc_bigint<128> x; // signed, 128 bit
```

The regular arithmetic operations can be performed on these types.

Fixed Point Representation

While the `float` data type can be used to model real numbers in the early stages of simulation, the hardware designer may have in mind an exact representation of such data in terms of the precision used for integral and fractional parts. The `sc_fixed` and `sc_ufixed` data types, which are used to represent such fixed point numbers in SystemC, are accompanied by the standard characteristics of fixed point arithmetic, such as quantization mode, overflow mode, and saturation bits.

```
sc_fixed<8, 5, SC_RND, SC_WRAP, 2> x;
```

defines a variable `x` with total word length: 8 bits; integer word length: 5 bits (left of decimal point); quantization mode: round to plus infinity; overflow mode: wrap around; and 2 saturation bits. The specified characteristics are used in all arithmetic for the fixed point variables. The fixed point data type is an important modeling feature of SystemC that is not found in HDLs.

The choice of data types has a significant impact on the simulation speed, and care must be taken to use the correct data types during modeling. For example, `sc_lv` should be used only in specific instances where either high impedance behavior is involved, or reset behavior in simulation is important; otherwise, the faster `sc_bv` type should be used. Similarly, if extensive arithmetic is performed, the `sc_int` and `sc_bigint` types should be preferred to `sc_bv` to prevent unnecessary type conversions. The fixed precision types (`sc_int`) should be used wherever possible (i.e., required bit width less than 64) instead of arbitrary precision (`sc_bigint`) for simulation efficiency. Finally, the native C++ types (`int`) are the most efficient.

The reader is referred to [2] for an exhaustive list of all the SystemC data types and the relevant operations.

4. SYSTEM LEVEL MODELING

The features of SystemC reviewed in the previous section make it a suitable hardware description language. However, the above mentioned capabilities would make SystemC only a minor improvement over the existing HDLs. The true advantage of SystemC as a specification language lies in the fact that it encompasses all the important hardware modeling features, as well as provides powerful modeling constructs for system level design. This ensures that the transition to a SystemC-based methodology entails no compromise in terms of expressive power at the lower levels of abstraction, and yet provides a useful framework for modeling at the higher levels. Current HDLs sorely lack the latter ability.

The system level modeling features introduced in SystemC 2.0 [3] mainly include the support of a much more general and abstract means of communication between processes and a more general mechanism for event synchronization.

4.1 Events and Sensitivity

SystemC 2.0 introduces a general mechanism for specification and notification of events. Events are no longer equated with the toggling of a single bit, but are abstract types that can be used for more general and complex interactions. The `sc_event` type can be used to declare events that can be created using the `notify` keyword and be synchronized with in `wait` statements, as shown below.

```
sc_event e1, e2; // declare events
sc_time t (5, SC_NS);
e1.notify (t); // notify event e1 after 5 ns
wait (e1); // suspend execution until
           // event e1 occurs
wait (); // wait until an event occurs
         // on the process sensitivity list
wait (10, SC_NS, e1 | e2);
     // wait for events e1 or e2 to occur
     // but for a maximum of 10 ns
```

4.2 Interfaces and Channels

In Section 3.1, we illustrated a simple example of modules connected using signals. This picture of communication, where interaction between modules is restricted to the passing of values on individual wires, is, however, at the lowest level of abstraction. At the system level, we need the ability to model more abstract, sophisticated, and intelligent communication paradigms. SystemC 2.0 introduces the notion of channels and interfaces which provide this modeling ability.

A system level SystemC design consists of a set of modules and channels at the top level. Loosely speaking, modules cover the functionality-related aspects of the system, and channels carry the communication-related aspects. Channels can be very general and implement complex algorithms within themselves, e.g., a complex bus protocol with arbitration; in fact channels can have hierarchical structure.

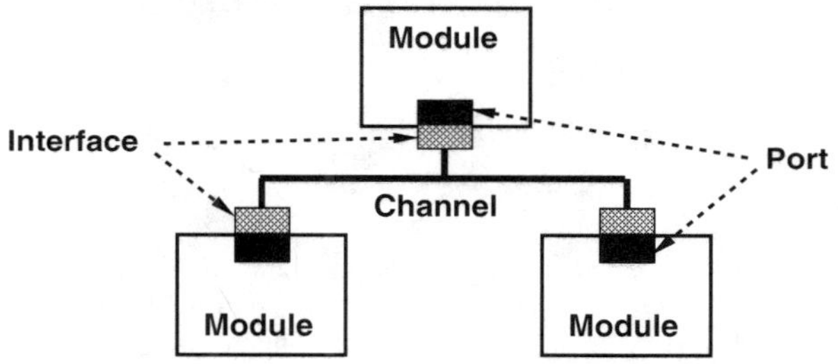

Figure 4: Interfaces and Channels. Ports of modules are connected to channels through interfaces.

Figure 4 shows a simple design with three modules connected to a channel. An interface consists of a set of method declarations (not related to SC_METHODs) implemented by the channel. These methods are visible to a port that is connected to the channel through the interface. Thus, the port (and consequently, the module) is insulated from the implementation details (such as local data) of the channel itself. This architecture helps keep the functionality-related parts of a design separate from communication, as far as possible, and allows the modification of one without affecting the other as long as the interface is unchanged.

The interface and channel constructs were inspired by similar concepts in the SpecC language [4].

4.3 Primitive and Hierarchical Channels

Channels in SystemC can be either *primitive* or *hierarchical.* Primitive channels are relatively simple; SystemC 2.0 provides a set of primitive channels which have wide applicability, such as `sc_signal` (classical signals discussed in Section 3.1), `sc_mutex` (used to model mutual exclusion) and `sc_fifo` (used for modeling queues). Hierarchical channels can exhibit structure; they are modules themselves, which in turn, can contain processes, and other channels and modules. Complex bus protocols which have several sub-tasks can be effectively modeled using hierarchical channels.

A simple example of two modules connected by a channel of type `sc_fifo` is shown below. A FIFO connection is established between the output port of module M1 and the input port of M2.

```
SC_MODULE (A) {
sc_fifo_in<int> in;
sc_fifo_out<int> out;
// rest omitted
};
...
A *M1, *M2;  // instances of module A
...
sc_fifo<int> q (5); // create FIFO channel
                    // with buffer size 5
M1->out (q); // connect port 'out' of M1 to q
M2->in (q); // connect port 'in' of M2 to q
```

4.4 Methodology-Specific Libraries

The modeling mechanism presented above is general enough for modeling many different models of communication and computation. Different communication methodologies could be built on this basic modeling infrastructure. A future release of SystemC will contain one such example - the master-slave communication library. The elements provided here can be used to easily model communication interfaces based on master-slave bus protocols.

5. SYSTEMC ARCHITECTURE

5.1 Language Design

The overall architecture of the SystemC class library is summarized in Figure 5. The simulation kernel, i.e., the lightweight scheduler that is responsible for activating and suspending the SystemC processes is at the heart of the implementation, and forms the base layer. The generalized event mechanism discussed in Section 4.1, which forms the basis of synchronization, is introduced in the next layer. With these layers as the foundation, the communication elements - interfaces, channels, and ports are defined in the next layer. The design is based on the *interface-method-call* (IMC) scheme: essentially, the ports access the channels only through the interfaces. The example primitive channels supplied by SystemC is built on this layer. Finally, the hierarchical and other user-defined channels are built on the top layer. The most important observation is that the upper layers are built cleanly on the lower ones, and the designer can use the modeling mechanisms at any of the levels.

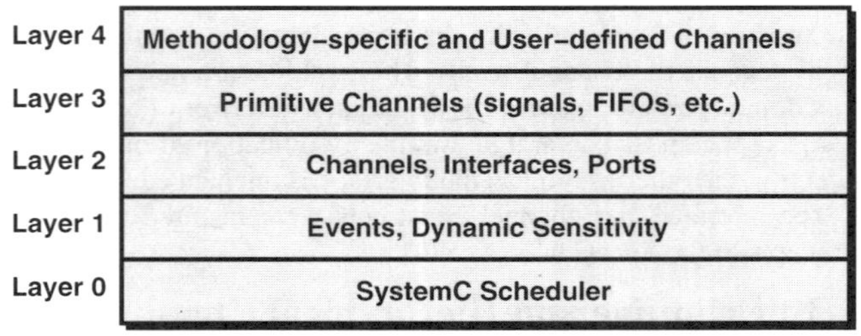

Figure 5: SystemC Language Architecture. Upper layers are built cleanly on top of lower layers.

5.2 Simulation Kernel

The simulation kernel for SystemC follows the evaluate-update paradigm that is common in HDLs. The concept of *delta cycles*, where multiple evaluate-update phases can occur at the same simulation time, is supported. A simplified version of the simulation algorithm is as follows:

1. *Initialization*: Execute all processes to initialize the system.
2. *Evaluate*: Execute a process that is ready to run. Iterate until all ready processes are executed. Events occurring during the execution could add new processes to the ready list.
3. *Update*: Execute any `update` calls made during step 2.
4. If delayed notifications are pending, determine list of ready processes and proceed to Evaluate phase (step 2).
5. Advance the simulation time to the earliest pending timed notification. If no such event exists, simulation is finished, else determine ready processes and proceed to step 2.

6. CONCLUSION

SystemC is a new modeling environment that is rapidly emerging as an industry standard for describing designs at the RTL, behavioral, and system levels. While including all the important hardware modeling capabilities offered by current generation HDLs, SystemC also provides a powerful mechanism for system level design, with the facility to specify abstract communication protocols that help model most known models of computation. The key advantage of a SystemC based design methodology is that the same language infrastructure is used for specifying the design at various levels of abstraction; thus, design refinement from abstract to detailed levels include only a change in data types and communication, and do not involve a switch of design language. All SystemC constructs have been implemented with standard C++, and no extensions to the C++ language were needed. The use of a standard C++ based framework for specifying both hardware and software parts of a design promises to smooth hardware-software co-design by bridging the long-standing specification language gap.

7. REFERENCES

[1] The Open SystemC Initiative. *http://www.systemc.org*.

[2] SystemC 1.0 user's guide. *http://www.systemc.org*, 2000.

[3] Functional specification for SystemC 2.0. *http://www.systemc.org*, Jan. 2001.

[4] D. Gajski, J. Zhu, R. Domer, A. Gerstlauer, and S. Zhao. *SpecC: Specification Language and Methodology*. Kluwer Academic Publishers, Norwell, U.S.A, 2000.

[5] J. Gerlach and W. Rosenstiel. System level design using the SystemC modeling platform. In *Workshop on System Design Automation*, pages 185-189, Rathen, Germany, Mar. 2000.

[6] R. K. Gupta. *Co-Synthesis of Hardware and Software for Digital Embedded Systems*. Kluwer Academic Publishers, Boston, U.S.A, 1995.

[7] S. Liao, S. Tjiang, and R. Gupta. An efficient implementation of reactivity for modeling hardware in the scenic design environment. In *Design Automation Conference*, pages 70-75, Anaheim, CA, June 1997.

[8] S. Swan. An introduction to system level modeling in SystemC 2.0. *http://www.systemc.org*, May 2001.

[9] Synopsys Inc., Mountain View, CA. *Describing Synthesizable RTL in SystemC*, May 2001.

The Standard SpecC Language

Masahiro Fujita
Department of Electronic Engineering
The University of Tokyo
3-8-1, Hongo, Bunkyo, Tokyo, 113-8656, JAPAN
+81-3-5841-6673
fujita@ee.t.u-tokyo.ac.jp

Hiroshi Nakamura
Research Center for Advanced Science and Technology
The University of Tokyo
4-6-1, Komaba, Meguro, Tokyo 153-8904, JAPAN
+81-3-5452-5162
nakamura@rcast.u-tokyo.ac.jp

ABSTRACT

This paper introduces SpecC language, a system level description language based on C, and its consortium, SpecC Technology Open Consortium (STOC). Currently SpecC language version 1.0 is publicly available. SpecC technology covers SpecC-based design "methodology" as well as SpecC language itself. In this paper not only SpecC language but also SpecC-based design methodology are briefly discussed. The SpecC language specification working group (LSWG) under STOC is discussing on SpecC version 2.0. We also give a summary of the discussions being made by LSWG targeting version 2.0. We plan to formally release version 2.0 in the beginning of 2002. The main goal is to precisely and exactly define the formal semantics of SpecC language especially on the semantics relating to parallel and concurrent statements and event control mechanisms. These are the issues on which SpecC version 1.0 does not give clear and concise semantics. With these clarifications given by SpecC version 2.0, varieties of supporting tools for SpecC can consistently and easily be developed.

Keywords: Hardware Description Language, System Level Design, C-based Hardware Description, Formal Semantics, System Synthesis, High-Level Synthesis, Formal Verification

1. Introduction and the SpecC design methodology

As semiconductor technology advances, entire systems can be realized within single LSIs as System-on-a-Chip (SoC). Designing a SoC is a process of entire system design from specification to implementation design and also a process of both hardware and software development. Performance of the designed systems fully depends on both hardware (LSI) and software on top of LSI. Correct partitioning between software execution and hardware execution must be taken for high performance with low implementation cost, and integrated specification for both software and hardware is indispensable. Therefore, in order to design SoC, specification process and implementation design process must be smoothly and tightly coupled.

ISSS '01, October 1-3, 2001, Montréal, Québec, Canada.

Figure 1 shows a design flow for SoC. Systems to be designed have both software and hardware, and IP in various design levels should be tried to be used as much as possible in order to shorten the design costs. In the right most part of the figure, the design levels that are covered by various languages are shown. SpecC is covering design levels from specification to behaviors. It can describe both software and hardware seamlessly and a good tool for rapid prototyping as well.

Two key elements to solve the integration of specification and design phases in the System-on-a-Chip (SoC) design process are: 1) a consistent and continuous design process from specification design to implementation design which covers both of software and hardware; and 2) design reuse, which means not only component IP but also specification IP and design IP. Over the years, many languages and data formats have been proposed. Recently, C/C++ based hardware (LSI) design methodologies are emerging. However, the current approaches do not efficiently cover these two key elements. Such approaches include UML, which is primarily used for specification design, and C/C++ and VHDL and/or Verilog, which are primarily used for implementation design.

SpecC-based design methodology is shown in Figure 2. SpecC covers specification model, architecture model, communication model, and implementation model with easy access and use of IP in corresponding design levels. Designers start their design processes with specification in SpecC. Then appropriate architectures that realize specifications are explored, and corresponding communications among components in architecture models are generated. Finally software models and hardware models as implementation models are the output of the SpecC design methodology.

In the following, we briefly review SpecC language version 1.0, which is currently available, and version 2.0 which is under discussion and will be available to the public by early next year. In section 2, we present key ideas of SpecC language version 1.0. Then in section 3, we give overview of SpecC Technology Open Consortium (STOC), which is an organization for promotion of SpecC language. In section 4, we give summary of the discussion points targeting SpecC version 2.0. Section 5 gives concluding remarks.

2. SpecC Language

SpecC methodology and language have been designed and implemented to integrate the specification and the design phases in the SOC design process. Originally developed at University of California, Irvine, with sponsorship from several companies,

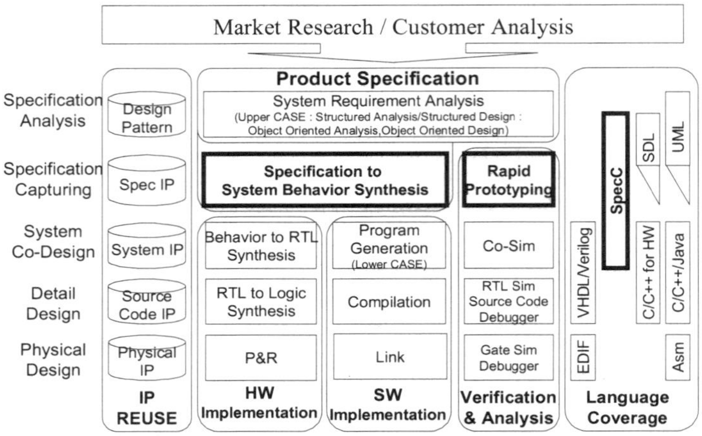

Figure 1. SOC Design Flow

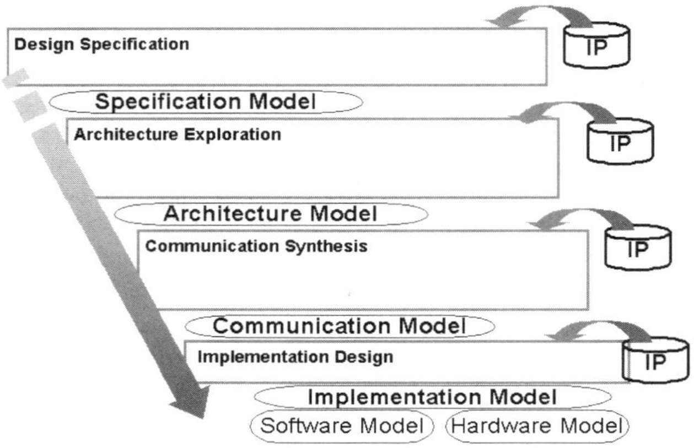

Figure 2. SpecC-based design methodology

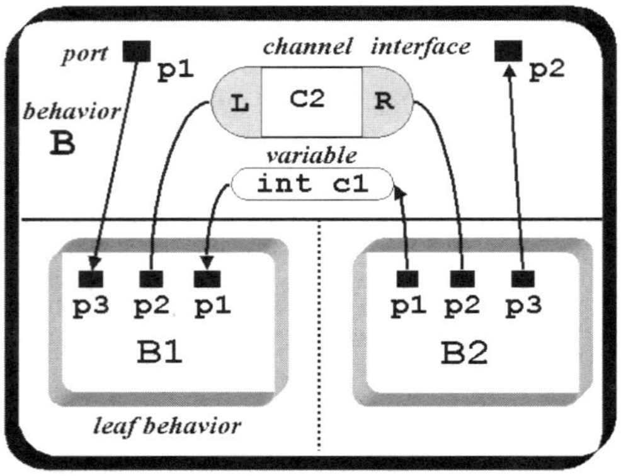

Figure 4. Communication between behaviors through channels

SpecC language is a system specification description language based on C. It allows the same semantics and syntax to be used to represent specifications for a system concept, hardware, software, and, most importantly, intermediate specification and information during hardware/software co-design stages.

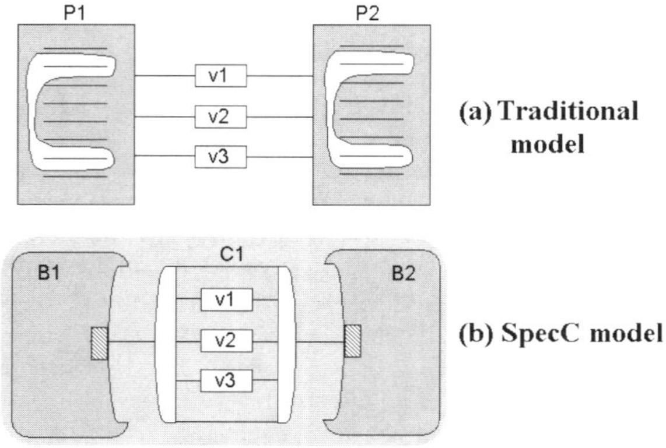

Figure 3. Communication through channels

Right now SpecC version 1.0 is publicly available. One key point in SpecC is the clear separation between communication and computation bodies in system level descriptions. With this clear separation, same descriptions can easily be used both for software and hardware (or both combined) development. As shown in Figure 3, in traditional approaches, communication among concurrent processes are just through shared variables, and control on the data transfer between the two processes are done by the statements which are in lined into the two process descriptions. Therefore, it is not easy or almost impossible to separate communication and the computation. In SpecC model, communications among processes are done through channels and control mechanisms for communication are described explicitly in the description of channels. This makes it very easy to explicit to separate the communication from the computation.

Structure hierarchy can also be described in SpecC as shown in Figure 4. In hierarchical designs, by using channels for communications, it can be easily seen how things are processed within a module in a hierarchical design as shown in the figure.

Also, SpecC has several ways to describe targeted control mechanisms:

(1) Sequential descriptions just like regular C

(2) Specialized syntax for finite state machine descriptions

(3) Explicit way to describe "parallel behaviors"

(4) Explicit way to describe "pipelined behaviors"

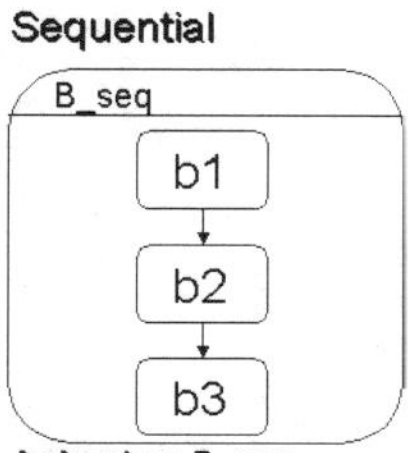


```
behavior B_seq
{
 B b1, b2, b3;
void main(void)
{
 b1.main();
 b2.main();
 b3.main();
 }
};
```

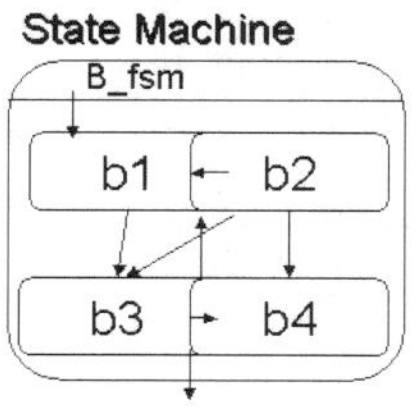


```
behavior B_fsm
{
 B b1, b2, b3, b4;
void main(void)
{
 fsm{ b1:{...}
      b2:{...}
      b3:{...}
      b4:{...}
    }
 }
};
```

Figure 5. Sequential and state machine description

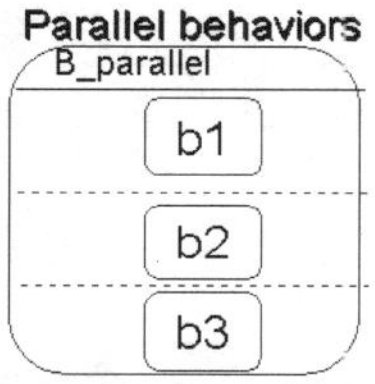


```
behavior B_parallel
{
 B b1, b2, b3;
void main(void)
{
 par { b1.main();
       b2.main();
       b3.main();
     }
 }
};
```

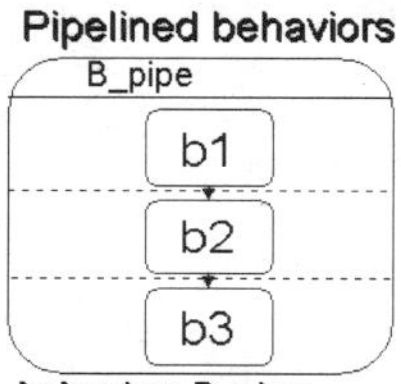


```
behavior B_pipe
{
 B b1, b2, b3;
void main(void)
{
 pipe{ b1.main();
       b2.main();
       b3.main();
     }
 }
};
```

Figure 6. Parallel and pipelined behaviors

Figure 5 and 6 give ideas on sequential, FSM, parallel, and pipeline statements. Sequential statements are just like regular C description. By using FSM statements, explicit state transitions can be clearly described. Parallel statements explicitly describe parallel execution of multiple processes whereas pipeline statements give parallel execution of multiple processes in pipelined ways.

With these flexible descriptions mechanisms, system level description targeting both software/hardware combined systems can be smoothly described. Here due to space limit, we briefly review (2)-(4) with illustrations, since those are main difference from regular C languages in terms of language constructs.

3. SpecC Technology Open Consortium (STOC)

STOC was established on November 10, 1999 by 24 companies and organizations worldwide for securing wide acceptance of a SpecC language-based methodology. Activities of STOC will be publicized at the consortium's web site (http://www.specc.gr.jp/eng), where the introduction of SpecC technology, the consortium's activities, and research results are available. Activities of the STOC include two technical working groups (WG).

- The Case Study WG that examines the ability of SpecC language through descriptions of real applications, and collects design knowledge to establish design guidelines or methodologies. According to the current schedule, a period of the WG activities is one year, and 14 members will exchange evaluation results of SpecC language ability and design know-how based on the specification description experiences.
- The Language Specification WG that maintains and establishes the specification of SpecC language while evaluating and enhancing the current specification to improve its efficiency and application scope. Members are recruited from worldwide STOC members, and the activity scope also includes standardization of relevant tools like SpecC Compiler.

Objectives and current activities of both WGs also can be tracked from the STOC web site.

4. Discussions for version 2.0

After releasing version 1.0 in early February 2001, LSWG has identified several issues to be clarified in the language. SpecC is under revision mainly on the following points:

- Clarification of detailed semantics of SpecC language
- Enhancement of usability by incorporating several syntax notations
- Others, such as tool friendly issues

Here we briefly summarize the discussions on detailed language semantics targeting SpecC version 2.0. Since this is under discussion, anything presented here could change in the future.

4.1 Why Semantics?

SpecC is a system level description language and a wide variety of designers are expected to use SpecC, including hardware designers and software designers. Since ways of thinking of hardware designers are sometimes significantly different from those of software designers, the semantics of SpecC should be clearly defined from the viewpoints of both hardware designers and software designers. The importance of formal semantics is emphasized also by the fact that varieties of design assistance will be required for system level design. Specifications in SpecC will be the input of not only simulation but also synthesis, verification, and others. As for the synthesis, it would be a case that the description is partitioned into hardware and software parts, and the former is then synthesized into RTL hardware. It would be another case of synthesis that they are bound with IP cores with modifying communications between cores. Thus, a wide variety of synthesis tools will emerge for system level design assistance. The same situation will occur in simulation and verification. Therefore, the semantics of SpecC should be defined independently from their execution engines.

The reference manual of SpecC Version 1.0 (LRM v1.0) [1] and its reference compiler [2] were already published and announced. Since the formal semantics is yet one of the most important issues, SpecC Language Specification Working Group [3] is trying to formalize its semantics, which will be included in the next version 2.0

4.2 Discussions items

One of the characteristics in SpecC is the separation of computation and communication. The communication can be specified by using either explicit channel or shared variables. Whereas the semantics of explicit channel is quite clear, that of shared variables currently contains ambiguity. This is because the semantics of parallel behaviors is not well defined. Thus, our discussion started from the semantics of "par" statement, which specifies parallel behaviors. SpecC also provides "pipe" statement to specify pipelined behaviors, which is of course a part of parallel behaviors. Though the semantics of "pipe" is also important, we focus on the semantics of "par" at first because "pipe" can be defined by using "par". Once the semantics of "par" is defined clearly, that of "pipe" will be clear.

Concerning to "par", the following items are picked up for the discussion.

- What order is permitted in the scheduling? : Is the scheduling non-preemptive or preemptive? Is it deterministic or not? If it is non-deterministic, then what degree of non-determinism is permitted?
- How to assure mutual exclusive access? : In SpecC, "wait/notify" is provided to support synchronization. However, no primitives are provided to support mutual exclusion. It will be helpful to introduce a primitive supporting for mutual exclusion which is well suited to "wait/notify".
- Semantics of synchronization primitives? : Synchronization of concurrent behaviors is a critical issue. However, some of the rules in LRM v1.0 are vague and the semantics can only be fully understood with the help of the examples and the *note* sections in LRM v1.0. The vague point is the propagation scope of notified event and the relationship between the scope and the "simulation time" in SpecC.
- How to disable exceptions temporarily? : In order to handle asynchronous exceptions correctly, it is required to disable other exceptions during the execution. Thus, it will be helpful to introduce some primitives that disable exceptions temporarily.
- When is variable assignment reflected to other concurrent behaviors? : This issue is closely related to the first issue. Without clear definition on the timing of variable assignments, it is hard to specify concurrent behaviors that share variables. Thus, it is highly recommended to establish well-defined semantics on this issue.

Since the first item of scheduling is the most fundamental among these issues and affects the discussions on the other items, we first started the discussion on scheduling.

4.3 Semantics of "par"

Figure 7 is an example of parallel behavior. In this example, behavior `a` and `b` are executed in parallel. Behavior `a` contains two sequential statements `st1` and `st2`, whereas behavior `b` contains one statement `st3`. The first question is, in which order these three statements are executed? Given the LRM v1.0, the scheduling is non-preemptive. Then, not only non-preemptive scheduling of "`st1` -> `st2` -> `st3`" and "`st3` -> `st1` -> `st2`", but also preemptive scheduling of "`st1` -> `st3` -> `st2`" are permitted.

```
main(){
par{  a.main();
      b.main();} }

behavior a{
main(){ z=y;        /*st1*/
        x=z+20;     /*st2*/ }}

behavior b{
main(){ y=x+z+1; /*st3*/ }}
```

Figure 7. Example of "par" statement

4.3.1 Sequentiality

Before clarifying the concurrency between statements, we have to define the semantics of sequentiality within a behavior. The definition is as follows. A behavior is defined on a time interval. Sequential statements in a behavior are also defined on time intervals which do not overlap one another and are within the behavior's interval.

For example, semantics of behavior `a` in Figure 7 is defined on time axis as shown in Figure 8. Suppose the beginning time and the ending time of behavior `a` are *Tas* and *Tae* respectively, and those for `st1` and `st2` are *T1s*, *T1e*, *T2s*, and *T2e*. Then, the only constraint which must be satisfied is;

$$Tas <= T1s < T1e <= T2s < T2e <= Tae$$

Statements in a behavior are executed sequentially but not always in continuous ways. That is, a gap may exist between *Tas* and *T1s*, *T1e* and *T2s*, and *T2e* and *Tae*. The lengths of these gaps are decided in non-deterministic way. Moreover, the lengths of intervals, (*T1e* – *T1s*) and (*T2e* – *T2s*) in Figure 8, are also non-deterministic.

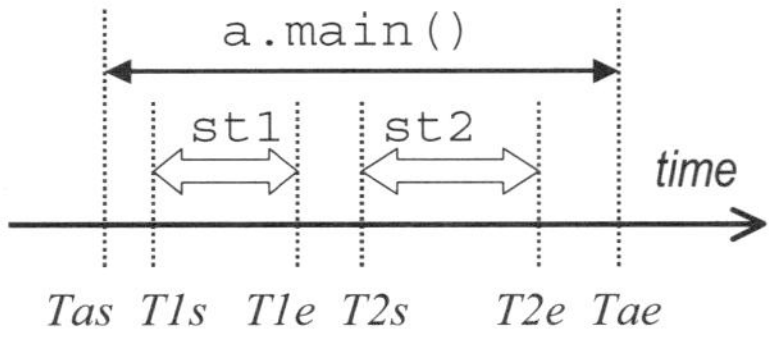

Figure 8. Semantics of Sequentiality

4.3.2 Concurrency

Behaviors invoked by "par" statement are executed concurrently. The definition of the concurrency is as follows. The beginning time of all the behaviors invoked by "par" statement are the same, and the ending time of all the behaviors invoked by "par" statement are also the same. For example, semantics of "par" statement in Figure 7 is defined on time axis as shown in Figure 9. Suppose the beginning time and the ending time of behavior a are *Tas* and *Tae* respectively, and those for behavior b are *Tbs*, *Tbe*. Then, the only constraint which must be satisfied is;

$$Tas = Tbs, \quad Tae = Tbe$$

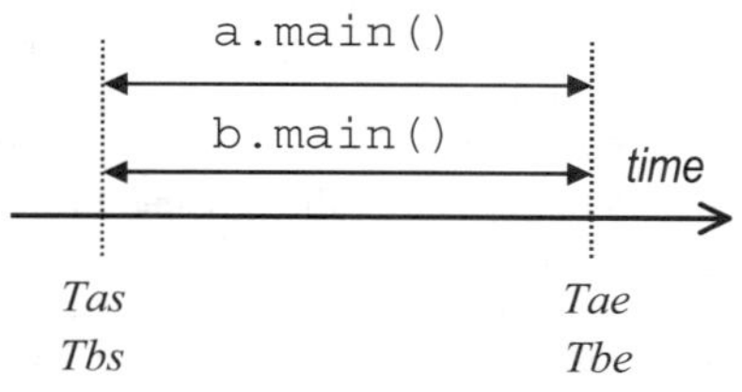

Figure 9. Semantics of Concurrency

Once the sequentiality and concurrency are defined, the semantics of the description in Figure 7 is clearly defined as illustrated in Figure 10. The followings are all the constraints to be satisfied.

- $Tas \le T1s < T1e \le T2s < T2e \le Tae$ (sequentiality in a)
- $Tbs \le T3s < T3e \le Tbe$ (sequentiality in b)
- $Tas = Tbs, \; Tae = Tbe$ (concurrency between a and b)

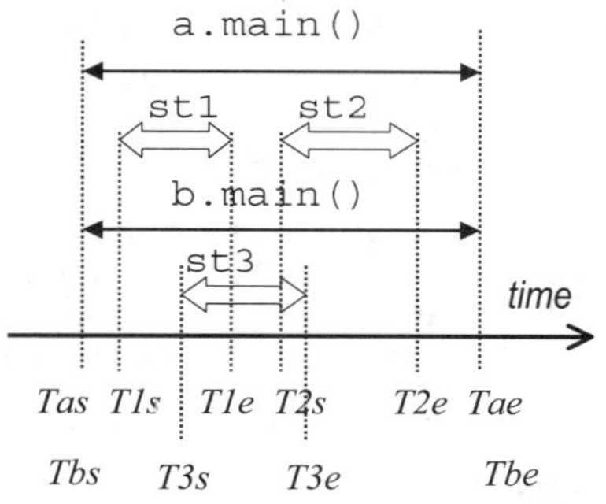

Figure 10. Scheduling for the example of Figure 7.

Note that there are no deterministic rules on the lengths of st3 st1, and st2, and on the lengths of the gap between statements, st3 may overlap with st1 and/or st2, or may not overlap with st1 or st2.

4.3.3 Atomicity

The next question is whether the overlaps between statements are permitted or not. The answer depends on the granularity of atomicity. In the LRM v1.0, atomicity is not described explicitly.

One policy is that each assignment statement is atomic. Under this policy, overlaps between statements are not permitted. Then, the statement of "y=x+x", for example, is always the same as "y=2*x" because x is not updated by any other statement during the execution of this statement. Thus, this policy will reduce the degree of non-determinism. On the other hand, this assumption is completely different from C language although SpecC is extended from C language, and thus it would be confusing. For instance, it is quite ambiguous what will happen if a function call is included in an assignment statement. Another disadvantage of this policy is that quality of synthesized hardware and/or software may be degraded because this atomicity should be guaranteed by hardware and/or software.

It would be another policy that no atomicity is assumed, which is opposite to the above policy.

We are also discussing this issue and going to reach the consensus that no atomicity is guaranteed in any operation, even in the memory access. Thus, statements may be preempted at any time in their execution. Due to this feature, overlaps between statements are permitted. Another result from this feature is "y=x+x" is not always the same as "y=2*x". This is because the first read of x may not be executed at the same time as the second read of x and because x may be updated by other parallel behaviors between the two reads. Therefore, if designers would like to use shared variables in a safe way, they should use those variables with explicit synchronization.

4.3.4 Relationship with Simulation Time

SpecC has two primitives to support the specification of timing called "simulation time": "waitfor" and "do-timing". Given the LRM v1.0, "waitfor" statement specifies execution time (or delay). Whenever the simulator reaches a waitfor statement, the execution of the current behavior is suspended for the specified amount of simulation time units. The do-timing construct is used to specify timing constraints in terms of minimum and maximum number of time units. The LRM v1.0 says the do-timing construct specifies synthesis constraints and the way that the simulator performs the constraint validation is implementation dependent.

In order to make the semantics of sequentiality and concurrency be sound with these primitives, the relationship between the length of each interval and the "simulation time" must be defined soundly. The definition is that the length of each interval on which a statement is defined is quite small and infinitely close to 0 in "simulation time"'. In other words, execution of each statement does not change the "simulation time". Going back to Figure 8, this definition is intuitively described as " $(T1e - T1s)$ and $(T2e - T2s)$, the lengths of statements' intervals, are infinitely close to 0". Note that this definition does allow that $(T1s - Tas)$, $(T2s - T1e)$, and/or $(Tae - T2e)$, the lengths of gaps, have non-zero value.

```
main(){
  par{ a.main();
       b.main();} }

behavior a{
  main(){ z=y;          /*st1*/
          waitfor(2);   /*NEW*/
          x=z+20;       /*st2*/ }}

behavior b{
  main(){ y=x+z+1; /*st3*/ }}
```

Figure 11. Example with "waitfor"

Figure 11 is an example where waitfor(2) statement is inserted between st1 and st2 of Figure 7. This waitfor(2) increments "simulation time" by 2. According to the above rule and the semantics of sequentiality and concurrency, there are three candidates on the timing when st3 is executed as shown Figure 12. Note that the length of the interval st3 is infinitely close to 0 whereas the interval of the behavior a and b has the length of 2.

Now, LRM v1.0 gives another rule that says that active threads are executed without changing the "simulation time". Thus, `st3` must be executed immediately without changing the "simulation time" before `waitfor(2)` as shown in Figure 13. Thus, `st3` must precede `st2` in this example.

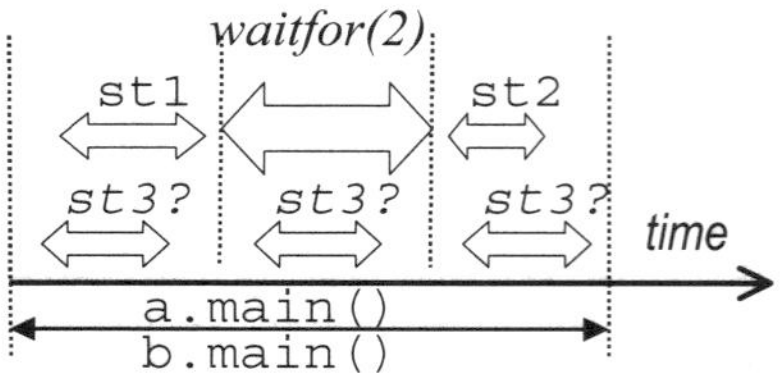

Figure 12. Candidates for Scheduling

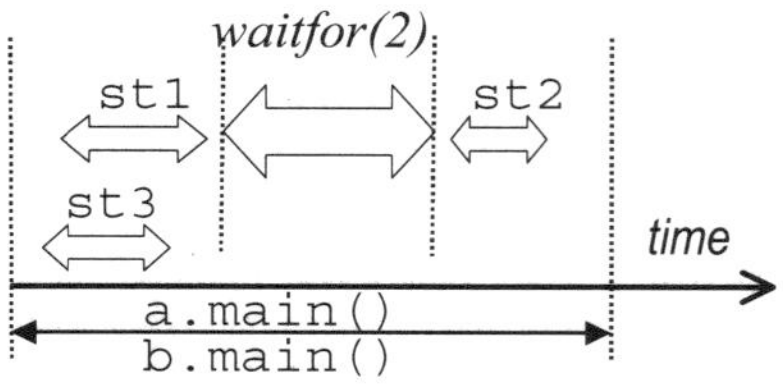

Figure 13. Scheduling for the example of Figure 6.

```
main(){
  par{ a.main();
       b.main();} }

behavior a{
  main(){ z=y;           /*st1*/
          waitfor(2);
          x=z+20;        /*st2*/
          notify e;      /*NEW*/}}

behavior b{
  main(){ wait e;        /*NEW*/}}
          y=x+z+1;       /*st3*/ }}
```

Figure 14. Example with "wait/notify"

Then, what will happen if `st3` is not an active thread?

In SpecC, "wait/notify" statements are used for synchronization. The semantics is that "wait" statement suspends the current thread from execution until one of the specified events is "notified". Since "wait" suspends a thread for a certain amount of "simulation time" unit, the next concern is how statements are scheduled if "wait" statements exist.

Suppose another example of Figure 14 where the synchronization statement of ``notify/wait'' is inserted into Figure 11. In this example, "`wait e`" suspends `st3` until the specified event `e` is notified by "`notify e`". Here, "`notify e`" is scheduled only after the completion of st2 due to the sequentiality in behavior a. Thus, it is guaranteed that `st3` is scheduled after `st2`. Consequently, the example of Figure 14 is executed as shown in Figure 15. Note that the scheduling of Figure 15 is one of the candidates shown in Figure 12.

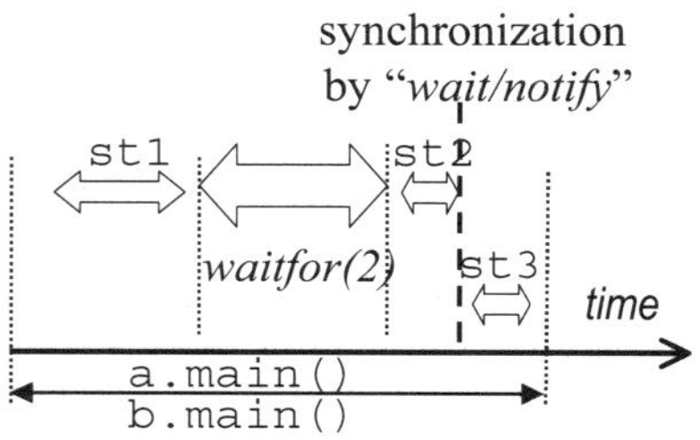

Figure 15. Scheduling for the example of Figure 8.

5. Concluding Remarks

In this paper we have reviewed the current status of SpecC languages emphasizing the issues being discussed by LSWG of STOC. We plan to formally release SpecC language version 2.0 in the beginning of 2002. Based on the formal semantics, many supporting tools for SpecC are expected to be available soon.

6. REFERENCES

[1] R. Doemer, A. Gerstlauer, and D. Gajski, "SpecC Language Reference Manual Version 1.0," http://www.specc.gr.jp/eng/tech/SpecC_LRM.pdf.

[2] http://www.ics.uci.edu/~specc/reference/

[3] http://www.specc.gr.jp/eng/wg_lang

Interoperability as a Design Issue in C++ Based Modeling Environments

Frederic Doucet
Center for Embedded Computer Systems
University of California
Irvine, CA 92697-3425
doucet@ics.uci.edu

Rajesh Gupta
Center for Embedded Computer Systems
University of California
Irvine, CA 92697-3425
gupta@uci.edu

Masato Otsuka
FUJITSU Ltd
Kawasaki, Japan
otsuka.masato@jp.fujitsu.com

Patrick Schaumont
Departement of Electrical Engineering
University of California
Los Angeles, CA 90095-1594
schaum@ee.ucla.edu

Sandeep Shukla
Center for Embedded Computer Systems
University of California
Irvine, CA 92697-3425
shshukla@ics.uci.edu

ABSTRACT

The increasing heterogeneity and complexity of VLSI systems has made the use of C++ popular for building simulation and synthesis models at higher levels of abstraction. Currently, there are several different embodiments of C++ based environments, mostly in the form of hardware modeling libraries built on top of C++. However, the *semantic gap* between hardware modeling concepts, and the software programming language constructs, poses several issues which require critical examination. In this paper, we address the issue of *interoperability* between models built using different C++ based modeling libraries, or even modeling "styles" including home-grown C++ models. Model interoperability is the ability to use C++ based descriptions across different C++ based modeling environments. Two important aspects of interoperability are model *composability*, and model *reusability*. In this paper we focus on model reusability, analyzing various dimensions of the reusability of C++ based models, in an integration environment for building SOC models. We show how an inheritance based composition may be used to make two distinct C++ based class libraries interoperate. We also outline the implementation of a dynamic composition environment, which allows automatic *run-time delegation* based composition, to achieve interoperability. These strategies allow system integrators to focus on design composition, rather than software programming details inherent in the current inheritance based solutions.

1. INTRODUCTION

System architects and verification engineers build C++ models of hardware systems, and testbenches, for architectural exploration, fast prototyping, hardware/software co-design, etc. C++ provides them with increased functionality/abstraction over other languages. Often these C++ based models need to express hardware concepts such as concurrency, structural hierarchy, and data types. The C++ syntax to express these hardware concepts vary from one environment to the other. In the transition of C++ from a software programming language to a language for high level modeling of micro-electronic systems various artifacts are introduced into the language, often in the form of library elements to express such hardware concepts. This is one of the major advantage of an extensible language like C++, but this also gives rise to the issue of semantic mismatch of the hardware concepts, and software programming artifacts. For instance, consider a hardware module with a 7-bit output, and another module with 7-bit input. From a hardware semantics perspective, they should be composable along their interfaces (provided the timing requirements are satisfied). However, in C++, 7 bits might be represented differently in the different modeling libraries. (For example, bit vector, or a parameterized class for a collection of n-bits.) To compose these two models, additional programming, or other modifications of the source code may be needed. The problem in this example is actually an easier one to solve than other problems germane in the semantic gap, such as differing models of concurrency in two modeling libraries, interfacing along combinational paths, differing functional accuracy in the models, differing timing accuracy in the models, and so on. Some of these problems might dictate imposition of methodological and notational requirements to high-level modeling styles using C++. We will not concern ourselves with those in this paper. For a treatment of methodological issues, the reader is referred to [5] [6].

The *interoperability* in the context of C++ models, means the ability to use C++ descriptions across different C++ based modeling environments. These may include interfacing of standard library based hardware models to legacy C++ code. Two major aspects of interoperability, are model *composability*, and model *reusability*. We want to construct models of a system, using components modeled in different libraries or different versions of the same library. However, we want the models to compose without having to change the models themselves. One can argue that composability, and reusability are the two sides of the same coin. Com-

ISSS'01, October 1-3, 2001, Montréal, Québec, Canada.

posability can be thought of as the problem of composing existing component models with maximal reuse of the components. Consequently, reusability is the main focus of our work. We often use the terms 'composability', and 'reusability' interchangeably in this paper, not to mean, that they are the same, but with the understanding that our objective is to achieve composability of C++ models, with maximum reuse of existing modules. Reusability is a major requirement due to the increased expectation of model integration in C++ (including *home grown* C++ models), and also due to extensive flexibility, and therefore diversity in modeling using C++ based libraries.

When building larger models by assembling smaller component models, the major technical challenges for achieving composability are: (1) Differing models of computation in the different models; (2) Differing levels of abstraction in the different models; (3) Different data types to represent the interfaces; (4) C++ being too flexible a language, the same hardware concepts can be programmed in completely different ways in the different models; (5) Differences in the notions and implementation of concurrency between hardware and software. Clearly not all these problems are related to the semantic gap problem. In fact, one major source of problems is differing models of computation in the models, which has been previously addressed extensively in the context of Ptolemy [14, 6, 7]. In this paper, we focus on the problems related to the semantic gap, because interoperability across differing models of computation, is not specific to C++ based modeling, and is present in most system modeling languages. This problem is important since software engineering and programming issues are becoming the problem of the hardware engineer when he/she uses C++ for modeling hardware systems. This also poses a difficult human resources challenge which is beyond the scope of this paper. However, ideally, the solutions to the problem of reusability should be such, that the hardware designers can focus on the hardware semantics, and design issues, rather than struggling with programming issues, and hacks in order to make a composed system work.

2. C++ BASED DESIGN ENVIRONMENTS

A number of C++ based micro-electronic high level modeling approaches have been proposed and discussed extensively in [10, 9, 12, 8, 13, 19, 20, 18]. C++ as a general syntax is often too complicated for a hardware designer. As a result, some environments are so designed that the models are expressed in a reduced syntax (like e.g. Cyn++ from Cynapps [19]) or a graphical one (like VCC from Cadence [18]). A preprocessor then translates the restricted syntax to C++, which is then linked with a modeling library. Consequently, a C++ design environment can have different embodiments that make it seem different from the traditional software development compile-link cycle. We want to stress however that this difference is mainly dependent on where one sees the interaction with the end-user. The core of the design environment can be a C++ modeling library even though the user writes a specialized language. Therefore, the interoperability problem extends into those environments as well, but rather from a tool API standardization perspective. Some examples are given in Table 1. This list is far from exhaustive and only targets to show that C++ is beginning to be used in a wide variety of environments.

Name	Origin	Embodiment
SystemC	OSCI	C++ library
Cynlib	Cynapps	C++ library
OCAPI	IMEC	C++ library
Cruise	Conexant	In-house C++ system simulation environment
Cyn++	Cynapps	Macro package on top of Cynlib
VCC	Cadence	Graphical notation using underlying C++ objects
SpecC	UC Irvine	Dedicated language compiled into C++ based simulation
ART/Library	Frontier Design	C++ Library (focus on datatypes)
Testbuilder	Cadence	C++ Library (focus on testbenches)

Table 1: C++ Based Design Environments

2.1 Modeling Dimensions

The complexity of the design modeling (and consequently the complexity of the C++ programs) quickly becomes clear by considering a system level design modeling taxonomy. The VSI SLD Taxonomy [15] is a good guideline to this. It distinguishes four orthogonal design model characteristics.

1. *Temporal detail*: which expresses the degree of precision of the ordering of the modeled events. This includes partial-ordered event accurate models, token-cycle accurate models, instruction-cycle accurate models, clock-cycle accurate models, clock-phase accurate models, and so on.
2. *Data value detail*: which expresses the representation or format of data values specified in a model. Data values could be enumerated values, word-level values, bit-true representations, etc.
3. *Functional detail*: which expresses the level of detail in the functionality of a model, ranging from mathematical formulae to detailed intermediate operations (gate-level or instruction level).
4. *Structural detail*: which expresses the level of detail in the structure of a model, ranging from single-block code to multiple levels.

While these are theoretically orthogonal design axes, in practice they are never described or explored separately. Instead, designers often use well-defined combinations of modeling precision to express a *model of computation*. For example, DSP hardware might be expressed using the data-flow model of computation, which expresses partial ordering (temporal level), actor-primitive code (functional level), flow-graphs (structural level). An executable simulation always fixes a "working point" on each of the four axes. Thus, if we want to simulate the dataflow computational model (that fixes temporal detail, functional detail and structural detail), we will also have to make a decision on the data value detail of the simulation by choosing the data type of the tokens.

2.2 Mapping of Modeling Dimensions

When a design model is constructed in C++, a supporting design model library is often used. This library contains a number of classes that allow expression of different modeling dimensions.

2.2.1 Temporal Detail

The standard C++ language is executed sequentially, with no notion of time. However, concurrency and parallelism are fundamental in hardware models. A modeling environment can explicitly

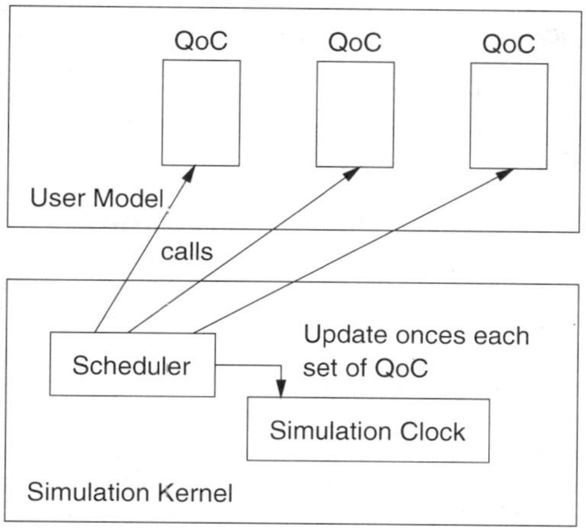

Figure 1: Generic Model of Concurrency in C++ Modeling Libraries

reference the time or else make it implicit through simulation cycles. Therefore, the introduction of concurrency and time characteristics always require specific classes and modeling support. The approaches used in C++ models are very often a derived form of Figure 1. The modeling library provides a *scheduler* that manages the simulation clock. The scheduler also decides when computation in the user model should be executed. The user model itself consists of several pieces of behavior called *Quantum of Computation*. A QoC is all activity in a user model that can happen in one step, without interaction with the simulation model environment. Concurrency is simulated in this model by calling several different QoC before updating the simulation clock. Thus, to the observer of the model, it looks like time has not advanced while several different QoC are executing: their activity seems concurrent. Cycle simulation is a frequently implemented time model in current C++ libraries and is often extended with the delta-cycle concept from HDL simulation. It works as follows. The QoC in the user model describe one cycle of processing. The QoC communicate through state variables or direct connections. Each state variable has a present- and a next-value. The overall simulation works in a two-phase approach. During the evaluate phase (phase 1), the execution of a QoC reads the present-value of the state variables and writes the next-value. During the update phase, next-value in state variables is copied to the present-value, and the simulation time is advanced. Additionally, the evaluate-phase might be driven by a value-change sensing mechanism (upon QoC inputs) to support relaxation-types of simulation (called the *delta cycle* in HDL simulation). This style of temporal modeling is reasonably simple, but yet many different approaches can be used in implementing it in C++. The actual implementation of a scheduler, of the simulation clock and the QoC can be done in a variety of ways: native execution or interpreter based, call-back mechanisms, multiple threads, etc.

While a detailed discussion of each of those approaches is beyond the scope here, it should be clear that there are can be as many implementations of the evaluate/update mechanism as there are C++ design environments. For example, different libraries can use different thread packages [4], and synchronization mechanisms. By itself, the synchronization interoperability can be very complex if it introduces many ordering protocols. Before two C++ environments can be interconnected, it must be clear how they implement the temporal axis in a model. The simulation detail (level of abstraction) should match, but in addition the implementation approach (API) must also match.

2.2.2 Data Value Detail

One of the big advantages in using C++ is the ability to introduce new data types (and classes). Most C++ design environments offer a wide spectrum of data representation and detail. Typically included are various types of scalar values with specific quantization characteristics. However, this kind of flexibility adversely affects interoperability. A common base of information representation is needed in order to transfer information from one environment to the other. There are three approaches in modeling data values.

1. Direct use of *built-in types*. C++ has a wide range of built-in types. Those values might be applicable for the model. In addition, the C++ built-in data types are interoperable by themselves.

2. We can use a *class model* of the actual representation of data values. For example, a bitvector can be modeled as an array of bits. This array can be stored as a private member of a class.

3. Sometimes an *abstracted representation of data values, with operational behavior* is used. For example, the operations on a bitvector (of limited word-length) might perfectly be done in terms of the built-in type "int" if we are only interested in the aggregate data value of the bitvector. Similarly, fixed point DSP calculations can perfectly be done using floating point C++ built-in types. In both cases, we need to take quantization effects (overflow and rounding) into account in the functional description.

The interoperability of (scalar) data values has been more successful than the other axes of modeling dimensions. A VSIA datatype standard [16] is under development as a reference for data values. Data types for which C++ libraries are available include 2-value and 4-value bits and bitvectors, arbitrary sized signed and unsigned integers, and fixed point values.

The interoperability of different C++ design environments implies that different data types can be cast across environments without loss of precision. If the target environment has no direct support for a particular datatype (for example, fixed point), then two situations can occur. First, there can be a data type in the target environment that has sufficient range. In that case a "converter stub" is needed to translate data values between the two environments. Second, the target environment can lack a type that has sufficient range. In that case, the target environment must be extended with an "emulator" that supports this data type. But, the interoperability problems can occur when this is to be specified, and checked. There is two approaches that can be used: (1) static type checks, and replacements in the compilation phase (2) dynamic conversions at runtime through stubs. Type systems have been used to infer types and provide some type looseness in programming languages such as ML or Ptolemy. As we discuss later in this paper, our solution is based on a run-time type inference and *delayed type instantiation*[2].

2.2.3 Functional Detail

The third axis of detail is the functional one. It expresses the precision of the model functionality. Each executable description implements the behavior of a model of computation.

The C++ Semantics: The C++ language uses a sequential consistency for correctness and composition. The language is designed for the implementation of software programs. The usage of classes makes C++ very convenient to capture real world structures as object in the software environment. The C++ language has no formal semantics, and is very flexible and extensible. In that sense, the usage of the syntactic constructs can be different from the original semantic intent. For example, the usage of exceptions is recommended for handling software error condition, but it has been used to model interrupt behavior in hardware systems. When different C++ environments are matched to each other, they will need similar styles of software design at their matching points.

Syntactic variations with C++: Modeling flexibility inherent in C++ often creates additional programming overhead for the IC designer. Consider, for instance, modeling of state machines, which of course, have a well understood semantic model. A common technique is to use a nested switch with a scalar state variable, or in more complex cases sparse arrays of actions and transitions for each state, with actions as function pointers. In object oriented modeling states are often treated as subclasses with common interface defined by a super class. Events are modeled as methods in the interface, and a separate "evaluate-class" is used to send events for processing to the current state object. Therefore, a state transition changes the current state object. Here inheritance is used for state addition to the model (by subclassing), and for adding events (by adding new functions to the subclass, or overwriting virtual methods of the super class). In order to execute the model correctly, the state machine needs to be integrated with other objects in the environment. This introduces *context dependencies* from the FSM to other software components, reducing the reusability. In other words, execution of the FSM model relies on the existence of other objects which are not a part of the FSM model. As a result, to use the FSM Model in different environments, one has to program the environment objects in the new environment again.

2.2.4 Structural Detail

The final modeling axis relates to structural detail. All modeling environments have the concept of a "block" that encapsulates other blocks or leaf behavior. In addition, the blocks recognize port and/or port lists that provide handles to express communication. The structural detail in a model allows relating it to an implementation view. Structural interoperability means that one environment is able to encapsulate a block from another environment.

However, structure can also include *design patterns* [3], which rely on C++ programming techniques such as polymorphism and component substitutability [11]. Organizing a C++ model at this level of abstraction provides a higher abstraction and flexibility than the entity-port-entity connection models. An open problem in this approach is how should these patterns be used in C++ hardware system modeling, and their impact on interoperability since the discrete event semantics rely on port-signal-port-process semantics.

3. INTEROPERABILITY STRATEGIES

Interoperability is often achieved, by creating *wrappers* around the existing C++ descriptions that allows communication of data values between different modules and co-ordination between them. However, wrappers can be implemented in many ways. The first and most common strategy is by using inheritance. In this approach, the wrapper is programmed by manually inserting code to align various design axes inside the inherited class. The component and the wrapper have a *common self* in this implementation [11]; i.e. the wrapper and the component are the same object. As a result, the the interoperability issues related to typing are resolved at compile time, and the wrapper and component have strong dependencies.

An alternative is to use wrappers that, if needed, *delegates* to the design component. In this case, the component is not modified, and the wrapper and the component are two distinct objects. Modules from different libraries can be imported as is, and dynamically placed in wrappers at runtime. Let us review both of these strategies in more details.

3.1 Interoperability with Inheritance

An example of inheritance based composition is shown in Figure 2. It shows how two models drawn from different C++ based libraries (in this case, Ocapi and Cynlib), can be composed in a single executable model. In Figure 2, the system shows a dataflow example where the modules are a mix of Cynlib and Ocapi-1 blocks. The system consists of four actors (active modules), three of which will be under the control of the Cynlib simulator, and one under control of the OCAPI simulator. For simplicity, all communications and data types are also taken from the Ocapi domain.

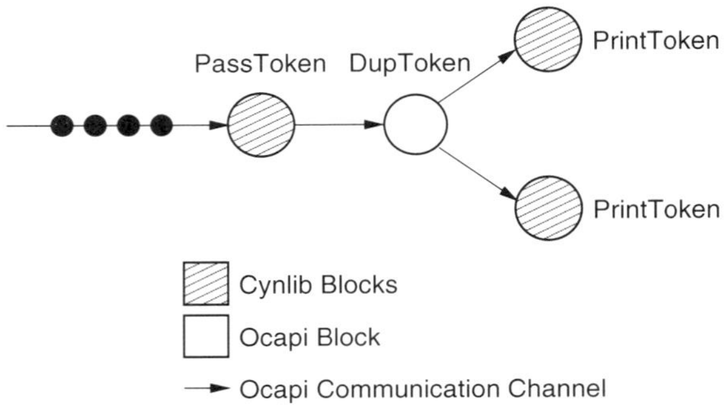

Figure 2: Example for Interoperability

As seen in the main function below, there is a main scheduling loop that calls the Cynlib and Ocapi schedulers in alternating fashion, until all dataflow tokens are consumed out of the system.

```
void main() {
  dfbfix Q1("queue1");     /* OCAPI data type */
  dfbfix Q2("queue2");
  dfbfix Q3("queue3");
  dfbfix Q4("queue4");
  PassToken2  P1(Q1, Q2);       // Cynlib block
  DupToken    P2(Q2, Q3, Q4); // Ocapi block
  PrintToken  P3(Q3);           // Cynlib block
  PrintToken  P4(Q4);           // Cynlib block
  sysgen ocapisystem("ocapisystem");   /* OCAPI */
  clk ocapiclk;  /* OCAPI clock */
  ocapisystem << P2;
  Q1.put(0.1);
  Q1.put(0.2);
  Q1.put(0.3);
  Q1.put(0.4);
  while ( Q1.getSize() > 0 ||
          Q2.getSize() > 0 ||
          Q3.getSize() > 0 ||
          Q4.getSize() > 0) {
    ocapisystem.run(ocapiclk);
    /* simulates one ocapi clock */
    CynTick();
    /* simulates one cynlib clock */
  }
  CynFinish(); /* clean up for cynlib */
}
```

In this example, PassToken, and PrintToken modules are derived from the `CynModule` class from Cynlib, and suitable code insertion has made it capable of accepting OCAPI datatypes such as `dfbfix`, while the DupToken inherits from the `base` OCAPI class for processes. Due to lack of space, we do not show the code, and necessary programming intervention into the modules from both domains, but is is available online [13]. Interoperability is achieved by making the two modeling environments match on the four dimensions by programming new classes via inheritance from the respective reactive class interfaces in OCAPI and Cynlib, and implementing call backs explicitly for the two simulation kernels as follows

1. On the temporal axis, the (untimed, partially ordered) dataflow model of computation was used. This is required to express the cycle simulation semantics of Cynlib in terms of a polling firing-rule check (DF_actor object). Note that because queues are used instead of signals, no delta events were exchanged between the two simulators. The simulation kernels cannot exchange delta events at this time because the event format is not interoperable, and the eval/update calls are not accessible to the programmer.
2. On the data value axis, interoperability was implicit since we used only the OCAPI-1 data type dfix for all calculations.
3. On the functional axis, we organized the processing of a token in a method, which was executed as native code. The method itself was slaved to a system scheduler (either Cynlib or Ocapi) that implemented dataflow semantics.
4. On the structural axis, the same approach was used as on the functional axis (since we did not consider synthesis of this model, only simulation).

While inheritance can quickly achieve interoperability in some cases, it is not a recommended approach for many reasons. For one, it may actually hinder reusability in the long term. Figure

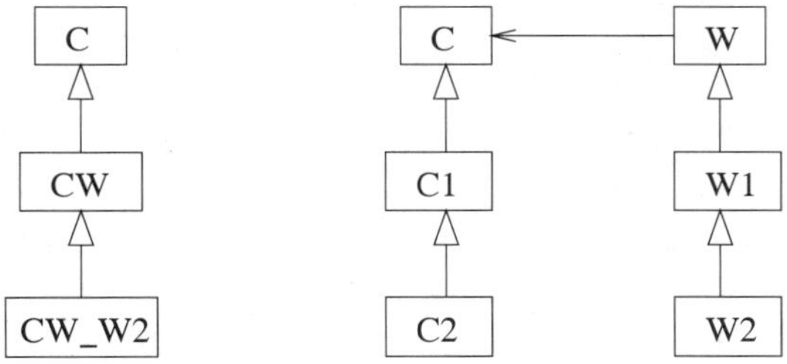

(a) (b)

Figure 3: Wrapper implementation strategies: (a) by inheritance (b) by composition

3(a) illustrates the UML class diagram of the typical problem of inheritance based composition (the *common-self* [11] problem). If a designer wants to reuse a component of class `C`, the class can be specialized by inheritance to a subclass `CW` to implement the wrapper functionality. Let us suppose that the behavior of the original class `C` is modified in the class `CW` by adding more functionality or by re-implementing a virtual function. If the class `CW` is to be reused in a different context, then it can be also inherited into a class `CW_W2` that implements more wrapper code to interoperate in the new integration context. The problem in this scenario is that all the three classes have a common self, and the original component has to be modified in every reuse context, via inheritance. Also, substituting an object of class `C` with a `CW` (which is legal in C++) may introduce subtle side effects. For instance, the wrapper code may modify the state of the component in ways that may not be obvious to the designer. If in a reuse environment, the original component being reused is unaltered, then it keeps its identity distinct from the identity of the wrapper that contains the code for the interoperability. Figure 3(b) shows the UML diagram of how a wrapper hierarchy can be built for composition (the open arrow indicates an association). In this case, the wrappers are separate from the component object hierarchy, and the interoperability interface remains separated in the wrappers, and any call to functionality of the original component is delegated from the wrapper to the component.

3.2 Interoperability with Dynamic Composition

To implement design interoperability and reuse with dynamic composition, wrappers can be individually implemented and used for each component. However, this is very difficult to perform on a large scale. A strategy to automate the interoperability is to use a wrapper generator. In our experiments, we built the BALBOA system [2] for dynamic composition. This environment is designed to relieve the system integrator from manually generating wrappers to align data-type detail axis, as well as the other axes of interoperability. This enables the system integrator to work with hardware semantics of components in their mind, and to compose components from a library, which makes sense from a hardware design stand point.

Our wrapper generator in BALBOA is a compiler, that parses component descriptions described in a special interface definition language (called BALBOA IDL or BIDL), and automatically builds smart customized wrappers. The use of BIDL is optional for the system designer since the description are automatically generated by the library builder. In addition to wrapper generation, the system also provides appropriate type determination in the context in which an object is used. Our dynamic typing mechanism, implements a delayed typing useful to compose objects since in some cases, in order to compose hardware and software objects, the designer may not know the exact object types used by the C++ libraries to implement the model. Our environment, upon getting a request for composition, enables the designer to figure out such details without having to go through the source code, and can rely on the tool to instantiate the types correctly for interoperability of the components. Note that it can also fail to instantiate the composition request due to incompatibilities in the designers choices.

BALBOA provides an interpretive command shell to instantiate and compose objects. The wrappers are visible from the user command shell. This visibility enable designers to manipulate the components by writing composition scripts. A composition language, called *Component Integration Language* is used to control the wrapper layer. In the current implementation, the interpreter is built using an extended OTcl interpreter. We call the wrappers *Split Level Interfaces*. This is because they are the link between the compiled C++ domain and the interpreted composition domain. Figure 4 shows the runtime view of the object interactions in the environment. The split level interfaces are in gray and execute composition commands. The simulation control flow is in the compiled hierarchy, from the discrete event simulator (DES) to the components C1, C2 and C3. Whenever possible, usually the interpreter is not involved in the simulation loop for efficiency reasons.

The split level interface allows *introspection*, or *reflection* [1], of the attributes of the component models from the component library layer to the command interpreter layer. As a result, the designer

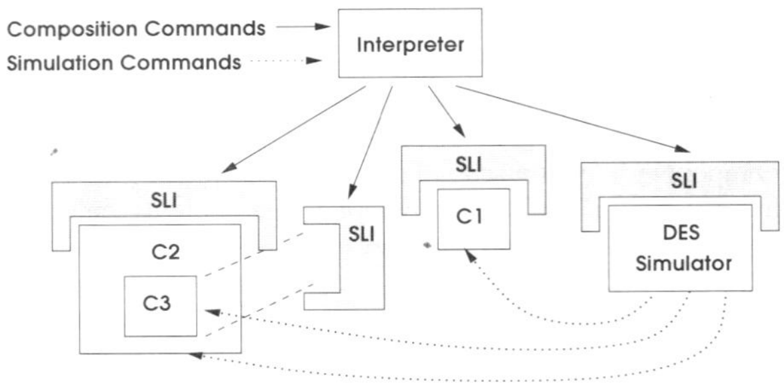

Figure 4: Layered composition with Split Level Interface wrappers (in gray) around design and tool components

or the tool can query a component for its characteristics (such as structural information, type, connectivity, attributes, methods), allowing dynamic composition decisions to be made. In BIDL, the component's exportable interface is described, along with certain other meta-level information about the component. For example, abstraction levels can be specified (behavioral, structural). The split level interface inheritance hierarchy, such as in Figure 3(b), is specified in this language. The BIDL compiler generates the C++ code for the split level interfaces, and the code is compiled into a library and loaded in the environment. The implementation of such a "smart" composition environment is quite challenging. However, this requires little (if any) changes in the existing C++ library environments.

Another possible approach to achieve interoperability is through interfacing the different simulators at the simulation run-time. The distinction from the approach just described, and this approach, is that in the first case, the interoperability is designed into the composed system at the environment run time, and in the latter case, it is achieved at simulation run-time. In the currently available C++ simulation libraries, there is no programming interface to the simulation kernels to make two distinct simulation kernels exchange delta cycle events, or synchronize the increment of the simulation clock. However, we can implement, or change existing simulation kernels to provide such APIs. If the purpose of system integration is to build a complete system simulation, this could be done by building a simulator by composing single or multiple simulation kernels through these APIs.

4. DISCUSSION AND FUTURE WORK

System level modeling and integration of components, using C++ models of micro-electronic systems can be decomposed in four different dimensions. Doing so, the problem of interoperability is divided in smaller chunks, such that each might be easier to conquer. In particular, the VSIA standards on data types [16] already have addressed the problem in the data value details axis. In this paper, we elaborate on the interoperability problem, in terms of composability, and reusability of existing models in an integration environment. We have presented the various solution strategies, and how they are implemented in C++. However, the extendibility of C++, and the sequential model of execution inherent in C++, lead to simulation and structural semantic gaps when composing models together. This is because of the possible different implementations of a component, and the use of inheritance to build wrappers around components that implement the function needed for the interoperability. We presented a solution for model interoperability using composition based techniques. We then extended our solution to create a dynamic composition environment that relies on composition and delegation. We also discussed the automatic wrapper generation, configured by a specific language to capture hardware semantics. Further experiments for matching different modeling dimensions and specifically their mapping to C++ are under way as a part of our ongoing research on C++ based hardware/system modeling issues [17].

5. ACKNOWLEDGMENTS

We gratefully acknowledge the support for this research from DARPA/ITO under contract DABT63-98-C-004, the National Science Foundation (NSF), the Semiconductor Research Corporation (SRC) and the Fond pour la Formation de Chercheurs et l'Aide à la Recherche (FCAR).

6. REFERENCES

[1] F. Buschmann, R. Meunier, H. Rohnert, P. Sommerlad, and M. Stal. *Pattern Oriented Software Architecture: A System of Patterns*. John Wiley and Sons, 1996.

[2] F. Doucet, M. Otsuka, R. Gupta, and S. Shukla. Efficient system level co-design environment for split-level programming. Technical Report TR-01-34, CECS, Univ. of California, Irvine, 2001.

[3] E. Gamma, R. Helm, R. Johnson, and J. Vlissides. *Design Patterns: Elements of Reusable Object-Oriented Software*. Addison-Wesley, 1995.

[4] P. Garg, S. Shukla, and R. Gupta. Efficient usage of concurrency models in an object-oriented co-design framework. In *DATE*, 2001.

[5] M. Keating and P. Bricaud. *Reuse Methodology Manual for System-on-a-Chip Designs*. Kluwer Academic Publishers, 1998.

[6] E. A. Lee. What's ahead for embedded software. *IEEE Computer*, September 2000.

[7] E. A. Lee and A. Sangiovanni-Vincentelli. A framework for comparing models of computation. *IEEE Trans. on CAD*, December 1998.

[8] S. Liao, S. Tjiang, and R. Gupta. An efficient implementation of reactivity in modeling hardware in the scenic synthesis and simulation environment. In *DAC*, 1997.

[9] G. D. Michelli. Hardware synthesis from C/C++ models. In *DATE*, 1999.

[10] L. Semeria and A. Ghosh. Methodology for hardware/ software co-verification in C/C++. In *HLDVT*, 1999.

[11] C. Szyperski. *Component Software: Beyond Object Oriented Programming*. Addison-Wesley, 1998.

[12] C. Weiler, U. Kebschull, and W. Rosenstiel. C++ base classes for specification, simulation and partitioning of a hardware/software system. In *CS Workshop on VLSI*, 1995.

[13] IEEE/DATC C++ Modeling Standardization Effort home page: http://www.ics.uci.edu/~rgupta/datc/.

[14] Ptolemy 2 project, UC Berkeley, home page: http://ptolemy.eecs.berkeley.edu/.

[15] VSI system level design taxonomy, v1.0, vsi alliance, http://www.vsi.org/library/specs/summary.htm#sldtax.

[16] VSIA data type standard, under development.

[17] BALBOA Project home page: http://www.ics.uci.edu/ balboa.

[18] Cadence VCC home page: http://www.cadence.com/eda_solutions/hcd_13_index.html.

[19] CynApps home page: http://www.cynapps.com.

[20] SystemC home page: http://www.systemc.org.

Bridging the Gap Between ISA Compilers and Silicon Compilers: A Challenge for Future SoC Design

Guang R. Gao
Department of Electrical and Computer Engineering
104 Evans Hall
University of Delaware
Newark, DE 19716
ggao@silvera.capsl.udel.edu

Abstract

The emerging technology of the System-on-Chip (SoC) is presenting new challenges at both the hardware and software stages of the design process. At present, system software engineers, e.g. high-level programming language (e.g. C/C++) compiler writers for processor cores, are working at the abstraction level of instruction set architecture (ISA) and its compiler optimization. On the other hand, the hardware engineers for the processor cores and other devices are working at a lower level abstraction level, e.g. RTL level, and using hardware description languages (e.g. VHDL, Verilog) and associated silicon compiler tools. Problems of communication gaps between the two world continue to exist due to the different abstraction levels, and the use of different design languages, incompatible tools and fragmented design flow, etc.

In this talk, we discuss such gaps with examples illustrating the limits of optimization that can be performed from the hardware/software alone. With the demand of aggressive exploitation of instruction-level parallelism with high-performance uniprocessor core as well as the need of multiprocessor cores — such gaps must be bridged. Such optimization includes instruction scheduling; register allocation, loop scheduling, locality optimization, etc. Such gaps also affect software debugging (including performance debugging) as well as hardware verification.

We briefly outline solution challenges and opportunities in this direction.

ISSS'01, October 1-3, 2001, Montréal, Québec, Canada.
ACM 1-58113-418-5/01/0010.

Panel

New Design Paradigms: What Needs to be Standardized?

Moderator: W. Rosenstiel
U. Tubingen, Germany

Panelists:

B. Bailey
Mentor Graphics, USA

M. Fujita
Tokyo U., Japan

G. Gao
University of Delaware, USA

R. Gupta
UC Irvine, USA

P. Panda
Synopsys, USA

NOTES

Loop Fusion for Memory Space Optimization

Antoine Fraboulet Karen Kodary Anne Mignotte
Institut National des Sciences Appliquées de Lyon
20 avenue Albert Einstein
69621 Villeurbanne, France
firstname.lastname@insa-lyon.fr

ABSTRACT

Portable or embedded systems as well as submicronic technologies have made the power consumption criterium crucial. Memory is known to be extremely power consuming. Moreover multimedia applications are memory intensive applications. Therefore, we propose new techniques to optimize a behavioral description of multimedia applications before the hardware/software partitioning (*Codesign*). These transformations are performed on "for" loops that constitute the main parts which handle the arrays of the multimedia code. This paper presents an optimal algorithm to reduce the use of temporary arrays by loop fusion. Although the algorithm is not polynomial, experiments have shown that it is very efficient.

1. INTRODUCTION

Code transformations for the design of an integrated system can be performed at several levels. For instance, Boolean functions minimization can be considered at the gate level. At the Register Transfer Level, transformations are performed on the control state charts by splitting or merging nodes. Moreover, at every stage of the design we can apply transformations used in software compilers [1, 2].

In this paper, we will focus on the design of data flow dominated embedded systems. These systems use signals and data stored in arrays such as images, video and sounds. This type of applications consumes memory for multidimensional data storage. More than a half of the surface of integrated systems of this kind is filled by memory. Memory is known to be power consuming. Therefore, this massive memory made power consumption criteria control compulsory. Power optimization by memory optimization can be done in several ways: the reduction of the size of the memory and improved data-movement strategies over the memory hierarchy.

Once the Hardware-Software partitioning is done, the memory has already been divided. It is therefore very important to make optimizations before this partitioning in order to deal with all the memory in homogeneous vision. Moreover, it allows to optimize both types of memories, the one that will be included in hardware and the one controlled by software.

ISSS'01, October 1-3, 2001, Montréal, Québec, Canada.

Methods and tools defined in this paper are specific to Codesign [3] because in the case of software-only compilation the memory is already instantiated in hardware and cannot be tuned. Moreover, the memory is rarely shared in software; a memory cell is used for only one array cell (unless explicitly stated when the designer uses the same name for two non-overlapping objects).

On the opposite, during silicon compilation the physical memory is optimized all along the design chain. In-Place Mapping [4] can allow to share memory by overlapping arrays when possible, memory allocation can select memory modules upon several criteria (size, number of ports) and assignment computes hardware addresses for accessing arrays in memory [5, 6, 7]. The memory is instantiated on-demand and specific modules can be used or even built specifically. This will be the main assumption for memory optimization by code transformations.

All the optimizations undertaken during silicon compilation improve the design starting from a given description. However, a preprocessing source-to-source code transformation similar to the one used in software compilation can be applied on the design in order to improve the efficiency, or enable, further optimizations. The source-to-source transformations we propose are target independent code optimizations. We do not consider specific modeling of the target except that it has, at least, two levels of memory [8], including a cache memory. These transformations are good on general principles and are a *complement* to transformations that are designed for a specific target platform on which more precise information, such as cache line size or number of registers, can be used to drive further loop transformations [9, 10].

The handling of arrays is done mainly through "for" loops in multimedia applications. These loops form the critical part of the optimizations we want to apply at the Codesign stage. We propose to transform the algorithmic description of a design by exploiting and adapting techniques similar to the ones used in automatic parallelization [2] so as to reduce the size of needed memory and the associated power consumption by enabling powerful optimizations. Further optimizations have to be applied later in the design flow when more architectural parameters are set for the design in order to complete the optimization process. However, these other steps and interactions between them are beyond the scope of this article.

In this paper, we will present a "for" loop transformation to optimize memory size. Loop fusion is a program transformation that collapses several loops into one. Memory minimization by loop fusion is obtained in our case by reducing the size of temporary arrays that are typically used to store intermediate results during multimedia processing.

An array written in a loop and read in another one must be stored in memory between these operations. In order to be removed from memory an array must be produced and used within the same loop nest and it must not be used elsewhere in the code. Once the statements that produce and consume values stored in an array have been merged within the same loop body several techniques can be used to reduce the size of this array or even to completely remove it.

For instance, *scalar replacement* [11] techniques can remove an entire array from the application's memory footprint as shown on Figure 1. *Scalar replacement* is a transformation that uses dependence information to find reuse of array values and expose it by replacing the references with scalar temporaries.

```
L1: for i=1 to n
   A[i] = ...
endfor
L2: for i=1 to n
   ... = f(A[i])
endfor
```

(a) source code

```
L12: for i=1 to n
   a = ...
   ... = f(a)
endfor
```

(b) after fusion

Figure 1: Scalar replacement after loop fusion

On Figure 1(a) the loop `L1` produces values stored in array `A` and the loop `L2` consumes these values. Merging these two loops (Figure 1(b)) allow to replace the array `A`, if not used elsewhere in the code, by a scalar `a` thus reducing the size of needed memory for the application.

Dependencies may not allow to remove completely an array by scalar replacement. In such cases we can apply intra-array storage order optimization [4]. This technique calculates an address reference window for a given storage order of a multi-dimensional array. Given the size of this window, we can "fold" array elements onto the same locations and hence increase the memory reuse. Intra array storage optimization is illustrated on Figure 2. The array `A` from source code on Figure 2(a) is replaced by a window of 2 values `a[0]` and `a[1]` on the fused code (Figure 2(b)).

```
L1: for i=1 to n
   A[i] = ...
endfor
L2: for i=1 to n
   ... = f(A[i-1],A[i])
endfor
```

(a) source code

```
L12: for i=1 to n
   a[i%2] = ...
   ... = f(a[i%2-1], a[i%2])
endfor
```

(b) after fusion

Figure 2: Intra-array storage optimization

Loop fusion increases the number of statements and accessed arrays within a loop nest. Sometimes loops access more data than can be handled by a cache. Further code transformations are needed to complete the optimization process once the *memory hierarchy parameters* such as the number of available registers or cache size and cache line size are known. In these cases, the iteration space of a loop can be blocked into sections whose reuse can be captured by the cache. Strip-mine-and-interchange [2] is a transformation that achieves this result. Its effect is to shorten the distance between the source and sink of a dependence so that it is more likely for data to reside in the cache when the reuse occurs. Extensive studies for cache optimizations can be found in [11, 9].

2. MEMORY MINIMIZATION BY LOOP FUSION

The algorithm we present in this section minimizes in an optimal way the size of the temporary arrays used in data dominated applications such as multimedia ones.

Previous algorithms for performing loop fusion have only considered the case when all loop headers are conformable [12, 13]. We consider a wider class of problems where the loops being considered for fusion need not have conformable headers. Loops with non conformable headers can be fused by using conditional statements to control the execution of operations within the loop nest. Both scalar replacement and intra array storage optimization techniques can handle conditional control flow.

The algorithm for maximal reuse by loop fusion proposed by McKinley and Kennedy in [12] has been proven NP-Hard. Our problem is different from *maximal reuse* because we do not constrain all edges to be maximaly fused but the complexity still remains exponential. We propose an algorithm that is efficient in practice and solves our problem with an optimal solution. A survey on loop fusion algorithms complexity can be found in [14].

2.1 Modeling the Problem

We approximate memory size requirement by the maximum size of time overlapping arrays. Memory used by non time overlapping arrays can be reused by inter storage optimization [4]. Our `Memory Cost` function is defined as following:

$$\text{MemoryCost} = \max_{\forall t} \left\{ \sum_{a_i \in \text{Live arrays}(t)} Size(a_i) \right\}$$

Where t is a time slot and $Size$ is the storage size of an array. Figure 3(b) represents the life time of arrays computed on Figure 3(a) source code. *MemoryCost* is maximized during loop `L4` (see figure 3(b)) and is equal to sum of the size of arrays `a1`, `a2`, `a3` and `a4`.

We use a *Data Flow Graph (DFG)* ($G = (V, E, A)$) representation for modeling the dependencies [2]. Graph nodes (V) represent the loop nests and edges (E) represent data dependences between these loops. A is the set of all arrays handled in the source code. Each array $a_i \in A$ has an associated weight $size(a_i)$.

A data dependence between two array references is represented by a hybrid distance/direction vector $\vec{\delta} = \{\delta_1 \dots \delta_n\}$ with the most precise information derivable. The vector component represents the data dependence corresponding left to right from the outermost loop to the innermost one enclosing the reference.

```
L1: for i=1 to n
    a1[i] = ...
endfor
L2: for i=1 to n
    a2[i] = f2(a1[i])
endfor
L3: for i=1 to n
    a3[i] = f3(a2[i+1])
endfor
L4: for i=1 to n
    a4[i] = f4(a1[i-1],a3[i])
endfor
L5: for i=1 to n
    ... = f5(a2[i],a3[i],a4[i])
endfor
```

(a) source code

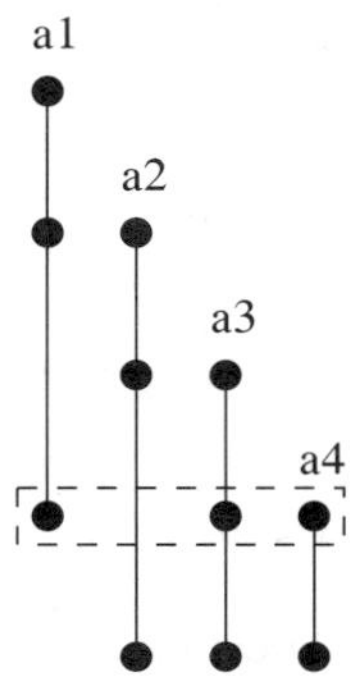

(b) array life time

Figure 3: Array variables life time

Figure 4 represents the dependence graph computed from the source code on Figure 3(a). Loops `L2` and `L3` cannot be fused due to the dependence carried by `a2`. If the loops were merged the code would read `a2[i+1]` (from `L3`) before its computation (from `L2`) in the same iteration.

Two nodes can be merged if and only if none of the dependence are reversed in the fuse loop compared to the original code. An edge that carries a dependency which prevents the fusion of its source node and its destination node is called a *fusion preventing edge (FPE)* and is marked with a slash.

Each edge is labeled by the name of the array $a_i \in A$ that carries the dependence and is weighted by the size of this array. An edge is labeled by only one array and if there are multiple array dependencies between two loops then the graph becomes a multigraph with potentially multiple edges between two nodes.

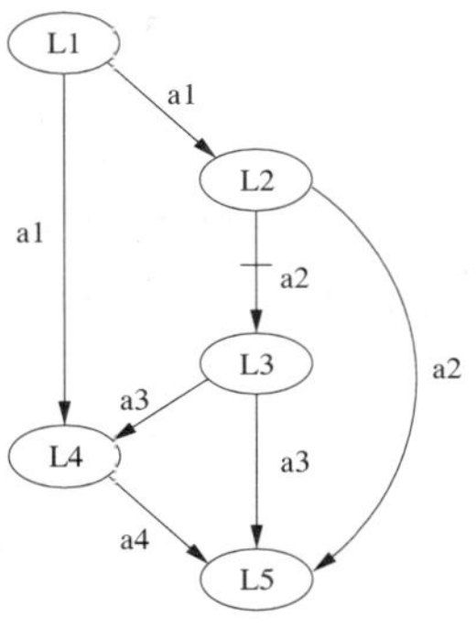

Figure 4: Modeling dependences

Isolated statements are also considered as nodes. Dependences between code statements and loops are preserved as we perform code reorganization during the transformation. An isolated statement will be represented in the graph as a regular node but all its incoming and outgoing edges will be marked as fusion-preventing ones.

An array can be removed from the memory, or at least minimized in size, if we can fuse all the loops that write into it with the loops that are reading its values. A removable array is marked with a star on the representations (see Figure 5).

2.2 Removable Arrays Detection

In order to remove an array from the program by fusion we need to fuse *all* the nodes connected by an edge which is labeled by this array in the DFG. An array cannot be removed by fusion there exists an edge $e = (u, v)$ labeled by this array and there exists a path from u to v in the DFG that contains a FPE.

In order to detect all the arrays that could be removed by loop fusion we perform a transitive closure on the DFG as can be seen on Figure 5.

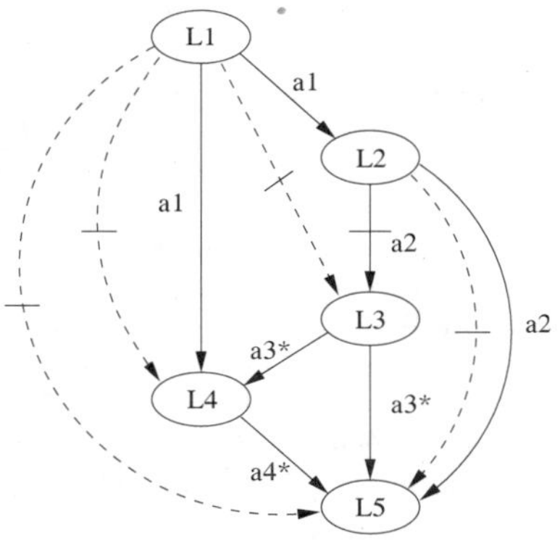

Figure 5: Transitive closure of the DFG for removable array detection

Array `a2` cannot be removed because there is a direct FPE between loops `L2` and `L3`. The same situation occurs for array `a1` where there is a path between `L1` and `L4` that goes through the FPE (`L2`,`L3`). Removing the array `a1` from the memory would require the fusion of loops `L1`, `L2` and `L4` and would create a cycle between the newly fused node `L124` and `L3` in the dependence graph. Such a cycle is not allowed in order to preserve the precedence constraints imposed by data dependencies.

Arrays `a3` and `a4` are marked with a star as they can be removed by merging loops `L3`, `L4` and `L5`. We call by extension *starred edges* an edge that carries a dependence on a removable array.

2.3 Conflicts Detection and Resolution

The previous step can detect if an array can be removed from the memory by loop fusion but the detection is local and some problems can arise when we consider the removable arrays altogether. For instance, on Figure 6(a) arrays `a` and `b` can be removed if we consider them separately. Unfortunately, removing both at the same time is not feasible. The situation can be more complicated as can be seen on Figure 6(b) where the fusion cannot be performed without creating a dependence cycle between loops (`L1`,`L3`,`L6`) and loops (`L2`,`L4`,`L5`).

In order to complete the fusion process we need to solve all possible conflicts by reducing the set of starred arrays without compromising the global optimality. This resolution is done in two steps, the first one identifies all possible conflicts in the graph and the second one solves all these conflicts in a global optimal way.

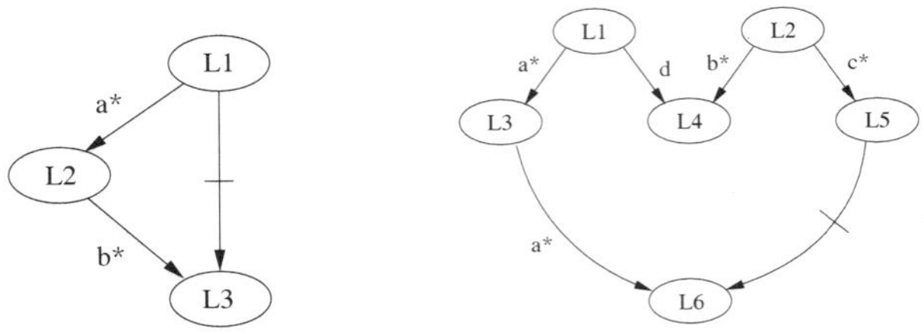

(a) direct conflict (b) conflict path

Figure 6: Conflict between removable arrays

2.3.1 *Con¤icts Detection*

Problems arise when several potential removable arrays are located on a cycle of the graph while part of this cycle contains a FPE. Given μ an elementary cycle of the graph with a given direction over this cycle we denote μ^+ the set of edges in the cycle oriented toward the cycle cover direction, μ^- is the set of edges oriented the other way round (see [15] for more details). We can associate to μ a vector $\vec{\mu} = (\mu_1, \mu_2, \ldots \mu_{|E|})$ such as:

$$\mu_u = \begin{cases} +1 & \text{if } u \in \mu^+ \\ -1 & \text{if } u \in \mu^- \\ 0 & \text{if } u \notin \mu^+ \cup \mu^- \end{cases}$$

Note that $-\vec{\mu}$ is also a vector associated to the cycle μ with a different cover direction.

PROPOSITION 1. *In order to solve all possible problems that would create an illegal fusion we need to detect all undirected elementary cycle μ of the graph such as $\vec{\mu}$ is composed in the following way:*

- *all +1 (resp. −1) are starred edges*
- *at least one −1 (resp. +1) is a FPE*

PROOF. Assume that we have a fused graph G that is illegal. We want to prove that this original (unfused) graph was composed of, at least, one cycle such as described in Proposition 1. A fused graph G is illegal if it contains an oriented dependence cycle μ_d. This dependence cycle is composed of FPE or unstarred edges since all the starred edges have been fused. As there was no dependence cycle before the fusion (the original graph is a DAG) the last edge e_s that has been fused is starred and is oriented in a direction that prevents the original graph from being cyclic. Thus, the vector $\vec{\mu'}$ associated with the undirected cycle composed of $\mu \cup e_s$ corresponds to the definition given in proposition 1.

Now we want to prove that if there exists a non oriented cycle in the original graph that follows the proposition 1 the graph resulting from the fusion of all the starred edges will produce an illegal fused graph. Let us suppose that we have fused all but one starred edges from an undirected cycle μ to produce a graph G'. The vector $\vec{\mu'}$ in G' has only one +1 (resp. −1) that corresponds to a starred edge and at least one −1 (resp. +1) that corresponds to a FPE. If we fuse the last starred edge then we produce a directed cycle in the resulting graph composed of all the edges, of which at least one was an FPE, that were marked −1 (resp. +1) in $\vec{\mu'}$. □

Cycle detection algorithm. We perform cycle detection by exploring the graph for each edge $e = (u, v)$ that is fusion preventing by looking for all cycles from u to v that follows the proposition 1. This implies that we will look for all the cycles μ for which $\vec{\mu}$ contains only starred edges in μ^+.

In order to speed up the exploration we use the property that we can stop the exploration on a path μ as soon as we encounter an edge in μ^+ that is not starred.

```
exploration(G = (V, E),k,u,v)
begin
  mark[k] ← true
  for all t ∈ V do
  begin
    if t = v and t ≠ u then
      C ← C ∪ {v ∈ V|mark[v] = true}
    else if e = (k, t) ∈ E and e is starred
                  and mark[t] = false
      exploration(G,t,u,v)
    else if e = (t, k) ∈ E and mark[t] = false
      exploration(G,t,u,v)
  end
  mark[k] ← false
end

begin
  C ← ∅
  for all e = (u, v) ∈ V
    exploration(C,u,u,v)
end
```

Figure 7: Graph exploration for conflict detection

We denote C the set of all cycles detected during the exploration of the graph. The next step will solve simultaneously all the dependency problems within these cycles.

2.3.2 *Integer Linear Programming Con¤ict Resolution*

In this section we present the ILP formulation [16] for solving dependency cycles conflicts detected in the previous step of the algorithm.

Once all the cycles have been detected we have to solve the global problem to decide which array will be taken out of the set of removable arrays.

We associate a binary variable x_{a_i} to each starred array a_i that could be removed but which has been included in a cycle during the previous step. If $x_{a_i} = 0$ then the array a_i will be considered for fusion otherwise ($x_{a_i} = 1$) the array will cease to be starred. For multi-graphs (for instance, k edges labeled $a_1, a_2, \ldots, a_k$) between two nodes u and v, a new variable x_{uv} is introduced to resume the arrays on this multi-edge. A variable x_{uv} will be set less or equal to each variable $x_{a_1} \ldots x_{a_k}$ associated with the arrays of the multi-edge. If x_{uv} is set to 1 (the multi-edge is removed from a path) then all associated variables will also be set to 1 and all arrays will be unstarred. Otherwise a variable x_{a_i} can be set to 1 without interfering with other arrays on the multi-edge (equation 3).

For each detected cycle $\mu \in C$ we need to decide which array carried by the edges in μ^+ will not be starred anymore. Thus the sum of all the variables x_{uv} in the μ^+ set of a cycle must be greater than or equal to 1 (equation 2).

The objective function of our ILP is thus to minimize the sum of the size of arrays that have to be removed from the set of all possible starred arrays detected in section 2.2 (equation 1).

$$\min \sum_{a_i \in A} size_{a_i} * x_{a_i} \quad (1)$$

$$\sum_{(u,v)\in\mu^+(c)} x_{uv} \geq 1, \qquad \forall \mu \in C \quad (2)$$

$$x_{uv} \leq x_{a_i}, \quad \forall a_i \in (u,v), \forall (u,v) \in E \quad (3)$$

$$x_{a_i} \in \{0,1\}, \qquad \forall a \in A \quad (4)$$

$$x_{uv} \in \{0,1\}, \qquad \forall (u,v) \in E \quad (5)$$

The ILP formulation given by (1), (2), (3), (4) and (5) minimizes the size that cannot be kept starred due to dependence constraints in a graph.

Values $x_{a_i} = 1, \forall i$ are always a feasible solution for the problem. Furthermore any feasible solution has a cost

$$\sum_{a_i \in A} size_{a_i} * x_{a_i} \geq 0$$

which ensures that an optimal solution always exists, because of this lower bound.

2.4 Graph Clustering and Fusion

All the edges that are still starred can now be fused. The only remaining step is to compute the clusters that will constitute the transformed dependence graph nodes. We have to ensure that if two nodes u and v will belong to the same cluster then all nodes that belong to a directed path from u to v will be also taken in the cluster. This step can be performed efficiently by computing a modified transitive closure in which if there is a path $u \stackrel{*}{\rightarrow} v$, a path $u \rightarrow w$ and a path $w \rightarrow v$ then u, v and w will be in the same cluster.

Code generation can be performed by writing the code for each loop following the numbering given by a simple order such as the height defined as follow:

$$h(x) = \begin{cases} 0 \text{ if } d^-(x) = 0 \\ \max\{h(y), y \rightarrow x \in E\} + 1 \text{ otherwise} \end{cases}$$

Figure 8 represents the modified dependence graph and the code corresponding to the loop fusion. Arrays `a3` and `a4` can be now replaced by scalars within the loop `L'3`.

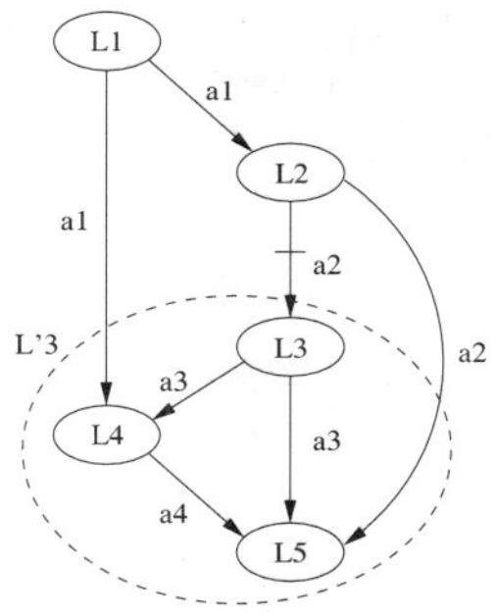

(a) clustered dependence graph

```
L1: for i=1 to n
   a1[i]=...
endfor
L2: for i=1 to n
   a2[i]=f2(a1[i])
   endfor
L'3: for i=1 to n
   a3[i]=f3(a2[i+1])
   a4[i]=f4(a1[i-1],
           a3[i])
     ...=f5(a2[i],
           a3[i],a4[i])
   endfor
```

(b) modified code

Figure 8: Clustering and code output

3. EXPERIMENTATIONS

We have implemented this algorithm and tested it using randomly generated graphs. We have chosen to generate graphs that are a lot more complex than graphs that can be found in real applications. Generated graphs were ranging from 10 to 30 nodes for which the number of edges was twice the number of nodes. Each edge has the probability of 1/3 to be fusion preventing and all weights were randomly chosen between 1 and 100. Arrays were constrained to belong to a path (writing in an array cannot be done by two potentially parallel loops). The number of in-edges (edges pointing to a node) was limited to 10 for each node as well as the number of out-edges (edges going out of a node). This limit is very high compared to real application codes and plays a major role for the cycle enumeration problem.

Tests were done on 21,000 different graphs. We used the ILP solver `LP_SOLVE` freely available from its ftp site [17]. Although the cycle enumeration step is exponential in theory as well as the ILP resolution, we achieved an average calculation time of 0.050 seconds per graph (including cycle enumeration and ILP resolution) on a Pentium II running at 450 MHz. The average potential gain in size (arrays that were completely fused) was 60.7% and the average number of fused arrays was 61.8%.

4. FUTURE WORK AND CONCLUSION

We have presented in this paper an optimal algorithm to minimize the memory size needed by temporary arrays in an application. This algorithm has a theoretical exponential complexity due to its cycle enumeration step and its Integer Linear Program but is very efficient in practice. Furthermore, real life problem size are usually small as the number of nodes in our graph represents the number of loop nests in a program.

Our memory optimization cost function, unlike many others in the literature, does not rely on any memory hierarchy parameter and loop fusion for memory minimization can be applied as a general preprocessing step before any other optimization.

As it is a source to source transformation it can be easily integrated to an existing CAD tool-chain as a design preprocessor that can be run prior the traditional design flow. Thus, it will enable new optimizations obtained using existing memory and power management techniques in CAD tools. The power and memory interest of this automatic approach is on the one hand to reduce the design time by extracting optimizations for the description and on the other hand to improve the development quality by a tool which will propose interactive transformations that a designer could have missed.

We would like to combine the present work with our loop alignment techniques developed for memory accesses optimization [18]. Loop alignment can help to remove FPE from the original graph and can also reduce the dependence distance between statements. Loop fusion combined with loop alignment improves data locality within a loop nest. Once a loop has been aligned, improved scalar replacement and intra array storage optimization results can be achieved over the data for both memory size and data locality.

5. REFERENCES

[1] Alfred Aho, Ravi Sethi, and Jeffrey Ullman, *Compilers: Principes, Techniques, and Tools*, Addison-Wesley, 1986.

[2] David F. Bacon, Susan L. Graham, and Oliver J. Sharp, "Compiler transformations for high-performance computing," *ACM Computing Surveys*, vol. 26, no. 4, pp. 345–420, Dec. 1994.

[3] Henry Chang, Larry Cooke, Merril Hunt, Grant Martin, Andrew McNelly, and Lee Todd, *Surviving the SOC Revolution: A Guide to Platform-Baased Design*, Kluwer Academic Publishers, 1999, ISBN 0–7923–8679–5.

[4] Eddy De Greef, *Storage Size Reduction for Multimedia Application*, Ph.D. thesis, Katholieke Universiteit Leuven – IMEC, Jan. 1998.

[5] M. Miranda, F. Catthoor, M. Janssen, and H.De Man, "Adopt: Efficient hardware address generation in distributed memory architectures," in *IEEE 9th International Symposium on System Synthesis, (ISSS'96)*, La Jolla, California, Nov. 1996, pp. 20–25.

[6] Preeti R. Panda, Nikil Dutt, and Alexandru Nicolau, "Architectural exploration and optimization of local memory in embedded systems," in *International Symposium on System Synthesis*, 1996.

[7] Preeti Ranjan Panda, Nikil Dutt, and Alexandru Nicolau, *Memory Issues in Embedded Systems-On-Chip*, Kluwer Academic Publishers, 1999, ISBN 0–7923–8362–1.

[8] Bowen Alpern, Larry Carter, Ephraim Feig, and Ted Selker, "The uniform memory hierarchy model of computation," *Algorithmica*, vol. 12, pp. 72–109, 1994.

[9] Chidamber Kulkarni, *Cache Optimization for Multimedia Applications*, Ph.D. thesis, Katholieke Universiteit Leuven – IMEC, Feb. 2001.

[10] Kathryn S. McKinley, Steve Carr, and Chau-Wen Tseng, "Improving Data Locality with Loop Transformations," *ACM Transactions on Programming Languages and Systems*, vol. 18, no. 4, pp. 424–453, July 1996.

[11] Steve Carr, *Memory-Hierarchy Management*, Ph.D. thesis, Rice University, Feb. 1993.

[12] Kathryn S. McKinley and Ken Kennedy, "Maximizing loop parallelism and improving data locality via loop fusion and distribution," in *The Sixth Annual Languages and Compiler for Parallelism Workshop*. 1993, pp. 301–320, Lecture Notes in Computer Science 768, Springer-Verlag.

[13] Guang R. Gao, Russ Olsen, Vivek Sarkar, and Radhika Thekkath, "Collective loop fusion for array contraction," in *1992 Workshop on Languages and Compilers for Parallel Computing*, New Haven, Conn., 1992, number 757, pp. 281–295, Berlin: Springer Verlag.

[14] Alain Darte, "On the complexity of loop fusion," *Parallel Computing*, vol. 26, no. 9, pp. 1175–1193, July 2000.

[15] M. Gondran and M. Minoux, *Graphs and Algorithms*, John Wiley, 1984.

[16] Alexander Schrijver, *Theory of Linear and Integer Programming*, John Wiley and Sons, New York, 1986.

[17] Michel Berkelaar, "Lp_solve Mixed Integer Linear Programming solver 3.2," Available at `ftp://ftp.es.ele.tue.nl/pub/lp_solve/`.

[18] Antoine Fraboulet, Guillaume Huard, and Anne Mignotte, "Loop Alignment for Memory Accesses Optimization," in *Twelfth International Symposium on System Synth esis Proceedings (ISSS'99)*. Nov. 1999, pp. 71–77, IEEE Computer Society Press.

Cache-efficient Memory Layout of Aggregate Data Structures

Preeti Ranjan Panda
Synopsys Inc.
700 E. Middlefield Rd.
Mountain View, CA 94043, USA
panda@synopsys.com

Luc Semeria
Clearwater Networks Inc.
160 Knowles Dr.
Los Gatos, CA 95023, USA
luc@clrw.net

Giovanni de Micheli
Computer System Laboratory
Stanford University
Stanford, CA 94305, USA
nanni@stanford.edu

ABSTRACT

We describe an important memory optimization that arises in the presence of aggregate data structures such as arrays and `structs` in a C/C++ based system design methodology. We present an algorithm for determining an optimized memory layout of such data. Our implementation consists of a pointer analysis and resolution phase, followed by memory layout optimization. Experiments on typical applications from the DSP domain result in up to 44% improvement in memory performance.

Categories and Subject Descriptors

B.3 [**Memory Structures**]; B.5.1 [**Register-Transfer-Level Implementation**]: Design—*Memory Design*; B.5.2 [**Register-Transfer-Level Implementation**]: Design Aids—*Automatic Synthesis, Optimization*; B.7.1 [**Integrated Circuits**]: Types and Design Styles—*Memory Technologies*; D.3.4 [**Programming Languages**]: Processors—*Compilers, Optimizations*

General Terms

Algorithms, Design, Experimentation, Performance

Keywords

Data Layout, Data Cache, Embedded Processors

1. INTRODUCTION

Since complex embedded applications are typically composed of both synthesized hardware blocks as well as application software executing on an embedded processor, the supporting design methodology has evolved to embrace several aspects of both hardware synthesis and software compilation of embedded code [6, 5, 4]. While Hardware Description Languages (HDLs) such as VHDL and Verilog were adequate to describe behavioral-level circuitry in the past, the push towards System-on-a-Chip level integration found them wanting in sufficiently high abstract modeling constructs. To alleviate the problem, the industry has been experimenting with replacing HDLs by C/C++ (e.g., [1]). In this design methodology, new optimization and exploration opportunities arise not only in the hardware synthesis side of the equation, but also on the compilation side. Many optimizations that are deemed computationally expensive for traditional compilers can now be performed in the embedded domain because a designer can afford to spend extra time to improve performance and power characteristics since there is only a single application.

Design of the memory subsystem needs careful attention because the same functionality can be implemented in several different ways, each with varying impact with respect to performance, area, and power consumption. In recent years, researchers have analyzed several different memory architectures and the impact of storage policies on these architectures in embedded systems. Among the earliest research efforts to study the memory allocation problem in the context of video data streams was the PHIDEO system [7]. Exploration environments for determining an optimized application specific on-chip memory architectures are studied in [9, 3]. More recently, in the context of C/C++ based synthesis, researchers have addressed the issue of finding reasonable hardware interpretations for dynamic memory allocation-related features [12, 10].

The work presented in this paper complements the *data layout* optimizations reported in works such as [8], where the focus is on the relative placement of user-declared data structures in memory so as to improve cache performance. We demonstrate that a significant amount of additional benefit can be obtained by either coalescing/merging different arrays or splitting an array of `structs` into separate arrays depending on the circumstances. The work also complements the memory synthesis techniques such as [11] by way of extending the analysis of aggregate data structures into the embedded processor-cache environment, thereby forming a more complete framework for hardware/software co-design.

2. OVERALL DESIGN FLOW

In typical programming languages such as C/C++, the relative placement of individual elements of an aggregate data structure is mandated by the language itself, and a compiler has no option but to obey the storage requirements, even if better alternatives are available from the performance point of view. This is because a C compiler typically sees only a part of the whole program at a time, and modifying the storage of data in non-trivial ways is unsafe in general. However, in embedded systems, where the entire application is usually visible to the compiler, an aggressive compiler can perform such structural transformations to the data after verifying

ISSS'01, October 1-3, 2001, Montréal, Québec, Canada.

the safety of the operation. Works such as [13] have investigated a general pointer analysis framework, which has been incorporated into techniques for hardware synthesis of pointers [10]. The same analysis information can be used to determine whether it is safe to transform the memory representation of data structures.

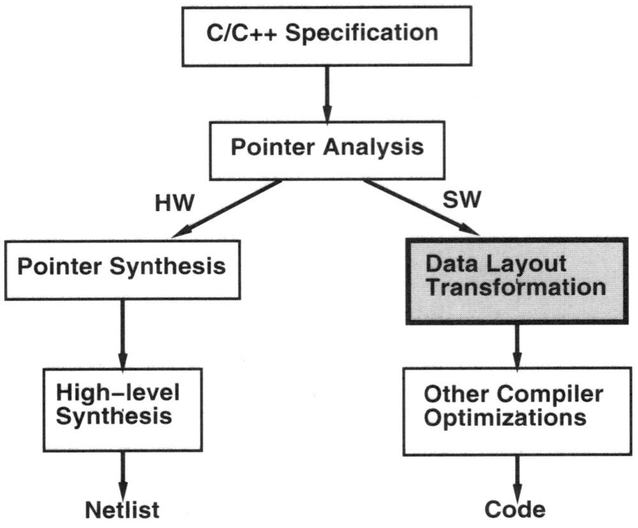

Figure 1: Where data layout transformation fits into the overall design flow

The overall framework is shown in Figure 1. The C/C++ specification is first analyzed for pointer arithmetic and the pointers are resolved. The pointer synthesis phase uses the result of the analysis to convert the original code into code with no pointers, which is then taken through a traditional hardware synthesis flow. In the software path, we perform the data layout transformation followed by the regular compiler optimizations and code generation phases. The hardware path may also have its own data layout transformations.

3. LAYOUT OF STRUCTS: AN EXAMPLE

The data restructuring optimization and its implications can be illustrated with the example shown in Figure 2(a). p is an array of `structs` with two fields (a and b) in each element, and q is an array of integers. The obvious way to store the data in memory is shown in Figure 3(a). Consider an example data cache with 4 lines; 2 words per line. When $p[0].a$ is accessed in the first iteration of Loop L1, the cache fills the entire line, thus fetching $p[0].b$ also. However, $p[0].b$ is never used in the loop, thus the cache subsystem is under-utilized. Similarly, in Loop 2, $p[0].a$ and $p[1].a$ are also unnecessarily fetched into the data cache (Figure 3(c)), thereby degrading performance.

The under-utilization problem can be solved by reorganizing the data based on an analysis of the memory accesses in the application. The transformed code is shown in Figure 2(b). The original $x.a$ has now become a, and the original $x.b$ and q have been merged into a new `struct` y. This ensures that spatial locality is maximized by storing consecutively accessed data in nearby locations. The storage strategy for the transformed code is shown in Figure 4(a). As shown in Figure 4(b) and (c), no useless data is fetched into the cache in any iteration of the two loops.

The data layout transformation results in the cache miss ratio decreasing from 62.5% to 37.5%. For a typical processor-memory

```
struct x {
   int a;
   int b;
} p[1000];
int q[1000];
...
avg = 0;
L1:  for (i = 0; i < 1000; i++)
   avg = avg + p[i].a;
avg = avg / 1000;
...
L2:  for (i = 0; i < 1000; i++)
{
   p[i].b = p[i].b + avg;
   q[i] = p[i].b + 1;
}
```

(a)

```
int a[1000]; // originally x.a
struct y {
   int q; // originally q
   int b; // originally x.b
} r[1000];
...
avg = 0;
L1:  for (i = 0; i < 1000; i++)
   avg = avg + a[i];
avg = avg / 1000;
...
L2:  for (i = 0; i < 1000; i++)
{
   r[i].b = r[i].b + avg;
   r[i].q = r[i].b + 1;
}
```

(b)

Figure 2: (a) Example code fragment (b) Transformed code

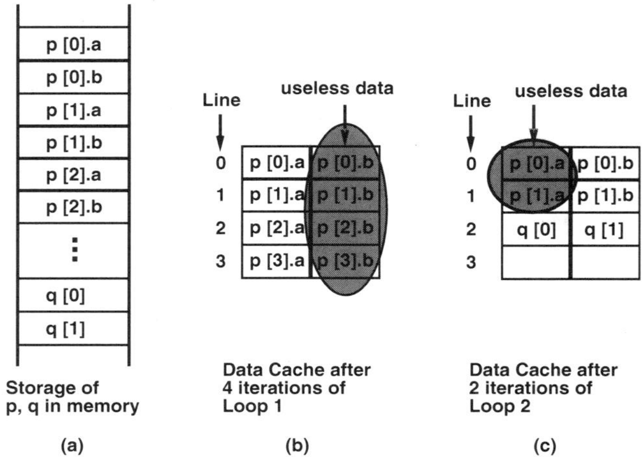

Figure 3: Cache behavior of original code

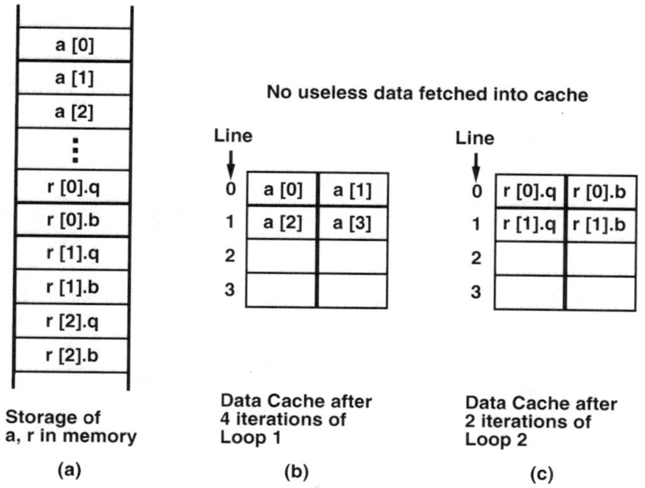

Figure 4: Cache behavior of transformed code.

system interface where a cache miss incurs a penalty of, say 15 processor cycles, and a cache hit results in a single cycle data access, this amounts to a cycle-count reduction of 34%.

The data restructuring transformation is not subsumed by other known optimizations in compiler/architecture and CAD literature. Data fetched into cache during Loop L1 is, in general, not present when L2 begins because of capacity misses. In the example of Figure 2(a), the *loop fusion* transformation does not apply because of data dependencies - *avg* needs to be computed before L2 begins. Finally, just splitting the arrays into individual components (without regrouping) is generally not sufficient because of the possibility of cache conflicts. Although the illustrative transformation of the code from Figure 2(a) to Figure 2(b) was simple, the general problem of deriving the most efficient data layout is non-trivial. In Section 4, we provide an algorithm for this transformation.

4. DATA LAYOUT TRANSFORMATION

The data layout problem is formulated as follows: given a set of arrays of either simple data types such as integer, or aggregate data types such as `structs`; and a set of innermost loops in a program accessing different arrays with different array index expressions, determine an efficient layout of the arrays in memory that maximizes the data cache utilization.

As a first step, we dismantle the user-specified grouping of data. For example, an array of `structs` may be split into separate arrays of its constituent fields.

4.1 Splitting into individual arrays

In the example code of Section 3, the splitting of the array of `structs` into two different arrays was trivial. However, in general, the task of splitting the address space while preserving the integrity of the code is rendered more complex by the presence of constructs such as the dereferencing, arithmetic, and type casting of pointers. The underlying memory representation in C (as in many other programming languages) is a continuous address space. Pointers represent addresses in this address space. However, to perform our optimizations, we need to map this address space into distinct sets of locations. For our memory representation, we use the notion of *location sets* introduced in [13]. Location sets support all C data structures including arrays, `structs`, arrays of `structs` and `structs` containing arrays. In order to handle large C programs efficiently, some memory data, such as the different elements of an array, are combined into a single location set. The representation of the memory into a set of distinct location sets is created by accurately analyzing how the different locations are being accessed in the code.

Pointer analysis [13] is a compiler pass to identify at compile-time the potential values of the pointers in the program. This information is used to determine the set of locations each pointer may point to at any point in a program. All memory data for a program can be arranged into a set of distinct location sets which can be mapped to separate arrays (or scalar variables).

After partitioning the memory into a set of arrays, we still need to resolve pointers. Since the underlying memory layout is changed, the behavior of pointers and more specifically of type casting and pointer arithmetic may be altered. The resolution of pointers consists of two passes. The first pass, where pointers are dereferenced, consists of replacing loads and stores by case statements in which the locations the pointer may access are explicitly read or written.

```
struct {
   int a;
   int b;
} ts[10];
int ti[20];
int *p;
...
if(...)
   p = (int *)ts;
else
   p = (int *)ti;

for(i=0; i<10; i++) {
   ...  = *p;
   p += 2;
}
```

(a) Original Code

```
int ts_a[10];
int ts_b[10];
int ti[10];
struct spc_pointer {
   short tag; short index;
} p;
...
if(...)
   p.tag = 0; p_index=0;
else
   p.tag = 1; p_index=0;

for(i=0; i<10; i++) {
   if(p.tag==0) // p→{ts[i].a}
     ...  = ts_a[p.index/2];
   else // p→{ti[i]}
     ...  = ti[p.index];
   p.index += 2;
}
```

(b) Transformed Code

Figure 5: Resolution of pointers

The value of the pointers are then encoded as they do not represent addresses in the original address space anymore.

Consider the code segment in Figure 5(a). After analyzing the code, the two fields of the `struct` are represented by two distinct location sets which can be mapped to two separate arrays `ts_a` and `ts_b`. In this example, the mapping of the array of `structs` `ts` onto `ts_a` and `ts_b` is not straightforward. Resolving pointers makes this mapping easier. The resulting code after removing pointers and mapping the two fields of the structure to separate arrays is the shown in Figure 5(b). We omit the details for brevity.

4.2 The clustering algorithm

Our objective is to regroup the split arrays based on their memory accesses. We represent the input specification as a bipartite graph with a set of *a-nodes* representing arrays in the specification and a set of *l-nodes* representing loops (Figure 6). Since most of the memory accesses and computations occur in the innermost loops, we consider only innermost loops out of nested loop structures. An a-node and an l-node are connected if the corresponding array is accessed in the loop. l-nodes have a weight equal to the number of times the loop is executed. If the loop bound cannot be established at compile-time, we assume that a profiler can supply that information. At this level of abstraction, we do not differentiate between memory read and write accesses. However, we do assume that register allocation has already been performed. For example, in Loop 2 of Figure 2, we assume that the statement "`q[i] = p[i].b + 1`" does not involve a memory read because `p[i].b`, which was written in the previous statement, could be stored in a register.

```
for i = 1 to 100 // Loop L1
    Read A [i]
    Read B [i]
    Read C [i]
for i = 1 to 2000 // Loop L2
    Read B [i]
    Read C [i]
for i = 1 to 500 // Loop L3
    Read A [i]
    Read D [i]
```

(a)

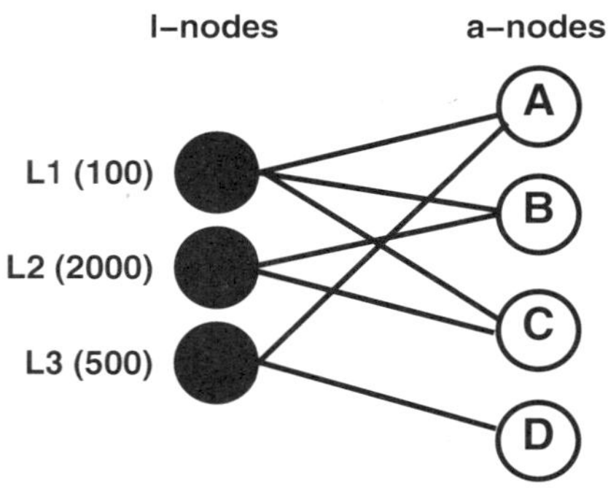

(b)

Figure 6: Sample memory access pattern in loops and the associated graph

```
Algorithm Cluster
Input: Specification represented as a series of loops and
array accesses
Output: Group of clusters CS

for all arrays j
    ASSIGNED [j] = FALSE
Set of clusters CS = φ
Sort all loops in decreasing order of total number of
array accesses
for all loops L
    for all arrays i in loop L with ASSIGNED [i] = FALSE
        min_cost = ∞
        for all existing clusters C (including φ)
            cost = find_cost (i, C);
            if (cost < min_cost)
                min_cost = cost
                best_cluster = C
        if best_cluster = φ
            Create new cluster C' = {i}
            CS = CS ∪C' // add C' to the set of clusters
        else
            best_cluster = best_cluster ∪{i}
        ASSIGNED [i] = TRUE
end Algorithm
```

Figure 7: Algorithm *Cluster*

Figure 6 shows a sample memory access pattern and the associated bipartite graph. For example, the l-node corresponding to Loop L1 is connected to a-nodes A, B, and C. Algorithm *Cluster* in Figure 7 shows the overall strategy involved in clustering the individual arrays of the graph into `structs`.

The vector ASSIGNED keeps track of whether each array is assigned to a cluster yet or not. CS is the set of generated clusters, each consisting of one or more arrays. CS is initialized to the empty set. Since the number of possible clusters is exponentially large, we devise a heuristic strategy where we first select the arrays in the most frequently executed loops for assignment to clusters. Further, the assignment decision, once made, is never altered in the interest of reducing computational complexity.

We begin with the loop with the maximum access count, and consider for assignment to clusters all the arrays accessed in the loop. For every array i that is unassigned, we compute the *cost* of assigning the array to each of the clusters in CS, including the null cluster ϕ (which corresponds to the creation of a new cluster). We discuss the actual cost computation in Section 4.3. In the overall strategy, we select for assignment the cluster C that minimizes the cost. If C is the null cluster ϕ, then we create a new cluster C' with i as the sole element. Otherwise, we add i to the cluster C. Finally, we mark array i assigned and continue our cluster assignment process.

4.3 Cost computation

The most important step in Algorithm *Cluster* is *find_cost* (C, i), the computation of the cost associated with assignment of array i to cluster C. In our model, the cost comprises two components:

- the penalty associated with assigning two correlated arrays into separate clusters
- the penalty associated with assigning two uncorrelated arrays into the same cluster

Algorithm *find_cost*
Input: cluster C, array i
Output: integer representing cost of assignment

```
cost = 0
// Part I: cost due to separating i from correlated arrays
for all edges e connected to array i (i.e., for all loops accessing i)
    penalty = TRUE
    for all arrays a accessed in loop e
        if a ≠ i
        and ASSIGNED [a] = TRUE
        and CLUSTER [a] = C
        and are_correlated (i, a, e)
            penalty = FALSE
    if penalty = TRUE
        cost = cost + EDGE_WEIGHT (e)

// Part II: cost due to clustering i with uncorrelated arrays
for all edges e such that ∃ j, j ∈ C and j ≠ i
    if are_correlated (i, j, e) = FALSE
        cost = cost + EDGE_WEIGHT (e)
end Algorithm
```

Figure 8: Algorithm *find_cost*

The components above are distinct; one does not subsume the other. Whether two arrays x and y are correlated or not is determined by a function *are_correlated* (x, y, l) which returns TRUE if x and y are different arrays with the same number of elements, and the index expressions of their accesses in loop l are *affine* (linear) and differ by a constant. This condition is essential to maintain spatial locality in the data cache, and is inherent to the definition of correlation for data layout. For example, if the respective index expressions are `a[2i]` and `b[2i+1]`, then upon clustering a and b, a fetch to `b[2i+1]` possibly brings `a[2i+1]` into the cache (assuming cache line size ≥ 2 and `a[2i+1]` lies on the line boundary), which is used in the next iteration. However, if the expressions are `a[i]` and `b[2i]`, then there is no spatial correlation as the distance between the two accesses increases with increasing iteration count. Function *are_correlated* detects a correlation when the expressions are affine.

The cost computation for assigning array i to cluster C is described in algorithm *find_cost* (C, i) in Figure 8. The first part computes the cost due to separating array i from other compatible arrays. This is done by checking all the loops accessing i to detect the existence of at least one other array a belonging to the same cluster C which is correlated to i. The *penalty* variable keeps track of this existence. If *penalty* is still TRUE at the end of the search, then we penalize the assignment, else, the incremental cost is zero. The amount of assigned cost is simply the loop count, since that is a measure of the extent to which the assignment proves costly.

In the second part, we compute the cost due to clustering i with uncorrelated arrays. For all other arrays j already assigned to cluster C, we check to see if i and j are uncorrelated in any loop; in such instances, we add the loop count as a penalty - the cost for clustering uncorrelated arrays together. Note that two arrays, while being correlated in one loop, may be uncorrelated in a different loop. This is how we handle conflicting array accesses in different loops. This completes the cost computation. The overall running time of the clustering algorithm, with n arrays and k array references in the program is $O(n^3k^2)$. We omit the details for brevity.

5. EXPERIMENTS

We implemented the clustering algorithm in the SUIF compiler framework [2]. After the pointer analysis phase, we split the aggregate data structures (e.g., arrays of `structs`) into individual arrays. We then executed the clustering algorithm and generated the transformed program with the revised data structures. Finally, we ran cache simulations using the SHADE simulator of the SPARC processor, with varying data cache parameters. We report the results in this section.

Figure 9 shows the applications on which we performed our experiments, on the x-axis. FFT (Fast Fourier Transformation), FIR (Finite Impulse Response), Kai-win (Kaiser Window-based coefficient computation), and RTPSE (Real-time power spectral estimation) are important signal processing applications. PIC-1-D (one dimensional particle-in-cell) and Disc-Ord (Discrete Ordinate Transport) are common in scientific computation.

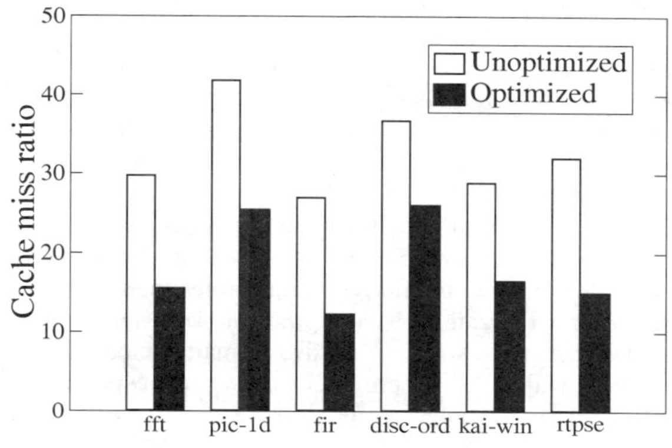

Figure 9: Data cache miss ratios

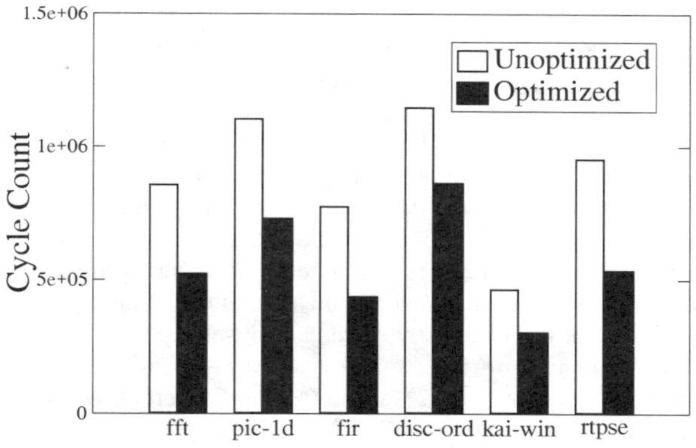

Figure 10: Comparison of cycle counts

Figure 9 shows the data cache miss ratio and after our data layout optimization. We observe a significant improvement in the cache performance. Figure 10 shows a comparison of the number of memory cycles computed assuming a cache miss penalty of 16 processor cycles. We observe an improvement of up to 44% on the original code. The measurements are taken on an architecture with a data cache size of 2 KB with a cache line size of 16 bytes. The run times of our algorithm are negligible (less than a second). In particular, since we rely on a static analysis of the application, the run time for data layout is not dependent on the array sizes, loop counts, and other dynamic run-time parameters.

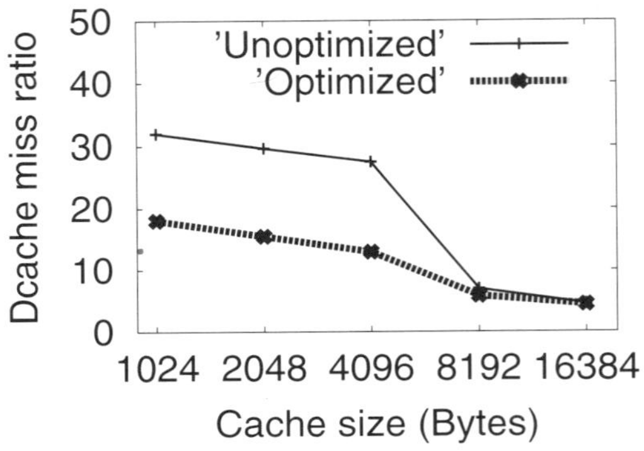

Figure 11: Variation of data cache miss ratio with cache size for FFT example

In Figure 11, we present the variation of the performance with increasing cache size keeping the line size constant for the FFT application. Note that beyond a cache size of 8 KB, there is no significant improvement in performance. This is expected, since, as mentioned in Section 3, if the cache is large enough to accommodate *all* the application data, then there is no useless data fetched into the cache; there are no capacity misses and the cache can be replaced by a simple on-chip RAM that stores the data. Our data restructuring optimization shows significant performance improvement when the cache sizes are relatively small compared to the total data size, which is the more realistic case, and especially useful in embedded applications, where chip area can be saved by using a smaller cache combined with aggressive compiler optimizations such as the one presented here.

6. CONCLUSION AND FUTURE WORK

We presented an algorithm for transforming the memory layout of aggregate data structures so as to improve the cache performance of embedded applications. The aggressive transformations are especially suited for embedded system design because we can assume that the entire application is visible to the compiler, thus making it possible to verify the safety of the data transformation operation. We presented an algorithm for automatically inferring the best clustering of individual fields of aggregate data structures such as arrays of `structs` based on the memory access patterns of the given application. Our experiments verify the soundness of the approach.

One area of refinement/improvement of the algorithm is the situation where an array is accessed with different index expressions in the same loop (e.g, `a[i]` and `a[2i]`). Currently, we consider array accesses to be correlated if there is at least one correlated access. We consider it beneficial to merge arrays `a` and `b` if accesses `a[i]`, `a[2i]`, `b[i]`, and `b[3i]` exist in a loop. However, this ignores the possible conflicts among the remaining accesses. The cost function could be refined to handle such cases. In addition, the greedy clustering algorithm could be improved by using better partitioning algorithms reported in CAD literature in various contexts.

7. REFERENCES

[1] The Open SystemC Initiative, http://www.systemc.org.

[2] The SUIF Compiler System, http://suif.stanford.edu.

[3] F. Catthoor, S. Wuytack, E. D. Greef, F. Balasa, L. Nachtergaele, and A. Vandecappelle. *Custom Memory Management Methodology*. Kluwer Academic Publishers, Dordrecht, June 1998.

[4] R. Ernst, J. Henkel, and T. Benner. Hardware-software co-synthesis of microcontrollers. *IEEE Design and Test of Computers*, 11(4):64–75, Dec. 1994.

[5] D. Gajski, F. Vahid, S. Narayan, and J. Gong. *Specification and Design of Embedded Systems*. Prentice Hall, 1994.

[6] R. K. Gupta. *Co-Synthesis of Hardware and Software for Digital Embedded Systems*. Kluwer Academic Publishers, Boston, 1995.

[7] P. E. R. Lippens, J. L. van Meerbergen, W. F. J. Verhaegh, and A. van der Werf. Allocation of multiport memories for hierarchical data streams. In *Proceedings of the IEEE International Conference on Computer Aided Design*, pages 728–735, Santa Clara, CA, Nov. 1993.

[8] P. R. Panda, N. D. Dutt, and A. Nicolau. Memory data organization for improved cache performance in embedded processor applications. *ACM Transactions on Design Automation of Electronic Systems*, 2(4):384–409, Oct. 1997.

[9] P. R. Panda, N. D. Dutt, and A. Nicolau. *Memory Issues in Embedded Systems-On-Chip: Optimizations and Exploration*. Kluwer Academic Publishers, Norwell, MA, 1999.

[10] L. Séméria, K. Sato, and G. D. Micheli. Resolution of dynamic memory allocation and pointers for the behavioral synthesis from C. In *Proceedings Design Automation and Test in Europe (DATE'00)*, pages 312–319, Paris, France, Mar. 2000.

[11] L. Séméria and G. D. Micheli. Resolution, optimization, and encoding of pointer variables for the behavioral synthesis from C. *IEEE Transactions on Computer Aided Design*, 20(2):213–233, Feb. 2001.

[12] S.Wuytack, J. L. da Silva, F.Catthoor, G. Jong, and C. Ykman-Couvreur. Memory management for embedded network applications. *IEEE Transactions on Computer Aided Design*, 18(5):533–544, May 1999.

[13] R. Wilson and M. Lam. Efficient context-sensitive analysis for C programs. In *Proceedings of the ACM SIGPLAN'95 Conference on Programming Language Design and Implementation*, pages 1–12, La Jolla, CA, June 1995.

Systematic Speed-Power Memory Data-Layout Exploration for Cache Controlled Embedded Multimedia Applications

M. Miranda C. Ghez C. Kulkarni F. Catthoor* D. Verkest

IMEC Lab., Kapeldreef 75, Leuven, Belgium
*Also Professor at the Katholieke Universiteit Leuven, Belgium

{miranda,ghez,kulkarni,catthoor,verkest}@imec.be

ABSTRACT

The ever increasing gap between processor and memory speeds has motivated the design of embedded systems with deeper cache hierarchies. To avoid excessive miss rates, instead of using bigger cache memories and more complex cache controllers, program transformations have been proposed to reduce the amount of capacity and conflict misses. This is achieved however by complicating the memory index arithmetic code which results in performance degradation when executing the code on programmable processors with limited address capabilities. However, when these are complemented by high-level address code transformations, the overhead introduced can be largely eliminated at compile time. In this paper, the clear benefits of the combined approach is illustrated on two real-life applications of industrial relevance, using popular programmable processor architectures and showing important gains in energy (a factor 2 less) with a relatively small penalty in execution time (8-25%) instead of factors overhead without the address optimisation stage. The results of this paper leads to a systematic Pareto optimal trade-off (supported by tools) between memory power and CPU cycles which has up to now not been feasible for the targeted systems.

Categories and Subject Descriptors

B.3.2 [**Hardware**]: Memory structures—*Cache memories*; D.3.4 [**Software**]: Programming languages—*Optimisation*

Keywords

Address generation, direct mapped cache, embedded systems, multimedia applications

1. INTRODUCTION

Multi-media systems such as medical image processing and video compression algorithms, typically use a very large amount of data storage and transfers. This is especially a problem for low-power embedded system realisations because the memories and bus transfers are responsible for most of system energy waste (between 50 and 80%). Therefore, optimising the global memory accesses of an application in a so-called Data Transfer and Storage Exploration (DTSE) [1] stages is a crucial task for achieving low power realisations. These optimisations have both platform independent and platform specific phases. The first phase has a positive influence on both energy and performance (irrespective of the architecture) since it removes redundant data transfer and storage and it improves the locality of production/consumption of the data. However, this phase need to be complemented by a platform specific one to exploit the opportunities created. This is especially true for highly constrained architectures like those found in programmable platforms due to resource limitations.

In multimedia, the vast majority of programmable processor use cache controllers to manage their on-chip memories. These controllers decide at run-time when and how the data is copied from the higher memory hierarchy layers to the cache architecture [2]. In this way the designer does not have to worry about managing the memory hierarchy, especially for the dynamic part of the application. However, this can become a run-time bottleneck especially due the cache misses when the required data is no longer present in the on-chip memory. These misses translates into an excess of system bus load and energy because of the traffic of data between main memory and the cache (hierarchies). This results into cycles wasted when the processor is stalled waiting for the data to arrive and in energy spent in reloading the cache. Moreover, it limits the performance of shared-memory multiprocessor based implementations.

All this unnecessary overhead can be avoided at the program level. However, it requires knowledge of the underlying platform architecture. This knowledge can be exploited using platform-aware transformations. Optimisations oriented to minimise the miss rate in the data cache (D-cache) are those exploiting the limited lifetime of the data during program execution (namely inplace optimisations which can reduce capacity misses [3, 4]) and those exploiting the memory data organisation freedom (to remove the conflict misses, e.g. [5, 6]). This reduction in miss rate leads to important savings in energy (see Section 3). However, they typically require to re-write the index expressions of the affected data arrays, thus resulting in a much more complex addressing functionality. This potentially large overhead in addressing can lead to factors overhead in execution time on programmable processors. In this way it can limit a more efficient cache utilisation.

After cache oriented code transformations, the new addressing code is dominated by index expressions of piece-wise linear nature and it becomes a bottleneck for the auto-increment nature of most commercial Address Calculation Unit (ACU) architectures. Therefore, it should be removed before going to the more pointer level

ISSS'01, October 1-3, 2001, Montréal, Québec, Canada

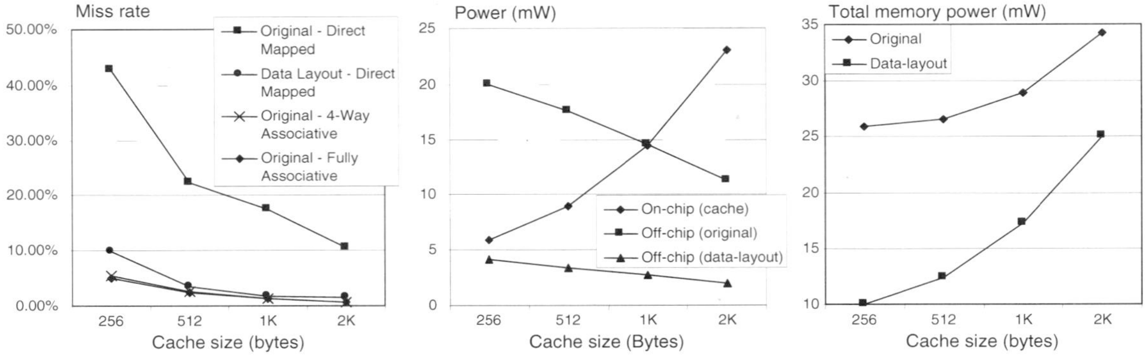

Figure 1: D-cache miss-rate evolution for the MPEG4 Motion Estimation driver for different cache sizes and controller types, including off-chip/on-chip power breakdown and total power evolution for different cache sizes (for a direct mapped cache controller).

specific address optimisation techniques like those found in conventional [7] or state-of-the-art compilers [8]. Moreover, conventional automated address optimisation approaches [9, 10, 11, 12, 13] do not allow this for address code containing modulo/division operations.

To remove this large bottleneck we have developed efficient address optimisation techniques. These are based on the use of program transformations which are largely independent of the targeted instruction-set architecture [14, 15], but which need also to be complemented by more architecture specific ones [16]. Using these techniques, the addressing code is globally optimised, resulting in factors overall improvement in execution cycles when compared to their original data-organised versions.

The clear benefits of the combined approach to aggressively improve cache utilisation by source code transformations which introduce complex addressing which is then reduced again by a high-level address optimisation stage, has to our knowledge not been studied in the literature. We will provide a systematic approach to achieve that in this paper. It leads to Pareto optimal speed power trade-off curves. That approach is illustrated on two real-life application drivers of industrial relevance, using three popular programmable processor architectures, showing important gains in cycle count and energy consumption.

2. EXPERIMENTAL SETUP

Due to flexibility requirements of the implementation an instruction-set processor architecture is preferred over a fully custom one. The architectures which we target in this paper, consist of multi-media (extended) processors (such as TriMedia's TM1000, Intel's Pentium-III MMX) but also more general RISC architectures such as Hewlett-Packard's PA800 architecture.

For realistic embedded implementation we assume their "core" versions which have a relatively small local (L1) on-chip cache memory to reduce the energy per L1 cache access (which is our focus here). These processors are connected to a (distributed) shared off-chip memory (hierarchy). Therefore, meeting real-time constraints in such architectures, requires an optimal mapping of the application onto the target platform.

For our experimental setup we have used the SimpleScalar simulator tool set [20] for simulating cache performance for varying cache sizes. The cache is simulated using the faster and functionally correct sim-cache simulator for measuring cache performance. Existing processors have been used to measure the performance values. The code versions have been compiled and run on the different platforms using the native compilers and enabling their most aggressive speed oriented optimisation features.

Our exploration approach is illustrated on two real-life application drivers: a Cavity Detector algorithm and MPEG4 Full Search Motion Estimation kernel for CIF video frames. The Cavity Detector is an image processing application used mainly in the medical field for detecting tumour cavities in computer tomography pictures (as large as 1280×1000 pixels) [17].

When these algorithms are mapped onto an embedded system, the system bus load and power requirements are quite high. At our laboratory, much effort has been already spent on optimising both drivers at the source-level code, mainly by applying the platform independent transformation stage of the DTSE methodology [18, 19]. In this paper we will focus only on the data cache related speed-power trade-offs during the platform specific mapping stage.

3. MEMORY DATA-LAYOUT OPTIMISATION FOR D-CACHES

A *cache miss* happens whenever a block of data requested by the CPU is not found in the cache. Therefore, the fist time a block has be copied into the cache can also be considered as a miss (namely a *compulsory miss*). However, only those misses related to blocks that have been previously allocated in the cache lead to an overhead. In this case, two possible situations exist [2]: (1) when the cache cannot contain all the blocks needed during execution, *capacity misses* will occur because of blocks being discarded and later retrieved; (2) if the block placement strategy is set associative or direct mapped, *conflict misses* (in addition to compulsory and capacity) will occur because a block can be discarded and later retrieved if too many blocks map to its set.

For the D-cache, optimisations are available which are oriented to minimise both capacity and conflict misses. Capacity misses can be greatly reduced by exploiting the limited life-time of the data (inplace oriented optimisations [3]) and the conflict misses by applying data-layout oriented transformations [6]. Using prototype tools supporting these techniques [21], we obtain the transformed C code. Thus, we now have the initial (reference) and the data layout transformed codes.

After cache simulations we have observed that both drivers are dominated by misses in the D-cache (the miss rate for I-cache is about three orders of magnitude smaller than for D-cache). Therefore, we have focused on optimising the D-cache miss rate by applying main memory data-layout oriented program code transfor-

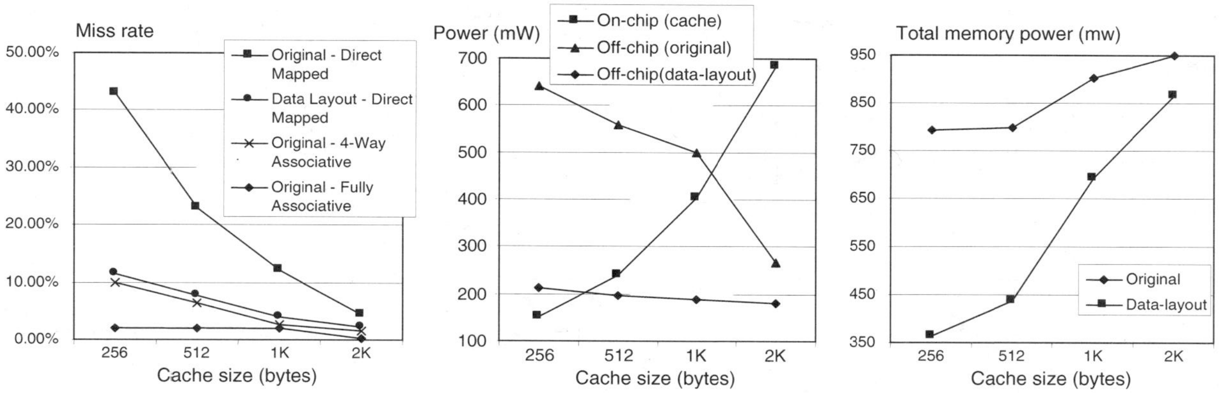

Figure 2: Data-cache miss-rate evolution for the Cavity Detector driver for different cache sizes and controller types, including off-chip/on-chip power breakdown and total power evolution for different cache sizes (for a direct mapped cache controller).

mations. Simulations have been performed using different cache controller types: a 4-way associative cache for the non optimised version and a direct mapped for both optimised and non-optimised versions. Also, different capacity sizes (with the number of cache lines ranging from 256 till 2024) have been evaluated. Figure 1 and 2 shows the miss rate after simulations for both drivers and controller types.

For the non-optimised code, the miss rate obtained using a direct mapped controller is rather large when we compare it to the one obtained when using 4-way associative controller. However, when using the cache optimised code, the miss rate behaves equally well for both controller types. This is clearly an important result because it enables the use of the simpler direct mapped cache controllers for embedded applications, instead of the more costly, and power hungry, set-associative controller types.

4. HIGH-LEVEL OPTIMISATION OF THE INDEX/ADDRESS COMPUTATION

Cache oriented transformations require the introduction of complex modulo and integer division operations in the index expressions. This is because, transformations exploiting the limited lifetime of the data requires complex modulo operations in the address code to express in time the folded nature of the relation between the original and the transformed address spaces in main memory.

On the other hand, data-layout oriented transformations require to create gaps of unused memory locations within array of data allocated in main memory, as well as to allocate in memory different arrays in an interleaved manner. Therefore, these data-layout oriented transformations also require modifications in the original addressing code by introducing complex modulo and integer division operations. Figure 3 illustrates the effect of such transformations on a piece of code representative of the Cavity Detector driver. The combined outcome is that even nested modulo expressions are present.

As a result, for both application drivers described in Section 3, a large overhead in addressing is created. For both drivers, this overhead is mostly due to the more complex index expressions (mainly of piece-wise linear nature) introduced during the inplace [3] and data-layout [6] DTSE oriented optimisation steps. Indeed, a considerable number of costly modulo operations are executed and traditional compilers completely fail to efficiently eliminate them. Hence, the execution time increases considerably: a factor between 2-20 depending on the application and the target processor architecture (see Section 5).

```
for(x=1; x<N-2; x++) {
  for(y=1; y<M-2; y++) {
    for(k=-1; k<1; k++) {
      ....
      A[x][y] += B[x+k][y]*C[abs(k)];
      ....
    }
    A[x][y] /= tot; }}
```
(a)

```
for(y=0;y<M+2;y++) {
  for(x=0;x<n+2;x++) {
    ....
    if(x>=0 && x<N && y>0 && y<M-1)
      D[x%3] = B[(y*N+x%3)%160+(y*N+x%3)/160*256+ 96];
    ....
    if(x-1>=1 && x-1<=N-2 && y>=1 && y<=M-2)
      for(k=-1;k<=1;k++)
        acc+=D[(x-1+k)%3]*C[abs(k)];
    acc/=tot; }}
```
(b)

Figure 3: Illustration of data cache oriented transformations in the Cavity Detector driver: (a) initial code; (b) transformed code.

Our novel design script allows to remove this overhead at the source-level code by reducing the complexity and the amount of address operations [16]. This high-level optimisation stage consists on two main stages.

The first one exploits algebraic and modulo properties to reduce the number operation instances. This stage does a re-factorisation of addressing expressions [22] (containing also modulo/division operations) that compilers are not capable to perform (see Fig 5b). This factorisation typically exposes more opportunities for common sub-expression elimination than those originally present in the initial code. When complementing this with aggressive code hoisting techniques across both loops and conditionals, the number of executed operations is minimised.

At that point, the second stage can focus on reducing the execution cost of the (remaining) modulo/division operations by transforming these onto a efficient combination of linear induction variables and conditional code (see Fig 5c) [16].

High-level address transformations also have a positive effect on

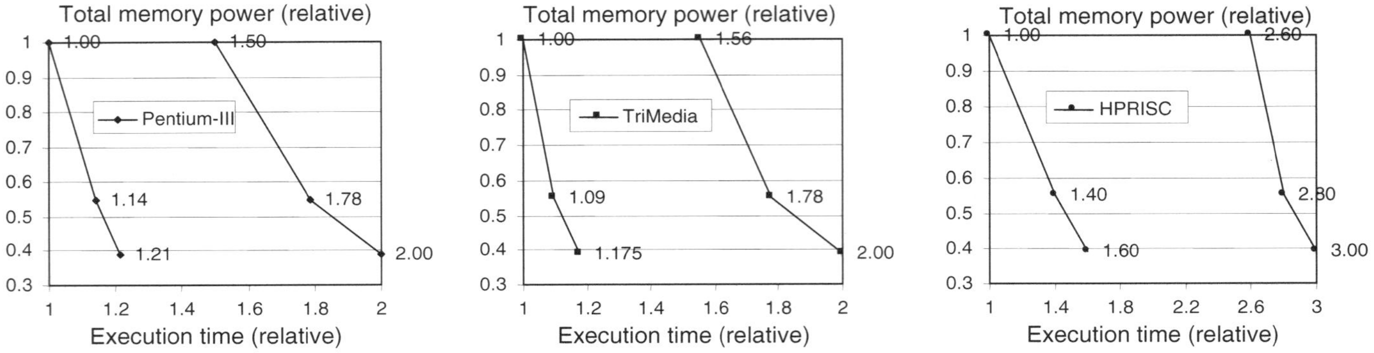

Figure 4: Power and performance trade-offs for the Motion Estimation kernel for different processors and memory data-layouts. Lines at the right represent trade-offs before the address optimisation phase and at the left after it.

memory accesses and in L1-misses both for I-caches and D-caches. For the D-cache, we have observed for both drivers (see Section 2) that the amount of data memory accesses as well the number of data misses decreases slightly ($\simeq < 10\%$). However, this improvement in data memory power is very limited when compared by the one achieved using the memory data-layout oriented transformations (see Section 5). For the I-cache, a larger reduction in instruction memory fetches ($>40\%$) is obtained (due to the more efficient addressing code) while the reduction in instruction fetch misses stays also limited ($\simeq < 10\%$). Still, in both drivers the miss-rate for the I-cache is about three orders of magnitude smaller than for the D-cache and so the off-chip memory related power.

```
for(y=0;y<10;y++){
  for(x=0;x<100;x++){
    if(x>1) A[(y%3)*3
                +(x-2)%3]=...
    if(x>4) ...=A[(y%3)*3
                + (x-5)%3]
}}
```

(a) Initial

```
for(y=0;y<10;y++){
  v_y = (y%3)*3;
  for(x=0;x<100;x++){
    v_yx = (x-2)%3 + v_y;
    if(x>1) A[v_yx] = ...
    if(x>4) ... = A[v_yx];
}}
```

(b) Index expression optimisation

```
for(y=0;y<10;y++){
  if(p_y>=9) p_y-=9;
  for(x=0;x<100;x++){
    if(p_x>=3) p_x-=3;
    v_yx = p_x + p_y;
    if(x>1) A[v_yx] =...
    if(x>4) ...= A[v_yx];
    p_x++;}
  p_y+=3;}
```

(c) Modulo operation sustitution

Figure 5: Illustration of processor independent address transformations for the Cavity Detector driver: (a) initial code; (b) after algebraic and modulo oriented transformations; (c) after modulo substitution transformations.

5. TRADE-OFF BETWEEN PERFORMANCE, POWER AND MAIN-MEMORY SIZE

We now discuss how the above technique can be applied to achieve important system level trade-off's. For both drivers we have started with an initial algorithm which has been optimised from a DTSE perspective.

In the first step, we obtain miss rates for different cache sizes when using a cost efficient direct mapped cache. This is shown in Figure 1 for the Motion Estimation and in Figure 2 for the Cavity Detector. Once we have obtained the miss rates for different cache sizes, we compute the total (off-chip plus on-chip) required power for each driver. We observe that for both drivers a cache size with 256 bytes consumes the least total power. For smaller cache sizes, the total consumed power would be dominated by the accesses (due to misses) to the off-chip memory. For larger sizes the accesses to the on-chip memory dominates the total power though.

In a next step, we choose the power optimal cache size of 256 bytes to decide on a trade-off between main-memory size (the overhead in memory space in the data layout optimisation process as compared to the initial algorithm) and the reduction in miss rate as shown in Tables 1 and 2. Thus depending on the design constraints, the designer can now either choose a lower power solution with some overhead in main-memory size and vice-versa. For the Cavity Detector algorithm we have decided to choose two versions representative of extreme points in the search space and observe the trade-offs: one with a 2% main-memory size overhead (labelled "Light") and one with a factor of 2 overhead (labelled "Aggressive"). For the Motion Estimation kernel the points selected are responsible for a 30% overhead in main-memory size (labelled "Light") and a much larger factor 3 overhead (labelled "Aggressive").

In the final stage, we perform address optimisations (also supported by prototype tools [16]) to remove the overhead in addressing operations introduced in the data layout optimisation process. Figures 4 and 6 show that we are able to largely remove this overhead in addressing. This is visible by comparing the projected values on the horizontal axis of the curve before the high-level address optimisation phase (right-hand side) and after it (left-hand side).

For both drivers, using their "Light" data-layout version, we are able to reduce memory related power by almost a factor 2. For the Motion Estimation, this is achieved by trading-off a 30% in main-memory size with a 14-40% in execution time (depending on the target processor), instead of the 80-280% CPU cycle overhead

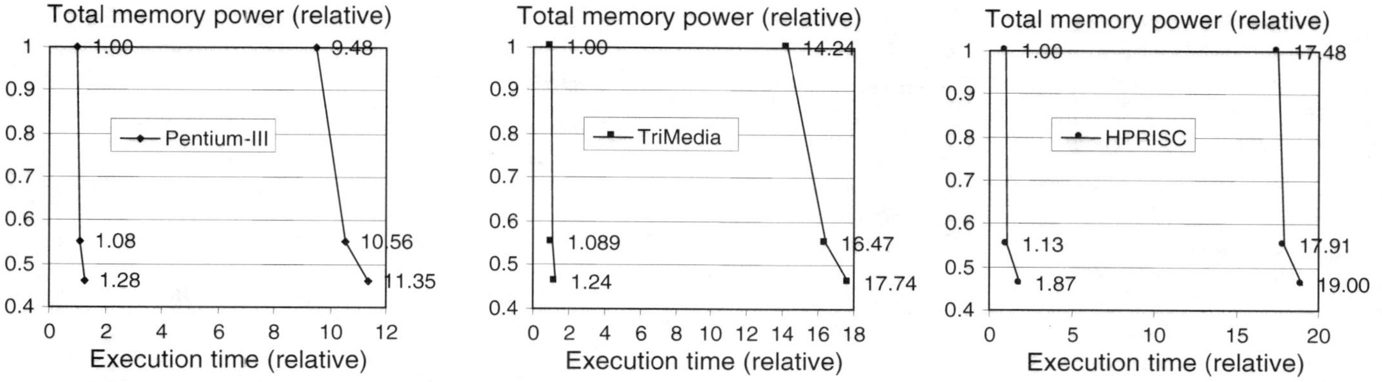

Figure 6: Power and performance trade-offs for the Cavity Detector algorithm for different processors and memory data-layouts. Lines at the right represent trade-offs before the address optimisation phase and at the left after it.

without the address post-processing stage (see Figure 4). For the Cavity Detector algorithm, main-memory size overhead is limited to just a 2% and the overhead in execution time is less 13% (irrespective of the target processor) instead of the factor 10-20 overhead in executed cycles when not using the address post-processing stage (see Figure 6). We assume that the data related memory power does not significantly change with the address code transformations stage but mainly with the memory data-layout stage as motivated in Section 4.

Table 1: main-memory size/power/speed trade-offs for the Motion Estimation.

Data-layout trade-off	Memory-size Overhead	Avrg.Power Gain	Avrg.Speed Degradation
Light	30 %	45 %	14-40 %
Aggressive	3X	60 %	18-60 %

Table 2: main-memory size/power/speed trade-offs for the Cavity Detector.

Data-layout trade-off	Memory-size Overhead	Avrg.Power Gain	Avrg.Speed Degradation
Light	2 %	45 %	8-13 %
Aggressive	2X	65 %	24-87 %

Note that the approach we have used in this work is mostly power centric namely, we first optimise for power (by selection the optimal cache size) then for main-memory size (by deciding the amount of data-layout) and lastly for performance (by optimising the addressing code). But the above technique can be used for a performance centric approach too. In this case, the designer should first choose the optimal cache size for data miss rate (e.g. by selecting the cache size from which the decrease in number of misses starts to saturate) and then select the amount of data-layout corresponding to the required trade-off between main-memory size and memory power. Following this approach, cache sizes of 512 bytes for the Motion Estimation and 1024 bytes for Cavity Detector would lead to better system performance (less data misses) at the expenses of higher data memory power (see total memory power evolution in Figures 1 and 2). Still, Pareto curves like those shown in Figure 4 and 6 can be used in both scenarios.

6. CONCLUSIONS

In this paper we have shown how to efficiently combine memory data-layout and address program transformations in a systematic way to trade-off speed and power when mapping data-intensive applications into architectures containing cache memories. The clear benefits of the combined approach have been illustrated by two real-life applications of industrial relevance, using popular programmable processor architectures. Important gains in energy (up to a factor 2 less) with very limited impact on execution time (<25%) are reported instead of the factors overhead in execution time without the address post-processing stage. Alternatively, execution time gains be achieved at the system level with a less aggressive power gain while trading-off main-memory size with total memory power.

7. REFERENCES

[1] F.Catthoor, K.Danckaert, C.Kulkarni, T.Omnes, *Data transfer and storage architecture issues and exploration in multimedia processors*, book chapter in "Programmable Digital Signal Processors: Architecture, Programming, and Applications" (ed. Y.H.Yu), Marcel Dekker, Inc., New York, 2000.

[2] D.Patterson, J.Hennessey, "Computer architecture : A quantitative approach", *Morgan Kaufmann Publ.*, San Francisco, 1996.

[3] E. De Greef, F. Catthoor, H. De Man, *Program Transformation Strategies for Memory Size and Power Reduction of Pseudo-regular Multimedia Subsystems* IEEE Trans. on Circuits and Systems for Video Technology Vol. 8, No. 6, pp. 719-733, October 1998.

[4] C.Kulkarni, F.Catthoor, H.De Man, "Hardware cache optimization for parallel multimedia applications", *Proc. EuroPar Conference*, Southampton, U.K.,pp.923-931, Sep. 1998.

[5] P.Panda, F.Catthoor, N.Dutt, K.Danckaert, E.Brockmeyer, C.Kulkarni, A.Vandecappelle, P.G.Kjeldsberg, "Data and Memory Optimizations for Embedded Systems", *ACM Trans. on Design Automation for Embedded Systems (TODAES)*, Vol.6, No.2, pp.142-206, April 2001.

[6] C.Kulkarni, F.Catthoor, H.De Man, Advanced Data Layout Optimization for Multimedia Applications, Proc. Workshop on Parallel and Distributed Computing in Image, Video and Multimedia Processing (PDIVM'00), IPDPS'2000, May 2000.

[7] A.V.Aho, R.Sethi, J.D.Ulmann, "Compilers: principles, techniques and tools", Addison-Wesley, 1986.

[8] S.Muchnick, *Advanced Compiler Design and Implementation* Morgan Kaufmann Publishers, 1997.

[9] R.Leupers, P.Marwedel, *Algorithms for Address Assignment in DSP Code Generation*. Proc. Intnl. Conf. on Computer-Aided Design (ICCAD), 1996.

[10] C.Liem, P.Pauling, A.Jerraya, *Address calculation for retargetable compilation and exploration for instruction-set architectures*. Proc. Design Automation Conference (DAC), pp. 597-600, 1996.

[11] C.Gebotys, *DSP address optimisation using a minimum cost circulation technique*. Proc. Intl. Conf. on Computer-Aided Design (ICCAD), pp. 100-104, 1997.

[12] A.Sudarsanam, S.Liao, S.Devadas, *Analysis and evaluation of address arithmetic capabilities in custom DSP architectures*. Proc. Design Automation Conference (DAC), 1997.

[13] S.Udayanarayanan, C.Chakrabarti, "Address Code Generation for Digital Signal Processors", *Proc. ACM Design Automation Conf.*, pp. 353-358, Las Vegas, June 2001.

[14] M.Miranda, F.Catthoor, M.Janssen, H.De Man, "High-level Address Optimisation and Synthesis Techniques for Data-Transfer Intensive Applications", *IEEE Trans. on VLSI Systems*, Vol.6, No.4, pp.677-686, Dec. 1998.

[15] S.Gupta, M.Miranda, F.Catthoor, R.Gupta, *Analysis of High-level Address Code Transformations for Programmable Processors*, In Proc. Design and Test in Europe Conf. (DATE), 2000.

[16] C.Ghez, M.Miranda, A.Vandecappelle, F.Catthoor and D.Verkest, Systematic high-level Address Code Transformations for Piece-wise Linear Indexing: Illustration on a Medical Imaging Algorithm, *In Proc. Workshop on Signal Processing Systems (SIPS)*, 2000.

[17] M.Bister, Y.Taeymans, J.Cornelis, "Automatic Segmentation of Cardiac MR Images", *Computers in Cardiology*, IEEE Computer Society Press, pp.215-218, 1989.

[18] K. Danckaert, F. Catthoor, H. De Man, *Platform independent data transfer and storage exploration illustrated on a parallel cavity detection algorithm*. Proc. PDPTA (CSREA Conf. on Parallel and Distributed Processing Techniques and Applications), 1999.

[19] Kristof Denolf, Peter Vos, Jan Bormans and Ivo Bolsens, Cost-efficient C-Level Design of an MPEG-4 Video Decoder *Proc. Workshop on Power and Timing Modeling, Optimization and Simulation*, 2000.

[20] D.Burger, T.Austin, "The Simplescalar Toolset", version 2.0, online document available at http://ww.cs.wisc.edu/ mscalar/simplescalar.html.

[21] C.Kulkarni, M.Miranda, C.Ghez, F.Catthoor, H.De Man, "Cache Conscious Data Layout Organization For Embedded Multimedia Applications", *Proc. 4th ACM/IEEE Design and Test in Europe Conf.*, Munich, Germany, March 2001.

[22] J.M.Janssen, F.Catthoor, H.De Man, *A specification invariant technique for operation cost minimisation in flow-graphs*, Proc. Intln. Symp. on High-level Synthesis, pp. 146-157, 1994.

Data Cache Energy Minimizations Through Programmable Tag Size Matching to the Applications*

Peter Petrov and Alex Orailoglu

Computer Science & Engineering Department
University of California, San Diego
(ppetrov,alex)@cs.ucsd.edu

ABSTRACT

An application-specific customization methodology for minimizing the energy dissipation in the data cache of embedded processors is presented in this paper. The data cache subsystem is one of the most power consuming microarchitectural parts of embedded processors. We target in this work particularly the data cache tag operations and show how an exceedingly small number of tag bits, if any, are needed to compute the miss/hit behavior for the vast majority of load/store instructions executed within application loops. The energy needed to perform the tag reads and comparisons can be thus dramatically reduced. We follow up this conceptual enhancement with a presentation of an efficient, reprogrammable implementation that utilizes application-specific information to apply the suggested energy minimization approach. The conducted experimental results confirm the expected significant decrease of energy dissipation for a set of important numerical kernels.

1. INTRODUCTION

An ever increasing and significant portion of the consumer electronic market nowadays is dominated by embedded systems. A large part of the functionality of such systems is typically implemented on a set of embedded processors. Major benefits of using embedded processors include improved time-to-market, flexible system implementation, and low-cost system design. The embedded processor cores impose though in turn significant penalties in terms of performance and power, mainly due to their generality.

With the advent of the mobile electronic system, such as cellphones, PDAs, and laptop computers, power consumption minimization is becoming one of the major quality requirements, since less power consumption of the product translates to longer battery life. Consequently, overall product quality is highly dependent on techniques for minimizing system power consumption. These techniques can be applied on various design abstraction levels, from circuit level to system architecture.

*This work is supported by an IBM Graduate Fellowship and NSF Grant 0082325.

ISSS'01, October 1-3, 2001, Montréal, Québec, Canada.

Circuit-level power minimization techniques have been the dominant approach in designing energy efficient designs so far [1, 2]. However, in recent years, architecture-level approaches have attained popularity due to their ability to eliminate redundancies on a higher, microarchitectural level, thus resulting in even larger power optimizations [3, 4]. In [5], a small and energy efficient L0 data cache has been introduced in order to reduce the power consumption of the memory hierarchy. The price paid is an increased miss rate and longer access time. A power optimization technique applied during behavioral synthesis for memory intensive applications has been presented in [6]. The behavior of the memory access patterns is utilized to minimize the number of transitions on the address bus and decoder, thus reducing power consumption. In [4] an L0 instruction cache has been proposed with run-time techniques for accommodating only the frequently executed basic blocks. The small size of this cache translates directly to power consumption reductions. The speculative execution in modern high-end processors results in high instruction execution overhead. In [3] a technique for speculation control and pipeline gating has been presented for energy reduction in speculative processors. A new energy estimation framework for microprocessors has been proposed recently in [7]. The simulation environment employs a transition based power model and quickly achieves very precise power estimations.

In this paper, we propose a technique for application-specific customization of the data cache (D-cache) subsystem of embedded processor cores, one of the most power devouring components of the processor architecture. The proposed technique is particularly suitable for applications that contain data-intensive, numerical loops, a trait shared by a variety of DSP applications. We describe an architecture, capable of utilizing application-specific information in a microarchitecturally reprogrammable way. The technique enables re-customization in a post-manufacturing fashion, thus effectively covering a large class of real-life applications with no need for spinning new silicon.

Application-specific customization of embedded processor architectures is a technique that transfers application information to the processor architecture [8]. In this case, the microarchitecture performs informed decisions as to how to handle various architecture-specific actions. Fundamentally, this approach extends the communication link between compiler and processor architecture by transferring application information directly to the microarchitecture, while keeping the traditional compiler techniques unaffected. The static analysis information transfer is accomplished by utilizing a reprogrammable hardware implementation. The architecture we propose allows application changes to be applied in field by loading the new application information, in a manner similar to program reloading.

The proposed methodology utilizes information about the placement of the data being accessed within the application loops and more specifically the possible D-Cache conflicts and the minimal number

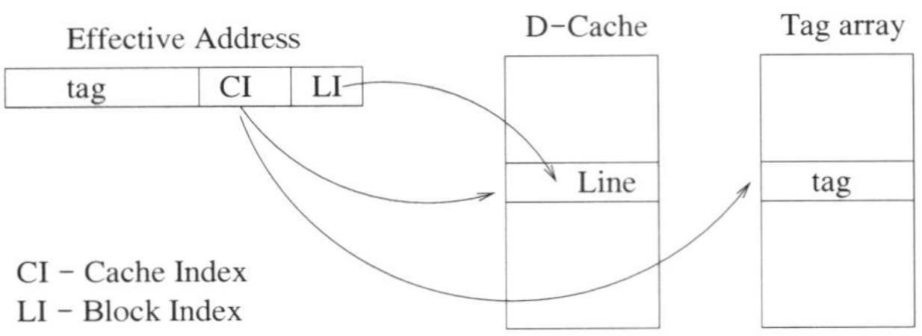

Figure 1: DM cache organization

```
for(i1=0;i1<64;i1++)
  for(i2=0;i2<64;i2++)
    for(i3=0;i3<64;i3++)
      C[i1][i3]+=A[i1][i2]*B[i2][i3];
```

Figure 2: Matrix multiplication code

of tag bits needed to identify these conflicts. The tag operations associated to the D-cache are designed for a worst case scenario and they utilize the entire effective address. These operations are very expensive in terms of power and usually carry a large amount of redundancy since conflicting references are frequently close to each other in the address space and a large part of their tags is identical. We show how the minimal necessary number of tag bits for identifying cache conflicts can be inferred from the data layout. In the extreme case of an application loop with a dataset that fits squarely in the D-cache, there would be no cache conflicts; hence no tag operations would be required at all. Only the cold misses when entering the loop require special attention. To handle the cold misses, the valid bits associated to the cache lines could be used. An efficient way of invalidating the cache lines corresponding to the loop prior to its execution is proposed, leading to a power efficient solution for handling the cold misses and enabling the application of the tag minimization framework that we propose.

We complement our methodology with a discussion of an efficient hardware implementation for the proposed D-cache customization. Not only is the hardware solution efficient, but is also reprogrammable, thus providing the flexibility to re-customize the embedded processor core in a post-manufacturing fashion. Consequently, the described hardware implementation constitutes a unified microarchitectural solution, capable of handling a large set of important applications through in-field re-customization, thus maintaining the market benefits of high-volume productions.

2. MOTIVATION

The D-cache is used to move the data closer to the processor core, so that the time needed to load data from memory is minimized and the performance gap between processor core and memory alleviated. A typical direct-mapped cache organization is shown in Figure 1. In this paper we consider only direct-mapped caches, but the approach can be easily extended to set-associative organizations. The referenced effective address is separated into *block index*, *cache index*, and *tag*. The block index is used to address a word within a cache line, while the cache index is used to address the cache line; the tag field checks whether there is a conflict with a memory location with the same cache index. The tag field of each cache line is stored in a separate tag memory array. Each time an access is performed to the D-cache, the tag associated to the cache line is read and compared to the tag of the effective address being referred. However, if the referred locations are close in the address space, a large part of these tag fields is identical. Consequently, a large amount of power is spent in reading, comparing and writing unnecessarily large tags.

In the domain of computationally intensive applications, such as DSP processing, application loops work on a set of data arrays. Performance considerations force manual optimization of these loops frequently. The loops rarely have any additional memory references, such as spill and fill code. The only data being addressed in the memory space is the actual data on which the loops operate. Figure 2 shows a matrix multiplication loop. The loop operates on three matrices and the only accesses to data memory consist of the array references.

Figures 3a and 3b depict the memory layout of the three matrices A, B, and C from the example. The data memory space is divided into regions that correspond to one D-cache size and for each of these memory regions the tag part of the address is a constant. We denote these memory regions as *0-tag regions*. The left part of Figure 3 shows a configuration in which the data set of the example resides within a single 0-tag region. It is evident that in such a case there will be no conflicts within the arrays of data in the D-cache and there is no need to perform any tag operations. This is a straightforward consequence of the fact that a tag region has size exactly equal to the D-cache size and the tag part of the address is a constant. Figure 3a depicts a configuration in which the dataset spans two tag regions. In this case there *will* be conflicts in the D-cache; nonetheless, the tag fields of two conflicting addresses will differ on average by an exceedingly small number of bits. If the least significant bit of the tag for a given tag region is 0, then the address tag associated with the subsequent tag region in the memory will differ only in the least significant bit, which will be 1. In this way the tag regions in neighboring pairs for which the address tag differs only by one bit, the least significant bit, can be grouped. Such pairs of 0-tag regions are denoted as *1-tag regions*. The entire memory space is covered by a set of disjoint 1-tag regions.

A straightforward inference that can be drawn from the above observations is that there typically exists a large amount of redundancy in reading the entire tag from the tag array and comparing it to the effective address tag, given the proximity of the dataset references; a large number of identical bits in the tag components is to be expected, consequently. Given that application-specific information about the application loop dataset layout in the data memory is present during program execution, a large part of the tag redundancy can be eliminated, resulting in significant energy savings. The application information can be obtained during compile time and provided to the D-Cache microarchitecture in a reprogrammable way. Furthermore, certain compile-time optimization techniques can be utilized, to ensure that the actual loop dataset layout minimizes the number of required tag bits for identifying D-cache conflicts. For example, if possible, the compiler could try to place the data within a 0-tag region. If the data does not fit, the compiler can try incrementaly larger tag regions until the required minimal number of tag bits is identified.

Subsequent sections in the paper present our methodology for eliminating the aforementioned tag redundancy in an application-specific

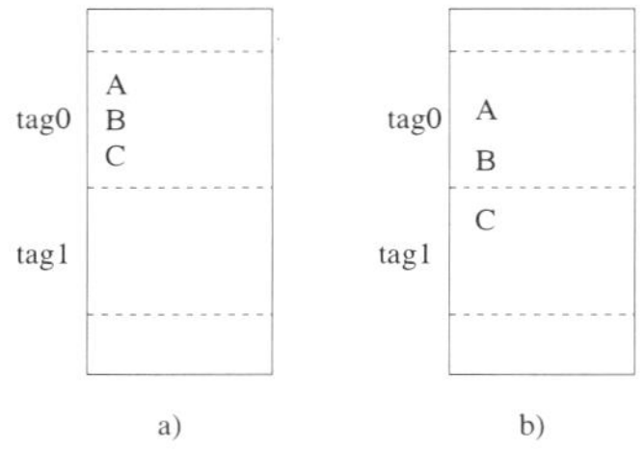

Figure 3: Memory layout

manner, thus achieving significant energy reductions. Since the flexibility of straightforward incorporation of application code changes is one of the paramount advantages of utilizing embedded processor cores, an efficient reprogrammable implementation that defines a unified architecture capable of capturing application information in-field is presented. This architecture preserves the generality of the embedded processor core in terms of functional programmability, while eliminating the inherent tag redundancy in the cache subsystem.

3. TAG UTILIZATION ANALYSIS

As demonstrated in the previous section, if the dataset of the frequently executed application fragments resides within a 0-tag region in the memory space, then no D-cache conflicts are possible; hence no tag operations are needed. When the loop dataset spans more than one tag region, a few tag bits are needed depending on the number and size of the tag regions the data spans. The structure and the position of the tag regions are determinative for extracting the redundancy in the tag fields. We explain subsequently the formation and structure of the tag regions within the main memory space.

3.1 Tag region formation

To understand the structure of the tag regions, let's consider a D-cache organization and memory address space that requires three bits of tag. This memory space can be divided into eight 0-tag regions with the tag field of the effective address a constant. A generalization of the 0-tag regions can be effected by noticing that all 0-tag regions can be grouped in pairs for which the tag field differs only in the least significant bit; for the first 0-tag region it contains the value of 0, while for the second one, the value is 1. We denote the region formed by the pair of such 0-tag regions as a 1-tag region. If a dataset resides within a 1-tag region, then only the least significant bit from the tag field needs to be used for conflict identification in the D-cache. In a similar vein, the 1-tag regions can be grouped into 2-tag regions. Generally, a $k+1$-tag region is formed by a pair of k-tag regions that differ in no more than the $k+1$ least significant bits of the tag field. All the tag regions are nested within each other; for example a $(k+1)$-tag region contains two k-tag regions and each of the k-tag regions contains two $(k-1)$-tag regions in turn. The set of all k-tag regions, for any value of k, covers the entire memory space. A k-tag region corresponds to a portion of the memory space with size equal to the size of 2^k D-caches and tags differing only in the least significant k bits. The n-tag region that covers the complete memory corresponds to a region that requires all the tag bits for detecting conflicts. The general-purpose caches operates under the extreme and general case assumption that all the application datasets reside in the n-tag memory region, which corresponds to the entire memory space. Their inability to incorporate application knowledge regarding the refinement of the tag regions within which the application data resides is the fundamental reason for the significant amount of tag operation redundancy.

Based on the above observations, it is evident that if the D-cache architecture incorporates application knowledge of the loop dataset layout, the energy expensive tag reads can be optimized to read only the minimum required number of tag bitlines from the tag SRAM array. At the same time, the compiler can try to ensure that the loop data are placed in such a way that they span the minimal tag region that corresponds to their size.

3.2 Dataset with no D-cache conflicts

If the dataset for the particular application loop has size smaller than the D-cache, then it can be placed within a 0-tag region. This size analysis is performed at compile time and the loop data is placed within a 0-tag region in the memory. In this case, no conflicts in the D-cache for the loop data are possible and hence no tag operations needed.

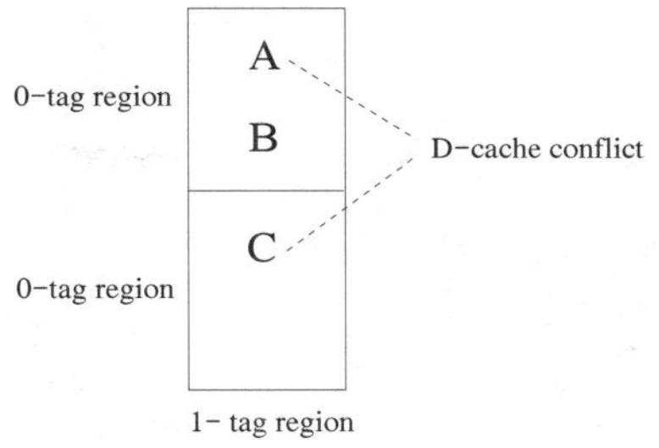

Figure 4: Loop dataset placement

Detection solely of the loop data cold cache misses is required for ensuring the correct D-cache operation. Detecting the cold cache misses can be achieved by invalidating the cache content in which the data resides; if the data spans the whole cache, then the cache needs to be invalidated completely. As the cache reuse across loops is negligible, if any, no performance penalty is incurred, or at worst in the case of data reuse between different loops, the insignificant penalty of the cold misses of the second loop data, constitutes the only performance penalty.

Once the cache part that will accommodate the loop data is invalidated, the cold misses are detected naturally through the usage of the valid bits of the cache lines. Noteworthy is that cold misses can occur not only in the first loop iteration but also in subsequent iterations, due to variantly traversed control paths in loop iterations. Consequently, the valid bit usage is a natural solution for detecting cold misses within the loop dataset.

3.3 Minimal tag usage for conflicting datasets

If the loop dataset cannot fit within a 0-tag region, then there will be D-cache conflicts and some tag bits will be needed for conflict identification. Since we want to minimize the number of tag bits needed for comparison, a compile time data placement algorithm is suggested in order to place the dataset within the boundaries of a k-tag region with minimal k.

An even further refinement of placing the dataset within the tag regions can be defined by observing that when placing a dataset within the boundaries of a $k+1$-tag region, for some of the data arrays only k tag bits might be enough to check for conflicts within the D-cache. Figure 4 depicts an example in which the dataset of the example from the previous section is placed into a 1-tag region and its size does not allow the dataset to fit within a 0-tag region. Since the 1-tag region comprises two 0-tag regions, part of the loop dataset (matrices A and B) is placed in the first 0-tag region, and another part (the matrix C) in the second 0-tag region. As the size of these matrices is identical, one can observe that matrix C overlaps in the D-cache with matrix A, while matrix B from the first 0-tag region does not overlap with any data in the second 0-tag region. Consequently, when accessing matrix B no tag bits would be needed for conflict checking, while in accessing A and C, one tag bit is required for detecting conflicts. This principle can be generalized to larger tag regions. If part of the loop dataset is placed into a k-tag region and the rest of it is placed into the next k-tag region, then for the components in the first k-tag region that do not conflict with the components in the second k-tag region, only k tag bits would be sufficient for D-cache conflict identification.

We can see that there are two different scenarios for the number of tag bits needed for the D-cache operations within a loop. If the entire dataset resides in a single k-tag region, with overlap possibilities for all data components, then only k tag bits are needed for this loop. If part of the data is placed in the next k-tag region as described in the previous paragraph, then for parts of the data components k tag bits would be enough, while for the remainder, $k + 1$ tag bits will be required.

The proposed methodology for energy reduction in the D-cache subsystem consists of two basic steps. The first step is the compile-time support that was presented in this section. This support includes placing the loop dataset within a tag region, or spanning more than one tag region by overlapping only some of the data arrays. During compile time, the minimal number of tag bits needed for each loop is determined and provided to the D-cache microarchitecture through the means outlined in the next section, wherein we describe the required hardware support.

4. IMPLEMENTATION

The proposed methodology requires a hardware support that would be able to dynamically enable only the minimum required number of bits from the tag array for the program loops. The hardware requires exact information as to how many tag bits are needed for a particular loop or functions within this loop.

First we present an efficient hardware for manipulating the tag memory array so that only the required minimal number of tag bits are used per application loop. The tag array in the cache subsystem is typically implemented as an SRAM array, possibly divided into multiple banks. The SRAM data array contains horizontal *wordlines* for each tag word and a vertical *bitline* for each bit within the tag word.

A read operation from the SRAM array is performed in the following way. The address decoder selects the wordline to be read from the array. All the bitlines are precharged and if the selected memory cell by the wordline contains logic zero, then the bitlines start to get discharged. Since the discharge is a quite slow process, a sense amplifier is utilized at the end of each bitline. If a small drop of the voltage level is detected, a logic zero is registered. The precharge and discharge of bitlines are the most energy consuming operations with SRAM data arrays [9].

By eliminating most of the bitline precharge and discharge operations, our approach greatly reduces the energy dissipation in the tag SRAM array. This is achieved by gating the bitlines according to the minimal number of tag bits required to check for D-cache conflicts. Only the needed bitlines, if any, are precharged and discharged, thus effectively eliminating the redundant reads. The sense amplifiers for the disabled bitlines are gated as well. Furthermore, the tag comparator cells are gated in order to perform the comparison only on the required tag bits.

The number of tag bits for each loop needs to be determined before entering the loop, so that the appropriate number of bitlines is enabled. Since this number is fixed for the loop, it can be stored in a special control register before entering the loop. Each bit in this special control register directly corresponds to an enable signal of bitline and sense amplifier. The default value of this register specifies that all tag bitlines are enabled. The current value of this register is used to determine the number of bitlines to enable. The only delay imposed by this implementation is the insignificant delay of the gating logic, which roughly corresponds to the delay of a simple *and* gate.

If there are data arrays placed in the next k-tag region with partial overlap with data arrays from the previous k-tag region, then the accesses to these arrays require only k tag bits. An identification mechanism is needed to distinguish the load instructions to these arrays from the others. One possible approach is the incorporation of an additional bit to the load instructions that will indicate whether an additional tag bit is needed. While highly cost effective in terms of hardware support, nonetheless, because of the optimized opcode size in most embedded processors, this approach might be infeasible. An alternative implementation consists of a small table, namely, a *Load Identification Table* (LIT). When a load instruction is encountered, the LIT is indexed by the PC of that load instruction and a bit in it specifies whether an additional tag bit is needed. Note that the size of these tables must be limited to a very small number of entries in order to keep the benefits of optimizing the additional tag bit. A reasonable solution would contain at most 8 entries, which compared to the bitline saved from the much larger tag array is negligible.

The proposed implementation is highly cost effective, while inherently reprogrammable. It does not impose a timing constraint to the D-cache organization and can be reprogrammed in a post-manufacturing fashion. The application information is provided by the LIT and by writing values to the special control register for fixing the minimal number of tag bits. This part is performed during compile time, by inserting an instruction for writing the correct value into the register before entering the loop, and an instruction for writing the default value after exiting the loop. The content of the LIT is loaded at the same time as loading the application code into the program memory. Since there might be multiple program loops, multiple LITs might be needed. This can be achieved in a practical way by implementing the LIT as a bigger table and parts of it treated as separate smaller tables. When switching program loops, a switch between these smaller tables needs to be effected. This can be done easily in software by writing a control information to a register that selects the LIT.

Another issue that needs to be addressed is the invalidation of the cache lines before entering a program loop so as to use the valid bits for detecting the cold cache misses for the loop dataset. Prior to entering the loop that is targeted for tag optimization, the data cache content needs to be invalidated. This can be effectively achieved by software in terms of setting a control bit just before entering the loop.

Setting the value for enabling the tag bitlines, switching the LITs, and invalidating the corresponding cache part are the operations that are performed in software. Noteworthy is that all of them are performed outside the loop, thus contributing no additional instructions (and no consequent delay) inside the loop. The lookup in the LIT is performed by hardware only for the *load* instructions; therefore, again no delay is added in executing the loop or accessing the D-cache.

5. EXPERIMENTAL RESULTS

In our experimental study we evaluate the ability of our methodology to reduce energy consumption by minimizing the number of tag bits used in the D-cache. The results demonstrate the proposed approach on 16K and 32K direct-mapped D-caches. Both D-cache configurations contain 4 instructions per cache line. We utilize four numerical computation applications: *Matrix multiplication (mmul)* of matrices with size 64x64; *LU decomposition (lu)* [10] on a matrix with size 64x64; *Extrapolated Jacobi-iterative method (ej)* [10] on a 64x64 grid; and *successive over-relaxation (sor)* [11] on a matrix with size 64x64.

Figures 5 and 6 show execution and power data for the benchmarks on general-purpose 16K and 32K direct-mapped instruction caches. The first row gives the number of D-cache hits. The second row of the tables corresponds to the number of D-cache misses, while the third row presents the energy dissipated in the D-cache in mJ. In order to generate the statistics for the D-cache behavior, we utilize the SimpleScalar [12] simulator. We utilize for the cache configuration power models obtained by using the Cacti tool [13] assuming 0.35um process technology. The total energy dissipation is computed by using the execution statistics from SimpleScalar and the static power model produced by Cacti. The energy for the main memory is based on the data presented in [14] and assumes 4.95nJ per access.

To evaluate the proposed power optimization technique we have identified the application loops and computed the size of the loop dataset and consequently, the k-tag region with minimal k, in which

	mmul	sor	ej	lu
#hits	1,003,006	46,556	563,849	126,884
#misses	45,570	1072	615,151	7,937
energy	2.31	0.102	4.21	0.302

Figure 5: Access and energy (mJ) statistics for 16K DM D-cache

	mmul	sor	ej	lu
#hits	1,011,904	46,588	808,529	132,930
#misses	36,672	1040	370,471	1,891
energy	3.17	0.143	4.22	0.352

Figure 6: Access and energy (mJ) statistics for 32K DM D-cache

	mmul	sor	ej	lu
tag bits	2	0	3	2
energy	2.06	0.143	4.08	0.271
reduction	0.25	0.021	0.13	0.031
reduction(%)	10.82%	20.59%	3.08%	10.26%

Figure 7: Energy (mJ) statistics for tag optimized 16K D-cache

	mmul	sor	ej	lu
tag bits	1	0	2	1
energy	2.79	0.117	3.94	0.352
reduction	0.38	0.026	0.28	0.05
reduction(%)	11.99%	18.18%	6.64%	12.44%

Figure 8: Energy (mJ) statistics for tag optimized 32K D-cache

the dataset can be placed. The subsequent computation of the D-cache access statistics for all the references within the application loops was performed by applying manual assembly level instrumentation of the applications and effecting the corresponding modifications to the simulator. Finally, using power models for the optimized tag array we compute the energy consumed in the D-cache subsystem after optimizing the number of tag bits required for D-cache conflict identification. By utilizing Cacti, we compute the energy dissipated per tag bitline, sense amp, and comparator cell, which allows computation of the energy dissipation for a tag array with only k tag bits enabled. Figures 7 and 8 show the results achieved for the benchmarks.

The first row in these tables shows the minimal number of tag bits required for D-cache conflict identification. The *sor* benchmark requires no tag bits, since it works on a single array that fits within both 16K and 32K D-caches. The second row of these tables shows the absolute amount of energy dissipation (in mJ) for the tag optimized D-caches. The third row corresponds to the absolute energy reduction compared to general-purpose D-cache configurations from Figures 5 and 6, while the fourth row shows the percentage improvement. One can observe that the improvements vary from 3% to above 20%. Of course, the relative energy reduction is a function not only of the number of tag bits utilized, but also of the miss rate. When the cache misses are considerable, the relative improvement is diminished, since the energy dissipated in the main memory due to misses overwhelms the energy saved from removing some of the tag bits.

In case no tag bits are needed whatsoever, which is the case for *sor*, then the tag subsystem is completely turned off, including the tag decoder and wordline selection, thus further decreasing the energy dissipation. Together with the insignificant miss rate, this complete absence of tag bits underlies the significant energy improvement for the *sor* benchmark.

6. CONCLUSION

We have presented an optimization methodology for reducing the energy for the data cache subsystem of embedded processors. The proposed framework consists of compile time support for placing the application loop's dataset into the memory in such a way that the required number of tag bits for accessing the D-cache are minimized. The approach transfers certain application information to the D-cache microarchitecture and dynamically utilizes it to further eliminate the redundancy in the tag operations. An efficient reprogrammable implementation has been proposed for the presented application-specific, power optimization technique. It preserves the fundamental advantage of processor-based implementations of flexibility, design reuse, and high-volume productions.

Power consumption is a crucial quality factor in numerous modern applications. Our experimental results demonstrate the strength of the proposed approach on a set of real-life applications and suggest the viability of the power minimization technique for a large range of important applications.

7. REFERENCES

[1] M. B. Kamble and K. Ghose, "Analytical energy dissipation models for low-power caches", in *ISLPED*, pp. 143–148, August 1997.

[2] K. Ghose and M. B. Kamble, "Reducing power in superscalar processor caches using subbanking, multiple line buffers and bit-line segmentation", in *ISLPED*, pp. 70–75, August 1999.

[3] S. Manne, A. Klauser and D. Grunwald, "Pipeline gating: speculation control for energy reduction", in *25th ISCA*, pp. 132–141, June 1998.

[4] N. Bellas, I. Hajj and C. Polychronopoulos, "Using dynamic cache management techniques to reduce energy in a high-performance processor", in *ISLPED*, pp. 64–69, August 1999.

[5] J. Kin, M. Gupta and W. H. Mangione-Smith, "The filter cache: an energy efficient memory structure", in *30th MICRO*, pp. 184–193, April 2001.

[6] P. R. Panda and N. D. Dutt, "Low-power memory mapping through reducing address bus activity", *IEEE Transactions on VLSI Systems*, vol. 7, pp. 309–320, 1999.

[7] N. Vijaykrishnan, M. Kandemir, M. J. Irwin, H. S. Kim and W. Ye, "Energy-driven integrated hardware-software optimizations using SimplePower", in *27th ISCA*, pp. 95–106, June 2000.

[8] P. Petrov and A. Orailoglu, "Towards effective embedded processors in codesigns: customizable partitioned caches", in *9th CODES*, pp. 79–84, April 2001.

[9] N. Bellas, I. Hajj and C. Polychronopoulos, "A detailed, transistor-level energy model for SRAM-based caches", in *ISCAS*, pp. 198–201, June 1999.

[10] S. Nakamura, *Applied Numerical Methods with Software*, Prentice-Hall, Englewood Cliffs, N.J., 1991.

[11] M. E. Wolf and M. S. Lam, "A Data Locality Optimizing Algorithm", in *PLDI*, pp. 30–44, June 1991.

[12] D. Burger and T. M. Austin, "The SimpleScalar Tool Set, Version 2.0", Technical Report 1342, University of Wisconsin-Madison, CS Department, June 1997.

[13] G. Reinman and N. Jouppi, "An Integrated Cache Timing and Power Model", Technical report, Western Research Lab, 1999.

[14] W-T. Shiue and C. Chakrabarti, "Memory exploration for low power, embedded systems", in *36th DAC*, pp. 140–145, June 1999.

Phase Coupled Operation Assignment for VLIW Processors with Distributed Register Files

Marco Bekooij
Philips Research
Prof. Holstlaan 4
Eindhoven, The Netherlands

Jochen Jess
University of Technology
Den Dolech 2
Eindhoven, The Netherlands

Jef van Meerbergen
Philips Research
Prof. Holstlaan 4
Eindhoven, The Netherlands

1. ABSTRACT

The ever increasing complexity of signal processing applications and the desire to reduce the time to market demands efficient compilation techniques for programmable Digital Signal Processors (DSPs). Because the instruction sets of VLIW processors are more regular and orthogonal then the instruction sets of the traditional DSPs, they tend to be more compiler friendly. However in order to improve the maximal clock frequency, the power efficiency and the code density, several register files are used in the newer generation of VLIW processors instead of just one large register file. The use of several register files and partial connected networks leads, for example, to the problem that a result stored in a register file can not be accessed by all the functional units in the processor. This makes the assignment of operations to functional units a difficult task for the compiler.

This paper describes the constraint analysis based operation assignment techniques intended to deal with processors with distributed register files and partially connected networks. The assignment techniques have been implemented in our code generation tool FACTS [8]. This tool is intended for the generation of an operation assignment, a register binding and a schedule of folded loops that satisfy the specified timing constraints. Our approach is based on satisfaction of constraints which makes it different from the optimisation based operation assignment techniques [4] [2] [3] which are known from literature. The operation assignment technique is based on the modeling of the assignment search space in a conflict graph. Pruning of this conflict graph prevents decisions that inevitably lead to solutions that do not satisfy the timing constraints. If after pruning infeasibility is detected, backtracking of assignment decisions is performed. In order to obtain a tight coupling between the assignment phase and the schedule phase information is derived from the conflict graph which is used to prune the schedule search space and information from the schedule search space is incorporated in the conflict graph. Automatic insertion of copy operations for moving intermediate values from one register file to another register files is not supported. However the use of a shared global bus in the processor guarantees that at least one direct communication path from a producing functional unit to a consuming functional unit exists and therefore the use of copy operations is not necessary.

ISSS'01, October 1-3, 2001, Montréal, Québec, Canada.

2. INTRODUCTION

In this section a motivating operation assignment example is described. Also the target processor family for which our operation assignment techniques are intended is defined. At the end of this section it is described how the assignment techniques are incorporated in our code generation tool FACTS.

2.1 Motivating example

In Figure 1 a Data Flow Graph (DFG) and a data-path of a processor is shown, which will be used to illustrate some aspects that make operation assignment a difficult task for the compiler. The shared resources in the data-path of this processor are the functional units (FUs), the registers in the register files, the connections in the connection network and the input ports and output ports of these building blocks. These resources can be used in parallel and are controlled by VLIW-instructions. In order to make the example easy to understand, the number of resources in the processor, and the number of operations and data-dependencies in the DFG, are kept small.

Assignment of the operations in the DFG to the functional units of the target processor should be done in such a way that a communication channel exists. A communication channel is a path from the output port of the functional unit that computes the result to the input port of the functional unit that uses this result. This path passes the connection network and a register file. For the DFG and the architecture in this example, the constraint that there must exist a communication path from the producing FU to the consuming FU, has consequences for the assignment of the operations $n0$ and $n1$ to the functional units. For example operation $n1$ must be assigned to FU_2 if operation $n0$ is assigned to FU_2. In the case that the DFG is folded and both operations $n0$ and $n1$ are executed in the same cycle then operation $n0$ can only be assigned to FU_1 because operation $n1$ must be executed on FU_2.

The basic block to be assigned and scheduled is represented by a DFG, which is defined as follows:

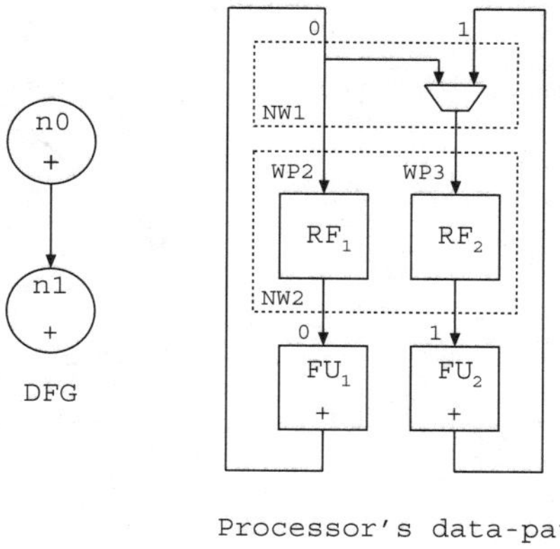

Figure 1: A example DFG and the data-path of the target VLIW-processor.

Definition 1: (Data Flow Graph). A data flow graph DFG is a triple $(V, E_d \cup E_s, w)$

- V is the set of vertices (operations),
- $E_d \subseteq V \times V$ is the set of data precedence edges,
- $E_s \subseteq V \times V$ is the set of sequence precedence edges, and
- $w : E_d \cup E_s \rightarrow Z$ is a function describing the timing delay (in clock cycles) associated with each precedence edge.

When an operation in the DFG is executed on an FU it consumes intermediate values via the input ports of this FU. In the case the input ports of the FU are not equivalent then the port via which the intermediate value must be consumed is specified. If the output ports of an FU are not equivalent the also the output port via which the intermediate value must be produced is specified.

The operation assignment problem that is addressed can be stated as follows:

Problem 1: Given a DFG and a port specification, find an assignment of operations to resources and intermediate values to register files in the target processor architecture such that a schedule can be constructed in which the specified global throughput and schedule length constraints are respected and, if required, loop-folding [5] is applied.

2.2 Processor template

The addressed operation assignment techniques are intended to be applied in a retargetable compiler for a family of DSP cores derived from the template shown in Figure 2.

The for operation assignment relevant characteristics of this template are:

- A distributed Register File (RF) architecture,
- Several potentially equivalent Functional Units (FU) that can execute an operation of a certain type,
- A partially connected Connection Network (CN) between the outputs of the unit clusters and the write ports of register files. This network may contain shared busses,
- An orthogonal instruction encoding.

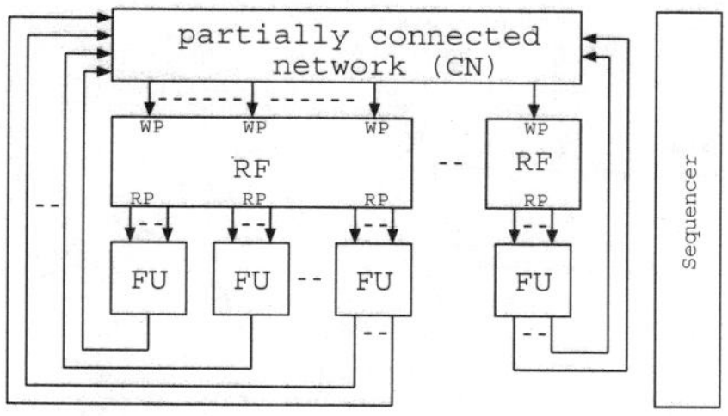

Figure 2: Target digital signal processor template

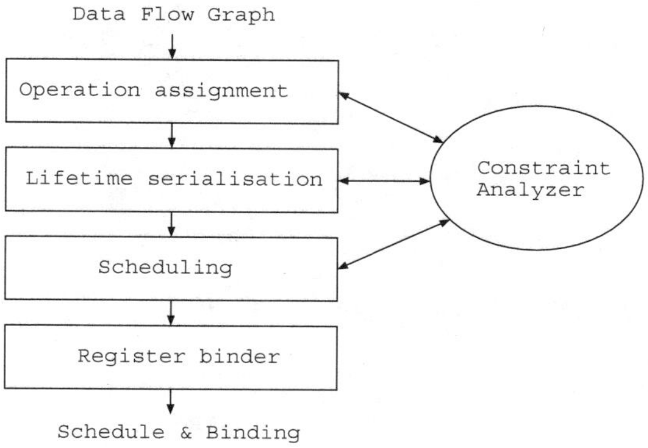

Figure 3: FACTS: Code generation phases

2.3 Code generation phases

The code generation techniques has been implemented in our research tool FACTS. Code generation takes place in an operation assignment phase, a register serialisation phase, a scheduling phase, and a register binding phase (see Figure 3). These code generation phases are re-targeted to a specific processor instance by means of a machine description file. During the operation assignment phase, operations are assigned to functional units. During the lifetime serialisation phase, operations are serialised in such a way that the register file capacity constraints are satisfied after scheduling [6]. During the scheduling phase the start times of operations are determined. After scheduling the register binder selects for every intermediate value a register in which it will be stored.

During the operation assignment phase it is for every operation in the data-flow graph decided, on which functional unit in the processor it will be executed. After an operation assignment decision is taken by the *operation assigner* (see Figure 4) the consequences of this decision are evaluated by the constraint analyzer. Back-tracking is performed in the case that the constraint analyzer detects infeasibility, where after another assignment decision is taken. In the case the constraint analyzer does not detect infeasibility the next operation is assigned till every operation is assigned to a functional unit.

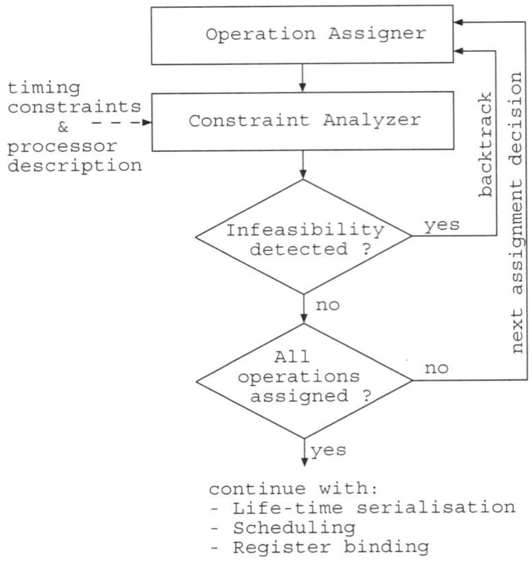

Figure 4: Operation assignment flow-diagram.

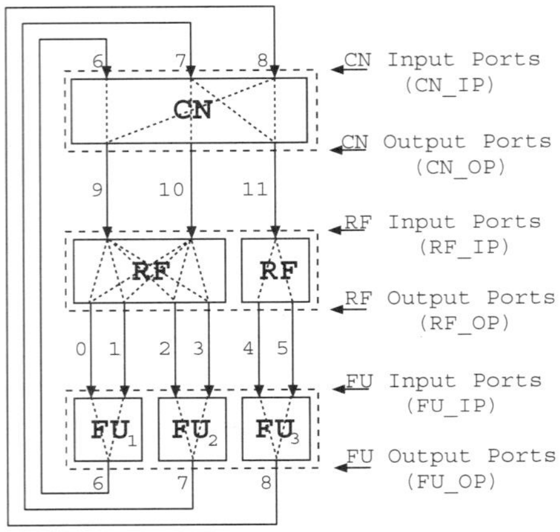

Figure 5: VLIW-Processor instance.

3. ASSIGNMENT SEARCH SPACE MODELING

Our operation assignment search space model is based on the notion that a processor architecture can be seen as a collection of networks (the dashed boxes in Figure 5). The output of a network in the processor is connected to the input of another network in the processor. The selection of a network input port determines the output ports through which potentially a result can be produced. The other way around is also true, that is, the selection of an output port through which a result must be produced determines through which ports the input data can be provided. These mutual dependencies between input ports and output ports can be modeled in a conflict graph. This conflict-graph is used to find an assignment of operations in a DFG to the functional units such that there exist a communication path, as specified by data dependency edges in the DFG, through the connection network and the register files in the target processor.

Figure 6 depicts a network in which there does not exist a connection between input port 0 and output port 3. This

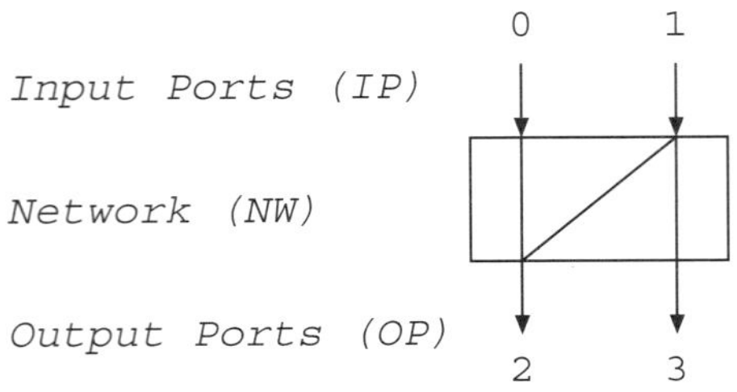

Figure 6: Network in which no connection exist between input port 0 and output port 3.

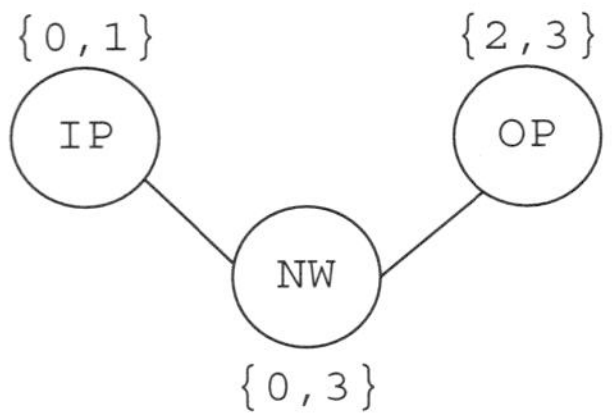

Figure 7: Conflict graph in which the same restrictions are expressed as in Figure 6.

has the consequence that if port 0 is chosen as input port then output port 3 is not reachable and vice versa. This restriction is modeled in the conflict graph shown in Figure 7. The IP and OP node in this graph are associated with respectively the input ports and the output ports of the network. The numbers in the sets next to the nodes indicate the ports that could be selected if there are no additional restrictions which is only the case if the network is fully connected. These numbers correspond also to the colors that potentially can be assigned to the nodes by the coloring algorithm. The third node in the graph, which is labeled with NW, enforces the restriction that the choice to color IP node with color 0 has as a consequence that OP node cannot be colored with color 3. All other combinations of colors can be assigned by a coloring algorithm. The restriction on the colors that can be assigned to the IP and OP node is enforced by the NW node in the following way. In the case the IP node is given color 1 then the edge between the IP and the NW node enforces that color 1 cannot be assigned to the NW node. The NW node must therefore be colored with 3. If the NW node is colored with 3 then the edge between the NW node and the OP node enforces that color 2 is the only color that can be assigned to the OP node. In a similar way the assignment of color 3 to the OP node has as consequence that color 0 cannot be assigned to the IP node. The NW nodes can be used in the same way to model in a conflict graph restrictions imposed by networks with an arbitrary interconnection pattern between a number of input ports and output ports. A NW node is needed for every combination of an input port and an output port for which there is no connection in the network. Therefore, the worst case number of needed NW nodes in the conflict graph per network equals $\#IP \times \#OP$ where #IP and #OP are respectively the number of input-, and output ports of the network.

A conflict graph can be used, as described above, to derive a valid assignment for the operations in the DFG and

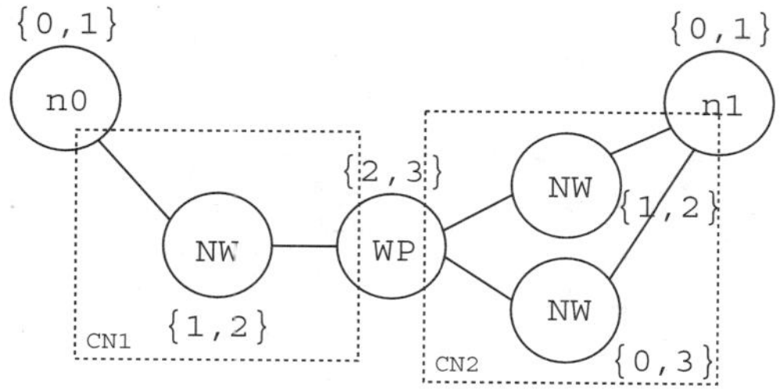

Figure 8: Conflict graph in which the communication paths in the architecture are modeled.

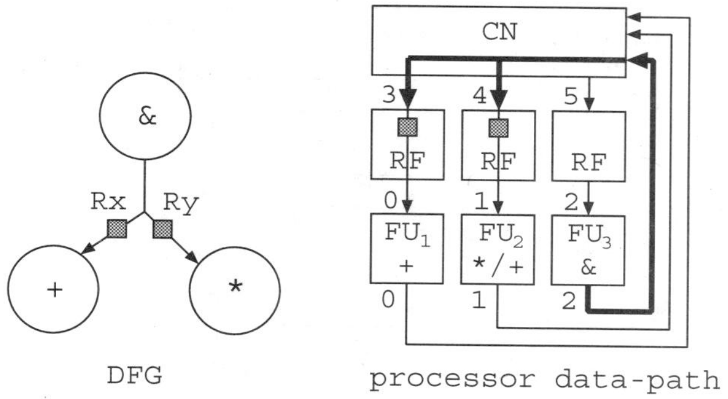

Figure 9: Multi-casting of an intermediate result to two register files

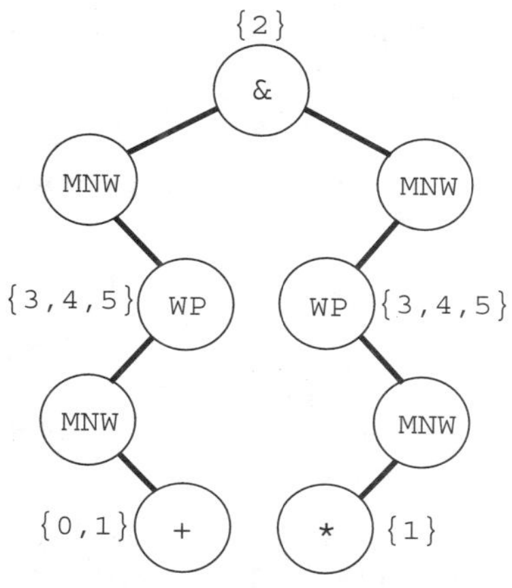

Figure 10: The conflict graph in which the communication paths from the producing operations to the consuming operations are modeled.

the processor shown in Figure 1. The nodes $n0$ and $n1$ in the conflict graph shown in Figure 8 correspond to operations $n0$ and $n1$ in the DFG. Every number in the depicted sets above these nodes correspond to one of the two output ports of network 2 (NW2) in Figure 1. Because both ports are connected to only one functional unit these numbers correspond also to a specific functional unit. The data produced by operation $n0$ should, according to the data edge in the DFG, be consumed by operation $n1$. A value produced by the functional unit on which $n0$ is executed should pass network 1 to a write port (WP) of a register file. In the conflict graph there is a node labeled with WP that corresponds to this write port. The write ports in the processor are numbered 2 and 3 which are also the numbers in the set above this WP node. The NW nodes in the conflict graph model that certain connections do not exist between the input ports and the output ports of NW1 or between the input ports and the output ports of network 2 (NW2). The existence of a valid coloring of this graph which only makes use of the colors in the sets, reveals that there exist an assignment which respects the constrains imposed by the interconnect. From the colors assigned by the graph coloring algorithm the assignment of the operations can be derived.

4. MULTI-CASTING

In Figure 9 a DFG is shown in which a value produced by an operation, is consumed by two operations. If these consuming operations are executed on functional units that do not have access to the same register file then the intermediate result must be stored in two register files. We assume that the target processor supports multi-casting that is the storage of an intermediate result that is produced by an functional unit in more than one register file in the same cycle. Multi-casting becomes a decision problem for the compiler if the number of register files in which an intermediate result must be stored depends on the assignment of the consuming operations. In that case the number of occupied register file write ports depends on the assignment of the consuming operations to the functional units. For example, if the consuming operations in Figure 9 are assigned to functional unit FU1 and FU2, multi-casting must be applied and two write ports are used while if both operations are assigned to functional unit FU2 the intermediate value must be stored once in the register file and only one write port is used. Whether multi-casting should be applied or not depends on the global timing constraints and the data-path of the processor.

Multi-casting is handled in our operation assignment technique as follows. In the conflict graph it is modeled that for every consumption of an intermediate result there must exist a connection between the output of the producing functional unit and the write port of the register file from which the intermediate value is consumed. The conflict graph for the DFG and architecture of Figure 9 is shown in Figure 10. The MNW nodes and the tick edges in this figure are used as short-hand notation and represent the necessary NW nodes with edges.

Care is taken that no conflicts are added between the write ports involved in multi-casting. This way the write port nodes in the conflict graph can get the same color which corresponds to the situation where both write port usage are assigned to the same write port in the processor. Only in the case that after pruning it is detected that different write ports must be used then the resource usage of the write ports is taken into account by timing constraint analysis.

5. SHARED GLOBAL BUS

In Figure 11a a DFG and a data path of a target processor is shown. In this processor a partial connected network is applied that connects the outputs of functional units to a write port of a register file. The DFG in this figure can not be executed on the target processor. The reason is that the multiply operation must be executed on FU2 and the

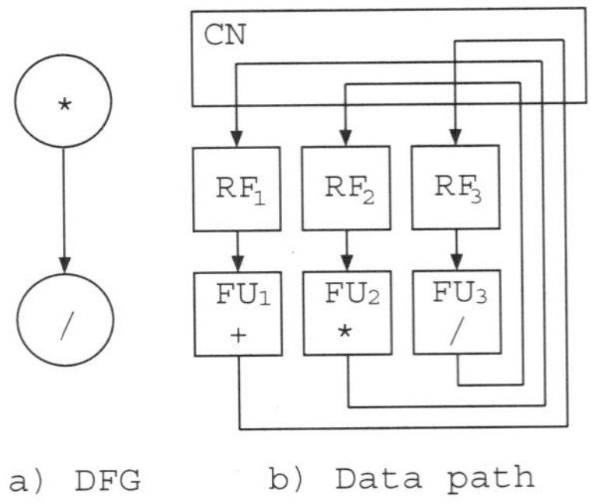

Figure 11: DFG (a) which can not be executed without an additional copy operation on the data path (b) of the target processor.

Figure 12: A DFG in which a copy operation is inserted such that it can be executed on the processor in Figure 11.

division operation on FU3. Therefore the result produced by FU2 must be stored in register file RF3 such that FU3 can read this result. However there is no connection in the network such that the value produced by FU2 can be stored in the register file RF3.

A solution is to modify the DFG by inserting an copy operation as shown in Figure 12. This copy operation is, for example, implemented as an addition with zero. It is used to copy the intermediate value from RF2 to RF3.

However the use of a copy operations was only possible because FU2 can execute operations that implement copying of an intermediate value without changing it. Also the insertion of the copy operation introduces latency and uses a functional unit during a cycle which can lead to violation of the global timing constraints.

An alternative for the use of copy operations is the use of a global shared bus as is shown in Figure 13. Via this bus the result produced by a functional unit can be stored in every register file. By applying multi-casting it is also possible to store the same intermediate value in several register files, if required.

Care should be taken that the global bus does not become the bottleneck that limits the computational performance of the processor. Therefore a network should be applied that contains an appropriate amount of other connections.

6. PRUNING AND PHASE-COUPLING

In order to prevent operation assignment decisions that inevitably lead to infeasibility, the colors in the sets of the nodes in the conflict graph are pruned. Pruning algorithms are used to remove the colors from the sets in the conflict graph, that given the colors that can be assigned to adjacent vertices, cannot be assigned to the vertex under consideration. A simple example of a pruning rule is that if only one color can be assigned to a vertex, then this color cannot be assigned to any adjacent vertex.

Pruning is also applied to establish a tight coupling between assignment and scheduling. If after pruning to a node only one color can be assigned, then the corresponding operation in the DFG can be executed by only one specific resource in the processor. If an operation can only be executed on one specific resource out of a set of equivalent resources in the processor's data-path then an additional resource usage is added in the internal DFG representation. An example of how the resource usage of one adder out of 4 adders is specialized to a specific adder in the data-path is shown in Figure 14. The dashed edges in this figure are sequence edges to enforce that the resource usage $+_A$ is scheduled in the same cycle as the addition. The additional resource usage is evaluated by the BSG constraint analysis technique [7] and potentially results in a reduction of the schedule search space.

In the case the constraint analyzer determines that two operations of the same type must be executed in the same cycle then an edge between the corresponding nodes in the conflict graph is added. This will guarantee that these nodes will be assigned a unique color which corresponds to the assignment of only one resource usage (e.g. an operation) to a resource (e.g. a functional unit). By adding these edges in the conflict graph, information from the schedule search space is modeled in the assignment search space.

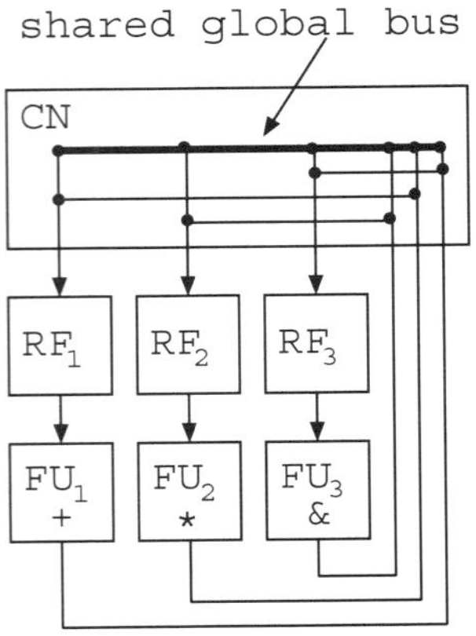

Figure 13: Processor with a shared global communication bus which guarantees the existence of a connections such that copy operations are not required.

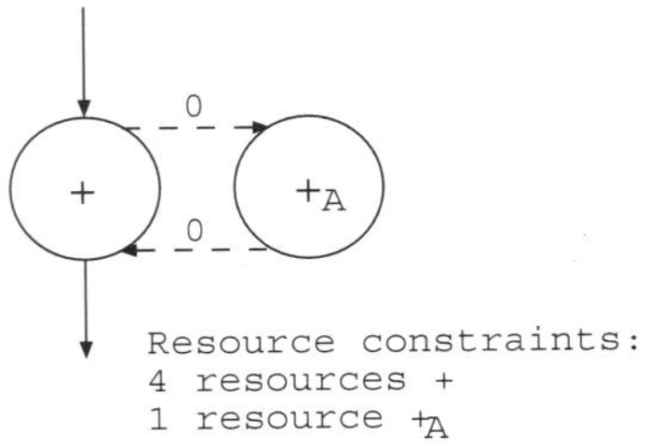

Figure 14: Resource usage specialization modeled in an internal DFG representation.

7. RESULTS

The template of the target architecture is shown in Figure 15 and the obtained results in Table 1. This table shows

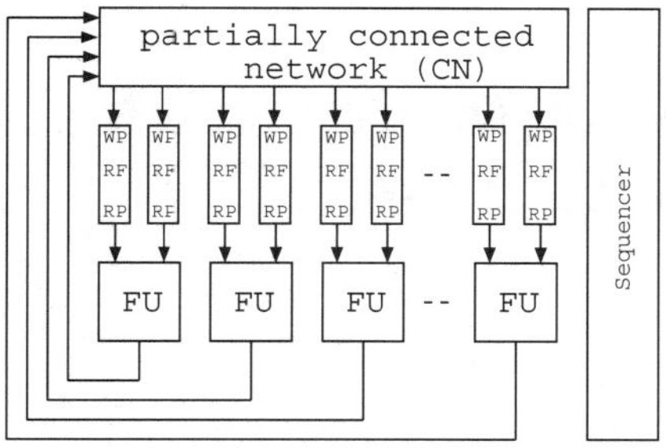

Figure 15: Template of the target VLIW-processor architecture.

no	Example	V_a	E_d	II lb.	II	L lb.	L	d.	b.
1	Fir	7	9	3	3	4	4	0	0
2	Fir	7	9	2	2	4	4	0	0
3	Fir	7	9	1	1	4	4	0	0
4	Sum	9	10	3	3	5	6	0	1
5	Biquad	15	19	7	7	8	8	0	0
6	Biquad	15	19	4	4	8	8	10	0
7	Mac-loop	25	31	9	9	10	10	0	0
8	Mac-loop	25	31	3	3	4	4	24	0
9	FFT	49	60	12	12	21	21	0	0
10	Fir	7	9	3	3	4	4	0	0
11	Biquad	15	19	7	10	8	13	0	30
12	Mac-loop	13	17	2	2	4	4	11	3
13	Mac-loop	13	17	1	1	3	3	5	2

Table 1: Operation assignment and scheduling results for inner-loops.

the number of operations V_a and data edges E_d in the DFG, the lower bound (lb.) estimates of the Initiation Interval (II) and Latency (L) and the obtained II and L. The lower bound estimates assume a fully connected processor network. The last two columns contain the number of assignment decisions and backtracks. In experiment 1,2,3 the number of unit clusters was increased such that an II of one was obtained. Experiment 6 and 8 shows that a relatively large number of decisions is needed to obtain an operation assignment. In experiment 10,11,12,13 a significant number of connections in the connection network of the processor were removed which causes an increases in the number of backtracks to obtain a feasible result.

The results in Table 1 indicate that the use of a strongly distribute register file architecture hardly effect the throughput of folded loops. The throughput is only reduced in the case a significant number of connections are remove from the connection network.

The results were obtained by appling FACTS in the A|RT designer environment of Frontier Design [1]. In order to evaluate only the effect of the use of a partially connected network and a distributed register file architecture on the schedule quality the number of registers in the register files were not taken into account in these experiments.

To obtain a compilation time of less than 10 seconds on a 600 MHz Pentium processor for our benchmark set, the assignment conflict graph was not colored but only pruned after every assignment decision. Backtracking was performed in the cases that after pruning it was detected that not any color could be assigned to a certain node in the conflict graph.

The effect on the schedule search space is taken into account during assignment, but because the schedule search space is only pruned there is no guarantee that after assignment a schedule, that satisfies the timing constraints, indeed exists. However our experience is that often a schedule does exist. This was also the case for the examples in Table 1.

8. FUTURE WORK

In the near future the effect of the number of registers and the number of read and write ports of the register files on the operation assignment and schedule quality will be evaluated. Techniques to reduce the size of the conflict graph will be implemented in order to reduce the compilation time for DFGs with more than 100 operations and processors with more than 20 functional units.

9. CONCLUSIONS

This paper describes how operation assignment is performed of potentially folded loops on VLIW processors with a distributed register file architecture and partially connected network under tight timing and resource constraints. Our method is based on the modeling of the assignment search space in a conflict graph. A tight coupling with the scheduling phase is obtained by the derivation of the usage of additional resources from a pruned conflict graph. Multi-casting of intermediate results can be modeled in the conflict graph and exploited by this operation assignment technique. The use of copy operations to move data values from one register file to another file is currently not supported but also not necessary in the case a global bus in the processor is applied.

10. REFERENCES

[1] *Frontier Design, http://www.frontierd.com.*

[2] S. Bashford and R. Leupers. Constraint driven code selection for fixed-point dsps. Proceedings Design Automation Conference.

[3] E. de Kock. *Video Signal Processor Mapping.* PhD thesis, Eindhoven University of Technology, 1995.

[4] J. Ellis. *Bulldog: A Compiler for VLIW Architectures.* ACM Doctor Dissertation Awards, MIT, Cambridge, 1986.

[5] G. Goossens. *Optimisation Techniques for Automated Synthesis of Application-Specific Signal-Processing Architectures.* PhD thesis, Katholieke Universiteit Leuven, 1989.

[6] B. Mesman, C. Alba-Pinto, and K. van Eijk. Efficient scheduling of dsp code on processors with distributed register files. San Jose, 1999. Int. Symp. on System Synthesis.

[7] A. Timmer. *From design space exploration to code generation.* PhD thesis, Eindhoven University of Technology, 1995.

[8] K. van Eijk, B. Mesman, C. Alba-Pinto, Q. Zhao, M. Bekooij, J. van Meerbergen, and J. Jess. Constraint analysis for code generation: Basic techniques and applications in facts. volume 5. ACM Transactions on Design Automation of Electronic Systems, 2000.

An Energy Efficient Rate Selection Algorithm for Voltage Quantized Dynamic Voltage Scaling

Lama H. Chandrasena
Dept. of E & E Engineering
Adelaide University
Adelaide, SA 5005, Australia
lama@eleceng.adelaide.edu.au

Priyadarshana Chandrasena
Dept. of E & E Engineering
Adelaide University
Adelaide, SA 5005, Australia
vpc@eleceng.adelaide.edu.au

Michael J. Liebelt
Dept. of E & E Engineering
Adelaide University
Adelaide, SA 5005, Australia
mike@eleceng.adelaide.edu.au

Abstract— This paper presents a highly energy efficient alternative algorithm to the conventional workload averaging technique for voltage quantized dynamic voltage scaling. This algorithm incorporates the strengths of the conventional workload averaging technique and our previously proposed Rate Selection Algorithm, resulting in higher energy savings while minimizing the buffer size requirement and improving the overall system stability by minimizing the number of voltage transitions. Our experimental work using the Forward Mapped Inverse Discrete Cosine Transform computation (FMIDCT) as the variable workload computation, nine 300-frame MPEG-2 video sequences as the test data, and a 4-level voltage quantization shows that our algorithm produces better energy savings in all test cases when compared to the workload averaging technique, and the maximum energy saving for the test cases was 23%.

1. INTRODUCTION

In CMOS circuits energy dissipation for processing a data sample is given by [2]:

$$E = nCV_{dd}^2 \tag{1}$$

where, n is the number of clock cycles per sample period, C is the averaged switched capacitance per clock period, and V_{dd} is the supply voltage. Due to this quadratic dependence of energy on voltage, supply voltage reduction is the most effective method of energy minimization. However, a reduction in supply voltage increases the circuit delays as shown by Equation 2[6]:

$$T_d = \frac{C_L V_{dd}}{\mu C_{ox}(W/L)(V_{dd} - V_t)^2} \tag{2}$$

where, T_d is the delay, V_{dd} is the supply voltage, C_L is the total node capacitance, μ is the mobility, C_{ox} is the oxide capacitance, V_t is the threshold voltage, and W/L is the width to length ratio of transistors.

ISSS '01 October 1-3, 2001, Montréal, Québec, Canada.

In highly sequential data-dependent computations, such as iterative variable workload computations, an increase in delay is acceptable provided the worst-case time constraint is not violated [6]. For such computations, the data samples with sub-optimal workload values can be processed at dynamically scaled down voltages without incurring a performance loss. As a result, the overall energy dissipation for the computation can be significantly reduced.

Even though the minimum energy dissipation in dynamic voltage scaling (DVS) is achieved with continuous voltage levels, it is impossible to prepare a stable supply voltage in such systems [3]; as an alternative, a small number of voltage quantizations has been proposed [2]. If the voltage can be dithered during a sample period, a 4-level voltage quantization produces a very good approximation to the continuous voltage level DVS. However, voltage dithering technique introduces additional voltage transitions, approximately doubling the total number of voltage transitions in the system.

The use of buffers and workload averaging has been shown to significantly improve energy savings in DVS [2]. The *Rate Selection Algorithm (RSA)* [1] demonstrates an alternative technique to the conventional workload averaging technique. This algorithm is specifically developed to minimize energy dissipation in voltage quantized DVS. This algorithm uses a single buffer, and where possible selects rates that are equal to quantized rate values. At quantized rate values the energy dissipation of voltage quantized DVS equals the energy dissipation of continuous voltage level DVS. However, the experimental results of [1] indicate that *RSA* only produces better energy savings than the conventional workload averaging technique if voltage is *not* dithered.

In this paper we present an improved rate selection algorithm named *Average-based Quantized Rate Selection (AQRS)* that produces better energy savings than the conventional workload averaging technique [2]. This algorithm uses the strengths of both the workload averaging technique and *RSA* in determining the rate. Moreover, this algorithm takes advantage of the convex nature of the energy versus rate relationship to improve energy savings by giving a higher priority to smaller quantized rates in its rate selection process. As a result the algorithm produces better energy savings, uses half the buffer size requirement of the conventional workload averaging technique, and improves overall system stability by eliminating the need for voltage dithering. To illustrate the performance of our algorithm we used nine 300-frame MPEG-2 video sequences as test data, the Forward Mapped Inverse Discrete Cosine Transform [4] as the variable workload computation, and a 4-level voltage quantization.

The rest of the paper is organized as follows. Section 2 presents the energy model, and section 3 describes the proposed *AQRS* algorithm. The experimental setup is given in section 4, and section 5 presents the results. Finally, section 6 presents the concluding remarks.

2. ENERGY MODEL

Combining Equations 1 and 2, energy per data sample is given by equation 3 [2]:

$$E(r) = E_0 r\left[\frac{V_t}{V_0} + \frac{r}{2} + \sqrt{r\frac{V_t}{V_0} + (\frac{r}{2})^2}\right]^2 \quad (3)$$

where, E_0 is a scaling factor with units of energy, $r = f/f_{ref}$ is the normalized processing rate ($0 \leq r \leq 1$), $V_0 = (V_{ref} - V_t)^2/V_{ref}$, V_t is the threshold voltage, and f_{ref} is the frequency at maximum voltage V_{ref}.

Using Equation 3, the normalized energy and rate relationship for the continuous voltage levels model and voltage quantized model using a 4-level voltage quantization corresponding to normalized rates of 0.25, 0.5, 0.75, and 1.0 is shown in Figure 1.

The ideal continuous voltage levels model requires the availability of unique supply voltages for all rate values. However, in voltage quantized DVS only a fixed number of quantized rates (voltage levels) are available. Therefore processing samples with rate values that do not equal to quantized rates can be handled by two different techniques:

The first technique is to process the sample at the next highest quantized rate. For example, if a sample has a normalized rate value of $r = 0.6$, the sample will be processed at $r = 0.75$ using the quantization shown in Figure 1. This technique is known as DVS *without* voltage dithering, and the energy dissipation for this model is represented by the *stair-step* curve in Figure 1.

The second technique processes part of the sample at one quantization and the remainder at another quantization. For example, the same sample above with the normalized rate value of $r = 0.6$ using this model would have 40% of the sample period processed at $r = 0.75$ and the remainder (60%) at $r = 0.5$. This technique is known as DVS *with* voltage dithering, and the energy dissipation for this model is represented by the *straight-line* curve in Figure 1.

As Figure 1 shows, the voltage dithering technique significantly improves the energy savings. However, these energy savings are achieved at the cost of increased voltage transitions in the system (approximately one additional transition per sample period), degrading the overall stability of the DVS system.

Finally, Figure 2 shows the energy difference between the voltage quantized DVS *with* voltage dithering and *without* voltage dithering, and the continuous voltage levels DVS.

3. AVERAGE-BASED QUANTIZED RATE SELECTION

3.1 AQRS Algorithm

The *RSA* algorithm in [1] uses buffered workload to where possible select rates that are equal to quantized rates. As Figure 2 demonstrates, the energy difference between the voltage quantized model and the continuous voltage levels model approaches zero at quantized rates. Although the *RSA* algorithm effectively selects the smallest quantized rate that always clears at least one buffer location, the experimental results demonstrate that the algorithm always produces a small percentage of rates corresponding to the highest quantized rate ($r = 1.0$ normalized). Because of the convex nature of the energy versus rate curve, even a small percentage of rates at the highest quantization can be detrimental to the overall energy savings. For example, the number of samples that can be processed at each quantization of Figure 1 for the same energy dissipation is given by Equation 4:

$$1 \cdot E_{r=1} = \begin{cases} 16.87 \cdot E_{r=0.25} \\ 4.49 \cdot E_{r=0.5} \\ 1.91 \cdot E_{r=0.75} \end{cases} \quad (4)$$

where, $n \cdot E_{r=i}$ represents the number of samples n and the normalized energy at normalized rate value of $r = i$. As this equation demonstrates, the comparative energy of a single sample processed at the highest quantized rate is

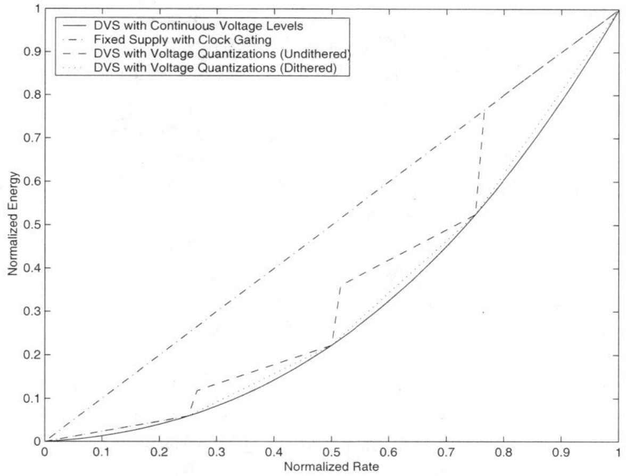

Figure 1: Energy vs. Rate

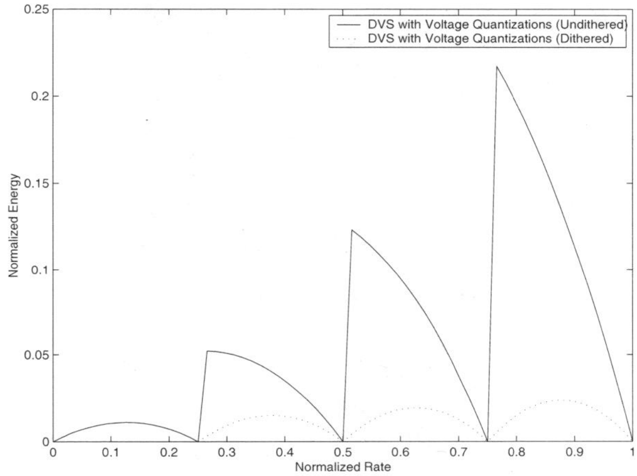

Figure 2: Energy Difference in Voltage Quantized Dynamic Voltage Scaling

approximately equivalent to 17 samples processed at $r = 0.25$, 5 samples at $r = 0.5$, and 2 samples at $r = 0.75$.

The *AQRS* algorithm uses the average buffered workload to estimate the required rate, and then selects the smallest quantized rate value that is sufficient to process the average buffered workload and at the same time empty one or more buffer locations. Because of this policy, the algorithm minimizes the rate values at the highest voltage quantization. Similar to the *RSA* algorithm, the *AQRS* algorithm prevents any buffer over-flow or under-flow conditions because the rate values are always selected from the actual total buffered workload.

The *AQRS* algorithm calculates the rate values in two steps: the first step calculates the average buffered workload (Equations 5 and 6), and the second step selects the smallest quantized rate value (Equation 7). The rate selection policy identifies the quantized rate r that is realistic ($\leq w_t$), clears the first buffer location ($\geq w[n]$), and satisfies the estimated average rate ($\geq r_a$). Equation 7 shows the details of the rate selection policy.

$$w_t = \sum_{k=0}^{B-1} w[n-k] \tag{5}$$

$$r_a = \frac{w_t}{B} \tag{6}$$

$$r = \begin{cases} r_0 & \text{if } w_t \geq r_0 \ \& \ w[n] \leq r_0 \ \& \ r_a \leq r_0 \\ r_1 & \text{if } w_t \geq r_1 \ \& \ w[n] \leq r_1 \ \& \ r_a \leq r_1 \\ \ldots\ldots & \\ r_{p-2} & \text{if } w_t \geq r_{p-2} \ \& \ w[n] \leq r_{p-2} \ \& \ r_a \leq r_{p-2} \\ r_{p-1} & \text{if } w_t \geq r_{p-1} \\ w_t & \text{otherwise} \end{cases} \tag{7}$$

where, w_t is the total buffered workload, r_a is the integer portion of the average buffered workload, r is the selected rate value, B is the buffer size, $p (\geq 2)$ is the number of quantized rates (voltage levels), and $r_0, .., r_{p-1}$ are quantized rate values ($0 < r_0 < r_1 < .. < r_{p-2} < r_{p-1}$). If the rate values are normalized $r_{p-1} = 1$.

3.2 Sample Calculations

Figure 3 demonstrates how the *AQRS* algorithm calculates the rate r for a hypothetical data sequence. For this example a buffer size of 3 and a 4-level voltage quantization is used. The four normalized quantized rates are 0.25, 0.5, 0.75, and 1.0, corresponding to 16, 32, 48, and 64 non-zero coefficients, respectively, for the FMIDCT computation [4]. The Equations 5, 6, and 7 modified to suit this example are given by Equations 8, 9, and 10, respectively.

In the zeroth sample period, the first workload (15) is buffered into buffer location $w[n-2]$ and Equation 8 produces 15 as the total buffered workload w_t for this period. Next, the evaluation of Equation 9 produces 5 as the average rate r_a for this sample period. Since w_t is less than the smallest quantized rate (16), all the *if* conditions in the Equation 10 are evaluated to *FALSE* and the *OTHERWISE* part of the *if* condition sets the rate r to w_t ($r = 15$). In the first sample period, the w_t is 16, r_a is 5, and $w[n]$ is 0, so Equation 10 evaluates to *TRUE* for the first *if* condition and hence produces 16 as the rate. Similarly in the second, third, fourth and fifth sample periods, the algorithm produces rates of 32, 32, 48, and 48, respectively.

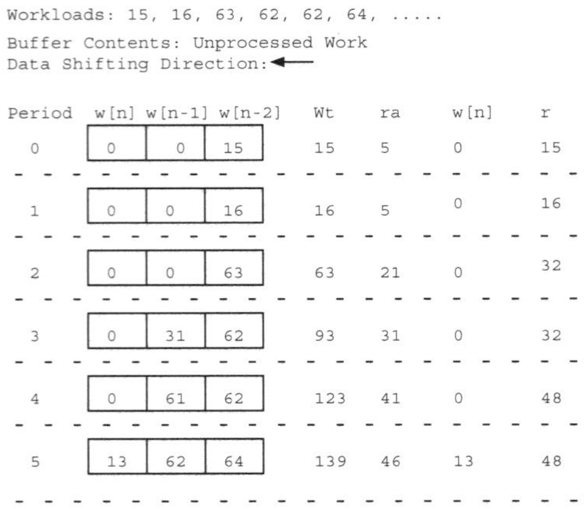

Figure 3: AQRS Algorithm Sample Calculations

$$w_t = \sum_{k=0}^{2} w[n-k] \tag{8}$$

$$r_a = \frac{w_t}{3} \tag{9}$$

$$r = \begin{cases} 16 & \text{if } w_t \geq 16 \ \& \ w[n] \leq 16 \ \& \ r_a \leq 16 \\ 32 & \text{if } w_t \geq 32 \ \& \ w[n] \leq 32 \ \& \ r_a \leq 32 \\ 48 & \text{if } w_t \geq 48 \ \& \ w[n] \leq 48 \ \& \ r_a \leq 48 \\ 64 & \text{if } w_t \geq 64 \\ w_t & \text{otherwise} \end{cases} \tag{10}$$

3.3 Complexity

The *AQRS* algorithm can be implemented by a constant number $(B-1)$ of *add* operations, a single *divide* operation, and a data-dependent number of *compare* (n_c) and *and* (n_a) operations. The constant B is the buffer size, and n_c and n_a are defined by Equations 11 and 12, respectively.

$$2 \leq n_c \leq 3p - 2 \tag{11}$$

$$2 \leq n_a \leq 2(p-1) \tag{12}$$

where, p is the number of quantized voltage levels. A comparison of the variation of operational complexity for *AQRS* algorithm, *RSA* algorithm, and the workload averaging technique as a function of buffer size is shown in Figure 4. Since the number of operations for *AQRS* algorithm and *RSA* algorithm are workload dependent, an upper and a lower bound for the number of operations have been plotted.

4. EXPERIMENTAL SETUP

To demonstrate the energy savings achievable with the *AQRS* algorithm we compare its energy dissipation results with the results of the conventional workload averaging technique [2]. For the energy analysis we use the Forward Mapped Inverse Discrete Cosine Transform (FMIDCT) algorithm [4] as the data-dependent computation and nine MPEG-2 compressed video sequences as test data. The video sequences

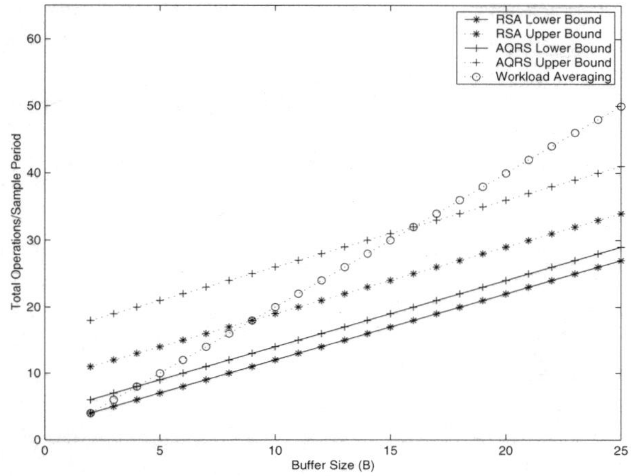

Figure 4: Operational Complexity vs. Buffer Size

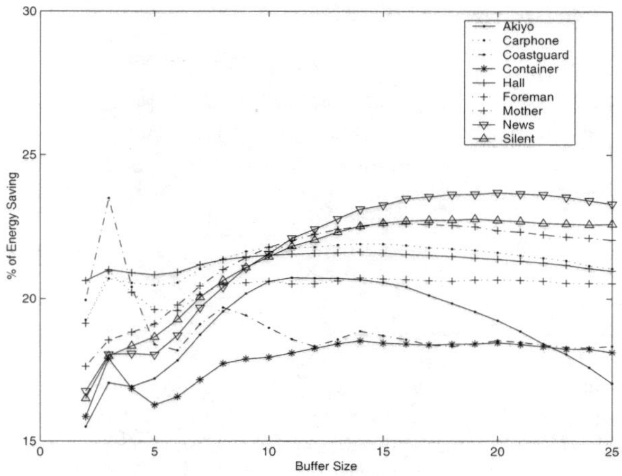

Figure 5: Energy Savings Comparison with Averaging (Undithered)

Parameter	Value
Frames in a GOP	15
I/P Frame Distance	3
Horizontal Picture Size (Pixels)	176
Vertical Picture Size (Pixels)	144
Frame Rate	30 frames/sec
Bit Rate	4 Mbits/sec
Profile	Main
Level	Low
Chroma Format	4:2:0

Table 1: MPEG-2 Compression Parameters

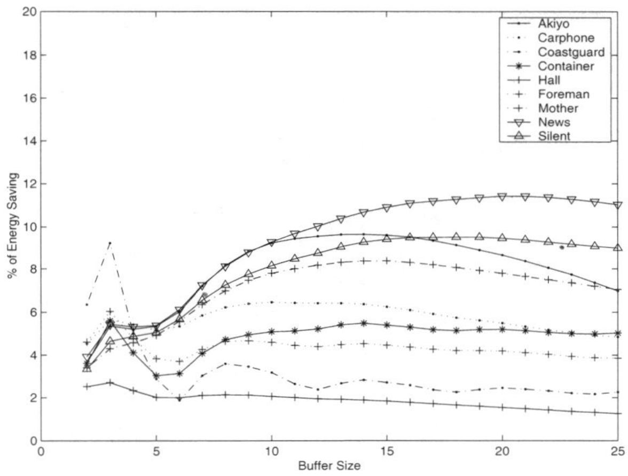

Figure 6: Energy Savings Comparison with Averaging (Dithered)

comprise of 300-frame color video sequences in QCIF format commonly used in the research community. More specifically, the names of the video sequences are Akiyo, Carphone, Coastguard, Container, Foreman, Hall, Mother, News, and Silent [7]. The MPEG-2 codec software used for video compression and decompression was acquired from the MPEG Software Simulation Group [5].

The MPEG-2 video compression parameters used in our experimental work are given in Table 1.

To study the impact of buffer size on the performance of the algorithm, we varied the buffer size from 2 to 25. For energy calculations, we assumed the maximum supply voltage and the threshold voltage (V_t) to be 3.3V and 0.7V, respectively. Moreover, we assumed that energy loss in the DC-DC converter to be negligible.

The simulation tool used for our energy analysis was MATLAB (Version 5) from MathWorks Inc.

5. RESULTS

Figures 5 and 6 show the energy savings achieved by the *AQRS* algorithm compared to the conventional workload averaging technique. For *all* nine test video sequences the algorithm produced better energy savings than the workload averaging technique, and the energy savings ranged from 1% to 23% for the 300-frame video sequences as the buffer size was varied from 2 to 25.

The *AQRS* algorithm achieves these energy savings by minimizing the higher quantized rates during rate selection. Table 2 demonstrates the changes in workload distribution compared to the corresponding distribution using the *RSA* algorithm. As this table shows, there is nearly a 100% reduction in workload distribution at $r = 1.0$ and a 75% or higher reduction for a majority of test cases at $r = 0.75$. Moreover, there is a small reduction in distribution at $r = 0.25$ and the majority of workload distributions are concentrated at $r = 0.5$. Finally Figure 7 shows the comparative workload distributions for all nine test video sequences using the workload averaging technique, the Rate Selection Algorithm [1], and the *AQRS* algorithm. For this comparison, a buffer size of 10 is used. This figure further highlights the efficiency of *AQRS* algorithm in reducing the higher quantized rates, particularly in the $0.5 > r \geq 1.0$ range as demonstrated in Table 2.

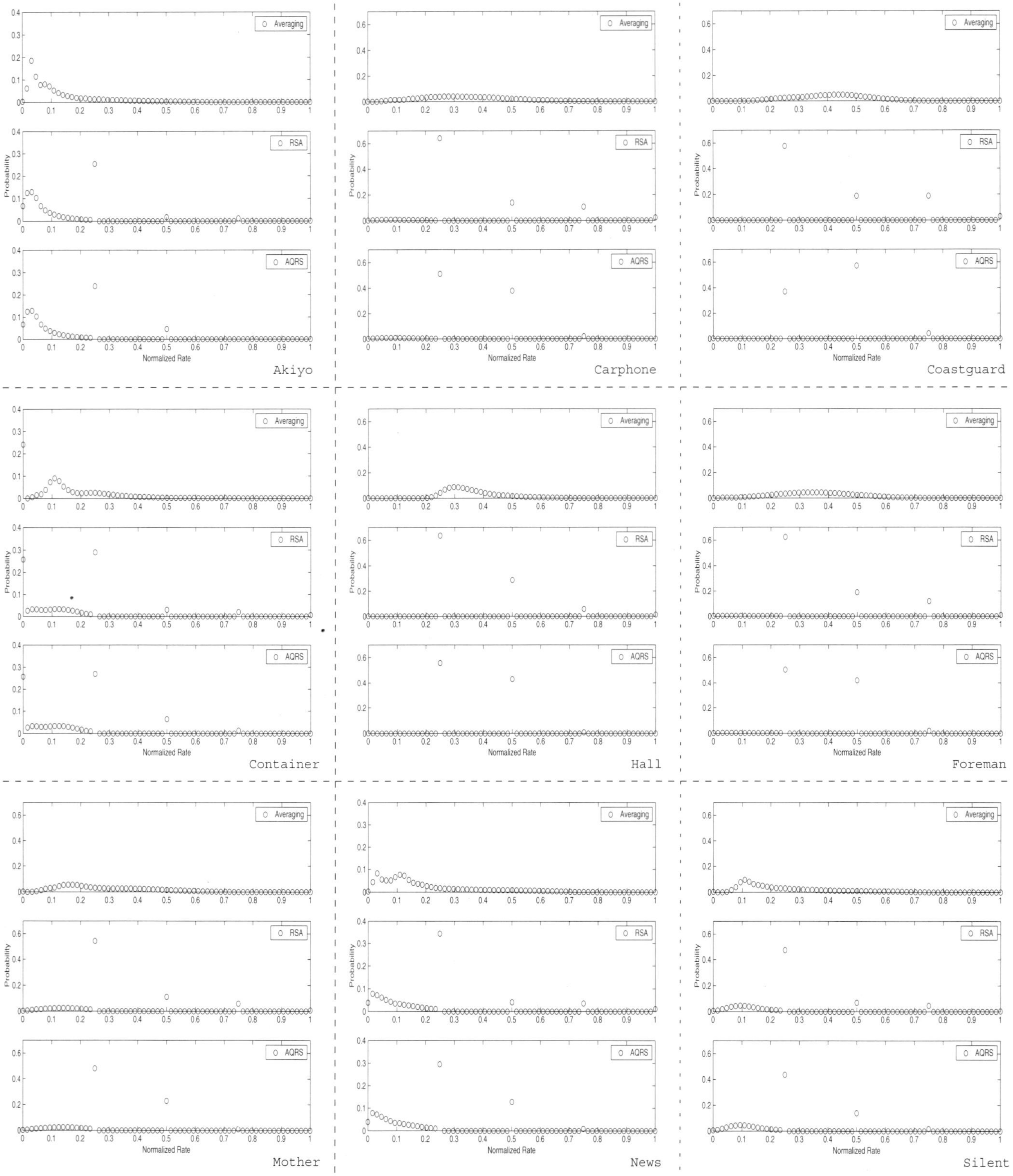

Figure 7: Rate Distribution Comparison for All Test Video Sequences

Sequence	r=0.25	r=0.5	r=0.75	r=1.0
Akiyo	-5.84%	155.78%	-96.76%	-100.0%
Carphone	-20.47%	172.18%	-80.69%	-99.48%
Coastguard	-35.91%	203.99%	-77.83%	-99.93%
Container	-6.82%	110.66%	-36.76%	-99.11%
Hall	-12.24%	49.07%	-85.61%	-99.96%
Foreman	-19.08%	119.55%	-82.73%	-99.82%
Mother	-11.36%	104.65%	-82.67%	-99.03%
News	-14.12%	209.67%	-75.21%	-99.26%
Silent	-7.59%	96.56%	-62.01%	-99.85%

Table 2: Workload Distribution Comparison - AQRS vs. RSA

6. CONCLUSION

In this paper we have presented a highly energy efficient alternative algorithm to the conventional workload averaging technique for voltage quantized dynamic voltage scaling. The algorithm named *Average-based Quantized Rate Selection* is based on the workload averaging technique [2] and our Rate Selection Algorithm [1]. The algorithm monitors the total buffered workload value, uses the average buffered workload to estimate the rate, and where possible *selects* rates that are equal to quantized rates. At quantized rates, the energy dissipation of voltage quantized DVS approaches the energy dissipation of continuous voltage level DVS. Moreover, the estimation of rate using the average buffered workload reduces higher quantized rates, there by reducing the overall energy dissipation. Our experimental work using the Forward Mapped Inverse Discrete Cosine Transform as the data-dependent computation for DVS, nine MPEG-2 test video sequences as test data, and a four-level voltage quantization shows that our algorithm produces better energy savings than the workload averaging technique for all test cases, and the energy savings achieved ranges from 1% to 23%.

Apart from the additional energy savings, our algorithm also has two key advantages over the averaging technique. First, the algorithm only requires one buffer or half the buffer size requirement of the averaging technique, making it very effective for applications with reduced memory and area requirements. Second, the algorithm eliminates the need for voltage dithering, there by improving the overall stability of the system by minimizing the number of voltage transitions.

Finally, as Figure 4 shows, the *AQRS* algorithm has a higher operational complexity compared to the *RSA* algorithm. However, comparison of the *AQRS* and the workload averaging technique shows that for buffer size $B > 15$, the overhead of the former (upper and lower bound) is smaller than the latter, making the *AQRS* algorithm a very energy efficient, low complexity replacement algorithm for the workload averaging technique in voltage quantized dynamic voltage scaling.

7. REFERENCES

[1] L. H. Chandrasena and M. J. Liebelt. A Rate Selection Algorithm for Quantized Undithered Dynamic Supply Voltage Scaling. In *International Symposium on Low Power Electronics and Design*, July 2000.

[2] V. Gutnik and A. P. Chandrakasan. Embedded Power Supply for Low-Power DSP. *IEEE Transactions on Very Large Scale Integration (VLSI) Systems*, 5(4):425–435, December 1997.

[3] T. Ishihara and H. Yasuura. Voltage Scheduling Problem for Dynamically Variable Voltage Processors. In *International Symposium on Low Power Electronics and Design*, August 1998.

[4] L. McMillan and L. Westover. A Forward-Mapping Realization of the Inverse Discrete Cosine Transform. In *Data Compression Conference*, pages 219–228, March 1992.

[5] http://www.bok.net/mpeg/MSSG/.

[6] L. S. Nielsen, C. Niessen, J. Sparsø, and K. van Berkel. Low-Power Operation Using Self-Timed Circuits and Adaptive Scaling of Supply Voltage. *IEEE Transactions on Very Large Scale Integration (VLSI) Systems*, 2(4):391–397, December 1994.

[7] Ftp://dspftp.ece.ubc.ca/pub/tmn/qcif_source/.

Current Consumption Dynamics at Instruction and Program Level for a *VLIW* DSP Processor

Radu Muresan, Catherine H. Gebotys
University of Waterloo
Department of Electrical and Computer Engineering
Waterloo, Ontario
Canada, N2L 3G1
rmuresan@dsp-cot.uwaterloo.ca, cgebotys@optimal.vlsi.uwaterloo.ca

ABSTRACT

This paper describes a new methodology for analyzing low-level current dynamics at the instruction level and the program level for a VLIW DSP processor core. An efficient methodology for software power analysis is presented which unlike other research supports dynamic current analysis and complex VLIW processor cores. Analysis of high bank register allocation, equivalent functional construct usage, and program-based current, power, and energy is presented. The basic principles and methods developed throughout this research are general and applicable to complex pipelined processors. This research is important for analyzing and designing secure power-efficient DSP embedded applications.

Categories and Subject Descriptors

C.3 [**Computer Systems Organization**]: Special-purpose and Application-based Systems; C.4 [**Computer Systems Organization**]: Performance of Systems

General Terms

Measurement, Experimentation

Keywords

DSP processors, current dynamics, methodology

1. INTRODUCTION

Power dissipation has become a critical factor in VLSI designs today impacting cost, reliability and security. As low power applications increase in number and grow in complexity, the power dissipation problem is expected to become a major barrier for designing reliable VLSI devices. Currently in many handheld devices, the DSP processor core dissipates a significant amount of power, due to it's highly compute intensive applications. Thus research in analyzing and understanding power dissipation in DSP processor cores is important. There is a need to perform in-depth detailed analysis of power dissipation, so that embedded designers will know how to optimize their applications for low power. Since modeling power dissipation of a VLIW processor core is a very complex problem, new methods for tracing power dynamically at program levels and lower instruction levels are important. Dynamic analysis of power is also crucial for verifying the security of wireless communication devices, which (en)decrypt video, audio or other data (before) after transmission. Since many wireless communications devices demand low power, low energy and the ability to encrypt, methodologies which support dynamic power measurement and analysis are important.

ISSS'01, October 1-3, 2001, Montréal, Québec, Canada.

2. POWER AND RELATED RESEARCH

The instantaneous power in a load is given by the following relation:

$$p(t) = v(t) * i(t) \qquad [Watts] \tag{1}$$

In Equation 1 $v(t)$ represents the time dependent function of the voltage applied to the load (measured in volts), and $i(t)$ represents the time dependent function of the current passing through the load (measured in amperes). The processor's power supply is a DC voltage and is constant during the execution of any program within the processor. The only time dependent component in this case is the current function. Given the instantaneous power function $p(t)$ of a load, the energy dissipated by the load during a period of time $[0, T]$ can be calculated as:

$$W_{load} = \int_0^T p(t)dt \tag{2}$$

Suppose that we can determine the current function $i(t)$ for a processor with a constant voltage supply V, while executing a program P which takes a total execution time equal to T. In this case the equation 2 becomes:

$$W_{program} = \int_0^T V * i(t)dt \tag{3}$$

Equation 3 represents the energy consumption of the processor while executing the program P. If programs are implemented such that this energy consumption is minimized then a power efficient implementation is achieved, which will guarantee an extended life time battery for the wireless applications. In order to implement power efficient programs it is important to determine the power consumption characteristics of the instruction set architecture and all their equivalent implementations. If program implementations are based upon low power consumption constructs the final program power consumption will be low and the energy $W_{program}$ consumed by the processor executing the program P will be minimized.

Previous research has studied lower level models for power as well as performed static power analysis. Transistor and module level power models have been developed as well as software techniques [11]. Recent research work is directed towards finding power consumption modeling techniques at the software level which will benefit the compilers for these DSP processors. [12, 11, 3] Power modeling at the instruction level for processors were investigated in [12]. However dynamic power simulation is not supported and only static single average power values are returned for a given software program running on a processor. Furthermore few researchers have examined complex VLIW processors where more than one instruction execute in parallel. Currently power attacks of cryptographic devices, have been analyzed using slow clock frequencies, non-VLIW processors in non-time critical applications, such as smart cards [6]. Future wireless communications devices such as encryption of voice and video will require time-critical (de)encryption and require VLIW processor implementation. In this paper a methodology for measuring the dynamic current, $i(t)$, of a complex VLIW core is presented, supporting instructions as well as entire programs. Analysis of these dynamic current traces are used to identify architectural and software techniques for low power. The next section will introduce the apparatus used in measuring dynamic power, followed by an introduction to the processor (the Starcore DSP processor core, SC140) used in our experiments.

3. SYNCHRONIZATION AND EXPERIMENTAL SETUP

There is no major problem in measuring the steady-state DC power consumption with a traditional mutimeter [10]. This implies a measure of the DC current drain and the battery voltage and multiply the two measurements. But most of the electronic devices specially the complex VLIW processors, switch between multitude of states even when under normal operating modes. Also the use of instruction constructs with a high level of current draw in loops or modules with repeated execution demands gives a dynamic characteristic to the processor's current draw during the program execution. Hence to understand the impact of the states and of the software used in these equipment on current consumption there is need to measure the dynamic current characteristics of the various states and modes using an oscilloscope. The usage of today's high-tech measuring equipment makes this problem fairly straight forward [10]. Nevertheless when dealing with complex DSP processors the measurement of the current dynamic at instruction or program level is very difficult. The difficulty relies on the type of the oscilloscope used and on the method of synchronizing the software with the measuring equipment. The current draw is not a regular pattern type waveform and even if the program under measurement (PUM) is looped in an infinite loop the measurement is not stable and is not accurate.

The problem of studying the current dynamics at instruction and program level is a three fold synchronization problem:

1. How can the software program be synchronized with the measuring equipment?

2. How the exact position of an instruction or of a set of instructions in the current waveform can be determined?

3. How does the current measurement take place for a program which does not execute in an infinite loop?

In solving the above problem for the particular processor under the test (SC140) we have created a work station composed of the following equipment:

1. StarCore 140 Software Development Platform (SC140 SDP) [5].

2. A signal/pattern generator ($HP81130A$) [4].

3. A sampling type oscilloscope ($TDS8000$) equipped with high frequency sampling heads, high frequency current probes and high frequency voltage probes [10].

Within this work station the synchronization problem was solved as follows:

- The processor's clock is externally provided at the processor speed by the pattern generator.
- The processor is kept in the wait state (a state that is equivalent with a standby state), were the state of the processor is preserved and the internal processor's clock is disabled. This state is a very low current consumption state for the SC140 processor [1].
- A non-maskable (or maskable) interrupt signal synchronous with the processor's clock is generated by the pattern generator at the NMI pin of the processor.
- The program or the instructions under measurement are boarded with a series of NOP instructions [1] before and after entering wait state.
- The NMI signal triggers the oscilloscope and causes the SC140 processor to come out of the wait state. As the processor comes out of the wait state the program execution is directed towards the program under measurement.
- At the end of the program execution the processor is introduced again in the wait state.

A signal diagram of the software synchronization process used in our measurements is presented in Figure 1. The generation of the NMI signal is periodic and the program under measurement is executed periodically at the NMI frequency. The difference between this method and the looping method is that the processor enters the wait state after each time the program is executed instead of looping to the beginning of the program. This method simulates more accurately the real dynamic behavior of the one run type DSP applications.

Synchronizing the processor's current draw measurement with the NMI signal provides an accurate data acquisition for the $TDS8000$ sampling oscilloscope. As a result the current waveforms display the true current dynamics within the processor while executing the program under measurement and give a stable waveform with true instantaneous values at each sample point in the T_{NMI} interval. Based on the synchronization principle presented in Figure 1 we incorporate our programs under measurement within a SC140 assembly language template. The template is designed as an interrupt service routine and the time periods TI_{nop} and TE_{nop} of Figure 1 are composed of 200 execution sets with a NOP instruction per execution set. Normally the processor enters into a wait state after each execution of the interrupt service routine until a new interrupt request comes. The use of the wait state and of the NOP instructions in the test-

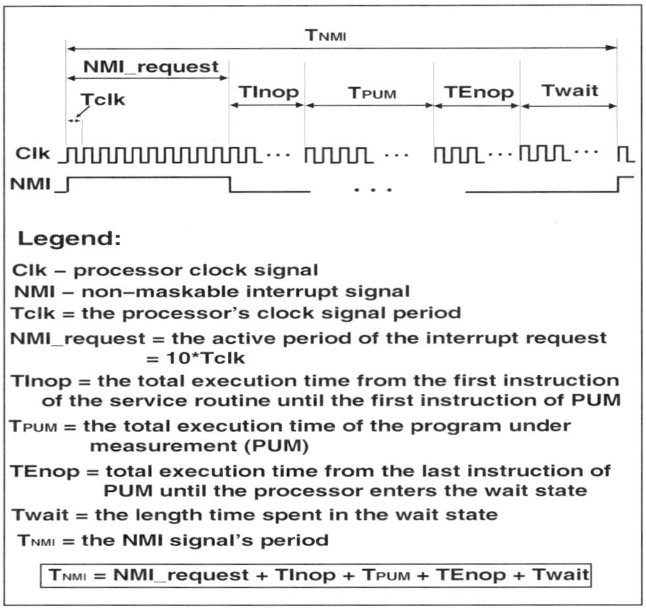

Figure 1: Software Synchronization Signal Diagram

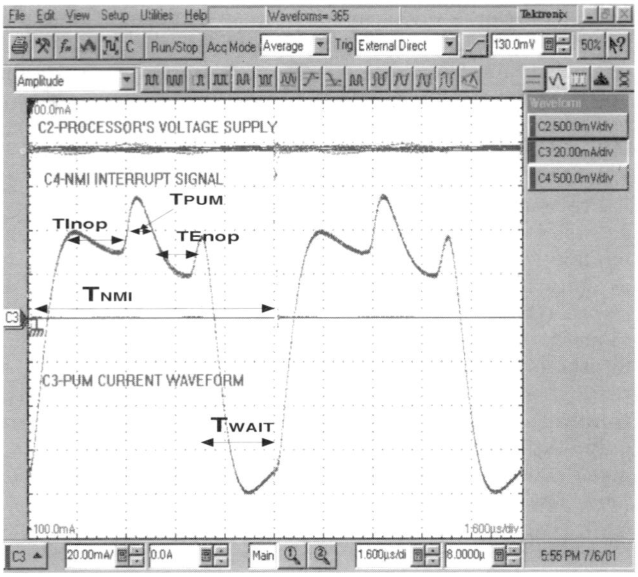

Figure 2: Oscilloscope Measurements, Example of Synchronized Waveform for a Short PUM.

ing template is important in generating the current draw variation necessary for the current probe to capture the real current draw of the program and in performing the software synchronization. The low current draw of the processor in the wait state and NOP state makes possible to visualize easily in the waveform diagrams the current draw waveform portion of the program under measurement.

In this experiment, our target processor is the SC140 Star Core processor developed by Motorola and Lucent Technology [1, 2]. The SC140 Star Core DSP processor is based on a Variable Length Execution Set (VLES) model and features multiple functional units that work in parallel [1]. All SC140 instruction words are 16-bit wide and each instruction encodes an atomic operation [1]. In order to execute signal processing operations, a set of atomic operations can be executed in parallel. An eight-word instruction set called a fetch set, is fetched from memory every clock cycle and the PSEQ unit detects the portion of this set that can be executed in parallel [1]. Here the VLES model is enforced, and based on grouping constraints the execution set, or the set of instructions that can be executed in parallel, varies from one to six atomic instructions [1]. The register file blocks within the SC140 DSP core are divided into two banks: bank 1 or low bank and bank 2 or high bank. Based on the instructions type and the usage of the upper bank registers within an execution set the instructions are serially grouped or prefix grouped by the assembler. The prefix grouping adds an extra 16-bit word to the execution set encoding [1]. The next section will present results using the SC140 processor along with the experimental setup described in this section.

4. RESULTS OF POWER AND ENERGY ANALYSIS

In this section we present a series of power consumption waveform analysis obtained using the work station and the template program described in Section 3. For each figure the programs or instruction sequences under measurement are executed under same conditions and the execution time in clock cycles of the equivalent programs is equal. In these figures we used the following shorted notations:

- 20x[$instruction$], 20x[$instruction1, instruction2$] - indicate a program under measurement composed of 20 execution sets [1] with instruction or instruction 1 and instruction 2 being the composing instructions for the each execution set.
- $0WP$, $2WP$ - serial grouping with no extra prefix words necessary in the execution sets and two-word prefix grouping which requires 2 extra instruction words for each execution set.
- $OP1, 2 = 00, FF, MIX$ - the instructions' operands one and two are filled with a sequence of bits equal with 0, 1 or a random combination of 0s and 1s.

Figures 2, 3, 4, 5 and 6 are all screen prints of real measurements produced by our workstation while executing real programs on the SC140 DSP core board at a frequency of $100MHz$. Basically at this frequency the SC140 DSP processor executes one cycle at every $10ns$ and for most of the ALU instructions the throughput will be one execution set at every $10ns$.

In all these figures the channels waveform distribution measurement is as follows:

- Channel $C2$ of the oscilloscope measures the voltage supply of the processor on a scale of $500mV/div$.
- Channel $C4$ of the oscilloscope measures the signal applied to the interrupt request input of the processor. This signal is also used to externally trigger the measurements.
- Channel $C3$ of the oscilloscope measures the instantaneous current draw of the processor as converted by a high frequency current transformer installed on the processor's power supply pin.
- Channel $C1$ of the oscilloscope measures the instantaneous

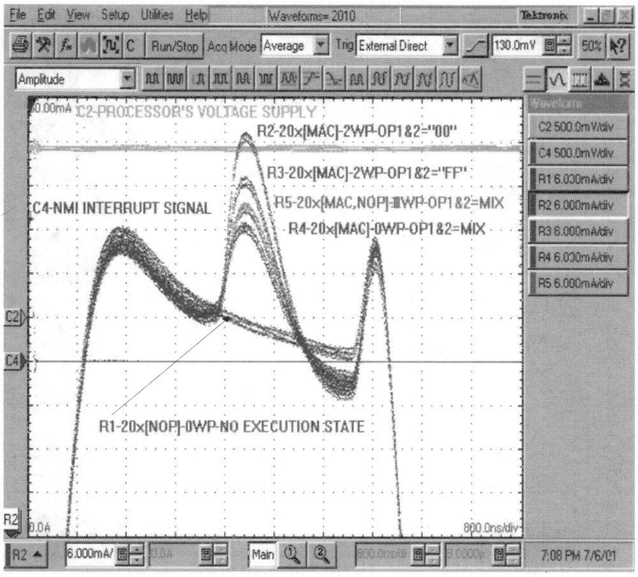

Figure 3: Current Waveform Analysis for High Bank Register Usage.

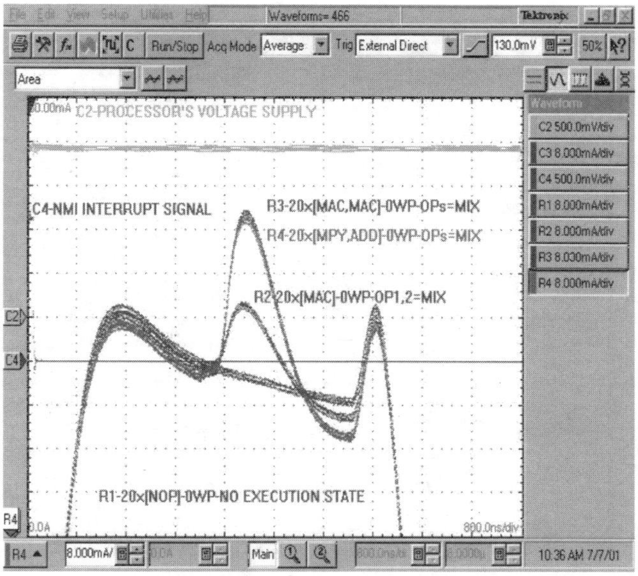

Figure 4: Current Consumption Analysis for Equivalent Constructs

current draw of the processor as converted by a DC current probe.

- The waveforms marked with Ri ($i \in \{1,2,3,4,5,6,7,8\}$) represent reference waveforms and are all obtained by storing instantaneous current waveform measurements produced by Channel $C3$ or Channel $C1$ of the oscilloscope.
- The waveforms marked with Mi ($i \in \{1,2,3,4,5,6,7,8\}$) represent mathematical waveforms and are obtained as a math combination of the active waveforms.

The right side of the oscilloscope print shows buttons with the name and the measuring scale for the displayed waveforms and presents all the measurements performed on these waveforms. The bottom part of the oscilloscope print shows the active measuring scale in $nano-seconds$ and the start position of the measurement taken from the rising edge of the synchronization signal.

Figure 2 presents a synchronized current waveform measurement for a short PUM composed of 20 execution sets and identifies the portions of the waveform that correspond to the time periods outlined in Figure 1 of Section 3. In this figure we can easily identify the processor's wait and NOP states and we can see the current measurement performed over two periods of the synchronization signal.

Figure 3 presents current consumption analysis for high bank register usage. The active scale for this print is $800ns$ per division and the period of the synchronization signal is $T_{NMI} = 8\mu s$. The PUM for each current waveform is composed of 20 identical execution sets which start executing at same point in time as referred to the synchronization signal. The figure presents the following measurements:

- $R1$ measures the current draw for a PUM composed of 20 execution sets with one NOP instruction per execution set. This waveform represents our base measuring waveform since the NOP instructions are encoded as a one-word prefix inside the execution set and they are not dispatched to any execution set [1].
- $R2$ measures the current draw for a PUM composed of 20 execution sets with one MAC (multiply accumulate) instruction per set (MAC $D3, D5, D13$) performing on two operands equal with zero. Each execution set has encoded a two-words prefix due to the usage of the register $D13$. The resulting current waveform for this setup shows the highest current consumption for this print.
- $R3$ measures the current draw for an identical PUM used for the $R2$ with the difference that the content of the registers $D3$ and $D5$ is equal with $(FFFFFFFF)_{16}$.
- $R5$ measures the current draw for PUM composed of 20 execution sets with one MAC instruction(MAC $D3, D5, D7$) and one NOP instruction per execution set. This setup for the execution set will actually be converted into one MAC instruction word end one-word prefix encoding. The content of the registers $D3$ and $D5$ is a mixed combination of 1s and 0s bits.
- $R4$ measures the current draw for an identical PUM used for the $R5$ with the difference that the NOP instruction is excluded from the execution set. As a result the encoding of the execution set contains only one instruction word.

The waveform relationship presented in this figure is common to other analyzed instructions of the SC140 architecture set. From this kind of current analysis we can conclude that for the particular processor under test, operations on data with more bits set to zero will increase the current consumption per execution set. Also an important observation is that the main current consumption increase per execution set is due to the usage of the high bank registers and of the parallel features of the processor. Typically regardless of the data handled by the execution sets and regardless of the number of high bank registers used within the execution sets the current draw is at maximum when the execution sets encode a two-word prefix. The current increase due to parallelism does not necessarily affects the total energy consumption per application. Using parallel structures increases the speed of execution and decreases the total execution time of the ap-

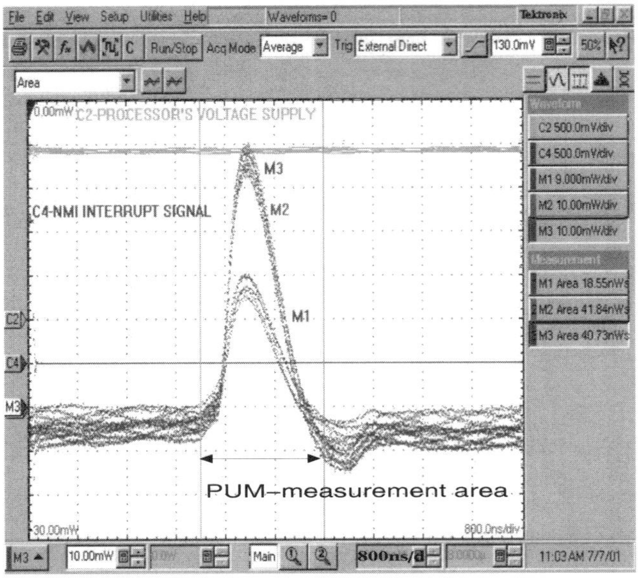

Figure 5: Instantaneous Power and Energy Consumption Analysis

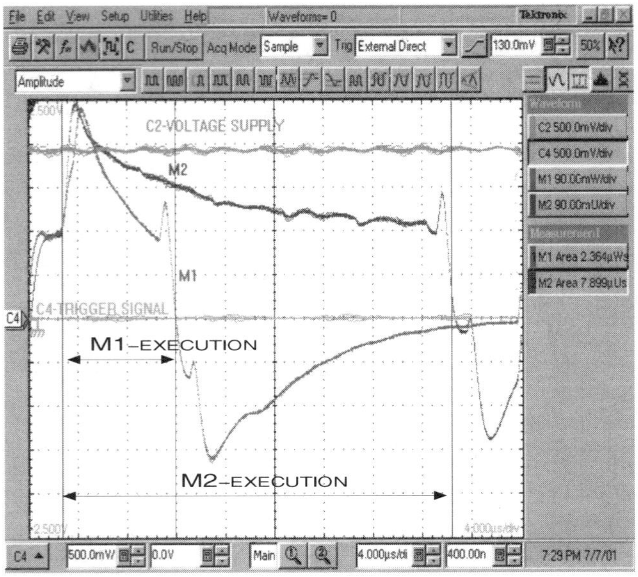

Figure 6: Instantaneous Power and Energy Consumption Analysis for Optimized Programs.

plication and as a result the integration period in Formula 3 decreases. Nevertheless a dynamic current waveform analysis is required to really be able to determine the effects of the parallel structures.

Figures 4 and 5 are part of the same oscilloscope print and are used to explain the procedure employed to accurately measure the variation of the instantaneous power and energy consumption at program and instruction level. The object of the analysis presented in these two figures is to determine the efficiency of using MAC instructions versus equivalent constructs composed of a separate multiply and addition operation. Figure 4 presents the following current measurements:

- $R1$ represents the base reference waveform and is identical with the $R1$ waveform of Figure 3.
- $R2$ is identical with the $R4$ waveform of Figure 3 but is displayed at a different scale.
- $R4$ and $R3$ represent the current measurements for a PUM composed of 20 execution sets with two instructions per execution set. $R3$ has two MAC instructions per execution set and $R4$ has one MPY (multiplication) and one ADD (addition) per execution set as equivalents for one MAC instruction.

As a current measurement principle we assume the current draw of a NOP instruction as a DC component for any instruction under measurement. Based on this principle in performing current measurements at program level for each PUM we perform a current measurement for an execution time equivalent PUM which has all the execution sets composed of a single NOP instruction. We call this program a $PUMnop$ program and we use the waveform generated by it as a base reference waveform.

Figure 5 represents the power waveform variation from the base reference waveform $R1$ for the current reference waveforms $R2$, $R3$ and $R4$ of Figure 4. The explicit instantaneous power consumption waveforms and energy consumption measurements were generated as follows:

- $M1[mW] = C2[mV] * (R2[mA] - R1[mA])$

  $M1_{Area} = \int_{2800ns}^{4800ns} *M1(t)dt = 18.55[nWs]$
- $M2[mW] = C2[mV] * (R3[mA] - R1[mA])$

  $M2_{Area}[nWs] = \int_{2800ns}^{4800ns} *M2(t)dt = 41.84[nWs]$
- $M3[mW] = C2[mV] * (R4[mA] - R1[mA])$

  $M3_{Area}[nWs] = \int_{2800ns}^{4800ns} *M3(t)dt = 40.73[nWs]$

The area measurements performed on these waveforms indicate the energy consumption increase due to executing non-NOP instructions. Comparing these area measurements we can deduce that a MAC instruction if used instead of a multiplication and addition construct is approximately two times less power consuming.

So far we presented experimental results of the current dynamic measurement approach performed on short programs. Performing current dynamic measurements for long programs becomes more challenging due to the limitations of the measuring equipment. As long as the execution time of the program under measurement is not out of the oscilloscope synchronization range we can perform measurements for the whole program by increasing the measuring scale and the period of the synchronization signal. Also we can refine and locate portions of the program under measurements by decreasing the measuring scale and adjusting the measuring start position time within the synchronization period. If the total execution time of the PUM is longer than the synchronization range of the oscilloscope the PUM must be divided into independent smaller portions and the current measurements must be performed separately on each portion.

Figure 6 presents an instantaneous power and energy consumption analysis performed for a cryptography application executing on two different sets of data. The cryptography application under analysis performs a polynomial multiplication operation on two large field elements using a shift and add algorithm [9]. The application is optimized for speed by using parallel constructs and by eliminating the leading zero bits of the multiplier operand. The SC140 assembly language program is composed of an outer loop which incorporates an inner loop. The outer loop executes at the most 6 times based on the number of non zero double words and the inner loop executes 32 times except for the last iteration of the outer loop where the total number of executions is based on the number of zero leading bits. The mathematical waveforms presented in Figure 6 have the following significance:

• $M2$ represents the instantaneous power measurement of the cryptography application while performing a polynomial multiplication on two field elements with no leading zero bits. In this situation the program execution takes its maximum time and the positions of each iteration of the outer loop can be visualized on the waveform.

• $M1$ represents the instantaneous power measurement of the cryptography application while performing a polynomial multiplication on two field elements with the multiplier having 5 of the leading double words equal with zero. As a result in this case the outer loop runs only for one iteration.

The energy consumption values for these waveforms were calculated as follows:

- $M1_{Area}[nWs] = \int_{3.2\mu s}^{34.8\mu s} *M1(t)dt = 2.364[\mu Ws]$
- $M2_{Area}[nWs] = \int_{3.2\mu s}^{12.4\mu s} *M1(t)dt = 7.899[\mu Ws]$

Performing these measurements by looping methods using static measurements will give unsatisfactory results due to the low frequency response of the static meters. Also for the one time run type applications using the looping method in current measurements needs a precise knowledge of the total execution time of the program for each separate data input otherwise erroneous energy measurements result.

5. CONCLUDING REMARKS

This study presents an important methodology for the analysis of dynamic characteristics of the current measurements in power efficient software implementations. The current dynamics obtained for the SC140 DSP processor show variations at a lower frequency than the processor's clock frequency and these variations are dictated by the internal constructs used within the programs. We have observed in our study that loops or portions of programs with high parallelism or computational activity can be easily located within the current waveform representations by the higher current draw jump. The wait, stop and low or no computational activity states can be located by the current draw fall. Also the current consumption per execution set is proportional with the number of ALU executing in parallel but the overall energy consumption per program is controlled by the total execution time. Another important observation provided by the current dynamics analysis is that the usage of the upper bank registers increases the current consumption not necessarily because of the extra prefix words used in the execution set but mainly because of the increased internal architectural activity within the processor. As a result an optimal register allocation should be an important feature of power efficient implementations for the SC140 DSP processor [8]. This methodology is unlike previous research which has used a static power analysis on a per instruction basis (unsuitable for VLIW processor analysis) or per program using an infinite loop. The new approach presented in this paper simplifies the power analysis for complex VLIW processors.

In summary this research contributes to analysis of power dynamics in complex VLIW processors. The methodology supports analysis of where in programs the power may vary and therefore helping to localize causes of this variation. This methodology can be used in generating accurate power measurements for a processor's instruction set and can generate data needed for developing power aware compilers. Another important application of this methodology would be to provide accurate current dynamic measurements for applications with security characteristics. Future research is directed towards finding efficient modeling techniques for power prediction at the software level using this methodology for current dynamics analysis [7] and is part of ongoing research that involves dynamic power efficient implementations at the software level for DSP processors [3].

This research was supported in part by grants from NSERC, Motorola (thanks to T.Tam, P.Marino) and CITO.

6. REFERENCES

[1] Alliance Group, Motorola and Lucent Technologies. *SC140 DSP Core Reference Manual*, 1999.

[2] C.H.Gebotys. Utilizing memory bandwidth. In *DAC*, pages 347–352, 2001.

[3] C.H.Gebotys and R.Gebotys. Statistically based prediction of power dissipation for complex embedded DSP processors. *Microprocessors and Microsystems*, (23):135–144, May 1999.

[4] Hewlett Packard. *HP 81130A Pulse/Data Generator, Reference Guide*, 1998.

[5] Motorola and Metrowerks Inc. *SC140 Software Development Platform (SDP) kit*, 2001. http://www1.motorola-dsp.com/software/sc140sdp.taf.

[6] P.Kocher, J.Jaffe, and B.Jun. Differential power analysis. *LNCS*, Vol.1666, 1999.

[7] R.Muresan and C.Gebotys. Dynamic power simulation model for VLIW DSP processor VLSI cores with secure applications. To appear in*11th IFIP VLSI-SOC 2001*, December 2001.

[8] R.Muresan and C.Gebotys. A dynamic programming approach to complex allocation in a DSP pipelined processor. In *CCECE 2001*, pages 1175–1183. IEEE Canada, May 2001.

[9] M. Rosing. *Implementing Elliptic Curve Cryptography.* MANNING, Greenwich, 1999.

[10] Tektronix Inc. *Application Note: Power-Electronics Measurements Made Easy with TDS Oscilloscopes*, 1996. Web Page: http://www.tektronix.com.

[11] V.Tiwari, D.Singh, S.Rajgopal, G.Mehta, R.Patel, and F.Baez. Reducing power in high-performance microprocessors. In *35th Design Automation Conference*, pages 732–737. ACM, Inc., June 1998.

[12] V.Tiwari, S.Malik, and A.Wolfe. Power analysis of embedded software: A first step towards software power minimization. *IEEE Transactions on VLSI*, 2(4):437–445, December 1994.

Dynamic Modeling of Inter–Instruction Effects for Execution Time Estimation

G. Beltrame[†], C. Brandolese[§], W. Fornaciari[§], F. Salice[§], D. Sciuto[§], V. Trianni[§]

[§] Politecnico di Milano, Piazza L. da Vinci, 32 - 20133 Milano, Italy

{brandole,fornacia,salice,sciuto,trianni}@elet.polimi.it

[†] CEFRIEL, Via R. Fucini, 2 - 20133 Milano, Italy

beltrami@cefriel.it

ABSTRACT

The market for embedded applications is facing a growing interest in power consumption issues: this work is intended to provide a new model to estimate software–level power consumption of 32-bit microprocessors. This model extends previous ones by considering dynamic inter–instruction effects that take place during code execution, providing a static means to characterize their energy consumption. The model is formally sound: it is conceived for a generic architecture and it has been preliminary validated on the Intel486™ architecture.

1. INTRODUCTION

While there has been a significant research effort in power estimation techniques and in low power design tailored for hardware systems, no EDA tools are available to help hardware/software embedded systems designers [4]. The main obstacle is an efficient analysis of the CPU power consumption, necessary to take into account also the software components during design–space exploration, while avoiding to rely with architectural or even layout–level simulation of the microprocessor. To fill such a gap, strategies working at the instruction–level recently appeared in literature. In fact, having a power model of assembly instructions is a value added for designers, since the increasing complexity of embedded systems software is evident and the need of early prototyping of embedded systems, in particular in terms of power consumption, is becoming a must. In [12][13][11] *a priori* knowledge of the current drawn by an instruction is obtained by executing an infinite loop of the target instruction in order to average out fine–grained fluctuations. These approaches are strongly processor–dependent and normally the statistical significance of power figures is not taken into account. A different approach, working on the concept of early *virtual* prototyping of the software for different target CPU cores has been proposed in [1]. This methodology abstracts from the architectural level and focuses on the *functionalities* involved during instruction execution. The resulting functional model decouples the execution time of an instruction from its average power consumption. This allows a *static* (data independent) characterization of each instruction in terms of the energy consumed together with a statistical validation of the resulting software power model. These assumptions are the basis for the work presented in this paper, which concentrates on timing aspects. To consider also the presence of *dynamic* inter–instruction effects such as pipeline interlocks or cache misses, which typically lead to an additional energy consumption not to be neglected in a overall system–level perspective, the previous approaches should be extended. In fact, even if estimates are accurate for the static microprocessor model, the introduction of dynamic inter–instruction effects may cause severe strays from reality for the entire system. The importance of this problem has been recognized in [10], where an instruction–level power model that considered dynamic effects is presented. The solution is based on a modification of the model proposed in [12][13] to obtain a more precise estimate for the base costs. Basically, the authors separated instructions with the same opcode but different addressing modes and added a statistical analysis of cache and pipeline interlock overheads. Unfortunately, this solution is still not general, in the sense that it needs measures for every processor it has to be applied to. The goal of this paper is to overcome the above limitations, providing a general model to describe interlock overheads for different types of processor cores, to complete the information provided via *static* analysis. This model is going to be implemented in a co-design flow in order to obtain a truly accurate and efficient software power estimation tool [9]. This paper is organized as follows: Section 2 defines the problem of considering inter–instruction effects in the scope of a static analysis; Section 3 introduces the mathematical and statistical models; Section 4 describes the methodology for model tuning, and Section 5 presents some experimental results. Finally, some conclusions are drawn in Section 6.

ISSS'01, October 1-3, 2001, Montréal, Québec, Canada.

2. PROBLEM DEFINITION

In this work, the model proposed in [1] is extended, taking into account inter–instruction effects related to pipelining. Interlocks are generally related to the execution of a particular sequence of instructions, thus they correspond to *dynamic* events. Taking into account such effects implies either a dynamic analysis, which requires an excessive computational complexity, or an accurate characterization of the computations made by the processor, which leads to a loss of generality [1].

When dealing with inter–instruction effects it is not possible to avoid a dynamic analysis. To recognize a hazard arising from the execution of a sequence of instructions, it is necessary to model the pipeline behavior of the target architecture and the instruction flow in the pipeline, thus leading to an excessive computational complexity. But if an *a priori* statistical characterization of the inter–instruction behavior of each instruction is known, then the static approach can still be applied: this correspond to a static representation of dynamic effects. The proposed approach is based on a *dynamic analysis* aimed at deriving a statistical model of the delay introduced by inter–instruction effects. Such model is then used *statically* during the estimation of the timing and energy requirements of each instruction. The dynamic analysis is made *once* for each target architecture, obtaining statistical information about the delay introduced in the execution time of each instruction due to pipeline interlocks. This temporal overhead is then combined with the purely static model [1], allowing an extension into the energy consumption domain, as detailed in the conclusion of Section 3.2. As mentioned above, the paper focuses on inter–instruction effects arising from a pipelined execution of the code. In this work pipeline stalls related to caches and memories are deliberately neglected. When a hazard is detected, the pipeline might be stalled for a given number of clock cycles. Three hazard types may arise [3]:

Structural hazards are due to limitations in the data–path, which cannot support certain instruction sequences.

Data hazards are related to the semi–parallel execution of the code, which may lead to an incorrect ordering of read/write operations.

Control hazards are related to the branch execution, since the pipeline generally needs to be stalled until the target address is calculated.

The present work analyzes the pipeline behavior of the two target architectures, namely the microSPARC™-IIep [6][7] an the Intel Embedded486™ [5]. Based on this analysis a general abstract model of the interlock behaviour has been derived and applied to a different microprocessor, as reported in Section 5. In general, a hazard may be associated with a couple of instructions occurring at a given distance in time; the penalty introduced by the resulting pipeline stall depends on both the specific hazard and the distance between the instructions. The former instruction in the pair is the cause of the interlock[1] while the latter the stalled one. For this reason the temporal overhead is conventionally associated with the latter. The proposed model estimates a statistical temporal overhead to be associated to an instruction pair and folds it on single instructions, as it will be presented in section 3. The estimates are obtained by means of a dynamic analysis carried out on a significant benchmark set; to this purpose, the *execution trace* of the chosen benchmarks is used. The trace carries the information of the instruction flow into the pipeline. The model is dynamic in the sense that it is tuned on execution traces rather than on the assembly source code but, once tuned, it is used statically to obtain the desired instruction characterization. However, an execution trace does not explicitly contain all the dynamic information on the processor state. For this reason, it is necessary to extract the implicit information from the trace, as it will be explained in section 4.

[1] In some uncommon cases the actual cause of a stall is a particular sequence of instructions rather than a single instruction.

3. MATHEMATICAL MODEL

For the purpose of producing a static estimation of the delay introduced by inter–instruction effects, a *taxonomy* of instruction sets has been proposed, which describes all possible hazards in an architecture independent manner. This taxonomy is essential to reduce model complexity and to allow a computationally feasible statistical analysis. Based on such a taxonomy, a mathematical model for the estimation of the temporal overhead caused by inter–instruction effects is then introduced.

3.1 Model Definition

The instruction set taxonomy provides some general architecture independent classes to be associated with architecture specific instructions. These classes are defined according to the type of hazard that an instruction may cause. Each instruction s of a given instruction set I is assigned to the class that best represents its dynamic behavior. Since three hazard types are possible, the taxonomy contains a maximum of eight classes c_h, each representing the set of instructions that may cause the same hazard type. The taxonomy $\mathcal{C}$ can be defined as:

$$\mathcal{C} = \{c_h \subseteq I | h \in [0,7]\}$$

To define the mathematical model of the temporal overhead, an assembly execution trace must be considered. Let Γ be an execution trace, i.e. an ordered sequence of instructions:

$$\Gamma = \{\gamma_1, \gamma_2, \ldots, \gamma_N\}, \quad \gamma_k \in I, \quad N, k \in \mathbb{N} \tag{1}$$

where N represents the execution trace size. To estimate the probability of finding a taxonomy class pair in the trace Γ, two operators have been introduced according to the following definitions.

Definition 1. *The **distance** $w(\gamma_{k_1}, \gamma_{k_2})$ between two instructions γ_{k_1} and γ_{k_2} is defined as the difference $|k_2 - k_1|$. The following notation is used to point out that two instruction γ_{k_1}, γ_{k_2} occur at a distance $\hat{w}$:*

$$\gamma_{k_1} \overset{\hat{w}}{\dashv} \gamma_{k_2}, \quad \hat{w} = w(\gamma_{k_1}, \gamma_{k_2})$$

The considered distances $\hat{w}$ should not be greater than the pipeline depth, i.e. 5-15, since farther instruction are almost independent in terms of interlock behavior.

Definition 2. *The **membership function** of instruction $\gamma_k \in \Gamma$ to $c_i \in \mathcal{C}$ is defined as:*

$$\langle k, i \rangle = \begin{cases} 1 & \text{if } \gamma_k \in c_i \\ 0 & \text{otherwise} \end{cases} \tag{2}$$

Definitions 1 and 2 can be then combined to introduce the concept of *event* as:

$$c_i \overset{\hat{w}}{\dashv} c_j \Leftrightarrow \exists (k_1, k_2) : \begin{cases} \langle k_1, i \rangle = 1 \\ \langle k_2, j \rangle = 1 \\ \gamma_{k_1} \overset{\hat{w}}{\dashv} \gamma_{k_2} \end{cases} \tag{3}$$

meaning that there exists in Γ two instructions $\gamma_{k_1} \in c_i$ and $\gamma_{k_2} \in c_j$ that occur at distance $\hat{w}$. Let us now introduce a statistical characterization of the events described above by examining the presence of particular classes of instructions in the execution traces. To this purpose, the frequency definition of probability is used [8].

DEFINITION 3. *The probability of finding class c_i in the execution trace is:*

$$P(c_i) = \frac{1}{N} \sum_{k=1}^{N} \langle k, i \rangle$$

where N is suitably large[2].

From this definition the relation $\sum_{i=0}^{7} P(c_i) = 1$ can be easily proved. Let us now consider class pairs statistics.

DEFINITION 4. *The probability of finding class c_i and class c_j at distance $\hat{w}$ in the execution trace is*

$$P(c_i \overset{\hat{w}}{\dashv} c_j) = \frac{1}{N} \sum_{k=1}^{N} \langle k, i \rangle \langle k + \hat{w}, j \rangle, \qquad N \gg \hat{w}$$

where N is, again, suitably large[3].

Definitions 3 and 4 are strictly linked; in fact, the following relation holds:

$$P(c_j) = \sum_{i=0}^{7} P(c_i \overset{\hat{w}}{\dashv} c_j), \tag{4}$$

This relation proves the consistency of the two definitions and thus, in turn, the soundness of the presented model.

3.2 Interlock Model

Thus far, a characterization of the frequencies of pairs of classes in the execution trace has been obtained while the properties of the interlocks that might arise have been neglected. It is worth noting that different pairs of instructions have different interlock behavior and latency, even if they are represented by the same couple of classes. In order to maintain both generality and accuracy it is thus necessary to consider the interlocks as produced by instructions pairs, and then to aggregate these figures up at class level. To do this it is necessary to abandon the exact, analytic view of the delay overhead introduced by single instruction pairs and rather consider such delays as random variables. The function $t(\gamma_k, \gamma_{k+\hat{w}}, \hat{w})$ that returns the *delay* introduced by the execution of an instruction pair $\gamma_k, \gamma_{k+\hat{w}}$ at a distance $\hat{w}$ is introduced. A delay of zero means that no interlock occurs. In order to take into account each possible interlock given a pair of classes at a distance $\hat{w}$, it is necessary defining the delay introduced by inter–instruction effects as a random variable.

DEFINITION 5. *The **class pair delay** is the delay introduced by the execution of a class pair (c_i, c_j) at a distance $\hat{w}$ and is modeled by the random variable $D_{i,j,\hat{w}}$. This variable is characterized by its density function:*

$$f_{D_{i,j,\hat{w}}}(d) = \frac{\sum_{k=1}^{N} \delta_{t(\gamma_k, \gamma_{k+\hat{w}}, \hat{w})=d} \langle k, i \rangle \langle k + \hat{w}, j \rangle}{\sum_{k=1}^{N} \langle k, i \rangle \langle k + \hat{w}, j \rangle}$$

where N is suitably large and $\delta_{t(\gamma_k, \gamma_{k+\hat{w}}, \hat{w})=d}$ is the Kronecker symbol, defined as:

$$\delta_{t(\gamma_k, \gamma_{k+\hat{w}}, \hat{w})=d} = \begin{cases} 1 & \text{if } t(\gamma_k, \gamma_{k+\hat{w}}, \hat{w}) = d \\ 0 & \text{otherwise} \end{cases}$$

Given i, j, $\hat{w}$, and d, $f_{D_{i,j,\hat{w}}}(d)$ represents the relative frequency of d-delay interlocks with respect to the class pair (c_i, c_j). Interlock latency associated with a single class—rather than a pair of classes—turns out to be particularly useful when a fast estimation, performed at source level, [2] is required.

Definition 6 formally introduces the idea of class delay.

DEFINITION 6. *The **class delay** is the delay associated with the execution of a class c_j paired with any other class at a distance $\hat{w}$, and is modeled by the stochastic variable $D_{j,\hat{w}}$. This variable is characterized by its density function:*

$$f_{D_{j,\hat{w}}}(d) = \frac{\sum_{k=1}^{N} \delta_{t(\gamma_k, \gamma_{k+\hat{w}}, \hat{w})=d} \langle k + \hat{w}, j \rangle}{\sum_{k=1}^{N} \langle k + \hat{w}, j \rangle}$$

Definitions 5 and 6 are bound by the relation:

$$f_{D_{j,\hat{w}}}(d) = \frac{\sum_{i=0}^{7} f_{D_{i,j,\hat{w}}}(d) P(c_i \overset{\hat{w}}{\dashv} c_j)}{\sum_{i=0}^{7} P(c_i \overset{\hat{w}}{\dashv} c_j)} \tag{5}$$

stating that the density function of the class delay $D_{j,\hat{w}}$ is equal to the sum of the density functions of the pair delays $D_{i,j,\hat{w}}$, weighted by the frequency of the corresponding pair. The importance of this relation is twofold: on one hand, it stresses the formal correctness of the model, as already stated by equation 4; on the other hand, it provides a means to estimate the class delays starting from class pair delays. Class delays can be used to obtain an energy consumption measure, by integrating them into the model described in [1]. According to the cited model, the energy consumption of an assembly instruction is expressed as the average current drawn by the processor during its execution and can be calculated as:

$$\mathbf{IN} = \mathbf{A} \times \mathbf{IF} \tag{6}$$

where **IN** is a vector collecting the total currents of all the instructions $s \in I$, **IF** is a vector storing the average currents per clock cycle associated to a predefined set of processor abstract functionalities and **A** is a matrix accounting for the execution times of each instruction s with respect to these functionalities. Since the main effect of interlocks is an increase of the execution time, a natural way to extend the power model is to add an overhead to the matrix **A**. The new model maintains the same algebraic form provided that **A** is substituted with $\mathbf{A}' = \mathbf{A} + \mathbf{OH}$, where **OH** stores the class overheads, suitably distributed over the different functionalities.

4. MODEL TUNING

This section presents the methodology adopted to tune the proposed model and to provide the estimates for the temporal overhead introduced by inter–instruction effects.

[2]The trace length N of a medium–sized assembly program is about $10^6 - 10^7$ instructions.

[3]Since $N \gg \hat{w}$ the upper limit of the summation $N - \hat{w}$, i.e. the total number of pairs, can be conveniently approximated with N.

Since timing and power effects are decoupled, as pointed out by equation (6), a first tuning phase can be performed considering timing properties only. A validation in terms of energy consumption is out of the scope of this paper. The model proposed in section 3 has been implemented by a tool to be integrated in a co–design environment for evaluating the energy consumption of embedded systems. Such a tool should consider different target architectures and thus its implementation must be as modular as possible. As mentioned above, hazards can be generally considered as particular *events* that occur during the code execution. The tool implementation consists of two portions:

- an architecture dependent inter–instruction model represented by a *list*. When a hazard condition arises (the event), it is detected by matching a corresponding *event model* in the list. This is the implementation of the delay function $t(\gamma_k, \gamma_{k+\hat{w}}, \hat{w})$ defined in section 3.2. Different architectures are characterized by means of a specific configuration file;
- an architecture–independent module responsible of providing a general representation of the assembly, and deriving the density functions associated with stochastic variables.

Estimation of the stochastic variables requires the three steps described below (see figure 1):

- produce an execution trace of a significant number of selected benchmarks;
- parse the assembly code and build an architecture–independent representation;
- check the hazards conditions and derive the distributions of the stochastic variables.

The first step of the tuning process is the generation of the execution trace which carries the dynamic information of the instruction flow into the processor pipeline. The main problem is the selection of a suitable set of benchmarks to be traced. Once a number of such execution traces has been created, the estimated densities of the random variables are assumed to represent a good statistic characterization of the temporal overhead associated with each instruction class pair at a given distance[4]. Creating a suitable execution trace is not trivial at all: the aim is to observe the real dynamic behavior of the pipelined execution, thus it is necessary to obtain data corresponding to a realistic computation. In fact, as pointed out in section 3.1, it is important not only to detect hazards, but also to know the actual probability of finding an instruction pair that flows in the pipeline at a given distance. The adopted approach consists thus in generating the execution traces of real programs operating on real data sets, in such a way to cover a sufficiently wide range of application typologies. The benchmarks used cover typical applications such as image processing, text manipulation and networking. Figure 2 shows the probability of finding all class pairs in the selected execution traces, and the corresponding aggregate values, calculated using equation (4). These values are assumed to represent all the available knowledge on the dynamic behaviour of typical programs. This assumption is justified by the fact that

[4]Distance is a fixed parameter

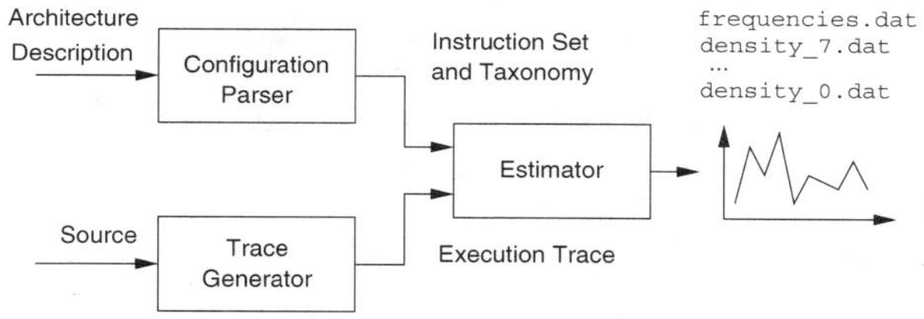

Figure 1: Model tuning execution flow

the obtained data do no exhibit any dependence on the specific benchmarks used. The size of the execution trace is in the range of 10^6-10^7 code lines, i.e. large enough to provide a satisfactory accuracy of the estimates. The second step of the tuning process is aimed at creating a general representation of the given architecture, with respect to both its instruction set and its dynamic behavior. The importance of this process is twofold: one one hand, it allows to apply the same methodology and perform an estimation of the dynamic behavior on different architectures; on the other hand, it is intended to be compatible with the static energy estimation model [1], which will be extended by considering inter–instruction effects. The last step is responsible of detecting hazards operating on an abstract representation of the execution trace. To this purpose, abstract models of the possible hazard conditions must be built. As an example, consider a typical RAW hazard of the Intel Embedded486™: the pipeline stalls for one clock cycle when an instruction that writes a register is immediately followed by an instruction that reads the same register; the following Boolean expression is the abstract model for this specific hazard:

$$(op_1 \equiv *) \wedge (op_2 \equiv *) \wedge ((rd_1 = rs_2[1]) \vee (rd_1 = rs_2[2])), \quad (7)$$

where op_1 is the op–code of the former instruction in the pair, op_2 the one of the latter instruction, rd_i is a register written by instruction i in the pair and $rs_i[j]$ is the jth source register of instruction i; the '$*$' is a wildcard, standing for any operation. This expression evaluates to true when

	C_0	C_1	C_2	C_3	C_4	C_5	C_6	C_7
C_0	0.03%	1.64%	10.53%	0%	0.03%	0%	0.32%	0.01%
C_1	12.14%	0.21%	2.09%	0%	3.23%	0%	0.08%	0.03%
C_2	0.26%	13.76%	36.68%	0%	1.24%	0.03%	2.8%	0.45%
C_3	0%	0%	0%	0%	0%	0%	0%	0%
C_4	0.04%	1.41%	2.84%	0%	2.97%	0.48%	0.11%	0.02%
C_5	0%	0.01%	0.16%	0%	0.32%	0%	0.02%	0%
C_6	0.09%	0.73%	2.89%	0%	0.09%	0.01%	1.69%	0.03%
C_7	0%	0.02%	0.02%	0%	0%	0%	0.49%	0%
Overall	12.56 %	17.78%	55.21%	0%	7.87%	0.52%	5.52%	0.54%

Figure 2: Class pair distance probabilities and aggregate class values

an interlock occurs. For the sake of clarity, consider the following instruction pair:

```
lea  0x4(%ebx,%esi,4),%eax
mov  %eax,0x8078eec
```

The pair will match the model, allowing the recognition of the interlock. For every instruction pair in the execution trace a delay value associated with a class pair can be computed; this process results in a number of random variables describing the statistical overhead introduced by each class pair. Using equation (5) these data can be folded on single classes, obtaining a set of random variables which can be statically used to estimate the timing requirements of each instruction. Table 1 shows the average value of the estimated temporal overheads for all classes, in clock cycles.

Table 1: Class temporal overhead introduced by inter–instruction effects

Class	Average delay	Class	Average delay
c_0	0.433673	c_4	0.515101
c_1	0.185519	c_5	0.108412
c_2	0.484779	c_6	0.499436
c_3	0.000000	c_7	0.042164

Once the random variables have been derived, two different estimation approaches can be devised. A first coarse analysis can be done by averaging the values of the class pair random variables and fold them to single classes. A finer analysis, on the other hand, might exploit all the information contained in the random variables by collecting and combining density functions rather than average values, leading to a statistical characterization of code portions or even entire functions.

5. EXPERIMENTAL RESULTS

The tuning of the model has been made by choosing $\hat{w} = 1$ because at this distance more hazards may arise. As figure 2, points out, class c_3 never appears and has thus an overall zero frequency in the code: in fact, such a class represents all the instructions that may cause both data and control hazards. This condition is never satisfied in the Intel486™. As table 1 shows, the average overhead introduced by each instruction class is generally significant. The model should be validated at two different levels: energy and time. In fact, the translation from the temporal overhead introduced by inter–instruction effects to the actual energy consumption associated with them introduces an additional level of abstraction that need to be confirmed by experimental data. Three solutions have been proposed:

- use an *Instruction Set Simulator* (ISS) which can produce exact timings for both activities of instruction execution and interlock management. This method refers only to timing measures and is only viable if a cycle–accurate instruction set simulator is available;
- simulate the code execution on a given architecture by means of its RTL–HDL model. Though such a solution offers a better accuracy, it is hardly applicable due to the scarce availability of RTL models of processor architectures and to the extremely high computational requirements;
- compute the timing on a test code directly during its execution, overriding delays due to the operating system and to interrupts. Though slightly less accurate, this approach is easily feasible.

The last approach has been adopted and the result obtained are presented in the remaining part of this section. The validation methodology has been applied as follows (see figure 3). A test program is first compiled, then executed and disassembled. The static data in the disassembled code is then combined with the dynamic information derived from the execution trace and then fed to an *annotation tool* which estimates—in an interlock–free manner—the timing of the code. The annotation is based on an *a priori* knowledge of the CPIs of every instruction, which typically depends on its operation code and its addressing modes. The same execution trace is analyzed by a dynamic effects estimator, which produces the total temporal overhead associated with the pipeline interlocks. Interlock–free timing data and temporal overheads are then added to obtain an overall estimate of the test program timing. The estimation of the interlock temporal overhead is performed based on the knowledge of the random variable associated with each instruction class: every instruction is contained in a taxonomy class, and thus inherits the class average temporal overhead which contributes to the total value. In this way, the contribution of the different classes is weighted by the actual frequencies of instructions in the traced code. The result is a more precise estimate of the timing that is then compared with the actual execution time. Five integer benchmark programs—not belonging to the tuning set—have been used to validate the model:

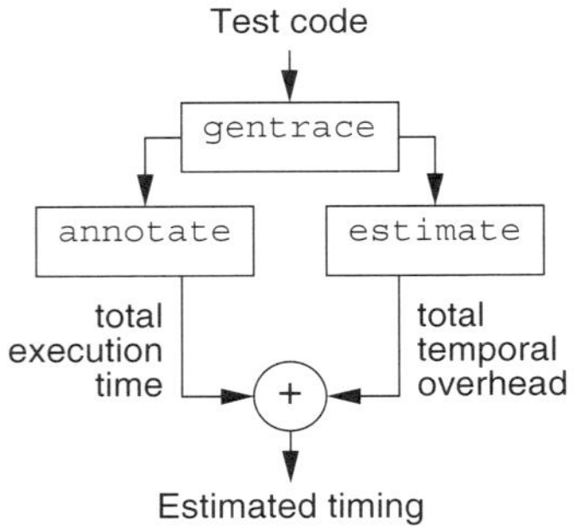

Figure 3: Code execution timing estimation

1. `genprim` generates a 3-digits prime number;
2. `rle` computes the run–length encoding of a string;
3. `crc16` computes the 16–bit CRC on strings;
4. `qsort` implements Quicksort for integers;
5. `md5` computes the digest of a given string.

Table 2 shows the relative errors obtained. The interlock–free static analysis obtained with the annotation tool has an average error around −24.1%, the reason being that it underestimates the clock cycles needed by the execution of each instruction. Considering the inter–instruction effects as well results in a considerable improvement: the error reduces to an average of −1.5%, indicating a much better overall estimation of the dynamic behavior of the processor.

Table 2: Relative errors of the interlock–free and interlock–aware models

Test case	Relative error interlock–free	Relative error interlock–aware
`genprim`	-32.1%	-9.4%
`rle`	-17.9%	+2.7%
`crc16`	-22.1%	+0.3%
`qsort`	-22.1%	-3.7%
`md5`	-26.5%	+2.5%
Overall	-24.1%	-1.5%
Overall (absolute)	24.1%	3.7%

It is important to remark that the applied analysis still ignores dynamic effects resulting from cache misses. For this reason all the benchmarks have been tailored in order to avoid or limit the number of cache misses. An accurate analysis of the results obtained has confirmed that the higher negative error obtained for `genprim` is mostly due to the presence of some uncommon complex addressing modes, currently ignored by the annotation tool.

6. CONCLUSIONS

In this paper a methodology for analyzing dynamic effects in pipelined architectures has been proposed. It is based on a rigorous mathematical model exhibiting satisfactory statistical properties. The results obtained suggest that the model is promising, while still in the early stages of validation. In particular the methodology has been applied to real cases and the estimated execution times have been proved to be much more accurate than those obtained neglecting timing dynamic components related to inter–instruction effects. Estimation errors are in the range of a few percent and are biased towards underestimation, as the model predicts. Such improved accuracy will enable a more precise energy estimation of embedded software programs. The timing model has been effortlessly integrated in a more general power estimation framework and preliminary results on the accuracy of the extended power model are under investigation. Future work will consider the integration of cache miss analysis or, more generally, of memory–related inter–instruction effects. The application of a better validation methodology and of a finer model tuning is currently in progress.

7. REFERENCES

[1] C. Brandolese, W. Fornaciari, F. Salice, and D. Sciuto. An instruction–level functionality–based energy estimation model for 32-bits microprocessors. In *Proceedings of 37th IEEE Design Automation Conference*, pages 346–351, Los Angeles, CA, June 2000.

[2] C. Brandolese, W. Fornaciari, F. Salice, and D. Sciuto. Source–level execution time estimation of c programs. In *Proceedings of International Workshop Hardware Software Codesign*, Copenhagen, Denmark, April 25-27 2001.

[3] J. Hennessy and D. A. Patterson. *Computer Architecture - A Quantitative Approach.* Morgan Kaufmann Publishers, San Mateo, II edition, 1996.

[4] E. Macii, M. Pedram, and F. Somenzi. High-level power modeling, estimation, and optimization. *IEEE Transactions on Computer-Aided Design of Integrated Circuits and Systems*, 17(11):1061–1079, November 1998.

[5] Intel Architecture Software Developer's Manual vol. 1. Technical report, Intel Corporation, 1997.

[6] The SPARC Architecture Manual, version 8. Technical report, Sun Microsystems, 1990.

[7] microSPARC™-IIep user's manual. Technical report, Sun Microsystems, 1997.

[8] A. Mood, F. Graybill, and D. Boes. *Introduction to the theory of statistics.* McGraw–Hill, New York, NY, 1988.

[9] PEOPLE. (Power Estimation for Fast Exploration of Embedded Systems). Technical Report D3.3.1, ESPRIT-ESD project n.26769, 1998.

[10] S. Ramalingam and K. Schindler. Instruction level power model and its application to general purpose processors. *IEEE Transactions on Computer-Aided Design of Integrated Circuits and Systems*, pages 753–756, 1998.

[11] J. Russell and M. Jacome. Software power estimation and optimization for high performance, 32-bit embedded processors. In *Proceedings of ICCD'98, International Conference on Computer Design*, pages 328–333, Austin, TX, October 1998.

[12] V. Tiwari, S. Malik, and A. Wolfe. Power analysis of embedded software: a first step towards software power minimization. *IEEE Transactions on VLSI Systems*, 2(4):437–445, December 1994.

[13] V. Tiwari, S. Malik, and A. Wolfe. Power Analysis of the Intel 486DX2. Computer Engineering Technical Report No. CE-M94-5, Princeton University, June 1994.

System Level Optimization and Design Space Exploration for Low Power

Ansgar Stammermann, Lars Kruse, Wolfgang Nebel, Alexander Pratsch, Eike Schmidt, Milan Schulte, and Arne Schulz
OFFIS Research Institute
Oldenburg, Germany
ansgar.stammermann@offis.de

ABSTRACT

We present a software tool for power dissipation analysis and optimization on the algorithmic abstraction level from C/C++ and VHDL descriptions. An analysis is most efficient on such a high level since the influence of design decisions on the power demand increases with increasing abstraction [1]. The ORINOCO® tool enables to compare different but functionally equivalent algorithms and bindings to RT-level architectures with respect to power consumption. The results of the optimized binding can be used to guide synthesis. In the experimental evaluation we compare the predicted optimization trend with synthesized implementations and prove the accuracy of our methodology and tool.

1. INTRODUCTION

Over the last few years, the integration density as well as the clock rate of microelectronic circuits have increased enormously. Today, a chip consists of several million gates. This development has led to the fact that the power dissipation of such systems has become an increasingly important criterion in the design process. A higher power dissipation reduces the battery operating time of mobile applications, raises the production costs and lessens the reliability of the circuit. A lot of techniques have already been proposed to take power consumption into account in high level synthesis. Among them are optimizations like algebraic transformations, usage of multiple supply voltages, loop transformations etc. See [2] for detailed overview.

In the extremely complex design of microelectronic circuits, the problem of estimating the effects of different design alternatives on the power dissipation arises. Design decisions made in a very early phase of the development process, in which the design consists of a yet very abstract description (algorithmic abstraction level), have the greatest influence on the power dissipation (Figure 1). Previously existing design tools require a highly advanced design process, however, in order to execute a power dissipation analysis. Consequently, nearly complete iterations through the development process are necessary in order to measure the power consumption and met power constraints. Such a procedure is time-consuming, cost-intensive and incompatible with the ever-shorter innovation cycles in circuit design.

The development of the software called ORINOCO® (OFFIS Research INstitute pOwer Characterizer, estimator and Optimizer) intends to create a power dissipation analysis and optimization on the algorithmic abstraction level. It allows for flexible treatment of different circuit variants and the ability to consider the influence of processed data on power dissipation.

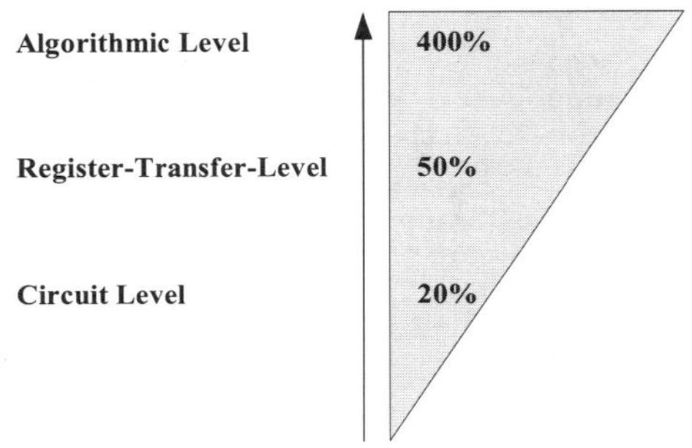

Figure 1. Influence of design decisions on the power dissipation at different levels of abstraction [1]

In Section 2 of the paper we describe the overall design flow for high level power optimization with ORINOCO®. The underlying analysis and optimization techniques are detailed in Section 3. An experimental evaluation is presented in Section 4 before providing a short summary in Section 5.

2. DESIGN FLOW

Our power dissipation analysis assumes the design flow depicted in Figure 2. The designer creates a system specification. This specification is subdivided into its different subtasks (tasks). For example, with an image processing chip, tasks could include motion estimation or a Fourier transform. For the realization of a task, several algorithms typically exist. As an example, a Fourier transform can be executed via a matrix multiplication or a fast Fourier transform. When an algorithm is found, the appurtenant

ISSS '01, October 1-3, 2001, Montreal, Quebec, Canada.

architecture is determined during the high-level synthesis (scheduling, allocation, binding), i.e. the algorithm is transformed into hardware. Again, there are many design decisions to be made. Scheduling determines during which clock cycle an operation will be executed. In the allocation task, the type and number of the components to be used (adders, multipliers etc.) is determined. In doing so, components are distinguished not only by their function, but also by their internal architecture. An adder can be realized as a carry-ripple or carry-select adder. "Binding" means the mapping of operations onto the components that were determined during allocation.

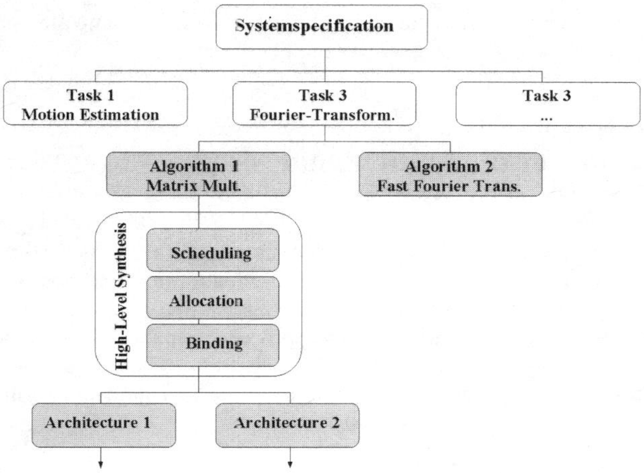

Figure 2. Design Flow

In regard to power dissipation, the designer must confront the following questions:

1. Which algorithm is the best?
2. What does the best architecture for an algorithm look like?
3. Which is the best architecture of a component?
4. How does the bit width of a component influence the power dissipation ?

It is the goal of the ORINOCO tool® to give the designer assistance in answering these questions.

3. UNDERLYING TECHNIQUE

The power dissipation analysis is based on simulation. A profiling of the hardware description, which can exist both in VHDL as well as in C/C++, is carried out in order to collect data statistics. At the same time, the expected circuit structure is derived from a control data flow graph, without carrying out a complete synthesis. Components of the RT level, upon which the design is later mapped, are first characterized [3]. The power assessment of the memory also takes place based on a characterization [4].

3.1 Model generation

For the power dissipation, analysis models are needed that describe the power dissipation of the individual components of the RT level. In general, the power dissipation depends on the input data, the characteristics of the components (e.g. bit width and architecture,) and the underlying cell library or technology.

The *Component Modeler* allows for the generation of such models (Figure 3). The models may contain parameters of both bit width and architecture. Once generated, models are stored in a library and are available for future analysis and optimization [3, 4].

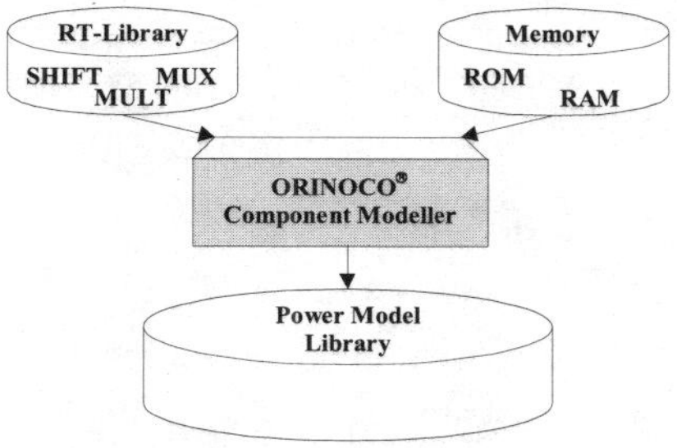

Figure 3. Model generation

Moreover, an open interface allows for the usage of user-defined components. This enables the simultaneous employment of IPs.

3.2 Low power allocation and binding

"Binding" concerns the mapping of operations or variables onto components during the high-level synthesis. A low power binding is a mapping in which the power dissipation of the components is minimal. Binding has a great influence on power dissipation, since different bindings lead to different input currents on the inputs of the components. Let's assume that two 1-bit variables with the input streams (1,1,0,0) and (1,1,0,0), respectively, are mapped to a register each (no resource sharing), thus leading to two transitions on the inputs. If the variables are mapped onto a single register (resource sharing), however, only one transition (1,1,1,1,0,0,0,0) arises. The data flows (1,1,0,0) and (0,0,1,1) on the other hand produce six transitions with only a single register and two transitions with two registers.

The basis for our calculation is a control data flow graph (CDFG) and simulation data. Through an analysis of the graph, a complete ordering of the execution sequence of operations of the same type (e.g. addition, multiplication) is determined (scheduling). This ordering determines which operations can be mapped together onto a component and which cannot. With the simulation data and the power dissipation models, the electric power consumption for a given binding of a component can be determined.

On the basis of these data, a lower and an upper bound to the power dissipation for each component type are calculated [5]. The problem is formulated as a bipartite-weighted matching problem, which is solvable in $O(n^3)$. The bounds calculated in this way do not necessarily correspond to a legal binding, i.e. no appropriate architecture can be synthesized. Therefore, heuristics are introduced in [6] that form a legal binding out of an illegal solution. A binding found in this way is not necessarily equal to the minimum or the maximum in regard to the power dissipation, but comes very close, as shown in our experimental evaluations.

3.3 Work flow

The starting point for the analysis is the hardware description and its test bench (Figure 4). Additionally, a few boundary conditions must be set by the user:

The technology must be determined. The appropriate power dissipation model for this technology is assigned to each component type. Additionally, a component type must be assigned to each operator in the description. This determines components upon which an operator of the description may be mapped. Operations on the critical path can thus be realized through high-consumption, fast components, while others can be realized through low-consumption, slow components.

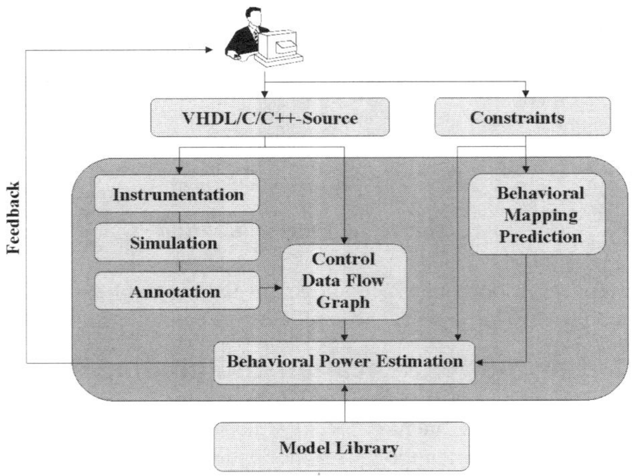

Figure 4. ORINOCO® Work flow

ORINOCO® is capable of reading in both VHDL as well as C/C++ descriptions. The work flow of the tool varies, however, depending on the language used. VHDL descriptions are simulated whereas C/C++ source code are translated and then executed.

3.3.1 VHDL description

The VHDL description is simulated in order to determine the input data streams on the individual operations. The description is automatically instrumented for that purpose. Special routines are inserted into the specification that write the input data streams of the individual operations into an activity file during a simulation. Simulation is possible with every commercial simulator (VSS, ModelSim, etc.). The work flow for VHDL descriptions is as follows:

1. The VHDL description is compiled and elaborated.
2. A control data flow graph is generated from the elaborated design.
3. The VHDL description is instrumented.
4. The modified VHDL description is simulated.
5. The input data streams from the activity file are annotated on the corresponding operations in the graph.
6. The order of execution of the operations is determined (scheduling).

3.3.2 C/C++ description

In contrast to VHDL, C/C++ descriptions are not simulated. They are translated and executed in order to determine the input data streams on the operations. During the translation, the generated program is automatically instrumented. Special test routines that write input data streams into an activity file during execution are inserted. At the same time, a structure file is created, from which a control data flow graph is later generated. The work flow for C/C++ descriptions is as follows:

1. The C/C++ description is translated. In doing so, the executable program is instrumented and at the same time a structure file is written.
2. The program is executed.
3. A control data flow graph is generated from the structure file.
4. The input data streams from the activity file are annotated on the corresponding operations in the graph.
5. The order of execution of the operations is determined.

3.4 Power dissipation analysis

A large part of the power dissipation analysis is based on the solution of the low power binding. For every employed component type, the binding is calculated with a minimal (light gray) and maximal (dark gray) power dissipation for each possible number of resources (allocation) (Figure 5). The difference between the bars corresponds to the power dissipation that can be influenced by the selection of the binding. The underlying reservation tables can be written to a file for later guidance of the synthesis tool.

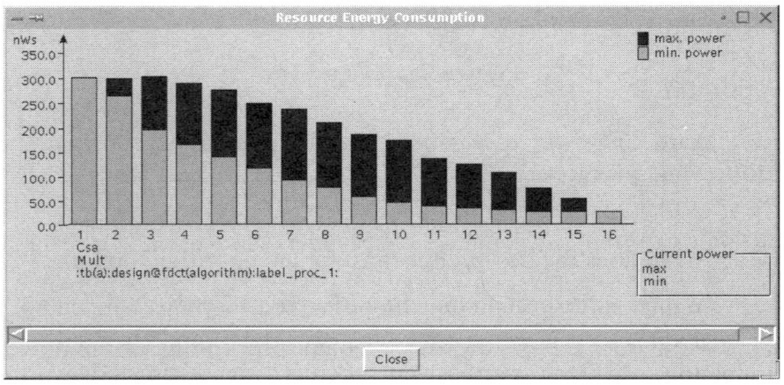

Figure 5. Minimal and maximal power dissipation of different bindings

The power dissipation assessment of the connecting structures, connecting wires and multiplexors is based on the power dissipation-optimal bindings. The interconnect structures are generated by a architecture extraction. For each input of a component that possesses two or more sources, a multiplexor is instantiated. This can emerge through control structures or resource sharing. The control structures are extracted from the control data flow graph. Resource sharing follows from the given binding. The power dissipation of the multiplexor is calculated from the simulation data and the corresponding power dissipation model. For the calculation of the power demand of the wires, their individual lengths must first be determined. The assessment of length is based on an extension of the Growth-Limited Multifold Clustering (GLMC) technique [7, 8]. This algorithm is based on clustering, a constructive placement algorithm. Together with simulation data and the wire model, the power dissipation for each wire is calculated. The power dissipation of memories and IO ports is also calculated on the basis of the power models. In contrast to the interconnect structures, their number and characteristics are, however, independent of the underlying binding.

4. RESULTS

For the evaluation, the degree to which ORINOCO® is capable of predicting the relative power consumption of different algorithms performing the same functionality was evaluated. In a further step, the capability to optimize the power demand of different architectures for a single algorithm was examined. For comparison of different architectures for a real life example please refer to [9].

4.1 Analysis of different algorithms

For the analysis of different algorithms, the DIFFEQ benchmark [10], an algorithm for the solution of a differential equation, was chosen. This benchmark is synthesizable with the Synopsys Behavioral Compiler® and an appurtenant test bench supplies the necessary input data for the simulation. In Table 1, a section of the original description of the algorithm is represented under algorithm 1. This part of the description was modified in algorithm 2 and 3 without changing the semantics. First the expression 3*d and next the variable u were factored out.

Table 1. Different algorithms for DIFFEQ benchmark

Algorithm 1	u := u - 3 * d * u * x - 3 * d * y
Algorithm 2	u := u - **3 * d** * (u * x + y)
Algorithm 3	u := **u** * (1 – 3 * d * x) - 3 * d * y

ORINOCO® first calculated the power dissipation for each algorithm. Subsequently, the algorithms were synthesized to gate level circuits. In the synthesis, the optimized bindings calculated by ORINOCO® were taken into consideration. The power dissipation of these synthesized circuits was estimated with Synopsys DesignPower®.

In Figure 7, the normalized results for each circuit are contrasted. The power dissipation increased due to the modification in circuit 2. In 3, on the other hand, the power demand could be lowered. In 2b the power optimized bindings calculated by ORINOCO® were not considered. For both tools, no resource sharing was permitted. The power demand increased as expected. In 3b the multiplication with the constant 3 was replaced by the following instructions:

u := u * (1 – **3** * d * x) - **3** * d * y

⇒ t := 2 * d

t := t + d

u := u * (1 – t * x) - t * y

Since a multiplication with the constant 2 is realized by a low-consumption shift, the power demand could thus be further lowered.

As is to be seen from the results, since the trend predicted by ORINOCO® from the algorithm could be confirmed by the synthesized circuit a prediction of the effects of different design alternatives is already possible with ORINOCO® at this point.

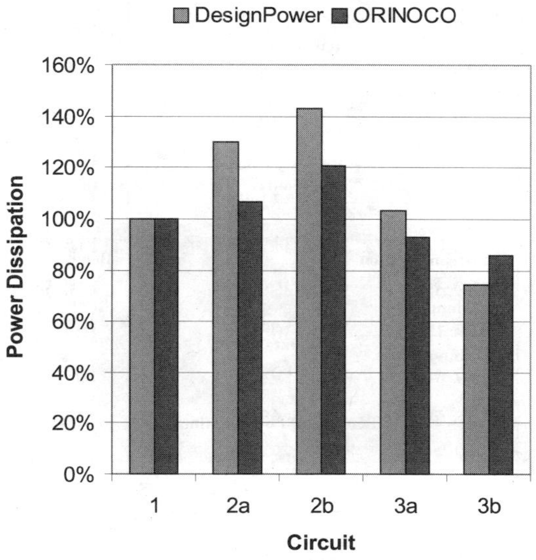

ORINOCO®

4.2 Analysis of different architectures for a single algorithm

As an example for the analysis of different architectures, a VHDL description of a FDCT was chosen. The circuit contains 16 multiplications that are considered in the following. Each multiplication is assigned to the component type CSA multiplier, i.e. all multiplications of the specification could be mapped onto a CSA multiplier.

ORINOCO® calculates the binding for each number of multipliers (1 to 16) with a minimal and maximal power dissipation. Subsequently, the circuit was synthesized for every number of multipliers with consideration to the best and worst binding for that gate level. The power dissipations for the synthesized architectures determined with Synopsys DesignPower® are entered in Table 2. No difference is present for 1 and 16 multipliers, since only one possible binding exists there.

The results reflect the trend predicted by ORINOCO®. The least power dissipation can be attained e.g. for a good binding with 14 or 15 multipliers (cf. Figure 5).

Table 2. Influence of the binding on the power dissipation

No. of mult.	Best binding [uW]	Worst binding [uW]	Difference
1	264,07	264,07	0,00
2	235,86	340,38	104,52
3	196,19	388,02	191,83
4	165,28	343,92	178,64
5	218,61	343,67	125,06
6	246,04	331,53	85,50
7	195,64	312,53	116,89
8	189,39	299,96	110,57
9	199,18	303,49	104,31
10	187,36	198,34	10,98
11	158,59	163,51	4,92
12	115,34	157,33	41,99
13	77,90	176,42	98,53
14	73,16	118,76	45,60
15	98,06	143,59	45,53
16	82,90	82,90	0,00

5. SUMMARY

ORINOCO® allows the designer to already make an efficient analysis and optimization of the design on the algorithmic level of abstraction. On this level, the influence of design decisions on the power dissipation increases considerably. It therefore makes possible decisive improvements in the design and compliance with given power consumption limits.

6. REFERENCES

[1] A. Raghunathan, N.K. Niraj, S. Dey, "High-Level Power Analysis and Optimization", Kluwer Academic Publishers, 1998

[2] E. Macii, M. Pedram, F. Somenzi, "High Level Power Modeling, Estimation, and Optimization", IEEE Transactions on Computer-Aided Design of Integrated Circuits and Systems, 17(11), pp. 1061 – 1079, November 1998

[3] G. Jochens, L. Kruse, E. Schmidt, W. Nebel, "A New Parameterizable Power Macro-Model for Datapath Components", in Proc. for DATE, pp. 29-36, 1999

[4] E. Schmidt, G. Jochens, L. Kruse, W. Nebel, "Automatic Nonlinear Memory Power Modelling", in Proc. for DATE, p. 808, 2001

[5] L. Kruse, E. Schmidt, G. Jochens, A. Stammermann, A. Schulz, E. Macii, and W. Nebel, "Estimation of Lower and Upper Bounds on the Power Consumption from Scheduled Data Flow Graphs", IEEE Transactions on Very Large Scale Integration (VLSI) Systems", pp. 3 – 14, February 2001

[6] L. Kruse, E. Schmidt, G. Jochens, A. Stammermann, W. Nebel, "Low Power Binding Heuristics", PATMOS-99, pp. 41-50, 1999

[7] A. Alvandpour, "Power Estimation and Low Power CMOS Circuit Techniques", Chapter 4, Linköping Studies in Science and Technology, Dissertation Nr. 587, 1999

[8] A. Alvandpour, P. Larsson-Edefors, C. Svenssons, "GLMC: Interconnect Length Estimation by Growth-Limited Multifold Clustering", Proceedings of IEEE International Symposium on Circuits and Systems, pp. V 465-8, Geneva, Switzerland, 2000

[9] A. Allara, M. Bombana, L. Kruse, E. Schmidt, A. Stammermann, "VHDL Behavioural Power Estimation for Telecom Devices", accepted at FDL, Lyon, September 2001

[10] N. Dutt and C. Ramachandran, Benchmarks for the 1992 high level synthesis workshop, Tech. Rep. #92-107, Dep. Inform. Comput. Sci., Univ. California, Irvine, 1992

Efficient Instruction-Level Optimization Methodology for Low-Power Embedded Systems*

Kyu-won Choi and Abhijit Chatterjee
School of Electrical and Computer Engineering
Georgia Institute of Technology
Atlanta, GA 30332
{kwchoi,.chat}@ece.gatech.edu

Abstract

In this paper, for low-power embedded systems, we solve the instruction scheduling and reordering problem as a Precedence Constrained Hamiltonian Path Problem for DAGs and the Traveling Salesman Problem (TSP), both of which are NP-Hard [1,2]. We propose an efficient instruction-level optimization algorithm for solving the NP-Hard problem. Minimum spanning tree (MST) and simulated annealing (SA) mechanisms are used for the optimization. We describe the methods for generating the control flow and data dependence graph (CDG), power dissipation table (PDT), and weighted strongly connected graph (SCG) for the instruction-level low-power analysis. In addition, confidence limits with error tolerance are considered for the validation of the optimization. Finally, experimental results that demonstrate the effectiveness and the efficiency of the proposed algorithms are shown.

1 Introduction and Previous Work

Recently, new research directions in reducing power consumptions for embedded systems have begun to address the issues of arranging software at the instruction level to control power dissipation [3,4,5,6,7,8,9,10]. The energy consumed by a processor depends on the previous state of the system and the current inputs. Therefore, it is clear that proper instruction choice and ordering should be considered for low-power embedded systems.

There has been previous research on instruction-level scheduling to reduce total power consumption. In [3], a technique called cold scheduling was combined with Gray code addressing to reduce the switching activity in the control path of high-performance processors. The cold scheduling algorithm works much the same way as traditional list scheduling with the exception that it schedules instructions based on a modified priority scheme.

Another scheduling technique for reducing power consumption is introduced in [4,5]. The goal here is to reschedule code such that instructions are more judiciously chosen as opposed to actually reordering instructions to reduce power. In order to achieve the goal of low-power scheduling, the authors implement a methodology for determining the energy consumption of a single instruction in which they measure the current through the processor when that instruction is executed, using hardware.

In [6], the authors introduce a redundant search space reduction scheme called BARS. Basically, BARS examines all possible schedules of a DAG, and finds the schedule with the lowest cost. The BARS algorithm employs two techniques for runtime efficiency. One technique avoids potentially redundant search, and another technique limits the number of sub-trees to be searched.

In this paper, we propose an efficient instruction-level optimization algorithm for low-power embedded systems. The proposed scheme has the following benefits:

1) The instruction-ordering problem for low power is formulated as a combinatorial graph-search optimization problem, yielding near-optimal results.
2) RTL-level power simulators are used to drive the optimization process.
3) A methodology for validating the results of the optimization process is presented.

2 Key Contributions

In this paper, we tackle the following problems with regard to instruction-level optimization:

1) The choice of instruction sequences is critical to reducing power consumption. The instruction scheduling or reordering problem is equivalent to the Precedence Constrained Hamiltonian Path problem for DAGs and the Traveling Salesman Problem in general, both of which are *NP-Hard.* With n instructions, there are (n-1)!/2 possible instruction sequences. For example, for 11 instructions, there are 16,314,400 possible combinations of the instruction sequences. For large numbers of instructions it is practically impossible to examine all possible instruction sequences to find the optimal sequence for low power. Recent research has demonstrated that design decisions made at the RTL level can have a dramatic impact on the overall power characteristics of the design [3,4.5,7,8]. Therefore, power estimation of assembly instructions at the RTL level is very useful, if accuracy is guaranteed within reasonable simulation time constraints.

* This work is sponsored by DARPA under the grant # E21-F48.

ISSS'01, October 1-3, 2001, Montréal, Québec, Canada.

2) Due to the large search space, the optimality of the search algorithm should be validated at the very least in a probabilistic sense.

3 Problem Description

The general procedure for instruction-level analysis is shown in Figure 1(a-d):

1) Assembly instructions are assembled from the source program.
2) The assembly code is decomposed into Basic Blocks (BB).
3) Control and data dependency graph (CDG) is constructed.

After obtaining the CDG, instruction scheduling is performed for each BB and optimal instruction code for low power is provided.

The main problem in instruction-level scheduling is that the search space of the possible instruction sequences is very large. The search space for six instructions of an FIR filter source code for one BB is shown in Figure 1(e). Even though only six instructions are considered, the search space is large.

Figure 2(a) shows a power dissipation table (PDT) which shows the average power consumed when an instruction in the left most column is followed by an instruction in the topmost rows. The control flow and data dependency graph (CDG) of Figure 2(b) shows the inter-dependency of instructions. For example, instruction ④ can be executed only after instruction ① and ② have both been executed, while instructions ①,②, and ③ may be executed in any order. The weighted strongly connected graph (SCG) of Figure 2(c) contains all the edges of the CDG of Figure 2(b) and some additional edges. If the order in which any two instructions are executed can be interchanged without violating the constraints of the CDG, then an additional edge is inserted between the graph nodes (vertices) corresponding to the two instructions. For example, the instruction ④ and ⑤ of the CDG in Figure 2(b) can be interchanged. Hence, in Figure 2(c), there is an edge between the nodes ④ and ⑤. Each edge of the SCG is assigned a weight corresponding to the power consumed by running the pair of instructions repeatedly. It is assumed that the order in which the instruction pair is executed does not matter.

Once the SCG is obtained, a minimum spanning tree algorithm in Figure 2(d) is used to obtain an initial sequence for the optimization. After the MST is performed, local improvement heuristics are conducted by using simulated annealing to obtain an optimal (least cost) Hamiltonian Tour of all the vertices of the SCG as shown in Figure 2(e). This tour gives the optimal sequence of instructions from the viewpoint of power. In this case, the optimal sequence is ③,②,①,④,⑤,⑥.

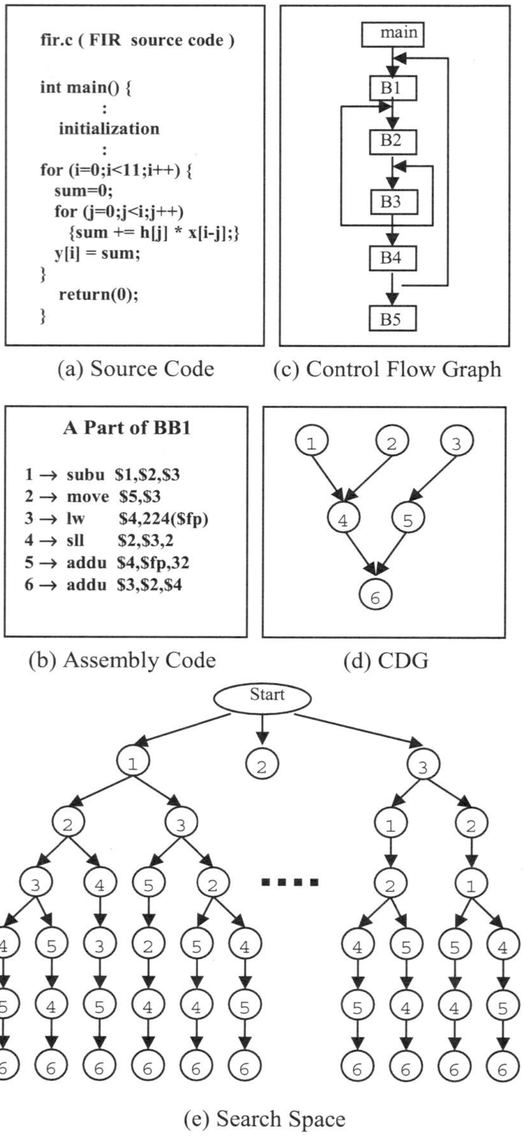

(a) Source Code (c) Control Flow Graph

(b) Assembly Code (d) CDG

(e) Search Space

Figure 1. CDG and Search Space Example

4 Optimization Procedure

The instruction-level optimization methodology is given below:

Step1: Assemble the source code
Step2: Decompose into basic blocks
Step3: Construct CDG for each basic block
Step4: Generate PDT from power simulation
Step5: Build weighted SCG from CDG and PDT
Step6: Solve TSP problem to find optimal or near optimal solution
Step7: Validate the optimization algorithm
Step8: Generate instruction sequence for low-power

	subu	move	lw	sll	addu
subu	5	1	5	3	6
move	1	2	3	9	2
lw	5	3	2	8	7
sll	3	9	8	2	1
addu	8	2	7	1	1

(a) PDT

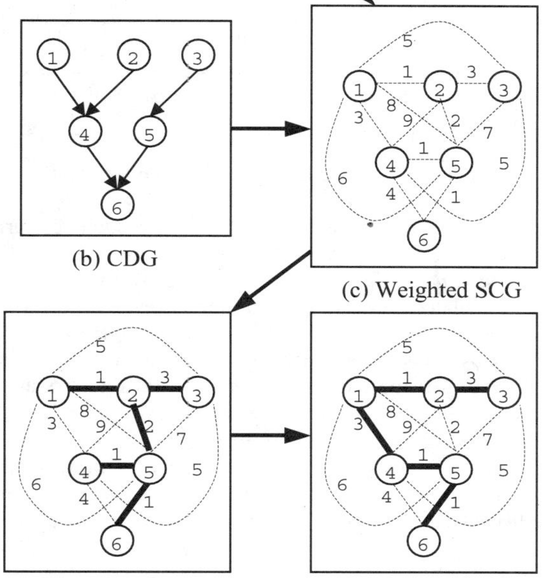

(b) CDG

(c) Weighted SCG

(d) After Minimum Spanning Tree

(e) After Simulated Annealing

Figure 2. Our Approach

In the following, we discuss specific steps of the optimization procedure.

4.1 CDG Construction

First, we review basic graph notations that are used in this paper. A graph ***G*** consists of a set of nodes ***V***, and a set of edges ***E***, ***G = <V,E>***. The degree of a node is the number of neighbors adjacent to it. We write ***X→Y*** when ***<X,Y> ∈ E*** in a directed graph. We define ***PRED(X)*** as the set of the all predecessors of node ***X***, and ***SUCC(X)*** as the set of all successors of ***X***. If ***X→Y***, then ***X ∈ PRED(Y)*** and ***Y ∈ SUCC(X)***. The ***indegree*** of a node ***X*** is the cardinality of ***PRED(X)*** and the ***outdegree*** of a node ***X*** is the cardinality of ***SUCC(X)***. The ***indegree(X)*** is the number of edges of the form ***W→X***, and the ***outdegree(X)*** is the number of edges ***X → Y***. If ***W→X*** , then ***W ∈ INDEG(X)*** and ***X ∈ OUTDEG(W)***. So, the ***OUTDEG(W)*** is a sub set of ***SUCC(W)***, and the ***INDEG(X)*** is the sub set of ***PRED(X)***. The notation ***X *→Y*** is to mean that there is a path from ***X*** to ***Y***. The control flow and data dependency graph specifies the execution order among the components for given instructions to obey the original program semantics. Figure 3 shows the CDG construction algorithm.

Algorithm 1 Algorithm for CDG Construction

Input: Instruction-level source code
Output: Control and Data flow DAG representation
Definition: **idn:x** : id number (**idn**) for each instruction **x**
src_pre(x) : source operands of previous instruction of **x**
des_pre(x) : destination operands of previous instruction of **x**
src(x) : current source operands of **x**
des(x) : current destination operand of **x**

step 0: Set identity number (**idn:x**) for each instruction **x**.
step 1: Calculate total BB number and store the start **idn** of each **BB**.
step 2: For each **x** in **BB**, visit **x**, identify **src_pre(x)**, **des_pre(x)**, **src(x)**, and **des(x)**.
step 3: IF there is any **y** in **des_pre(x)** associated with **src(x)**, THEN create an **<x,y>∈E** in **G=<V,E>** and remove **y** from **des_pre(x)**
step 4: IF there is any **y** in **des_pre(x)** associated with **des(x)**, THEN create an **<x,y>∈E** in **G=<V,E>** and remove **y** from **des_pre(x)**
step 5: IF there is any **y** in **src_pre(x)** associated with **des(x)**, THEN create an **<x,y>∈E** in **G=<V,E>** and remove **y** from **src_pre(x)**
step 6: IF there is any **x** in **BB** to be scheduled, THEN go to **step 2**. ELSE generate CDG graph and return.

Figure 3. CDG Construction Algorithm

4.2 PDT Generation

The power dissipation table describes the power consumption due to the execution of an instruction itself and a pair of instructions. We use a cycle-accurate data path energy model at the RTL level. A cycle-by-cycle instruction-level simulator is used to collect the switching activity at all latches in the data path during execution of the program. The SimpleScalar tool set [11], version 3.0 with RTL level power model is used. Our target machine has a five-stage pipelined data path and the functional units are 32-32bit general registers, I-cache, D-cache, divider, multiplier, ALU, shifter, and control units.

Details of generating infinite loops to measure the power dissipation due to an instruction itself and an instruction pair are shown in Figure 4. To avoid any corruption due to loop overhead, we repeat the instruction pair 200,000 times with a *nop* operation.

```
main:
:
lw    $2,228($fp)  }
move  $5,$4        }
nop                }
lw    $2,228($fp)  }
move  $5,$4        }
nop                }
lw    $2,228($fp)  }
move  $5,$4        }
nop                }
... 200,000 times
:
```

Figure 4. PDT Generation Example

4.3 SCG Generation

We define a strongly connected graph that is a set of nodes S such that there is $S_1 *\!\!\rightarrow S_2$ for any two nodes $S_1, S_2 \in S$. As shown in Figure 2(c) in Section 3, the weighted SCG is a sub set of all possible instructions corresponding to the CDG. The SCG Generation algorithm is shown in Figure 5.

Algorithm 2 Algorithm for SCG Generation

Input: CDG stream
Output: SCG DAG representation (summation of **SCCs**)
Definition: indegree(X) : the number of edges of **W→X**
outdegree(X) : the number of edges of **X→Y**
INDEG(X) : If W→X , then W ∈ INDEG(X)
OUTDEG(X) : If X→Y , then Y ∈ OUTDEG(X)
SCC(X) : strongly connected components of **X** means that the components in **SCC(X)** may be followed by an instruction **X** (i.e., **SCC(X)= [Y, Z]:Y,Z** can be followed by **X**)

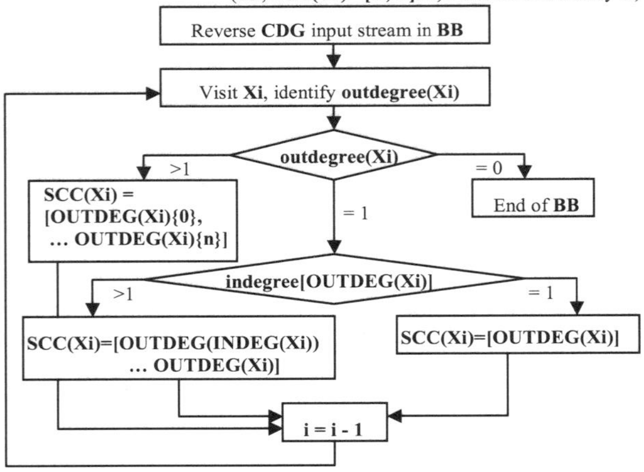

Figure 5. SCG Generation Algorithm

4.4 TSP Realization

In the general form of the *traveling salesman problem*, we are given a finite set of points V and a cost c_{uv} of travel between each pair $u.v \in V$. A tour is a circuit that passes exactly once through each point in V. The TSP is to find a tour of minimal cost. The TSP can be modeled as a graph problem by considering a complete graph $G = <V,E>$, and assigning each edge $u.v \in E$ the cost c_{uv}. A tour is then a circuit in G that meets every node. The tours are sometimes called *Hamiltonian Circuits*. The TSP is one of the best-known problems of combinatorial optimization. A nice collection of papers tracing the history and research on the problem can be found in [12]. No polynomial-time algorithm is known for solving the TSP in general. Indeed, it belongs to the class of *NP-Hard* problems.

Heuristics are methods that cannot be guaranteed to produce optimal solutions, but which produce fairly good solutions at least some of the time. For the TSP, there are two different types of heuristics. The first attempts to construct a good tour from scratch. The second tries to improve an existing tour, by means of local improvements. In practice it seems very difficult to get a really good tour construction method [12]. In this paper, as a construction method, we use a minimum-cost spanning tree by using Prim's Algorithm [13], and as a improvement method, we use ***2-optimal*** and ***3-optimal*** local search heuristics by using simulated annealing. Prim's algorithm is used for computing a minimum spanning tree. It builds upon a single partial minimum spanning tree, at each step adding an edge connecting the vertex nearest to but not already in the current partial minimum spanning tree. If Prim's Algorithm is applied to the graph of Figure 6(a) with starting vertex ***a***, edges are chosen in the order ***ab***, ***af***, ***ac***, ***cd***, ***dg***, ***de*** as shown in Figure 6(b).

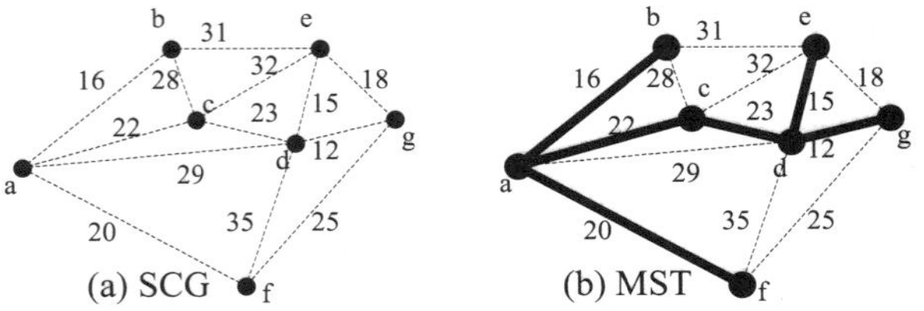

Figure 6. Prim's Algorithm Example for MST

The MST solution is used as a starting point for further optimization using heuristics. In this paper, we use ***2-optimal*** and ***3-optimal*** mechanisms for the improvement heuristic, using simulated annealing with the reasonable cooling parameters as the optimization engine. The ***2-optimal*** heuristic proceeds by considering each non-adjacent pair of edges of tree T in turn. If these edges are deleted, the T breaks up into two paths T_1 and T_2. There is a unique way that these two paths can be recombined to form a new tour T'. If $c(T') < c(T)$, then we replace T with T' and repeat the procedure. As shown in Figure 7, if $c(T') > c(T)$ for every choice of pairs of nonadjacent edges, then T is ***2-optimal*** and we terminate the procedure.

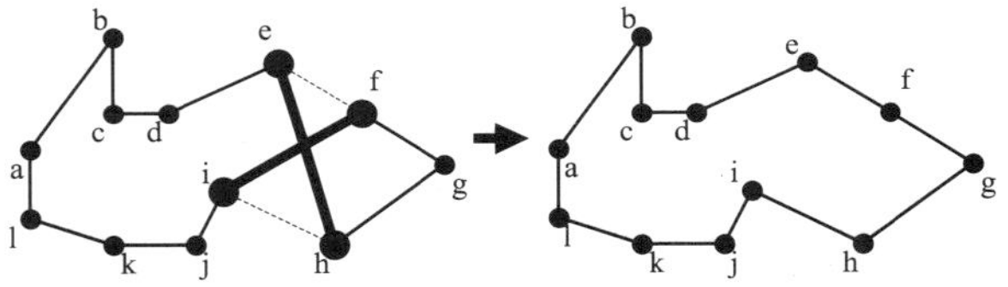

Figure 7. 2-Interchange Local Search Heuristics

The ***2-optimal*** algorithm can be generalized naturally to a ***k-optimal*** algorithm, wherein we consider all subsets of the edge-set of a tour of size of k, or size at most k, remove each subset in turn, then see if the resulting paths can be recombined to form a tour of lesser cost. The problem is that the number of subsets grows exponentially with k, and we soon reach a point of diminishing return. For this reason, ***k-optimal*** for $k>3$ is rarely used. Figure 8 shows ***3-optimal*** example. In this paper we use both the ***2-optimal*** and the ***3-optimal*** heuristics for optimization.

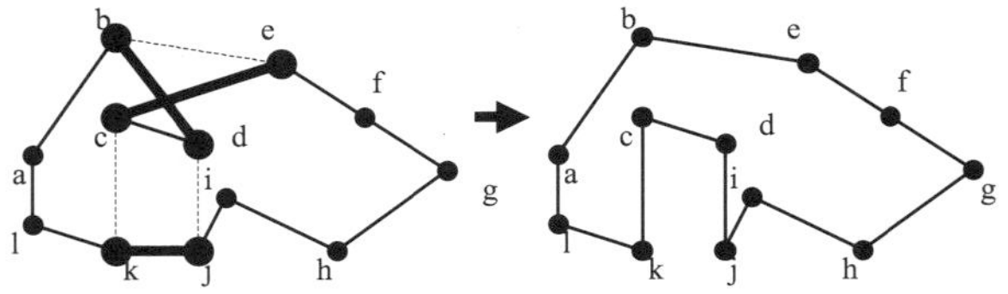

Figure 8. 3-Interchange Local Search Heuristics

5 Validation of Optimization Methodology

Let us designate the sample space $n=(k-1)!/2$ for k instructions in a **BB**. Let us define v as an input vector for an instruction sequence, define random variable $W(v)$ to be the power dissipation of the system when v is applied. If we choose j input vectors $v_1, v_2,\ldots,v_j$ randomly and exclusively, the power dissipation obtained in each trial is also an independent random variable (RV) $W_j=W(v_j)$, $j=1,\ldots,n$. Since the W_j are independent, the set $\{W_1, W_2,\ldots,W_j\}$ constitutes a random sample. We define a new RV $X_j=min(W_1, W_2,\ldots,W_j)$, so that X_j is the minimum power dissipation over j trials.

Let us designate the jth ordered observation oX_j and the fraction of the population below this observation as $P_j=F(_oX_j)$. Since the value of oX_j varies from sample to sample, P_j is a random variable. Thus we must consider the distribution of P_j. We will now proceed with the development of the distribution for P_j.

Given an ordered random sample $_oX_1$, $_oX_2$, ..., $_oX_n$ of size n from a population having a cumulative distribution function $F(X)$, where X is continuous, we try to find estimators for $F(_oX_1)$, $F(_oX_1)$, ... , $F(_oX_n)$. Let us define $_nP_j=F(_oX_j)$, where $_nP_j$ is the probability of failing to find an optimal minimum sequence X_n prior to the jth ordered observation in a sample space n. Then, we have the $F(_oX_j)$ probability for $j-1$ outcomes, $f(_oX_j)dX$ for 1 outcome, and $1- F(_oX_j)$for $n-j$ outcomes. Clearly, the multinomial distribution is applicable in this situation. Recall that the multinomial distribution is given by

$$P(y_1,y_2,\ldots,y_k)=\frac{m!}{y_1!y_2!\ldots y_k!}(\Theta_1)^{y_1}(\Theta_2)^{y_2}\ldots(\Theta_k)^{y_k} \quad (1)$$

Where, the Θ_i is the probability of obtaining the ith outcome and y_i is the RV representing the number of outcomes of the ith type.

Therefore, the probability of $j-1$ outcomes with $F(_oX_j)$, 1 outcome with $f(_oX_j)dX$, and $n-j$ outcomes with $1- F(_oX_j)$is given by

$$\frac{n!}{(j-1)!1!(n-j)!}[F(_oX_j)]^{j-1}f(_oX_j)dX[1-F(_oX_j)]^{n-j} \quad (2)$$

This is precisely the distribution of $_oX_j$, the value of the jth odered observation.

Now we know that

$$dF(_oX_j)=f(_oX_j)dX=d_nP_j \quad (3)$$

Hence the probability element becomes

$$g(_nP_j)d_nP_j=\frac{n!}{(j-1)!(n-j)!}{}_nP_j^{\,j-1}(1-{}_nP_j)^{n-j}d_nP_j(0\leq{}_nP_j\leq 1) \quad (4)$$

This distribution is commonly termed the rank distribution. Actually the p.d.f. of the RV $_nP_j$ is the well-known beta distribution [14]. Figure 9 shows the p.d.f. for different values of j for a sample of size n=10.

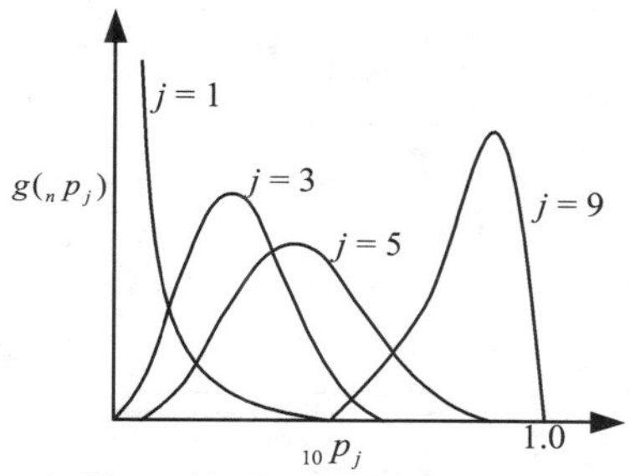

Figure 9. The rank distribution for a sample of size 10

Recall that the $_nP_j$ is the probability of failing to find an optimal minimum sequence X_n prior to the jth ordered observation in a sample space n. Let us define that ε is the error tolerance with a range of $0\leq \varepsilon \leq 1$and α is confidence limit with range $0\leq \alpha \leq 1$.

$$P\{_nP_j\leq\varepsilon\}\geq\alpha \quad (5)$$

This equation describes the method used to estimate the confidence limit of the optimization with error tolerance ε. For example, in order to get 95% confidence with less than 5% error tolerance for any optimization value, it is estimated as follows:

1) Estimate j trial number from the $P\{_nP_j\leq 0.05\}\geq 0.95$ in the sample space n
2) Generate j input instruction sequences randomly and exclusively
3) Find the minimum value among all j trial sequences
4) Compare the minimum value (minimum power) and TSP optimized value
5) If two values are close, we can say that the TSP optimization has 95% confidence limit with 5% error tolerance.

6 Experiments and Results

All simulations are done by using the SimpleScalar tool set [11], version 3.0 with RTL level power model. The target machine includes a five-stage pipelined data path, 32-32bit general registers, I-cache, D-cache, divider, multiplier, ALU, shifter, and control units. The simulated annealing parameters are tuned for 95% confidence limit and 5% error in Equation (5). We assume a fixed clock frequency, fixed supply voltage, and 0.35 micron technology. So, the terms "power" and "energy" can be used interchangeably because the clock frequency is fixed. Moreover, the power is almost proportional to the switching capacitance, due to the fact that over 90% of the total power dissipation is the switching power in well-designed circuits [15]. We analyze the power consumption without any schedule and with the optimal schedule when running several embedded applications. Figure 10 shows an optimal instruction sequence example for an FIR filter application. When one basic block is optimized, 8.5 % of the total power can be reduced with our scheme. Figure 11 presents power savings in each component of the target system. Table 1 shows that a maximum 29% of the total power can be saved with our algorithm for about 95% confidence limit with 5 % error tolerance.

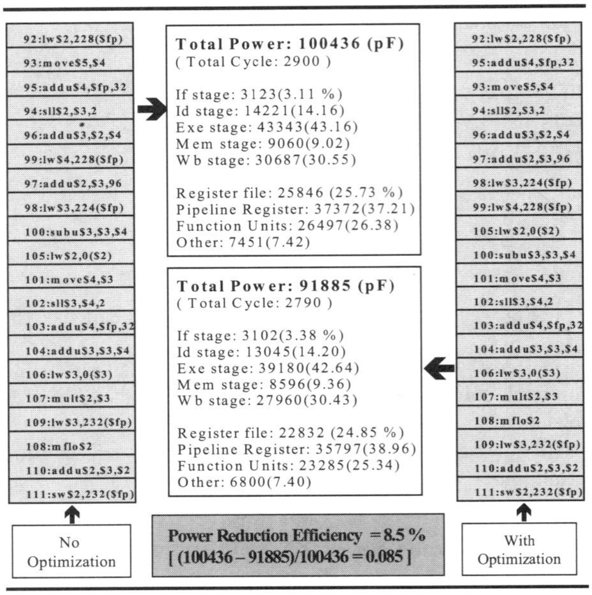

Figure 10. Scheduling Example for one BB of FIR Source

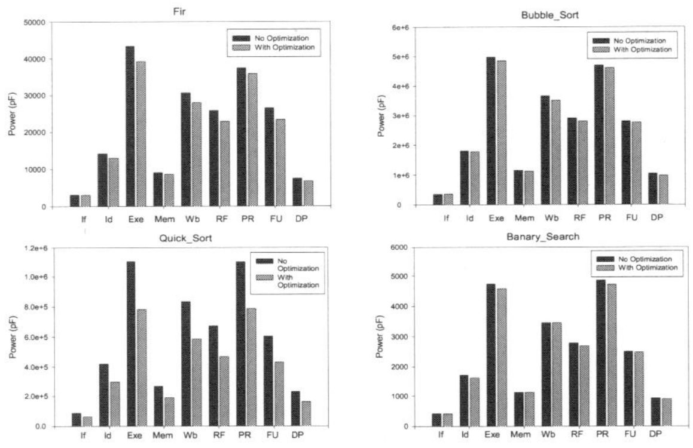

Note: If: Instruction Fetch, Id: Instruction Decode, Exe: Execution, Mem: Memory access, Wb: Wright back, RF: Register file, PR: Pipeline Register, FU: Functional Units, DP: Other Data Paths

Figure 11. Power Savings for Each Component

Table 1. Total Power Saving Results for Some Applications

	Total Power / (Cycles) without Scheduling (pF)	Total Power / (Cycles) with Scheduling (pF)	Confidence Limit / Error Rate (%)	Power Reduction (%)
FIR Filter	100436.35 / (2900)	91885.50 / (2790)	≈ 95 / ≈ 5	**8.52**
Bubble Sort (100 Samples)	11948917.22 / (368100)	11627652.60 / (360675)	≈ 95 / ≈ 5	**2.68**
Quick Sort (100 Samples)	2711445.75 / (85502)	1919845.60 / (61170)	≈ 95 / ≈ 5	**29.19**
Heap Sort (100 Samples)	3615121.35 / (101136)	3373014.48 / (96329)	≈ 95 / ≈ 5	**6.69**

7 Conclusion and Future Work

In this paper, we show that the instruction-level optimization problem can be solved using combinatorial methods. An efficient instruction-level optimization methodology and a validation method for the optimization are proposed. Experimental results show the effectiveness of the new approach.

The goal of this paper is to present a methodology for developing and validating an instruction-level low-power optimization framework for a given instruction set architecture. Future work will include global compiler-directed solutions for low-power embedded systems that will also consider the power benefits of voltage and frequency scaling.

References

[1] W.J. Cook, W.H. Cunningham, W.R. Pulleyblank, and A. Schrijver, *Combinatorial Optimization*, Wiley-Interscience Series in Discrete Mathematics and Optimization, pp241-271, 1998.

[2] V. Jain, S. Rele, S. Pande, and J. Ramanujam "Code restructuring for improving execution efficiency, code size and power consumption for embedded DSPs", *12th International Workshop on Languages and Compilers for Parallel Computing*, 1999.

[3] C.-L. Su, C.-Y. Tsui, and A. M. Despain, "Low power architecture design and compilation techniques for high-performance processors," *Proc. IEEE CompCon'94*, pp. 489-498. Feb., 1994.

[4] V. Tiwari, S. Malik, and A. Wolfe, "Instruction Level Power Analysis and Optimization of Software," *Journal of VLSI Signal Processing*, pp.1-18, 1996.

[5] V. Tiwari, S. Malik, and A. Wolfe, "Compilation Techniques for Low Energy: An Overview," *IEEE Symposium on Low Power Electronics*, October 1994.

[6] H. Tomiyama, T. Ishihara, A. inoue, and H. Yasuura, "Instruction Scheduling to Ruduce Switching Activity of Off-Chip Busses for Low-Power Systems with Caches," *Proc. IEICE*, pp. 2621-2629. Dec., 1998.

[7] C. Lee, J.K. Lee, and T.T. Hwang, "Compiler optimization on Instruction Scheduling for Low Power," *ISSS2000*, pp.20-22, Oct., 2000.

[8] K.Roy and M.C. Johnson, "Software design for low power," *Technical report at Purdue Univ.*, 1996.

[9] C.-L. Su, C.-Y. Tsui, and A. M. Despain, "Low power architecture design and compilation techniques for high-performance processors," *Proc. IEEE CompCon'94*, pp. 489-498. Feb., 1994.

[10] G. Lakshminarayana, A. Raghunathan, N.K. Jha, "Incorporating Speculative Execution into Scheduling of Control-Flow-Intensive Designs," *IEEE Transaction on Computer-Aided Design of Integrated Circuits and Systems*, vol., 19, no. 3, pp. 308-324Mar., 2000.

[11] D. Burger and T.M. Austin, "SimpleScalar Tool Set," *Univ. of Wisconsin-Madison Computer Science Dept., Tech. Teport #1342*, Jun., 1997.

[12] E.L. Lawler, J.K. Lenstra, A.H.G. Rinnooy Kan, and D. Shmoys, *The Traveling Salesman Problem*, Wiley, Chichester, 1985.

[13] R.C. Prim, "Shortest connection networks and some generalizations," *Bell System Technical Journal36*, pp1389-1401, 1957.

[14] K.C. Kapur and L.R. Lamberson, *Reliability in Engineering Design*, John Wiley & Sons, 1977.

[15] T.D. Burd and R.W. Brodersen, "Energy efficient CMOS microprocessor design," *Proceedings 28th HICSS Conference*, vol. I, pp. 288-297, Jan., 1995.

Source Code Transformation based on Software Cost Analysis *

Eui-Young Chung
CSL, Stanford Univ., USA
eychung@stanford.edu

Luca Benini
DEIS, Univ. di Bologna, Italy
lbenini@deis.unibo.it

Giovanni De Micheli
CSL, Stanford Univ., USA
nanni@stanford.edu

ABSTRACT

This paper presents a model and a strategy for source-code transformation applied to software application programs to reduce their energy cost. We propose a flexible performance and energy model for a processor-memory system. The benefit of the model is generality (it is not tied to a single memory and processor architecture) and effectiveness of evaluation. With this model, we first estimate the effects of source-code transformations (called transformation cost), representing the improvement ratios of processor cycles, I-cache misses, and D-cache misses. Next, we combine the transformation cost model with hardware parameters to estimate the actual effect of a transformation on performance and energy. The model can be used to guide software transformation selection for power and performance. The experimental results show that the proposed approach finds the optimal transformation in 95% of the cases, and that the penalty when the non-optimal transformation is selected is within 5%.

1. INTRODUCTION

Most electronic systems execute software programs on processor chips or cores. Energy-efficiency of the overall system depends heavily on software design [4]. Low-energy software design can be achieved in different ways, namely by energy-aware selection of the algorithms [15], code restructuring [7, 8] and instruction-level optimizations [3]. While algorithm selection has the highest potential, it is hard to automate, and its impact strongly depends on programmer's ingenuity. In contrast, instruction-level approaches can be automated (performance-oriented optimizations are available in the back-end of most compilers), but their impact on energy is local, and strongly tied to a given target architecture. Code restructuring techniques lie in between, since they can be automated to some degree [12], but they have global impact and they are not strictly architecture-dependent. This paper addresses strategies for source-code restructuring. The critical issue in code restructuring for low energy is the estimation of the impact of a given transformation. A straightforward approach (which we call *iterative-ISS*) is to compile the restructured code, generate an executable and run it either on the target hardware, or on a power-aware instruction simulator [14], to measure energy savings. This estimation flow goes through several time-consuming steps and it ultimately prevents fast, iterative exploration of many alternative transforms. Hence, more abstract and computationally-efficient energy estimation metrics are needed to support optimization.

A traditional abstract code metric is compactness. The most compact code for a program uses the least instruction memory. Moreover, if the program represents pure data flow, (i.e., no branching and iteration is involved), it executes in the shortest time and consumes the least energy. (This holds under the assumptions of constant energy cost of the instructions and if we neglect specific architectural features of processors, that may favor some instructions over some others.) This argument breaks down when considering processor-memory systems, and in particular the fact that accessing memory may consume a significant amount of energy. More refined abstract metrics rely on profiling[1, 2]. In these cases, the effects of branching/iteration may have significant impact on performance/energy. However, profiling relies on instruction simulation, which is too time consuming to be repeated for every possible transformation.

In previous work on source-code transformations, the estimation issue has been partially bypassed by focusing on hardware targets and application domains where some simplifying assumptions hold. Catthoor and coauthors [8], assume that the data memory access cost is the dominant factor for both energy and performance. Therefore, they apply extensive loop transformations for reducing data accesses and improving their locality. Other approaches [7] focused instead on the number of processor cycles, implicitly assuming that the processor is the most energy-critical system component. Thus, loop unrolling and procedure inlining were used to reduce the number of processor cycles, while data locality was improved by cache size optimization. Several papers have addressed the problem of assessing the impact of source code transformations on families of hardware architectures [5, 6, 7]. In these works, instruction-level simulation is employed to measure the effects of code transformation on energy. Without exception, these works have concluded that the optimal transformation depends on the characteristics of the processor and of the memory system.

On the other hand, pure analytical models were proposed especially for memory oriented transformations [9, 16]. These approaches estimate the effect of transformation very fast, but the accuracy is lower than the *iterative-ISS* approaches.

This paper introduces an abstract hardware model that makes it possible to take into account hardware characteristics when assessing the effectiveness of code transformations, at a fraction of the computational effort that would be required by the straightforward *iterative-ISS* approach. Bene-

*This work was supported by NSF (CCR-9901190), MARCO, ARPA, and GSRC.

ISSS'01, October 1-3, 2001, Montréal, Québec, Canada

fits of using this model include generality and speed of evaluation, since a drastically reduced number of instruction-level simulations is required. Thus, our work is in the middle of the previous two approaches - *iterative ISS* approaches and pure analytical approaches.

We apply our techniques to tune and select two well-known transformations, namely *loop unrolling* and *loop blocking* for several target programs. Results show that our technique is accurate in predicting the impact of code transformations. Interestingly, our analysis also demonstrates that a program should be transformed in different ways depending on the target cost metrics (energy and performance) as well as on hardware configuration (processor and memory). As a consequence, we give further evidence of the fact that energy and performance are not always optimized jointly.

2. SOFTWARE COST MODEL AND OVERALL FLOW

In this section, we introduce the abstract system performance and energy model at the basis of our approach, and we describe a computationally-efficient estimation flow for transformation analysis and exploration. It is important to stress that the abstract model should not be used for estimating power and performance of a program in an absolute sense, but it should be intended as a selection criterion to choose among alternatives. Thus, the emphasis is not on absolute accuracy, but on reliable selection guidance.

2.1 System Model

The proposed technique adopts a general system model which consists of a processor and an external memory. The processor is modeled as three major components - processor core, I-cache, and D-cache. The processor core includes all other components such as ALU, branch prediction unit, etc.

Based on this simple system model, we relate the software behavior to component usage. In other words, during software execution, the system is in one of three possible states: *i)* only processor is in working state (the processor is processing instructions and data stored in caches or registers), *ii)* only memory system is in working state (the processor stalls while external memory is accessed), *iii)* both processor and memory system are in working state (the processor does not immediately stall during external memory accesses). The third state can be omitted for simple processors which are completely stalled during memory access. For the memory system, we consider two different sub-states of its working state to distinguish its triggering sources - I-cache or D-cache misses.

2.2 Simplified Software Cost Model

For the sake of explanation, in this section we describe a simplified system model, assuming that - *i)* processor cycle and memory activity are completely non-overlapping. *ii)* the memory accesses are mostly due to D-cache miss, *i.e.* I-cache miss is negligible compared to D-cache miss. These simplifying assumptions will be removed in Section 2.4. The hardware parameters used in our cost model are shown in Table 1. For the given system, we perform instruction-level simulation for the target software to obtain the usage of each component. We denote the number of clock cycles devoted to processor as N_p and the number of accesses to memory system as N_m. Thus, execution time of the target program

parameter	meaning
T_p	processor cycle time
T_m	memory cycle time
P_{ap}	average active power of processor
P_{ip}	average idle power of processor
P_{am}	average active power of memory
P_{im}	average idle power of memory

Table 1: Hardware parameters of the system model

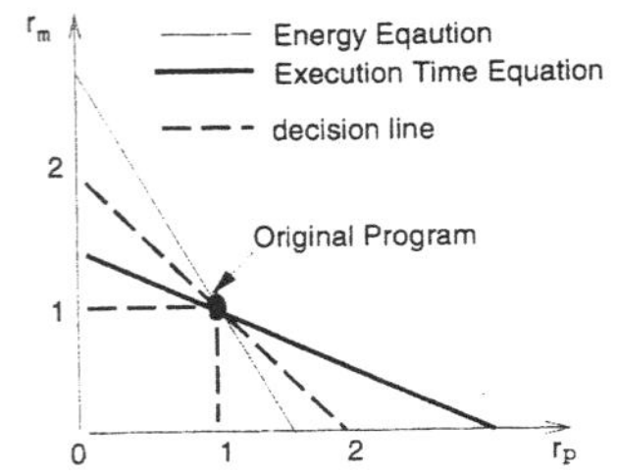

Figure 1: 2D representation of Equation 5 and 6

can be simply represented as Equation 1.

$$T_{exe} = N_p * T_p + N_m * T_m \quad (1)$$

Similarly, the energy consumption is:

$$E = (P_{ap} + P_{im}) * N_p * T_p + (P_{ip} + P_{am}) * N_m * T_m \quad (2)$$

Suppose we have a set of transformation techniques, $\mathcal{T}_i, i = 0, 1, \cdots, K-1$, and each of them changes N_p and N_m to $r_p(i) * N_p$ and $r_m(i) * N_m$, respectively. We call $r_p(i)$ ($r_m(i)$) *transformation cost of processor cycle (memory access) ratio* of transformation $\mathcal{T}_i$. Thus, Equation 1 and 2 can be rewritten as Equation 3 and 4, respectively to consider the effect of the transformation.

$$T(i)_{exe} = r_p(i) * N_p * T_p + r_m(i) * N_m * T_m \quad (3)$$

$$\begin{aligned} E(i) =& (P_{ap} + P_{im}) * r_p(i) * N_p * T_p \\ &+ (P_{ip} + P_{am}) * r_m(i) * N_m * T_m \end{aligned} \quad (4)$$

where, $T(i)_{exe}$ and $E(i)$ represent the execution time and energy consumption of the code transformed by $\mathcal{T}_i$.

Obviously, $\mathcal{T}_i$ is only effective when $T_{exe} > T(\mathcal{T}_i)_{exe}$ if the target objective is performance. Similarly, it is only effective when $E > E(\mathcal{T}_i)$ if the target objective is energy. These two inequalities can be rearranged with respect to r_p and r_m as shown in next.

$$(r_m(i) - 1) \leq (1 - r_p(i)) * \frac{N_p * T_p}{N_m * T_m} \quad (5)$$

$$(r_m(i) - 1) \leq (1 - r_p(i)) * \frac{N_p * T_p}{N_m * T_m} * \frac{P_{ap} + P_{im}}{P_{am} + P_{ip}} \quad (6)$$

These two equations characterize the software cost (energy and performance) relations in terms of r_m and r_p when a general transformation technique is applied. Each equation is represented as a line in a two-dimensional space, as shown in Figure 1. First, each equation defines the boundary conditions for r_p and r_m that can be acceptable after the transformation. Only when r_p and r_m are in the region below the line (the triangle formed by two axes and the line itself), the transformation is effective for the given cost metric. We call this region *effective region*.

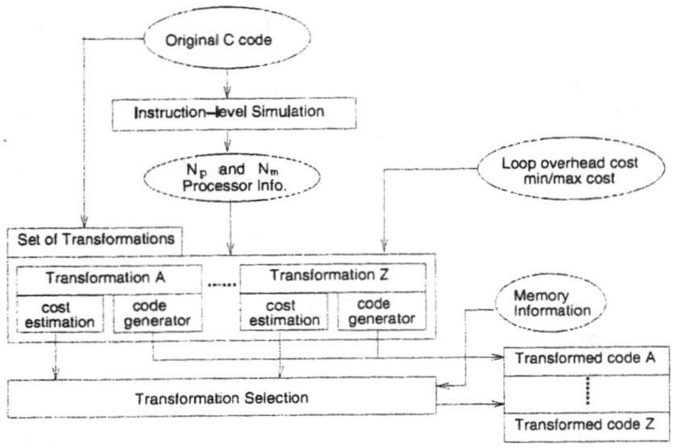

Figure 2: Overall transformation flow

Second, the slope of the line indicates the relative importance of r_p and r_m. In detail, r_p (r_m) is more important than r_m (r_p) if the slope is greater (smaller) than 1 (the slope of decision line) because the given cost metric is more heavily affected by $r_p(r_m)$. Thus, performance and energy may require different transformations.

Both equations can be generalized to directly compare two arbitrary transformations - $\mathcal{T}_i$ and $\mathcal{T}_j$ as follows.

$$(r_m(i) - r_m(j)) \leq (r_p(j) - r_p(i)) * \frac{N_p * T_p}{N_m * T_m} \quad (7)$$

$$(r_m(i) - r_m(j)) \leq (r_p(j) - r_p(i)) * \frac{N_p * T_p}{N_m * T_m} * \frac{P_{ap} + P_{im}}{P_{am} + P_{ip}} \quad (8)$$

The condition which minimizes the energy-delay product can be simply obtained by multiplying Inequalities 7 and 8 because each of them is the condition for execution time and energy, respectively. Also, notice that the left hand side terms of Inequalities 7 and 8 are identical, thus they always have the same polarity and the right hand side terms of these two equations are always positive. Thus, the inequality for energy-delay product is:

$$(r_m(i) - r_m(j)) \leq (r_p(j) - r_p(i)) * \frac{N_p * T_p}{N_m * T_m} * \sqrt{\frac{P_{ap} + P_{im}}{P_{am} + P_{ip}}} \quad (9)$$

For each inequality (7, 8, 9), if the condition is satisfied, then $\mathcal{T}_i$ is superior to $\mathcal{T}_j$ for the corresponding cost metric. Otherwise, $\mathcal{T}_j$ improves the original program more than $\mathcal{T}_i$. Note that for each transformation $\mathcal{T}_i$ we need to provide a value for the transformation cost $r_p(i)$ and $r_m(i)$. Estimation of transformation cost is discussed in Section 3.

We can use these inequalities for two different purposes. First, for a system with a fixed external memory, we use these inequalities to find the optimal transformation among a set of transformations by estimating $r_m(i)$ and $r_p(i)$ of each transformation. Second, when there exist multiple choices of external memories, we can find the optimal transformation for various external memory configurations. Then, the impact of external memory selection and optimal transformation can be evaluated by Equation 3 and 4, thus optimal pair of external memory and transformation can be obtained.

2.3 Overall Transformation Flow

The proposed transformation flow is illustrated in Figure 2. The flow requires a single instruction-level simulation for the original source code, before transformations, to extract parameters useful for both transformation and cost estimation such as N_p, N_m, P_{ap}, P_{ip}. Currently, the WATTCH simulator [14] is used in the initial instruction-level simulation step. Also, P_{am} and P_{im} can be obtained from the data book or real measurement.

The transformation costs (r_p and r_m) are estimated by the dedicated cost estimators of each transformation. Each cost estimator requires additional information such as loop overhead and min/max operation cost which are independent of the characteristics of each program. Techniques for cost estimation, and their computational cost, are described in Section 3.

In the transformation selection phase, we evaluate two well-known high-level transformation techniques - *loop unrolling* and *loop blocking*. *Loop unrolling* is implemented under *SUIF* environment and *loop blocking* is performed by another *SUIF* package called *skweel* [13]. Notice that our framework can encapsulate any other class of transformations, provided that a cost estimator is available. In the next section, we illustrate the cost estimators we developed for *loop unrolling* and *loop blocking*.

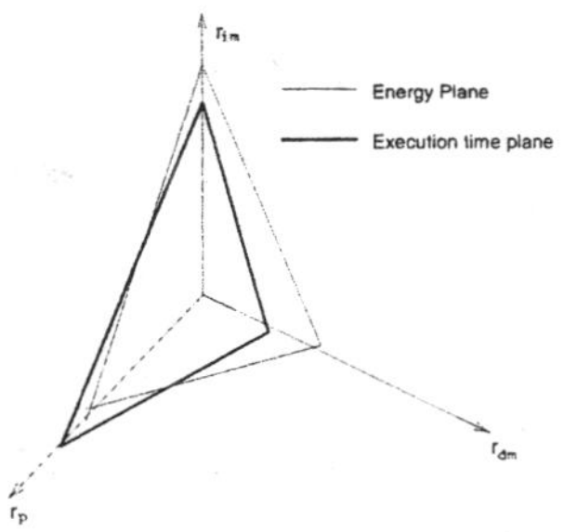

Figure 3: 3D representation of critical parameters

2.4 General Cost Model

In Section 2.2, we ignored the effect of I-cache. Also, we assumed external memory accesses are never overlapped with processor cycles. We now extend the simplified model to consider these effects.

I-cache effects can be simply considered by breaking N_m into $N_{dm} + N_{im}$ which are number of memory accesses due to D-cache miss and I-cache miss respectively. The graph shown in Figure 1 becomes 3-dimensional as shown in Figure 3. We can still use the inequalities introduced in Section 2.2 by choosing the most critical plane. The most critical plane has the smallest *effective region* and the parameters consisting of the plane replace the parameters appearing in each equation.

Finally, the overlapping between memory access and processor operation for processors with non-blocking caches is considered by scaling the memory cycle time. The scaling factor can be achieved by performing instruction-level simulation twice. The first simulation is performed with zero-latency (ideal) memory system and the second simulation is performed with non-ideal memory system. The scaling factor is the difference in execution time divided by the product of the latency of the non-ideal memory system and N_m. It is a measure of the aggressiveness of the non-blocking cache implementation, rather than a property of software execution. Thus, we compute the factor for a set of programs and use the average value for all other programs.

```
for (i = 0; i < TC; i++)
  X[i] = Y[i]*Z[i];
```

(a) Original version

```
for (i = 0; i < TC-1; i++) {
  X[i] = Y[i]*Z[i];
  i++;
  X[i] = Y[i]*Z[i];
}
for (; i < TC; i++)
  X[i] = Y[i]*Z[i];
```

(b) Unrolled version (u = 2)

Figure 4: An example of loop unrolling

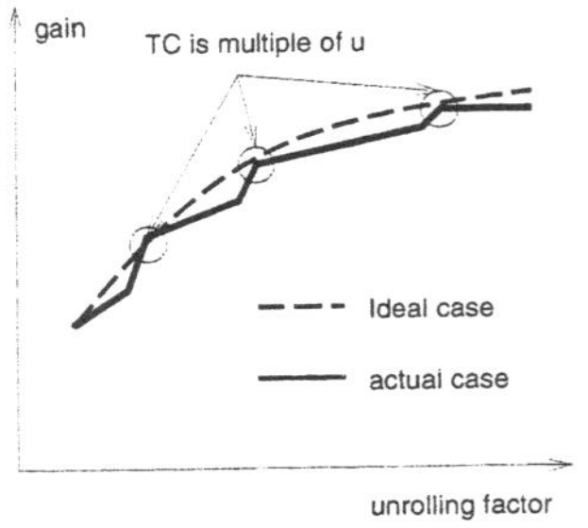

Figure 5: Gain variation with unrolling factor

3. TRANSFORMATION COST ANALYSIS

In this section, we describe the cost estimators of the transformation techniques which estimate r_p and r_m. We consider two well-known transformation techniques - *loop unrolling* and *loop blocking(tiling)*. *Loop unrolling* aims at reducing the number of processor cycles by eliminating the loop overheads. Also, it provides a better starting point to the conventional optimization techniques by enlarging the basic block size. This technique improves the number of processor cycles (N_p), but it also increases I-cache misses (N_{im}). N_{dm} is rarely sensitive to this technique because it does not change the data access behavior.

Loop blocking breaks large arrays into several pieces (tiles smaller than cache size) and reuses each piece without self-interference. Thus N_{dm} can be effectively reduced. But it may cause significant increase of N_p because the depth of loop nesting is increased and min/max operations are required to compute the lower and upper bounds of the blocked loop. The variation of N_{im} can be ignored in this approach because the code size increase is marginal.

3.1 Loop Unrolling

Loop unrolling is controlled by the *unrolling factor*, u which is the number of duplications of the body statements inside the loop. If $u = 1$, the original loop is kept without any change. Even though it is well-known that *loop unrolling* is effective to reduce N_p, there is no obvious method to determine this factor. Thus, typically *iterative-ISS* is required with the change of the unrolling factor to find the optimal one. We propose a new unrolling strategy to find the optimal unrolling factor with a single *ISS*.

An example of *loop unrolling* is shown in Figure 4 ($u = 2$). The gain of loop unrolling is achieved by the first loop of Figure 4 (b), while the second loop is same to the original loop and its number of iterations is (TC *modulo* u).

We denote the gain of loop unrolling as $gain(u)$ when the unrolling factor is u. The $gain(u)$ can be graphically represented as shown in Figure 5. In Figure 5, the solid line (actual case) is when the number of loop iterations is limited to integer numbers (the second loop in Figure 4 (b) is iterated by (TC *modulo* u) times), while the dotted line (ideal case) is when the number of loop iterations can be non-integer numbers, which is not possible in practice (the second loop in Figure 4 (b) is never executed) . Thus, when u is selected as a multiple of TC, the unrolling effect becomes as same as the ideal case. Also, u should be selected as large as possible to maximize the gain. But, as u increases, the I-cache miss rate also increases and will eventually decrease the gain achieved by loop unrolling.

Without the estimations of both gain and I-cache miss rate, it is unavoidable to perform *iterative-ISS* with the change of u.

Instead of measuring I-cache miss rate directly, we estimate the code size increased by loop unrolling. Based on the code size estimation, we decide the maximum unrolling factor, u_{max}. u_{max} is the largest unrolling factor not to increase code size larger than I-cache size and is shown next.

$$u_{max} = \frac{size\ of\ instruction\ cache}{I_{org} * size\ of\ instruction} \qquad (10)$$

where, I_{org} is the number of instructions of the loop body and is estimated in either front-end (SUIF) or back-end part.

Thus, the optimal unrolling factor u_{opt} is the greatest divisor of TC, but smaller than u_{max}. By finding u_{opt}, we can replace *iterative-ISS* by single ISS to obtain $gain(u_{opt})$.

The transformation costs of loop unrolling are computed using u_{opt} and shown next.

$$\begin{aligned} r_p &= (N_p - gain(u_{opt}))/N_p \\ r_{im} &= (N_{im} + (I_{org} * u_{opt}))/N_{im} \\ r_{dm} &= 1 \end{aligned} \qquad (11)$$

Notice that r_{dm} is set to 1 without loss of generality because its effect on data access behavior is relatively small.

3.2 Loop Blocking

This technique is very effective to reduce the number of D-cache misses, but it often increases N_p largely due to the overhead of loop bound decision. To estimate r_{dm}, we propose an estimation technique for the number of misses caused by *loop blocking*. An example of loop blocking is shown in Figure 6. Two innermost loops (loop k and j) in the original version are blocked to avoid self-interference and the graphical representation is shown in Figure 7. One tile of array `Z` (BxB words) is fully used during the iteration of two innermost loops in the tiled version (loop k and j), whereas only B words of array `Y` and `X` are used, respectively. Also, loop i uses the same tile of array `Z` used in two innermost loops, while each iteration uses different B words of array `X` and `Y`. Therefore, unavoidable misses to complete one iteration of loop i, namely intrinsic misses are:

$$M_{intrinsic} = \frac{B^2}{CL}(array\ \mathtt{Z}) + 2\frac{N * B}{CL}(array\ \mathtt{X}\ and\ \mathtt{Y}) \qquad (12)$$

where CL is the cache line size in terms of words.

Notice that the tile size B can be chosen such that there is no self-interference using the tile size selection algorithms presented in [9, 10, 11]. Among them, we use the algorithm proposed in [10].

The misses due to cross interference can be estimated using the `footprint` of arrays in loop k. The ratio of the space occupied by array `Z` over the cache size, CS is $B * B/CS$.

```
for (i = 0; i < N; i++)
  for (k = 0; k < N; k++)
    r0 = Y[i][k];
    for (j = 0; k < N; k++)
      X[i][j] += r0*Z[k][j];
```

(a) Original version

```
for (kk = 0; kk < N; kk+=B)
  for (jj = 0; jj < N; jj+=B)
    for (i = 0; i < N; i++)
      for (k = max(0, kk) < min(N, kk+B-1); k++)
        if (jj = 0)
          r0 = Y[i][k];
        for (j = max(0, jj); j < min(N, jj+B-1); j++)
          X[i][j] += r0*Z[k][j];
```

(b) Tiled version

Figure 6: An example of loop blocking (Tiling)

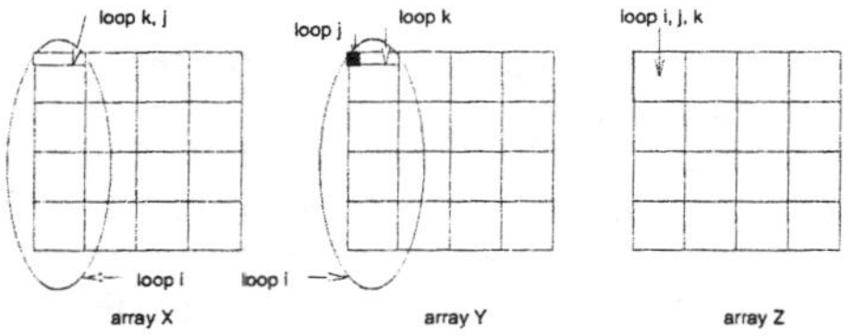

Figure 7: Data access pattern of loop blocking

Similarly, the ratio for array X and Y over the cache size is commonly B/CS. Thus, the probability that two or more references will access the same cache line is:

$$P_{cross} = \frac{2*B^2}{CS} * \frac{B}{CS} + (\frac{B}{CS})^2 + \frac{B^2}{CS} * (\frac{B}{CS})^2 \quad (13)$$

and total cross-interference occurred per iteration of *loop i* is $M_{cross} = P_{cross} * B^2$, where B is the trip count of loop k and j. Therefore, total misses to complete the whole loop nest is shown next and r_{dm} is simply M_{total_block}/N_{dm}.

$$M_{total\_block} = (M_{intrinsic} + M_{cross} * N) * (\frac{N}{B})^2 \quad (14)$$

On the other hand, r_{im} can be set to 1 because the code size increase is trivial, but r_p should be carefully analyzed.

$$N_p(blocking) = N_p + \sum_{i=0}^{N}(\prod_{l=0}^{k} TC_l * T_{mo}) \quad (15)$$

where, N is the total number of *min* and *max* operations appearing in the tiled version and k is the loop level that each *min* or *max* operation can be moved without destroying the dependency. Also, T_{mo} is the cost of *min* or *max* operation. Notice that the cost of *min/max* operation can be characterized by simulating a simple program which only includes *min/max* operation and the cost can be generally used for all other programs.

In Figure 6 the *min* and *max* operations in *level j* can be moved up to *level jj*, thus its impact on N_p is marginal. But if the tiled version is skewed or has triangle-shape tile, these operations cannot be moved, thus its impact cannot be neglected. Finally, r_p is simply $N_p(blocking)/N_p$.

4. EXPERIMENTAL RESULTS

The experiment was conducted based on WATTCH simulator. The processor was configured such that it had one arithmetic unit for both integer and floating point operation without L2-cache. Also, both D-cache and I-cache were 4K and their associativity was 2.

external memory	latency	power
M1	30	0.1
M2	50	0.1
M3	30	0.5
M4	50	0.5

Table 2: Four different memory configurations

M	pgm	cost metrics					
		performance		energy		perf. * energy	
		unroll	block	unroll	block	unroll	block
1	m100	0.82	0.75*	0.80*	0.91	0.66	0.68+
1	m200	0.85	0.74*	0.80*	0.90	0.68	0.67*
1	l100	0.82*	0.89	0.81*	1.00	0.66*	0.89
1	l200	0.84*	0.90	0.84*	0.96	0.73*	0.86
1	sub	0.88*	1.02	0.77*	1.02	0.68*	1.04
1	idct	0.82*	1.06	0.69*	1.06	0.56*	1.12
2	m100	0.85	0.63*	0.82	0.82*	0.70	0.52*
2	m200	0.85	0.62*	0.82	0.82*	0.70	0.51*
2	l100	0.85	0.80*	0.82*	0.93	0.70*	0.74
2	l200	0.89	0.83*	0.87*	0.96	0.77*	0.80
2	sub	0.91*	1.01	0.80*	1.00	0.73*	1.01
2	idct	0.85*	1.07	0.72*	1.07	0.61*	1.12
3	m100	0.82	0.75*	0.83	0.78*	0.71	0.59*
3	m200	0.85	0.74*	0.83	0.78*	0.71	0.58*
3	l100	0.82*	0.89	0.84*	0.95	0.70*	0.76
3	l200	0.84*	0.90	0.85*	0.93	0.72*	0.84
3	sub	0.88*	1.02	0.82*	1.02	0.72*	1.04
3	idct	0.82*	1.06	0.72*	1.06	0.59*	1.12
4	m100	0.85	0.63*	0.86	0.67*	0.73	0.42*
4	m200	0.85	0.62*	0.86	0.67*	0.73	0.42*
4	l100	0.85	0.80*	0.85	0.84*	0.72	0.67*
4	l200	0.86	0.83*	0.87	0.85*	0.75	0.71*
4	sub	0.91*	1.01	0.85*	1.00	0.77*	1.01
4	idct	0.85*	1.07	0.77*	1.01	0.77*	1.08

Table 3: Decision accuracy of the proposed approach

We used four different external memory configurations shown in Table 2. Note that latency is in terms of processor cycle and the power consumption is normalized to the average power consumption of processor.

We applied our technique to two well-known programs used for loop-blocking - matrix multiplication (m100, m200) and LU-decomposition (lu100, lu200). Also, it was applied to two kernels of mp3 decoder - subbandSynthesis (sub) and inverse discrete cosine transform(idct) [15].

First, instruction-level simulation was performed for each program to extract necessary parameters - N_p, N_m, P_{ap}, and P_{ip}. Then, each program was transformed into two versions (unrolled version and tiled version) and transformation cost was estimated without considering specific memory configuration. Next, we performed the transformation selection step for each program by applying a set of Inequalities(7, 8, 9) to decide the most effective transformation. This step was repeated four times with four different different external memories shown in Table 2. To measure the accuracy of the selection step, the optimal transformation of each program was searched by performing the simulation for each transformed version. Table 3 shows the comparison between the decisions made by our technique and simulation results.

The numbers in Table 3 were obtained from the simulation and normalized to the original program. Notice that we marked our decisions with "*" and "+" in Table 3. "*" represents the correct decision, while "+" represents the wrong decision. The proposed technique achieves about 95% accuracy and the penalty due to wrong decisions was less than 5% over the correct decisions (For example, a wrong decision marked by a + sign was the case for the program $m100$ with memory configuration $M1$ for energy-delay product). Furthermore, our approach found the optimal transformation, even when the best execution time and best energy consumption were found in different versions ($m100$ and $m200$ in $M1$, $l100$ and $l200$ in $M2$).

Notice that this situation usually happens when the power consumption ratio of processor over the external memory is large. In this case, the slope difference of energy and execution time equations in Figure 1 becomes larger and each equation has different dominant factor.

Two kernels from mp3 decoders were not suitable for *loop blocking* due to small array size and complex array indexing, even though program *sub* suffers from data cache misses. Thus, more aggressive and general transformations for data locality improvement are required. It is also worthwhile to mention that the instruction-level simulation was performed twice (one for parameter extraction, one for loop unrolling) for each program to make a decision.

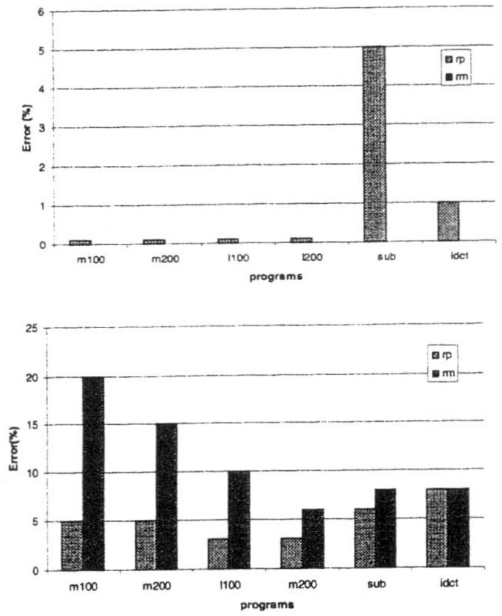

Figure 8: Transformation cost estimation error of loop unrolling (top) and loop blocking(bottom)

We also show the transformation cost estimation error of each transformation in Figure 8. On average, the estimation accuracy of *loop unrolling* is about 95% for r_p and 99% for r_m (almost invisible in Figure 8 (top) because the error is too small), while the estimation error of *loop blocking* is about 11.5% for r_{dm} and 4% for r_p.

5. CONCLUSION AND FUTURE WORK

We proposed an abstract software performance and energy estimation when multiple transformations are available. This approach greatly reduces the time required for code quality assessment compared to traditional approaches by avoiding *iterative-ISS*. The proposed approach found the optimal transformation with 95% accuracy and the penalty when the non-optimal transformation is selected is within 5%. Also, the proposed technique can easily reselect the optimal transformation when the memory configuration is changed. With this strategy, we were able to reduce the energy consumption in average by 20% and also improve the performance in average by 21%. It was also shown that both optimal performance and optimal energy consumption were not always found by single transformation because their improvement ratio is different depending on the power consumption ratio between the processor and memory.

Finally, we would like to address three limitations of our approach which will be enhanced in the future. First, our technique is limited to single-stage optimization, namely each optimization is considered independently. The reason is that the present tool has as a main objective the comparisons of transformations for different hardware parameters. We will extend our technique to support multi-stage optimization which may provide better quality of transformed code. Second, there are only two transformations are available, but we will encapsulate more high-level transformations such as *in-lining* in our framework. Third, the metric for the transformation is two-dimensional *i.e.* processor cycles and external memory cycles which are known as the most dominant factors in performance and energy consumption. But our appoarch can be extended to consider another metric such as on-chip memory cycles (by considering caches as separate components) using the similar concept.

6. REFERENCES

[1] T. Ball and J. Larus, "Optimally Profiling and Tracing Programs", Proceedings of the 19th Annual Symposium on Principles of Programming Languages, Jan., 1992

[2] E.-Y. Chung, L. Benini, and G. De Micheli, "Energy Efficient Source Code Transformation based on Value Profiling", *1st workshop for Compilers and Operating Systems for Low-Power*, pp. D-1-D.7, Philadelphia, PA, 2000

[3] V. Tiwari, S. Malik, A. Wolfe, "Instruction Level Power Analysis and Optimization of Software", *Journal of VLSI Signal Processing Systems*, vol. 13, pp.223-233, 1996

[4] L. Benini and G. De Micheli, "System-Level Power Optimization Techniques and Tools", *ACM TODAES*, vol. 5, issue 2, pp.115-192, Apr. 2000

[5] H. Mehta, R. Owens, M. Irwin, R. Chen, and D. Ghosh, "Techniques for Low Energy Software", *ISLPED*, pp.72-75, 1997

[6] G. Esakkimuthu, N. Vijaykrishnan, M. Kandemir, M. Irwin, "Memory system energy: influence of hardware-software optimizations," *ISLPED*, pp. 244-246, 2000.

[7] Y. Li and J. Henkel, "A Framework for Estimating and Minimizing Energy Dissipation of Embedded HW/SW Systems", *Design Automation Conference*, pp.188-193, 1997

[8] F. Cathoor, S. Wuytack, E. De Greef, F. Balasa, L. Nachtergaele, and A. Vandecappelle, *Custom Memory Management Methodology: Exploration of Memory Organization for Embedded Multimedia System Design*, Kluwer, 1998

[9] M. Wolfe, *High Performance Compilers for Parallel Computing*, Addison-Wesley, 1996

[10] M.S. Lam, E.E. Rothberg, and M.E. Wolf, "The Cache Performance and Optimizations of Blocked Algorithms", *ASPLOS*, pp. 63-74, 1991

[11] P.Panda, H. Nakamura, N. Dutt, and A. Nicolau, "Augmenting Loop Tiling with Data Alignment for Improved Cache Performance", *IEEE trans. on Computers*, vol. 48, No. 2, pp. 142-148, 1999

[12] D. Bacon, S, Graham, and O. Sharp, "Compiler Transformation for High-Perforamnce Computing", *ACM Computing Surveys*, pp.345-420, vol26, No. 4, Dec. 1994

[13] Stanford Compiler Group, The SUIF Library: A set of core routines for manipulating SUIF data structures, Stanford University, 1994

[14] D. Brooks, V. Tiwari, and M. Martonosi, "Wattch: a framework for architectural-level power analysis and optimizations", ISCA, pp. 83-94, 2000

[15] T. Simunic, L. Benini, G. De Micheli, and M. Hans, "Source Code Optimization and Profiling of Energy Consumption in Embedded Systems", *ISSS*, pp. 193-198, 2000.

[16] P. R. Panda, N. Dutt, and A. Nicolau. Memory Issues in Embedded Systems-on-Chip: Optimizations and Exploration. Kluwer, 1999.

Static Resource Models of Instruction Sets

Q. Zhao
Dept. of Elec. Eng.
Eindhoven University of Technology
NL-5600 MB Eindhoven
The Netherlands
q.zhao@tue.nl

T. Basten
Dept. of Elec. Eng.
Eindhoven University of Technology
NL-5600 MB Eindhoven
The Netherlands
a.a.basten@tue.nl

B. Mesman*
Philips Research Laboratories
Prof. Holstlaan 4
NL-5656 AA Eindhoven
The Netherlands
bart.mesman@philips.com

ABSTRACT

Due to an increasing need for flexibility, embedded systems embody more and more programmable processors as their core components. Because of silicon area and power considerations, the corresponding instruction sets are often highly encoded to minimize code size for given performance requirements. This has hampered the development of robust optimizing compilers because the resulting irregular instruction set architectures are far from convenient compiler targets. Among others, they introduce a strong phase coupling between the tasks of instruction selection and scheduling. Traditional methods perform these tasks in different phases, thereby yielding inferior schedules. In this paper, we present an approach that reduces the need for explicit instruction selection by transferring constraints implied by the instruction set to static resource constraints. All resulting schedules are then guaranteed to correspond to a valid implementation with available instructions. We demonstrate a practical way to identify and construct a static resource model from a given instruction set. Experimental results show the efficacy of our approach.

Keywords

code generation, high-level synthesis, instruction set constraints

1. INTRODUCTION

The combined issues of performance requirements for meeting real-time constraints on the one hand, and code size requirements on the other hand, have led embedded DSP vendors to focus on the "expressive power" of the associated instruction sets. The resulting instruction sets are highly encoded and have an irregular structure, making them inconvenient compiler targets. Overheads in cycle time and code size have been reported in the order of 800% [10] when compared to manually written assembly. As a result, these embedded DSP processors are most often programmed in assembly, which is painstaking, labour intensive, and requires expert knowledge of the processor architecture and instruction set. Furthermore, the resulting code is not portable to other platforms, difficult to debug, maintain and update, etc.

The task of instruction selection is to *cover* a data flow graph (DFG), like the one depicted in Figure 1, with processor instructions that implement the individual operations in the DFG. The main issue introduced by an irregular instruction set is the issue of *phase coupling*: On the one hand, if instruction selection is performed prior to scheduling, the optimal schedule can easily be eliminated as a result of the choices made during instruction selection. On the other hand, if scheduling is performed first, the available instructions may not be able to implement the schedule. Traditional methods perform these tasks in different phases, thereby yielding inferior schedules. This point is illustrated in Figure 1. The DFG on the left hand side has been covered with machine instructions. The associated optimal schedule (6 clock cycles) for this selection of instructions is given in the right hand side of Figure 1. The imposed instruction selection is rather unfortunate, however, because Figure 2 depicts a valid schedule requiring only 5 clock cycles.

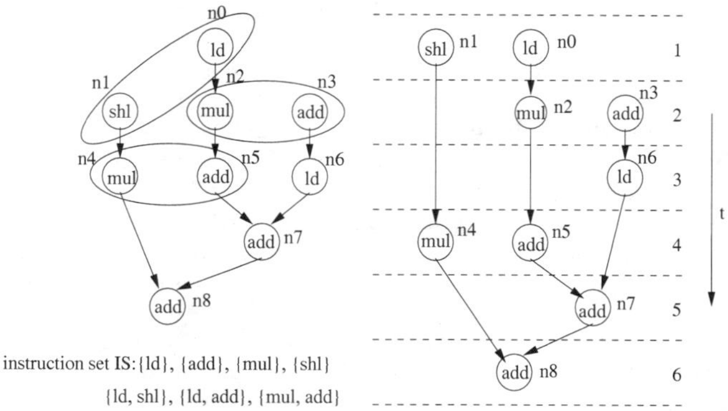

Figure 1: *Instruction selection prior to scheduling may yield inferior results*

In this paper, we present a new approach that eliminates the need for explicit instruction selection by transferring the

*See Section 7 for additional authors.

ISSS'01, October 1-3, 2001, Montréal, Québec, Canada.

constraints from the instruction set to static resource constraints. All resulting schedules are then guaranteed to correspond to a valid implementation with instructions. This is illustrated in Figure 2. The instruction set IS of Figure 1 has been augumented with virtual resources $\{ld, mul\}$, $\{mul, shl\}$ and $\{shl, add\}$, which are abbreviated as LM, MS and SA. Each of these virtual resources has one instance. Each operation uses all the virtual resources that it is contained in, e.g., operation mul uses virtual resources LM and MS. For this so called *static resource model* (SRM), a straightforward list scheduler generates the schedule on the right hand side of Figure 2. The reader can verify that the operations at each clock cycle can be implemented with instructions from the original instruction set IS. This example demonstrates that better schedules can be obtained using a static resource model thereby reducing the need for explicit instruction selection.

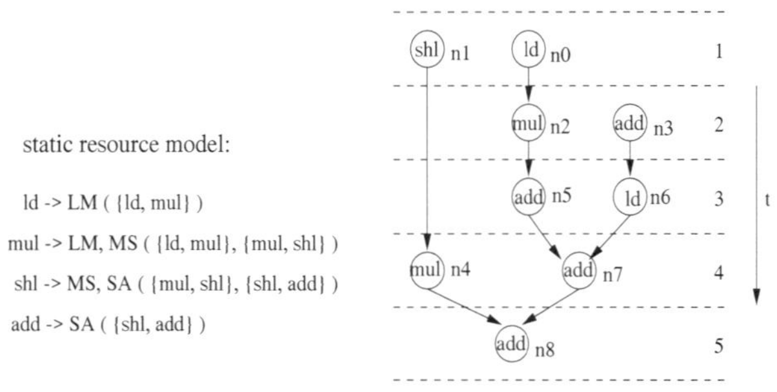

Figure 2: *With a static resource model optimal results can be obtained*

Much work has been done on exploiting instruction selection. Most compilers use template pattern bases and tree-covering techniques to partition the instruction selection problem in a stepwise fashion [1, 5, 8]. Such methods often split the DFG into expression trees and perform tree-covering on each tree separately, demonstrated by the example in Figure 1. In *Chess* [13], the target processor is described in the nML language [3] and is translated into an Instruction-Set-Graph (ISG), which models connectivity, encoding restrictions and structural hazards. Code selection covers the control-data flow graph with partial instructions (bundles) by searching valid paths in the ISG. Such a method adds a complex step to the compiler chain and eliminates potentially interesting solutions from the schedule and register binding search spaces. In [4, 14], code generation tasks are performed by imposing constraints and the complete solution space is explored while all the constraints are considered. This approach can only deal with small applications and a restricted set of architectures.

Another approach to tackle the code generation problem is to exploit the instruction set constraints statically. Eisenbeis [2] starts from the placement conflicts by using reservation tables for VLIW architectures, such as the Trimedia processor. Timmer et al. [12] discusses the modeling of instruction set constraints together with resource constraints for instruction scheduling, but the assumption that all the instruction set constraints can be transferred to resource constraints targets mostly instruction sets with a structure associated with so called Issue-Slot machines. The virtue of these orthogonal instruction sets, like VLIW instruction sets [11], is that they allow to a large extent the modeling of the instruction set constraints by means of a model like [2], [12], or a static resource model, as proposed in this paper. These models offer the scheduler more opportunity to satisfy the timing and resource constraints than with the use of an explicit instruction selection step. The scheduler rather than the instruction selector is considered the designated place for handling these constraints. The disadvantage of the orthogonal processors (especially VLIW processors) is the inherent problem of code size due to their associated instruction word widths. The focus of this paper is on replacing the instruction set constraints of highly encoded instruction sets with a static resource model, allowing the use of code size efficient processors in combination with efficient compilation tools. In this paper we do not consider the strong phase coupling between scheduling and register binding; for that, we use the method described in [9].

This paper is organized as follows. Section 2 details the problem statement and approach. Section 3 addresses the identification and construction of an SRM of an instruction set. In Section 4, some rules are provided for the minimization of SRMs. In Section 5, experimental results are given for benchmarks as well as real applications. Conclusions and future work are discussed in Section 6.

2. PROBLEM STATEMENT AND APPROACH

A DSP algorithm can be expressed as a data flow graph, which describes the primitive operations performed in an algorithm and the dependencies between those operations.

Definition 1. A *data flow graph* (DFG) is a tuple (V, E), where V is the set of vertices (operations) and $E \subseteq V \times V$ is the set of precedence edges.

In a processor architecture, a functional resource can be used in different ways. E.g., a functional resource ALU can execute an operation *add* or a *subtract*, etc. For reasons of complexity, we do not wish to enumerate all possible uses of a functional resource in an instruction set. Therefore, we consider the collection of these uses of a functional resource and associate with it an *operation type*. E.g., on the functional resource ALU, operations *add* and *subtract* can be executed, which are associated with the operation type *alu*. We denote the set of operation types with T. An *instruction* is now defined as a combination of operation types that can be executed in a single clock cycle.

An operation type can appear multiple times in an instruction (multiple *alu*s can be present in the data path). For an operation type op in an instruction I, we denote this number by $I(op)$. If for two instructions I_0 and I_1, $I_0(op)$ is always at most equal to $I_1(op)$ for each operation type op, we say that instruction I_0 is *contained* in instruction I_1. In this paper we consider instruction sets IS where for each instruction all contained instructions are also in IS. We call these instruction sets *prefix closed*.

The code generation problem is to find a schedule of a DFG, i.e., to determine a start time $s(v)$ for each operation $v \in V$, that satisfies precedence constraints and architectural constraints. These architectural constraints can be modeled either as an instruction set or by introducing functional resources and associating a certain resource usage with each operation. The corresponding resource constraints are *static* in the sense that they only provide a fixed upper limit and any usage within the limit is valid.

Definition 2. A *Static Resource Model* (SRM) is a model generating static resource constraints that defines three aspects:

−a set of resources R,

−a mapping that associates each operation type with the resources in R that it needs, and

−the number of instances of each resource $r \in R$, denoted by $\#r$.

Our approach is motivated by the observation that both resource constraints and instruction set constraints can be expressed as inequalities. For example, if an architecture contains two ALUs and each ALU can be used as an adder or a subtractor, then the resource constraints can be expressed as the following inequality: $N(ALU) \leq 2$, which is equal to: $N(A) + N(S) \leq 2$, where $N(A)$ and $N(S)$ denotes the number of adders and subtractors in use. Any schedule satisfying at any time the above inequality indicates a valid resource usage. Similarly, if an instruction set contains instructions $\{add, add\}$, $\{add, sub\}$ and $\{sub, sub\}$, the operation type usage can also be expressed as an inequality: $N(add) + N(sub) \leq 2$, assuming any subinstruction is also a valid instruction.

Problem Statement: The general problem can be defined as mapping a given instruction set to an SRM such that for any schedule for a DFG satisfying the functional resource constraints posed by the SRM, a corresponding valid instruction selection exists. We say that the instruction set *has* an SRM. This problem can be separated into two subproblems.

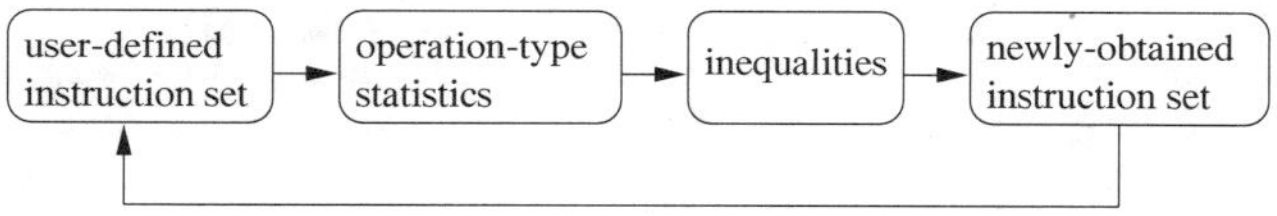

Figure 3: *Overview of the approach*

Problem 1. Given an instruction set, determine whether it has an SRM.

We propose a solution strategy based on expressing the instruction set constraints as inequalities, like $N(add) + N(sub) \leq 2$ in the example above. These inequalities follow from the *operation-type statistics*, as explained in the next section. We then search for an SRM that implies the same set of inequalities. The equivalence of the instruction set constraints and the SRM is verified by comparing the original instruction set to the instruction set that is implied by the SRM. The procedure is illustrated in Figure 3.

Because the run-time performance of a scheduler depends heavily on the complexity of the SRM, we also consider the following problem.

Problem 2. For an instruction set having an SRM, construct the SRM with minimal resources.

The resources can be obtained directly from the inequalities when deriving an SRM. Section 4 provides three rules for reducing the number of resources by analyzing potential redundancy in the generated inequalities.

3. IDENTIFICATION AND CONSTRUCTION OF AN SRM

In this section, we present a method based on inequalities for verifying whether an instruction set IS has an equivalent SRM. If it has, the method also gives this SRM.

3.1 Deriving inequalities

Consider the instruction set of Figure 4(a). The desired inequalities are derived from the *operation-type statistics* of the instruction set, depicted in the table in Figure 4(b). In the table, rows correspond to the individual instructions in Figure 4(a), and columns correspond to (combinations) of operation types. The numbers in the table indicate how many times an operation type is present in an instruction. For example, the operation type *add* occurs twice in instruction (1), and the operation types *shift* and *mul* together occur three times in instruction (3). By looking at the largest frequency within each column, the inequalities in Figure 4(c) are derived. Each inequality corresponds to one column.

(1) {add,add,mul,shift}

(2) {add,add,shift,shift}

(3) {add,mul,mul,shift}

(4) {add,mul,shift,shift}

(a) user-defined instruction set

	add	mul	shift	add mul	add shift	shift mul	add shift mul
(1)	2	1	1	3	3	2	4
(2)	2	0	2	2	4	2	4
(3)	1	2	1	3	2	3	4
(4)	1	1	2	2	3	3	4

(b) operation-type statistics

(1) N(a) <= 2

(2) N(m) <= 2

(3) N(s) <= 2

(4) N(a)+N(m) <= 3

(5) N(a)+N(s) <= 4

(6) N(m)+N(s) <= 3

(7) N(a)+N(m)+N(s) <= 4

(c) inequalities

#A = 2, #M = 2, #S = 2,

#AM = 3, #MS = 3, #AMS = 4

add -> A, AM, AMS

mul -> M, AM, MS, AMS

shift -> S, MS, AMS

(d) static resource model

Figure 4: *Example of an instruction set with an SRM*

In general, given some instruction set IS, we have one inequality for each set of operation types $S = \{op_1, \cdots, op_n\}$:

$$N(op_1) + \cdots + N(op_n) \leq \underset{I \in IS}{\text{MAX}}\Big(\sum_{op \in I \cap S} I(op)\Big) \qquad (1)$$

where $N(op_i)$ is the number of times an operation type appears in an instruction.

The instruction set constraints have now been replaced by a set of inequalities, denoted by $InEq(IS)$. This set often contains redundancy; in the example of Figure 4, inequality (5) can be removed because it is implied by inequality (7). Removing inequalities is advantageous because the complexity of the derived SRM is determined by the number of inequalities in $InEq(IS)$.

3.2 Deriving an SRM

The desired SRM can be derived from the inequalities obtained from the operation-type statistics. Our choice to consider prefix closed instruction sets is motivated by the following corollary, which follows from the containment relationship of instructions.

Corollary. If instruction I_1 contains instruction I_0, and I_1 satisfies $InEq(IS)$, then I_0 also satisfies $InEq(IS)$.

This corollary implies that we can construct an SRM by limiting our observation to the "largest" instructions that are not contained in any other instruction.

Theorem. If S is the set of all the instructions satisfying $InEq(IS)$ and S is equal to the original IS, then IS has an SRM.

We prove this theorem by giving the following SRM:

- R equals the *sets* of operation types,
- each operation type needs all the resources that it is contained in, and
- the number of instances of a resource equals the bound in the corresponding inequality defined by (1).

For example, inequality (4) in Figure 4(c) translates to a virtual resource $\{add, mul\}$, which is abbreviated as AM, with three instances available. For reasons of convenience, we represent a virtual resource by combining the first letters of all those operation types which compose the virtual resource. This will be used throughout the paper. Thus AM is used by operation types *add* and *mul*, as indicated in Figure 4(d).

In order to close the loop in Figure 3 and to prove the above theorem, we need to verify that the given SRM models the original instruction set. We do this by implicitly enumerating the instructions that are valid given the SRM. If this newly-obtained instruction set is the same as the original instruction set, then we may conclude that the original instruction set has an SRM. It is not difficult to see that a schedule of a DFG constrained via the above SRM satisfies all the instruction set constraints.

Our method does not always give an SRM. For example, if we omit instruction (4) in the above example, we obtain the same seven inequalities as before and thus also the same SRM. However, this SRM is not an SRM for instruction set IS = {(1), (2), (3)} because it allows instruction (4) which is not an element of IS.

Note that for certain important classes of instruction sets, it is always possible to derive an SRM using our method. One such class are the VLIW instruction sets, which serve as the interface for VLIW architectures that are used quite often in media processing. Our method is a generalization of the methods presented in [2] and [12].

4. MINIMIZATION OF AN SRM

As we have seen in the example of Figure 4, sometimes some of the inequalities derived via our method are redundant. If we can remove an inequality, we can also remove the corresponding resource from the derived SRM. However, the general problem of minimizing a set of inequalities is intractable. Thus, we resort to heuristics. We summarize three rules for minimizing an SRM. For simplicity, the rules are presented only for two operation types op_i and op_j. Assume that the usage constraints for virtual resources $\{op_i\}$, $\{op_j\}$ and $\{op_i, op_j\}$ are given as follows: $N(\{op_i\}) = n_i$, $N(\{op_j\}) = n_j$ and $N(\{op_i, op_j\}) = n_{ij}$.

Rule 1. If $n_i = n_j = n_{ij}$, then operation types op_i and op_j are *totally overlapping*, which means that they share the same resource instances at any time for any usage. Virtual resources $\{op_i\}$ and $\{op_j\}$ can be removed from the SRM, because the constraint on $\{op_i, op_j\}$ makes the constraints on these two resources redundant.

Rule 2. If $n_i < n_j$ and $n_j = n_{ij}$ then operation type op_j *fully covers* op_i, or operation type op_i is *fully covered* by op_j. Each execution of op_i will occupy the resource instances for executing op_j, but not all the usage of op_j will be restricted by op_i. In this case, resource $\{op_j\}$ is redundant since the constraint imposed by resource $\{op_i, op_j\}$ already enforces the constraint imposed by $\{op_j\}$.

Rule 3. If $n_i + n_j = n_{ij}$, then operation types op_i and op_j are *non-overlapping*, which means they don't share any resource instances at all. In this case, resource $\{op_i, op_j\}$ is redundant. For instance, in Figure 4, resources $\{add\}$ and $\{shift\}$ are non-overlapping, which indicates that inequality (5) can be removed.

Note that if $n_i + n_j > n_{ij}$, then operation types op_i and op_j are *partly overlapping*. Part but not all of the resource instances which can execute op_i can also be used for op_j, and vice versa. In this case, we cannot remove any resources.

Reconsider the example in Figures 1 and 2. The minimized SRM of Figure 2 has been obtained by repeatedly applying rules 1 and 3.

5. EXPERIMENTAL RESULTS

The first example shows that our method can also deal with very flexible designs using complex instructions. The task to be scheduled is a slightly adapted example taken from [7]:

$$e = m_1 * m_2 + m_3 * m_4 + (m_5 * m_6 + m_7 * m_8) * m_9$$

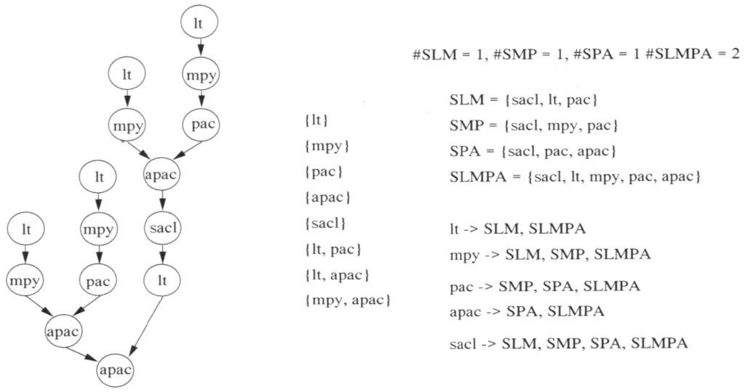

(a) an example of a DFG (b) instruction set (c) minimal SRM

Figure 5: *Complex instructions and the SRM*

Complex instructions for the TMS320C25 processor are shown in Figure 5(b). They indicate potential parallelism to be exploited. This instruction set can be proven to have an SRM and this SRM can be minimized by applying the rules in Section 4. Thus the minimized SRM is given in Figure 5(c). Scheduling the DFG in Figure 5 with this SRM gives us a latency of 12, which equals the optimal result.

One of the merits of the SRM approach is that by performing instruction scheduling for applications with different SRMs, one can directly see from the results how restrictive an IS is. Experiments below perform the scheduling and register binding for benchmarks with two instruction sets. IS1 is the instruction set in Figure 4, IS2 is the set $\{\{add, add, shift, shift\}$, $\{mul, mul, shift, shift\}$, $\{add, mul, shift, shift\}\}$. Assume that the hardware resources are ALU, MUL and $SHIFT$, each with two instances and one cycle delay. Table 1 lists the results for 'fdct', 'idct', 'ar' for AR filter and 'wdf' for fifth-order digital elliptical wave filter. The second and third columns show the latency and register requirements (assuming one register file for all the variables) with given functional resources, the fourth and fifth give latency and registe requirements for IS1 and the sixth and seventh for IS2. #in is the number of minimized inequalities.

Table 1: Scheduling and register binding results

	FS		IS1		IS2	
	L	RF	L_{SRM}	RF_{SRM}	L_{SRM}	RF_{SRM}
fdct	13	12	16	12	21	14
idct	14	11	15	11	20	13
ar	10	6	11	7	14	8
wdf	16	8	16	8	19	11
#in	3		6		4	

From this table we can see that the latency and register requirements with only the functional resource restrictions are minimal for all the examples. This is because we assume that all the functional resources can be exploited maximally. Instruction set constraints usually increase the latency and register requirements. Although using the same resouces, IS2 is obviously more restrictive than IS1, since all latencies are increased. Register requirements are also increased because when some operations are postponed in order to meet the instruction set constraints, the values they consume have to be stored in registers for a longer time, which increases the register pressure.

Table 2: TMS320C62x instruction set

	L	S	D	M
Integer Adder	add	add	add	
	sub	sub	sub	
	mov	mov	mov	
	cmpgt			
	cmplt			
Logic	and	and	and	
	or	or	or	
	not	not	not	
Shift		shl		
		shr		
			ld	
			st	
Multiplier				mpy

VLIW instruction sets have an SRM because of their orthogonal instruction format, such as the TMS320C62x architecture. The C62x has two identical data paths with four functional units each. Each data path has 16 32-bit registers. Table 2 shows part of the instructions for one group of the data path supported by TMS320C62x.

Before computing operation-type statistics, some optimization can be performed to operation types which have exactly the same usage in the instruction set. For example, *add*, *sub* and *mov* can be collected in one group A, *comgt* and *comlt* in group C, *and*, *or* and *not* in group L, *shl* and *shr* in group S, *ld* and *st* in group D. Now virtual resources can be created and they can be minimized by applying the rules in Section 4. The resulting SRM can be summerized as follows: $\#M = 1, \#C = 1, \#S = 1, \#D = 1, \#CLS = 2, \#ACLSD = 3$. Table 3 shows the scheduling and register binding results for GSM speech-coding algorithms. 'Convolution' and 'viterbi' are the half-rate convolutional encoder and one_viterbi_step procedure for the viterbi decoder in channel codec. 'weight', 'inverse' and 'quant' are the weighting_filter, APCM_inverse_quantization and APCM_quantization algorithms for regular pulse exitation encoding in speech codec. SRMs can also be applied to software pipelining, since it only provides a static boundary without modifying the scheduling and register binding algorithm themselves. In Table 3, L and RF are the latency and register requirements with instruction-set constraints within one iteration. II is the minimal initiation interval when software pipelining is applied. L' and RF' are the latency and register requirements under the minimal initiation interval restrictions. This is not performed for 'quant' because it costs too much time to obtain the minimal initiation interval.

Table 3: Scheduling and register binding results for GSM speech-coding algorithms

	L	RF	II	L'	RF'
convol	5	8	5	5	8
viterbi	21	10	18	33	10
weight	18	7	11	20	7
invers	7	4	2	8	5
quant	89	16	-	-	-

6. CONCLUSIONS

In this paper, we propose a method for code generation for highly encoded instruction set processors. The purpose of the method is to deal with the strong phase coupling between instruction selection and scheduling, caused by the instruction set. We replace the instruction set with a set of virtual resources that implement the individual operations contained in the instruction set. This reduces the need for explicit instruction selection, because any schedule satisfying the virtual resource constraints can be implemented by the instruction set. With this static resource model, the scheduler has the opportunity to generate better schedules in terms of timing and register requirements. Furthermore, software pipelining can be applied more effectively to exploit the available ILP.

Our experiments demonstrate that a static resource model of an instruction set offers the possibility to measure the effectiveness of an instruction set with respect to exploiting the processor resources. This enables instruction set designers to make tradeoffs between the performance and the code size associated with an instruction set.

We plan to extend our method to support more versatile instruction sets. In addition, the heuristics to remove the redundancies from an SRM need more investigation. We also intend to study special features of instruction sets used in media processors, such as SIMD instructions [6].

7. ADDITIONAL AUTHORS

C.A.J. van Eijk (Magma Design Automation BV, email: koen@Magma-DA.com) and J.A.G. Jess (Eindhoven University of Technology, email: J.A.G.Jess@ele.tue.nl).

8. REFERENCES

[1] G. Araujo, S. Marlik, and M. Lee. Using Register-Transfer Paths in Code Generation for Heterogeneous Memory-Register Architectures. In *33rd Design Automation Conference Proceedings*, pages 591–596, June 1996.

[2] C. Eisenbeis, Z. Chamski, and E. Rohou. Flexible Issue Slot Assignment for VLIW Architectures. In *Proceedings of the 4th Int. Workshop on Software and Compilers for Embedded Systems*, March 1999.

[3] A. Fauth et al. Describing Instruction Set Processors Using nML. In *European Design and Test Conference Proceedings*, pages 503–507, March 1995.

[4] S. Hanono, G. Hadjiyiannis, and S. Devadas. Aviv: A Retargetable Code Generator Using ISDL. In *34th Design Automation Conference Proceedings*, pages 299–302, June 1997.

[5] R. Leupers. *Retargetable Code Generation for Digital Signal Processors*. Kluwer Academic Publishers, Amsterdam, 1997.

[6] R. Leupers. Code Selection for Media Processors with SIMD Instructions. In *Design, Automation and Test in Europe Conference Proceedings*, pages 4–8, March 2000.

[7] R. Leupers and P. Marwedel. Instruction Selection for Embedded DSPs with Complex Instructions. In *Europe Design Automation Conference*, 1996.

[8] C. Liem, T. May, and P. Paulin. Instruction-Set Matching and Selection for DSP and ASIP Code Generation. In *Proceedings of the Int. Symposium on System Synthesis*, 1994.

[9] B. Mesman, C. Alba-Pinto, and C. van Eijk. Efficient Scheduling of DSP Code on Processors with Distributed Register Files. In *Proceedings of the Int. Symposium on System Synthesis*, November 1999.

[10] P. Paulin and C. Liem. Embedded Systems: Tools and Trends. In *European Design and Test Conference Proceedings*, March 1996.

[11] B. Rau and C. Glaeser. Some Scheduling Techniques and An Easily Schedulable Horizontal Architecture for High Performance Scientific Computing. In *Proceedings of the 14th Workshop on Microprogramming*, pages 183–198, 1981.

[12] A. Timmer, M. Strik, J. van Meerbergen, and J. Jess. Conflict Modeling and Instruction Scheduling in Code Generation for In-House DSP Cores. In *32nd Design Automation Conference Proceedings*, pages 593–598, June 1995.

[13] J. van Praet, G. Goossens, D. Lanner, and H. De Man. Instruction Set Definition and Instruction Selection for ASIPs. In *Proceedings of the Int. Symposium on System Synthesis*, 1994.

[14] T. Wilson, G. Grewal, B. Halley, and D. Banerji. An Integrated Approach to Retargetable Code Generation. In *Proceedings of the Int. Symposium on System Synthesis*, 1994.

Combined Instruction and Loop Parallelism in Array Synthesis for FPGAs*

Steven Derrien
IRISA
Rennes, France
sderrien@irisa.fr

Sanjay Rajopadhye
IRISA
Rennes, France
rajopadhye@irisa.fr

Susmita Sur Kolay
Indian Statistical Institute
Calcutta, India
ssk@isical.ac.in

ABSTRACT

Compiling perfect, uniform dependence loops to FPGA based co-processors normally yields processor (PE) arrays where a PE executes one instance of the loop body per clock cycle. We develop a transformation framework in which the derived PE can be systematically and automatically pipelined through retiming. We use well known transformations—**skewing** and **serialization**, by which an arbitrary number of registers may be placed at the PE outputs. They are then moved into the PE data-path using standard commerecial circuit retimers. Our experiments (based on performance estimates after place-and-route) have been very encouraging. For a number of examples we have seen dramatic performance improvements: speed increases of an order of magnitude with relatively little (always less than 100%) area overhead.

Keywords

Instruction Level Parallelism, Programmable Logic, Retiming, Regular Processors Arrays

1. INTRODUCTION

High-performance embedded systems are an exploding market, with many applications. These systems often have to deal with very stringent performance (both speed as well as area and power) constraints. Hence, their design is a real challenge, especially in the context of current time to market pressure. Automating the design requires that (i) the application is specified at a high level through standard languages (such as C or MATLAB), (ii) the generated system is formally correct with respect to the initial specification, and (iii) the design tool is flexible enough to allow a relatively wide user-driven design-space exploration.

*Supported in part by IFCPAR project 1802-1: CORCoP Compilation and Optimization for Reconfigurable Co-Processors

Critical portions of embedded applications often consist of regular computations generally expressed as nested loops. Hence, the ability to compile loops to specialized parallel circuits should help attain the above objectives and meet performance and power consumption constraints. Several such tools exist in the research community some of which have reached a relative maturity [1, 5]. These tools act as specialized silicon compilers: they generate a structural description (RTL level) of a regular (systolic) array and its associated control from a loop description expressed in a high level specification language. The RTL description can then be used by standard CAD tools to target either an ASIC or an FPGA.

Choosing an adequate target technology is not straightforward. Although some applications still require an ASIC implementation, the advent of dense and cheap FPGAs has made them a viable alternative. However, FPGAs are not as efficient as ASICs, leading to disappointing performance. This is especially true when operations involved in the loop are complex and/or numerous: since traditional array synthesis algorithms implement the loop body as a combinational data-path, the critical path of the resulting design tends to be large, leading to low clock frequency.

However, it is also well known that hand tuned FPGA designs can compete and sometimes even beat ASIC implementations (see [7]). These high performance designs usually take advantage of very fine grain parallelism for which recent FPGA architectures are very well suited: large number of flip-flops, and programmable delay-lines with small area cost. By exploiting similar techniques, we may expect to improve FPGA processing power by pipelining the internal PE structure, so that performance would benefit from intra as well as inter PE parallelism. Our objective is thus to provide tools which will automatically transform a given processor array architecture to take advantage of fine grain pipeline, while preserving its functionality.

In this paper, we propose high-level architectural transformations, which enable very fine grain pipelining in processor arrays. We also propose a heuristic to choose the transformation parameters. Since our transformations are based on the formal foundations of space-time mappings, we can ensure their correctness and incorporate them at a higher level of the design flow, within an array synthesis tool. Our approach is validated experimentally on several examples and shows very encouraging results.

2. BACKGROUND

We now recap the techniques of array processor synthesis,

develop some constraints that we impose on the derived architecture and the corresponding transformations. In doing so we also introduce our notations and conventions.

2.1 Loop parallelization

We only consider a restricted class of loop nests, for which well established methodologies exist. Specifically, we assume perfectly nested loops with uniform flow dependences and statically known bounds. Let I denote the loop domain defined by a set of linear inequalities. Let $\overrightarrow{x}$ denote the loop index vector $[\ x_1\ \ \ldots\ \ x_n\ ]$. The computation of the loop body is characterized by m data dependence vectors represented as a matrix $D = [\ \overrightarrow{d_1}\ \ \ldots\ \ \overrightarrow{d_m}\ ]$. Consider the loop nest description for $N \times N$ matrix multiplication:

```
for(i=0;i<N;i++)
  for(j=0;j<N;j++)
  {
    c[i][j]=0;
    for(k=0;k<N;k++)
      c[i][j]=a[i][k]*b[k][j]+c[i][j];
  }
```

The dependencies are the unit vectors $\overrightarrow{i}$, $\overrightarrow{j}$, and $\overrightarrow{k}$, and the iteration space is a three-dimensional cube in the $(\overrightarrow{i}, \overrightarrow{j}, \overrightarrow{k})$ index space. Following well established methods [8], the parallelization of such a loop nest consists of two steps, namely scheduling and allocation.

The *scheduling* function maps iteration $\overrightarrow{x}$ to time instant $t = \tau(\overrightarrow{x})$, this function must ensure that all data dependencies are satisfied. The schedule is normally an affine function, and we have $t = \overrightarrow{\tau}\overrightarrow{x} + c_0$. The condition for the schedule to be valid (with respect to the data dependencies) can be written as $\overrightarrow{\tau}\overrightarrow{d_k} > 0$ where d_k is the kth data dependence vector.

The *allocation* function assigns iteration $\overrightarrow{x}$ to a PE $\overrightarrow{p}$ in the processor index space. As with scheduling, we consider linear allocation functions (specified by a projection vector $\overrightarrow{v}$). They map the n-dimensional iteration space to an $(n-1)$-dimensional processor space. Let π denote this projection matrix, so that $\overrightarrow{p} = \pi\overrightarrow{x}$. The whole transformation is expressed as $\overrightarrow{x'} = \Pi\overrightarrow{x} + \overrightarrow{c}$, where $\Pi = \left[\frac{\tau}{\pi}\right]$. For the transformation to be valid, there should be no conflicts (i.e., only one iteration allocated to a PE at any time), and it is well known that this implies that Π should be non-singular.

Note that for each dependence, d_k, the vector $\pi\overrightarrow{d_k}$ gives the corresponding interconnection link in the architecture and τd_k gives its associated delay (in terms of clock cycles).

In addition to the standard constraints described above, we impose two restrictions over π and $\overrightarrow{\tau}$ (for a formal justification please refer to the extented version of this paper [10].

- We only allow unidirectional communications in our array, which translates as $\pi\overrightarrow{d_k} \succeq 0$.
- We only allow nearest neighbor interconnections, which trasnlates as $\forall k,\ \overrightarrow{\tau}\overrightarrow{d_k} \geq \left|\pi\overrightarrow{d_k}\right|$.

2.2 Resulting hardware characteristics

The scheduling and allocation functions yield a processor array where each PE consists of a data-path connected to a set of registers (see Fig. 1 which we shall use as a running example). There are two types of registers in the PE.

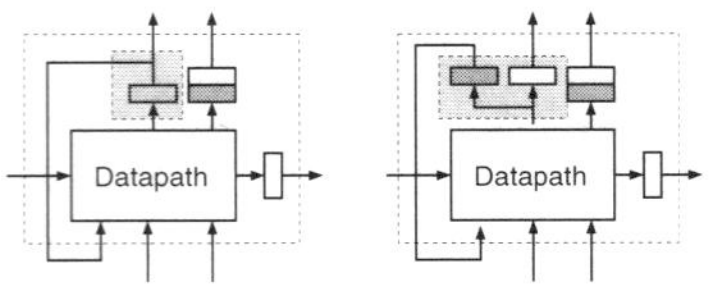

(a) (b)

Figure 1: (a) Spatio-Temporal registers in the original architecture (b) modified architecture with non ambiguous register type.

- *Temporal registers* act as local memory within the PE data-path.
- *Spatial registers* connect two PEs along one processor space dimension (for $i = 1 \ldots n-1$).

When a register drives both a local (i.e, *temporal*) register and a neighboring PE, It can be considered as both spatial and temporal. In such a case we choose to duplicate this register (by means of retiming) such that the resulting registers are either *spatial* or *temporal* but not both (see figure 1).

The data-path is modeled as a directed acyclic graph of combinational operators, and performs the computations associated with the loop body. It contains n different types of paths (n being the loop dimension).

- A spatial path in the ith dimension ($i = 1 \ldots n-1$) is a path starting from any register output or PE input, and driving a spatial register in this dimension.
- A temporal path (i.e., a path in the n-th or the time dimension) is a path starting from any register output or PE input and driving a temporal register.

Note that it is the register at the *end* of the path that determines its dimension.

2.3 Improving Array performance

Obviously, a large combinational path in the data-path is a performance bottleneck, especially for floating point implementations, where FPGAs clock speed implementations can not go beyond 12MHz, although conventional microprocessors attain GHz frequencies. We therefore seek to to pipeline our data-path whenever possible. There are three reasons for this: (i) we expect significant gains in clock speed, (ii) FPGA register resources are generally underutilized, and (iii) in our context, we expect to pipeline aggressively, and tuned to the application at hand.

The pipelining is achieved by "retiming", a technique originally introduced by Leiserson and Saxe [2]. It is a synchronous circuit transformation preserving the behavior of the design while permitting to reorganize the registers of the circuit.

Our goal is here to increase the array achievable clock frequency through retiming. We assume that the PE data-path is represented as a net-list of standard FPGA combinational primitives (each with a predefined delay), so that we can estimate the delay along all combinational paths. Since interconnect delay cannot be estimated prior to the place and route phase, we base our delay estimation on the number of combinational primitives in a path. As in Section 2.2, we partition the PE paths into n subsets, one per dimension.

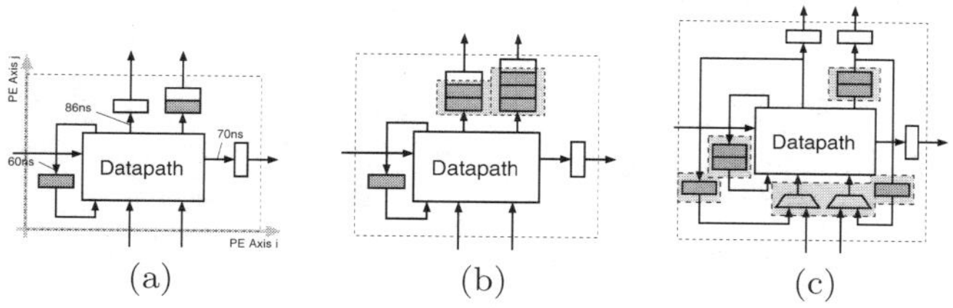

Figure 2: Impact of skewing and serialization. The original PE (a), skewed along the j axis with $\lambda_j = 2$ (b), and then serialized along the j axis with $\sigma_j = 2$.

If we can arbitrarily increase the number of its registers in any dimension, we can pipeline this large combinational path to an arbitrary degree. Of course, the more the registers that we create in a given dimension, the smaller will be the final critical path.

3. TRANSFORMATIONS

We now present two space-time transformations (*skewing* and *serialization*) which allow us to tune the number of registers in the various paths of the PE architecture by affecting both the scheduling and mapping functions.

3.1 Skewing

The **skewing transformation** increases latency between iterations mapped to neighboring PEs. Since this additional latency materializes as registers, which can be used for retiming, we can expect this transformation to allow some clock speed improvement.

The skewing transformation is specified by a vector $\overrightarrow{\lambda}$, its component λ_i being the latency between computations mapped to neighboring PEs along the ith processor index axis;

The modified schedule is then given below. Note that this transformation is only valid for arrays with unidirectional connections (i.e., where $\pi.\overrightarrow{d_k} > 0$, the restriction we imposed in 2.1).

$$\tau'(\overrightarrow{x}) = \tau(\overrightarrow{x}) + \overrightarrow{\lambda}.\pi(\overrightarrow{x})$$

It is easy to show that after skewing, a *spatial* register along a given processor axis i is appended at its input by λ_i temporal registers. This transformation hence increases the number of registers associated with all original spatial paths. However, *skewing* does not affect temporal registers, hence in architectures with temporal loops, *skewing* alone cannot provide registers at appropriate places for retiming. An example of *skewing* is shown figure 2.b.

3.2 Serialization (Clustering)

The **serialization transformation** is well known space-time transformation that has been widely studied [3, 4, 6, 11]. As opposed to classic systolic synthesis, it is non-linear. The key idea is to group PEs derived from the systolisation process into "clusters" in which the original PE's iterations are performed sequentially. The virtual array obtained from the systolisation is hence transformed into a smaller physical array.

Serialization has been used for parallelizing loops on fixed size arrays [6] (also called *active clustering*) or for improving the efficiency of arrays obtained by non-unimodular space-time mappings [3] (called *passive clustering*). Finally, it is also useful for IO bandwidth adaptation [12, 9] and data reuse.

Clustering consists of two coupled sub-problems (i) defining the cluster geometry (ii) specifying the schedule within and between clusters. In the scope of this paper, to ease the derivation and to simplify the control of the serialized architecture, we choose rectangular cluster shape with edges parallel to the communication channels.

Let H be a diagonal rational matrix $[\sigma_1^{-1} \ldots \sigma_p^{-1}]$, in which σ_i are positive integers. The clustered processor mapping is then $\overrightarrow{p} = \lfloor H\pi\overrightarrow{x} \rfloor$, and the number of iterations to be performed in a cluster is given by $\Pi_{i=0}^{n}\sigma_i$.

Once the cluster geometry is set, iterations within this cluster have to be scheduled. Finding the optimal schedule within a cluster has been studied by several authors, either in the scope of resource constraints (minimizing memory requirements, adequate use of functional units [11]) or to provide simple control logic while preserving the scheduling efficiency [4]. To ease the derivation of the clustered architecture (and hence be able to predict the number and position of all registers), we restrict ourselves to simple scheduling, knowing that (i) cluster boundaries are parallel to the processor space index axes, and (ii) all virtual PEs (i.e., before clustering) are active in a given clock cycle.

For active clustering, these concerns are not relevant. We therefore use a very simple local schedule: iterations are executed in an axis-major order as if our p-dimensional clustering consisted of a sequence of uni-dimensional *serializations* along each dimension of the cluster. Of course, since such serializations are quasi-linear transformations, the order in which they are performed is crucial.

To determine the resulting architecture, we just need to understand the impact of a *serialization* along a given cluster axis. The following rules which can be used to build a serialized architecture

- All temporal registers are duplicated by a factor σ_i. The number of registers associated with the temporal paths (i.e., the depth of the delay line driven by the path output) is thus increased.
- If *serialization* is done along i^{th} processor axis, feed back loops (and their associated multiplexers) are created (as shown in figure 2.b) for all spatial registers along the corresponding dimension.
- The control logic commanding the feed-back loop multiplexer associated to dimension i hence simply consists of a periodically active signal (the signal period is a simple function of the order of serializations and the cluster dimensions).

3.3 Combining all transformations

It is possible to apply these transformations in any order and along any space dimension. However the order in which they are applied has a strong impact on the resulting architecture. This is easy to understand: *skewing* adds temporal registers in all spatial paths, and *serialization* duplicates these temporal registers. If *skewing* is performed before *serialization* its additional registers will be duplicated by serialization, if *skewing* is performed after serialization, its additional register will not get affected. This leads to the following transformation rules for a $p = n - 1$ dimensional processor space.

- A *skewing* transformation performed along i^{th} cluster axis induces λ_i additional temporal registers on all paths in the ith processor space axis. These additional registers (which are temporal) will hence be duplicated by all subsequent *serializations*. Assuming that all *serializations* are performed in the lexicographic order of the PE space (starting with dimension $\overrightarrow{k}$), we can write the succession of serializations as $\sigma_k, \sigma_{k+1}, \ldots, \sigma_p$. Since all the temporal registers due to *skewing* will be duplicated by each subsequent *serialization*, the number of registers generated in the final architecture is $\lambda_i \Pi_{n=k}^{p} \sigma_i$ (see figure 3.a for the impact of a *skewing* with $\lambda_j = 1$, and figures 3.b and 3.c for the effect of subsequent serializations).
- A *serialization* transformation along the ith cluster axis has two effects: (i) it duplicates all temporal registers by the *serialization* factor σ_i, and (ii) it creates feed-back loops (with one temporal register and a multiplexer) for all spatial paths along the ith processor axis. These temporal registers will not be affected by subsequent skewing, but they will be duplicated by all subsequent serializations. Again, if $\sigma_k, \sigma_{k+1}, \ldots, \sigma_p$ is the sequence of transformations following our initial *serialization* (assuming $i \notin [k, p]$), the number of registers present in the final PE i^{th} axis feed-back loop is $\Pi_{i=k}^{p} \sigma_i$ (eg. the feed-back registers that appeared in 3.b are duplicated by $\sigma_i = 2$ as shown in 3.c)
- When, for a given index i, *skewing* is performed after all serializations, all the λ_i new temporal registers appear outside the feed-back loop induced by the preceding serializations. They can then moved within the data-path if and only if there are enough registers associated to the *serialization* feed-back loop at that time. In other words, since $\Pi_{i=k}^{p} \sigma_i$ denotes the delay-line depth associated with these registers, the number of registers that can be used for pipelining is then $\min(\Pi_{i=k}^{p} \sigma_i, \lambda_i)$ (see figure 3.e for the *skewing* and 3.f for the register factorization).

We now describe some of our assumptions about the order of application of our transformations. First, we will make a distinction between two kinds of skewing. Let λ_i^{pre} denote a dimension-i *skewing* operation performed just before the σ_i transformation and λ_i^{post} denote a *skewing* operation performed after all serializations. We impose the following restrictions.

1. We choose a sequence of axes in the processor space, and for each dimension i in this sequence we execute a pre-σ *skewing* λ_i^{pre}, followed by the σ_i transformation.
2. After step 1 is executed for all dimensions, we perform a succession of post-σ *skewings* by λ_i^{post} for each dimension i.

We now express the number of registers available for pipelining in each dimension: after all the serialization steps, all our initial temporal paths now have $\Pi_{i=1}^{p} \sigma_i$ available registers. We can also formulate the number of registers on the ith spatial path: (i) the combination of pre-σ skew λ_i^{pre} and all

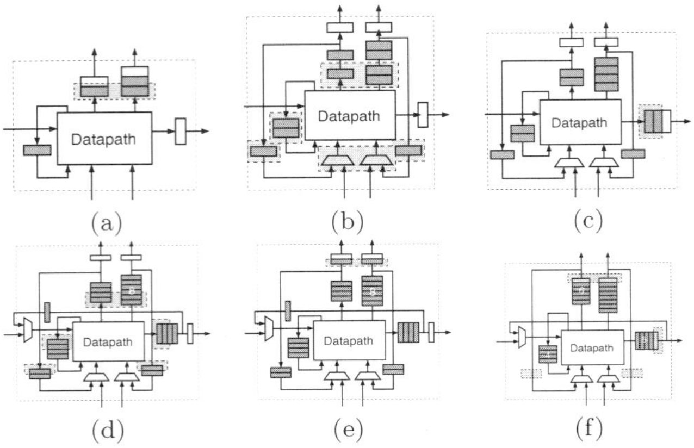

(a) (b) (c) (d) (e) (f)

Figure 3: Successive transformations for the PE of Fig. 2.a: (a) Skewing $\lambda_j^{pre} = 1$; (b) Serialization $\sigma_j = 2$; (c) Skewing $\lambda_i^{pre} = 2$; (d) Serialization $\sigma_i = 2$; (e) Skewing $\lambda_j^{post} = 1$; (f) final architecture.

its subsequent serializations provides $\lambda_i^{pre} \Pi_{k=i}^{p} \sigma_k$ additional registers along i^{th} spatial axis (ii) the post-σ skew λ_i^{post} provides λ_i^{post} registers, from which only $\min(\Pi_{k=i+1}^{p} \sigma_k, \lambda_i^{post})$ can be used for pipelining. The number of registers along spatial axis i is then $\lambda_i^{pre} \Pi_{k=i}^{p} \sigma_k + \min(\Pi_{k=i+1}^{p} \sigma_k, \lambda_i^{post})$.

3.4 Choice of tranformations

There is considerable freedom in choosing the order and parameters of the transformations, and we seek one which satisfies the constraints for a given desired throughput. Although several transformations may satisfy these constraints, they are not necessarily equivalent in terms of total register cost. In this paper we use simple pragmatic heuristic to determine a satisfactory, but not necessarily optimal solution. Let d_i denote the given constraints on the minimum number of pipeline stage along dimension i (with d_n for the temporal dimesion).

Generally the cluster dimensions are either set to specific values or (more generally) have lower bounds, so that they can match external (eg. bandwidth and resource) constraints. Hence we will assume that the cluster dimensions are given and are chosen such that $\Pi_{i=1}^{p} \sigma_i > d_n$. The problem is then to choose (i) the order of serializations, and (ii) the values of λ_i^{pre},λ_i^{post}.

For (i), we propose the following: sort space indices in the decreasing order of T_{path_i} and execute the serializations according to this order. This allows the most critical spatial path to benefit most from the additional registers provided by the subsequent serializations.

For (ii), we define $\Delta = \Pi_{k=i+1}^{p} \sigma_k$ if $i < p$, $\Delta = 1$ otherwise. The *skewing* parameters are then given by $\lambda_i^{pre} = \min\left(0, \left\lceil \frac{d_i - \Delta}{\Pi_{k=i}^{p} \sigma_k} \right\rceil\right)$ and $\lambda_i^{post} = \min(d_i, \Delta) - 1$.

3.5 Example

To illustrate the transformation flow, consider the PE whose architecture is shown in figure 2. Assume that we need to meet the following set of inequality constraints over the number of registers required along each dimension of its datapath. We set $d_3 \geq 4$ (4 stages along the temporal axis), $d_1 \geq 5$ (5 stages along processor axis i) and $d_2 \geq 6$ (6 stages along processor axis j). Given these constraints, the next step is to choose the cluster size. In our case we will only consider constraints over the clock period, hence any cluster shape should be valid provided that the constraint on the number of registers in the temporal paths is satisfied (in other words, $d_3 \geq 4$ stages with $\sigma_i \sigma_j = d_3$). To keep our choice simple we will take $\sigma_i = 2$ and $\sigma_j = 2$. Since the number of required stages along j axis dominates that for i axis, serialization along j is performed before i. Let us determine our transformation parameters:

- For axis $\overrightarrow{j}$, we have $\Pi_{k=i+1}^{p} \sigma_k = 2$. Since we need at least 6 stages along this dimension, we need a pre-serialization *skewing* transformation. Our heuristic gives us the following values: $\lambda_j^{pre} = \lceil \frac{6-2}{4} \rceil = 2$ and $\lambda_j^{post} = 0$.

- For axis $\overrightarrow{i}$, there are no subsequent serializations. Since we need at least 5 pipeline stages along this dimension, we need both a pre and post-skewing transformation along axis $\overrightarrow{i}$ to provide additional registers. We then have $\lambda_i^{pre} = \lceil \frac{5-1}{4} \rceil = 1$ and $\lambda_i^{post} = 1$.

Our resulting architecture is shown in figure 3.f, we see that in all dimensions, the number of registers available for pipeline matches our requirements. The data-path can hence now be pipelined using a retiming tool to move these registers so that the global critical path is reduced down to the estimated target clock period.

4. EXPERIMENTAL RESULTS

Given our framework to exploit fine grain parallelism in processor array compilation, we must study experimentally how these transformations effectively impact (i) clock speed, and (ii) area. To do so, we took several loop nest examples and applied our transformations on them, and then used existing retiming capabilities of commercial CAD tools (Synopsys FPGA compiler II). All PE architectures were described in standard synthesizable VHDL, either using available existing IP modules or the CAD tool arithmetic inference capabilities (as for integer operations). The following loop examples were used as benchmarks.

- Adaptive filter (`DLMS`) for 8 and 16 bit integer and 32 bit floating point.

- Biological sequence comparison (best alignment score) for amino acid (`AA`) and `DNA` sequences

- Matrix multiplication (`MatMul`) for 8 and 16 bit integer and 32 bit floating point.

A key hypothesis in our work is that the area overhead caused by the additional pipeline registers will not impact the total area too strongly. We propose to experimentally validate this hypothesis, by observing the relation between (i) pipeline level, (ii) maximum operating frequency, (iii) PE area cost and (iv) overall raw performance improvement. Our target architecture is a VirtexE-8 from Xilinx. Results, in terms of area use (Virtex Slices) and achievable clock period (in MHz) are those predicted by Xilinx place and route tools and are shown in figure 4.

DLMS-float

Stages	Slices	ns	MHz	ρ
1	1444	85,00	11,76	8,1
2	1413	48,50	20,62	14,5
3	1520	34,00	29,41	19,3
4	1556	27,50	36,36	23,3
5	1587	24,50	40,82	25,7
7	1588	20,00	50,00	31,4
11	1654	18,00	55,56	33,5

DLMS-16bits

Stages	Slices	ns	MHz	ρ
1	353	21,00	47,62	134,9
2	419	13,00	76,92	183,5
3	414	11,50	86,96	210,0
4	421	10,50	95,24	226,2
5	441	9,70	103,09	233,7
7	449	10,00	100,00	222,7
9	452	10,50	95,24	210,7

DLMS-8bits

Stages	Slices	ns	MHz	ρ
1	123	17,40	57,47	467,2
2	147	9,00	111,11	755,8
3	147	8,50	117,65	800,3
4	147	8,50	117,65	800,3
5	147	8,20	121,95	829,6

(a)

MatMul-float

Stages	Slices	ns	MHz	ρ
1	704	85,00	11,76	16,71
2	707	55,00	18,18	25,72
3	713	36,00	27,78	38,96
5	725	24,00	41,67	57,47
7	728	21,00	47,62	65,41
9	748	17,50	57,14	76,39
11	749	16,00	62,50	83,44
13	738	15,50	64,52	87,42
17	766	12,50	80,00	104,4
21	781	13,00	76,92	98,49
25	781	12,50	80,00	102,4

MatMul-16bits

Stages	Slices	ns	MHz	ρ
1	154	17,00	58,82	381,9
2	164	12,50	80,00	487,8
3	194	10,00	100,00	515,4
4	194	9,50	105,26	542,5
5	195	9,00	111,11	569,8
9	206	8,50	117,65	571,1

MatMul-8bits

Stages	Slices	ns	MHz	ρ
1	55	14,00	71,43	1298,7
2	55	7,50	133,33	2424,2
3	70	6,50	153,85	2197,8
4	63	7,00	142,86	2267,5
5	74	6,00	166,67	2252,2

(b)

ADN

Stages	Slices	ns	MHz	ρ
1	57	15,00	66,67	1169,5
2	57	13,71	72,94	1279,6
3	84	8,50	117,65	1400,5
4	90	9,50	105,26	1169,5
5	120	7,00	142,86	1190,4

AA

Stages	Slices	ns	MHz	ρ
1	193	32,00	31,25	161,9
2	197	20,00	50,00	254,1
3	206	18,00	55,56	269,6
4	231	14,50	68,97	298,2
5	232	12,50	80,00	344,4

(c)

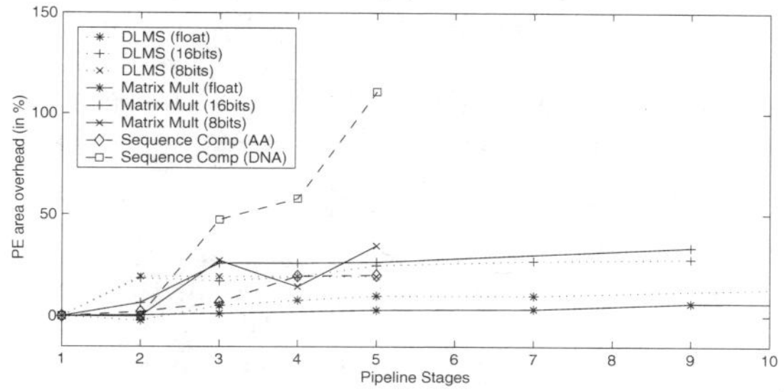

(d)

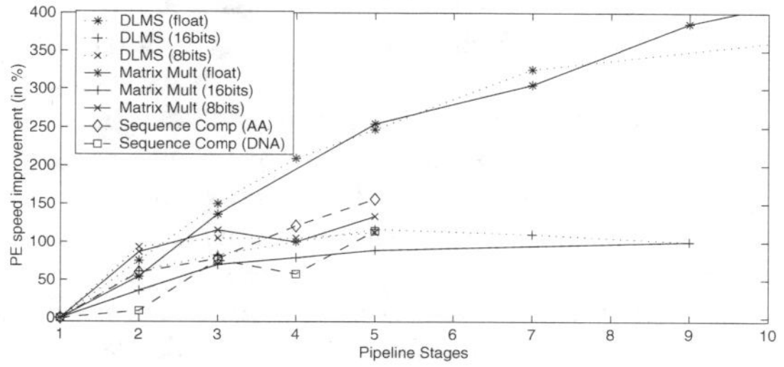

(e)

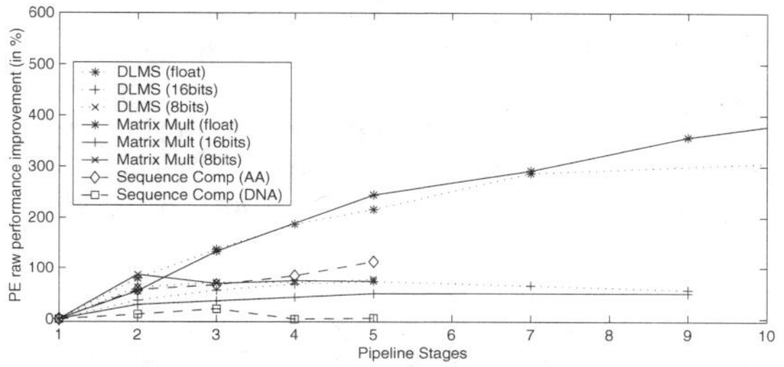

(f)

Figure 4: Experimental results (area, speed and raw performance) for all targeted loop nests

4.1 Area/Clock speed trade-off

Our goal here is to quantify the effective performance improvement induced by our transformation. Specifically, we have shown that deep pipelining requires a lot of registers, which will use more of the available real estate. This leads to a trade-off between area and clock speed: the more registers we use, the better is the clock speed, but the fewer are the PEs that we can fit on the reconfigurable resource. The area overhead due to the pipeline registers is difficult to evaluate analytically, and quantifying the effective performance improvement is not trivial.

In the scope of systolic array implementations, we consider that the array performance is mostly dictated by two parameters: (i) n_{PEs} the number of PEs in the array (i.e., the degree of parallelism) (ii) f_c, the PE speed. We introduce a raw performance metric $\rho = f_c n_{PEs}$ for our architecture. Since n_{PE} is roughly inversely proportional to the PE area (we have $n_{PE} \approx \left\lfloor \frac{A_{fpga}}{A_{pe}} \right\rfloor$ where A_{PE} is the PE area cost and A_{fpga} the target FPGA density), we can also estimate the raw performance by using $\rho' \approx f_c A_{PE}^{-1}$, where A_{PE} is the area cost of the transformed PE. Our results are shown in figure 4. It appears that the raw performance is improved (up to an order of magnitude for complex data-path) but there is also noticeable gain for simpler ones (between 50 to 100%).

We also observed that even by providing a large number of registers, the maximum achievable clock frequency is very dependent on the complexity and regularity of the data-path. We could not get more than 50MHz for a floating point DLMS, while we almost reached 120MHz for a 16 bit integer Matrix multiplication cell. These figures are of course to be compared to the bound for the internal frequency of the target FPGA (130 MHz, as per the device data-sheet).

4.2 Performance limitations

From our experiments, it seems that two factors limit the benefit of using very fine grain parallelism (in other words pipelining down to the logic cell level).

First, it seems that the commercial retiming tool we have been using during our experimentations does not try to reduce the critical path below 5 logic levels. This poses bounds over the minimum achievable combinational path within a pipeline stage, and prevents us from fully exploring the trade-off between area, routability and clock speed for very fine grain pipelined designs. Note that this is a limitation inherent to the CAD tool itself, which could be bypassed, either by using other tools, or by implementing a custom retimer.

Second, routing delays severely impact the minimum achievable clock period. Depending on the regularity (and complexity of the data-path) they represent between 30% (for a 8-bits integer matrix multiplication) and 80% (DLMS with floating point data) of the critical path delay. Since retiming only operates on the combinational delay elements of the path, it cannot take into consideration the impact routing delays. This poses the question of the efficiency of existing retiming algorithm with respect to modern FPGA architectures, in which routing delays are likely to become the performance bottleneck.

5. CONCLUSION AND FUTURE WORK

In this paper, we provided a framework to allow automatic and efficient integration of pipelined data-path for processor array synthesis tools. This framework is based on well-established space-time transformations which ensure the correctness of the pipelined circuit. Although this transformation is not restricted to FPGA implementations, we observed that these types of architectures are very well suited to such transformations which can increase the raw-power of the synthesized architecture by factors up to 6.

Although the results are very encouraging we believe that there is need to further explore the trade-off involved with very fine grain pipelined designs. Specifically since routing delay is likely to have a major influence on such designs, we believe that there is some need for a layout-aware retiming tool which would be able to compensate the routing influence by exploiting placement information. This is the subject of our ongoing investigations.

6. REFERENCES

[1] The MMAlpha Environment. COSI Website, IRISA http://www.irisa.fr/COSI/ALPHA.

[2] J.B. Saxe and C.E. Leiserson. Optimizing synchronous systems. In *J. VLSI and Computer systems*, 1983.

[3] A. Darte. Regular Partitioning for Synthesizing fixed-size Systolic Arrays. In *INTEGRATION, the VLSI journal*, 1991.

[4] A. Darte et al. A Contructive Solution to the Juggling Problem. In *International Conference on Application Specific Processor Arrays (ASAP)*, 2000.

[5] R. Schreiber et al. High-level Synthesis of Non-programmable Hardware Accelerators. In *IEEE conference on Application Specific Array Processor*, 2000.

[6] E.F. Depreterre P. Dewilde and J. Bu. A Design Methodology for Partitioning Systolic Arrays. In *IEEE conference on Application Specific Array Processor*, 1990.

[7] C. Patterson. High performance DES encryption in Virtex FPGAs using JBits. In Kenneth L. Pocek and Jeffrey Arnold, editors, *IEEE Symposium on FPGAs for Custom Computing Machines*. IEEE Computer Society Press, 2000.

[8] P. Quinton. Automatic Synthesis of Systolic arrays from Recurrent Uniform Equations. In *International Conference on Computer Architecture*, pages 208–214, 1984.

[9] S. Derrien S. Rajopadhye and S. Sur-Kolay. Optimal partitionning for FPGA based regular array implementations. In *IEEE PARELEC'00*, August 2000.

[10] S. Derrien S. Rajopadhye and S. Sur-Kolay. Combining Instruction and Loop Level Parrallelism for FPGAs. *IRISA Research report N1376*, 2001.

[11] L. Thiele J. Teich and L. Zhang. Scheduling of Partitioned Regular Algorithms on Processor Arrays with Contrained Resources. In *International Conference on Application Specific Processor Arrays (ASAP)*, 1996.

[12] Renate Merker and Uwe Eckhardt. Co-Partitionning - A Method for Hardware/Software design for scalable Systolic Arrays. In *Reconfigurable Architectures, ITPress*, 1997.

Conditional Speculation and its Effects on Performance and Area for High-Level Synthesis*

Sumit Gupta Nick Savoiu Nikil Dutt Rajesh Gupta Alex Nicolau

Center for Embedded Computer Systems
Dept. of Information and Computer Science
University of California at Irvine
http://www.cecs.uci.edu/~spark
{sumitg,savoiu,dutt,rgupta,nicolau}@cecs.uci.edu

ABSTRACT

We introduce a code transformation technique, "conditional speculation", that speculates operations by duplicating them into preceding conditional blocks. This form of speculation belongs to a class of aggressive code motion techniques that enable movement of operations through and beyond conditionals and loops. We show that, when used during scheduling in a high-level synthesis system, this particular code motion has positive effect on latency and controller complexity, e.g., up to 35 % reduction in longest path cycles and the number of states in the finite state machine (FSM) of the controller. However, it is not enough to determine complexity by the number of states in the control FSM. Indeed, the greater resource sharing opportunities afforded by speculation actually increase the total control cost (in terms of multiplexing and steering logic). This also adversely affects the clock period. We examine the effect of the various code motions on the total synthesis cost and propose techniques to reduce costs to make the transformations useful in real-life behavioral design descriptions. Using the MPEG-1 and ADPCM benchmarks, we show total reductions in schedule lengths of up to 50 % while keeping control and area costs down.

1. INTRODUCTION

High-level synthesis is the automated synthesis of a digital design from its behavioral description [1, 2]. There has been a large body of research on high-level synthesis (HLS) which has concentrated on reducing schedule lengths of a design by improved scheduling techniques. However, the presence of complex control flow significantly affects the quality of synthesis results. Hence, several beyond-basic-block code motion techniques such as speculation have been used to extract the inherent parallelism in designs and increase resource utilization.

Generally, speculation refers to the unconditional execution of operations that were originally supposed to have executed conditionally. Conversely, in reverse speculation, which we introduced in previous work [3], operations before conditionals are moved into *subsequent* conditional blocks and hence, executed conditionally.

*This work is supported by the Semiconductor Research Corporation: Task I.D. 781.001

ISSS'01, October 1-3, 2001, Montréal, Québec, Canada.

In this paper, we present a variant of speculation where an operation from after the conditional block is duplicated *up* into preceding conditional branches and executed conditionally. Hence, this code motion is called *conditional speculation*.

These kind of aggressive generalized code motions lead to significant reductions in schedule lengths and controller complexity. However, the effects of code transformations on synthesis costs, particularly control and multiplexing costs are poorly understood. In order to better understand these effects, we have taken the VHDL generated after scheduling by our high-level synthesis system and synthesized it using logic synthesis tools. We find that if left unchecked, these code motions can lead to substantial area and clock period overheads.

This leads us to believe that although these type of speculative code motions are useful, there needs to be a judicious balance between when to speculate, reverse speculate or conditionally speculate. Based on our experiments, we have developed simple heuristic cost models for the code motions and use them to guide a priority-list scheduling algorithm. This heuristic uses information on which code motions are allowed, and the cost of each code motion, to determine the most favorable operation to schedule on a given resource at a given time step.

However, the higher resource utilization and sharing caused by these code motions still lead to higher area and control costs. The control-intensive nature of the "real-life" benchmarks we have considered, further adds to these costs due to increased resource sharing among mutually exclusive operations, which leads to larger interconnect and associated control logic. Interconnect, here, refers to the multiplexors and buses that connect components together.

To address the complexity of the interconnect, this paper also presents an interconnect minimization approach based on a resource binding methodology. This methodology attempts to first bind operations with the same inputs or outputs to the same functional unit. The variable to register binding then takes advantage of this by trying to map variables which are inputs or outputs to the same functional units to the same register. In this way, the number of registers feeding the inputs and storing the outputs of functional units is reduced, in effect, reducing the size of the multiplexors and demultiplexors connected to the functional units. Our results demonstrate the effectiveness of this approach in reducing area costs without adversely effecting performance.

The rest of this paper is organized as follows. We first discuss related work and then present the conditional speculation code motion. Section 4 outlines the scheduling heuristic which guides the various code motions within a synthesis framework. Section 5 studies the effects of the various code motions on the quality of synthesis results. Finally, an interconnect minimization strategy is outlined along with a study of its effectiveness on synthesis results.

2. RELATED WORK

Initial high-level synthesis work concentrated on data-flow designs and applied optimizations such as algebraic transformations, retiming and code motions across multiplexors for improved synthesis results [4, 5]. Subsequent work has presented speculative code motions for mixed control-data flow type of designs and demonstrated their effects on schedule lengths. CVLS [6] uses condition vectors to improve resource sharing among mutually exclusive operations. Radivojevic et al [7] present an exact symbolic formulation which generates an ensemble schedule of valid, scheduled traces. The "Waveschedule" approach [8] incorporates speculative execution into high-level synthesis (HLS) to achieve its objective of minimizing the expected number of cycles. Santos et al [9] and Rim et al [10] support generalized code motions, taken from software compilers, for scheduling in HLS.

However, most previous works compare the effectiveness of their algorithms in terms of only schedule lengths. This has prevented a clear analysis of the effects of scheduling and code motions on the area and latency of the final hardware generated, since control logic overheads are usually ignored. To this end, Rim et al [10] use an analytical cost model for interconnect and control while applying code motions and Bergamaschi [11] proposes the behavioral network graph to bridge the gap between high-level and logic-level synthesis.

A range of code motion techniques similar to those presented in our work have also been previously developed for high-level language software compilers (especially parallelizing compilers) [12, 13, 14]. Although the basic transformations (e.g. dead code elimination, copy propagation) can be used in synthesis as well, other transformations need to be re-instrumented for synthesis. This is usually because the cost models in compilers and synthesis tools are different. For example, in compilers there is generally a uniform push towards executing operations as soon as possible by speculative code motions. However, in synthesis, the additional hardware costs associated with code motions must be taken into account while making scheduling decisions.

Reducing interconnect using binding techniques has also been studied before [1, 2]. Stok et al [15] use a network flow formulation for minimum module allocation while minimizing interconnect. Paulin et al [16] perform exhaustive weight-directed clique partitioning to find the lowest combined register and interconnect costs. Mujumdar et al [17] use a network flow formulation to bind operations and registers in each time-step one at a time.

However, several of these approaches have been tested using data dominated designs with little or no control flow. Many moderately complex benchmarks extracted from industrial design descriptions such as ADPCM and parts of MPEG are control-intensive designs. This adds a new dimension to the complexity of the problem due to the presence of mutually exclusive operations on different branches of conditionals which share resources. Code motions during scheduling also lead to higher resource utilization and code duplication. This leads to added control logic both in terms of control signal generation and interconnect complexity.

The contributions of this paper include a presentation of conditional speculation which is another code motion in a class of code motions presented earlier [3] followed by a comparative study of these code motions. Then, a simple scheduling heuristic which directs these code motions is outlined. Finally, an interconnect reduction methodology is presented to reduce the higher control costs due to these aggressive code motions. This work has been implemented within a high-level synthesis framework called *Spark* which provides a path from a behavioral input description down to synthesizable register-transfer level code.

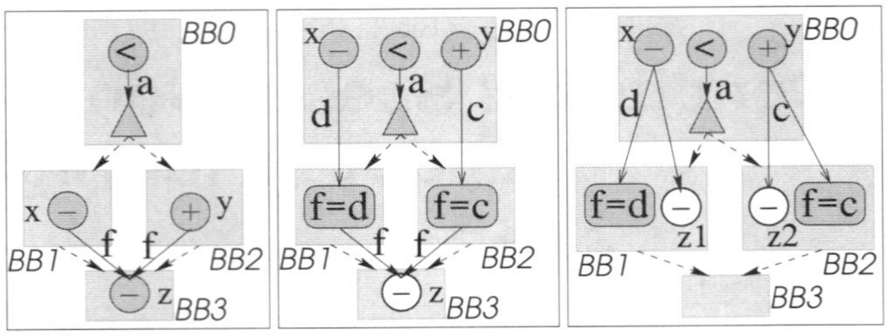

Figure 1: (a) A sample control-data flow graph (b) Operations x and y are speculated leaving idle slots in the conditional branches (c) Operation z is *conditionally speculated* into conditionals BB_1 and BB_2

3. CONDITIONAL SPECULATION

There are often instances in the input description where the basic blocks that comprise the branches of a conditional do not have enough operations to fully utilize the resources allocated to the design. Speculation also creates such "idle slots" on resources by moving operations out of conditionals. These idle slots can be filled or utilized by scheduling operations which lie in basic blocks *after* the conditional blocks. These operations can be *duplicated up* into both branches of the conditional and executed speculatively. We call this code motion, *conditional speculation* (CS). This is similar to the duplication-up code motion used in compilers and the node duplication transformation discussed by Wakabayashi et al [6].

Figure 1 demonstrates how such idle slots are created by speculation and how conditional speculation can be used to fill them. In the example in Figure 1(a), consider that the operations x and y both write to the variable f in their respective conditional branches BB_1 and BB_2. Now, consider that this design is allocated one adder, one subtracter and one comparator. Then operations x and y can be speculatively executed as shown in Figure 1(b). As shown in this figure, the results of the speculated operations are written into new destination variables, d and c, which are not committed until the corresponding condition is evaluated, i.e., the results of the speculated operations are *written back* to the variable f only within the conditional blocks.

Figure 1(b) demonstrates that the speculation of these operations leaves "idle" slots in which no operations have been scheduled on the resources. Furthermore, in this example, operation z is dependent on either the result of operation x or operation y depending on how the condition evaluates (i.e. operation z is dependent on the variable f). Operations such as z, which lie in basic blocks after the conditional blocks, can be duplicated up or *conditionally speculated* into both branches of the conditional to fill idle slots as illustrated in Figure 1(c).

Note that condition speculation does not necessarily need speculation to be done first to activate it as shown in the example. As stated earlier, there are often empty slots within conditional branches, which go unused unless operations are conditionally speculated from after the conditional block.

A scheduling heuristic which guides conditional speculation along with other code motions in the *Spark* high-level synthesis system is presented next.

4. PRIORITY-BASED GLOBAL LIST SCHEDULING HEURISTIC

For the purpose of evaluating the various code motion transformations, we have chosen a *priority-based* global list scheduling heuristic. Since we have chosen the objective of minimizing the *longest delay* through the design, hence, the priorities are assigned

MPEG Prediction Block; Resources = 3*ALU*,2[ ],3 <<,2 ==,1*(2-cycle); BBs = non-empty Basic Blocks						
Type of Code Motion	*calc_forw* (73 Ops, 31 BBs) # States	Long Path	*pred*2 (217 Ops, 45 BBs) # States	Long Path	*pred*0_1 (101 Ops, 26 BBs) # States	Long Path
Within basic blocks	37	37	182	6359	187	3072
+across hier blocks	28(-24%)	28(-24%)	157(-14%)	5956(-6%)	162(-13%)	2871(-7%)
+speculation	26(-7%)	26(-7%)	102(-35%)	4263(-28%)	137(-15%)	2177(-24%)
+early cond exec	24(-8%)	24(-8%)	100(-2%)	4261(-0%)	134(-2%)	2174(0%)
+cond speculation	**22(-8%)**	**22(-8%)**	**92(-8%)**	**3945(-7%)**	**122(-9%)**	**1910(-12%)**
Total Reduction	40.5 %	43.2 %	49.5 %	38.0 %	34.8 %	37.8 %

Table 1: Comparison of various types of code motion for the MPEG Pred benchmark

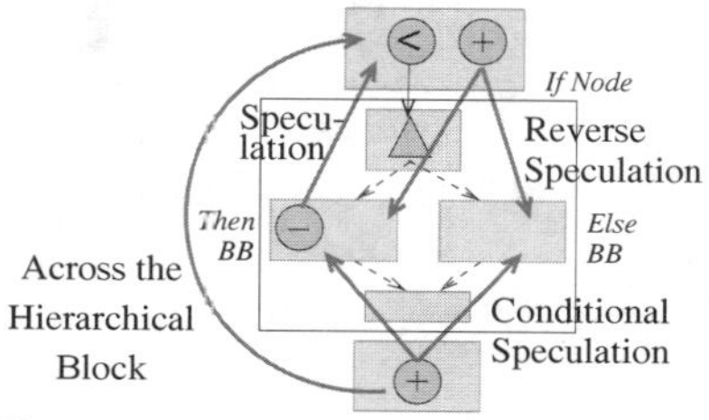

Figure 2: Various types of code motions

ADPCM Encoder(65 Ops, 38 non-empty BBs)		
Type of Code Motion	1*ALU*,2 ==,2[ ],1 << # States	Long Path
Within basic blocks	33	313
+across hier blocks	28(-15%)	273(-13%)
+speculation	26(-7%)	253(-7%)
+early cond exec	24(-8%)	233(-12%)
+cond speculation	**16(-33%)**	**152(-35%)**
Total Reduction	51.5 %	51.4 %

Table 2: Comparison of various types of code motion for the ADPCM Encoder benchmark

to each operation based on their distance from the primary outputs of the design. The priority of an operation is calculated as one more than the maximum of the priorities of all the operations that use its result with output operations having a priority of one [3].

The scheduling heuristic works as follows: first, a priority is assigned to each operation as explained above. Then scheduling is done one control (or scheduling) step at a time while traversing the control-data flow graph (CDFG). At each time step, for each idle resource, a list of *available* operations is collected [14]. Available operations are operations which can be scheduled on the current resource type and whose data dependencies are either satisfied or can be eliminated by dynamic renaming [18].

For each operation in the available operations list, the code motion technique determines if there is a path from the operation's current location to the scheduling step under consideration and the code motions that will be required to move the operation. The heuristic checks the code motions required to schedule the operation against a user specified list of code motions (i.e. speculation, reverse speculation, conditional speculation et cetera), and removes the operation from the available list if it requires a code motion that is not enabled.

The heuristic then assigns a cost to each operation based on metrics such as priority of the operation, cost of code motions and their effects on control logic. It then instructs the code motion technique to schedule the operation with the *lowest* cost from the list of remaining available operations. This is repeated for all resources in each scheduling step as the basic blocks in the CDFG are traversed from top to bottom. Operations left unscheduled at the end of a basic block are moved down into the next basic block or reverse speculated into the conditional branches, as the case may be.

Costs are assigned to each operation in the available list as:

$$Cost_{op} = -Priority * K_{CodeMotion1} * \ldots * K_{CodeMotionN}$$

where $K_{CodeMotion1}$ to $K_{CodeMotionN}$ are the multiplication factors ($<= 1$) associated with each code motion required to schedule the operation at the scheduling step under consideration. Since we found that except for conditional speculation, all the code motions are equally useful, we assigned them a multiplication factor of one. However, unchecked application of conditional speculation (CS) can lead to poor scheduling results since this code motion involves code duplication.

Hence, we developed a three-fold strategy to guide this code motion. Firstly, $K_{CodeMotion}$ for CS is set to 0.5. Next, we allow CS only after the "then" conditional branch has already been scheduled, i.e., in Figure 1, we would allow consideration of operations which require CS only while scheduling basic block BB_2 (after BB_1 has been scheduled). This gives us a better picture of available idle slots. Lastly, we do not allow CS if it leads to an increase in the maximum number of cycles through the conditional node. This means, in Figure 1, if CS would lead to an additional cycle being required in either the "then" (BB_1) or the "else" (BB_2) basic blocks, then the code motion would not be allowed.

These cost models have been developed as first-cut heuristic rules to guide the scheduling heuristic. The next section presents results which compare the effectiveness of the various code motions when guided by this scheduling heuristic.

5. EFFECTS OF CODE MOTIONS ON QUALITY OF SYNTHESIS RESULTS

The various code motions presented earlier [3] along with conditional speculation are shown again in Figure 2. In addition to this, early condition execution is a code motion technique which executes conditional checks as soon as possible by reverse speculating unscheduled operations before the conditional, into the conditional's branches.

The two benchmarks used for the experiments in this paper are the *Encoder* block from the ADPCM algorithm and the *calc_forw*, *pred*0_1 and *pred*2 functions from the *Prediction* block of the MPEG-1 algorithm[1] [19].

5.1 Effects on Performance

The effects of these code motions on the number of states in the finite state machine (FSM) and the cycles on the longest path in the design are presented in Tables 1 and 2. The percentage reductions of each row over the previous row are in parentheses. The number of states denotes the controller complexity and the longest path length is equivalent to the execution cycles of the design. For loops, the longest path length of the loop body is multiplied by the number of loop iterations. The resources used are indicated in the tables; *ALU* does add and subtract, $*$ is a multiplier, $==$ is a comparator, $[]$ is an array address decoder and $<<$ is a shifter. The multiplier is

[1]Although both benchmarks have loops, no loop transformations have been applied for these experiments

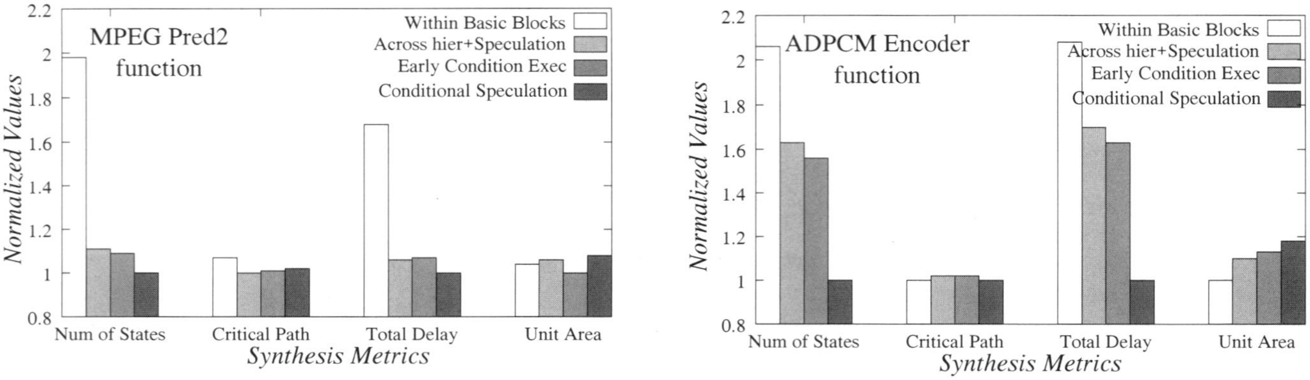

Figure 3: Effects of code motions on various metrics for the MPEG *pred*2 and the ADPCM Encoder

a 2-cycle resource and all other resources have single cycle execution time. The number of non-empty basic blocks and operations are also given in these tables.

The rows in the tables present results with each code motion enabled incrementally, i.e., these signify the allowed code motions while determining the available operations (see Section 4) and do *not* represent an ordering of code motions. We first allow code motions only within basic blocks (first row) and then, in the second row, we also allow code motions across hierarchical blocks, i.e., across entire if-then-else conditionals and loops. The third row allows speculation too, the fourth row has early condition execution enabled as well and the final row has the conditional speculation code motion also enabled.

The fifth row in these tables demonstrate that enabling conditional speculation leads to reductions of 33-35 % in the number of states and the longest path cycles for the ADPCM encoder and between 7-12 % for the MPEG algorithm. This code motion is more effective for the ADPCM benchmark since this benchmark is highly control intensive with nearly as many conditional checks as operations. Hence, moving operations into its conditional branches significantly improves resource utilization. The functions in the MPEG Prediction block on the other hand have a more mixed distribution of data and control operations. Hence, the improvements due to the various code motions is more uniform for the MPEG functions (see Table 1).

These observations and the results in Tables 1 and 2 demonstrate that the effectiveness of a particular code motion is heavily dependent on the characteristics of the behavioral description being synthesized. Control-intensive designs (such as *calc_forw* and ADPCM Encoder) benefit more from code motions that move operations into conditional branches (such as early condition execution and condition speculation), whereas designs which have more data operations than conditionals (such as *pred*0_1 and *pred*2) benefit more from code motions such as speculation.

Also, while experimenting with different resource constraints, we found that opportunities for conditional speculation increase with increasing resources, leading to up to 30 % reductions for the MPEG benchmark. This goes towards showing that resources are most idle within conditional branches, especially as more resources are allocated.

These tables show that these kind of speculative code motions lead to substantial improvements in the latency of the design and complexity of the controller. The total reduction in execution cycles and number of states achieved with all the transformations enabled over code motion only within basic blocks ranges between 35 % to 51 % (last row in the tables).

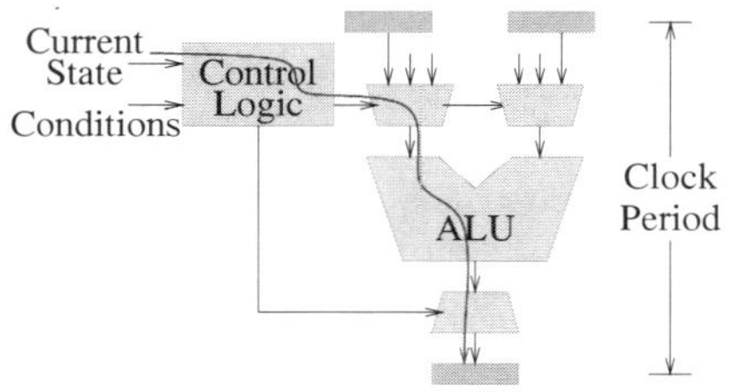

Figure 4: Typical critical paths in control-intensive designs

5.2 Effects on Area and Clock Period

Although aggressive code motions lead to significant reductions in the execution cycles of a design, their overall effects on synthesis results should take into account the control costs. These are not obvious until the design is synthesized to the gate level. Hence, to further evaluate the effects of the various types of code motions, we synthesized the register-transfer level VHDL, generated after scheduling by the Spark synthesis system, using the Synopsys *Design Compiler* logic synthesis tool. The LSI-10K synthesis library was used for technology mapping.

The results for the MPEG *pred*2 function and ADPCM Encoder are presented in the graphs in Figure 3. In these graphs, four metrics are mapped: the number of states in the FSM, the critical path length (in nanoseconds), the unit area and the maximum delay through the design. The critical path length is the length of the longest combinational path in the netlist as determined by static timing analysis. The critical path length dictates the clock period of the final design. The unit area is in terms of the synthesis library used (the LSI-10K library). The maximum delay is the product of the longest path length (in cycles) and the critical path length (in ns) and signifies the maximum input to output latency of the design.

The values of each metric are normalized by the lowest value for that metric. They are mapped for code motions allowed only within basic blocks, then with across hierarchical block code motions and speculation also allowed, with early condition execution as well and finally with conditional speculation enabled too. We synthesized these designs with a simple, naive binding of operations to functional units so as to ensure that the number of resources synthesized are as per the resources allocated during scheduling by the high-level synthesis system.

These graphs demonstrate that as we apply more and more aggressive code motions, the size of the controller (number of states) decreases and the performance of the design increases, i.e. total delay decreases. These values are almost halved when all the code motions are enabled over when code motions only within basic blocks are allowed.

These graphs also demonstrate that the critical path lengths in

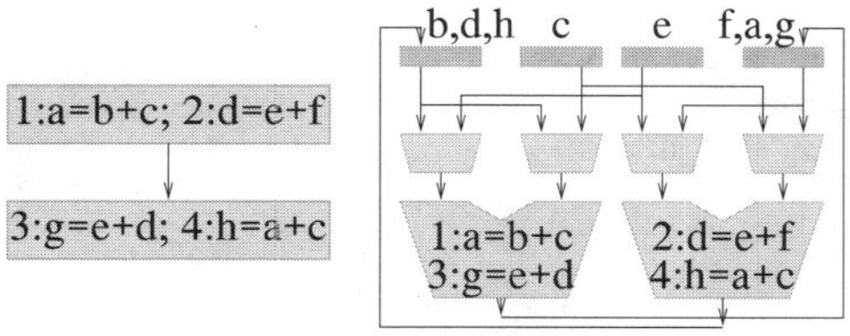

Figure 5: An example of binding leading to a large number of interconnections

the designs remain fairly constant, while the area increases steadily. This area increase is due to increasing complexity of the steering logic and associated control logic caused by resource sharing. Critical paths also typically pass through this steering logic. A typical critical path in the synthesized designs is shown in Figure 4. It starts in the control logic that generates the select signals for the multiplexors connected to the functional units. The path continues through the multiplexors, through the functional unit and then through another multiplexor, which finally writes to the output register. As the resource utilization and sharing increases, due to aggressive speculative code motions, the size of these interconnects (multiplexors and demultiplexors) gets increasingly large, leading to increased area.

As noted above, the critical path length does not change significantly as more and more code motions are enabled. This is because although aggressive code motions affect critical path lengths adversely due to higher resource utilization and sharing, they also lead to reduced number of states in the FSM and shorter schedule lengths. This leads to smaller controllers which counter balance the effects of the increased interconnect and effectively leads to negligible affect of the code motions on critical path lengths.

6. REDUCING INTERCONNECT

The very resource sharing that is leading to increases in circuit complexity, also provides an opportunity to minimize interconnect. Since the resources have several operations and variables mapped to them, there exist opportunities to reduce the number of inputs to, and hence, the complexity of, the (de)multiplexors between these resources by resource binding techniques. Fewer inputs not only mean smaller interconnects but also simpler associated control logic. The next two sections describe a resource binding methodology to minimize these interconnect and control costs.

6.1 Operation to Functional Unit Binding

The number of interconnections required to connect modules to each other and to registers can be reduced by combining operations which have the same inputs and/or same outputs. This can be intuitively understood by considering the classical example of binding and resultant hardware shown in Figure 5 [1]. The interconnect can be simplified by exchanging the functional units that operations 3 and 4 are bound to, as shown in Figure 7(a). This is because operations 1 and 4 have the input variable *c* in common and operations 2 and 3 have *e* in common.

Hence, the operation binding problem can be defined as follows: given a scheduled control data flow graph (CDFG) and a set of resource constraints, map each operation to a functional unit from among the given resources, such that the interconnect is minimized.

We formulate this problem by creating an operation compatibility graph for each type of resource in the resource list. Each operation in the design of the resource type under consideration has a node in the graph. Compatibility edges are created between nodes corresponding to operations which are scheduled in either different control steps or execute under a different set of conditions. This means that mutually exclusive operations (and their variables) scheduled in the same time step are compatible with each other.

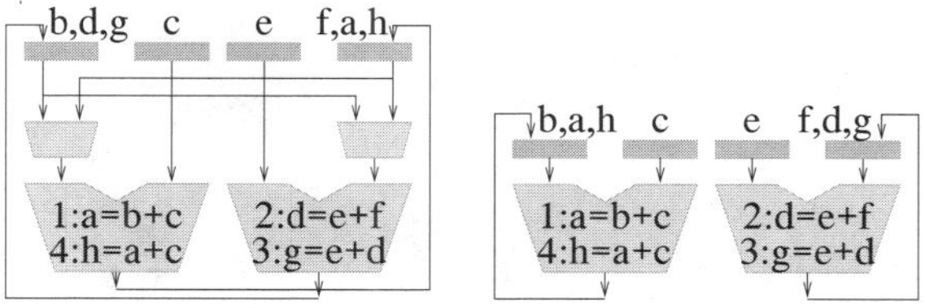

(a) (b)

Figure 7: Reducing interconnections by improved (a) operation binding (b) variable binding

For reducing interconnect, we add additional edge weights between operations for each instance of common inputs or outputs between them. A maximally weighted clique cover of this graph will lead to binding that reduces interconnect. The constraint on the number of resources means that the number of cliques cannot exceed the number of resources of each type. To solve this problem, we formulate it as a multi-commodity network flow problem and find the max-cost flow [20, 21]. Chang et al [20] use the same formulation for module allocation but their objective is to minimize power consumption.

6.2 Variable to Register Binding

Variable to register binding can take advantage of the improved operation binding by mapping variables that are inputs or outputs to the same port of the same functional unit to the same registers. Hence, the result obtained after operation binding shown in Figure 7(a) can be further improved by changing the variable binding as shown in Figure 7(b). In this binding, variables *b* and *a*, which are inputs to operations 1 and 4 (which are bound to the same functional unit), have been bound to the same register. Similarly, variables *f* and *d* are bound to the same register.

The formulation of this problem is similar to the operation binding problem, except that we do not place a constraint on the number of registers. A compatibility graph is created with a node corresponding to a write to a variable in the CDFG. Compatibility edges are added between nodes corresponding to variables which do not have overlapping lifetimes or are created under a different set of conditions.

Edge weights are added between variables for each instance of them being inputs or outputs to the same port of the same functional unit. A maximally weighted clique cover represents a valid variable to register binding with minimal interconnect . This is solved by formulating it as a min-cost max-flow network problem. This formulation has been used earlier to solve similar problems in [15] and [22].

7. RESULTS OF RESOURCE BINDING

We synthesized the various designs with a naive resource binding ("Unbound" case) and with the interconnect minimization methodology outlined above ("Bound" case). The results for the MPEG *pred*2 and the ADPCM Encoder designs are summarized in the graphs in Figure 6. The metrics compared in these graphs are the critical path length, total delay and the unit area. The values for each metric are normalized to the minimum value for that metric among all its values (before and after binding).

The reductions in area of the "Bound" case over the "Unbound" case are significant, especially for the *pred*2 function. These improvements are despite the fact that in our interconnect minimization strategy, we sometimes choose to allocate more registers if this leads to a reduction in the steering logic. Hence, the reductions in interconnect complexity dominate any increases due to higher reg-

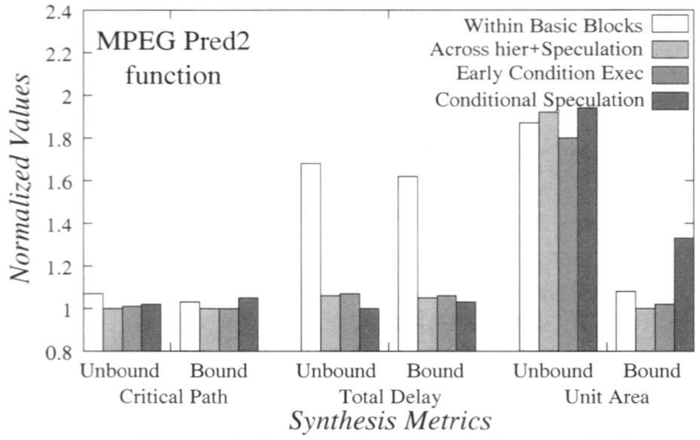

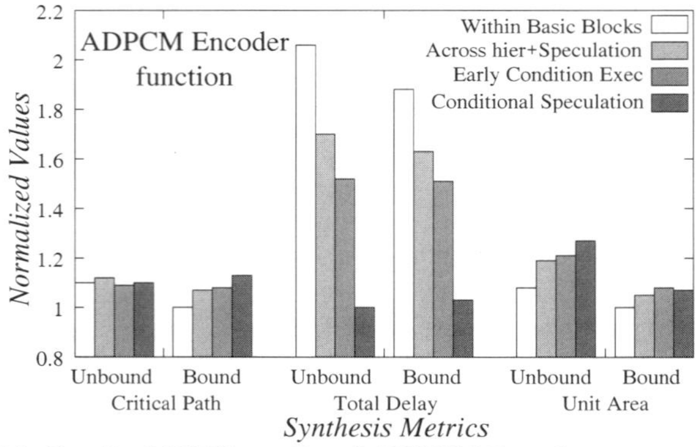

Figure 6: Synthesis results before and after resource binding for MPEG *pred2* and ADPCM Encoder

ister requirements. Furthermore, we found that although synthesis using a binding methodology, which minimizes only registers, leads to fewer registers, the total area of the design is worse, since the interconnect sizes are not reduced.

The graphs show that critical path lengths remain fairly constant in all the designs, hence, barely leading to any changes in delay through the circuit. These results demonstrate that the interconnect methodology is able to achieve more area efficient designs without sacrificing performance.

For both the bound and unbound cases, we find that applying the conditional speculation transformation can lead to an increase in the critical path lengths and area of the synthesized circuit. This is due to the higher resource sharing and code duplication that this code motion leads to. Hence, there is a need to develop more accurate control cost models, which the scheduling heuristic can use while deciding which code motions to apply.

8. CONCLUSIONS

In this paper, we have presented a new code motion for synthesis, called conditional speculation. This code motion is particularly effective for control-intensive behaviors where more opportunities exist to move operations into otherwise idle slots in conditional branches. We have shown that these kind of aggressive code motions can be directed to obtain significant reductions in the execution cycles of a design and also the number of states in the controller for large control-intensive segments of industrial strength benchmarks. Furthermore, the control and interconnect overheads incurred due to these code motions can be minimized by resource binding targeted at interconnect minimization. This leads to lower area, without adversely effecting the latency of the final hardware generated by logic synthesis tools. Future work will involve developing more elaborate cost models that will help in guiding when to apply the various code motions.

9. REFERENCES

[1] D. D. Gajski, N. D. Dutt, A. C-H. Wu, and S. Y-L. Lin. *High-Level Synthesis: Introduction to Chip and System Design.* Kluwer Academic, 1992.

[2] R. Camposano and W. Wolf. *High Level VLSI Synthesis.* Kluwer Academic, 1991.

[3] S. Gupta, N. Savoiu, S. Kim, N.D. Dutt, R.K. Gupta, and A. Nicolau. Speculation techniques for high level synthesis of control intensive designs. In *Design Automation Conf.*, 2001.

[4] M. Potkonjak and J. Rabaey. Optimizing resource utlization using tranformations. *IEEE Transactions on CAD*, March 1994.

[5] R. Walker and D. Thomas. Behavioral transformation for algorithmic level ic design. *IEEE Transactions on CAD*, October 1989.

[6] K. Wakabayashi and H. Tanaka. Global scheduling independent of control dependencies based on condition vectors. In *Design Automation Conference*, 1992.

[7] I. Radivojevic and F. Brewer. A new symbolic technique for control-dependent scheduling. *IEEE Transactions on CAD*, January 1996.

[8] G. Lakshminarayana, A. Raghunathan, and N.K. Jha. Incorporating speculative execution into scheduling of control-flow intensive behavioral descriptions. In *Design Automation Conference*, 1998.

[9] L.C.V. dos Santos and J.A.G. Jess. A reordering technique for efficient code motion. In *Design Automation Conf.*, 1999.

[10] M. Rim, Y. Fann, and R. Jain. Global scheduling with code-motions for high-level synthesis applications. *IEEE Transactions on VLSI Systems*, September 1995.

[11] R.A. Bergamaschi. Behavioral network graph unifying the domains of high-level and logic synthesis. In *Design Automation Conference*, 1999.

[12] J. Fisher. Trace scheduling: A technique for global microcode compaction. *IEEE Transactions on Computers*, 7, July 1981.

[13] A. Nicolau. Uniform parallelism exploitation in ordinary programs. In *International Conf. on Parallel Processing*, 1985.

[14] K. Ebcioglu and A. Nicolau. A global resource-constrained parallelization technique. In *3rd International Conference on Supercomputing*, 1989.

[15] L. Stok and W.J.M. Philipsen. Module allocation and comparability graphs. In *IEEE International Sympoisum on Circuits and Systems*, 1991.

[16] P. G. Paulin and J. P. Knight. Scheduling and Binding Algorithms for High-Level Synthesis. In *Design Automation Conference*, 1989.

[17] A. Mujumdar, R. Jain, and K. Saluja. Incorporating performance and testability constraints during binding in high-level synthesis. *IEEE Trans. on CAD*, 1996.

[18] S.-M. Moon and K. Ebcioglu. An efficient resource-constrained global scheduling technique for superscalar and vliw processors. In *International Symposium on Microarchitecture*, 1992.

[19] Spark Synthesis Benchmarks FTP site. ftp://ftp.ics.uci.edu/pub/spark/benchmarks.

[20] J.-M. Chang and M. Pedram. Module assignment for low power. In *European Design Automation Conference*, 1996.

[21] L. Stok. Transfer free register allocation in cyclic data flow graphs. In *European Conf. on Design Automation*, 1992.

[22] J.-M. Chang and M. Pedram. Register allocation and binding low power. In *Design Automation Conf.*, 1995.

A Data Scheduler for Multi-Context Reconfigurable Architectures

Marcos Sanchez-Elez, Milagros Fernández, Roman Hermida, Rafael Maestre
Dept. de Arquitectura de Computadores y Automatica
Universidad Complutense
28040 Madrid, SPAIN
Tel: (+34) 91 394 70 70
marcos@eucmos.sim.ucm.es
mila45 | rhermida | maestre@dacya.ucm.es

Fadi Kurdahi, Nader Bagherzadeh
Dept. of Electrical and Computer Engineering
University of California, Irvine.
California 92697, USA
Tel: (+1) 949 824 8104
kurdahi | nader@ece.uci.edu

ABSTRACT
In this paper, we present an approach to the problem of data scheduling for multi-context reconfigurable architectures targeting DSP applications. The main goal is to improve applications execution time, through the integration of the data scheduler within a compilation framework specifically conceived for these architectures. Some amount of on-chip data storage is assumed to be available in the reconfigurable architecture. Therefore the data scheduler tries to optimally exploit this storage, saving data transfers between on-chip and external memories. In order to do this, specific algorithms for data placement and replacement have been designed. We also show that a suitable data scheduling could decrease the number of operations required to implement the dynamic reconfiguration of the system.

1. INTRODUCTION
Reconfigurable computing systems are systems that combine programmable hardware with programmable processors. They are an alternative for implementing a wide range of computationally intensive applications such as DSP and multimedia. The most common devices used for reconfigurable computing are FPGAs [1]. However, the reconfiguration time has a negative effect on system performance. In this respect, dynamic reconfiguration has emerged as a particularly attractive technique for minimizing this negative effect [2].

An example of dynamic reconfiguration are multi-context architectures, which may store a set of different configuration planes (contexts) in a context memory. A context is a complete configuration for the entire reconfigurable chip. When a new configuration is needed, it is downloaded from the context memory, if available. As the context memory is on chip, this operation is faster than the reconfiguration from the external memory.

ISSS'01, October 1-3, 2001, Montréal, Québec, Canada.

Previous work [3][4] discussed scheduling for multi-context architectures, in particular with MorphoSys [5] as the target architecture. This architecture has been developed for applications with a considerable amount of potential parallelism such as multimedia and DSP, which are typically composed of a group of macro-tasks that are repeatedly executed within a loop. We will use the term kernel to refer to one of these macro-tasks. At the abstraction level on which we are working a kernel is characterized by its contexts as well as its input and output data. A kernel scheduling technique was proposed in [6] to generate a kernel sequence that estimates the execution time through tentative context and data schedules. Context scheduling is further refined in [4] and its goal is to minimize the number of context loads that do not overlap with computation. Data scheduling has not been dealt with in detail previously, however it has an important influence on system performance. Every time a kernel sequence (generated by kernel scheduling) is executed, its data and results have to be transferred from/to the external memory. An improvement in data scheduling decreases data transfers. Moreover, as will be shown below, an optimal management of the internal memory can increase context reuse. Therefore, a good data scheduler can achieve a decrease in overall execution time.

Data scheduling in reconfigurable computing systems has not been discussed in detail by other authors. In [7] a data scheduler for dynamic architectures is proposed, though it does not optimize memory management. Data scheduling is addressed in the memory management area for general purpose processors [8]. Unlike these cases, many multimedia applications are periodical and their input data could be statically considered.

The paper begins with an overview of MorphoSys and its compilation framework. Section III intuitively describes the problem. In section IV we discuss the fundamental aspects of data management within a cluster (subset of kernels of the whole application), and present a new methodology to deal with this issue. In section V we show how data reuse among clusters reduces data transfers. Experimental results are presented in section VI. Finally, we present some conclusions from our research in section VII.

2. ARCHITECTURE AND FRAMEWORK OVERVIEW

This section briefly describes the target system M1, which is the first implementation of MorphoSys. We also present the development framework that integrates the data scheduling methodology presented in this paper with other compilation tasks.

MorphoSys (Figure 1) is composed of an 8x8 array of reconfigurable cells (RC). Its functionality and interconnection network are configured through 32-bit context words, which are stored in a Context Memory (CM). RC array input data and results are stored in the frame buffer (FB) which is an internal data memory. The DMA controller establishes the bridge that connects the external memory to either the FB or the CM. Thus simultaneous transfers of data and contexts are not possible. The MorphoSys system operation is controlled by a RISC processor.

The data scheduler optimizes FB utilization. Organizing FB into two sets allows overlapping of computation and data transfers. One of the two sets provides computation data for the RC Array and also stores processed data and results, whereas the other set stores results in the external memory through the DMA controller and reloads data for the next round of computations. The data scheduler reduces data transfers to each set and optimizes data and results allocation.

The data scheduler has been developed for MorphoSys architecture. However, it can be applied to any system that allows overlapping of computation and data transfers between an external memory and an internal memory organized into two sets.

An overview of the proposed framework is shown in Figure 2. The application description is given in C code. This code is written in terms of kernels that are available in a kernel library.

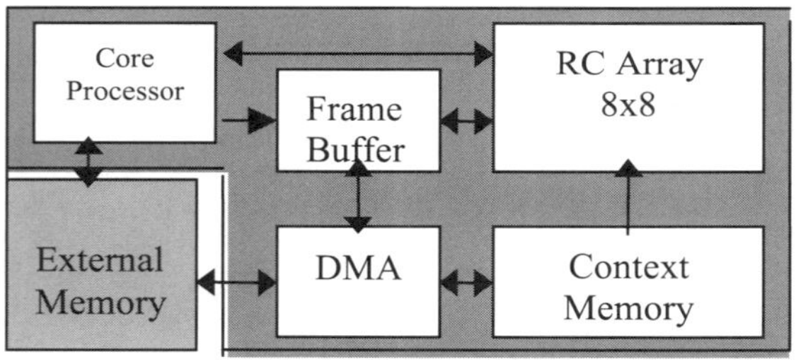

Figure 1. M1 chip.

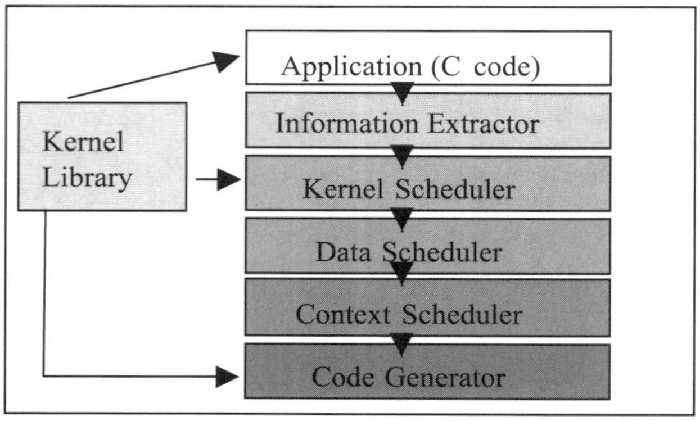

Figure 2. Compilation Framework.

The kernel programming is equivalent to specifying the mapping of computations to the target architecture, and is done only once.

The information extractor generates the information needed by the compilation tasks that follow it, including kernel execution times, data reuse among kernels, as well as data and context sizes for each kernel.

The kernel scheduler [6] explores the design space to find a sequence of kernels that minimizes the execution time. The kernel scheduler decides which is the best sequence of kernels and performs clusters. The term cluster is used here to refer to a set of kernels that is assigned to the same FB set and whose components are consecutively executed. If we suppose an application is composed of kernels k_1, k_2, k_3 and k_4, the kernel scheduler could assign k_1 to one FB set, and k_2, k_3 and k_4 to the other set. This would imply the existence of two clusters $\{k_1\}$ and $\{k_2, k_3, k_4\}$. While the first cluster is being executed using data of one FB set, the data and contexts of the other cluster are being transferred to the other FB set and CM.

The kernel scheduler generates one kernel sequence that minimizes the overall execution time, estimating data and context transfers. The context scheduler and data scheduler specify how and when each transfer is performed.

3. PROBLEM OVERVIEW

We propose a methodology to perform data scheduling on a given ordered set of clusters.

The problem could be defined as: *Given an ordered set of clusters and its data and results sizes, find the data scheduling that minimizes the overall execution time".*

The target reconfigurable system allows overlapping contexts and data transfers with system computation. Therefore execution time for cluster C_c is:

$$ET(C_c) = MAX\left[\sum_{i=1}^{n} K_i, \sum_{i=1}^{n}(D_i + R_i) + t(C_c)\right]$$

Where K_i stands for computation time, D_i for data loading time, R_i for results storing time, for kernel i of C_c and $t(C_c)$ for C_c contexts loading time.

The data scheduler cannot minimize computation time, it can only decrease data and context loading time from external memory and results storing time to external memory.

Then the time for context and data transfers for C_c is :

$$TT(C_c) = \sum_{i=1}^{n}(D_i + R_i) + t(C_c)$$

We can improve data management within a cluster or among clusters because :

- An optimal data and results management within a cluster improves FB use. It allows the number of consecutive iterations of kernel execution (RF) to be increased, as will be shown in section IV. If one kernel is consecutively executed RF times, its contexts have to be loaded only once. Therefore, RF is defined as the Context Reuse Factor. The data scheduler minimizes context transfers, and thus, execution time.
- An optimal data management among clusters reduces data transfers with the external memory. If a cluster data are later used by other clusters and kept in FB then reloading of these data is avoided.

4. DATA MANAGEMENT WITHIN A CLUSTER

The first step towards optimizing data scheduling is to manage data within a cluster. The kernel scheduler generates clusters whose data fit into one FB set. Furthermore, before cluster execution begins, data have to be transferred to FB. For this reason, we may consider clusters as data management units and we begin by optimizing data management within a cluster.

Data management computes the maximum RF value such the cluster data and results fit into one FB set.

4.1 Data Size

A basic data scheduling within a cluster was proposed by the kernel scheduler [6].

We consider that all cluster data have to be loaded before cluster execution begins. $DS(C_c)$ stands for the maximum data size used by C_c. This may be obtained by summing all input data and results generated by all the kernels in the cluster. When a kernel has already been executed, data that are not used by the following kernels can be replaced by generated results.

Let $C_c = \{k_1, k_2, .., k_n\}$ be a cluster, then the data size may be expressed as:

$$DS(C_c) = \underset{i \in \{1,\dots,n\}}{MAX}\left[\sum_{j=i}^{n} d_j + \sum_{j=1}^{i} r_j\right]$$

d_j = size of input data for kernel k_j except those shared with a kernel that belongs to $\{k_{j-1},..,k_n\}$, which are executed later.

r_j = size of the results of kernel k_j

The kernel scheduler provides a set of clusters that fulfills $DS(C_c) \leq$ FBS (Frame buffer size of one set) for this basic scheduling.

The data scheduler improves on this basic scheduling if it takes into account the fact that the results are not used by all kernels. If results of one kernel are data for some kernels executed later, these results may be replaced when the last kernel, that uses them as data, has been executed (Figure 3).

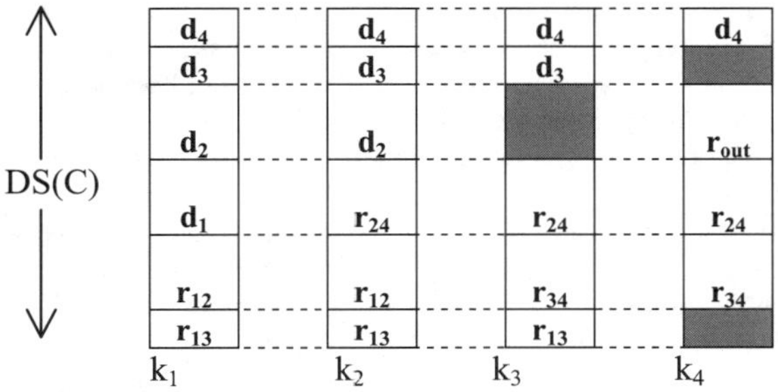

Figure 3: Data scheduling

This achieves the minimum data and results space necessary for cluster execution. In this case, the data size may be expressed as:

$$DS(C_c) = \underset{i \in \{1,\dots,n\}}{MAX}\left[\sum_{j=i}^{n} d_j + \sum_{j=1}^{i}\left(rout_j + \sum_{t=i}^{n} r_{jt}\right)\right]$$

d_j = size of the input data for kernel k_j except those shared with kernels executed later $\{k_{j+1},..,k_n\}$.

$rout_j$ = size of the results of kernel k_j that will be used as data by kernels of clusters executed later or as results of the application.

r_{jt} = size of the results of kernel k_j, which are data for k_t and not for any kernel executed after t. Obviously $r_{jj} = 0$.

The kernel scheduler generates a cluster sequence and a kernel sequence within a cluster. The data scheduler can reorder this kernel sequence (when data and control dependencies allow it) to find the sequence that minimizes $DS(C_c)$.

Multimedia applications, such as DSP or MPEG, are composed of a sequence of kernels that are consecutively executed over a part of the input data, until all the data are processed. If the kernels of the applications may be executed 'n' times to process the total amount of data, their contexts may be loaded to CM 'n' times. However sometimes loop-fission may be applied, so that every kernel can process the total amount of data before executing the next one. The number of consecutive executions of one kernel (RF) is limited by the internal memory size. In this case their contexts are only loaded n/RF times, achieving a decrease in overall execution time.

This data scheduling maximizes free space in the FB, that could be used to store all the cluster data for RF consecutive iterations.

Data and results have the same size regardless of the iteration. In order to find data size, data used or produced are multiplied by RF (number of consecutive iterations) for all kernels in the previous expression, except one of them, say k_i. If k_i is going to be executed RF times, the first execution of k_i requires a data size of $RF \cdot d_i + \sum_{j=1}^{i-1} RF \cdot r_{ji} + rout_i + \sum_{j=i+1}^{n} r_{ij}$, the second one $(RF-1) \cdot d_i + (RF-1) \cdot \sum_{j=1}^{i-1} r_{ji} + 2 \cdot rout_i + 2 \cdot \sum_{j=i+1}^{n} r_{ij}$, and so on.

Therefore, the maximum value obtained is the true data size used by k_i :

$$SZ(i) = \underset{l \in \{1,..,x\}}{MAX}\left[(RF - l + 1) \cdot \left(d_i + \sum_{j=1}^{i-1} r_{ji}\right) + l \cdot \left(rout_i + \sum_{j=i+1}^{n} r_{ij}\right)\right] =$$

$$= MAX\left[RF \cdot \left(d_i + \sum_{j=1}^{i-1} r_{ji}\right) + \left(rout_i + \sum_{j=i+1}^{n} r_{ij}\right), \left(d_i + \sum_{j=1}^{i-1} r_{ji}\right) + RF \cdot \left(rout_i + \sum_{j=i+1}^{n} r_{ij}\right)\right]$$

In addition, $DS(C_c)$ may be expressed as:

$$DS(C_c) = \underset{i \in \{1,\dots,n\}}{MAX}\left[\sum_{j=i+1}^{n} RF \cdot d_j + \sum_{j=1}^{i-1}\left(RF \cdot rout_j + \sum_{t=i+1}^{n} RF \cdot r_{jt}\right) + SZ(i)\right]$$

By solving the previous equation, the data scheduler finds the maximum RF value that fulfills $DS(C_c) \leq$ FBS, for the cluster that has the maximum amount of data and results. RF may be the same for all clusters on account of data and results dependencies.

The data scheduler improves data management within a cluster by considering result reuse. It achieves the maximum available free space and, therefore, the maximum RF value. However, results reuse makes data and results assignment complex.

4.1 Data and results allocation

Data scheduling is static because data and results sizes are known at computation time and it is periodical in time. Therefore data scheduling has to be performed only once.

As FB is not a large memory and as data and results sizes are similar, the chosen allocation method is first-fit. It keeps track of which parts of the memory (FB) are in use and which parts are free through a linear list of all free blocks.

All input data of the cluster have to be loaded into FB at the same time before its execution starts. To minimize fragmentation, the data scheduler allocates to upper free addresses those data that will remain in memory longer.

First the procedure (Algorithm I) ***Data_allocate*** places data following the first-fit algorithm from ***address*** to lower addresses.Then results are placed following the procedure ***result_allocate*** from ***address*** to upper addresses.

The data scheduler starts placing at the lowest address the results of kernel ***kernel*** that are going to remain longest in memory. Then it places the next result that is going to remain longest. The process is repeated for the non-allocating results.

To make addressing easier, data and results allocation should be periodical. The data scheduler stores in the FB data of all kernels in the application for RF consecutive iterations. To maintain periodicity, data and results are allocated from the address where previous data or results were addressed (Figure 4).

The procedure ***release()*** adds to ***FB_list()*** the free space generated by results and data no longer used when one kernel iteration finishes.

Sometimes a result does not fit into any free block, so to improve memory use ***data_allocate*** and ***result_allocate*** split it

```
Kernel_list(c);                    Ordered kernel list to cluster c
FB_list();                                   Free space list into FB
kernel = last kernel in Kernel_list;
data_result_allocator{
while kernel≠ 0 {                 If k=0 there are not any kernel
    for(iteration=1;iteration++;iteration≤RF){
    if(iteration=1) then address=upper free address
    address=data_allocate(kernel,address,FB_lista())
    data(kernel,iteration)=address;   Load data position.
    }
  kernel=previous kernel in Kernel_list(c)
}
kernel= first kernel in Ker_list;
while k≠ 0{                       If k=0 there are not any kernel
 q= last kernel in Ker_list(c);                         q kernel
 for(iteration=1;iteration++;iteration≤RF){
if(iteration=1) then  address=lower free address
 address=result_allocate(kernel,address,FB_lista())
                                          This places output result
   while q≠ k;{
address(q)=result_allocate(kernel,address(q),FB_lista())
     result(kernel,q,iteration)=address(q);
     q=previouss kernel in Kernel_list(c);
    }
  release(kernel,iteration)
 }
kernel=next kernel in Kernel_list(c)
}}
```

Algorithm I

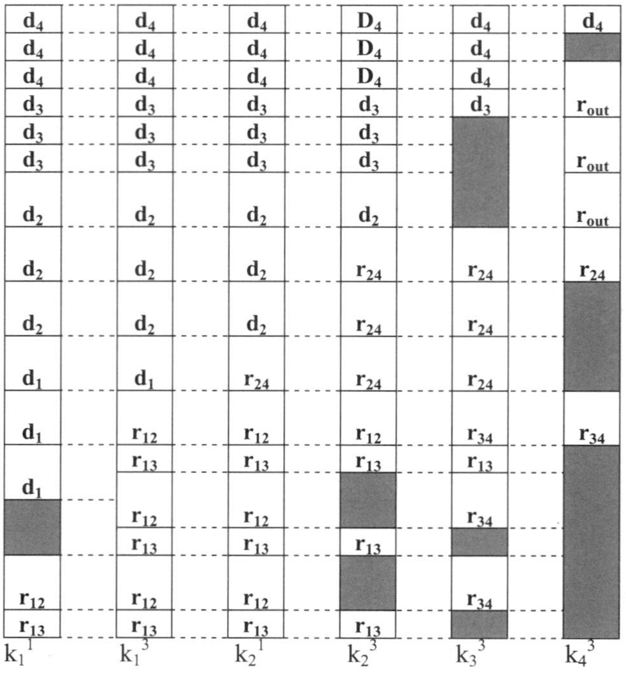

Figure 4. Data scheduling with RF = 3

into two or more parts, and as a consequence the access to this result is more complex.

This algorithm achieves a periodical data and results allocation with low memory fragmentation. Figure 4 shows figure 3 example for RF=3.

5. DATA REUSE AMONG CLUSTERS.

We can improve data scheduler because there might be free space in some clusters. This may happen because the cluster with the highest data size determines the maximum value of RF. This fact implies that the available memory during execution of the others clusters is certainly higher than that which is available when executing the cluster that has the highest data size. This free space can be used to keep data shared with following clusters, which are assigned to the same FB set. Thus these data will not be reloaded. Therefore, as many data are not reloaded data transfers from external memory are reduced, which reduces the overall execution time.

The data scheduler finds n_c which is the number of clusters assigned to the same FB set that can share data. It starts checking if shared data with the next cluster fit in FB ($DS(C_c) \leq FBS$). Then if there is still free space in FB, it checks the data shared with the following cluster, and so on, until there is not enough free space to store shared data with more clusters.

Data management among clusters entails computations of the maximum available memory space and the allocation of the shared data into this space. As FB is divided into two sets, data scheduler can manage both independently.

Let $\{C_1, C_2, \ldots, C_N\}$ be a set of clusters of our application, where $\{C_1, C_3, \ldots, C_N\}$ are assigned to one FB set and $\{C_2, C_4, \ldots, C_{N-1}\}$ are assigned to the other set. Then the maximum data size for a cluster C_c considering data shared among n_c clusters may be expressed as:

$$
\begin{aligned}
DS(C_c) = \max_{i \in \{1..n(c)\}} \Bigg\{ & \sum_{l=i+1}^{n(c)} \left(RF \cdot d_l - \sum_{j=1,v=c+2}^{c-2,N} RF \cdot D^{l}_{j...c...v} \right) + \\
+ & \sum_{l=1}^{i-1} \left(RF \cdot rout_l + \sum_{j=i+1}^{n(c)} RF \cdot r_{lj} \right) + \\
+ \mathrm{MAX} \Bigg[& RF \cdot \left(d_i - \sum_{j=1,v=c+2}^{c-2,N} D^{i}_{j...c...v} + \sum_{j=1}^{i-1} r_{ji} \right) + \left(rout_i + \sum_{j=i+1}^{n} r_{ij} \right), \\
, & \left(d_i - \sum_{j=1,v=c+2}^{c-2,N} D^{i}_{j...c...v} + \sum_{j=1}^{i-1} r_{ji} \right) + RF \cdot \left(rout_i + \sum_{j=i+1}^{n} r_{ij} \right) \Bigg] \Bigg\} + \\
+ & \sum_{j=1,v=c+2}^{,c,N} RF \cdot D_{j...v}
\end{aligned}
$$

$D_{j,...,v}$ is the size of shared data with clusters j , ... , v , that are assigned to the same FB set. As only data shared by n_c fit into the FB then some of them must belong to $\{C_{c+2}, ..., C_{c+(2nc-2)}, C_{c+2nc}\}$. And there are some b > c and a ≤ c that fulfill b – a ≤ $2n_c$, therefore, there are no data shared among clusters more than $2n_c$ which is the maximum clusters distance for their data to fit into one FB set. Thereby, $\sum_{j=1,v=c+2}^{c,N} D_{j...v}$ are the shared data among clusters that were stored in FB from cluster C_j .These data will be released when the last cluster which uses these data C_v, has been executed.

$D^{i}_{j,...,c,...v}$ is the size of input data for kernel i of cluster c shared with cluster j, ..., c, ..., v (which are not data for following kernels), that are assigned to the same FB set. As only data shared by n_c clusters fit into the FB, some of them belong to $\{C_{c-2nc}, C_{c-(2nc-2)}, ..., C_{c-2}, C_{c+2}, ..., C_{c+(2nc-2)}, C_{c+2nc}\}$. As d_i is the total data used by k_i and data shared among clusters do not release FB space until the last cluster that uses them is executed, then $d_i - \sum_{j=1,v=c+2}^{c-2,N} D^{i}_{j...c...v}$ gives us the space that will be released when k_i execution ends.

The algorithm first allocates data of one cluster, that are shared with the next furthest cluster, and repeats the process for the rest of the clusters.

The procedure ***cluster_data_shared(c,v,RF)*** places data shared between cluster c and cluster v for the iteration RF.

After shared data among clusters are placed, the data scheduler allocates data that belong only to cluster c, following the algorithm explained in section IV. The procedure ***data_result_allocate*** performs the placement for the kernels

```
Clusters_list();
FB_list();
nc;
c=first cluster in Cl_list;
while c≠ 0 {
  v=nc cluster in CL_list then c;
  while v>c{
 cluster_data_shared(c,v,RF);
  v=previous cluster in CL list;
  }
data_result_allocate(c);
c=next cluster in CL_list;
}
```

Algorithm II.

6. EXPERIMENTAL RESULTS

In this section we present the experimental results for a group of synthetic and real experiments, in order to demonstrate the quality of the proposed methodology.

The experiments differ in data dependencies, number of kernels and kernel information as shown in Table 1. All data sizes are in bytes.

Finding the execution time as was explained in section III, for the sequence that minimizes data and results space, we can compare the basic scheduler (developing the method suggested in the kernel scheduler to find RF) and the data scheduler with the basic scheduler (without RF), as shown in figure 5. Where the first column is the basic scheduler with context reuse and the second is the data scheduler.

As shown, the proposed methodology always finds a good solution, minimizing overall execution time and maximizing the reuse factor.

The kernel scheduling depends on data and context sizes and available internal memory. We analyze different kernel scheduler for MPEG and ATR as shown in Table 1. If a cluster contains few kernels, data reuse among clusters is improved. However, if a cluster contains many kernels, this improves data and results reuse within a cluster. The data scheduler reuses data among clusters and data and results within a cluster, maximizing the RF value as shown in Table 1.

Table 1. Experimental results.

(N: total number of cluster; n maximum number of kernels; d input data size per iteration; D shared data size per iteration; r kernel result size per iteration; r_{out} output result size per iteration; n_c number of cluster that can share data;RF number of consecutive iterations: RF_s with basic scheduler, RF_s with data scheduler).

	N	**n**	**d**	**D**	**r**	**r_{out}**	**n_c**	**RF_B**	**RF_S**
E1	6	5	540	60	408	244	2	6	7
E2	5	5	1080	176	1500	548	2	3	6
E3	4	7	444	20	796	196	1	3	5
MPEG	3	3	1344	0	768	768	0	1	2
MPEG	2	6	1344	0	1920	384	0	2	2
ATR-FI	1	4	256	0	256	128	0	5	7
ATR-FI	3	2	384	128	128	256	1	2	2
ATR-SLD	4	1	8192	8192	8192	4096	1	2	2

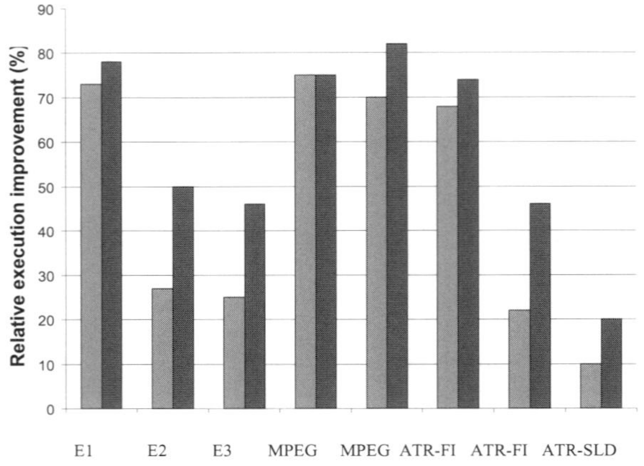

Figure 5. Experimental results.

7. CONCLUSION

In this paper we have shown that using a suitable strategy to minimize data and context transfers contributes to the reduction of the execution time in multi-context reconfigurable architectures.

The proposed data scheduler enables the reuse of results within a cluster, releasing results and data that will not be used later. As this maximizes the available free space in the FB, the data scheduler can increase the number of consecutive iterations (RF). As a consequence, kernel contexts are reused for an increased number of iterations, so reducing context reloading and minimizing execution time.

Data reuse is not limited to operations within a cluster. If the FB has sufficient free space, data to be used by other clusters can be retained, so allowing further reduction of data transfers and execution time.

The work of the data scheduler is based on a specific data placement policy that tries to simplify accesses to the FB, as well as promote periodicity in both time and space.

Future work will address the reuse of results among clusters. However this possibility may complicate the placement policy. Alternative placement policies have to be studied more in depth.

8. ACKNOWLEDGMENTS

This research is supported by the Spanish Grant CICYT TIC 99-0474, and the Commission for Scientific Exchange between USA and Spain.

9. REFERENCES

[1] S. Brown, J. Rose, "Architecture of FPGAs and CPLDs: A Tutorial," IEEE Design and Test of Computer, Vol. 13, No 2, pp. 42-57, 1996.

[2] E. Tau, D. Chen, I Eslick, J Brown and A. DeHon, "A First Generation DPGA Implementation", FDP'95, Canadian Workshop of Field-Programmable Devices, May 29-Jun1,1995.

[3] R. Maestre, F.J. Kurdahi, N. Bagherzadeh, H. Singh, R. Hermida, M. Fernandez "Kernel Scheduling in Reconfigurables Architectures", DATE Proceedings pp 90-96, 1999.

[4] R. Maestre, F. Kurdahi, N. Bagherzadeh, M. Fernandez, R. Hermida, H. Singh "Analysis and Evaluation of Context Scheduling Heuristic for Multi-Context Reconfigurables Architectures", 2000 IEEE International Conference on Computer Design. VLSI in Computer & Processors (ICCD'00), Austin, Texas, Sept 2000

[5] H. Singh, M. Lee, G. Lu, F.J. Kurdahi, N. Bagherzadeh and E. Filho, R. Maestre "MorphoSys: Case study of a reconfigurable Computing System Targeting Multimedia Applications"" Proc. Design Automation Conference Proceedings (DAC'00) pp 573-578, Los Angeles, Californis; May 2000.

[6] R. Maestre, F. Kurdahi, M. Fernandez, R. Hermida, N. Bagherzadeh "A Framework for Scheduling and Context Allocation in Reconfigurable Computing", Proc International Symposium on System Sybthesis (ISSS'99) pp 134-140 San Jose, California, 1999.

[7] M. Kaul, R. Vemuri, S. Govindarajan I. Ouaiss "An Automated Temporal Partitioning and Loop Fission approach for FPGA based reconfigurable synthesis of DSP applications" Proc. 36th ACM/IEEE Design automation conference, *1999, Pages 616 - 622*

[8] P.R. Wilson, M.S. Johnstone, M Neely, and D Boles "Dynamic Storage Application A Survey and Critical Review" IWMM 1995: 1-116

Scheduling and Partitioning for Multiple Loop Nests*

Zhong Wang
Dept of Comp Sci & Engr
University of Notre Dame
Notre Dame, IN 46556
zwang1@cse.nd.edu

Qingfeng Zhuge
Department of Comp Sci
University of Texas at Dallas
Richardson, TX 75083
qfzhuge@utdallas.edu

Edwin H.-M. Sha
Department of Comp Sci
University of Texas at Dallas
Richardson, TX 75083
edsha@utdallas.edu

ABSTRACT

This paper presents the multiple loop partition scheduling technique, which combines the loop partition and prefetching. It can exploit the data locality better than the traditional loop partition, which only focus on a singleton nested loop, and loop fusion. Moreover, multiple loop partition scheduling balances the computation and memory loading, such that the long memory latency can be hidden effectively. The experiments shows that multiple loop partition scheduling can achieve the significant improvement over the existed methods.

1. INTRODUCTION

Multi-dimensional applications on image processing, DSP processing, etc, comprise of lots of computation in the form of multi-dimensional loops. These loops access the array data in rather regular patterns. The time cost for loading the data from the memory plays an important role in determining the overall performance. To reduce the inefficiency caused by the long memory access time, two methods can be applied: use prefetching to hide the memory access time by computation, and enhance the data locality to reduce the number of memory references. In this paper, we propose a new technique base on loop partition. This multiple loop partition scheduling technique combines the above two approaches. The experiments show that it can achieve the improvement over the traditional methods by about 15% to 45% for different benchmarks.

The traditional loop partition technique [1, 10] is an effective method to exploit the data locality in a singleton nested loop. However, it is usual that a program includes several loop nests in the consecutive order. A lot of computational overhead is caused by the repetitive access to array data elements. Separately partitioning each loop will not take full advantage of the data reuse occurred between different loop nests, thereby incur much more memory reference than multiple loop partition scheduling. This is demonstrated by the experiments in Section 5. Therefore, the traditional loop partition technique may be achieve a good result for a singleton nested loop, it cannot perform well to multiple loop nests. Multiple loop partition scheduling technique deal with multiple loop nests together and partition them at the same time, such that the data locality can be exploited to the largest extent.

Our technique can be used in the architecture with multiple processors or a processor with multiple function units. They shared a memory hierarchy. We assume two levels memory in this paper, in which the first and second levels memory can be regarded as the on-chip and off-chip memories, respectively. The model consists of multiple ALU and memory units. The ALU units are for computation, while the memory units execute the memory operations to prepare the data in the first level memory. Two kinds of memory operation are supported by the memory units. *Prefetch* operation is used to load the data in advance, and *keep* operation is used to keep the data in the first level memory for the near future use. The objective of keep operation is to prevent unnecessary long time data swapping. It is needed when the first level memory is really restrictive. When the first level memory is large enough, the keep operation can be neglected because such data still remain in the first level memory. The overall schedule includes the memory schedule and ALU schedule, corresponding to arranging the memory and ALU operations in the respective units. This model can be found in DSP processors, embedded system and shared-memory multiprocessors computer systems. For example, separated ALU and memory units exist in TMS320C64x.

In the past, a lot of work has been done on loop fusion [4] and loop tiling [8, 2]. Loop fusion is used to fuse the consecutive loops into a single loop to exploit the data locality and reduce the additional synchronization. However, the memory reference maybe too much to be hidden efficiently even after the loops are fused. Therefore, we use multiple loop partition scheduling in order to exploit more data locality. Moreover, the partition size is carefully selected such that the computation time and memory loading time are balanced and memory latency is tolerated effectively. In fact, loop fusion can be thought of as a special case of our technique when the partition size is 1. Loop tiling is a technique for grouping elemental computation points so as to increase computation granularity and thereby reduce communication time. The traditional loop tiling only considers the singleton loop and lack of the consideration of prefetching and scheduling.

*This work is partially supported by Graduate Fellowship of the Center for Applied Mathematics

Another technique related to the memory access latency is data layout optimizations [3]. They modify the memory storage order of multi-dimensional arrays so as to reduce the cache miss rate. Loop partition is in the higher level above the data layout transformation. We assume full associativity in the first level memory. For the lower associativity, data layout transformation can be applied first to prevent the cache conflict.

The rest of the paper is organized as follows. In Section 2, the program models and their representation are introduced. Section 3 presents the concept of partition. Section 4 describe multiple loop partition scheduling in detail and Section 5 is the experimental results.

2. PROGRAM MODEL

Multiple loop nests are represented by *Loop Dependence Graph* (LDG), as defined below.

DEFINITION 1. *A loop dependence graph (LDG) $G = (V, E, D_L)$ is an edge-weighted directed multigraph, where V is the set of loop nests, $E \in V \times V$ is the set of dependence edges between the loop nests, and D_L is a function from E to Z^n, representing the set of loop dependency vectors between two nodes, where n is the number of loop dimension.*

The LDG is a directed multigraph because multiple dependences can exist from one loop nest to another arising from different variables. Figure 1(a) shows an example of LDG and Figure 1(b) shows the corresponding code segment. In this example, $V = \{A, B, C, D\}$ and $E = \{e_1, e_2 : (A, B), e_3, e_4 : (B, C), e_5 : (C, C), e_6 : (C, D), e_7 : (A, C), e_8 : (D, A)\}$ where, $D_L(e_1) = (2, 1)$, $D_L(e_2) = (1, 1)$, $D_L(e_3) = (0, 1)$, $D_L(e_4) = (0, -2)$, $D_L(e_5) = (1, 0)$, $D_L(e_6) = (0, -1)$, $D_L(e_7) = (0, 1)$, $D_L(e_8) = (2, 1)$. Note that multiple edges exist between nodes A, B and B, C, due to the different array elements access.

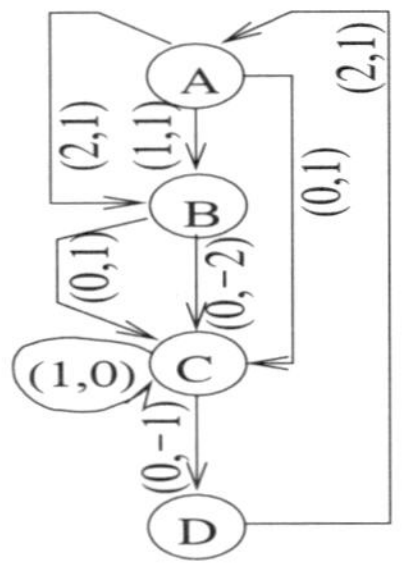

(a) LDG

```
      DO   10   i = 0, n
   A: DO   20   j=0, m
        a[i][j] =        e[i-2][j-1]
20      CONTINUE
   B: DO   30   j= 0,m
        b[i][j] = a[i-1][j-1]
                  +a[i-2][j-1]
30      CONTINUE
   C: DO   40   j= 0,m
        c[i][j] = b[i][j+2] - a[i][j-1]
                  +b[i][j-1]
        d[i][j] = c[i-1][j]
40      CONTINUE
   D: DO   50   j= 0,m
        e[i][j] = c[i][j+1]
50      CONTINUE
10    CONTINUE
```

(b) Program segment

Figure 1: The code and its LDG

In this paper, we only consider the loops with uniform data dependence. A lot of applications in DSP and image processing fit in this category. Also the importance can be justified by the fact that affine index access can be uniformized first [9]. The idea of multiple loop partition scheduling is illustrated with multiple two-dimensional nested loops. The weight of edges in the corresponding LDG can be written as $D_L = (D_L[1], D_L[2])$. The two different target program models are shown in the Figures 2(a) and 2(b), respectively.

```
     DO  K1   i = 0, n
         DO  K2  j=0, m
         ...
K2       CONTINUE

         DO  K3  j= 0,m
         ...
K3       CONTINUE
         .
         .
         .
K1   CONTINUE
```

(a) Nested Multiple Loops

```
     DO  K1   i = 0, n
         DO  K2  j=0, m
         ...
K2       CONTINUE
K1   CONTINUE
     DO  K3   j= 0,m
         DO  K4  j=0, m
         ...
K4       CONTINUE
K3   CONTINUE
         .
         .
         .
```

(b) Multiple Nested Loops

Figure 2: Program Model

Both two models comprise of several uniform loop nests without the intervening code between them. All the loop nests are *conformable* with each other. Conformability is a binary equivalence relation. Two loop nests are said to be conformable if their corresponding loops have the same type (serial in this paper) and identical iteration space size (loop bounds). The data dependences between loop nests are constant, as well as lexically forward (from the earlier loop to the later). Program transformations may be used to obtain a program segment that belongs to the above models. For instance, code motion may be employed to obtain a sequence of loops with no intervening code. Loop permutation may be used to ensures that loop nests are conformable.

The difference between two models is that multiple sequential loops have the same outer-most loop in the nested multiple loops program model, while the loops in the multiple nested loops model are realatively independent. Thus, there will be some loop-carried data dependence introduced by the outer-most loop in the first model, which may cause a dependence cycle in the corresponding LDG. To guarantee the correctness of the execution order, there should not exist the dependence that flows backwards with respect to the iteration execution order. A set of nested multiple loops is illegal if no execution order exists to sastify all the data dependence. The following lemma ensure the legality in the first program model.

LEMMA 1. *A set of nested multiple loops is legal if each cycle in its corresponding LDG sastify $W(c) \geq (1, -\infty)$ [1] and $D_L(e)[1] >= 0, \forall e \in E$, where $W(c)$ is the weight summation for all edges in a cycle.*

On the contrary, there is no data dependence from a loop nest to its ancester in the second program model. Its LDG is always acyclic. The existence of cycle in LDG brings a little more complication on the in-partition execution order, which is discussed in the next section.

[1]In this paper, all the comparsion between two vectors is based on the lexicographic order

3. CONCEPT OF PARTITION SCHEDULING

Partitioning is an effective technique to improve the data locality. Due to the general short data dependence relative to the iteration space size, grouping several iteration executions can increase both the cache and register locality. The partitioning of multiple loop nests is built upon the partitioning of an individual loop nest. The former is the extension of the latter, taking the data dependence between loop nests into consideration. It is necessary to review the partitioning technique for an individual loop nest.

An individual nested loop can be described by a *multi-dimensional data flow graph (MDFG)* [6]. Each node in the MDFG corresponds to a computation. An edge between two nodes represents that these two nodes have a data dependence. Its weight (d_e) is the data dependence vector between these two nodes. A partition is a parallelogram in the iteration space. All iterations with integer index vectors which lie in this parallelogram belong to the same partition. A partition is characterized by its shape and size. Its shape is delimited by two direction vectors: P_x and P_y, where P_y is anti-clockwise to P_x. The following property guarantees all the data dependence vectors lie between P_x and P_y, such that the data dependence for a singleton nested loop can be maintained after partition.

PROPERTY 1. *It is a legal partition shape if and only if the cross products* $d_e \times P_x \leq 0$, $d_e \times P_y \geq 0$, $\forall$ *data dependence* d_e *in MDFG.*

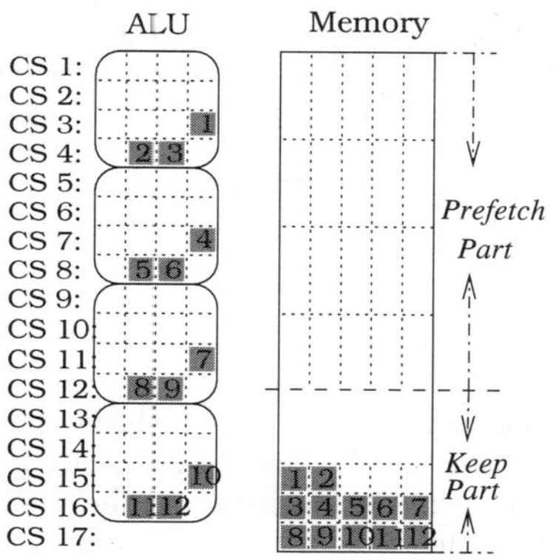

Figure 3: Partition schedule

A partition schedule, as shown in Figure 3, is made up of the ALU schedule, which schedules the ALU operations, and memory schedule, which schedules the prefetch and keep operations. The ALU schedule is formed by Multi-dimensional Rotation Scheduling Algorithm [7]. In fact, any loop pipelining scheme can be used to schedule the ALU operation. The reason we use this algorithm is that it is proven to be optimal [7]. The entire ALU schedule is the simple duplication of a single iteration schedule achieved by Rotation Scheduling Algorithm for each iteration in the partition. To arrange the memory operation, the data dependence is analyzed to collect the prefetch and keep operations for a partition. These operations are scheduled in the sequence of prefetch, keep operations, as well as maintain the time relation between the ALU execution and memory operation i.e., the keep operations must be issued after the corresponding execution. A partition size is determined to make the ALU and memory schedules *balanced*, such that the large memory access latency can be tolerated by the ALU operations. A *balanced partition schedule* is defined to be a partition schedule in which the memory schedule is at most one keep operation time longer than the ALU schedule length.

Another important aspect of partitioning technique is the partition execution order. Instead of the general row-wise order along X axis or column-wise order along Y axis in the unit of iterations, the loop nest is executed in the unit of partitions in the row-wise manner: execute all the first line of partitions along X, then the second line, the third line, etc.

In the case of partitioning multiple loop nests, A partition consists of several *subpartitions*. Figure 4 plots an example of a single partitoin. In a partition, all the iterations which belong to the same iteration space constitute a subpartition. In this figure, L_1, L_2 and L_3 are the iteration spaces for the first, second and third loop nests, respectively. SP_1, SP_2 and SP_3 are the subpartitions in L_1, L_2 and L_3, respectively.

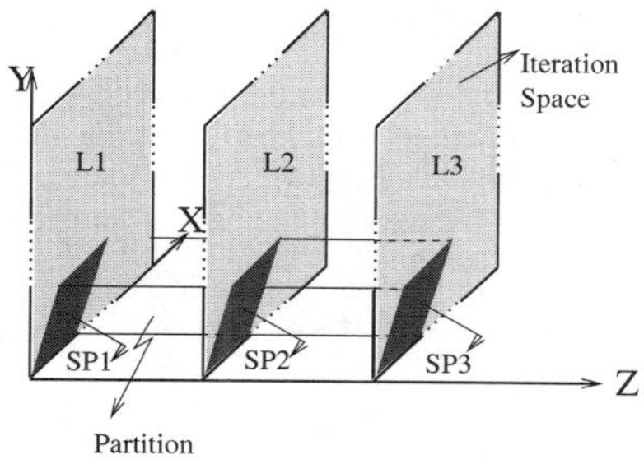

Figure 4: Partition and subpartitions

Multiple loop partition exploits not only the data locality inside each iteration space, but also the data locality among different loop nests. Take Figure 5 as an example, $SP1$ and $SP2$ represent the subpartitions in iteration space L1 and L2, respectively. The dark circles denote the iterations. Iterations $I1$, $I2$, and $I3$ lie in $SP1$, while iterations $I4$ and $I5$ lie in $SP2$. Therefore, data dependences $d1$ and $d2$ belong to the dependences inside a single loop nest, $d3$ and $d4$ belong to the dependence between different loop nests. Assuming iterations $I2$ and $I3$ are in different rows, so do iterations $I4$ and $I5$. They all need the outcome from the computation of iteration $I1$. According to the general row-wise order, the result of iteration $I1$ will be fetched from the memory for 4 times. On the contrary, this result is still in the first level memory and no fetch is needed with the multiple loop partition scheduling technique. With the row-wise partition execution order, different grained in-partition execution order can be applied. The coarse-grained in-partition execution order is shown in Fig 6(a). The first subpartition is finished first, then the second subpartition, until the last subpartition's execution ends. On the other hand, we can execute the iterations alternatively in the loop nests. Figure 6(b) shows this fine-grained in-partition execution order. After the execution of the first line of iterations in each subpartition along loop sequence, we jump to the first subpartition and begin to execute the second line. A partition is finished

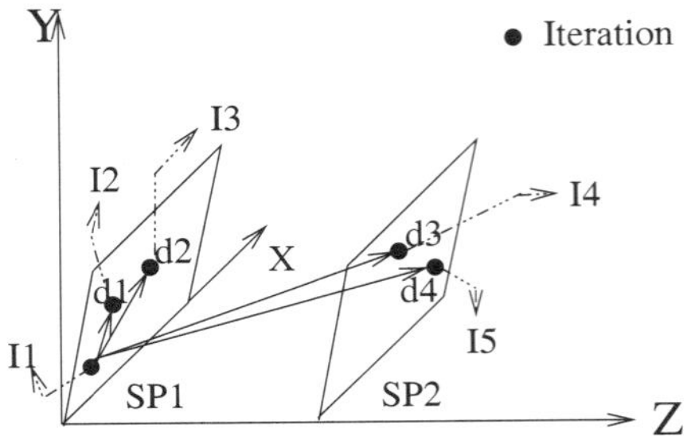

Figure 5: Different data dependences

until all the lines of iterations are executed in this manner.

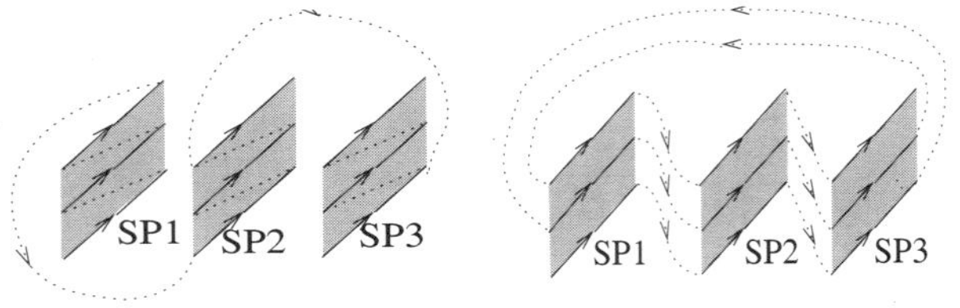

(a) Coarse-grained (b) Fine-grained

Figure 6: In-partition execution order

The first principle of the selection of in-partition execution order is that such order cannot violate the data dependence. For the multiple loop nests program model, both orders are feasible because of the acyclic lexically forward dependence. This is not the case for the nested multiple loops program model. Some data dependence cannot be satisfied by the coarse-grained execution order due to the cycle in LDG.

There are also some other considerations on the in-partition execution order. For example, different efficiency can be achieved for the different data access patterns in the loops. The coarse-grained order performs better when each loop nest has its own input data set, while fine-grained order is preferred when the loop nests have a common input data set. In such case, some compiler switches can be used to designate a better in-partition execution order.

4. MULTIPLE LOOP PARTITION SCHEDULING

Multi-dimensional retiming technique [6] is used in multiple loop partition to transform the iteration space, such that the iteration space can be partitioned legally. A *multi-dimensional retiming* r is a function that redistributes the nodes in the iteration space. A new LDG is created after the retiming. The retiming vector $r(u)$ of a node $u \in V$ represents the offset between the original iteration containing u, and the one after retiming. The weight of the edge changes accordingly to preserve dependence, i.e., $D_L^r(u,v) = D_L(u,v) + r(u) - r(v)$, where D_L^r and D_L is the weight after and before retiming, respectively. Also, $D_L^r(c) = D_L^r(c)$ for each cycle $c \in LDG$.

In the nested multiple loops program model, it is stated in Lemma 1 that $D_L[1]$ element of the weight in LDG should be no less than zero for any edge in LDG. Provided the fine-grained execution order is used, there are two cases for the data dependences. If $D_L[1] > 0$ or $D_L[1] = 0, D_L[2] \geq 0$, these data dependences can be preserved using the fine-grained execution order. If $D_L[1] = 0, D_L[2] < 0$, it is reverse to the flow of execution along X axis and will be violated after the partition. Therefore, we should eliminate all the data dependence that belong to the second case. This can be accomplished by the retiming technique [6]proved by the following theorem.

THEOREM 2. *Given a legal LDG, there exists a set of retiming vector r such that a legal retimed LDG is obtained with $D_l \geq (0,0)$ for any edge in this graph.*

PROOF. Assuming an edge $e : u \to v$, its weight after retiming is $D_L^r = D_L + r(u) - r(v)$, The inequality $r(v) - r(u) \leq D_L$ must be true to make $D_L^r \succeq (0,0)$ Therefore, a feasible solution of the following integer programming problem can serve as a retiming vector set, where r_n denote the retiming vector on n^{th} node.

ILP:
$$
\begin{aligned}
& r_1 - r_2 \leq D_L(1,2) \\
& r_2 - r_3 \leq D_L(2,3) \\
& \vdots \\
& r_{n-1} - r_n \leq D_L(n, n-1)
\end{aligned}
$$

This specical IP problem can be solved using graph theory. A directed graph can be constructed with each node denoting a variable, and edges between the corresponding nodes whose weight equal to D_L. An additional source node is also added. This node has a zero weight edge to any node in the original graph. If there is no cycle with weight less than $(0,0)$, The single source shortest path is a feasible solution. Lemma 1 has shown that for all cycle in the graph, $W \geq (1, -\infty)$, which ensure the existence of a feasible solution.

□

A retiming vector set can be obtained using Bellman-Ford single source shortest path algorithm. The only modification is to replace all the weights, real numbers in the original algorithm, by weight vectors i.e., D_L in the LDG.

In the multiple loop nests program model, there is no certainty that $D_L[1] \geq 0$. The data dependence with $D_L[1] < 0$ will also be voilated after the partition. This voilation can still be overcome by retiming. Because the LDG for this program model is acyclic, Algorithm 1 can be used to get rid of all of the violiations.

After applying the retiming vectors obtained above, all the data dependences sastify $D_L \geq (0,0)$, thereby are automatically preserved by the partition execution order. The partition shape is only determined by the data dependence d_e in the MDFG of each loop nest. Therefore, we can find a legal subpartition shape for each loop based on Property 1. Due to the lexically forward data dependence, vector $(1,0)$ can always serve as P_x for each subpartition, thereby the P_x of the partition. As about P_y, it is one of P_y of all the subpartitions, which has the largest angle with vector $(1,0)$. It is not difficult to verify that all the data dependences conform to Property 1 under such partition shape.

Algorithm 1 Find a feasible retiming vector set

Input: An LDG graph
Output: A retiming vector set of LDG
  Sort the nodes in topological order
  FOREACH Node i in LDG **do**
    $r(i) = (0, 0)$
  ENDFOR
  FOREACH Node i in LDG **do**
    Construct a vector $NV = (NV[1], NV[2])$, which sastisfy $NV[1] \leq D_L[1], NV[2] \leq D_L[2]$, $\forall$ incoming edges with weight D_L.
    IF $NV \geq 0$ **THEN** $r(i) = (0, 0)$ **ELSE** $r(i) = NV$ **ENDIF**
    Update all the outgoing edges' weigt to $D_L^r = D_L + r(i)$.
  ENDFOR

As the same principle of partitioning an individual nested loop, the determination of the partition size depends on the relation between the memory and ALU schedules. A partition size which can balance the ALU and memory schedules is a prefered size. To derive the memory scheudle, all the memory operations need to be identified.

The number of these memory operations depends on the data dependence distance and the partition size. A certain data dependence decide a perfetch region, in which all data need to be prefetched in advance, and a keep region, in which all data will be kept in the first level memory. All the data in the keep region will be reused soon (in the next partition along the execution sequence), while the data in the prefetch region will be reused in a relatively long time. The Figure 7 shows two adjacent partitions along the partittion execution direction and two different data dependences. $d1$ is a data dependence between two loop nests, and $d2$ is a dependence inside a loop. Each of them deicde a prefetch region and a keep region in the partition, as shown in the figure. For the keep region determined by a data dependence, we can see that this dependence occurs between two adjacent partition. while it is not true for the prefetch region.

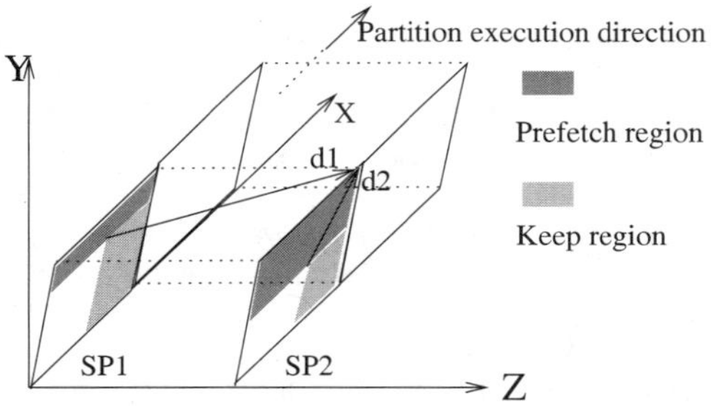

Figure 7: Prefetch and keep regions

In the algorithm to decide the partition size, a partition size is denoted by f_x and f_y. Then the actual partition size is f_x along X axis and $||f_y \times P_y||$ along the P_y direction. The lengths of memory and ALU schedules are denoted by L_{mem} and L_{ALU} respectively. T_{keep} represents the time for a keep operation. The first "for" loop in the algorithm calculates the minimum partition size requirement. This requirement means that no data dependence will span two or more partitions. This constraint is used to reduce the computation and simplify the analysis. The "while" loop in the algorithm calculates the partition size which can achieve a balanced partition schedule. The theory behind these steps is: increase the partition size along P_y direction can maintain the number of prefetch operation. If the memory schedule is longer than ALU schedule at the start step, enlarge the partition along P_y direction only increases the number of keep operations and the number of iterations in the partition, which imply the ALU schedule will increase faster than the memory schedule if the partition size along P_x direction is large enough. It is this theory that guarantee the existence of the balanced partition schedule and the termination of the algorithm. In the algorithm, we use the variable "icount" and a predefined constant "MI" to ensure the f_x is large enough to find a balanced partition schedule.

Algorithm 2 Multiple loop partition scheduling

Input: The data dependences d (including both d_e in MDFG and D_l in LDG) in multiple loop nests
Output: The partition size
  /*find the partition shape*/
  For each loop nest, find the subpartition shape P_{x_s}, P_{y_s}
  Set $P_x = (1, 0)$. Choose P_y as the most anti-clockwise vector relative to P_x in all P_{y_s}.
  /*find the minimum f_x and f_y*/
  $f_x = 0, f_y = 0$.
  FOREACH $d = (d[1], d[2])$ **do**
    if $fx < (d[1] - d[2] * p_y[1]/p_y[2])$ **then**
      $fx = \lceil d[1] - d[2] * p_y[1]/p_y[2] \rceil$
    end if
    if $fy * P_y[2] < d[2]$ **then**
      $f_y = \lceil d[2]/P_y[2] \rceil$
    end if
  ENDFOR
  /*determine the partition size*/
  Calculate L_{mem} and L_{ALU} under the partition size f_x, f_y.
  icount = 0
  WHILE $L_{mem} \geq L_{ALU} + T_{keep}$ **do**
    f_y++;
    icount ++;
    Calculate L_{mem} and L_{ALU} under the partition size f_x, f_y.
    if icount $\geq$ MI **then**
      fx++;
    end if
  ENDWHILE
  Schedule the ALU and memory operations in ALU and memory units, respectively.

5. EXPERIMENTAL RESULTS

In this section, the effectiveness of multiple loop partition scheduling technique is evaluated by running a set of simulations on four benchmarks. *Example* is the example code shown in Figure 1(b). *Jacobi* is a PDE solver. *LL18* is the eighteenth kernel from the Livermore Loops benchmark. *Tomcatv* is extracted from the 101.tomcatv in SPEC95 benchmark. We compared the *AET/Iter* by applied three different schemes on these benchmarks. *AET/Iter* (Average execution time per iteration) is the summation of all the average execution times for one iteration in each loop nest. Because of the comfortability of the loop nests, AET/Iter reflects the overall effectiveness of each scheme.

In the simulation, we assume 4 ALU units and 4 memory units. The first level memory is 32KB in size and full associative. Each data is float type which consumes 8 bytes. The computation time for each operation is simplified as one unit time. The data are prefetched in block with size 64 bytes. This operation take 10 units time while keep operation take one unit time. The assumption is reasonable considering the big gap between the CPU and memory speeds.

We first compare multiple loop partition scheduling and partitioning each loop nest separately, the former is superior to the latter, due to the fact that the better data locality is exploited and the repetitive array elements access are re-

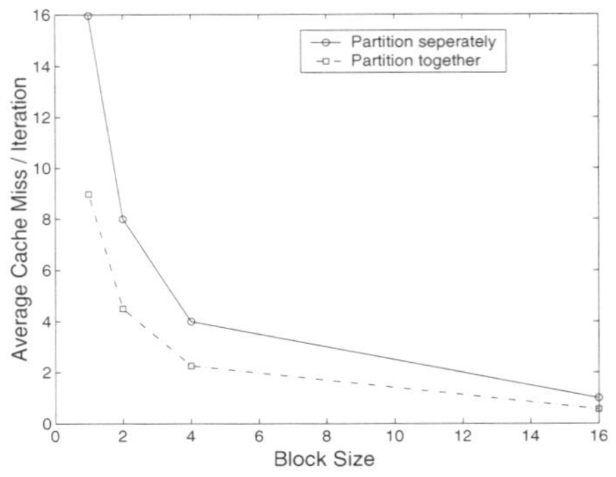

Figure 8: LL18 Kernel

duced. Figures 5 shows how *average cache miss/ Iteration* change with the cache block size (denoted by the number of float data in a block) for LL18 kernel under the above simulation environment. We can see that the number of average cache miss for partitioning separately is always two times the number of our technique. This observation can be explained by the number of array reference per iteration. Partitioning separately has two times memory reference as many as multiple loop partition. Since the overall execution time is mainly decided by the memory access time, much more number of memory references mean the longer execution time. Therefore, multiple loop partition scheduling can get better performance than the traditional partitioning technique.

The simulation results are listed in Table 1. Three methods compared are *Original*, which is the original loop without any transformation, *Fusion*, which applied the loop fusion on the benchmarks, and *MLP*, which is multiple loop partition. Because it has been shown in [10] that software pipelining and loop tiling cannot perform better than the traditional separately partitioning, we didn't compare their results. The column *#loop nests* denotes the number of loop nests in each benchmarks. The *size* column is the partition size. We also list the theoretic lower bound in the L_b column. The ALU schedule is obtained without the consideration of the memory load latency. Thus, the ALU schedule length per iteration provides the lower bound for computation under the resource constraints. Compare the AET/Iter, we can find that partitioning technique can achieve the best performance. Accredit to increasing the data locality appeared between different loop nests, the loop fusion perform better than the original loop. The multiple loop partitioning not only takes advantage of the benefit of loop fusion, but also explores more data reuses which exist in the different iterations. Moreover, it takes the balance of computation and memory reference into consideration, thereby prevent the wasted time caused by the dominated memory reference time. Therefore, the multiple loop partition scheduling technique can efficiently exploit the data locality and hide the memory access.

The performance of multiple loop partition is very close to the lower bound, which demonstrates that the memory latency is hidden very efficiently. Their difference is mainly due to the iterations lie on the boundary of iteration space. These iterations can be regarded as the preface, which is the preparation stage of the normal partition execution. Also,

	#loop nests	Original	Fusion	MLP	size	L_b
Example	4	8.5	5.41	**2.34**	8×8	2
Jacobi	2	5.25	4.0	**2.16**	4×8	2
LL18	3	20.85	13.44	**11.5**	4×4	11
Tomcatv	5	25.25	20.38	**18.26**	4×4	18

Table 1: Experiment result of average execution time

the extra keep operations by which the memory schedule is longer than the ALU schedule play a minor role in this difference.

In tomcatv benchmark, there are five loop nests with the same iteration space size. However, the first three and the last two loop nests should be thought of as in two independent groups, since the step direction is contrary in different groups. The first group is in the form as *do* 10 $i = 1, N, 1$, while the second group is in the form of *do* 10 $i = N, 1, -1$. Because loop fusion can be regarded as a special case of multiple loop partition when the partition size is 1, The problem to group loop nests is the same as the fusible loop problem [5] in essence.

6. REFERENCES

[1] F. Chen and E.H.-M.Sha. Loop scheduling and partitions for hiding memory latencies. In *Proc. IEEE 12th International Symposium on System Synthesis*, pages 64–70, San Jose, November 1999.

[2] J. Chame and S. Moon. A tile selection algorithm for data locality and cache interference. In *Proc. of the 1999 ACM International Conference on Supercomputing*, Rhodes, Greece, June 1999.

[3] M. Kandemir, A. Choudhary, and N. Shenoy. A linear algebra framework for automatic determination of optimal data layouts. *IEEE Transactions on Parallel and Distributed Systems*, 10(2), Feb 1999.

[4] Naraig Manjikian and Tarek S. Abdelrahman. Fusion of loops for parallelism and locality. *IEEE Transactions on Parallel and Distributed Systems*, 8(2), Feb 1997.

[5] N. Megiddo and V. Sarkar. Optimal weighted loop fusion for parallel programs. In *Proceedings of 9th ACM symposium on Parallel algorithms and architectures*, pages 282–291, Newport, RI, June 1997.

[6] N. Passos and E.H.-M.Sha. Achieving full parallelism using multi-dimensional retiming. *IEEE Transactions on Parallel and Distributed Systems*, 7(11), November 1996.

[7] N. Passos and E.H.-M.Sha. Scheduling of uniform multi-dimensioanl systems under resource constraints. *Journal of IEEE Transactions on VLSI Systems*, 6(4), December 1998.

[8] P. Bouilet, A.Darte, T.Risset, and Y.Robert. (pen)-ultimate tiling. In *Scalable High-Performance Computing Conference*, pages 568–576, May 1994.

[9] W. Shang, E. Hodzic, and Z. Chen. On uniformization of affine dependence algorithms. *IEEE Transactions on Computers*, 45(7), 1996.

[10] Z. Wang, M. Kirkpatrick, and E.H.-M.Sha. Optimal two level partitioning and loop scheduling for hiding memory latency for dsp applications. In *Proc. ACM 37th Design Automation Conference*, pages 540–545, Los Angeles, California, June 2000.

Object Oriented Hardware Synthesis and Verification

T. Kuhn, T. Oppold,
C. Schulz-Key,
M. Winterholer,
W. Rosenstiel
Univ. of Tuebingen, Sand 13
72076 Tuebingen, Germany
oase,rosen@informatik.uni-tuebingen.de

M. Edwards
Cisco Systems, Inc.
7025 Kit Creek Road
RTP, NC 27709
jme@cisco.com

Y. Kashai
Verisity Design, Inc.
2041 Landings Drive
Mountain View, CA 94043
yaron@verisity.com

ABSTRACT

The synthesis of hardware from object oriented specifications is presented. Our approach utilizes the *e* language that has been proven to be highly efficient for the verification of hardware. The *e* language is similar to Java and provides additional constructs for specification and verification of hardware. We describe an automated design flow for the synthesis of object oriented descriptions that tightly integrates simulation based verification. The usability of our approach is demonstrated by real-world examples.

Keywords

Object oriented hardware modeling, verification, high-level synthesis.

1. INTRODUCTION

There is a growing gap between the number of gates that can be implemented on a single chip and the number of gates that can be designed by one person in one day. Additionally, short product life cycles, time to market, and changing standards require shorter design times. Therefore, new design methodologies must be applied. By specifying on a higher level of abstraction the productivity can be increased enormously. Commercial tools for synthesizing algorithmic descriptions are available already and gain more and more acceptance. Newer approaches raise the abstraction level even more by synthesizing object oriented descriptions. The object oriented paradigm can be applied in order to cope with the complexity of system-level designs. This paradigm also simplifies re-use of IP.

Since hardware description languages like VHDL and Verilog are more suitable for RT level design than for higher levels of abstraction, software languages like C/C++ or Java are recently deployed for synthesis. These languages are already widely used for specifications that can be executed. Furthermore, hardware/software co-design can be simplified by using a single language for both domains.

ISSS'01, October 1-3, 2001, Montréal, Québec, Canada.

Verification typically consumes over half of the design effort. The languages currently used for synthesis provide only insufficient support for verification. Therefore languages like Verisity's *e* (www.verisity.com) or Synopsys' Vera (www. open-vera.com) hardware verification language are deployed within a dedicated environment to improve the verification task. The *e* language is similar to Java enhanced by various verification and hardware related constructs. *e* provides all basic object oriented constructs, supports *multi-threading*, and it can be executed in the Specman™ environment. Therefore it is also well suited for specification.

Synthesis on the system-level requires support for multi-threaded descriptions. Due to the complexity of such designs, we want to support verification appropriately in our approach. The powerful verification features of *e* and its capability for object oriented specification, encouraged us to investigate the applicability of the *e* language for synthesis. By making the synthesis of *e* descriptions possible, we allow to use one single language for specification, verification, and synthesis.

The remainder of the paper is organized as follows: In Section 2, we will present an overview of related work. Section 3 describes object oriented synthesis and details of the synthesis from *e* descriptions. In Section 4, we present verification within the Specman environment and the integration of this environment in our design flow. Section 5 presents examples and discusses the results. Section 6 concludes this paper and gives an outlook on further work.

2. PREVIOUS WORK

In the past, various approaches have been made to specify hardware and hardware/software systems on the basis of objects. Object oriented VHDL [1, 2] enhances VHDL with object oriented concepts. SystemC [3] is based on C++ class libraries and is intended for design at the system/algorithmic and register-transfer levels. Recently, successful efforts have been made to specify [4, 5, 6] and to synthesize [7, 8] from Java.

For validation, simulation and formal verification have a long tradition and various commercial tools are provided by major EDA companies, e. g., Cadence, Mentor Graphics, and Synopsys.

3. OBJECT ORIENTED SYNTHESIS

The object oriented design paradigm has already gained broad acceptance in software engineering for the design of large systems. Object oriented synthesis allows hardware modeling on an abstraction level above the behavioral level. Designers can express their ideas in a very natural way by thinking of classes rather than of data and procedures. Encapsulating things that belong together and having data and behavior within one entity also simplifies re-use.

We developed an object oriented analysis system (OOAS) that allows to synthesize object oriented hardware descriptions. Our OOAS can be used to read in descriptions written in different languages. Currently we support Java, SystemC, and *e* as input languages. In this paper we describe the synthesis from *e*.

There is already a variety of good synthesis tools on the market. These tools provide an automated design flow for RT and algorithmic descriptions, but they do not support object oriented concepts like object references, inheritance, or polymorphism. We utilize the algorithms deployed by these tools for the synthesis of object oriented descriptions by transforming such descriptions into equivalent descriptions on a lower level of abstraction that can be handled by commercial tools. The formats that we generate for those descriptions are VHDL, Verilog, and SystemC (figure 1). For the sake of simplicity this paper refers only to the output of Verilog.

3.1 Synthesis from *e*

Using one single object oriented language for specification, verification, and synthesis simplifies the design process. There is a variety of languages that could be used as such an unified language, each of them having advantages and disadvantages. Most of the languages do not support verification adequately. Verification of multi-threaded descriptions is mandatory for hardware design and particularly challenging. The *e* language is therefore especially suited as an unified language for hardware design. Today *e* is not only used for verifying hardware descriptions written in VHDL or Verilog, it is already used for writing a *golden model* of the hardware in an object oriented high-level language. This model is then manually translated into a synthesizable HDL description. The advantage of *e* over software languages like C/C++ or Java is that hardware related constructs like bit accurate data types, clocks, etc. are part of the language.

For the transformation from an object oriented description in *e* into an equivalent description in Verilog, the meta data that describe the object oriented structure is generated. The number and structure of objects have to be static in the realization in hardware. This should be considered in the description and is checked by preallocation during the analysis. Objects have to be allocated for variables and parameters of methods which reference sets of objects. The identification of such sets of static references is done during an alias analysis, which is part of the OOAS.

In *e* concurrent threads of control are described by so called *Time Consuming Methods* (TCMs). TCMs are similar to Threads in Java. TCMs are triggered by events. Events can be defined by temporal expressions that are part of the *e* language. TCMs have to be handled separately from the regular methods (non-TCMs) during the transformation process. Conflicts resulting from concurrent access to variables by different TCMs must be detected by a concurrency analysis and then be resolved. We now describe the control data flow analysis that is performed for the sequential case and the concurrency analysis that is performed for the parallel case.

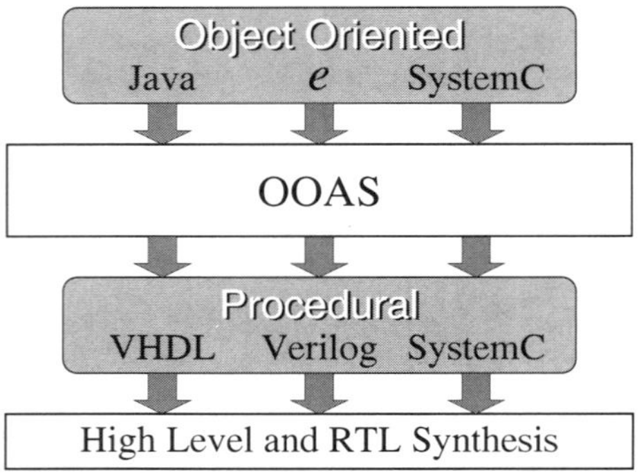

Figure 1: Languages supported by OOAS

3.2 Control Data Flow Analysis

The control data flow analysis applies techniques known from software compiler design [9] to the synthesis of hardware.

After the lexical and semantical analysis done by the scanner and parser for *e*, a static control and data flow analysis is performed on the set of syntax trees for each *e* object. The result of the analysis is a control flow graph (CFG) where the data flow information is stored in a scope table within each node of the graph. Because of the combination of data and control flow information, no separate data flow graph has to be generated and the analysis traverses the syntax tree only once. The CFG has two different types of nodes. The control flow nodes divide the CFG in multiple sub-trees if a node has multiple children. This is the case for nodes representing, e.g., *while* loops or *if* statements. The second type of nodes in the CFG are the data flow nodes, which do not change the control flow, like arithmetic operations or assignments.

The main problem of the transformation is the usage of references. Deciding which object is accessed when a method is called on a variable can only be done at runtime. Objects may have several references, or aliases at the same time, so it is hard to tell which statements affect which object.

The analysis determines a set of possible objects for each variable within the scope of a statement. Each node of the CFG has one scope table, where all variables in the scope of the node are stored together with a set of objects that may be referenced by this variable. The scope tables are built together with the whole CFG. When a new node is created, the scope table of the parent node is cloned and the set of references ('reference set') of each variable changed by the statement is updated.

A reference set $R_s(a)$ is the maximal set of all references on objects, which can be hidden by the alias a after the execution of statement s under consideration of the type of the variable and the preceding control flow. All reference sets $R_s(a)$ of variables accessible in a CFG node n, build the scope table $S(n)$.

Figure 2 shows an example of a hardware component written in *e*. Classes are described using the keyword *struct*. A struct declares data fields and methods. Inheritance is supported by the keyword *like*. The *init* method is similar to the constructor in Java. Instances of a struct are made by using the keyword *new*. A detailed description of the *e* language can be found in [10]. The constructs that we use for the specification of hardware components are described in [11].

The analysis for the TCM *runHWO* of the example code results in the CFG shown in figure 3. At node 5 in the CFG, the scope table includes three reference sets $R_5(x)$, $R_5(y)$ and $R_5(z)$. Each reference set has been initialized in the init method, where three objects of the struct S have been instantiated. The objects *S_1*, *S_2* and *S_3* are labeled with subsequent numbers.

For each type of statement, a different algorithm is implemented to update the scope table of a node in the CFG. The algorithm for loop statements, used for the determination of the scope table for node number 7 in figure 3 is described in algorithm 1.

Table 1 shows the evolution of the reference sets for each iteration of the algorithm. The body of the *while* loop has to be reanalyzed four times to get the final reference sets for the *while* loop node (without determining the exact number of iterations during execution).

```
struct Test like HWO {
    x : S; y : S; z : S;

    init() is {
        x = new S;
        y = new S;
        z = new S;
    };

    runHWO() @clk is {
        var i : uint;
        i = 0;
        while (i < 10)
        {
            z = x;
            x = y;
            i = i + 1;
        };
        z.foo();
    };
};
```

```
struct S {
    foo() is {
        ...
    };
};
```

Figure 2: Struct *Test* and struct *S*

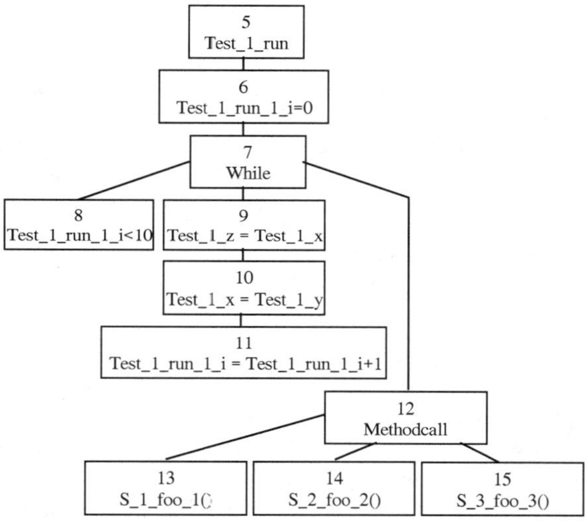

Figure 3: CFG for the TCM *runHWO*

The analysis terminates because there are no changes in the reference sets of step three and four. The merged reference sets in the last column of table 1 are the resulting sets contained in the scope table *S(7)* of node 7.

Input: CFG node *n*, statement *s* of *n*, scope table *S(p)* where *p* is the predecessor node of *n*
Output: Updated scope table *S(n)*
begin
  S(n) ← copy of *S(p)*
  S(tmp) ← copy of *S(p)*
  repeat
    S(n) ← *S(n)* ∪ *S(tmp)*
    S(tmp) ← analyze the block statements of the loop
  until *S(n)* = *S(tmp)*
end

Algorithm 1: Analysis of loops

Table 1: Reference sets for the while loop

	1.	2.	3.	4.	result
$R_7(x)$	{S_1}	{S_2}	{S_2}	{S_2}	{S_1, S_2}
$R_7(y)$	{S_2}	{S_2}	{S_2}	{S_2}	{S_2}
$R_7(z)$	{S_3}	{S_1}	{S_2}	{S_2}	{S_3, S_1, S_2}

The scope table *S(7)* is the input for the analysis of node 12. The method call *z.foo()* uses variable z where $R_{12(z)}$ contains the objects *S_3*, *S_1* and *S_2*. On which object the method *foo()* will be called depends on how often the *while* loop has been iterated at runtime. The analysis splits the CFG into three sub-trees, one for each object that may be referenced by the variable z.

For each method call, a new node in the CFG is created. The body of the method builds a sub-tree of the node. When the method is a TCM, the new CFG node builds an independent CFG with the method call node as root node. A copy of the reference sets of the actual scope is the initial scope of the new CFG. The analysis always terminates because of the constant number of objects in the whole system. The number of objects in a reference set can not exceed the maximum number of objects instantiated in the whole system. The constant number of objects instantiated in the *e* program is guaranteed since the instantiation of objects in loops is only allowed if the number of iterations can be determined at compile time. The instantiation of objects is not allowed within cyclic or recursive method calls.

When the analysis terminates, the CFG is used as input for the concurrency analysis, which is described in the next section.

3.3 Concurrency Analysis

During the concurrency analysis, the reference sets and the CFGs of the data and control flow analysis are used for creating a set of variables which are accessed by different TCMs. A variable can be accessed by a TCM in two different ways:

- **write access:** The variable is on the left hand side of an assignment and becomes an alias for another object.
- **read access:** The variable is on the right hand side of an assignment or is passed to another method as parameter or a method is called on the variable.

If a node in the CFG accesses a variable the following cases have to be handled by the analysis:

1. There is no other TCM which reads or writes the variable. The variable is a normal variable that does not require any special treatment.
2. At most one TCM has write access to the variable and multiple TCMs have read access. This variable has to be declared in a global scope to enable multiple TCMs to access the referenced object.
3. More than one TCM writes to the variable. This case is reported to the user of the system. An arbiter to resolve the access must then be inserted. This arbiter is an adapted variation of the arbiter described in [12].

For the variables which are accessed by multiple TCMs (case 2) the CFG is extended by a set of global variables called *global*. To build up this set, the CFG is traversed to build a set of variables read by the TCM t called $read_t$ and a set of variables written by t, called $write_t$. When a read access occurs in a node of the TCM t, the variable v is added to the set $read_t$. If v is in the set $write_m$ or $read_m$, where m is an already analyzed TCM, v becomes element of *global*. In case of a write access, v is added to the set $write_t$. If v is already element of the set $write_m$ an error state is reached. When v is member of $read_m$ v becomes element of the set *global*. The actual TCMs are stored on a stack because a TCM can start another TCM. The actual TCM where a read or write access is executed, is always the top element of a stack called *tcmStack*. The described method that creates the global set of shared variables is shown in algorithm 2.

```
Input: node {root node of the CFG}
Output: global {set of global references}
begin
  tcmStack ← empty {stack with actual analyzed TCMs}
  tcmSet ← empty {set of already analyzed TCMs}
  repeat
    switch node
    case start of TCM t
      tcmSet ← tcmSet ∪ tcmStack.top
      tcmStack.push(t)
    case end of TCM t
      tcmSet ← tcmSet ∪ tcmStack.pop
    case statement reads variable v
      TCM t ← tcmStack.top
      read_t ← read_t ∪ v
      for all TCM m in tcmSet do
        if v ∈ read_m or write_m then
          global ← global ∪ v
        end if
      end for
    case statement writes variable v
      TCM t ← tcmStack.top
      write_t ← write_t ∪ v
      for all TCM m in tcmSet do
        if v ∈ read_m then
          global ← global ∪ v
        end if
        if v ∈ write_m then
          report write access to the user
        end if
      end for
    end switch
    node ← node.next
  until node is empty
end
```

Algorithm 2: Concurrency analysis

After the complete concurrency analysis, the set *global* is added to the root node of the CFG. The CFG is traversed by the Verilog code generator that uses the scope information to generate the appropriate Verilog constructs. The TCMs that are used in *e* to specify multiple threads of control are transformed into Verilog *always* blocks. Each *always* block is initially idle and starts its actual execution at the same time as the corresponding TCM is started in the *e* specification. In order to obtain this behavior and to ensure a correct reset behavior of the circuit, a skeleton is built implicitly around the actual description. Within that skeleton, the Verilog statements are generated according to the information in the CFG.

4. VERIFICATION WITH *e* AND SPECMAN

Closely related to *e* is the verification environment Specman, both developed by Verisity Design. Simulation based verification requires the introduction of stimuli to the Device Under Test (DUT) being simulated, as well as the collection of DUT responses for

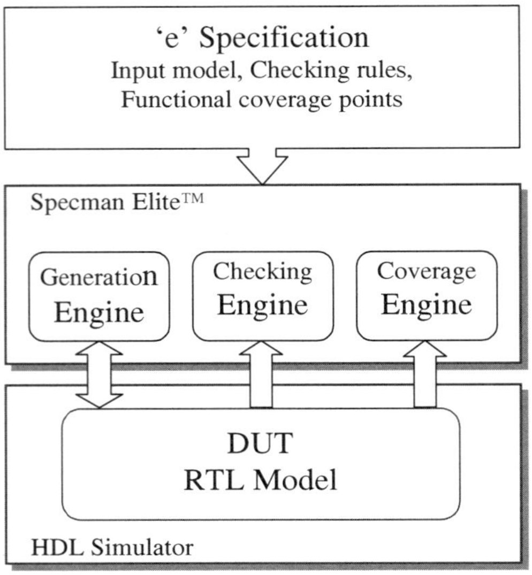

Figure 4: A typical *e* driven testbench

the purpose of checking and coverage analysis (figure 4). Specman and the *e* language provide powerful support for these verification tasks. The supported verification methodology can be applied to DUTs implemented in *e*, those implemented in HDLs such as Verilog and VHDL as well as numerous other modeling languages.

We use this verification environment in three different phases of the design process depicted in figure 5.

First, the design flow starts with the specification of the hardware module in *e*. This system specification may contain algorithmic descriptions as well as descriptions at the register-transfer level. The correctness of the specification can be verified by executing the *e* code in the Specman environment.

Second, existing Verilog IP can be included for verification by attaching a simulator. The results of this first step in the verification process can be used to refine the test bench, also written in *e*, around the hardware module.

Third, the *e* specification of the hardware module is processed by our object oriented analysis system. Depending on the description style used in the specification (algorithmic or register-transfer level) the generated code is either behavioral Verilog, suitable for high-level synthesis with Synopsys Behavioral Compiler™/Design Compiler™, or a Verilog description at the register-transfer level that can be synthesized by Design Compiler. Additionally, the OOAS generates Verilog code that comprises several enhancements for simulation. The generated Verilog can be verified by attaching a simulator the same way as for the simulation of Verilog IP. The same environment is used for the verification of the results of the commercial tools.

All steps of the verification task are supported by Specman's sophisticated verification methodologies and the test bench can be re-used easily.

4.1 Input Modeling and Generation

In *e*, input stimuli are modeled as a hierarchy of objects with inter relating constraints. By defining object types the user specifies the universe of data elements or an alphabet for an input sequence. Constraints can both remove parts of the alphabet and restrict the composition of members of the alphabet into sequences. Constraints may depend on the state of the system.

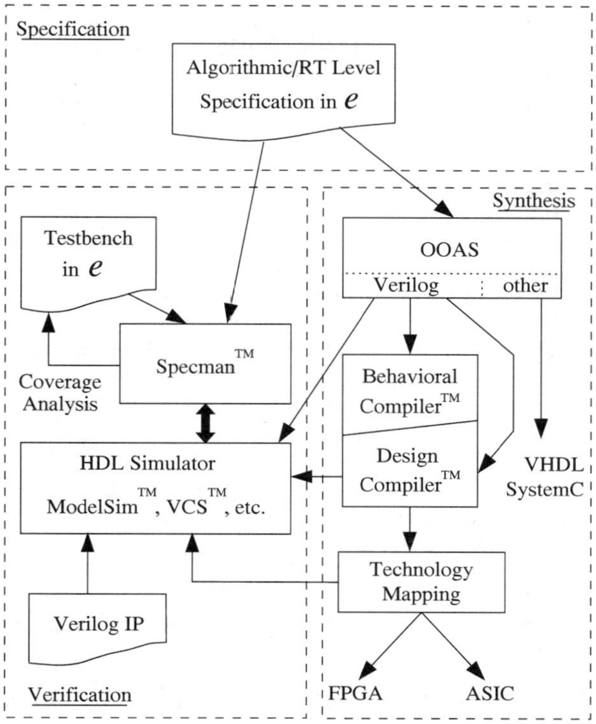

Figure 5: Design flow

In contrast to deterministic test inputs, the *e* input model normally contains degrees of freedom. The Specman test generation engine uncovers these degrees of freedom and creates input sequences using a controlled pseudo-random process.

Constraints are conjunctive by nature, hence one can direct the generated input sequence by addition of constraints. These additions can be made per feature to be tested, or as a way to avoid areas of known defects and work in progress.

4.2 Driving and Checking

A directed random input generation methodology requires automated checking, since the input model does not predict a unique response. The *e* language offers three major features in support of driving and checking: Events, TCMs, and a complete temporal language. The temporal language uses events and state formulae as atomic entities. Temporal and logical operators are used for expressing protocol rules the DUT must adhere to. Specman features a temporal engine that interprets temporal expressions as runtime checkers.

4.3 Functional Coverage

The generation process ensures non-zero probability for any legal input sequence. However, given the huge input space and state space of modern devices, a practical approach would control the distribution of input sequences in view of the accumulated coverage.

The *e* language provides a way to define functional coverage metrics. Functional coverage points are user defined combinations of states, or sequences of states that have some architectural or micro-architectural significance. Because of its sequential nature, functional coverage is a more rigorous metric than code coverage.

The accumulated functional coverage and its breakdown to architectural and micro-architectural features provide status information about the verification effort. This information is used for steering the process and to eventually certify that the DUT has a high probability of being functional.

4.4 Hardware/software Co-Verification

A key aspect of verifying SoC designs, which typically have one or more processors on board, is verifying the embedded software together with the hardware. This will flush out integration errors, beside hardware only and software only defects. In order to apply the same methodology to the integrated system it is crucial that generation, coverage, and checking are applied to the software part, as well as to the hardware part. This will facilitate tests, checks, and coverage metrics that capture hardware and software dependencies.

This requirement is achieved by the combination of Specman with a hardware/software co-verification tool, which is running the software components. Such deep integration exists for the Mentor Graphics Seamless™ tool. This integration provides Specman with the capability of reading and writing to any variable and memory location. This is the support required for the application of generated stimuli to the software parts, checking based in part on the state of the software and collecting functional coverage while taking into account the state of the software along with the hardware components.

5. EXAMPLES AND RESULTS

We used our object oriented analysis system for synthesizing several examples. One example is a part of an ATM header translator (AHT) another one is the Rana interface. The Rana interface represents a typical 'receive' direction, FIFO buffering scheme between three proprietary data communication interfaces. The primary incoming data interface is being buffered into two distinct FIFOs that are then being transmitted to two identical transmit interfaces. Thus the data stream is being de-multiplexed from the incoming data stream into two separate data streams. On all three interfaces handshake flow control is implemented. The Rana interface was developed by Cisco Systems [13] and is presently successfully in production.

The results of the synthesis are depicted in table 2. For each module, the number of non-comment lines of code (ncloc) of both the *e* specification and the resulting Verilog code, and the time needed by the OOAS for the translation from *e* to Verilog are given. The execution time of the OOAS, as well as the time spent by Behavioral Compiler and Design Compiler for the synthesis (BC/DC), were measured on a 360MHz Sun Ultra-5 with 256 MBytes RAM. The clock rate for which the module was synthesized and the area of the resulting circuit are also given in the table. The area is composed of the cell area and the net interconnect area. It is estimated by Design Compiler and given in units of the used library. We used the lca300k library, where one unit is the area of one basic cell of the LCA.

The AHT module contains almost no object oriented constructs and therefore the translation of the *e* specification into Verilog results in a description of nearly equal size. In contrast to that, there is a great number of objects involved in the Rana module. One of these objects is a FIFO buffer used to store other objects. We have synthesized the Rana module with three different sizes for the FIFO buffer. The depth of the FIFO (i.e., the number of objects that can be stored in the buffer) is appended to the module names in table 2. While the *e* specifications differ only in the declaration of the FIFO depth and therefore have the same size, the resulting Verilog code is growing considerably. The reason for that is, that polymorphic method calls have to be resolved to enable the transformation from an object oriented specification into procedural code.

Table 2: Results of the synthesized examples

Module	ncloc e	ncloc Verilog	OO AS	BC/ DC	Clk	Area
AHT	134	132	11 sec	92 sec	40 MHz	1426
Rana3	945	1535	48 sec	32 min	20 MHz	17239
Rana8	945	1920	55 sec	1h 24m	20 MHz	24707
Rana16	945	2536	68 sec	5h 36m	20 MHz	36707

The control data flow analysis therefore determines statically for each method call on an object all possible references the variable can hold during run-time and a case statement with branches for all possible values is inserted in the Verilog code. Since the number of possible objects grows with the depth of the FIFO, the size of the generated Verilog code also increases with the FIFO depth. This effect is even more drastic as we use the technique of inlining method calls in the calling method.

6. CONCLUSIONS AND FUTURE WORK

This paper presented results from the DFG project OASE and a cooperation between Cisco Systems, Verisity Design, and the Computer Engineering Department from the University of Tuebingen. Our approach provides an automated design flow for synthesis of object oriented specifications. Verification is tightly integrated in the design flow and all the design tasks can be carried out using the object oriented language e. This contribution shows that synthesis from high-level models written in e is practical and that the presented analysis system is capable of dealing with real-world applications.

At present, no extensions have been made to the e language in order to distinguish hardware and software objects or to define the interfaces between them. Instead inheritance was used to augment object semantics as needed. We consider adding proper constructs to the e language to simplify the specification task for the designer.

Further research will be done in the area of optimization of multiple concurrent tasks within the same hardware object and hierarchies of hardware objects with no formal interface between them.

So far we have deployed our synthesis system to improve and speed up the implementation flow. When applied to the verification flow, some components of the test environment may be subject to synthesis which may facilitate test bench acceleration and post silicon validation.

We also investigate the application of object oriented concepts for hardware/software co-design partitioning[14].

7. ACKNOWLEDGMENTS

This work is funded by CISCO and DFG project No. RO 1030/8-1.

8. REFERENCES

[1] S. Swamy, A. Molin, and B. Covnot. OO-VHDL: Object-oriented extensions to VHDL. IEEE Computer, 1995.

[2] M. Radetzki, W. Putzke-Röming, and W. Nebel. Objective VHDL: The object-oriented approach to hardware reuse. In *Advances in Information Technologies: The Business Challenge*, 1997.

[3] www.systemc.org.

[4] R. Helaihel and K. Olukotun. Java as a specification language for hardware-software systems. In *IEEE/ACM International Conference on Computer-Aided Design*, 1997.

[5] J. S. Young, J. MacDonald, M. Shilman, P. H. Tabbara, and A. R. Newton. Design and specification of embedded systems in Java using successive formal refinement. In *Proceedings of the Design Automation Conference (DAC'1998)*, 1998.

[6] T. Kuhn, W. Rosenstiel, and U. Kebschull. Description and simulation of hardware/software systems with Java. In *Proceedings of the Design Automation Conference (DAC'1999)*, 1999.

[7] LavaLogic. Forge-J: Fast Java to Verilog-HDL Compiler. http://www.lavalogic.com, 1999.

[8] T. Kuhn and W. Rosenstiel. Java based object oriented hardware specification and synthesis. In *Proceedings of ASP-DAC*, 2000.

[9] R. Wilson and M. Lam. Efficient context sensitive pointer analysis for C programs. In *Proceedings of the ACM SIGPLAN Conference on Programming Languages Design and Implementation*, 1995.

[10] Y. Hollander, M. Morley, and A. Noy. The e language: A fresh separation of concerns. In *Proceedings of TOOLS-38*, 2001.

[11] T. Kuhn, T. Oppold, M. Winterholer, W. Rosenstiel, M. Edwards, and Y. Kashai. A framework for object oriented hardware specification, verification, and synthesis. In *Proceedings of the Design Automation Conference (DAC'2001)*, 2001.

[12] J. Madsen and J.P. Brage. Modeling shared variables in VHDL. *Transactions on the ACM*, 1994.

[13] www.cisco.com.

[14] C. Schulz-Key, T. Kuhn, and W. Rosenstiel. A framework for system-level partitioning of object-oriented specifications. In *Proceedings of the tenth workshop on Synthesis and System Integration of Mixed Technologies (SASIMI'2001)*, Nara, Japan, 2001.

Embedded Systems Technologies for Application-Specific Architecture Platforms

Pierre G. Paulin

STMicroelectronics
Central R&D, SoC Platform Automation
16 Fitzgerald Rd. Suite 300,
Nepean, Ontario, K2H 8R6, Canada
pierre.paulin@st.com

Extended Abstract

This talk addresses the emerging architectural platform approach to improve time-to-market, and the design automation technologies needed to support it. Architectural platforms can be defined as a domain- or application-specific base design which is easily configured to the specific needs of a given market. An experimental network processing platform developed at STMicroelectronics [1] will be presented to illustrate the concept. Key platform automation challenges will be introduced.

In order to best exploit the inherent capabilities of a network processor architecture, a powerful embedded software development toolset is required in order to support high-level descriptions of the algorithms running on the processor. This ensures time-to-market, code readability and easy portability. Moreover, the toolset must support the rapid platform and/or processor configuration.

We have based the network processor's toolset on STMicroelectronics internal "FlexWare" [2] embedded software development environment, already used at ST for a wide range of application-specific DSP's and MCU's used in consumer audio [3], wireless telecom, video processing [4] and other applications [5], [6].

The current FlexWare environment is a retargettable suite of four tools:

1. FlexCC: High-performance C compiler technology
2. FlexSim: High-speed instruction-set simulator model generator
3. FlexGdb: Source-level debug toolset
4. FlexPerf: Performance analysis of the embedded S/W and processor pair.

We present the technical characteristics of the FlexWare technologies and demonstrate their application on the ST experimental network processor. In particular, we emphasize the architecture exploration capability that is supported by the retargettability of the FlexWare tools. This will allow customers to fine tune the architecture to their specific needs. This flexibility is a key requirement in the fast changing network processor market environment.

References

[1] P. G. Paulin, F. Karim, P. Bromley, "Network Processors: A Perspective on Market Requirements, Processor Architectures and Embedded S/W Tools", Proc. of Design Automation and Test in Europe (DATE), Munich, March 2001.

[2] C. Liem, P. G. Paulin, "Compilation Techniques and Tools for Embedded Processor Architectures", in Hardware/ Software Co-Design: Principles and Practice, J. Staunstrup, W. Wolf (editors), Kluwer Academic Publishers, 1997.

[3] L. Bergher, X. Figari, F. Frederikson, M. Froidevaux, "MPEG Audio Decoder for Consumer Applications", *Proc. Of CICC*, 1995.

[4] M. Harrand et al, "A Single Chip Videophone Video Encoder/Decoder", *International Solid State Circuits Conference*, Feb. 1995, pp. 292-293.

[5] C. Liem, P. G. Paulin, A. Jerraya, "Industrial Experience Using Rule-Driven Retargetable Code Generation for Multimedia Applications", *Intl. Symposium on System-Level Synthesis*, Cannes, Sept. 1995.

[6] P. G. Paulin, "A Flexible HW/SW Development Environment and its Application to Consumer Multimedia Product Designs", *Presented at.CODES/CASHE*, Seattle, Jan. 1999.

ISSS'01, October 1-3, 2001, Montréal, Québec, Canada.
ACM 1-58113-418-5/01/0010.

System Design of a Telecommunication Router

Richard Norman
President & CTO, Hyperchip
1800 René Levesque West
Montreal, Quebec, H3H 2H2, Canada
rnorman@hyperchip.com

Extended Abstract

The demand for telecommunication bandwidth continues to grow rapidly, fuelled by increasing numbers of users, increasing time per user, and increasing connection speeds. Optical fibres can cope with this bandwidth explosion; the fastest links deployed today pack 3.2 terabits down a hair-thin glass fiber, and a modern bundle has hundreds of fiber strands. With ultra-long-haul optics driving photons across the continent without regeneration, lighting petabits per bundle will soon be practical.

But while the optics can handle petabits of traffic, today's routers still require converting the traffic to electrons to re-route the traffic at each hop, an average of ten times across the network core. If a router could scale to match the optics, packets could be routed only once onto a wavelength that would be optically transported to its destination city with no need for intermediate electronics. Hyperchip has developed such a router based on a system architecture that scales to support up to petabits of aggregate bandwidth.

A router consists of complex software for maintaining routing and forwarding tables, dedicated hardware to parse packets and forward them according to those tables, a switch fabric to transfer packets from interface card to interface card, and traffic managers to optimise traffic flow through the switch fabric. While some hardware is implemented in reprogrammable logic, the switch fabric hardware must be in leading edge ASICs for performance, density and minimal power consumption.

In Hyperchip's case the switch fabric ASICs have 4.3 million gates with 3.2 million bits of embedded dual-port SRAM. Although these Matrix ASICs are large, their complexity and size are manageable as long as the design tools can handle multiple levels of hierarchy; the design has 100,000 unique gates in 5 blocks, and the entire 16.6mmX16.6mm die is built from cookie-cutter repetition of these blocks. The largest blocks are 16 identical customized ARC microprocessor cores that control the configuration and monitoring of the 300 dedicated packet processing pipelines.

These switch fabric chips gain their throughput through parallelism rather than through speed; the entire Matrix ASIC runs only at 155 MHz, but with 16 complete datapaths with 32 bits in each direction, the total I/O bandwidth is 160 Gb/sec per chip. The peak internal bandwidth is even higher; in the most extreme case, over 300 reads and 300 writes can occur simultaneously within a chip, for a total internal memory bandwidth of over 3 terabits/second. The matrix chips can be run in parallel planes to increase channel speeds, and can be arrayed in multiple stages to scale to 65,536 ports of any channel speed. Because each matrix chip is self-buffering and self-scheduling, packets can be starting on any port at any time.

Such ASICs are not easy to design, especially with their complex interaction with FPGA-based firmware and complex control software. Large (and dense) designs are also not easy to implement in deep-sub-micron technology. Therefore it was essential to start with a high-level architectural description and proceed toward a gate-level implementation, with optimisation and validation at every step of the way. A full suite of synthesis tools proved essential to the task, including:

For FPGA design: Mentor Modelsim for RTL and gate level simulation; Mentor Leonardo for synthesis; Xilinx place and route tools

For ASIC design: Mentor Modelsim for RTL and sometime gate level, Synopsys VCS is also use; Synopsys SysOpp for synthesis; Mentor FormalPro for netlist equivalency checking; IBM suite of tools for timing, floorplaning, Scan insertion, etc.

Other tools where used at IBM associate with their design process like rules checking and margin analysis. Some drivers analysis where done with Hspice analog simulator

Extensive use of synthesis tools allowed a very aggressive schedule to be met; from ASIC design freeze June to ASICs in April, and from an FPGA design freeze in November to product in the lab in May. Dealing with a higher level of abstraction as long as possible in the design phase also allowed numerous possibilities to be explored quickly; for example, the 16x1 logical cell vector was initially intended to be implemented as a 4x4 physical cell array, whereas a 2x8 physical array proved significantly more practical.

Even with synthesis from a high-level design, extra validation at the gate level was needed before committing to silicon. Because the interaction of several hundred fast pipelines per chip is incredibly demanding for a gate-level simulation, an array of Xilinx FPGAs was used for additional gate-level design validation (this reduced the time to run 1 million packets per port from 28 days to ½ second!). Of course shifting between FPGA and ASIC designs as the system was tested and tuned put even more emphasis onto the synthesis tools to allow maximal reuse of the detailed designs.

This paper will cover the techniques used and the lessons learned in bringing such a large ASIC and such complex FPGAs to fruition on such a short timetable, and how synthesis and simulation were aggressively employed to ensure first-pass silicon and system success.

ISSS'01, October 1-3, 2001, Montréal, Québec, Canada.
ACM 1-58113-418-5/01/0010.

Network Processing in Content Inspection Applications

Feliks Welfeld
Solidum Systems
1575 Carling Avenue, Ottawa, ON K1Z 7M3
613-724-6004
Feliks.welfeld@solidum.com

ABSTRACT

This paper will show how NP can be used for complicated tasks including advanced classification of packets. Advanced classification requires the NP to look beyond the layer 3-4 header of the protocol, deep into the session and application layer payload. Dubbed "content inspection", such advanced classification requires specialized high-performance ICs, and a powerful and sophisticated set of tools for programming the ICs. These tools enable users of advanced classifiers to describe protocols using a high-level formal language, and then build classification policy with the help of an API. Complimented by policy verification and system simulation tools, content inspection will bring the required ease of use and processing power into the hands of communication systems designers.

1. INTRODUCTION

Network Processing is a new and rapidly growing sector of the communications integrated circuit (IC) industry. It is defined as a system of interconnected programmable devices performing wire speed processing of Protocol Data Units (PDUs) on the forwarding plane of a data communication device. And it has emerged as a direct result of the growing demand for enhanced, next generation communication services.

Network processing consists of four primary functions:

- **Classification**, which establishes a relationship between a PDU and one or many members of a finite set of classes. Class is an abstract that can be expressed as an action or as a number;
- **Modification**, which changes the contents of a PDU. In this case, by modification we mean PDU header editing, not massive payload modifications. Header editing involves insertion, removal and replacing of header fields;
- **Traffic Management**, which shapes PDU traffic. This involves queuing PDUs for transmission with potential discard of PDUs based on a pre-defined discard policy; and
- **Encryption**, which encrypts and decrypts the PDU payload.

These functions are usually managed in network edge hardware such as switches, routers and gateways.

ISSS'01, October 1-3, 2001, Montréal, Québec, Canada.

2. THE NETWORK PROCESSING CHALLENGE

To deliver enhanced, next generation services like converged voice and data, streaming video, point-and-click calling, secure virtual private networks, and differentiated Quality of Service (QoS) levels, system designers must address the challenge of building a network processing architecture that efficiently executes each network processing function. That architecture must be fast enough to process traffic, flexible enough to allow for application specific functions and future upgrades, and reliable enough to provide an opportunity to guarantee service quality.

The first network processing solutions emerged as highly integrated functional ICs called Network Processors, which were designed to manage all network processing functions. But as the data rates in the network continued to grow, surpassing the scaling capabilities of semiconductor devices, it became obvious that disintegration in the functional capability built into a semiconductor device would have to happen in order for it to cope with the growing demand for speed. This disintegration occurred along the lines of the logical network processing functions, commonly referred to as functional blocks.

As a result system designers are now addressing the network processing challenge by mating a network processor with a co-processor that is designed to perform a specific network processing function.

A co-processor is usually designed to perform a specific task and it offloads that task from the network processor. In most cases a co-processor can offer higher performance at reduced power levels when compared to a network processor. Some co-processors are fully programmable, while others are only configurable. Both result in reduced development time for the system designer.

There are ASICs today that are custom-designed to perform all network processing functions. But the demand for enhanced communication services has put a strain on traditional network processing methods. And the difference between these devices and network processing devices is programmability, a critical consideration for next generation network systems.

3. NETWORK PROCESSING IN NEXT GENERATION NETWORKS

Carrier data networks have evolved as a non-homogenous set of end-user stations, servers and communication devices connected by electrical, optical and wireless links. There are many different classification schemes and criteria used to define different segments or areas of the network. For our purposes we are interested in considering two distinct segments of the network: the edge and the core.

The edge of the network is where the subscriber connects to the service provider and where the service provider connects to the carrier. The core of the network is where service providers connect to each other through a carrier network.

The core of the network deals with aggregated and faster traffic. Therefore, the ability to perform sophisticated processing in the core is limited. But given the reliance of core equipment vendors on custom silicon, the relative simplicity of processing, and the high data rates, we can expect that network processing in the core will take place later.

Meanwhile, the network processing approach to the management of traffic will be more widely used at the edge. Network devices on the edge often work at an aggregation point where all the information that is needed to determine Quality-of-Service levels and application processing criteria is available. Therefore, it is logical to examine different types of traffic and decide how this traffic will traverse the rest of the network. And if these decisions are made at the edge, then the processing of PDUs in the core will be easier.

4. THE ROLE OF CLASSIFICATION

Out of the four key functions of network processing—classification, modification, encryption and traffic management—one stands aside. It is PDU classification.
Based on the definitions of the four functions outlined above, it is logical to conclude that classification is the first function that must be performed when a PDU enters the system. Classification drives the rest of the network processing functions. It tells them what needs to be done with the PDU, depending on the class to which it belongs.

Therefore, the granularity of classification that is performed and the complexity of classification criteria that the network processing solution can handle, will determine how intelligent and powerful the networking device will be.

There are three types of classification that can be performed by networking devices:

- single-field (SF) classification;
- multi-field (MF) classification; and
- content inspection

Single field classification, which looks at a single field in the protocol header, is the most rudimentary and well-understood type of classification. It is typically performed in MAC bridging and IP routing. In these applications one field is being extracted from the protocol header and its value is usually looked up in a table. The result of the look-up determines what happens to the PDU. As long as the field in not too wide existing hardware solutions can handle the processing required and a co-processor approach to classification is not needed.

Multi-field classification is more complicated. With this type of classification the lookup key is more complex (longer and composite), the set of values is richer, and the process of forming the key is more complicated. In these applications, the ability to extract a field's values—to parse the field—is more important.

In a fixed protocol environment, where all protocol headers have a well-known fixed offset from the beginning of a PDU, parsing is relatively easy—IPv4 over 802.3 is a good example. But in multi-protocol environments, where PDUs are often encapsulated in protocols such as L2TP, PPP, IPsec, with MPLS shims—complex parsing operations are required in order to get to desired fields in the PDU.

Typical applications for this type of classification are IP services devices and multi-service switches with features such as DiffServ and Access Control List (ACL). For these types of applications a classification co-processor is ideal.

But it is still difficult to perform multi-field classification in protocol environments such as IPv6, where headers have a variable length.

Given the tendency for edge devices to provide increasingly intelligent traffic management capabilities, there is a need for more granular and powerful classification. That classification capability is provided by content inspection.

Content inspection classification refers to the ability to examine deeply into packet content in order to make classification decisions based on long character string values (i.e. hundreds of characters).

For example, this content inspection can be used to locate the Uniform Resource Locator (URL) and the cookie in a Hypertext Transfer Protocol (HTTP) header.

This is particularly useful for networking equipment deployed in front of large and very busy Web server farms, such as server load balancers and URL switches.

In order to perform content inspection the processor must parse five layers of protocol headers and then perform regular expression matching. This type of classification is best performed by a classification processor, which can look for patterns that involve hundreds of characters anywhere in the packet.

5. THE MECHANICS OF CONTENT INSPECTION

The HTTP is an application-level, request/response type protocol for distributed hypermedia information systems. It facilitates an open-ended set of methods and headers that indicate the purpose of a request.

The URL is the basis of an information request and subsequent interchange of data or metadata.

Additionally, a token or "cookie" provides a mechanism for maintaining a stateful HTTP stream between a client and a Web switch or origin server.

How does the server keep track of a particular customer?

It tracks the customer through the use of the cookie. The URL addresses a particular Web page or other information on the network. The way to distinguish between customers that at any given moment in time use the URL page is to issue a cookie, which is planted on the client machine.

Each HTTP request from the customer may also contain this cookie. The load balancer may use the cookie to direct requests to an appropriate server based on URL and cookie values contained in the HTTP header.

URLs take the form of an arbitrary text string such as h*ttp://*

Cookies usually take the form of *name* = *value* where *name* is an arbitrary string and the value is a string as well, representing a unique customer identification. Both URL field and the cookie field can have an arbitrary offset from the beginning of the packet. Both fields have arbitrary length.

As shown below, HTTP is an application layer encapsulated protocol. The HTTP protocol is based on a request/response paradigm.

A client establishes a connection with a web switch or server and sends a request to the server in the form of a request method, URL, and protocol version followed by a MIME-like message containing request modifiers, client information, and possible body content.

The server responds with a status line including the message's protocol version and a success or error code followed by a MIME-like message containing server information, entity meta-information, and possible body content. The response may also contain a cookie.

Most HTTP communication is initiated by a user agent and consists of a request to be applied to a resource on some origin server or web switch. For example:

Example 1
Ethernet II layer
Internet Protocol layer
Transmission Control Protocol layer
Hypertext Transfer Protocol Layer
GET /docs/products/index.html HTTP/1.0\r\n
User-Agent: Mozilla/4.72 [en] (X11; U; Linux 2.2.16 i586)\r\n
Host: www.solidum.com\r\n
Accept: text/html, text/plain, audio/mod, image/*, video/*, vi
Accept: x-sun-attachment, audio-file, postscript-file, default
Accept: application/postscript, */*;q=0.01\r\n
Accept-Encoding: gzip, compress\r\n
Accept-Language: en\r\n\r\n

A content inspection classification processor applies predefined and programmed filters and policies against the HTTP protocol stream received. It separates the HTTP protocol into fields and then applies a set of rules against the fields.

The following example illustrates how the HTTP input stream depicted in the previous section is broken into manageable fields to be operated upon by a classification processor.

Example 2
String "GET "
Prefix "/docs/products/"
Wildcard "*" (Random amount of characters)
Suffix ".html "
Random amount of characters
String "\r\nHost: "
Host "www.solidum.com"
String "\r\n"

6. PROGRAMMING CLASSIFICATION

There are new non-procedural languages such as XML or well known languages such as SQL that reduce the complexity of classification programming significantly while still being formal enough to be easily translatable or interpretable into machine instructions. One such language is Solidum's PAX Pattern Description Language (PDL).

Solidum's PDL is a fourth-generation language used to describe data structures or patterns that need to be recognized in bit streams or PDUs. It enables the user to describe protocol headers as patterns. A pattern is represented as a list of fields and each field is identified by its name and specific type in order to allow conditions to be imposed upon it:

Example 3
For example, an Ethernet header can be described as
```
PATTERN Ethernet_Hdr {
DestMACAddr BIT 48;/* 48 bit MAC Destination address */
SrcMACAddr  BIT 48;/* 48 bit MAC Source address */
Ethertype   UINT 16 == 0x0800/* 16-bit Ethertype, with */
                        /*condition - *//* indicates IP protocol*/
}
```

The language provides the ability of describing an arbitrary string as part of the pattern:

Example 4
```
PATTERN HelloString {
string ASCII "Hello, World"; /*string field */
}
```

Parametric patterns can be defined where values of certain fields are not known, ahead of time. This feature enables the specification of run-time parameters such as IP addresses, TCP/UDP ports and values of URL and cookies. For example, the previous pattern could be defined as:

Example 5
```
PATTERN ParametricString  (regEX STRING){
String          ASCII 12 == regEx;  /* contents of the field must match the regular expression passed as parameter */
}
```

In this case, the following pattern would be equivalent to the original one:

```
HellloString
ParametricString ("Hello, World");
```

The following example shows how the HTTP request header is coded using PAX PDL.

Example 6

```
/* first the request line of the header */
PATTERN HTTP_REQUEST_LINE (url STRING )
{
  method [
    method_get  ASCII "GET ";
    method_post ASCII "POST ";
  ];
  request_url TOKEN_AFTER_SPACES( url );
  rest_of_line ASCII "[^\n]*\n"
};

/* and now the whole request header including the request
line and a cookie */

PATTERN HTTP_REQUEST ( url STRING,
                    cookie_name STRING,
                    cookie_value STRING )
{
  request_line    HTTP_REQUEST_LINE ( url );
  request_headers HTTP_HEADERS ( cookie_name,
                       cookie_value );
};
```

This example describes the generic parametric pattern for an HTTP request. This pattern is used to match packets that contain specific values in place of parameters. One way to create a pattern with specific values is to substitute parameters at compile time:

```
HTTP_REQUEST ("/docs/products/index.html",
                  "ISON",
              "yes")
```

In most cases, however, parameters will be substituted at run-time when the application is running. It is done by run-time API, once the application gathers parameters from the management plane.

7. COMPILATION

Patterns need to be compiled ahead of time in order to minimize the run-time processing. All patterns for a cookie-switching application are known while the application is being developed, thus the compilation never needs to happen at run-time. The compiler creates a binary object that we call a filter. In this case, since the pattern contains parameters for the URL, the cookie name and the cookie value, the result of compilation will be a set of "parametric filters".

8. BUILDING THE APPLICATION

In order for the application to control the classification processor at run-time, a run-time library of functions is required. This library is accessed through the Application Program Interface (API). The API uses the library of filters in order to build a classifier. There are three steps involved:

1. Installation of a parametric filter from the library;
2. Creation of a filter instance by substituting parameters to the parametric filter;
3. Creation of a classifier by assigning the actions or tags to the filter instances, and combining together a number of such filter/action pairs.

Once the classification processor is loaded into the co-processor pattern memory, it can be executed.

Solidum's PAX.port family of classification processors employ a programmable state machine architecture. The program is represented in the form of a state graph. Each bit or group of bits in the packet causes a state transition. All possible state transitions that will match various patterns are built into the graph during compilation and subsequent run-time construction of classification on the control plane. Therefore, the data plane performance of the processor is invariant of the number of patterns that it matches.

Once the pattern match is found, the processor produces the tag that was specified by the application when the classifier was built. The tag represents a unique identifier of either URL or URL and cookie combination.

9. THE ROLE OF STANDARDS IN NETWORK PROCESSING

Where do standards fit into all this?

As the industry evolves into a multi-vendor, multi-part environment, it will be necessary to ensure that all co-processors can interface and work with each other.

A typical architecture of a network processing-based networking device contains hardware devices implementing different functional blocks and software pieces from a variety of vendors. The only way for these products to be delivered to the market in time is to base them on standard interfaces—both hardware interfaces between the parts and software interfaces to these parts.

Semiconductor and networking equipment vendors are putting a significant effort on standardization. And there are a number of standards organizations working on network processing and adjacent standards.

The Network Processing Forum (NPF – www.npforum.org) is the major industry organization working on standardization of all aspects of network processing. And the Optical Internetworking Forum (OIF – www.oiforum.com) in its Physical and Link Layer (PLL) working group is doing work on inter-chip communications that is closely related to the work being done by the NPF.

Hardware interfaces are being specified at two levels:

- electrical interconnect between chips; and
- logical protocols for passing information between chips

There are three areas where interfaces are being standardized:

- between a framer and a network processor;
- between different parts (or functional blocks) of a network processor; and
- between a network processor and the switch fabric.

The focus of these efforts is on ensuring that there is as much commonality in these interfaces as possible. The strong preference is to have the same electrical interface in all three areas. Logical protocols are being layered, so that the differences between the interfaces appear at the highest possible layer, leaving the lower layers as similar as possible.

In addition, software interfaces are being specified to allow applications to be independent of the hardware implementations of IP.

10. THE NEED FOR CLASSIFICATION PROCESSING

It is clear that a classification processor is the key element in any network processing architecture. High level languages like PAX PDL are being proposed by several vendors for use with a classification processor. Making such a language standard will help to promote the use of classification co-processors for performing content inspection in policy-based communications equipment.

Those processors in turn, will enable the delivery of enhanced, next generation services like converged voice and data, streaming video, point-and-click calling, secure virtual private networks, and differentiated Quality of Service (QoS) levels.

They will allow system designers to address the challenge of building a network processing architecture that efficiently executes each network processing function. An architecture that is fast enough to process traffic, flexible enough to allow for application specific functions and future upgrades, and reliable enough to provide an opportunity to guarantee service quality.

Panel

Programming Models for Network Processors

Moderator: A.A. Jerraya
TIMA, France

Panelists:

P. Paulin
STMicroelectronics - Ottawa
Canada

R. Norman
Hyperchip Inc.- Montreal
Canada

Feliks J. Welfeld
Solidum Systems - Ottawa
Canada

NOTES

Synthesis of Configurable Linear Feedback Shifter Registers for Detecting Random-Pattern-Resistant Faults

Chien-In Henry Chen
Department of Electrical Engineering
Wright State University
Dayton, Ohio 45435 U.S.A.
E-mail: cihchen@cs.wright.du

ABSTRACT

In this paper we describe an optimized BIST scheme which has a configurable 2-D LFSR structure. A synthesis procedure for this test generator is presented. Experimental results show that the hardware overhead is considerably reduced compared with 2-D LFSR generators. The experiment result shows that compared with the non-configurable 2-D LFSR, the average number of flip-flops is reduced by 79% for five benchmark circuits. The average number of faults detected by the configurable 2-D LFSR is 9.27% higher than that of the conventional LFSR and 0.57% higher than that of the non-configurable 2-D LFSR.

1. INTRODUCTION

Ever-increasing VLSI circuit density has made today's chip testing more complicated and costly. Built-in self-test (BIST) has been proven to be an effective approach to achieve sufficiently high, if not complete, fault coverage without any external automatic test equipment on site. It has revolutionized the way the integrated circuit chips can be tested by 1) reducing the cost of manufacturing testing by shortening the test application time, 2) minimizing the amount of test data stored, and 3) lowing the cost of test equipment. The implementation of BIST can result in a reduction of the product development cycle and cost, and the cost of system maintenance can be significantly reduced by testing chips, boards, and the entire system virtually using BIST.

Typical BIST architecture consists of a test pattern generator and a test response analyzer. The efficiency of BIST implementation can be characterized by test length and hardware overhead for a given fault coverage requirement which is defined as the ratio of the number of faults that can be detected to the total number of faults in the assumed fault domain. It is expected that BIST insertion to integrated circuit chips will result in high fault coverage, small volume of test data, at-system test speed, and compatibility with the design for testability techniques.

There have been various BIST techniques based on pseudo-random testing [1,9], pseudo-exhaustive testing [2,10,11], weighted random testing [3,12,13], and reseeding of LFSR [5-7]. These approaches offer different trade-off among test data volume, test application time, hardware overhead and fault coverage. One of the most popular approaches is the pseudo-random BIST, which employs an LFSR to generate a large number of test patterns with small hardware overhead. The major limitations with this method are the long test time and low fault coverage. Several approaches have been proposed to overcome these disadvantages, most of which embed a set of pre-computed test vectors, called deterministic patterns, to reach high fault coverage within a shorter time. Such deterministic patterns can be obtained by an automatic test pattern generation (ATPG) and implemented with a ROM to store the patterns, or the traditional LFSRs with pre-designed seeds to generate the patterns.

Recently, another method was presented to realize both pseudo-random pattern generation and deterministic pattern embedding using a 2-D LFSR [8]. With the two-dimensional feedback algorithm, it can achieve higher fault coverage than the conventional LFSR due to improved randomness. In this paper, our focus is to reduce the hardware overhead by proposing a configurable 2-D LSFR based BIST scheme.

2. 2-D LFSR

A conventional LFSR can be used to generate a large number of pseudo-random test patterns with very small area overhead that is composed of exclusive-or gates (XORs) and flip-flops (FFs). The general structure is shown in Fig. 1, which can be expressed with the polynomial in Eq. (1). The coefficients *Ci (i = 1~M-1)* are zero or one.

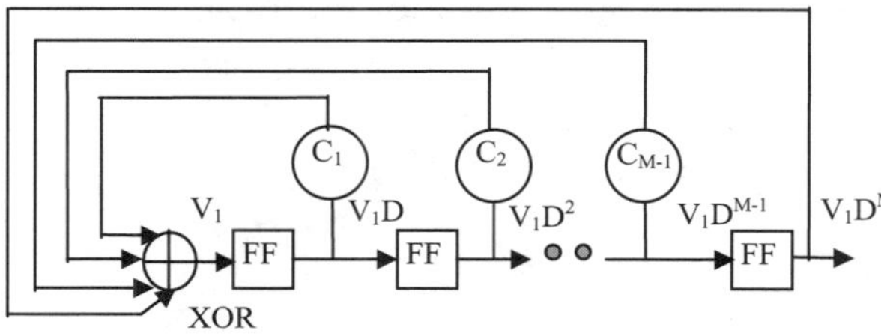

Figure 1. A conventional LFSR.

$$P(V) = 1 + C_1V + C_2V^2 + \ldots + C_{M-1}V^{M-1} \quad (1)$$

An LFSR goes through a cyclic sequence of states and the outputs produced are also periodic. The maximum length of this period is $2^M - 1$, where M is the number of stages. So the patterns generated by an LFSR are pseudo-random and the random properties depend on its initial state and its generating function $P(V)$. Once the generating function and the initial state are fixed, the patterns produced are also determined. It also can not produce a sequence of deterministic ordered patterns that are required to detect the random-pattern-resistant faults. A number of the LFSR based techniques [5-7] have been developed to generate deterministic ordered test patterns but the encoding and decoding procedures and the implementation of control logic are relatively complex. A 2-D LFSR structure was presented in [8]. This generator can generate a set of pre-computed test vectors for detecting random-pattern-resistant faults. In addition, it can generate better random patterns than a conventional LFSR. Fig. 2 shows the general representation of a 2-D LFSR based on N primitive polynomials:

$$V_i = \sum_{j=1}^{N} \sum_{k=1}^{M} a_{ijk} V_j D^k + C_i \ , \quad i = 1 \sim N \qquad (2)$$

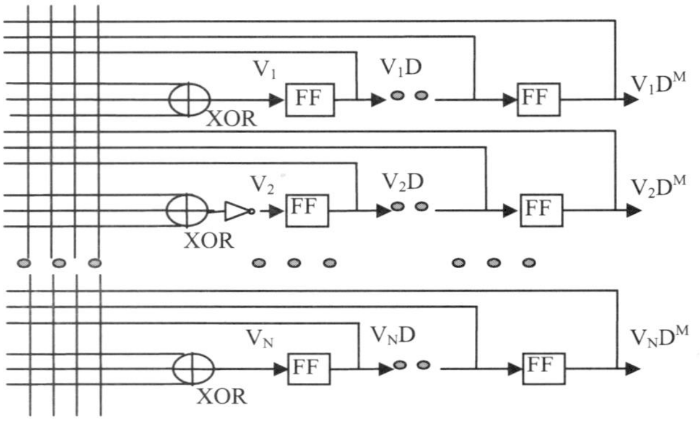

Figure 2: 2-D LFSR.

This circuit consists of N shift registers, each of which has M stages. V_i $(i=1 \sim N)$ represents an N-bit vector, and V_iD^k $(k=1 \sim M)$ represents the kth delay of a vector V_i. V_i is generated by the feedback network given by Eq. (2). If $a_{ijk}=1$, the signal V_jD^k is connected to the XOR gate to generate V_i. Otherwise, there is no connection. If $C_i=0$, the output of the XOR gate is connected to the shift register directly. If $C_i=1$, then an inverter is added to the input of the shift register for generating a complementary feedback signal. Given L vectors with a length of N-bit,

V_1: $b_{11}, b_{12}, b_{13}, \ldots, b_{1L}$

V_2: $b_{21}, b_{22}, b_{23}, \ldots, b_{2L}$

...

...

V_N: $b_{N1}, b_{N2}, b_{N3}, \ldots, b_{NL}$.

To generate these vectors in a 2-D LFSR with minimum stage M, we construct Eq. (3) and obtain the solutions by determining the minimum value of M.

$$V_i(n) = \sum_{j=1}^{N} \sum_{k=1}^{M} a_{ijk} V_j(n-k) + C_i \qquad (3)$$

where $V_i(n) = b_{i,n}$, $V_j(n-k) = V_j(n)D^k = b_{j,(n-k)}$, $i = 1 \sim N$ and $n = 1 \sim L$. When solving the first vector $V_i(1)$, $V_j(1-k)$ represents the initial states of the 2-D LFSR. An optimization to Eq. (3) is described below:

```
{ M = 1; /* M is the no. of FF stages of 2-D LFSR */

    Set initial states of 1st stage FF's;
    Given all Vi's(i=1~N); /* each Vi represents an N-bit
                                       vector*/

    While ( a_ijk for all Vi's are not solved ) {

        if ( a_ijk for V_i is solved) return;

        for (each unsolved V_i ) {
            Formulate Eq. (3) and set C_i = 0 ;
            Assign a_ijk values to Eq. (3);
            if ( a_ijk values are valid)
                mark signal V_i SOLVED;
            else {
              use branch & bound method to obtain a
                    new set of a_ijk values;
              if ( a_ijk values are valid) {
                  mark signal V_i SOLVED;
              }
            }

         if ( V_i is not SOLVED ) {
           Formulate Eq. (3) and set C_i = 1 ;
           Assign a set of a_ijk values to Eq. (3);
           if ( a_ijk values are valid)
              mark signal V_i SOLVED;
           else {
               use branch & bound method to obtain
                   a new set of a_ijk values;
               if ( a_ijk values are valid) {
                   mark signal V_i SOLVED;
               }
           }
         }
        } /* unsolved signal Vi */

      M = M+1;
      Set initial states of M-th stage FF's;

    } /* time frame */
} /* end */
```

In addition to embed the deterministic sequence, the 2-D LFSR can generate better pseudo-random patterns than a conventional LFSR according to the experimental results in [8]. The longer the deterministic sequence is, the more stages of a 2-D LFSR are required, which means more hardware required. For some practical circuits, a large overhead is unacceptable. In the next section, a feasible configuration scheme based on a 2-D LFSR to reduce the overhead is proposed.

3. CONFIGURABLE 2-D LFSR

A configurable 2-D LFSR based test pattern generator is proposed to generate an embedded deterministic sequence of test patterns followed by pseudo-random patterns. The generator mainly consists of four types of function blocks – the flip-flop array (FFA), the configuration networks (CN), the multiplexers (MUXs), and the control unit (CU) as shown in Fig. 3. The FFA is an $N \times M$ flip-flop array, where N is the number of inputs of a circuit under test (CUT) and M is the number of stages of the 2-D LFSR. To reduce the hardware, M is usually a small number. If Eq. (3) cannot be solved with a small value of M, the embedded test sequence is then partitioned into multiple subsequences embedded by a configurable scheme. Each CN consists of XOR gates and an inverter if necessary. The MUX selects one of the p configuration networks to feed the feedback signals to the FFA. The MUX is controlled by the CU. When resetting the generator, the initial states of FFA are set to <1010...>, alternating 1 and 0, in each column of the FFA.

The synthesis procedure for a configurable 2-D LFSR is shown in Fig. 4 with two main tasks: (1) find a set of deterministic ordered patterns and (2) embed these patterns to the configurable 2-D LFSR. HITEC [4] is used as an ATPG to generate a set of test patterns for detecting random-pattern-resistant faults. With the deterministic sequence of test patterns generated by the ATPG, all coefficients a_{ijk}'s of Eq. (3) are to be obtained by the optimization procedures. The number of stages, M, in the 2-D LFSR reflects the hardware complexity. Given a small value of M, the solution space may not be large enough to obtain all a_{ijk}'s of Eq. (3); therefore, partitioning the original sequence of test patterns into consecutive multiple subsequences are required. As the length of each subsequence decreases, Eq. (3) can be solved with a small M.

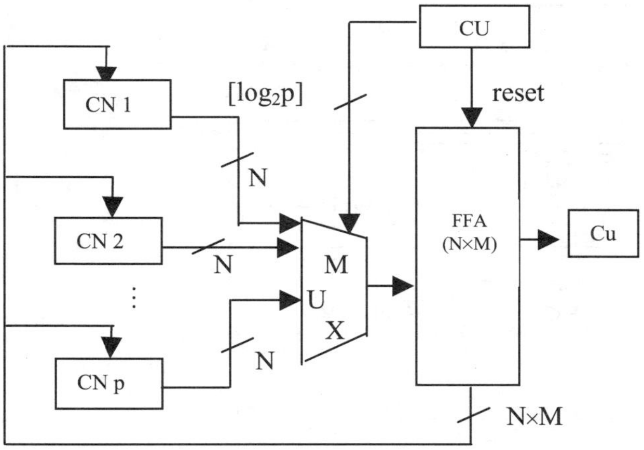

Figure 3: Configurable 2-D LFSR.

The following is an example to show the effectiveness of the configurable 2-D LFSR based generator. Given a deterministic sequence of 18 6-bit patterns with the initial seed <101010>, both a configurable and a non-configurable 2-D LFSRs are generated. Fig. 5 shows the configurable 2-D LFSR with $M = 1$ and $p = 2$ and Fig. 6 shows the non-configurable 2-D LFSR with $M = 5$. In Fig. 5, feeding the initial seed <101010> back to

t →

	t1	t2	t3	t4	t5	t6	t7	t8	t9	t10	t11	t12	t13	t14	t15	t16	t17	t18
1:	1	0	1	0	0	0	0	1	1	1	0	0	1	0	1	1	1	0
2:	0	1	1	0	1	0	1	1	1	0	0	0	1	0	0	0	0	1
3:	1	1	1	1	0	0	0	1	0	0	1	1	0	0	0	1	0	0
4:	0	1	1	1	1	0	0	0	1	0	0	1	1	0	0	0	1	0
5:	0	0	1	1	1	0	1	1	0	1	0	1	1	1	0	0	1	0
6:	1	0	1	1	1	1	0	0	0	1	1	1	1	1	0	1	0	1

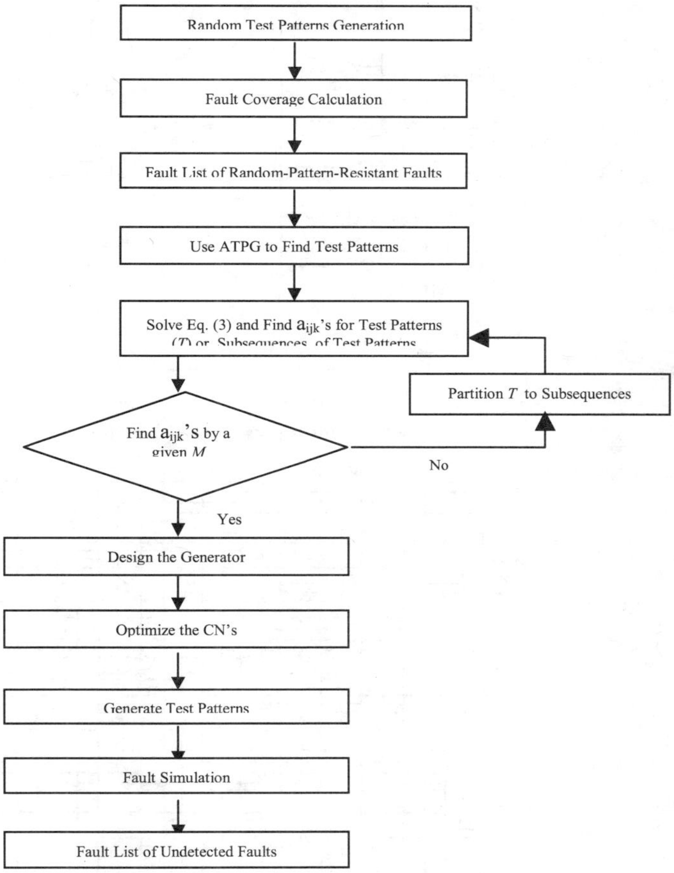

Figure 4: Synthesis of a configurable 2-D LFSR.

FFA through the configuration network CN1 generates the first test pattern <101001>. Other patterns are generated in sequence by following the same procedures until the ninth pattern <110100> are generated. In this configurable generator, the CN1 generates the first 9 patterns, <101001>, <011100>, <111111>, <001111>, <010111>, <000001>, <010010>, <111010> and <110100>. The CN2 generates the other 9 patterns, <100011>, <001001>, <001111>, <110111>, <000011>, <100000>, <101001>, <100110> and <010001>. The tenth pattern is generated with the ninth pattern <110100> feeding through the CN2. The CU with a modulo-9 counter controls this switch. With the optimization on the feedback network of Fig. 5 by assigning minimal number of 1's to a_{ijk}'s of Eq. (3), an optimized configurable 2-D LFSR is shown in Fig. 7.

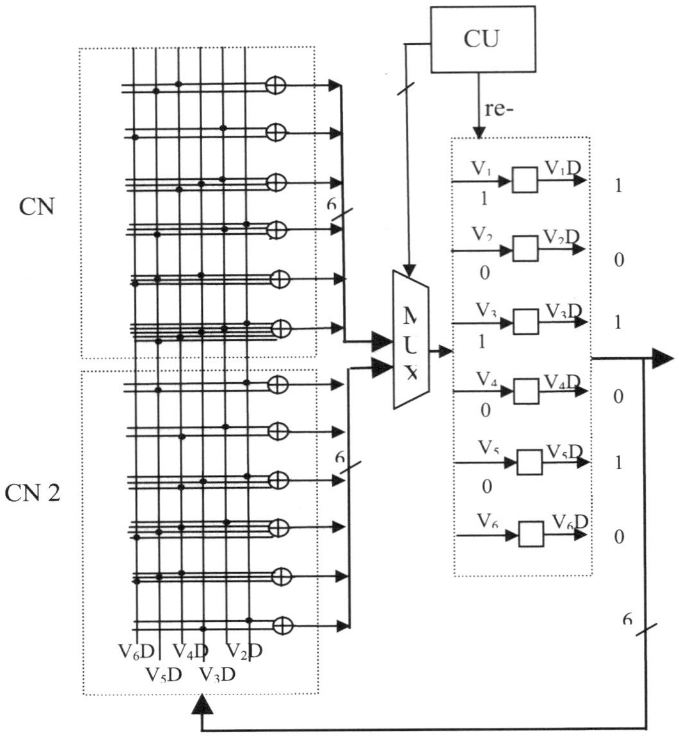

Figure 5: A configurable 2-D LFSR.

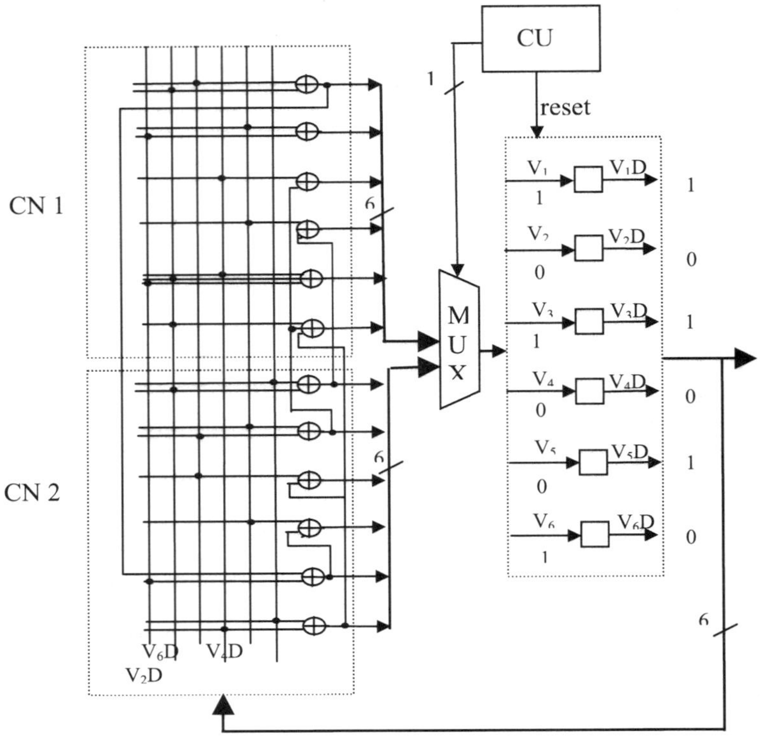

Figure 7: An optimized configurable 2-D LFSR.

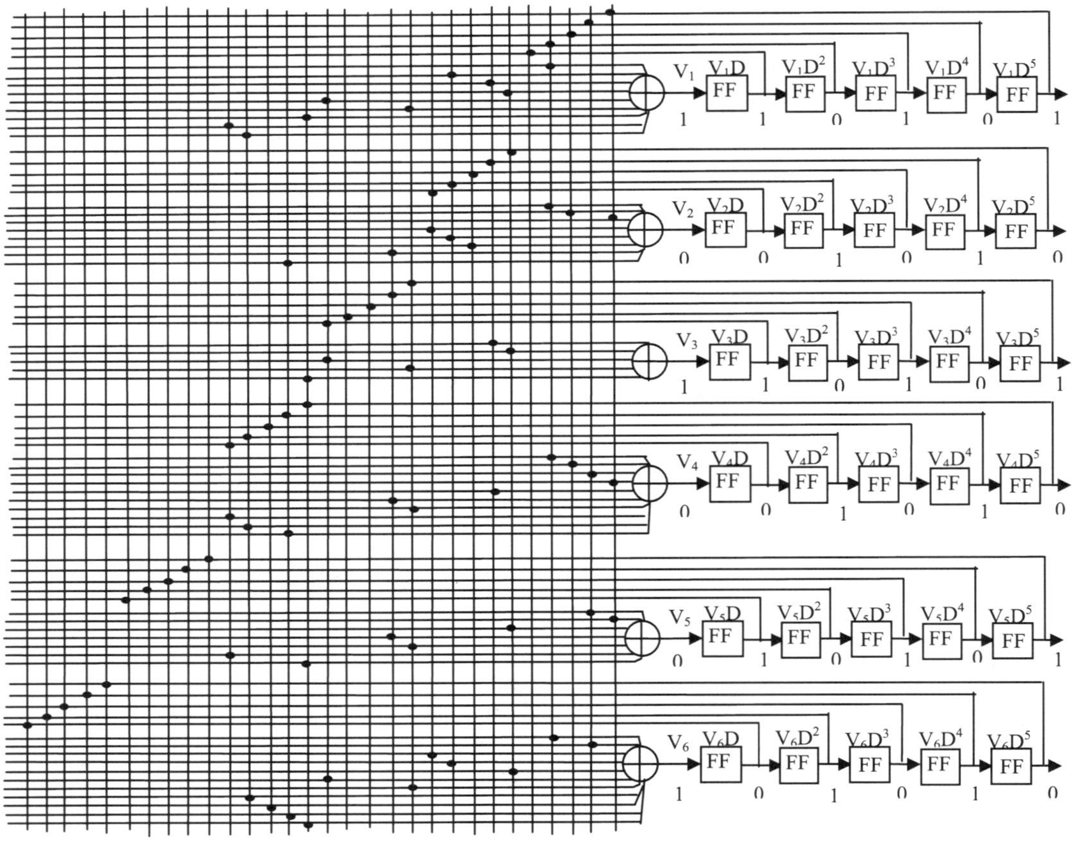

Figure 6: A 2-D LFSR test pattern generator.

4. EXPERIMENTAL RESULTS

Five synthesized circuits are used as benchmark circuits to evaluate the configuration structure of the 2-D LFSR scheme. The characteristics of the five circuits are summarized in Table 1. *Am2910* is a 12-bit microprogram sequencer, which has a stack of depth 5, a stack pointer, a microprogram counter, and a register counter (down counter). A 4-to-1 multiplexer selects the next microprogram address from either the input data bus, the stack, the register counter, or the microprogram counter. *Mult16* is a 16-bit 2's complement multiplier, which uses a shift-and-add algorithm. The control unit has been implemented using 3-bit and 4-bit counters. There is one start instruction. *Div16* is a 16-bit divider that uses repeated subtraction to perform division. A zero-detect unit checks for the divide-overflow condition and flags the termination of the repeated subtraction loop. *Pcont2* is an 8-bit parallel controller used in DSP applications. This circuit is composed of 8 adders, 2 fixed-point multipliers, and 3 MUXs -- all combinational logic. Three registers serve as delay elements. A global reset line resets all the registers, and new data is input at every clock cycle. There is no control unit. *Piir8* is an 8-point infinite impulse response (IIR) filter for DSP applications. It has a very regular structure with 7 adders, 8 fixed-point multipliers, 7 8-bit registers, and 7 2-to-1 MUXs. The data input and output buses are 8 bits wide. There is no control unit. A global reset line is the only control signal. In Table 2, the configuration and the original non-configuration results of 2-D LFSR for the five benchmark circuits are compared. The first column is the number of embedded deterministic patterns detecting the random-pattern-resistant faults for each circuit. The second and third columns give the stage number of shift registers and the total number of flip-flops for the non-configurable test generator. The number of configurations, the stage number of shift registers and the total number of flip-flops for the configurable 2-D LFSR are given in the fourth, fifth and sixth columns. The synthesis results of *am2910* and *mul16* in Table 2 show the number of flip-flops are significantly reduced from 260 to 40 (84.62%) and from 252 to 36 (85.71%), respectively. Because the number of embedded patterns for *div16*, *pcont2* and *piir8* is small, the synthesis procedure results in no reconfiguration. Among the benchmark circuits, *div16* require the largest number of flip-flops (330) due to its large number of primary inputs (33) which makes the Eq. (3) difficult to be solved. The number of flip-flop's stage (M) for *div16* can be reduced from 10 to 2 by increasing the number of interative loops in the branch and bound algorithm while solving Eq. (3). The number of flip-flop's is also reduced from 330 to 60 (81.82%). Table 3 shows the comparison of the test generation and fault simulation. The first and second columns show the number of equivalent single stuck-at faults and ATPG results of HITEC where "Det" represents the number of detected faults and "Vec" represents the number of test patterns. The fault simulation of the conventional LFSR is summarized in the third column. Column four "LFSR+Add" gives the fault simulation results of the conventional LFSR plus the deterministic sequence of test patterns that detect the random-pattern-resistant faults. The fault simulation results of the non-configurable 2-D LFSR and the configurable 2-D LFSR are summarized in the fifth and sixth columns. From Table 3 the average number of equivalent faults is 9,441 where 3,955 faults are detected by "HITEC." Comparing "LFSR," "LFSR+Add," and "2-D LFSR," the experimental results show that the average detected faults by "2-D LFSR" is 5,952 which is 5.08 % higher than 5,664 of"LFSR+Add" and 8.65 % higher than 5,478 of "LFSR" and 50.49% higher than 3,955 of "HITEC." The average number of faults detected by "Configurable 2-D LFSR" is 5,986, which is 0.57% higher than 5,952 of the 2-D LFSR. The average number of flip-flop's required by "Configurable 2-D LFSR" is 187 which is reduced by 78.92% in comparison with 887 flip-flop's required by "2-D LFSR."

Table 1: Characteristics of five synthesized circuits

Circuits	Seq. Depth	FFs	PIs	POs
am2910	4	87	20	16
mult16	9	55	18	33
div16	19	50	33	34
pcont2	3	24	9	8
piir8	5	56	9	8

Table 2: Hardware comparison of 2-D LFSR and configurable 2-D LFSR

		2D LFSR		Configurable 2D LFSR		
		Stgs (M)	Flip-flops	Cnfg. (P)	Stgs (M)	Flip-flops
am291	30	13	260	2	2	40
mul16	72	14	252	4	2	36
div16	21	10	330	1	2	66
pcont2	7	2	18	1	2	18
piir8	19	3	27	1	3	27
Total	149	-	887	-	-	187

Table 3. Test generation and fault simulation of five synthesized circuits

Ckts	Total Faults	HITEC		LFSR		LFSR + Add		2-D LFSR		Configurable 2-D LFSR	
		Det	Vec	Det	Vec	Det	Vec	Det	Vec	Det	Vec
Am2910	**2391**	2142	726	2126	2^{17}	2166	2^{17}+30	2188	2^{17}	2179	2^{17}
mult16	**1708**	1568	89	665	2^{17}	1395	2^{17}+89	1605	2^{17}	1605	2^{17}
div16	**2147**	1676	190	1679	2^{17}	1702	2^{17}+21	1705	2^{17}	1719	2^{17}
pcont2	**11272**	3147	7	6727	2^{17}	6727	2^{17}+7	6336	2^{17}	6518	2^{17}
piir8	**29689**	11234	19	16195	2^{17}	16331	2^{17}+19	17925	2^{17}	17913	2^{17}
Avg.	**9441**	3955	209	5478	2^{17}	5664	~2^{17}	5952	2^{17}	5986	2^{17}

5. CONCLUSION

A BIST scheme based on a configurable 2-D LFSR and procedures to design a test pattern generator has been presented. Without storage of test patterns and seeds, the 2-D LFSR test pattern generator can generate a sequence of deterministic test patterns as well as pseudo-random patterns. The hardware overhead of this BIST scheme decreased considerably through configuration. The experiment result shows that compared with the non-configurable 2-D LFSR, the average number of flip-flops is reduced by 78.21% for five synthesized circuits. The average number of faults detected by the configurable 2-D LFSR is 5,986 which is 51.35% higher than 3,955 of HITEC; 9.27% higher than 5,478 of the conventional LFSR; 5.69% higher than 5,664 of the "LFSR+ADD"; and 0.57% higher than 5,952 of the non-configurable 2-D LFSR.

In order to improve the fault coverage of the configurable 2-D LFSR, a minimal set of deterministic test patterns detecting random-pattern-resistant faults is needed. Logic optimization is also necessary to further reduce the hardware of the configuration networks.

6. REFERENCES

[1] P. Bardell, W.H. McAnney and J. Savir, Built-in Test for VLSI: Pseudorandom Techniques, Wiley & Sons, New York, 1987.

[2] C.-I. H. Chen and J. Yuen, "Automated Synthesis of Pseudo-Exhaustive Test Generator in VLSI BIST Design," *IEEE Trans. on VLSI Systems*, Vol. 2, No. 3, pp. 273-291, Sept. 1994.

[3] F. Brglez, et al., "Hardware-Based Weighted Random Pattern Generation for Boundary-Scan," *Proc. IEEE Int. Test Conf.*, pp. 264-274, 1989.

[4] T. M. Niermann and J. H. Patel, "HITEC: A Test Generation Package for Sequential Circuits," *Proc. European Conf. on Design Automation*, pp. 213-218, 1991.

[5] S. Hellebrand, S. Tarnick, J. Rajski, and B. Courtois, "Generation of Vector Patterns through Reseeding of Multiple-Polynomial Linear Feedback Shift Registers," *Proc. IEEE Int. Test Conf.*, pp. 120-129, 1992.

[6] S. Venkataraman, J. Rajski, S. Hellebrand, and S. Tarnick, "An Efficient BIST Scheme Based on Reseeding of Multiple Polynomial Linear Feedback Shift Registers," *Proc. Int. Conf. on Computer-Aided Design*, pp. 572-577, 1993.

[7] S. Hellebrand, et al., "Built-In Test for Circuits with Scan Based on Reseeding of Multiple-Polynomial Linear Feed-back Shift Registers," *IEEE Trans. on Comp.*, Vol. 44, No. 2, pp. 223-233, Feb. 1995.

[8] X. Yuan and C.-I. H. Chen, "Automated Synthesis of a Multiple-Sequence Test Generator Using 2-D LFSR," *Proc. IEEE International ASIC Conf.*, pp. 75-79, 1998.

[9] K. D. Wagner, C. K. Chin, and E. J. McCluskey, "Pseudorandom Testing," *IEEE Trans. on Comp.*, Vol. 36, No. 3, pp. 332-343, 1987.

[10] D. Kagaris, F. Makedon, and S. Tragoudas, "A Method for Pseudo-Exhaustive Test Pattern Generation," *IEEE Trans. on CAD*, Vol. 13, No. 9, pp. 1170-1178, 1994.

[11] H.-J. Wunderlich and S. Hellebrand, "The Pseudoexhaustive Test for Sequential Circuits," *IEEE Trans. on CAD*, Vol. 11, No. 1, pp. 26-32, 1992.

[12] R. Kapur, S. Patil, T. J. Snethen, and T. W. Williams, "Design of an Efficient Weighted Random Pattern Generation System," *Proc. ITC*, pp. 491-500, 1994.

[13] F. Muradali, V. K. Agarwal, and B. Nadeau-Dostie, "A New Procedure for Weighted Random Built-In Self-Test," *Proc. ITC*, pp. 660-669, 1990.

Methods for Optimizing Register Placement in Synchronous Circuits Derived Using Software Pipelining Techniques

Noureddine Chabini
LASSO, DIRO, Université de Montréal, C.P. 6128, Suc. Centre-ville, Montréal, Qc, Canada, H3C 3J7.
Email: chabinin@iro.umontreal.ca

Yvon Savaria
GRM, DGEGI, École Polytechnique de Montréal, C.P. 6079, Suc. Centre-ville, Montréal, Qc, Canada, H3C 3A7.
Email: savaria@vlsi.polymtl.ca

ABSTRACT

A method based on software pipelining has been recently proposed to optimize mono-phase clocked sequential circuits. The resulting circuits are multi-phase clocked sequential circuits, where all clocks have the same period. To preserve functionality of the original circuit, registers must be placed according to a correct schedule. This schedule also ensures the maximum throughput. In that method, it is question of (1) how to determine a schedule that requires the minimum number of registers, and (2) how to place these registers optimally. In this paper, problems (1) and (2) are tackled simultaneously. More precisely, we deal with the problem of determining schedules with the minimum register requirements, where the optimal register placement is done during the schedule determination. To optimally solve that problem, we provide a mixed integer linear program that we use to derive a linear program, which is polynomial-time solvable. We show that the dual of this linear program can be transformed to a minimum cost network flow problem, which can be solved more efficiently. Experimental results confirm the effectiveness of the approach, and show that significant reductions of the number of registers can be obtained. Also, they confirm that the obtained dual formulation can be solved much faster than its primal.

Keywords

Retiming, software pipelining, mono-phase, multi-phase, sequential circuits, scheduling, register, linear program, network flow.

1. INTRODUCTION

Basic Retiming has been proposed as an optimization technique for synchronous circuits [15]. This technique changes the location of registers in the circuit in order to achieve one of the following goals: (i) minimizing the clock period, (ii) minimizing the number of registers, or (iii) minimizing the number of registers for a target clock period. It can guarantee the determination of the optimal clock period only for single-phase edge-trigged clocked circuits. To deal with the case of multi-phase, methods based on basic retiming have been proposed [9, 14, 16]. In [14], retiming has ben extended to deal with circuits whose registers are not enabled at the same time. The main idea is that registers controlled by the same phase can be moved across combinational blocks.

It is known that with level-sensitive storage elements (latches), clocked circuits can be made faster and smaller [9, 16] than with edge triggered flip-flops. In [9], methods to minimize the clock period of multi-phase level-sensitive clocked circuits are provided. Also, procedures to derive that kind of circuits from edge-trigged ones are presented. In [16], retiming with multi-phase clocks was proposed. With this method, the phases are fixed before retiming, which can give an optimal clock period if good phases are chosen.

Software pipelining is a powerful technique for increasing the instruction-level parallelism for parallel processors. This method overlaps the execution of successive iterations. It has recently been used to develop a method for optimizing mono-phase clocked sequential circuits [3]. The resulting circuit is a multi-phase clocked circuit, where all clocks have the same period. That method may be described as follows. First, the optimal clock period is determined, and a schedule of all the functional elements of the circuit is computed. Second, in order to preserve the behavior of the original circuit, registers are placed, independently of their initial placement, according to that schedule. Finally, once the registers are placed, the phases are determined.

With this method, it is question of (1) how to determine a schedule that produces the minimum number of required registers, and (2) how to place the minimum number of registers even if that schedule is already determined. Solving (1) and (2) is of great interest, since reducing the number of registers allows to reduce the number of control signals, the area of the circuit, and the power consumption.

In [5], the authors have provided two polynomial-time solvable methods to determine schedules for reducing register requirements, and the number of the required phases. Compared to the original method [3], these methods proved very efficient in reducing the number of registers and the number of the required phases. Nevertheless, the problem of how to efficiently place registers in the circuit is not addressed.

Scheduling under register constraints has been examined in the literature to generate the code for parallel processors. But, it was assumed that processors are single-phase clocked circuits.

In this paper, we focus on solving simultaneously (1) and (2) that are outlined above. More precisely, we tackle the problem of determining schedules that yields the minimum number of registers, where the optimal register placement is done during the schedule determination. To optimally solve that problem, we provide a mixed integer linear program (MILP), which we use to derive a linear program (LP) that is polynomial-time solvable. Also, we transform the dual of this linear program to a formulation of a minimum cost network flow problem that can be solved more efficiently. To test the effectiveness of the approach, we experiment the MILP and the LP on well known benchmarks, and we show the superiority of that approach over the original method [3]. The comparison of the run-time of both the LP and its transformed dual is also done.

This paper is organized as follows. The next section gives some notations and definitions used in this article. Section 3 briefly reviews the registers placement step in the method based on software pipelining, which was outlined above. Also, it shows that the algorithm used to place registers is greedy. The problem we tackle and its optimal solution are presented in Section 4, and a linear program for that problem is given in Section 5. The transformation of the dual of this linear program to a formulation of a minimum cost network flow problem is presented in Section 6. Section 7 provides experimental results and Section 8 concludes the paper.

2. PRELIMINARIES

2.1. The Cyclic Graph Model

In order to minimize the clock period of a synchronous sequential circuit, it is modeled (as in [3]) as a directed cyclic graph $G = (V, E, d, w)$, where V is the set of functional elements in the circuit, and E is the set of edges which represent interconnections between vertices. Each vertex v in V has a non-negative integer propagation delay $d(v) \in N$, which is assumed to be fixed. Each edge $e_{u,v}$, from u to v, in E is weighted with a register count $w(e_{u,v}) \in N$, representing the number of registers on the wire between u and v.

Figure 1 presents an example of a circuit and its directed cyclic graph model. In this figure, large rectangles represent functional elements, and small rectangles represent registers. Wires are oriented to show the propagation direction of the signals. The propagation delay of each functional element of this circuit is specified as a label on the left of each large rectangle. This example will be used through this paper, and will serve to illustrate the initial specification for the problem to optimize. The initial specification is in general a synchronous circuit with a single-phase clock. The minimum clock period of the circuit in Figure 1 as specified is 7, which is equal to $d(v_5) + d(v_1)$.

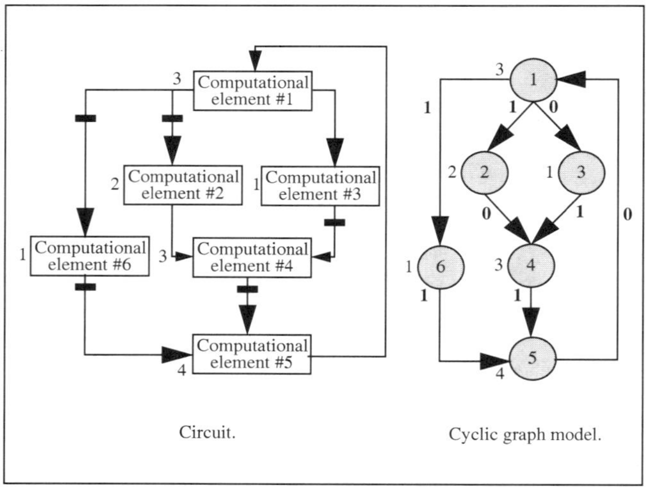

Figure 1. Sample circuit and its directed cyclic graph model.

2.2. Periodic Schedules

We define a schedule s [2, 3] as a function $s : N \times V \rightarrow Q$, where $s_n(v) \equiv s(n, v)$ denotes the schedule time of the nth iteration of operation v. In multi-phase flip-flop based circuits, the schedule time is the start time of the operation. A schedule s is called periodic with period P, if: $\forall n \in N, \forall v \in V: s_{n+1}(v) = s_n(v) + P$. (1)

When there is no resource constraint, a schedule s is said to be valid if and only if the operations terminate before their results are needed. In this case, we say that data dependencies are satisfied, which is equivalent to the following mathematical inequality:

$$\forall n \in N, \forall e_{u,v} \in E : s_{n + w(e_{u,v})}(v) \geq s_n(u) + d(u). \quad (2)$$

2.3. Maximum Throughput of Synchronous Sequential Circuits

The throughput, T, of a synchronous sequential circuit is bounded by the inverse of the length, P, of the critical paths in the circuit. Based on data dependencies constraints only, the maximum throughput is [2]:

$$T = Min_{c \in C}\left(\left(\sum_{e_{u,v} \in c} w(e_{u,v})\right) / \left(\sum_{\forall v \in V \text{ and } e_{u,v} \in c} d(u)\right)\right), \quad (3)$$

where C is the set of directed cycles in the directed cyclic graph modeling the circuit. Determining the maximum throughput is a Minimal Cost-to-Time Ratio Cycle Problem [7, 13], which can be solved in the general case in $O(|V| \cdot |E| \cdot \log(|V| \cdot d_{max}))$ [13], where $d_{max} = Max_{v \in V}(d(v))$. A possible method to solve this problem is to iteratively apply Bellman-Ford's algorithm [6] for longest paths on the graph $G_P = (V, E, d, w_P)$ derived from G by letting:

$$w_P(e_{u,v}) = d(u) - P \cdot w(e_{u,v}), \quad (4)$$

where $e_{u,v} \in E$ and $P = 1/T$. A binary search may be used to find the minimal value of P for which there is no positive cycle in G_P [2]. Without loss of generality, we assume that P is greater than or equal to the execution delay of each computational element in the circuit.

For the example in Figure 1, we have that $P = 6$. This value corresponds to the cycle defined by vertices v_1, v_2, v_4, and v_5.

2.4. Schedule for a Given Throughput

From equation (1) and inequality (2), we have that:

$$\forall e_{u,v} \in E, s_0(v) - s_0(u) \geq d(u) - P \cdot w(e_{u,v}). \quad (5)$$

In the case of periodic schedules, determining a valid schedule of all the instances of each vertex v in V is equivalent to determining $s_0(v)$ for each v in V, which is also equivalent to determining solutions to the system of inequalities described by (5). To solve this system, the graph G_P, previously described, may be used. To find an ASAP schedule, Bellman-Ford's algorithm [6] for longest paths, from a chosen vertex v_x to the others, may be applied on the graph G_P. Finding an ALAP schedule may be done as follows. Step 1, a graph G' has to be derived from G_P by inverting the direction of each edge in G_P. Step 2, Bellman-Ford's algorithm for longest paths, from the vertex v_x to the others, has to be applied on the graph G', where the weights of its edges are defined by equation (4). Finally, step 3, the ALAP schedule is obtained by multiplying each result in step 2 by -1. Relatively to $v_x = v_1$, the ASAP schedules of vertices v_1, v_2, v_3, v_4, v_5, and v_6 of the circuit in Figure 1 are 0, -3, 3, -1, -4, and -3, respectively. Their ALAP schedules are 0, -3, 4, -1, -4, and 1, respectively.

2.5. Schedule Graph

As in [3], a periodic schedule, with period P, is expressed by a schedule graph $G_s = (V, E, d, w_s, P)$. Here V, E and d have the same definition given for the case of the graph G previously defined, and $w_s : E \rightarrow Q$ is a weight function, which associates to each edge $e_{u,v}$ in E the time distance between the schedule times of u and v. Mathematically, $w_s(e_{u,v})$ is defined as follows:

$$\forall e_{u,v} \in E, w_s(e_{u,v}) = s_{w(e_{u,v})}(v) - s_0(u). \quad (6)$$

Because s is periodic with period P, equation (6) may be written as follows: $\forall e_{u,v} \in E, w_s(e_{u,v}) = s_0(v) - s_0(u) + P \cdot w(e_{u,v})$ (7)

The graph G_s is consistent if and only if for each edge $e_{u,v}$ in E, $w_s(e_{u,v}) \geq d(u)$. This is derived from equation (2). Figure 2 shows a consistent schedule graph, where edges are labeled with w_s values, for the circuit in Figure 1, using the ASAP schedule determined in Section 2.4.

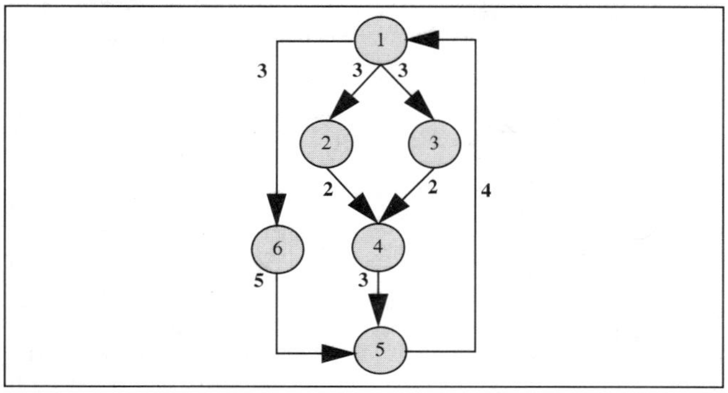

Figure 2. Schedule graph.

3. REGISTER PLACEMENT

In the method proposed in [3], which was outlined in Section 1, a register placement step is needed in order to preserve the behavior of the original circuit. The placement of registers is derived from a schedule graph G_s, by breaking every path in G_s that is longer than the optimal clock period P. For paths having a length less than P, no register is required because operations chaining is assumed.

For the circuit in Figure 1, applying the algorithm in [3] for register placement on the schedule graph G_s in Figure 2, starting from v_1, gives the placement of registers and their schedules as depicted by Figure 3. The number of registers that are placed is 6 and the number of phases is 4.

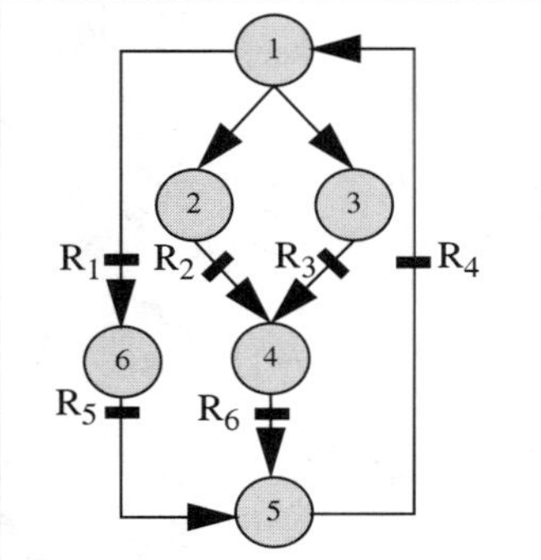

Register	Schedule
R_1	3
R_2	5
R_3	5
R_4	0
R_5	2
R_6	2

Figure 3. Register placement an their schedules.

The algorithm for register placement in [3] is not exact. Indeed, for Figure 3, R_1 can be omitted.

4. PROBLEM FORMULATION AND OPTIMAL SOLUTION

As mentioned in Section 1, two problems arise in the method based on software pipelining proposed in [3]: the first one is how to determine a schedule that yields the minimum number of required registers, and the second one is how to place the minimum number of required registers even if that schedule is already determined. Our focus in this paper is to simultaneously solve these two problems. More precisely, the problem (*Prob*) we tackle is to determine a schedule with the minimum register requirements, where the register placement is done during the schedule determination. To optimally solve *Prob*, we provide a mixed integer linear program (MILP), and use it to derive a linear program which is polynomial-time solvable.

Before presenting that MILP, let us first give some requirements. Figure 4 gives a portion of the cyclic graph modeling the circuit, where i and j are two computational elements. $x_{i,j}$ denotes the number of registers that must be placed on the arc $e_{i,j}$ to guarantee that the length, $l_{i,j}$, of every path that goes to j via i, is less than or equal to the optimal clock period P. $l_{i,j}$ will be defined in the following. Note that as in [3], operation chaining is assumed, and hence no register is required if $l_{i,j} \leq P$. Suppose that paths that go to j via i are already examined in order to determine if some registers must be placed on them or not. Let m_i be a no-negative real greater than or equal to each rest obtained by dividing the length of each one of those paths by P. The length $l_{i,j}$ of every path that goes to j via i is the sum of m_i and $w_s(e_{i,j})$, where $w_s(e_{i,j})$ is defined by equation (7). $y_{i,j}$ is the rest of the division of $l_{i,j}$ by P. We require that $m_i \leq (P - d(i))$, which guarantee that if a register R is on the output of computational element i, then its schedule will be after i finishes its execution.

Figure 5 presents a mathematical formulation to *Prob*. The objective function expresses the number of registers to be placed in the circuit. Equations (8), (9), and (10) are equivalent to the definition of $x_{i,j}$, $y_{i,j}$, and m_i, respectively. Inequality (11) is equivalent to (5). (13) is required, since the number of registers must be an integer. In this formulation, the variables are $x_{i,j}$, $y_{i,j}$, m_i and the schedule $s_0(u)$ for each computational element u.

The formulation in Figure 5 can be linearized as follows. Using the fact that $\lfloor x \rfloor \leq x < \lfloor x \rfloor + 1$, and that no register is required if the length of a path is less than or equal P, equation (8) can be replaced by:

$$\forall e_{i,j} \in E, x_{i,j} \leq (s_0(j) - s_0(i) + P \cdot w(e_{i,j}) + m_i)/P \leq x_{i,j} + 1 \quad (14)$$

Equations (9) and (10) together can be replaced by

$$\forall e_{k,i} \in E, m_i \geq (s_0(i) - s_0(k) + P \cdot w(e_{k,i}) + m_k) - P \cdot x_{k,i} \quad (15)$$

After linearizing the formulation in Figure 5, we obtain the MILP to optimally solve *Prob* as presented in Figure 6. In this figure, equations (16) and (17) are equivalent to (14). (18) is equivalent to (15). (19), (20) and (21) are equivalent to (12), (11) and (13), respectively.

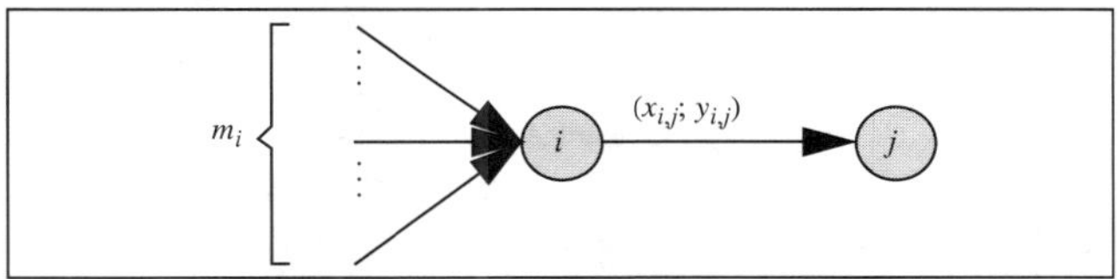

Figure 4. Illustration of the variables of the MILP.

$$Minimize\left(\sum_{\forall e_{i,j}\in E} x_{i,j}\right)$$

Subject to:

$$\forall e_{i,j}\in E,\ x_{i,j} = \lfloor (s_0(j) - s_0(i) + P\cdot w(e_{i,j}) + m_i)/P \rfloor \quad (8)$$

$$\forall e_{i,j}\in E,\ y_{i,j} = (s_0(j) - s_0(i) + P\cdot w(e_{i,j}) + m_i) - P\cdot x_{i,j} \quad (9)$$

$$\forall i\in V,\ m_i \geq (y_{k,i})_{k\in Fanin(i)} \quad (10)$$

$$\forall e_{i,j}\in E,\ s_0(j) - s_0(i) \geq d(i) - P\cdot w(e_{i,j}) \quad (11)$$

$$\forall i\in V,\ m_i \leq P - d(i) \quad (12)$$

$$\forall e_{i,j}\in E,\ x_{i,j} \text{ is integer} \quad (13)$$

Figure 5. A mathematical formulation to solve *Prob*.

$$Minimize\left(\sum_{\forall e_{i,j}\in E} x_{i,j}\right)$$

Subject to:

$$\forall e_{i,j}\in E,\ -P\cdot x_{i,j} - s_0(i) + s_0(j) + m_i \geq -P\cdot w(e_{i,j}) \quad (16)$$

$$\forall e_{i,j}\in E,\ P\cdot x_{i,j} + s_0(i) - s_0(j) - m_i \geq P\cdot w(e_{i,j}) - P \quad (17)$$

$$\forall e_{k,i}\in E,\ P\cdot x_{k,i} + s_0(k) - s_0(i) + m_i - m_k \geq P\cdot w(e_{k,i}) \quad (18)$$

$$\forall i\in V,\ m_i \leq P - d(i) \quad (19)$$

$$\forall e_{i,j}\in E,\ s_0(j) - s_0(i) \geq d(i) - P\cdot w(e_{i,j}) \quad (20)$$

$$\forall e_{i,j}\in E,\ x_{i,j} \text{ is integer} \quad (21)$$

Figure 6. A MILP to optimally solve *Prob*.

5. A LINEAR PROGRAM FOR SOLVING *PROB*

Linear programs are polynomial-time solvable [10, 11]. A linear program for solving *Prob* can be obtained by deleting the constraint that $x_{i,j}$ is integer in Figure 6. In this case, once the linear program is solved, the number of registers to be placed on the arc $e_{i,j}$ is $\lceil x_{i,j} \rceil$. Due the space limitation, details on why it is possible to place $\lceil x_{i,j} \rceil$ registers on the arc $e_{i,j}$ can be found in [4].

6. A MINIMUM COST NETWORK FLOW FORMULATION

In this section, we focus on transforming the dual of the linear program (LP) in Section 5 to a formulation of a minimum cost network flow problem, since this latter can be solved more efficiently [1, 8, 13].

By replacing $P\cdot x_{i,j}$ with $X_{i,j}$. The LP can be written as in Figure 7.

$$Minimize\left(\sum_{\forall e_{i,j}\in E} X_{i,j}\right)$$

Subject to:

$$\forall e_{i,j}\in E,\ -X_{i,j} - s_0(i) + s_0(j) + m_i \geq -P\cdot w(e_{i,j}) \quad (22)$$

$$\forall e_{i,j}\in E,\ X_{i,j} + s_0(i) - s_0(j) - m_i \geq P\cdot w(e_{i,j}) - P \quad (23)$$

$$\forall e_{k,i}\in E,\ X_{k,i} + s_0(k) - s_0(i) + m_i - m_k \geq P\cdot w(e_{k,i}) \quad (24)$$

$$\forall e_{k,i}\in E,\ -m_i \geq -(P - d(i)) \quad (25)$$

$$\forall e_{i,j}\in E,\ s_0(j) - s_0(i) \geq d(i) - P\cdot w(e_{i,j}) \quad (26)$$

Figure 7. A linear program to solve *Prob*.

For each i in V, let $\delta^+(i)$ be the set of immediate successors of i and $\delta^-(i)$ be its set of immediate predecessors. The dual of the linear program in Figure 7 can be written as in Figure 8. In this figure, the variables are: $A_{i,j}$'s, $B_{i,j}$'s, $C_{i,j}$'s $D_{i,j}$'s and $E_{i,j}$'s.

$$Max\left(\begin{array}{l}\sum_{\forall e_{i,j}\in E} -P\cdot w(e_{i,j})\cdot A_{i,j} \\ +\sum_{\forall e_{i,j}\in E} (P\cdot w(e_{i,j}) - P)\cdot B_{i,j} \\ +\sum_{\forall e_{i,j}\in E} P\cdot w(e_{i,j})\cdot C_{i,j} \\ +\sum_{\forall e_{i,j}\in E} d(i) - P\cdot w(e_{i,j})\cdot D_{i,j} - (P - d(i))\cdot E_{i,j}\end{array}\right) \quad (27)$$

Subject to:

$$\forall e_{i,j}\in E,\ -A_{i,j} + B_{i,j} + C_{i,j} = 1 \quad (28)$$

$$\forall i\in V,\ \begin{array}{l}\sum_{j\in\delta^+(i)} (-A_{i,j} + B_{i,j} + C_{i,j} - D_{i,j}) \\ -\sum_{j\in\delta^-(i)} (-A_{j,i} + B_{j,i} + C_{j,i} - D_{j,i}) = 0\end{array} \quad (29)$$

$$\forall i\in V,\ \sum_{j\in\delta^+(i)} (A_{i,j} - B_{i,j} - C_{i,j}) + \sum_{j\in\delta^-(i)} C_{j,i} + E_{j,i} = 0 \quad (30)$$

$$\forall e_{i,j}\in E,\ A_{i,j}\geq 0,\ B_{i,j}\geq 0,\ C_{i,j}\geq 0,\ D_{i,j}\geq 0,\ E_{i,j}\geq 0 \quad (31)$$

Figure 8. The dual of the formulation in Figure 7.

Equation (29) can be written as follows:

$$\forall i\in V,\ \sum_{j\in\delta^+(i)} D_{i,j} - \sum_{j\in\delta^-(i)} D_{j,i} = \sum_{j\in\delta^+(i)} (-A_{i,j} + B_{i,j} + C_{i,j}) - \sum_{j\in\delta^-(i)} (-A_{j,i} + B_{j,i} + C_{j,i}) . \quad (33)$$

For each i in V, let $f_i = |\delta^+(i)| - |\delta^-(i)|$. Using equations (28) and (33), equation (29) can be replaced by:

$$\forall i\in V,\ \sum_{j\in\delta^+(i)} D_{i,j} - \sum_{j\in\delta^-(i)} D_{j,i} = |\delta^+(i)| - |\delta^-(i)| = f_i . \quad (34)$$

Using equation (28), equation (30) can be transformed to:

$$\forall i\in V,\ \sum_{j\in\delta^-(i)} C_{j,i} + E_{j,i} = \sum_{j\in\delta^+(i)} -A_{i,j} + B_{i,j} + C_{i,j} = |\delta^+(i)| \quad (35)$$

Using equation (28), we can transform formula (27) to:

$$Maximize\left(\begin{array}{l}\sum_{\forall e_{i,j}\in E} -(P - d(i))\cdot E_{i,j} - (P\cdot B_{i,j}) \\ +\sum_{\forall e_{i,j}\in E} (d(i) - P\cdot w(e_{i,j}))\cdot D_{i,j}\end{array}\right). \quad (36)$$

Formula (36) can be rewritten as follows:

$$Minimize\left(\begin{array}{l}\sum_{\forall e_{i,j}\in E} (P - d(i))\cdot E_{i,j} + P\cdot B_{i,j} \\ +\sum_{\forall e\ \in E} (P\cdot w(e_{i,j}) - d(i))\cdot D_{i,j}\end{array}\right). \quad (37)$$

Now, let us put all the above modifications together. Using (37) instead of (27), (34) instead of (29), and (35) instead of (30), we obtain the formulation in Figure 9.

$$Minimize \left(\sum_{\forall e_{i,j} \in E} (P - d(i)) \cdot E_{i,j} + P \cdot B_{i,j} + \sum_{\forall e_{i,j} \in E} (P \cdot w(e_{i,j}) - d(i)) \cdot D_{i,j} \right) \quad (39)$$

Subject to:

$$\forall e_{i,j} \in E, -A_{i,j} + B_{i,j} + C_{i,j} = 1 \quad (40)$$

$$\forall i \in V, \sum_{j \in \delta^+(i)} D_{i,j} - \sum_{j \in \delta^-(i)} D_{j,i} = f_i \quad (41)$$

$$\forall i \in V, \sum_{j \in \delta^-(i)} C_{j,i} + E_{j,i} = |\delta^+(i)| \quad (42)$$

$$\forall e_{i,j} \in E, A_{i,j} \geq 0, B_{i,j} \geq 0, C_{i,j} \geq 0, D_{i,j} \geq 0, E_{i,j} \geq 0 \quad (43)$$

Figure 9. Formulation after modifying Figure 8.

Since, $\forall e_{i,j} \in E, B_{i,j} \geq 0$, $E_{i,j} \geq 0$ and considering that constraints on $D_{i,j}$'s are independent of constraints on $B_{i,j}$'s and on $E_{i,j}$'s, then we can always select all $B_{i,j} = 0$ and $E_{i,j} = 0$. Hence, formula (39) can be reduced to:

$$Minimize \left(\sum_{\forall e_{i,j} \in E} (P \cdot w(e_{i,j}) - d(i)) \cdot D_{i,j} \right). \quad (44)$$

Due to the fact that the variables $A_{i,j}$'s, $B_{i,j}$'s, $C_{i,j}$'s and $E_{i,j}$'s do not appear in formula (44), then they can be removed from the constraints. The final form of the transformed dual of the linear program in Figure 7 is presented in Figure 10, which is a formulation of a minimum cost network flow problem, and hence it can be solved more efficiently using, for instance, algorithms provided in [1, 8, 13].

$$Minimize \left(\sum_{\forall e_{i,j} \in E} (P \cdot w(e_{i,j}) - d(i)) \cdot D_{i,j} \right)$$

Subject to:

$$\forall i \in V, \sum_{j \in \delta^+(i)} D_{i,j} - \sum_{j \in \delta^-(i)} D_{j,i} = f_i \quad (45)$$

$$\forall e_{i,j} \in E, D_{i,j} \geq 0 \quad (46)$$

Figure 10. The transformed dual of Figure 7.

7. EXPERIMENTAL RESULTS

To test the effectiveness of our approach, the MILP in Figure 6 and the corresponding linear program (LP), obtained by ignoring the constraint *integer* in (21), are experimented on well known benchmarks. Circuits from the ISCAS89 benchmark suite are used to test the efficiency of the LP in terms of the run-time and of the reduction of the number of registers inserted in the circuit. The mathematical formulations for each circuit are automatically generated by a module we coded in C++ and integrated in a tool we developed in [5]. We did not implement the cited polynomial-time algorithms for linear programs, but the Lp_Solve tool [17] (in the public domain) is used to solve the generated mathematical formulations. Obtained results are given in Tables 1 and 2, where the first column gives the name of the circuit and the second column presents the number, N_1, of registers placed using the algorithm in [3] that uses ALAP as a schedule. The number, N_2, of registers placed by MILP or by LP are presented in the third column. The fourth column gives the relative gain defined as $((N_1 - N_2)/N_1) \times 100\%$. For Table 2, the fifth column gives the run-time in seconds on an UltraSparc 10 with 1GB RAM. As Table 1 reports, significant reductions of the number of required registers are obtained. Substantial reductions are also obtained using the LP. Indeed, as summarized by Table 2, reductions as high as 77.46% are obtained in less than 181.4s.

To test the efficiency of the transformed dual of the LP, we used the two formulations to solve a few benchmarks as given in Table 3. In this table, we present the run time (RT_1) of the LP, and the run time (RT_2) of its transformed dual, in the second and third columns respectively. The fourth column presents the speedup defined as RT_1/RT_2. As Table 3 reports, speedup factors ranging from 1 to 16.47 have been achieved, although we have not used specialized algorithms for minimum cost network flow problems to solve the transformed dual.

Table 1. Register placement by [3] vs. by MILP.

	#registers placed by [3]	#registers placed using Figure 6	Relative gain
Figure 1	6*	5	16.66%
SOIIR Filter [2]	3	2	23.33%
Polynomial Div. [2]	9	4	55.55
Correlator [3]	6	6	0%
FOWDEF [12]	14	8	42.85%

Table 2. Register placement by [3] vs. by LP.

	#registers placed by [3]	#registers placed using the LP	Relative gain	Run-time (s)
Figure 1	6*	5	16.66%	0.01
SOIIR Filter [2]	3	3	0%	0.02
Polynomial Div. [2]	9	4	55.55%	0.02
Correlator [3]	6	6	0%	0.01
FOWDEF [12]	14	12	14.28%	0.06
S344	131	53	59.54%	1.63
S641	142	32	77.46	1.25
S1423	422	216	48.81%	17.31
S5378	1033	581	43.75%	181.4
S9234	1042	466	55.27%	93.29

*: ASAP schedule is used.

Table 3. Run times of the LP and Figure 10.

	Run-time of the LP (s)	Run-time using Figure 10 (s)	Speed up
Figure 1	0.01	0.01	1
SOIIR Filter [2]	0.02	0.01	2
Polynomial Div. [2]	0.02	0.01	2
Correlator [3]	0.01	0.01	1
FOWDEF [12]	0.06	0.01	6
S344	1.63	0.11	14.81
S641	1.25	0.19	6.57
S1423	17.31	1.55	11.16
S5378	181.4	11.01	16.47
S9234	93.29	6.4	14.57

8. CONCLUSIONS

A method based on software pipelining has recently been proposed to optimize mono-phase clocked sequential circuit. The resulting circuit is a multi-phase clocked circuit, where all clocks have the same period. To preserve the behavior of the original circuit, registers are placed according to a schedule, which has the maximum throughput.

In that method, two problems arise: how to determine schedules that lead to a minimal register requirements, and how to place the minimum number of required registers even if these schedules are already determined.

In this paper, we have simultaneously tackled these two problems. We have provided a mixed integer linear program and used it to derive a linear program, which is polynomial-time solvable. Also, we have transformed the dual of this linear program to a formulation of minimum cost network flow problem, which can be solved more efficiently. Experimental results on well known benchmarks confirmed the effectiveness of the approach we propose. Indeed, significant reductions of the number of required registers have been obtained in very short run-time. The run time to solve the transformed dual of the linear program was very small compared to the one of the primal.

ACKNOWLEDGMENTS

The authors would like to thank El Mostapha Aboulhamid for useful discussions and suggestions. This work was partly supported by Micronet.

REFERENCES

[1] R.-K. Ahuja, T.-L. Magnanti, and J.-B. Orlin., *Network Flows: Theory, Algorithms, and Applications*, Prentice Hall, Englewood Cliffs, NJ, 1993.

[2] I.-E. Bennour, *Estimation de la performance et méthodes d'allocation dans la synthèse de systèmes numériques, Thèse de doctorat*, DIRO, Université de Montréal, 1996.

[3] F.-R. Boyer, E.-M. Aboulhamid, Y. Savaria and M. Boyer, "Optimal Design of Synchronous Circuits Using Software Pipelining Techniques", *ACM Trans. on Design Aut. of Elec. Systems*, Vo. 7, Num. 2, 2002.

[4] F.-R. Boyer, E.-M. Aboulhamid and Y. Savaria, "An Efficient Verification Method for a Class of Multi-phase Sequential Circuits", *The 7th IEEE International Conference on Electronics, Circuits & Systems*, Lebanon, December 17-20, 2000.

[5] N. Chabini, E.-M. Aboulhamid and Y. Savaria, "Reducing Register and Phase Requirements for Synchronous Circuits Derived Using Software Pipelining Techniques", *Proceedings of the IEEE Computer Society Annual Workshop on VLSI*, Orlando, Florida, April, 2001.

[6] T. H. Cormen, C. E. Leiserson, and R. L. Rivest, *Introduction to Algorithms*, New York, NY: McGraw-Hill, 1990.

[7] S.-H. Gerez, S.-M.-H. de Groot, and O.-E. Herrmann, "A Polynomial-Time Algorithm for the Computation of the Iteration-Period Bound in Recursive Data- Flow Graphs", *IEEE Trans. on Circuits and Syst.-1*, No. 1, Vo. 39, Jan. 1992.

[8] A.-V. Goldberg and R.-E. Tarjan, "Solving Minimum-Cost Flow Problems by Successive Approximation," *Proceedings of the 19th Annual ACM Symposium on Theory of Computing*, New York City, May 25-27, 1987.

[9] A.-T. Ishii, C.-E. Leiserson, and M.-C. Papaefthymiou, "Optimizing two-phase, level-clocked circuitry," *Journal of the ACM* 44, 1 (Jan.), 1997, 148-199.

[10] N. Karmakar, "A New Polynomial-Time Algorithm for Linear Programming", *Combinatorica*, Vo. 4, 1984.

[11] L.-G. Khachian, "A Polynomial Algorithm in Linear Programming", *Soviet Math. Doklady*, Vo. 20, 1979.

[12] S. Y. Kung, H. J. Whitehouse and T. Kailath, *VLSI and Modern Signal Processing*, Prentice-Hall, Inc., Englewood Cliffs, NJ, 1985, pages: 259-60.

[13] E.-L. Lawler, *Combinatorial Optimization: Networks and Matroids*, Holt, Reinhart, and Winston, New York, NY, USA, 1976.

[14] C. Legl, P. Vanbekbergen, and A. Wang, "Retiming of edge-triggered circuits with multiple clocks and load enables," *IWLS'97*, 1997.

[15] C.-E. Leiserson, and J.-B. Saxe, "Retiming synchronous circuitry", *Algorithmica* 6, 1, 1991.

[16] B. Lockyear, and C. Ebeling, "Optimal retiming of level-clocked circuits using symmetric clock schedules," *IEEE Transactions on Computer-Aided Design of Integrated Circuits and Systems* 13, 9 (Sept.), 1994, pages: 1097-1109.

[17] The LP_Solve Tool: ftp://ftp.ics.ele.tue.nl/pub/lp_solve/

High-level Automatic Pipelining for Sequential Circuits *

Maria-Cristina V. Marinescu
Laboratory for Computer Science
Massachusetts Institute of Technology
Cambridge, MA 02139
cristina@lcs.mit.edu

Martin Rinard
Laboratory for Computer Science
Massachusetts Institute of Technology
Cambridge, MA 02139
rinard@lcs.mit.edu

ABSTRACT

This paper presents a new approach for automatically pipelining sequential circuits. The approach repeatedly extracts a computation from the critical path, moves it into a new stage, then uses speculation to generate a stream of values that keep the pipeline full. The newly generated circuit retains enough state to recover from incorrect speculations by flushing the incorrect values from the pipeline, restoring the correct state, then restarting the computation.

We also implement two extensions to this basic approach: stalling, which minimizes circuit area by eliminating speculation, and forwarding, which increases the throughput of the generated circuit by forwarding correct values to preceding pipeline stages. We have implemented a prototype synthesizer based on this approach. Our experimental results show that, starting with a non-pipelined or insufficiently pipelined specification, this synthesizer can effectively reduce the clock cycle time and improve the throughput of the generated circuit.

Keywords

Pipeline, modular, speculation, stall, forward

1. INTRODUCTION

This paper presents a new algorithm for automatically pipelining sequential circuits. The algorithm is based on speculation and uses state retention and recovery to respond to incorrect speculations. The paper also presents two extensions to the basic approach: generating stall logic to avoid incorrect speculations and the associated area penalty, and generating forwarding logic to increase the throughput of the resulting circuit.

Our algorithm starts with a non-pipelined or insufficiently pipelined specification of a circuit and repeatedly shortens its clock cycle by extracting a computation from the critical path and moving it into a new pipeline stage. The new stage precomputes the result of the selected expression and passes it to the computation of the next stage that uses it. To keep the pipeline full, the new stage must produce the next value of the expression before the final values of the variables it accesses become available. Our algorithm achieves this goal by speculating on the values of these variables. If the speculation is incorrect, the circuit restores its state to match the state before the speculation, flushes the incorrect values from the pipeline, then restarts the computation.

Our algorithm uses several techniques to improve the quality of the pipelined circuit. If the amount of state necessary to recover from an incorrect speculation is excessive, our algorithm can generate stall logic that causes the pipeline stage to stall until the new values are available. This technique eliminates the need for retaining recovery state, as the execution of the pipeline stage will never need to roll back. Our algorithm also generates circuits that forward the correct value to preceding pipeline stages. This technique increases the throughput of the circuit by reducing the amount of time that the circuit spends recovering from incorrect speculations or waiting for correct values to become available.

We have built a prototype implementation of our algorithm. Using our synthesizer [13] as backend, this implementation generates synthesizable Verilog at the RTL level. We have used our implementation to automatically generate pipelined versions of several circuits. Our results show that our automatically generated pipelined circuits are competitive with hand-generated versions.

This paper makes the following contributions:

- **Approach:** It presents a new approach for automatically pipelining sequential circuits. This approach repeatedly extracts a computation from the critical path and moves it into a new stage. This stage uses speculation to generate a stream of values that keep the pipeline full. The approach reduces the clock cycle and increases the throughput of a circuit.
- **Algorithm:** It presents a pipelining algorithm that implements our approach. It also presents two extensions to the approach: stalling, which reduces the amount of area that would otherwise be required to respond to incorrect speculations; and forwarding, which increases throughput either by replacing values produced by incorrect speculations with correct values or by making new values available earlier to the stall logic.
- **Experimental Results:** It presents experimental results that prove the viability of the approach in practice.

The remainder of the paper is organized as follows. Section 2 discusses related work. Section 3 illustrates how a system is specified using rewrite rules and gives an example

*This research was supported in part by NSF Grant CCR-9702297.

ISSS'01, October 1-3, 2001, Montréal, Québec, Canada.

of what the starting and derived circuit specifications may look like. Section 4 presents the pipelining algorithm. Section 5 presents the experimental results. Section 6 draws the conclusions.

2. RELATED WORK

Many high-level synthesis systems focus on the automatic generation of highly efficient pipelined designs. Most of this work is primarily concerned with functional pipelining. Many synthesis tools target instruction-set architectures[10, 4, 3, 14, 15, 1, 9, 2]; our tool, on the other hand, targets the more general class of sequential circuits. Other approaches start with a C program [8, 5].

Kroening and Paul [11] describe a method of automating the generation of stall and forward logic starting from a given sequential machine. Starting from hardware that is initially partitioned into pipeline stages, the algorithm produces a circuit that can stall in any arbitrary stage while keeping the other stages running, if possible. To implement forwarding, the designer has to specify the registers holding intermediate results that need to be forwarded to previous stages in the pipeline. The goal of our research, in contrast, is to completely automate the pipelining transformation starting from a non-pipelined or insufficiently pipelined specification.

Retiming [12] optimally pipelines combinatorial circuitry. Architectural retiming [6] adds a negative/normal register pair on a latency-constrained path, effectively pipelining the logic without adding latency. It implements the negative register by either precomputation or prediction of the value that it produces.

Research by Hoe and Arvind [7] and Shen and Arvind [16] has introduced an approach to describe, verify and synthesize processors based on term rewriting systems (TRS). They do not implement automatic pipelining, but their specification language offers comparable capabilities in this direction as our language.

3. EXAMPLE

The text inside the boxes in Figure 2 and Figure 1 presents a specification written in our high-level description language. The figures also contain a graphical representation that we find useful in explaining our example. We first present a non-pipelined datapath, then a simple, three-stage, linear pipelined datapath that our algorithm can automatically derive from the non-pipelined specification. Section 4 shows the intermediate specifications at each step of the algorithm. We chose to present this three-stage linear pipeline because of its simplicity; our algorithm is capable of generating deep pipelines and is not specific to this particular class of circuits.

The designer specifies the circuit using two kinds of information:

- **State Declarations:** The designer specifies the state of the system as a set of typed variable declarations.
- **Module Specification:** The designer specifies the behavior of each module as a set of update rules. Modules communicate by reading and writing shared state and particularly using FIFO queues.

3.1 Modules

Figure 2 and Figure 1 show the functional modules in our non-pipelined and respectively, pipelined, examples and the queues that interconnect them. Each module consists of a set of *update rules*. An update rule has an enabling condition and a set of updates to the state. When the enabling condition evaluates to `true`, the rule is enabled and can execute, in which case its updates are *atomically* applied to the state. Conceptually, the execution of the system repeatedly chooses an enabled rule and executes it. In practice, our backend synthesizer analyzes and transforms the specification to execute multiple rules in parallel in the same clock cycle, even when they do not necessarily access disjunct state [13].

Queues provide buffered, first-in, first-out connections between modules. Modules can perform several operations on a queue `q`:

- `head(q)`: Retrieves the first element in the queue.
- `tail(q)`: Returns the rest of `q` after the first element.
- `insert(q,e)`: Returns the queue `q` after inserting the element `e` at the end of `q`.
- `replace(e1,e2,q)`: Returns `q` after replacing all entries `e1` by `e2`.
- `notin(q,e)`: Returns *true* if the element `e` is not in `q`; otherwise returns *false*.
- `q = nil`: Resets the queue to be empty.

We next illustrate the conceptual model of execution in our system by discussing the operation of the rules in our example. The rules describe the structure of the hardware pipeline and *not* the program that executes on it.

3.1.1 Non-pipelined Speci£cation

```
<INC r> = im(pc) ->
    rf = rf(r->rf(r)+1), pc = pc+1;
<JRZ r l> = im(pc) and rf(r) = 0 ->
    pc = l;
<JRZ r l> = im(pc) and rf(r) != 0 ->
    pc = pc+1;
```

Figure 2: Non-pipelined Specification

The first rule in Figure 2 processes `INC` instructions. The rules use a form of pattern matching similar to that found in ML and Haskell. If the rule's enabling condition is true, the clause matches and binds the variable `r` to the register name argument of the `INC` instruction. The rule can then use `r` to refer to this argument. If enabled, the rule atomically executes the block in the right-hand-side of the arrow. The update `rf = rf[r->rf[r]+1]` sets element `r` of the register file to be `rf[r]+1`. The other rules perform similar actions. To keep the example clear, the instruction set contains only an `INC` instruction, which increments the value in its single register argument, and a `JRZ` instruction, which tests the value in its register argument and, if the value is zero, jumps to the location in its location argument.

3.1.2 Three-stage Pipelined Speci£cation

The condition for the rule in module IFM of Figure 1 is `true`, which means that the rule is always enabled. When it executes, it fetches an instruction from the instruction memory and inserts it into the instruction queue `iq`. It also increments the program counter `pc` to set up the next fetch.

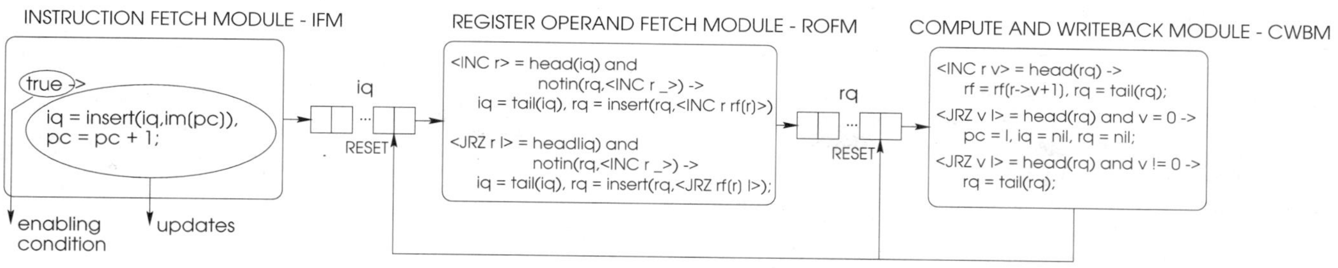

Figure 1: Three-stage Pipelined Specification

The two rules in the module ROFM remove instructions from `iq`, fetch the register operands, and insert them into `rq`. The enabling condition of the first rule is `<INC r> = head(iq) and notin(rq, <INC r _>)`. If the instruction at the head of `iq` is an `INC`, the clause matches and binds `r` to the register name argument of the `INC` instruction. The second clause, `notin(rq, <INC r _>)` uses the binding `r` to check for a read after write (RAW) hazard caused by a pending instruction in `rq` that will write the register `r`. In this case, the machine delays the operand fetch so that it fetches the value after the write (this translates into `stalling`[1]). The clause `notin(rq, <INC r _>)` checks to make sure that there is no such instruction in `rq`, and the rule as a whole is enabled and can execute only if there is no hazard.

The other rules perform similar actions. The update `iq/rq = nil` clears the queue(s) `iq/rq`.

3.2 State

3.2.1 *Non-pipelined Specification*

Figure 3 presents the state and type declarations for Figure 2.

```
1 type reg = int(3), val = int(8), loc = int(8);
2 type ins = <INC reg> | <JRZ reg loc>;

4 var pc :  loc, im :  ins[N], rf :  val[8];
```

Figure 3: State Variables and Type Declarations for Example in Figure 2

Line 4 in Figure 3 presents the state declarations, which consist of the following state variables: a program counter `pc`, an instruction memory `im` and a register file `rf`. Lines 1 and 2 contain the type declarations for these variables. The type declarations include a 3 bit register name type `reg`, an 8 bit integer type `val`, an 8 bit integer type `loc` which represents the locations of instructions in the instruction memory and an instruction type `ins`. The instruction type is a tagged union type, similar to those found in ML and Haskell and contains only an `INC` and a `JRZ` instruction.

3.2.2 *Three-stage Pipelined Specification*

Figure 4 presents the state and type declarations for Figure 1. Line 5 in Figure 4 declares the two queues, `iq` and `rq`. Line 3 contains the type declaration for instructions whose register operands have been fetched from the register file. The rest of the declarations are identical to the ones in Figure 3.

```
1 type reg = int(3), val = int(8), loc = int(8);
2 type ins = <INC reg> | <JRZ reg loc>;
3 type irf = <INC reg val> | <JRZ val loc>;

4 var pc :  loc, im :  ins[N], rf :  val[8];
5 var iq = queue(ins), rq = queue(irf);
```

Figure 4: State Variables and Type Declarations for Example in Figure 1

4. PIPELINING ALGORITHM

4.1 Basic Approach

The pipelining algorithm starts with a non-pipelined or insufficiently pipelined specification and automatically generates a highly-pipelined, functionally equivalent specification. The algorithm repeatedly extracts an expression from a target module and creates a new module to compute the value of the expression at each clock cycle. It then uses a stream to transport the computed values from the new module into the target module from which the expression was extracted. The length of the stream is conceptually unbounded. The synthesis algorithm we developed in [13] implements all the streams in the final specification as finite hardware buffers. This algorithm operates on the resulting specification once the pipelining algorithm has finished. Our pipelining algorithm transforms the target module so that it reads the value of the expression from the stream instead of computing its value. Because this transformation splits computations across multiple clock cycles, it may reduce the clock cycle of the circuit and increase its throughput.

In general, the extracted subcomputation may depend on values that are not available until after it must produce the new value. The compiler therefore speculates on the values that the subcomputation uses. If the speculation is incorrect, the circuit restores the values of any incorrectly updated variables and restarts the computation from the restored state. To enable the restoration, the transformed specification inserts the old values of any potentially incorrectly updated variables into the new stream. When the circuit encounters an incorrect speculation, it extracts these values from the stream and uses them to restore any incorrectly updated variables to their correct values. The algorithm consists of seven phases for each further pipelining decision. The steps are illustrated using Figure 2, Figure 1 and Figure 6. Figure 6 is the intermediate two-stage pipelined

[1]We chose here to present stalling for the sake of simplicity of the presentation.

specification derived from Figure 2 by applying the algorithm once.

- **Select Target Expression:** The selection of the target expression is driven by an analysis of the combinational path lengths in the circuit. The algorithm repeatedly determines the critical path, then chooses a target expression on this critical path. Inserting the computation of the target expression into a different stage of the pipeline removes the expression from the critical path, shortening its length. A more general approach could be implemented that uses a wider set of paths than the critical one(s) in deciding which expression to select as target. In addition to selecting the target expression automatically, our implemented system also allows the designer to drive the pipelining process by manually selecting the target expression. For Figure 2 the algorithm selects `im[pc]`; for Figure 6 the target expression is `rf[r]`.
- **Compute All Involved Variables:** The value of the target expression depends on the variables that it references. This set of variables is called the *set of involved variables.*
  For the specification in Figure 2, the set of all involved variables of `im[pc]` is {`im,pc`}. For Figure 6, the set of all involved variables of `rf[r]` is {`rf,head(iq)`}.
- **Speculate on New Values of Involved Variables:** The pipelining algorithm will move the computation of the target expression into a new module. This module will compute the value of the target expression in a clock cycle before the final values of the involved variables have been determined. The module therefore speculates on the final values of these variables, using the speculated values to compute the value of the target expression. There are two kinds of speculation:
  - **Control:** Speculate on which rule will fire. For the involved variable `pc` in Figure 2 we speculate that the first rule will fire. This choice implies that the new value of `pc` is `pc+1`. For `iq` in Figure 6 we speculate that the first rule in the rightmost box will fire, so `iq`'s new speculated value is `tail(iq)`.
  - **Data Hazard:** Speculate on the absence of data hazards. For involved variable `rf` in Figure 6, we speculate that there will be no writes to `rf[r]`.
- **Generate a Stream of Values:** Generate a stream containing the sequence of values of the target expression and transform the specification to use these values. For each rule that originally read the target expression:
  - Modify the rule so that it now reads from the head of the new stream.
  - Replace all occurrences of the expression with the value read from the stream.
- **Update Involved Variables:** Augment the new module to update the involved variables with their speculated values. This operation ensures that, during the next clock cycle, the specification will generate an appropriate next value for the target expression.
  Figure 6 presents the results of this transformation for the specification in Figure 2 and target expression `im[pc]`. Figure 1 presents the results of this transformation for the specification in Figure 6 and target expression `rf[r]`.
- **Augment Stream to Handle Failed Speculations:** If the speculation is incorrect, the specification must restore the *updated variables* (the set of all variables updated as a result of the speculation) to their correct values. The algorithm therefore augments the generated stream with the values of the updated variables before the speculation. The set of updated variables for `im[pc]` is {`pc`}. The set of updated variables for `rf[r]` is {`rf,iq`}.
  The algorithm transforms the specification to detect incorrect speculations and, when necessary, use the values in the stream to restore the correct state of the system and clear the stream. The system will therefore restart from a consistent state.
  For the non-pipelined example in Figure 2, Figure 5 shows the resulting specification after the algorithm executes this step.

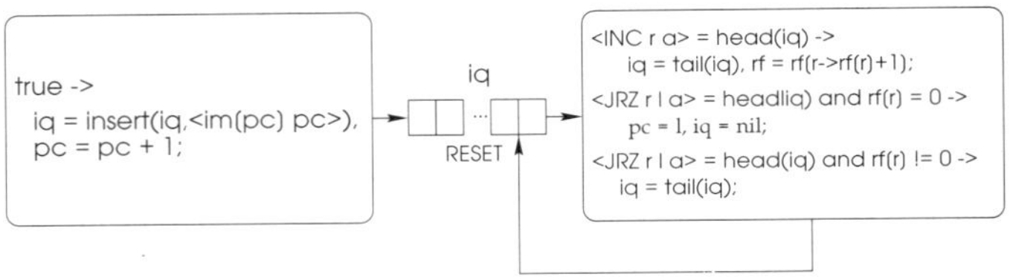

Figure 5: Specification After Stream Augmentation for Handling Failed Speculations

- **Remove Unused Values from Stream:** After updating all the rules that read the target expression, eliminate all the fields of stream entries that were saved and never used again.
  As we notice in Figure 5, field `a` of `iq` is never used, so we can safely remove it from the stream to obtain the specification in Figure 6.

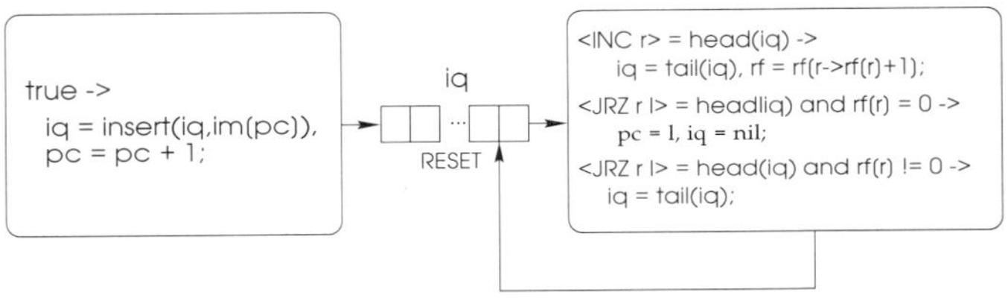

Figure 6: 2-stage Intermediate Specification

4.2 Optimizations

We next present how our algorithm generates logic that implements two techniques — stalling and forwarding — which can improve the quality and performance of the automatically pipelined circuit.

We first present the circuit that responds to incorrect speculations by restoring saved state. Figure 7 shows the transformation schema for a rule R_i

R_i: `e = head(str) and` $P_i \rightarrow A_i$

that reads some target expression `TE`. `e = head(str) and` P_i is the enabling condition of R_i; both clauses are optional. A missing clause reads as a true clause. A_i consists of all the updates performed by rule R_i.

In Figure 7, `IV` stands for the set of involved variables of `TE` and `UV` for the corresponding set of updated variables. `IV` is the disjunct union of two subsets: IV_{ctrl} — the set of involved variables on which the algorithm applies control speculation, and IV_{DH} — the set of involved variables on which it applies data hazard speculation. The speculated value of `TE` is `TE'`, and the set of speculated values for the elements of IV_{ctrl} is IV'_{ctrl}. A_i.upd(IV) returns the set of values that A_i updates the involved variables in IV to. A_i(IV) returns the updates in A_i that write the involved variables in IV. newstr is the newly generated stream of values for target expression TE. dataHazard(E) returns **true** if head(newstr) writes the expression E in the current clock cycle and at least one entry in tail(newstr) reads it.

```
R_i1:  e1 = head(str) -->
     newstr = insert(newstr,<e1 TE[IV'_ctrl/IV_ctrl] UV>),
     IV_ctrl = IV'_ctrl;
If control speculation:
If A_i.upd(IV) = IV'_ctrl then:
  R_i2:  <e2 TE2 UV2> = head(newstr) and
                      P_i[UV2/UV,TE2/TE] -->
       newstr = tail(newstr),
       A_i[UV2/UV,TE2/TE] \ A_i(IV);
Otherwise:
  R_i2:  <e2 TE2 UV2> = head(newstr) and
                      P_i[UV2/UV,TE2/TE] -->
       UV = UV2,          // restore UV
       newstr = nil,      // clear stream
       A_i;               // update
If data hazard speculation:
  R'_i2:  <e2 TE2 UV2> = head(newstr) and
                      P_i[UV2/UV,TE2/TE] and
                      no dataHazard(TE ∪ IV_DH) -->
       newstr = tail(newstr),
       A_i[UV2/UV,TE2/TE] \ A_i(IV);
  R''_i2: <e2 TE2 UV2> = head(newstr) and
                      P_i[UV2/UV,TE2/TE] and
                      dataHazard(TE ∪ IV_DH) -->
       UV = UV2,          // restore UV
       newstr = nil,      // clear stream
       A_i;               // update
```

Figure 7: Restoration Schema

Assume we apply this transformation to the specification in Figure 6, for TE = rf[r]. Figure 8 presents the INC instruction that this transformation generates. The first clause of each newly derived rule reads the head of rq and binds r, x and s to the arguments of the INC instruction. The clause notin(tail(rq),<_ r _ _>) checks if there is an entry in tail(rq) that reads rf[r]. This is the check for a data hazard on rf[r] for the INC instruction. In case of a hazard — second rule in Figure 8 — all the updated variables, in our case iq, have to be restored to their old values. We would like to avoid having to store and carry the whole instruction stream iq along, up to the restoration point. In this case, a viable approach is stalling the pipeline stage that reads rf[r] until all data hazards are cleared.

```
<INC r x s> = head(rq) and
              notin(tail(rq),<_ r _ _>) -->
    rf = rf[r->x+1], rq = tail(rq);
<INC r x s> = head(rq) and
              ~notin(tail(rq),<_ r _ _>) -->
    iq = tail(s), rq = nil, rf = rf[r->x+1];
```

Figure 8: Roll-back Scheme for INC instructions

4.2.1 *Stalling*

Let S be the set of all target expressions on which the algorithm speculates. For TE ∈ S, let $\{R_i\}$ be the set of rules that generate the speculated values of TE and let this stream be Q_1. Let $\{Q_n\}$ be the set of streams that the rules that write TE read from. To eliminate the need to restore state in case of a failed speculation on TE, the algorithm modifies the preconditions of all rules in $\{R_i\}$ to check that either 1) no item in any stream from Q_1 to $\{Q_n\}$ will generate a write to TE or 2) all items that update TE write the same known value. This approach implements the *stalling* mechanism; Figure 1 presents its results for our example.

Let R_{21} and R_{22} be the two resulting rules from splitting the rule in Figure 6 handling INC instructions. The check for data hazards is now handled by R_{21}, which will not fire and read the target expression rf[r] until all the previous rules writing rf[r] did so:

```
R21:<INC r> = head(iq) and notin(rq,<INC r _>) -->
        iq = tail(iq),
        rq = insert(rq,<INC r rf[r]>);
```

Rule R_{22} does not anymore need to check for data hazards for the current target expression — in our example rf[r]. There is no speculation on fly regarding the absence of a data hazard and therefore no need to save the instruction queue in the newly generated stream of values for rf[r]. The derived R_{22} will have the form below:

```
R22:<INC r v> = head(rq) -->
        rf = rf[r->v+1], rq = tail(rq);
```

Stalling trades the potentially higher throughput of speculative execution for a smaller circuit area. This trade-off requires a policy to decide when it is better to stall the pipeline or when it is better to speculate. The decision depends primarily on the accuracy of the predictions and the amount of state that needs to be saved for restoration purposes. Also, if all all the rules ahead in the pipeline will update TE with the same known value, the circuit can safely generate the next value of TE even if some rule will write TE. Therefore, a stalling check replacing a data hazard speculation waits until TE is hazard-free; a stalling check replacing a control speculation waits until all the previous rules in the pipeline can only update TE with the same known value.

4.2.2 *Forwarding*

Regardless of whether the algorithm speculates on the value of TE or stalls the pipeline, waiting for its correct value to become available, generating *forwarding* logic may increase the throughput of the circuit. To implement forwarding, the algorithm replaces the obsolete values of TE in Q_1 with their correct, updated values. Figure 10 shows how the technique updates a rule to implement the bypass. updatedTE stands for the newly computed, correct value of TE.

```
<INC r x> = head(rq) -->
    rq = replace (<INC r _>,<INC r x+1>,
         replace (<JRZ r _ _>,<JRZ r _ x+1>,
         tail(rq))),
    rf = rf[r->x+1];
```

Figure 9: Forward Scheme for INC instructions

Forwarding transforms the two rules handling INC instructions in Figure 8 into the single new rule in Figure 9. This rule produces a circuit that updates all of the entries in `rq` produced by rules that accessed `rf[r]` with the new correct value `x+1`.

```
R'_i1:  e1= head(str) and dataHazard(TE) →
      newstr = insert(newstr,<e1 updatedTE UV>),
      IV_ctrl = IV'_ctrl;
R''_i1:  e1 = head(str) and no dataHazard(TE) →
      newstr = insert(newstr,<e1 TE[IV'_ctrl/IV_ctrl] UV>),
      IV_ctrl = IV'_ctrl;
If control speculation:
If A_i.upd(IV) = IV'_ctrl then:
  R_i2:  <e2 TE2 UV2> = head(newstr) and
                        P_i[UV2/UV,TE2/TE] →
       newstr = tail(newstr)[updatedTE/TE2],
       A_i[UV2/UV,TE2/TE] \ A_i(IV);
Otherwise:
  R_i2:  <e2 TE2 UV2> = head(newstr) and
                        P_i[UV2/UV,TE2/TE] →
       UV = UV2,          // restore UV
       newstr = nil,      // clear stream
       A_i;               // update
If data hazard speculation:
  R'_i2:  <e2 TE2 UV2> = head(newstr) and
                        P_i[UV2/UV,TE2/TE] and
                        no dataHazard(IV_DH) →
       newstr = tail(newstr)[updatedTE/TE2],
       A_i[UV2/UV,TE2/TE] \ A_i(IV);
  R''_i2:  <e2 TE2 UV2> = head(newstr) and
                        P_i[UV2/UV,TE2/TE] and
                        dataHazard(IV_DH) →
       UV = UV2,          // restore UV
       newstr = nil,      // clear stream
       A_i;               // update
```

Figure 10: Forward Scheme

Forwarding reduces the amount of time that the circuit spends recovering from incorrect speculations or waiting for correct values to become available. It may therefore increase the throughput of the circuit.

5. EXPERIMENTAL RESULTS

We have implemented the pipelining algorithm within our prototype synthesizer, which generates synthesizable Verilog implementations at the RTL level. We then by compared the results obtained by our algorithm against a hand-written version that implements the same basic functionality with our example processor. We wrote a non-pipelined specification of a 32-bit datapath processor with a complete instruction set[2] and ran it through our pipelining algorithm for all the pipeline buffers of depth one. The resulting pipelined specification was then fed into the synthesizer to obtain a Verilog model for it. This model was then synthesized using the Synopsis Design Compiler to an industry standard .25 micron standard cell process. To serve as a reference point, we also synthesized, in the same environment, the Santa Clara University SCU RTL 98 DSP, a hand-written (in Verilog), standard 32-bit fixed point DSP that implements the same basic functionality. Our automatically pipelined version had a cycle time of 88.9 MHz as opposed to a 90.9 MHz cycle time for the hand-pipelined version; the synthesized areas were virtually identical.

It took us approximately fifteen minutes to write the specification for the non-pipelined processor and less than one minute to run it through our pipeline algorithm. Our specification contains 7 lines for state declarations and 10 lines of rule definitions for module specifications. Our automatically generated implementation consists of about 1200 lines of synthesizable Verilog. We tested the generated Verilog model using the Cadence NCVerilog simulator.

[2]The instruction set contains load, store, jump, ALU, multiply and variable shift operations, but no division.

6. CONCLUSIONS

This paper presents a new approach for automatically pipelining sequential circuits: repeatedly extract a computation from the critical path, move it into a new stage, then use speculation to generate a stream of values that keep the pipeline full. We also present extensions that integrate stalling and forwarding into this basic approach. Our experimental results provide encouraging evidence that the approach can deliver efficient pipelined implementations.

7. REFERENCES

[1] M. Breternitz and J. P. Shen. Architecture synthesis of high-performance application-specific processors. In *Proceedings of the 27th ACM/IEEE Design Automation Conference*, 1990.

[2] F. Chang and A. Hu. Fast specification of cycle-accurate processor models. *To appear in ICCD 2001*, 2001.

[3] R. J. Cloutier and D. E. Thomas. Synthesis of pipelined instruction set processors. In *Proceedings of the 30th ACM/IEEE Design Automation Conference*, 1993.

[4] H. D. M. G. Goossens, J. Rabaey and J. Vandewalle. An efficient microcode-compiler for custom DSP-processors. *IEEE Transactions on Computer-Aided Design*, 9:925–937, 1990.

[5] G. Goossens, J. Vandewalle, and H. DeMan. Loop optimization in register-transfer scheduling for DSP-systems. In *Proceedings of the 26th ACM/IEEE Design Automation Conference*, 1989.

[6] S. Hassoun and C. Ebeling. Architectural retiming: Pipelining latency-constrained circuits. In *Proceedings of the 33rd ACM/IEEE Design Automation Conference*.

[7] J. Hoe and Arvind. Hardware synthesis from term rewriting systems. In *VLSI: Systems on a chip*, Lisbon, Portugal, Dec. 1999.

[8] U. Holtmann and R. Ernst. Combining MBP-speculative computation and loop pipelining in high-level synthesis. In *ED & TC*, 1995.

[9] I.-J. Huang and A. M. Despain. High level synthesis of pipelined instruction set processors and back-end compilers. In *Proceedings of the 29th ACM/IEEE Design Automation Conference*, 1992.

[10] C.-T. Hwang, Y.-C. Hsu, and Y.-L. Lin. Scheduling for functional pipelining and loop winding. In *Proceedings of the 28th ACM/IEEE Design Automation Conference*.

[11] D. Kroening and W. Paul. Automated pipeline design. In *Proceedings of the 38th ACM/IEEE Design Automation Conference*, Las Vegas, 2001.

[12] C. E. Leiserson, F. Rose, and J. Saxe. Optimizing synchronous circuitry by retiming. In *Proceedings of the 3rd Caltech Conference on VLSI*.

[13] M.-C. Marinescu and M. C. Rinard. High-level specification and efficient implementation of pipelined circuits. In *Proceedings of the ASP-DAC*, 2001.

[14] N. Park and A. C. Parker. Sehwa: A software package for synthesis of pipelines from behavioral specifications. *IEEE Transactions on Computer-Aided Design*, 7:356–370, 1988.

[15] P. B. Paulin and J. P. Knight. Force-directed scheduling for the behavioral synthesis of ASIC's. *IEEE Transactions on Computer-Aided Design*, 8:661–679, 1989.

[16] X. Shen and Arvind. Using term rewriting systems to design and verify processors. *IEEE Micro Special Issue on "Modeling and Validation of Microprocessors"*, 1999.

Synthesis of Pipelined Memory Access Controllers for Streamed Data Applications on FPGA-based Computing Engines

Joonseok Park and Pedro C. Diniz
University of Southern California / Information Sciences Institute
4676 Admiralty Way, Suite 1001
Marina del Rey, California 90292
{joonseok, pedro}@isi.edu

ABSTRACT

Commercially available behavioral synthesis tools do not adequately support FPGA vendor-specific external memory interfaces making it extremely difficult to exploit pipelined memory access modes as well as application specific memory operations scheduling critical for high-performance solutions. This lack of support substantially increases the complexity and the burden on designers in the mapping of applications to FPGA-based computing engines. In this paper we address the problem of external memory interfacing and aggressive scheduling of memory operations by proposing a decoupled architecture with two components - one component captures the specific target architecture timing while the other component uses application specific memory access pattern information. Our results support the claim that it is possible to exploit application specific information and integrate that knowledge into custom schedulers that mix pipelined and non-pipelined access modes aimed at reducing the overhead associated with external memory accesses. The results also reveal that the additional design complexity of the scheduler, and its impact in the overall design is minimal.

Keywords: FPGA-based configurable computing; Scheduling of Memory Accesses; Hardware Interfaces and Customizable Memory Controllers.

1. INTRODUCTION

Commercially available synthesis tools for FPGAs have mostly ignored system level issues when dealing with external memories. While some tools now incorporate internal RAM modules and the mapping of array variables to them, they have avoided all external memory interfacing issues. Even for internal memories, the current tools require specific syntax and synthesis expertise precluding the interfacing with third party vendors for which timing information is either unavailable or cannot fit into the timing model of the tool. In addition most, if not all, behavioral synthesis tools do not support pipelined modes further restricting an important source of performance improvement. As a result designers must engage in laborious and error-prone matching and synthesis of interface signals.

Configurable architectures offer a unique opportunity to address the memory access and interfacing issues via customization. Improvements can be achieved by creating specialized hardware components for generating addresses and packing and unpacking data items. Compiler analysis can provide application knowledge as to the memory access patterns for pipelining of data references corresponding to array references across multiple iterations of loops. Furthermore the compiler can derive information about the relative rate among various array references and embed that knowledge into the scheduling of memory operations.

In this paper we focus on the design, implementation and validation of external memory interfacing modules that are generated by a compiler and behavioral synthesis tool that translate high-level computations directly to FPGA hardware. For maximum generality, we have separated the memory interface into two components. The first component is target-dependent and captures the specific target architecture timing requirements for accessing memory. The second component is architecture-independent and provides a set of channels and memory access modes abstractions for the application to store and retrieve data from memory. In particular the designs we have implemented allow compiler-generated designs to exploit pipelined access modes and mix both pipelined and non-pipelined memory accesses modes.

We used the interfaces described in this paper to develop application specific scheduling strategies for a set of four digital image-processing applications. The experimental results reveal that while the designs do not exploit all of the available external memory bandwidth, they achieve respectable performance at a reasonable implementation and generality cost.

ISSS'01, October 1-3, 2001, Montréal, Québec, Canada,

This paper makes the following contributions:

- Describes an abstract memory channel architecture with the concepts of channels, FIFOs and schedulers for managing memory accesses. This architecture decouples the target-dependent from the application-specific implementation knowledge thereby decreasing the complexity of interfacing with commercially available target architectures.
- Describes a suite of simple memory access schedulers for both pipelined and non-pipelined access modes for statically schedule streamed data access patterns. The schedulers are parameterizable and interface with behavioral code for the core datapath to generate complete designs.
- Describes an optimization in the definition of the memory controller scheduler that exploits application specific knowledge. This optimization reduces the number of controller cycles improving the overall design's performance.
- Presents experimental results of the application of distinct scheduling strategies for a small set of kernel applications on a commercial FPGA-based computing engine. For these kernels pipelined access mode improves the performance up to twofold while the controller FSM optimization further improves up to 10%.

The results presented in this paper support the claim that it is possible to exploit application specific information and integrate that knowledge in a custom scheduler for reducing the overhead associated with external memory accesses. The results also reveal that the additional design complexity of the scheduler, and its impact in the overall design is minimal.

While generality and performance are often conflicting goals, the complexity reduction, faster and more robust mapping of applications to FPGA-based hardware, are non-negligible factors in fast-prototyping settings. We believe that the simple abstract memory architecture with the interfaces presented in this paper are fundamental concepts that allow the easy integration of high-level analysis and program transformations in the mapping of applications to configurable computing architectures.

The rest of this paper is organized as follows. In the next section we describe the proposed external memory interface and its underlying abstractions. Next we describe the opportunities for application specific memory channel scheduling strategies. In section 3 we describe the basic analysis our compiler uses to generate the memory interfaces by analysis of the application programs. Section 4 presents a set of experimental results. We survey related work in section 5 and conclude in section 6.

2. EXTERNAL MEMORY INTERFACING

The proposed external memory interface is defined around a target-dependent interface and a target-independent interface. The target-dependent interface takes into account the specific timing requirements of the target hardware architecture and for practical reasons is tightly coupled to the vendor-supplied memory interface. This interface includes strict requirements that every memory access must meet such as the relative timing of memory operations; clock cycle counts for each type of access; and binding of pins in the design. The target-independent interface allows the core datapath that implements the computation in hardware to interface with input/output FIFO queues using a simple, timing-independent protocol.

2.1 Streamed Execution Model

To support the operation of streamed applications we have defined several memory access abstractions to exploit application-specific knowledge and advanced memory access modes, respectively, an **address generation unit (AGU)**, a **memory access scheduler (MAS)** and **FIFO queues** (see Figure 1).

The core of the computation is carried out by a datapath with input and output ports. These ports are physically bound to FIFO queues to retrieve and store data from memory. As computation progresses the datapath issues requests for data from the FIFO queues associated with its ports. These requests are then translated into low-level signals via the target-dependent interface. A simple handshaking protocol allows the design control to be informed about when the data has been deposited into the FIFO queue.

2.2 Memory Architecture Abstractions

Associated with each FIFO queue there is the notion of a **channel** and a **data stream**. A data stream defines a sequence of addresses and is identified by the tuple *(base_address, offset, stride)*. A channel binds a port, the corresponding FIFO queue in time, by the contents of specific hardware resources in the address generation unit (AGU). The AGU consists of a register table with one entry per data stream supported. Each entry has a set of programmable fields to keep physical address data, an arithmetic unit to update and generate physical addresses, and a FSM to generate control signals. The details of the implementation are described in [4].

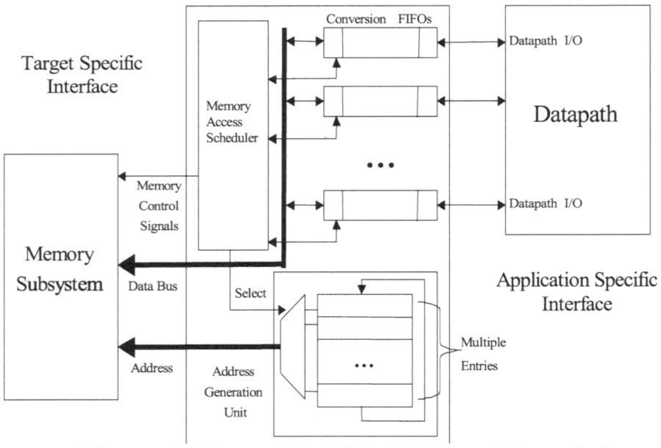

Figure 1. Memory Architecture and Interfacing.

We have defined and implemented both interfaces and hardware abstractions to support the data stream execution model of this approach for designs with a single computation task and with both single and multiple external memories.

2.3 Application Specific Scheduling

In the simpler case where the memory accesses can be determined statically, the compiler can **schedule** the order in which the accesses should occur. The scheduler, implemented in hardware via a FSM, should avoid deadlocking due to internal state transition conditions of multiple outstanding memory operations that can be dependent on each other. The memory access scheduler is defined by three hardware processes. A process checks which of the channels needing service by checking if the corresponding FIFO is empty (or full); a process to issue memory requests and a process to synchronize the transactions of the other two processes.

A simple scheduling calls for the handling of each memory channel corresponding to the datapath input/output ports in a **round-robin** fashion. For each computation, typically an iteration of a loop, the scheduler checks whether or not a given channel needs to access memory by inspecting the FIFO queue associated with it. To be able to handle conditional memory accesses we convert all conditional accesses to non-conditional accesses by speculatively fetching all of the potentially required. This approach, while wasteful of memory bandwidth allows for a much simpler memory controller. An alternative would be to implement a memory controller with the possibility of aborting memory accesses. This approach however would require timing the signals that dictate which memory references to abort, in the core datapath with the memory controller at the appropriate time. In the presence of pipelined execution modes this design would clearly become more sophisticated most likely leading to a reduced overall design performance.

Despite its apparent simplicity, this strategy interacts with other techniques common in synthesis such as loop pipelining. Using pipelining, loop prologues and loop epilogues do not exhibit all of the memory operations of the regular, steady state bodies of the loop. Typically the prologue generates no write operations and the epilogue requires no additional input data. The information about the scheduling of prologues and epilogues must be encoded in the scheduler's FSM, therefore increasing its complexity. In addition, round-robin works well if all of the channels have the same rate, that is, they produce/consume the same number of data items per cycle of the computation. If different channels have distinct rates, the scheduler must check for every computation, whether or not a memory operation is required. Again, because the FSM uses a larger number of predicates to determine its appropriate action, the implementation complexity increases.

A way to eliminate the overhead associated with the checking of which channels need to access memory is to embed information about several channels whose data access exhibit the same pattern. For example, if at every iteration of the computation there are three channels that need to access memory, testing for a single channel, is equivalent to test for any of them. Using this approach the number of FSM states, and therefore, cycles dedicated to hardware checks is substantially reduced. We call this approach a round-robin **group** scheduling strategy. Clearly, this group strategy can only be applied when the compiler can determine the exact relationship between memory accesses of the channels.

3. COMPILER ANALYSIS AND SUPPORT

We have integrated the synthesis of pipelined memory access controllers described in the previous sections in the DEFACTO compilation and synthesis system [3]. The current implementation analyzes source C programs in the intermediate SUIF representation format [10] and identifies opportunities for simple data reuse using tapped-delay lines. The analysis focuses on loop nests with array references using affine index functions (e.g., pixel[2*i + j +1]). While the analysis, as described in detail in [4] is capable of handling indexed for loops with compile-time unknown bounds, the current code generation phase must rely on known bounds to perform loop unrolling of inner that are to be mapped to hardware.

Given a set of array references in a loop nest that exhibit temporal reuse the compiler analyzes the reference index functions and the loop bounds to determine the *base address*, *offset* of the array being accessed as well as the *stride* of consecutive accesses. Figure 2 below illustrates the extraction of a single data stream corresponding to the accesses and data reuse of the array references in a loop.

```
for(i=1; i <= N; i++){                        // Compiler extracts
  tmp = 2*a[i] + a[i+1] + 2*a[i+2];           // stream 0 = (a, 1, 1) in
  if(tmp < threshold){
    e[2i-2] = 0;                              // stream 1 = (e,0,2) out
  } else {
    e[2i-2] = 1;
  }
}
```

Figure 2. Temporal Data Reuse and Stream Extraction.

Using the information about data streams the compiler uses library functions to define a data stream and programs an entry in the address generation unit (AGU) that will generate the sequence of addresses that correspond to the consecutive array accesses. The compiler also determines, using a very simple algorithm, the placement of the data in the FPGA's external memories, so that it can generate the base addresses for each of the data streams. In addition the compiler generates source C code, via a predefined set of library functions, that map the data to and from the host processor on the target FPGA's external memories.

As part of the DEFACTO code generation phase the compiler emits structural VHDL code that implements all of the functionality of the memory interface and corresponding abstractions using predefined VHDL parameterizable templates. This structural code is then "linked" automatically with the behavioral code that describes the code of the datapath computation by via a naming scheme for the individual datapath ports and corresponding streams.

4. EXPERIMENTAL RESULTS

We now present experimental results for the application of distinct memory access channel scheduling strategies as described in Section 2. We first describe the methodology used in these experiments and then present the results obtained for three image processing kernel computations running on a real FPGA-based computing board.

4.1 Methodology

We have mapped three (3) computation kernels from C to VHDL using the DEFACTO design system [3]. The DEFACTO mapping process generates behavioral VHDL specifications for computations in the body of loop nests it finds to be profitable to execute on an FPGA-based computing engine – the Annapolis WildStar™ [13] FPGA-based board.

Next, we have manually modified the memory channel interface for the target architecture to allow the implementation of two distinct flavors of the round-robin memory access scheduling strategy, namely **naïve (N)**, **pipelined(P)**, **group (G)** and **pipelined with grouping(P+G)** scheduling. We then compare the performance of the designs using the different strategies. This performance comparison was carried out in a functional simulator, ModelSim™[7], where we are able to extract more precise clock cycle counts. We also confirmed the performance improvements via real executions on the WildStar™ board.

The WildStar™ board has three Xilinx® [15] Virtex 1000BG560 parts each of which is connected to two SRAM memory modules with 4Mbytes capacity. We have used Synplicity® Synplify® 5.1.5 and Xilinx® M1 place & route tool to generate the bitmap file for the Virtex parts. To exacerbate the problems of memory access scheduling, we mapped all of the applications data onto a single memory module. This approach allowed us to determine the severity of the memory scheduling issue. Techniques such as stripping data arrays onto different memory banks (see for example [5]) are orthogonal to the scheduling approach presented in this paper.

4.2 Applications

Sobel Edge Detection (SOBEL)

This application implements a simple eight point computations based on a 3-by-3 window of a 128-by-128 image of pixels. Each iteration of the inner most loop of the code's main loop nest consumes 8 data items from the input array variable and produces 1 item of the output array variable. The number of operations can be reduced significantly to 3 read and 1 write stream operations exploiting data reuse using tapped-delay lines across iterations of the main computation loop.

Automatic Target Recognition (ATR)

This application computes a binary image correlation using a binary mask array variable and a scalar accumulation variable. Because the compiler has aggressively exploited loop unrolling it generates a design with vast amount of parallelism and data reuse. Due to the unrolling, however, the number of data memory accesses per iteration of the inner loop is substantial. To study the impact of the number of memory accesses and hardware support for a varying number of channels we have implemented two variants of this application. One variant called ATR-4 uses 4 input channels and corresponds to using a fixed mask variable for the correlation computation. The other variant, called ATR-8 uses 8 input channels, 4 channels for the input image variable and another 4 for the binary mask.

Multiply-Accumulate-Zero (MAZ)

This computation computes the sums of the product of every pair of adjacent array values if the first value of the pair is smaller then the current running sum. For every addition, the computation zeros out the first element of the pair in the array. Because the accumulation and multiplication (16 bits output) is conditional and data dependent on the running sum of the computation, we call this computation multiply-accumulate-zero (MAZ). From the standpoint of the memory controller this computation exhibits a more irregular memory access pattern as some of the write operations are dependent not on an input values but rather on the value of an internal computation.

4.3 Results

We begin this discussion by first characterizing the execution of each of the applications using the default round-robin naive memory access scheduling strategy. Figure 3 below presents a breakdown of the execution time for the steady state of the main computation loop in each of these applications for a single memory bank implementation.

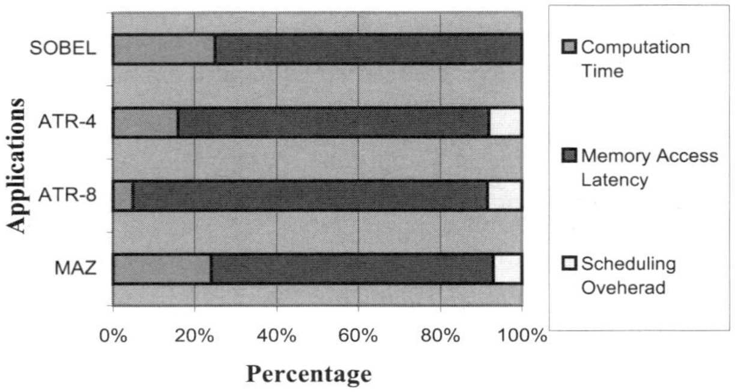

Figure 3. Execution Time Breakdown for Tested Applications.

As expected, and given that in these experiments memory accesses are blocking, the bulk of the execution time (60% to 80%) is spent stalling on memory accesses. Approximately 8% to 9% is spent checking the status of the input/output FIFO queues.

Table 1 shows the performance results for all applications for the different scheduling strategies. These results exclude the initial data loading and final data retrieval from the board. We report the overall design size in terms of FPGA slices; the maximum allowed clock rate for the design; the simulated execution time using a 25 MHz clock and the speedup measured as the ratio of the execution time of each version with respect to the computation using the **naïve** scheduling strategy.

Table 1 reveals that all designs are small (12.5% maximum FPGA occupancy) and therefore exhibit good performance characteristics in terms of maximum attainable clock rates. Table 1 also reveals the performance advantages of pipeline with an average speedup of 1.9 over the four tested kernels. Group scheduling by itself yields modest performance improvement with an average speedup of 1.1. When combined with pipelined, group scheduling boosts the average speedup to 2.05. This improvement is most noticeable for ATR-8 where the number of channels with the same input/output behavior is the largest.

Table 1. Synthesis and Timing Results.

Applications		Slices (out of 12,288)	Max. Freq. (MHz)	Simulation Time (nsecs)	Speedup
SOBEL	N	1,144	30.1	1,312,020	1.00
	P	1,061	31.5	738,540	1.78
	G	1,160	31.7	1,312,140	1.00
	P+G	1,068	31.6	697,660	**1.88**
ATR-4	N	1,968	25.9	120,040	1.00
	P	1,980	25.6	66,600	1.82
	G	1,974	33.9	102,280	1.17
	P+G	1,984	26.9	59,600	**2.00**
ATR-8	N	2,771	25.9	188,440	1.00
	P	2,707	25.9	71,840	2.62
	G	2,718	30.8	163,440	1.15
	P+G	2,730	25.9	69,480	**2.71**
MAZ	N	1,027	30.4	85,760	1.00
	P	1,191	36.2	62,360	1.38
	G	1,226	31.5	78,680	1.09
	P+G	1,003	29.6	55,520	**1.55**

Table 2 shows the synthesis metrics for the synthesis of the channel controllers for each design. Overall the more sophisticated group-scheduling controller has clock rates in the 100MHz range and therefore appears not to impact the critical path of the whole design. By itself, the implementation of the group-scheduling controller requires no more than 21 additional slices than the simpler naïve controller does for a total a maximum of 75 slices barely 5% of the designs.

Table 2 Synthesis Metrics for Channel Controller (N: Naïve, P: Pipelined, G: Group P+G: Pipelined with Grouping).

Applications		CLBs	Gates	Clock Rate (MHz)
SOBEL	N	29	381	140.1
	P	25	333	130.3
	G	35	431	87.5
	P+G	35	448	134,7
ATR-4	N	35	458	127.3
	P	42	568	125.0
	G	40	531	105.2
	P+G	46	635	120.7
ATR-8	N	54	679	106.2
	P	74	937	82.2
	G	57	758	77.9
	P+G	75	1,010	69.4
MAZ	N	30	383	120.5
	P	34	450	112.8
	G	36	450	115.6
	P+G	45	559	116.4

4.4 Discussion

The experimental results, not surprisingly, reveal that pipelining techniques substantially improve the overall design performance. The implementation of group-scheduling techniques marginally increases the performance for the whole design with negligible impact in terms of area and very little influence on the maximum clock rate.

While we are able to eliminate almost all the memory overhead by pipelining and aggressive group scheduling there are several techniques that have been explored in other contexts and could be explore for the context of FPGA-based designs, namely:

- Reducing the sharing of physical bus channels will reduce the memory latency.
- Assigning multiple memory modules to disjoint input array for concurrent accesses.
- Aggressive pre-fetching and overlapping memory accesses with computations.

In this work we have focused exclusively on application level techniques that impact the design of the memory controller, rather than on architecture related approaches for reducing memory latency. We focused on the scheduling of memory accesses within a single computational task where memory accesses are statically scheduled. The scheduling in the context of multiple tasks may require a more flexible run-time scheduling strategy to minimize memory access contention. In the future we plan to address the implementation of dynamic, run-time scheduling implementation techniques where a schedule is setup only at run-time rather than statically for both single and multiple tasks.

Given the trade-off between generality and performance we have estimated the performance gap between the currently automated applications in this empirical study and what a designer could achieve exploiting the overlapping of computation in the core datapath with the communication with external memory. In Table 3 we compare the performance of the generated designs against an optimal solution where the memory accesses are perfectly scheduled and are fully overlapped with the computation in a zero latency scenario.

Table 3. Performance Expectation for Hand Designs (P+G+O: Pipelined with Grouping and Overlapping, OPT: Optimal Scheduling Design).

Applications		Speedup	Applications		Speedup
SOBEL	N	1.00	ATR-8	N	1.00
	P+G	**1.88**		P+G	**2.71**
	P+G+O	3.60		P+G+O	4.41
	OPT	7.99		OPT	7.00
ATR-4	N	1.00	MAZ	N	1.00
	P+G	**2.00**		P+G	**1.55**
	P+G+O	3.56		P+G+O	2.91
	OPT	7.50		OPT	6.48

While Table 3 reveals there is still a substantial performance gap between the automatically generated codes and the possibly infeasible optimal version, the effort and time investment for a hand design is still substantial, in particular for a novice programmer. While our designs take a few seconds to generate and about 30 minutes to synthesize and download onto the board, a hand design can take days if not weeks to design and verify its correctness.

5. RELATED WORK

Other researchers have addressed the issues memory operations scheduling in the context of application specific implementations.

Weinhardt and Luk developed memory access optimizations for pipeline vectorization in RAM interface [12] using a scheme to reduce consecutive memory accesses of array data using shift registers but accessing only on-chip RAM modules. Gokhale and Stone [5] proposed an automatic array allocation compile-time algorithm for multi-level memory subsystem. They attempt to allocate array variables to memories based on the memory latency, data access frequency and execution schedule. Schmit [11] developed a mapping scheme for mapping datapaths with memory operations directly to hardware. His approach uses a centralized memory controller scheme where the scheduling of the operations is done in conjunction with the execution of the datapath computation. Panda et. al. [8,9] refined this approach by defining a time-constrained based specification of the a centralized scheduler for handling external memory operations. Catthoor, Balasa et. al. developed and evaluated memory optimizations for embedded systems for a particular application set [1,2,6]. This research focuses on optimizations to minimize memory area and power consumption. Catthoor also proposed a data packing scheme to reduce memory bandwidth requirements for dynamic data structure. Wuytack et al. suggested minimizing memory bandwidth requirements [14] by mapping highly accessed array variables to fast hierarchy storage.

The research described in this paper differs from these efforts in several aspects. The common approach to memory scheduling operations has been to develop, based on a specification for the dependences of the operations, a centralized memory scheduler that fetches the data from an external memory into the datapath. Our approach provides an architecture independent view of the datapath and a memory controller that is decoupled from the datapath execution controller. This scheme has several advantages over the centralized control schemes proposed by previous researchers. First, in designs where pipelined memory accesses are desirable, the implementation complexity of a centralized scheme substantially increases. The scheduler needs to generate a controller that obeys the timing constrains for all the memory accesses in the pipeline. Second, our approach makes it easier to incorporate several tasks into the same design allowing them to share physical memory ports. A centralized memory controller scheme would require the description of a joint behavior for all the tasks a proposition that is hardly extensible and scalable.

6. CONCLUSION

The performance of FPGA-based computing platforms depends critically on the performance of external memory interface. In this paper we have described an approach to decouple the concerns of memory interfacing and static scheduling of possible memory accesses for applications with streamed data. We described the application of simple scheduling strategies to three kernel computations. The experimental results reveal that we are able to significantly increase the performance (speedup of two) of the overall design by using pipelined memory accesses. We further improve the performance by eliminating almost all of the latency due internal memory controller optimization resulting in a further 10% performance increase. The experiments reveal that the added complexity of the resulting designs is minimal.

7. REFERENCES

[1] F. Balasa, F. Catthoor, and H. De Man “"Dataflow-driven Memory Allocation for Multi-dimensional Signal Processing Systems", Proceedings of the IEEE International Conference on Computer Aided Design, Santa Jose, Calif., Nov. 1994, pp. 31-34.

[2] F. Catthoor, F. Franssen, S. Wuytack, L. Nachtergaele, and H. DeMan "Global communication and memory optimizing transformations for low power signal processing systems", IEEE workshop on VLSI signal processing, La Jolla, Calif., Oct. 1994.

[3] P. Diniz, M. Hall, J. Park, B. So and H. Ziegler, “Bridging the gap between Compilation and Behavioral Synthesis in the DEFACTO System”, To appear in the Proc. of the workshop on Languages and Compilers for Parallel Computing, (LCPC’2001).

[4] P. Diniz and J. Park, "Automatic Synthesis of Data Storage and Control Structures for FPGA-based Computing Machines", In Proc. of the IEEE Symp. on FPGAs for Custom Computing Machines (FCCM'00), IEEE Computer Society Press, Los Alamitos, Calif., Oct. 2000, pp. 91-100.

[5] M. Gokhale and J. Stone “Automatic Allocation of Arrays to Memories in FPGA Processors With Multiple Memory Banks” Proc. of IEEE Symp. on FPGAs for Custom Computing Machines (FCCM’99), IEEE Computer Society Press, Los Alamitos, Calif. Oct. 1999, pp. 63-69.

[6] M. Miranda, F.Catthoor, M. Janssen and H. DeMan, “High-level address optimization and synthesis techniques for data-transfer-intensive applications”, IEEE Transactions on Very Large Scale Integration (VLSI) Systems, 6(4), Dec. 1998, pp. 677 –686.

[7] Monet™ User’s and Reference Manual Software Release R42, Mentor Graphics Inc., 1999.

[8] P. Panda, F. Catthoor, N. Dutt, K. Danckaert, E. Brockmeyer, C. Kulkarni, A. Vandercappelle and P. Kjeldsberg. “Data and memory optimization techniques for embedded systems”, ACM Transactions on Design Automation of Electronic System, 6(2), Apr. 2001.

[9] P. Panda, N. Dutt and A. Nicolau, “Exploiting off-chip memory access modes in high-level synthesis” Proceedings of the 1997 IEEE/ACM International Conference on Computer-Aided Design (ICCAD’97), 1997, pp. 333 – 340.

[10] “The Stanford SUIF Compilation System”, version 1.1.2 Public domain software and documentation available at http://suif.stanford.edu.

[11] H. Schmit and D. Thomas, "Synthesis of Applications-Specific Memory Designs," IEEE Transactions on VLSI Systems, 5(1), Mar. 1997, pp. 101-111.

[12] M. Weinhardt and W. Luk “Memory Access Optimization and RAM interface for Pipeline Vectorization”, In Proc. of Symp. on Field Programmable Logic (FPL’99), Springer-Verlag, 1999, pp. 61-70.

[13] WildStar™ Reference Manual revision 4.0, Annapolis MicroSystems Inc., 1999.

[14] S.Wuytack, F.Catthoor, G.De Jong, and H.De Man. “Minimizing the required memory bandwidth in VLSI system realizations”, IEEE Transactions on Very Large Scale Integration (VLSI) Systems, 7(4), Dec. 1999, pp. 433 –441.

[15] Xilinx, Inc. Virtex™ 2.5V Filed Programmable Gate Arrays Product Specification. DS003(v2.4), 2000.

Soft-Cores Generation by Instruction Set Analysis

Alessandro Fin Franco Fummi Giovanni Perbellini

Universitá di Verona
Dipartimento di Informatica
Verona, ITALY

Abstract

The popularity of Soft Cores *is rapidly increasing. Their integration in a design requires their synthesis and optimization, thus their application is more complex than the use of* Hard Cores. *However,* Soft Cores *can be customized to the design constraints, thus promising to lead to more efficient designs. The decision of using* Soft *or* Hard Cores *is difficult since it is a trade-off between performance, cost and design time. The parametrization methodology presented in this paper gives to the* Soft Core *providers the possibility of putting on the market easily customizable versions of their* Cores. *Moreover, the proposed* Soft-Cores *generator helps the designer to select between the* Soft *and the* Hard-Core *version of a processor.*

Keywords: soft IP-core, microprocessor customization

1. INTRODUCTION

The definition of standard interfaces and the *IP-core* based design are some of the solutions adopted by VLSI companies to speed up the design. The market window for a new chip is getting smaller and smaller and missing it can imply no revenues. The processor market is one of the more challenging markets and processor design is complex and expensive. Moreover, it requires to foresee the exact date for the final release, in order to not miss the time to market.

The popularity of *Soft Cores* is rapidly increasing. Their integration in a design requires their synthesis and optimization, thus their use is more complex than the design of *Hard Cores*. However, the final design is more flexible and it can be easily adapted to different design configurations. The development of a *Soft Core* allows core providers to put on the market several different *Cores* based on the same original design. Thus, the same basic design can be exploited for a wider range of products (i.e., complete or reduced instruction set, different data size, etc.). The down-side of this approach is the longer and more complex design process. In fact, VLSI designers have to apply specific design rules to obtain a configurable *Core*. The decision of using *Soft* or *Hard Cores* is difficult since it is a trade-off between performance, cost and design time. The customization methodology presented in this paper tries to help the designer in this decision.

ISSS'01, October 1-3, 2001, Montréal, Québec, Canada.

Reusing *IP-cores* is becoming more and more popular, especially for large Systems on a Chip [3, 4]. Famous commercial examples (e.g., [5, 6]) have fixed I/O interfaces, no configurable instruction set and register data size. They are well known examples of *Hard Cores* available on the market. These designs are not configurable, but this feature allows to optimize the performance of these processors. In fact, many design optimizations (i.e., architectural optimizations) can be easily applied only if the structural description of the processor is the same during the whole design work-flow. On the contrary, the customizable design can offer different kind of optimizations and advantages: area saving for design based on FPGA, memory saving implied by smaller instruction sets (i.e. the OP code is shorter) and fast development of processor families based on the common original design. Another commercial tool is [2]. It offers a very complete tool suite to customize a base CPU considering the required instruction set. A different example is the VHDL IP library (VIP [7]): a library of parametric IP modules from CSELT. Each design in the library can be configured to match the final design requirements. The general component descriptions are adapted to the design specifications by invoking configuration functions of the VIP package. The parametric methodology is based on the *Generic* VHDL statement. On one hand, this statement allows a structural parametrization of one entity, but on the other hand it makes impossible to define constraints between design components and to state how these components are affected by the processor's instruction set. [8] is a *Soft Core* generator for RISC processors. This solution produces RT level configurable descriptions. In fact, it is possible to set: instruction size (from 8 to 32 bit), ALU dimension (from 8 to 64 bit) and the instruction set can be restricted to a subset of the original set. This solution, even if highly flexible, has been designed for a precise architecture describing a unique RISC processor. PEAS-III [1, 8] is another efficient tool to parametrize pipelined processors. As for the previous example, it is an architecture-specific tool.

The aim of this paper is to present a parametric *Core* generation methodology applicable to any kind of processor. It is able to produce an *ad-hoc Core* description given the complete VHDL description at the RT level of the processor and the requirements list. This allows the *Core* vendor to supply several version of the same main design by varying: instruction set and data size. The automatic customization process is guided by the user requirements. A large number of different processor descriptions can be generated. By performing a rapid synthesis, the user can easily measure if the customized processor is convenient, in terms of area and delay, with respect to the general processor. If the analysis is positive, the user can decide to accurately synthesize and optimize the customized processor (by following the *Soft Core* design strategy), otherwise the general processor is selected, thus following the *Hard Core* design strategy. The presented methodology does not exploit any architecture specific feature as [1, 8], thus it can be applied to any architecture expressed by a controller and data-path schema. This feature allows to apply the customization proposed methodology to a wider set of Cores.

The rest of the paper is organized as follow. Section 2 describes the features of the adopted methodology to customize the processor description. More information about controller and data-path parametrization and synchronization are presented in Section 3. The parametrization of a couple of example processors is presented in Section 4, while the last section is devoted to concluding remarks and future works.

2. METHODOLOGY

The parametric generation of VHDL processor descriptions allows to obtain several different versions of the same processor. The main differences among them are the instruction set and data size. In order to produce the customized descriptions, the RT-level description of the full processor is elaborated considering the list of customization requirements.

```
-- <DUPLICATE α,instr_x,instr_y,instr_z >
    component COMP1
        port(i0: in bit_32;
             i1: in bit_32;
             i2: in bit;
             o0: out bit_32);
    end component;
-- </DUPLICATE>
```

Figure 1: Command-comment DUPLICATE example.

Figure 2 shows the differences between the generic and the parametric design work-flow. The list of customization requirements is an input supplied either by the *Core* manufacturer or by the customer. The application of the customization requirements can produced a high application-oriented *Core* modifying the main features of the original description.

A wide adopted technique to describe the functionalities of a general sequential circuit uses the concept of Finite State Machine with Data-path (FSMD) [9] where two main parts can be identifies:

- **Controller.** It is composed of the state register and some combinational logic to evaluate the next state to control the data-path. It is modeled by using a FSM.
- **Data-path.** It contains the execution unit, its inputs and outputs are connected with either the controller or the input/output ports. It is modeled by connecting structural components.

The customization process requires the modification of both parts: controller and data-path. Moreover, the synchronization between them has to be preserved after the customization process, in order to guarantee the correct functionality of the final description, as described in Section 3.3. This kind of representation can be considered as a design rule. The designer has to adopt this rule in order to allow the automatic generation of customized version of the processor by automatic generator. Note that, the FSMD model can be applied to complex systems by accordingly interfacing some FSMDs.

In order to obtain a configurable description, the original VHDL description has to be enriched with some *command-comments*. This *command-comments*, see Figure 1, are inserted by the designer before each component declaration in the RT-level description. We selected the comment method to annotate the VHDL code, thus the inserted commands for parametrization do not conflict with other tools analyzing VHDL code. There are two kind of *command-comments*:

- `CUT`. The list of instructions using the declared component is the only parameter of this comment. The generator uses this information to check if the commented component can be removed from the data-path description with respect of the required instruction set.
- `DUPLICATE`. This comment needs two parameters: the number of instances of the component in the original description and the list of instructions using the component. The first parameter allows the automatic generator to increase or reduce the number of instances of the component conforming to the data size specifications, while the second one is useful for the instruction set customization.

The *command-comments* are only inserted in the data-path description of the processor, the automatic parametrization of the controller is implicitly derived by the customization of the data-path, as described in Section 3.

The proposed methodology can be applied both to ex-novo *and already designed architectures. The parametrization of a new* Core is easier if it has been designed to be parametrizable. Thus, the designer has focused his attention on the parametrization process instead of the high architecture optimization. In fact, generally customization and optimization are two diverging design requirements and to achieve good results on one aspect implies a penalty on the other requirement.

3. PARAMETRIZATION

The customized description of the processor is obtained by a three-step procedure:

- data-path parametrization,
- extrapolation of the parametrized controller,
- mutual synchronization of these components.

3.1 Data-path parametrization

This task produces either an extension or a reduction of the original description. The generator completes this phase by elaborating the *command-comments*. The data-path is expressed as:

$$DP = \{C, S, PMF\}$$

C is the no empty list of components in the data-path RT-level description, S is the no empty list of connecting signals

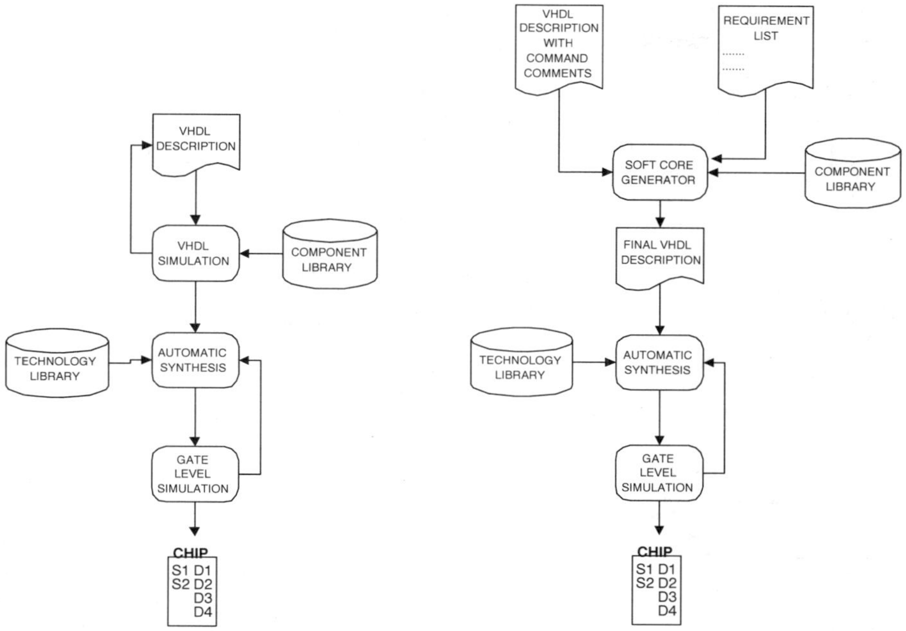

Figure 2: Fixed and parametric design work-flows.

and *PMF* is a function mapping component ports and connecting signals. This formal representation of the data-path is extracted by the generator by reading the VHDL data-path file. The generator, applying the *command-comments* to this representation, produces a customized formal version of the original data-path. The translation of the customized formal representation to VHDL is the last step of the data-path parametrization.

The components of the data-path can be categorized as: duplicable (DP) and no duplicable (NDP). In fact, the *command-comment* `DUPLICATE` can not be applied to any component in the RT-level description. For instance, the modification of the number of components connected to the data-path outputs could also imply the modification of the number of data-path output ports. Thus, this design rule has to be checked during the design of the parametric *Soft Core.*

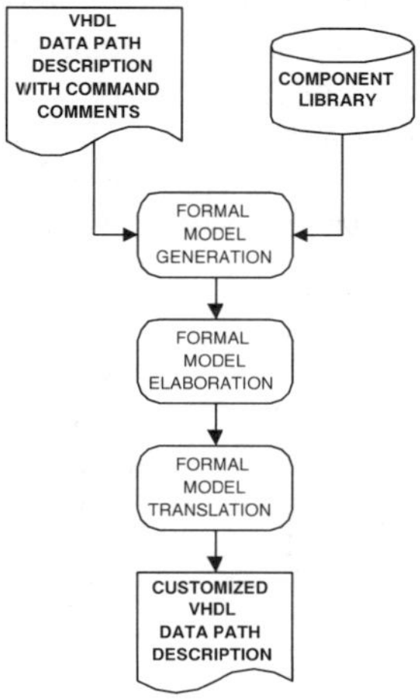

Figure 3: Parametrized data-path generation process.

The generator has to check the input/output signals to duplicate a DP component. Figure 2 shows three different connection structures:

- **DP to NDP.** To manage this kind of connection, a *tristate* has to be inserted between the NDP and DP components. The C and S are extended with new elements as shown in Figure 4A.
- **DP to DP.** The set S must be enriched with extra connection signals, to allow the extension of the C set with new instances of the DP component (see Figure 4B).
- **NDP to DP.** The extension of this connection structure can be obtained by adding new elements to set C and S (see Figure 4C).

The customization procedure for the data-path is summarized in Figure 3.

3.2 Controller parametrization

The original RT-level description and the formal representation of the customized data-path are inputs for the controller parametrization. The corresponding *Finite State Machine*(*FSM*) has to be modified in order to produce the correct control signals to execute the selected instructions subset. The modified next state function of the customized *FSM* ($\delta(s, x)$) has to preserve the FSM determinism and the data-path synchronization. The controller parametrization is a three-step procedure as for the data-path:

- A formal representation of the controller, based on the Mealy *FSM* model, is extracted from the RT-level VHDL description.
- The formal customized controller representation is generated and checked accordingly to the customized formal data-path representation. In fact, the removal of data-path components can imply the modification of the overall architecture (i.e. internal signals, controller), see Figure 6.
- The translation of the formal modified description to VHDL is the last step of the parametrization.

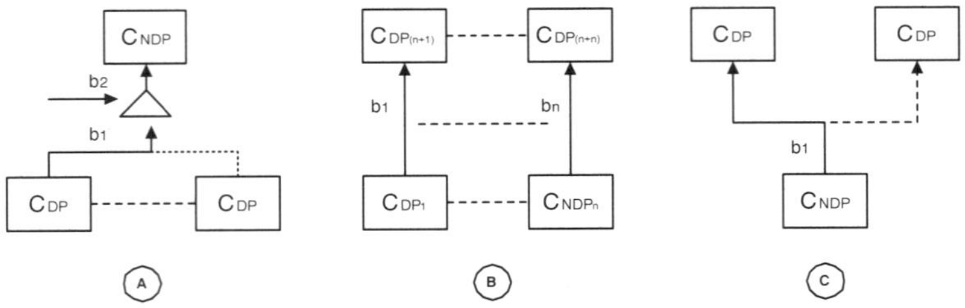

Figure 4: Different connection structures.

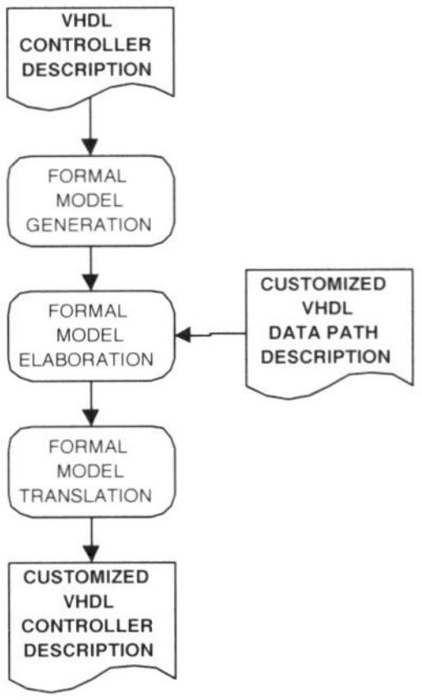

Figure 5: Parametrized controller generation process.

Figure 5 shows the parametrization process for the controller.

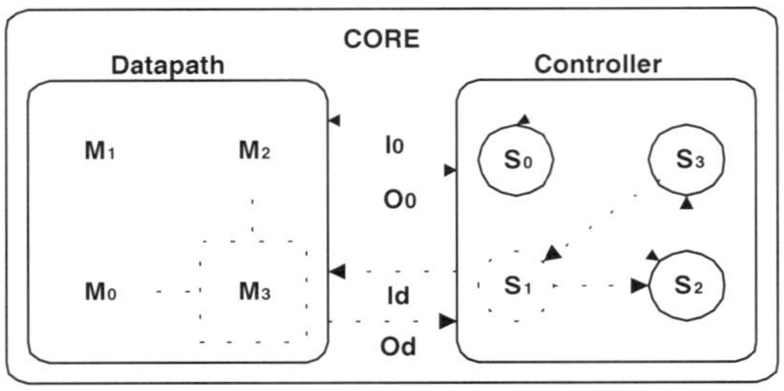

Figure 6: Customized architecture.

3.3 Synchronization

The customized controller, described as

$$FSM = < S_c, I_c, O_c, \delta_c, \lambda_c >$$

has to be checked for verifying the correct synchronization with the customized data-path. This problem can arise after the automatic synthesis process if the customized *FSM* is not minimal. To prove the correct synchronization of the customized data-path and controller, some definitions have to be introduced.

Definition 1. *Given a state-minimal FSM M_1 defined as*

$$M_1 = < S_1, I_1, O_1, \delta_1, \lambda_1 >$$

all states $s_i \in S_1$ can not be distinguished. A FSM

$$M_2 = < S_2, I_2, O_2, \delta_2, \lambda_2 >$$

is a sub-machine *of M_1 if*

$$S_2 \subseteq S_1, I_2 \subseteq I_1, O_2 \subseteq O_1, \delta_2 \subseteq \delta_1 \text{ and } \lambda_2 \subseteq \lambda_1.$$

Definition 2. *Given two FSMs*

$$M_1 = < S_1, I_1, O_1, \delta_1, \lambda_1 >$$
$$M_2 = < S_2, I_2, O_2, \delta_2, \lambda_2 >$$

such that M_2 is a sub-machine of M_1, M_2 is sub equivalent *of M_1 if*

$$\forall I_\alpha \in I_2 | M_1(I_\alpha) = O_\alpha \Rightarrow M_2(I_\alpha) = O_\alpha$$

If M_2 is *sub equivalent* of M_1 with respect to the set $I_2 \subseteq I_1$, then M_2 can produce the same outputs of M_1 for I_2.

Let M_1 be the state-minimal *FSM* describing the original complete controller, M_2 the customized *FSM* produced by the generator and M_2^1 the *FSM* obtained from the automatic minimization and synthesis of M_2. To guarantee the synchronization, after the customization process, between the *FSM* and *data-path*, it is necessary to prove the *sub equivalence* for the input set I_2 of M_2^1 and M_1. In fact, M_2^1 is the state-minimal and equivalent *FSM* of M_2, therefore, proving the *sub equivalence* of M_2 and M_1 proves the *sub equivalence* of M_2^1 and M_1.

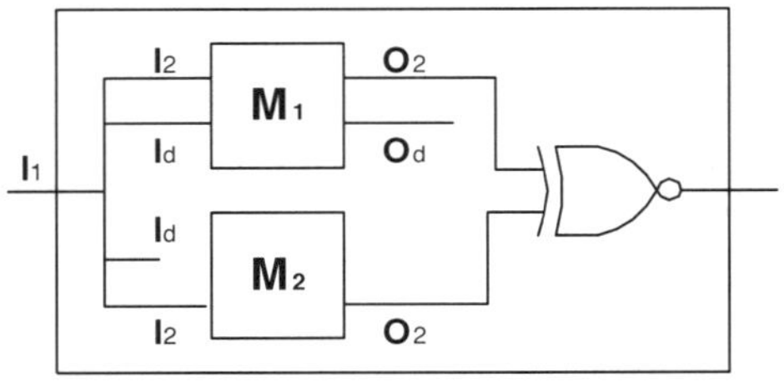

Figure 7: Sub equivalence check.

Let $I_1 = I_2 \cup I_d$ be the M_1 set of inputs, I_2 is the set of inputs of M_2 and I_d is the set of inputs removed due to the data-path parametrization. I_d is applied only to M_1 as shown in Figure 7. Let $O_1 = O_2 \cup O_d$ be the M_1 set of outputs and O_2 is the M_2 set of outputs. The *sub equivalence* of M_2 and M_1 is proven if set O_2 generated by M_1 is not affected by inputs I_d, but depends only on I_2. The verification of this property guarantees the correct parametrization of the *Core*, that is, it guarantees that the customized *Core* behaves as the complete *Core* concerning the selected instructions subset. This verification can be proven by applying equivalence checking algorithms (e.g.,[10, 11]) to the FSMs composition shown in Figure 7. However, it can be modeled also in terms of verification of the *FSM* determinism. To show this verification we use the state-transition table model of a *FSM*.

Let $I_1 = \{j_i \mid i = 1...2^n$ and where n are the input line$\}$ be the set of M_1 inputs.

Let D_k:

$$D_k = ((d_{ij}, p_{ij}), ...) = ((\delta_1(s_i, j), \lambda_1(s_i, j)), ...)$$

where $j = j_k$ and $i = 1... \mid S \mid$, be the ordered set of the next state-output pairs for a given input configuration j_k. The set D_k is the *k-th* column of the M_1 state-transition table, for the configuration j_k.
Let $I_{DC} = \{j = \langle x_1, ..., x_i, ..., x_n \rangle \in I_1\}$ be the set of I_1 input configurations which have an undefined value (don't care) in the *i-th* position.
Let's suppose we want to eliminate the *i-th* input symbol x_i from the *FSM* due to the data-path customization. The input configuration of M_2, that satisfies the scheme in Figure 7, is the set $I_2 \subseteq I_{DC}$, where the input configuration $j_{DC} \in I_{DC}$ satisfies the condition:
for all values assigned to $x_i \in j_{DC}$, *if all the ordered sets* D_k *obtained by configuration* j_{DC} *are equals, then* $j_{DC} \in I_2$, *otherwise* $j_{DC} \notin I_2$. This guarantees that, for each value assigned to the eliminated input symbol, the generated pair $(\delta_1(s_i, j), \lambda_1(s_i, j))$, for the *i-th* state of machine M_1 coupled with j_{DC}, is not affected by the eliminated input symbol, thus producing the same output and an equivalent next state of M_2. Thus, applying the input sequences $j_{DC} \in I_2$ to both M_1 and M_2 will produce the same output sequences.

The presented analysis allows to check the correct parametrization of the *Core* obtained by inserting *command comments.* The verification of the determinism of the customized FSM is sufficient to verify that the customized *Core* behaves as the complete *Core* concerning the selected instructions subset.

4. EXPERIMENTAL RESULTS

The developed *Soft Core* generator has been applied to two public domain processor descriptions [12, 13]. The general features of such processors are presented in Table 1.

DP32 is a 32-bit processor with a small instruction set: *Add, Sub, Mult* and *Branch.* Two different configurations have been produced from the original processor description:

- **Customization 1.** The *Branch* instruction has been removed from the instruction set. The total number of gates of the generated description remains close to the number of the full processor. This customization allows to save a large area for the controller, but the it produces only a limited reduction for the data-path. In fact, most of the data-path components are shared by all the instructions. In this case the *hard core*-based design strategy seems to be more effective.

- **Customization 2.** The instruction set is reduced to: *Add* and *Sub.* This allows a larger area reduction than previous customization, thus making this choice suitable for the *soft core*-based design.

CPU16 is a 16-bit processor with a quite rich instruction set: *Load, Indirect Load, Store, Indirect Store, Add, Indirect Add, Diff, Jmp, Jne* and *Halt.* Two parametric descriptions have been generated:

- **Customization 1.** The instruction set is reduced to: *Load, Store, Add, Diff, Jmp, Jne* and *Halt.* Removing all the instructions with an indirect access to the memory can save 6.5% on total number of gates.

- **Customization 2.** This configuration is obtained shrinking further the instruction set: *Load, Store, Add, Jne.* The results confirm a larger save on the controller description than on the data-path.

Table 2 summarizes the results on parametric generation of the two different configurations for both processors. Rapid synthesis has been performed by using Exemplar Leonardo Spectrum, an automatic synthesis tool targeted to fast prototyping. These results have been obtained adding a small number of *command-comments* (from 7 to 13) on the already designed VHDL descriptions. There is on average a high reduction on the controller size, whereas the same result is not achieved by the data-path customization. This depends on the original VHDL descriptions which have a high degree of shared components. The overall performance could be improved by adopting a configurable-oriented design methodology with a decreased number of shared components. In this case a larger complete processor is created, but several smaller high customized processors can be obtained. In any case the application of the proposed methodology to these examples allows to measure the potential advantages and drawbacks to use them as *soft cores* and to spend further design time for their custom synthesis and optimization.

5. CONCLUDING REMARKS

An efficient automatic *Soft Core* generator has been presented in this paper. It can be easily applied for parametrizating and designing any kind of processor which can be described by using FSMD(s). The parametrization of the full processor is obtained by inserting few *command-comments* in the description of the data-path, while the reduced controller is automatically inferred. The formal proof of the correctness of the produced descriptions has been presented concerning the correct synchronization between controller and data-path. This check allows to verify the correct parametrization of the core, thus ensuring the user that the customized *Core* behaves as the complete *Core* reduced to the selected instructions subset. Finally, the application of the customization procedure allows to estimate the potential area reduction of the customized *Soft Core*, with respect to the original *Core.* This information allows the design team to decide if the *Soft Core* design strategy must be further exploited, until the customized *Core* is completely designed and optimized, or if a larger, but highly optimized and ready-to-use *Hard Core* must be adopted.

6. REFERENCES

[1] A. Kitajima, M. Itoh, J. Sato, A. Shiomi, V. Takeuchi, M. Ima. Effectiveness of the ASIP design system PEAS-III in design of pipelined processors. *Proc. Conference on Asia South Pacific Design Automation Conference*, pp.649–654, 2001.

[2] Tensilica, Inc. xtensa Processor Generator. *http://www.tensilica.com.*

[3] S. Pees, M. Vaupel, V. Zivojnovic, H. Meyr. On core and more: A design perspective for systems-on-a-chip. *Proc. International Conference on Application-Specific Systems, Architectures and Processors*, pp.448–457, 1997.

[4] R.K. Gupta, Y. Zorian. Introducing core-based System Design. *Proc. IEEE Design & Test of Computers*, pp.15-25, 1997.

[5] ARM Processors and Peripherals. http://www.arm.com.

Processor	#Instructions	#Gates DP	#Gates Ctrl	#Gates	#command-comments	#VHDL Lines
DP32	4	54171	741	54912	13	6612
CPU16	11	12484	551	13035	7	38025

Table 1: Benchmark features.

Configuration	#Instr.	#Gates DP	%Save	#Gates Ctrl	% Save	%Tot. Save	#VHDL lines	% Save
DP32 Cust.1	3	52169	3.7	390	47.4	4.5	3462	47.5
DP32 Cust.2	2	48762	10.0	288	61.1	12.0	2157	67.4
CPU16 Cust.1	7	11828	5.3	409	25.8	6.5	5630	85.2
CPU16 Cust.2	5	11637	6.8	360	34.7	9.0	2336	93.4

Table 2: Parametrization and synthesis results.

[6] Atmel Corporation. http://www.atmel.com.

[7] E. Filippi, L. Licciardi, A. Montanaro, M. Paolini, M. Turolla, M. Taliercio. The Virtual Chip Set: a Parametric IP Library for System-on-a-Chip Design. *Proc. IEEE Custom Integrated Circuits Conference (CICC)*, pp.97–100, 1998.

[8] M. Berekovic, M. Heistermann, P. Pirsch. A Core Generator for Fully Synthesizable and Highly Parameterizable Risc-Cores for System-on-a-Chip Designs. *Proc. IEEE Workshop on Signal Processing Systems*, pp.561-568, 1998.

[9] D.D. Gajskj, N.D. Dutt, A.C-H. Wu. High-Level Synthesis, Introduction to Chip and System Design. *Kluwer Academic Publisher*, 1992.

[10] O. Coudert, C. Berthet, J.C. Madre. Verification of Sequential Machines Using Boolean Functions Vectors. *Proc. Workshop on Applied Formal Methods for Correct VLSI Design*, 1989.

[11] H. Cho, G.D. Hachtel, E. Macii, B. Plessier, F. Somenzi. Algorithms for Approximate FSM Traversal Based on Space State Decomposition. *Proc. Design Automation Conference*, pp.25-30, 1993.

[12] P.J. Ashenden. The VHDL Cookbook. *Dept. Computer Science University of Adelaide South Australia*, 1990.

[13] J.S. Turner. http://www.arl.wustl.edu/~jst/cs/260/hw/cpu.html. Washington University, St. Louis, Missouri.

Concurrent-Simulation-Based Remote IP Evaluation over the Internet for System-on-a-Chip Design*

Hung-Pin Wen, Chien-Yu Lin, Youn-Long Lin
Department of Computer Science
National Tsing Hua University
Hsinchu 30043, Taiwan, R.O.C.
ylin@cs.nthu.edu.tw

ABSTRACT
We propose an Internet-based concurrent-simulation scheme to ease IP evaluation process between IP vendors and users. Complex system-on-a-chip design requires more and more IP modules from 3rd party vendors. What can be disclosed by the vendor without impairing its trade secrete and what needs to be examined by the user to gain satisfactory level of confidence are contradictory of each other. Via PLI interface functions and Internet protocol, our proposed software enables HDL simulators (Verilog) residing in both the vendor and user's sites to concurrently simulate the IP and SOC together. Only stimulus and response defined in the IP's I/O are exchanged between the sites. Therefore, the vendor need not to create a functional model (or encrypted code) for the IP while the user is assured what he/she simulates is what he will purchase. Beside simulation speed degradation due to communication overhead, the SOC design/debug process is exactly same as if the IP is in the user's hand. Our contribution will help all IP providers expose their IPs to all potential users without human intervention and IP right infringement concern.

Keywords
Concurrent Simulation, Intellectual Property (IP), IP Evaluation, System-on-a-Chip.

1. INTRODUCTION
Ever increasing functionality demand from the application side and exponentially growing integration capability from the technology side together steer system implementation targeted towards system-on-a-chip (SOC) realization. Nowadays we, the system synthesis community, encounter the problems of large productivity gap, shorter time-to-market and more serious designer shortage. IP (intellectual property) reuse has been considered one of the most feasible methodologies for the above predicaments. Intuitively, integrating existing designs to form an SOC design can bridge the productivity gap. Many ASIC design house/divisions also try to repackage their existing designs in to IPs. In the mean time, most SOC design companies (IC or system houses) are willing to adopt external IPs. These lead to an IP business segment in the semiconductor industry.

However, the integration of IPs into an SOC design is not trivial. Unlike evaluating IC samples in the system-on-a-board era, IP evaluation requires not only data sheet but also simulatable models. Once the user is interested in a particular IP, he wants to verify its functionality first. Further, they would like to integrate the IPs into their complete SOC design and test for speed, area, and power ... etc for comparing with other alternatives. Until making sure of the accuracy of the entire design, users will not purchase the IP designs. During the evaluation process, vendors must provide a model of its IP that demonstrates the capability but hides the real design from being stolen. The further the evaluation process goes, the more resource the vendor has to spend.

Presently, two approaches are employed. First, the vendor would provide a fake model, called bus transaction model or functional model, for evaluation purpose. Second, some encryption is performed on the design data. The fake model approach requires extra effort and is very difficult to guarantee the complete match between the real and fake model. The encryption approach cannot assure 100% safety and would limit certain description power of the HDL.

The widespread use of the Internet has affected the VLSI design community. Several previous researches [1,2,3] have been proposed to exploit the power of the Internet. They make CAD tool usage one kind of service through WWW. In [4,5], the JAVA language is used to model an IP design. Additional IP-remodeling from HDL is needed. An HDL-based methodology is proposed in [6]. But, it needs usage of a commercial tool and suffers from the abortion problem of its synchronization scheme and the speed problem due to socket conversion.

We envision a more perfect scenario. The entire design system can be more automatic and take advantage of the Internet more effectively. We develop a concurrent simulation framework for remote IP evaluation. Our method is based on a client–server architecture [7] where the client and the server stand for IP users and vendors, respectively. This architecture has been employed by many Internet-based applications. We focus on the automatic generation of wrapper programs for remote concurrent simulation.

ISSS'01, October 1-3, 2001, Montréal, Québec, Canada.

* supported in part by a grant from the National Science Council, R.O.C., under contract no. NSC 89-2218-E-007-054 and NSC 89-2218-E-007-054

An AES (Advanced Encryption Standard) Rijndael cipher case study presented herein demonstrates our proposed scheme's effectiveness and efficiency. Experimental results show the viability of our technique.

The rest of the paper is organized as follows. In Section 2, we describe how our tool will be used. Section 3 describes and analyzes the technical detail. The case study is presented in Section 4. Finally, in Section 5 we draw conclusions and point to possible directions for future research.

2. PROPOSED APPROACH

We propose for the IP vendor a software system that takes as its input the IP description and generates two Verilog modules and two C programs. The usage of these modules and programs in the user's site and vendor's site are illustrated in **Figure 1** and **Figure 2**, respectively. When the user wants to evaluate a remote IP within the context of its SOC design, he just instantiates the module (*RemoteIP()* in the illustration) as any other local module and include the vendor provided shell file, which is generated automatically by our tool. The shell file describes the callee module, which uses PLI interface (*$RemoteIP_clt*) to communicate with the vendor site. The communication consists of four major functions in the automatically generated C program (*PLI_routines*). They will be presented in the next section.

```
/*============================================*/
/*    This part is original user design.      */
/*============================================*/
module SOC()
   :
   RemoteIP();     /* Instantiation of the IP under
                      evaluation */
   :
endmodule          /* End of module SOC */
```

```
/*============================================*/
/*    This part is automatically generated.   */
/*    It is included into SOC simulation.     */
/*============================================*/
module RemoteIP()
   :
   $RemoteIP_clt(···); /* This will call compiled C
                          function thru PLI */
   :
endmodule          /* End of module RemoteIP */
```

```
/*============================================*/
/* This is automatically generated and compiled */
/* into object code to be called by           */
/* $RemoteIP_clt() during Verilog simulation  */
/* thru PLI.                                   */
/* It consists of four main functions.        */
/*============================================*/
PLI_routines()
{
   function socket_initialization()
   function port_updating()
   function data_transfer()
   function socket_closing()
}
```

Figure 1. The usage of generated modules and programs in the user's site

We have also developed a WWW-based user interface so that the IP user can use a browser to download the Verilog module and C program as well as invoking the simulator in the IP vendor's site.

```
/*============================================*/
/*    This part is automatically generated.   */
/*    It includes real IP into SOC simulation */
/*============================================*/
module RemoteIP()
   :
   RemoteIP();      /* Instantiation of the IP under
                       evaluation */
   :
   $RemoteIP_svr(···); /* This will call compiled C
                          function thru PLI */
   :
endmodule          /* End of module RemoteIP */
```

```
/*============================================*/
/*    This part is original vendor' s real IP */
/*============================================*/
module RemoteIP()
   :
   :
endmodule          /* End of module IP */
```

```
/*============================================*/
/* This is automatically generated and compiled */
/* into object code to be called by           */
/* $RemoteIP_clt() during Verilog simulation  */
/* thru PLI.                                   */
/* It consists of four main functions.        */
/*============================================*/
PLI_routines()
{
   function socket_initialization()
   function port_updating()
   function data_transfer()
   function socket_closing()
}
```

Figure 2. The usage of generated modules and programs in the vendor's site

3. REMOTE CONCURRENT SIMULATION

In order to exchange data across the Internet, we apply the client/server paradigm to every concurrent simulation session. An IP vendor is the server side while the user is the client side. Our client/server architecture is composed of the Verilog Programming Language Interface [8,9] functions and a pair of shell modules built on the basis of the original design system. The details are described below：

3.1 PLI Function Implementation

The PLI functions, named *$modulename_clt* and *$modulename_svr*, are programmed for interprocess communication using the TCP/IP. IEEE 1364 standard provides the TF/ACC routines and the VPI routines (referred to as PLI1.0 and PLI2.0) for calling a C function from Verilog codes. We use PLI1.0/2.0 to accomplish four main operations: (1) opening and initializing a socket, (2) updating values for the input/output ports, (3) transferring data using the socket, and (4) closing the socket. The PLI functions (*$modulename_clt* and *$modulename_svr*) has re-ordered module ports as their arguments. We order them such that all input ports appear before output ports to ease encoding and decoding of signal values.

3.2 Remote Shell Module Implementation

We program the client/server shell modules in Verilog and use them to call PLI functions. IP users include the client shell module as if the real IP is at hand. Each time when a user instantiates the name of the IP in his SOC design, upon executing *$modulename_clt* the client site simulator sends input values to the server site before output values are received from the vendor's real IP. The server shell module behaves similarly, but it will send output values after receiving input values. The server shell module is responsible for invoking the server site simulator to evaluate the real IP while the client site simulator is invoked by user's testbench or design. In the vendor site, because the real design can be viewed as an external module, it's quite simple to provide different abstraction levels like behavioral or netlist for remote simulation by changing the included IP filename in the server shell module. The other primary advantage of shell module implementation is that once the users obtain the real Verilog code for the IP, no alteration is necessary besides replacing the file name of the client shell module with that of the real IP. Integrating the entire SOC design becomes effortless.

Current Time Step:

Slot 1:

All actions in a slot are intermixed in any order!
- Evaluate RHS of non-blocking assignments
- Evaluate RHS & change LHS of blocking assignments
- Evaluate RHS & change LHS of continuous assignments
- Evaluate output from $display and $write
- ***Call PLI calltf routines for system tasks and system functions***

Slot 2:

Change LHS of non-blocking assignments evaluated in slot 1

Slot 3:

Call registered simulation callbacks which have cbReadWriteSybch reason

Slot 4:

Print output from $monitor and $strobe

Call registered simulation callbacks which have cbReadOnlySybch reason

Next Time Step:

...

Figure 3. The activity in a Verilog simulation time step

3.3 Synchronization Scheme

The synchronization scheme must guarantee the correctness of remote concurrent simulation. To avoid the abortion problem in [6], we utilize a cycle-evaluation technique. Because a socket is message driven through the client and the server, the packaged data should be synchronized to the socket. A naive way is to transmit every input/output value within a socket to the opposite side in every time step, and then decide the related port update and new event schedule.

In the IEEE 1364 Verilog standard, the activity in a Verilog simulation time step is conceptually illustrated in **Figure 3**. Simulation will not proceed to the next slot until it has executed all scheduled events within the current slot. In the beginning, *$modulename_svr* is called to wait at time step 0. For each time step, all valid input values can be read during slot 3 after all known events are executed in the client and transmitted to the server at slot 0, which is not defined in the original organization but a means to hold the time wheel before any event is executed in this time step. Afterwards, the server proceeds to process the scheduled events and finally the valid output values can be accessed during slot 4 and sent back to the client. Then the time wheels of both sides go forward to the next time step. The scheme is shown as **Figure 4**. Note that the server does not start to evaluate in slot 0 because the PLI interface function is just invoked in slot 1 at time step 0.

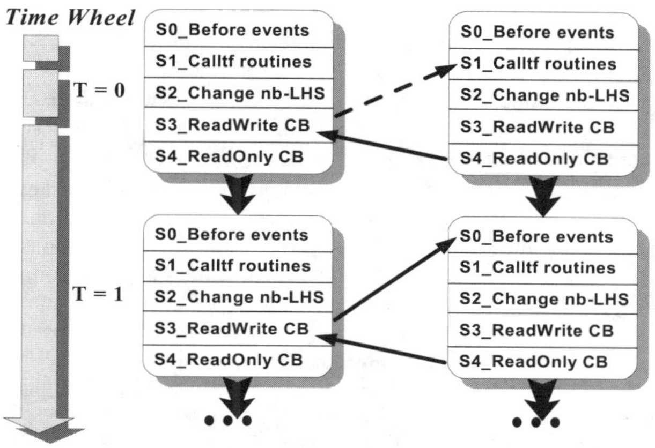

Figure 4. The cycle-evaluation technique

3.4 Packet Packing Scheme

The speed problem of remote simulation is also a great concern to the user. The conversion between input/output values and data packets may dominate the total run time more than the transmission rate. However, owing to the cycle-evaluation technique, in every time step we have to send/receive port values back and forth between the client and the server. It seems that we deteriorate the speed problem. Actually, the packet conversion will not restrict the total run time too badly as long as no extra control messages are attached and a packet packing scheme is applied properly.

Our cycle-evaluation technique guarantees the correctness of synchronization so that only the input/output values need to transmit. We encode a character (one byte) for each bit of the input/output ports. The Verilog 4-state logic values are represented with "0", "1", "x" and "z" in C strings. Since the total bits of input/output ports are usually far shorter than the longest data that a packet can carry, we make use of this feature to reduce a great number of packet conversions. We have mentioned the rearranging technique for the order of input/output ports. Now we can concatenate all input bits or output bits into one data stream by this order. Then in every time step, only one packet is sent and the other one is received. Once the total number of input/output ports is larger than two, our packet packing scheme will take effect. For instance, if an IP has N inputs and M outputs, we convert only two packets instead of (M+N) packets. The time for (M+N-2) packet conversion is therefore saved.

3.5 IP Protection Scheme

IP protection is a key issue of SOC business. The dilemma originates from how to keep the evaluation of a real IP from revealing its content to IP users. A common way is rewriting a new simulation model in C or encrypting IP's content. However, our remote IP co-simulation method does require neither of them. Our client/server shell modules separate the user's design and IP.

Furthermore, PLI interface functions permits our socket protocol only, and any intention to access the real IP will be blocked. Both the client and server sides can only see the interfaces of each other, and therefore, a user can really evaluate an IP but can't catch any detail information about it except the output values.

3.6 Performance Analysis

The total simulation time is composed of total evaluation time for all events in the timing wheel. Therefore, we create a model to analyze the performance of our scheme. First, we assume that the simulation time for an IP and its interface to the rest SOC contributes respectively 100α and 100β percent of total time (T) simulated on a single local machine while the remaining SOC consumes $(1-\alpha-\beta)T$. The transmission rate is γ times slower than that on the single local machine. Table 1 depicts the comparison of total simulation time between our scheme and the origin.

Table 1. Simulation time comparison between our scheme and the origin

Design Part	IP	IP/SOC interface	Remaining SOC	Total
Original local simulation	α	β	$(1-\alpha-\beta)T$	T
Concurrent simulation	αT	γ	$(1-\alpha-\beta)T$	$(1+(\gamma-1)\beta)T$
Ratio	1	γ	1	$(1+(\gamma-1)\beta)$

For example: If an MAC consumes 10% and it interface with the outer DSP design consumes 1% of total simulation time, the Internet transmission rate (assume @1KB/sec) is now 1600X slower than that on the single local machine, and the original simulation time is 1,000,000 ms, then

$$\alpha = 10\%,\quad \beta = 1\%,\quad \gamma = 1600,\ \text{and}\ T = 1000000$$

We can calculate the new simulation time and the slow-down ratio (φ)

$$T' = (1+(\gamma-1)\beta)T = (1 + (1600-1)\times 1\%)\times 1{,}000{,}000$$
$$= 16{,}990{,}000 \text{ ms}$$
$$\varphi = (1+(\gamma-1)\beta) = (1 + (1600-1)\times 1\%) = 16.99$$

We can see that our new simulation time is dominated by two factors: one is the percentage of simulation time for IP/SOC interface and the other is the transmission rate. In this example, the 1600X Internet delay is hidden by multiplying the small proportion for simulating on the IP/SOC interface, and finally we only get approximately 17X total simulation time. Putting the possible improvement of the Internet speed aside, the total delay will be hidden more along with larger SOC design. The larger the SOC design becomes, the smaller proportion of total simulation time the IP/SOC interface occupies. Therefore, for evaluating an IP in an SOC design, the delay due to our scheme will be confined to a reasonable range.

4. CASE STUDY

We use a synchronous AES Rijndael cipher chip at the RTL level [10] to test the proposed approach. This cipher IP module has 6 input and 3 output ports. **Figure 5** and **Figure 6** give the program listing of the generated modules for the client and server site, respectively. The generated C programs are too long (527 lines) to be included here. The simulation is performed on a SUN ULTRA SPARC60 equipped with Cadence Verilog-XL. **Table 2** shows the effectiveness of packet packing scheme. At first, the synchronous AES Rijndael cipher encrypts input data. Then the encrypted output data can be obtained. The single process, method 1 and method 2 in the second column stand for the simulations on the same workstation by one process, two processes without packet packing scheme and two processes with packet packing scheme. Column 3, 4 and 5 represent the user CPU time, system CPU time and total run time in second respectively. The final column shows the normalized total run time. It is clear that our packet packing scheme reduces the total run time significantly for the client/server concurrent simulation.

Table 2. Simulation with different synchronization schemes

Pattern Length	Synchronization Scheme		User CPU Time	System CPU Time	Total Run Time	Normalized Total Run Time
160	Single Process		7.00	0.23	8.00	1.00
	Two-processes w/o packet packing	Client	0.00	0.00	1236.00	154.50
		Server	3.00	0.00	1241.00	155.13
	Two-processes w/ packet packing	Client	2.94	0.83	13.02	1.63
		Server	9.75	0.90	13.48	1.69
1600	Single Process		31.46	0.28	32.91	1.00
	Two-processes w/o packet packing	Client	0.00	0.00	2676.00	81.31
		Server	17.00	0.00	2676.00	81.31
	Two-processes w/ packet packing	Client	6.60	1.75	46.57	1.42
		Server	37.46	1.92	47.12	1.43
16000	Single Process		275.59	0.50	279.22	1.00
	Two-processes w/o packet packing	Client	4.00	9.00	15738.00	56.36
		Server	165.00	27.00	15739.00	56.37
	Two-processes w/ packet packing	Client	41.25	12.16	363.01	1.30
		Server	315.72	12.36	363.58	1.30

Moreover, we use this cipher to establish an encrypt/decrypt system. Encryption is done on the server while decryption is done on the client. This remote concurrent simulation is analyzed under three different conditions:

- **Single machine with single process**
  Both encryption and decryption are executed on the same local machine. The simulation ran on one SUN ULTRA SPARC60 called IC6 with Cadence Verilog-XL.
- **Intranet with two processes**
  The client sent out the input data and ran the decryption on a SUN ULTRA SPARC60 called IC5 while the server ran encryption on IC6. The client/server machines communicate with sockets through a 100Mbit Ethernet LAN connection. This result exhibits the effectiveness of packet packing scheme. The transmission delay influence the total run time slightly.
- **Internet with two processes**
  The client sent out the input data and ran the decryption on a SUN ULTRA SPARC30 called Gucsun01 while the server ran encryption on IC6, and they communicate with sockets through different ISPs with about 6.0Kbyte/sec traffic under

normal network loading. This environment measures the most practical Internet environment.

Table 3 shows the results. Intranet with two processes is the fastest. In this condition, the packet conversion and transmission rate do not limit the speed of concurrent simulation and take advantage of distributed computation. However, the results in the Internet with two processes interest us most. Our remote IP concurrent simulation method is only constrained by the transmission rate, which may vary under different situations. We can see that the Internet condition consumes 10 to 36 times more total run time. This result is acceptable to both the IP vendor and the IP user given the convenience it brings to the party. We expect the total run time will significantly reduce when video-grade bandwidth is available.

Table 3. Remote IP concurrent simulation under different network conditions

Pattern Length	Simulation Type	Machine	User CPU Time	System CPU Time	Total Run Time	Normalized Total Run Time
160	Single machine	*IC6*	13.13	0.32	14.62	1.00
	Intranet	*IC5* (Client)	2.66	1.09	12.00	0.82
		IC6 (Server)	9.48	0.87	12.26	0.84
	Internet	*Gucsun01* (Client)	6.95	1.78	546.66	37.39
		IC6 (Server)	10.04	1.40	547.49	37.45
1600	Single machine	*IC6*	64.67	0.47	67.27	1.00
	Intranet	*IC5* (Client)	6.02	2.19	44.13	0.66
		IC6 (Server)	36.45	1.92	44.56	0.66
	Internet	*Gucsun01* (Client)	25.40	1.86	780.01	11.60
		IC6 (Server)	41.84	2.49	781.62	11.62
16000	Single machine	*IC6*	579.57	0.93	589.73	1.00
	Intranet	*IC5* (Client)	36.76	13.38	363.64	0.62
		IC6 (Server)	308.51	12.54	363.97	0.62
	Internet	*Gucsun01* (Client)	225.09	13.29	7235.84	12.27
		IC6 (Server)	337.02	13.84	7240.15	12.28

5. CONCLUSIONS AND FUTURE WORK

We have demonstrated the feasibility of remote IP evaluation using an Internet-based concurrent simulation scheme. Our software can automatically generated wrapper programs and modules for remote exchange of simulation data. Our contribution will help both the IP vendor and user. Therefore, it will ease the adoption of external IP during SOC design project.

Our proposed system is built on a client/server architecture. This architecture mainly comprises some PLI functions and a pair of shell modules. They also provide the security and only permit to access the interface values of each other. Cycle-evaluation technique is responsible to timing synchronization and guarantees the correctness. However, packet packing scheme reduces a lot of conversion overhead and the total run time can be in the reasonable range of tolerance.

Our scheme also provides thousands of client evaluating multiple IPs in vendor's machine if the vendor has enough licenses. It eases the concurrent simulation of multiple IPs for SOC design. Many kinds of simulator are developed in the market. To provide a standard interface, we support all kinds of simulator that are conforming to IEEE 1364. Thus, any simulator conforming to IEEE 1364 can be applied with our method.

Internet bandwidth is the only major bottleneck on our proposed scheme. Although we expect it will be solved in the broadband era, we would like to study whether the amount of communication can be further reduced.

6. REFERENCES

[1] F. Chan, M. Spiller and R. Newton, "WELD-An environment for Web-based electronic design", Proc. of the Design Automation Conference, 1998, pp. 146-151.

[2] L. Benini, A. Bogliolo and G. De Micheli, "Distributed EDA tool integration: the PPP diagram", Proc. of the International Conference on Computer Design, 1996, pp. 448-453.

[3] Y.L. Lin, "Computing Brokerage and Its Application in VLSI Design", Proc. of Asia and South Pacific Design Automation Conference '97, 1997.

[4] M. Dalpasso, A. Bogliolo and L. Benini, "Specification and Validation of distributed IP-based designs with JavaCAD", Proc. of Design, Automation and Test in Europe Conference &Exhibition, 1999, pp. 684-688

[5] M. Dalpasso, A. Bogliolo and L. Benini, "Virtual Simulation of distributed IP-based designs", Proc. of the Design Automation Conference, 1999, pp. 50-55.

[6] A. Fin and F. Fummi, "A Web-CAD Methodology for IP-Core Analysis and Simulation", Proc. of the Design Automation Conference, 2000, pp. 597-600.

[7] D.E. Comer and D.L. Stevens, Internetworking With TCP/IP Volume III: Client-Server Programming and Application, Prentice-Hall, Inc., 1996, pp. 9-19.

[8] S. Mittra, Principles Of Verilog PLI, Kluwer Academic Publishers, 1999.

[9] S. Sutherland, The Verilog PLI Handbook: a user's guide and comprehensive reference on the Verilog programming language interface, Kluwer Academic Publishers, 1999.

[10] An AES Rijndael Cipher Design, refer to AES web page: http://csrc.nist.gov/encryption/aes/rijndael.

```
module  top          // rij_shell_clt.v shell
(
            clk,                    // clock : CLK
            reset,                  // reset : RST
            mode,                   // mode : Mode
            en_de,                  // encrypt or decrypt
            key_length,             // length of key:128 192 256
            din,                    // data input : Din

            ready,                  // ready : Ready
            dout,                   // data output : Dout
            sftout
);

// declaration of i/o type and width
input       clk, reset, en_de;
input       [1:0] mode, key_length;
input       [7:0] din;
output      ready;
output      [7:0] dout;
output  [127:0] sftout;

// declaration of variable type and width
wire        clk;
wire        reset, en_de;
wire        [1:0]  mode, key_length;
wire        [7:0]  din;
wire   [7:0]   din_d;
wire               ready;
wire   [7:0]   dout;
wire        [127:0] sftout;

assign  din_in = din;
initial begin
 $rijndael_clt(clk,
        reset,
        mode,
        en_de,
        key_length,
        din_d,
        ready,
        dout,
        sftout);
end

endmodule
```

Figure 5: The generated shell module for client site

```
`include "rijndael.v"
module rij_shell_svr_vpi;
parameter ClkRateOfRijndael = 5;
parameter EndofCoSimulation = 175000;

// declaration of i/o type and width
/*
input       clk, reset, en_de;
input       [1:0] mode, key_length;
input       [7:0] din;
output      ready;
output      [7:0] dout;
output  [127:0] sftout;
*/
// declaration of variable type and width
reg         clk;
wire         reset, en_de;
wire        [1:0] mode, key_length;
wire        ready;
wire   [7:0]   din;
wire   [7:0]   dout;
wire        [127:0] sftout;
reg         clk_r,reset_r, en_de_r;
reg    [1:0]   mode_r, key_length_r;
reg    [7:0]   din_r;

top    u1(
            clk,
            reset,
            mode,
            en_de,
            key_length,
            din,

            ready,
            dout,
            sftout
        );
always
        #(ClkRateOfRijndael) clk = ~clk;
assign  clk   = clk_r;
assign  reset = reset_r;
assign  mode  = mode_r;
assign  en_de = en_de_r;
assign  key_length = key_length_r;
assign  din   = din_r;

initial begin
 $rijndael_svr(
        clk_r,
        reset_r,
        mode_r,
        en_de_r,
        key_length_r,
        din_r,
        ready,
        dout,
        sftout
        );
end
initial begin
        #(EndofCoSimulation)  $finish;
end

endmodule
```

Figure 6: The generated shell module for server site

Application of Software design patterns to DSP library design

Pontus Åström
Dept. of Electroscience
Lund University
P.O Box 118
SE-221 00 Lund, Sweden
Pontus.Astrom@es.lth.se

Stefan Johansson
Turin Networks
Petaluma, CA, USA
SJohansson@turinnetworks.com

Peter Nilsson
Dept. of Electroscience
Lund University
P.O Box 118
SE-221 00 Lund, Sweden
Peter.Nilsson@es.lth.se

ABSTRACT

The design of a hardware data path library is one of the harder problems in design for reuse. Thanks to the appearance of hardware modeling libraries based on C++, it is possible to apply advanced software techniques to design such a library. This paper shows how software design patterns can be applied to hardware design. Design patterns yield a twofold advantage: a faster design process, and a library that is more extensible and modular than an equivalent HDL counterpart. From a VHDL–C++ design comparison we have found that those factors might result in a reduction of the code size by a factor of two.

1. INTRODUCTION

The software community has been the source for many of the larger productivity leaps in hardware design for the last two decades. Two of the major transfers have been procedural programming and object-oriented design (OOD). Procedural programming appeared with the advent of the HDLs Verilog and VHDL, both derived from the procedural software languages C respectively ADA. Several proposals have been given for how to add support for the OOD methodology to hardware design [1]. Another recent idea to benefit from the strengths of the object-oriented paradigm is to move the hardware design to a suitable software language like C++ [2, 3].

Hardware design in C++ is promising as it simplifies the application of good software design techniques to hardware designs. Design by reuse of *design patterns* is one such technique. It will be shown here that software design patterns can be applied to hardware designs.

A design pattern can be thought of as the skeleton of a good design that can be reused in new designs in different fields and over time. In hardware design typical examples of design patterns are finite state machines (FSM) or communication protocols. With the availability of a public pattern catalog with good and well proven patterns, design by reuse of design patterns will boost the productivity in several areas. It will result in faster and less error prone design processes. It will give designs that are more modular and extensible. Finally, it results in a higher abstraction level as the design can be explained and understood in terms of the applied patterns.

Currently there exist very few public design patterns aimed specifically for hardware design. However, in the software domain and particularly in the OOD area, design patterns have had a big impact over the last few years. Several public software pattern catalogue exist [4, 5, 6] and a large productivity boost has been observed from pattern usage [7].

It will be shown that several design patterns from the software pattern catalog [4] easily can be applied to the design of a hardware data path library in C++, designed with aid of the library Ocapi [3]. In total four patterns have been applied. The patterns are: Composite, Object Adaptor, Abstract Factory and Decorator.

The usability of those patterns is demonstrated by the design of a synchronizer for a mobile radio system. The design is compared to an equivalent VHDL design. The results show that the C++ design has half the code size compared to the VHDL design.

2. MOTIVATION FOR USING DESIGN PATTERNS

Every experienced designer/programmer reuses structures and designs that have worked well in the past more or less without thinking. Previously, the reused patterns were seldom put in print, the patterns therefore were spread very slowly or not at all. Learning patterns was thus a question of getting experience, to recognize the patterns that repeat over time. Unfortunately, gathering experience takes long time.

By writing down good design patterns in a structured way that clearly states the intention, usage and implementation, much is won in terms of reuse, learning and abstraction. Three advantages can be seen:

- Novice designers get a much steeper learning curve. They can quickly acquire the experience gathered by expert programmers over many years to write robust, well partitioned and error free code.
- Design discussions can be performed at a much higher level of abstraction. Instead of discussing how indi-

ISSS'01, October 1-3, 2001, Montréal, Québec, Canada.

vidual classes should be arranged, the discussion can revolve around whether a particular pattern is a good way to structure a given problem.

- Better documentation. It can be written in terms of patterns to give the reader a direct understanding of how the code is organized.

A study of applying patterns in the software domain have verified the above points [7]. We can not see any fundamental differences between the software and hardware design processes, that would invalidate the results for hardware designs. However, the advantages will not show up until there is a public design catalog and an educated community that can communicate in terms of patterns.

3. HARDWARE DESIGN IN C++

Hardware design has essentially become a software activity. For many projects the hardware part is minor in terms of code size and work force. As there are benefits in a uniform development environment for hardware-software co-design, there is a motivation to move hardware design to a software language like C++. However, the move can be motivated for hardware-only designs were the corresponding simulation model is written in a software language. A few of the advantages are:

- Promotes design by stepwise refinement. Small hardware units can fast and easily be verified in the simulation program by simply being exchanged with the corresponding software units. This speeds up the development process as the dedicated test benches need to test fewer cases.
- Higher abstraction level due to the object oriented features of C++.
- Access to several useful software libraries including the standard C and C++ libraries.
- Simplified usage of several well proven design paradigms including the mentioned object oriented paradigm with use of design patterns.

There are disadvantages in designing with C++ too. The larger part of the hardware design community is still used to traditional HDL such as VHDL and Verilog. We believe however that moving to C++ offers a set of design techniques that matches well up against the learning curve of moving to another language.

4. THE TOOL OCAPI

Ocapi [3, 8] is a C++ tool aimed for design and simulation of hardware according to the data flow paradigm. Ocapi provides an object-oriented design library for data path designs and takes full advantage of the language C++.

With Ocapi it is feasible to encapsulate a data path component with a finite state machine (FSM) completely in a C++ class. Ocapi defines a bus object `busTp` (Tp for type) for transport of fixed point data between two data path objects. In hardware the object busTp translates into plain wiring.

It is easy to raise the abstraction level by defining new bus types. Bus types for complex numbers and vectors are used by the data path library. With the container classes of

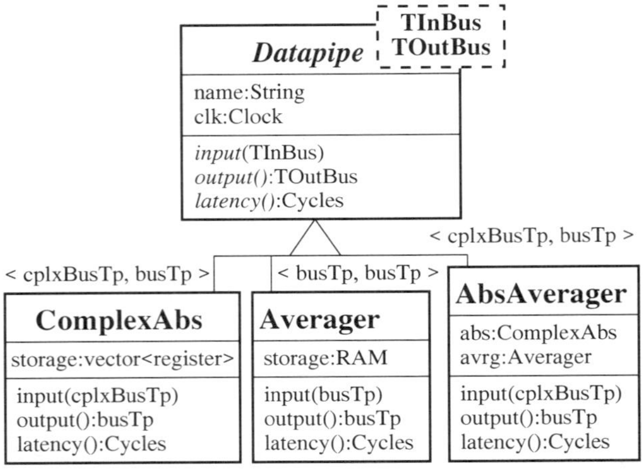

Figure 1: The data path storage composition.

the standard template library (STL) [9] it is easy to define the desired buses.

```
typedef std::pair<busTp, busTp > cplxBusTp;
typedef std::vector<busTp >       vecBusTp;
```

5. THE DATA PATH LIBRARY

The library is intended for data path design and matured in parallel with a custom DSP implementation. Currently the library contains about 20 data path objects ranging from simple FIFOs to a complete channel synchronizer[10]. All data path objects are currently in the hardware mapped algorithm form. This kind of data paths are fast, have a high throughput and require little control. The drawback is that the data path objects might have low utilization and thus the silicon usage might be excessive. In section 5.2 it is shown how the data path library can be extended to better adapt to different requirements.

5.1 The repository

The composite pattern is chosen as base to arrange the data path objects in a tree-like, hierarchical structure. This arrangement has two benefits. First, it allows the data path objects to be treated uniformly with no difference between leaf objects designed from scratch and compositions of objects. Second, the user can easily extend the library by defining new composite objects from the existing leafs and composites.

Figure 1 shows a small example of the composite pattern in UML (Unified Modeling Language) notation[11]. The root class is named *Datapipe*, it defines the interface for the data path objects. Three concrete data path objects are inherited form the root class.

The Datapipe class is an abstract base class that defines the type of the data path objects, i.e. the names of the method calls, the input and return types of those calls and so on. Three abstract methods are defined. `latency():Cycles` returns the delay in clock cycles from input to output, `input(TInBus)` and `output():TOutBus` connects the data path object to an input and an output bus. `TInBus` and `TOutBus` are parameters, or templates in C++ notation,

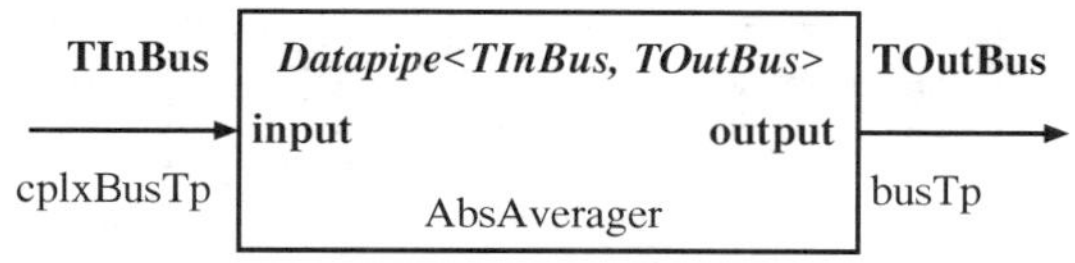

Figure 2: A structural view of a data path component.

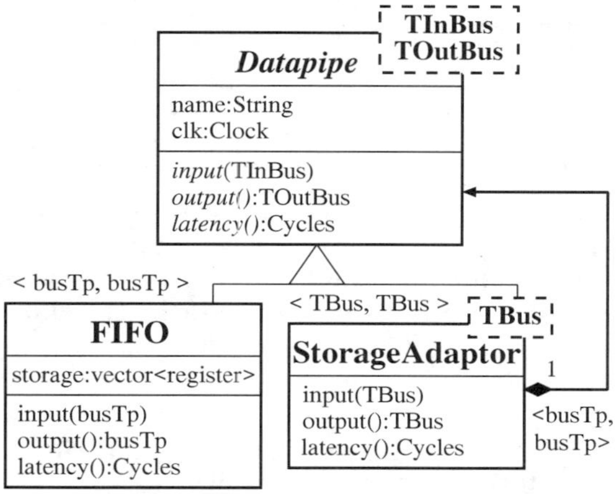

Figure 3: Application of the adaptor to the composite pattern.

whose exact types is specified in each subclass. For example, the `ComplexAbs` object specifies the type of `TInBus` to `cplxBusTp` and the type of `TOutBus` to `busTp`.

The concrete data path objects derived from the class Datapipe are of two kinds, leafs and composites. Leafs are designed from scratch while composites are compositions of leafs and other composites. In figure 1 `ComplexAbs` and `Averager` are leafs and the `AbsAverager` object is a composite. `AbsAverager` is composed of the data path objects `ComplexAbs` and `Averager`.

The interface defined by the Datapipe class maps to a component with a structural view as shown in Figure 2 with one input and one output. Text in boldface describes the component as defined by the Datapipe class. Each concrete class that inherits from the Datapipe class maps the parameterized types `TInBus` and `TOutBus` to real bus types. `AbsAverager` is used as an example. It maps the input and the output to the bus types `cplxBusTp` respectively `busTp`.

5.2 Interface adaptation

The library defines several data path objects related to storage which all have the input and output type `busTp`. Thus, storage objects only store signed or unsigned integers. There are reasons to be able to store data of other types as well, for instance complex and vector data of the types `cplxBusTp` and `vecBusTp`. The *object adaptor* pattern can be used to change the interfaces of an existing object without touching it. In Figure 3 the adaptor StorageAdaptor that adapts a given type to `busTp` is shown. Within the adaptor a mapping to `busTp` is defined for each other bus type. As an example, the mapping from `cplxBusTp` is shown in

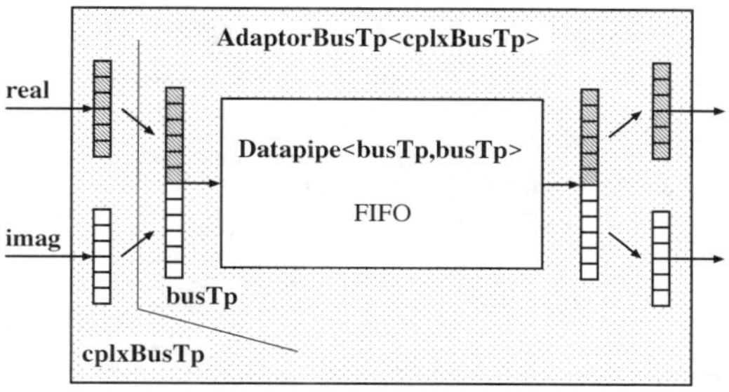

Figure 4: A structural view of the adaptation of `cplxBusTp` to `busTp`.

Figure 4. In this particular example the adaptee is a FIFO. The corresponding code to instantiate a FIFO for complex numbers and connect it to two buses is shown below.

```
1  cplxBusTp inBus, outBus;
2  Adaptor<cplxBusTp> cplxFIFO
3    ( new FIFO( FIFOsize ));
4  cplxFIFO.input( inBus );
5  outBus = cplxFIFO.output();
```

The adaptor is instantiated on lines 2 and 3. The constructor takes a pointer to the adaptee as an argument, which here is a newly created instance of FIFO. At the instantiation the whole data path required for the adaptation is created. The data path is connected to external buses on lines 4 and 5.

The advantage with this solution is that only one adaptor object has to be implemented. If it is desirable to utilize the storage objects for new bus types the only code that has to be written is a new bus type map within StorageAdaptor.

5.3 Dynamic data path creation

The current implementation of the library is targeted to one particular DSP implementation with a specific need of high throughput. To be useful for a broad range of DSP implementation it has to support other optimization constraints as well. One extension has been designed to allow the library to better adapt to varying requirements of different designs. The extension utilizes the pattern *Abstract factory*. It is used to implement a similar structure to the entity–architecture–composition structure in VHDL.

Consider the design of an IP data path block utilizing a module that can be designed according to different tradeoffs. Which version to choose depends partly on end user requirements that not are known at the design time of the IP block. What is needed is a mechanism to let the user decide the implementation of some modules within the IP block.

A pattern that matches the specification is the Abstract Factory pattern. A possible implementation with two concrete factories for low power and small area respectively, is shown in Figure 5. The abstract data path object `ComplexAbs` has one implementation targeted for each concrete factory. In the figure the client is the IP-block. The user of the IP-block gives a concrete factory as argument at the instantiation of the IP-block/client. In this case it is either a HighThroughput or a LowPower factory. Depending on which, either the Cordic or the LockUp module gets instantiated in the IP-block.

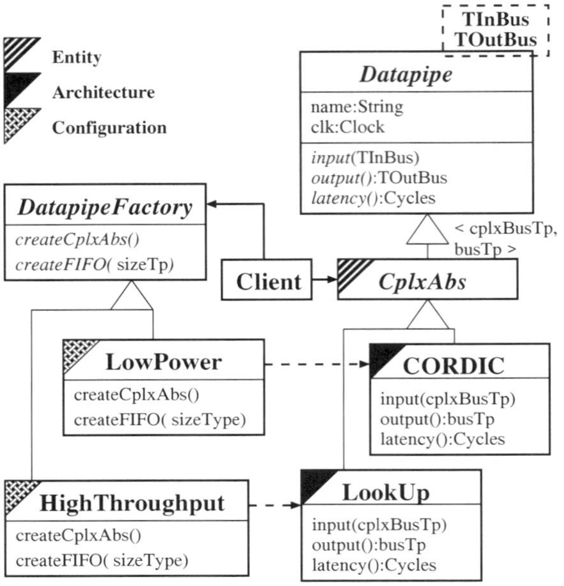

Figure 5: The abstract factory pattern. Triangular shaded areas indicate the corresponding structure in VHDL.

Note the close ties to the VHDL composition in an entity, an architecture and a configuration. The entity corresponds to the `ComplexAbs` object, the architectures are the concrete classes inheriting from `ComplexAbs` and finally the configurations corresponds to the concrete DatapathFactory objects which connects an interface to an implementation. The design shows that particular design features of the current HDLs not have to be lost by a move to an object-oriented design environment like C++.

5.4 Handshaking

Consider the problem of connecting a data path object, processing data in blocks, like a FFT, to a source that cannot guarantee a continuous data stream, like a multitasking processor. This communication channel requires a handshaking protocol and a data queue to buffer incoming data as shown in Figure 6.

The *Decorator* pattern provides a object composition for this problem. The idea of the pattern is to decorate the data path object with the extra functionality, in his case the handshaking protocol. In Figure 7 the object structure for the handshaking decorator is shown. The buses ack and req are used by the handshaking protocol. The Queue class buffers incoming data and forwards it to the decorated data path object when a whole block of data has been received.

The advantage of this pattern is that only one implementation is needed to add handshaking to all different block processing data path objects.

6. EVALUATION OF LIBRARY

The library has been evaluated with a frame synchronization algorithm for an Orthogonal frequency division multiplexing (OFDM) mobile radio system [10]. In Figure 8 the data flow of the algorithm is shown. As the algorithm is

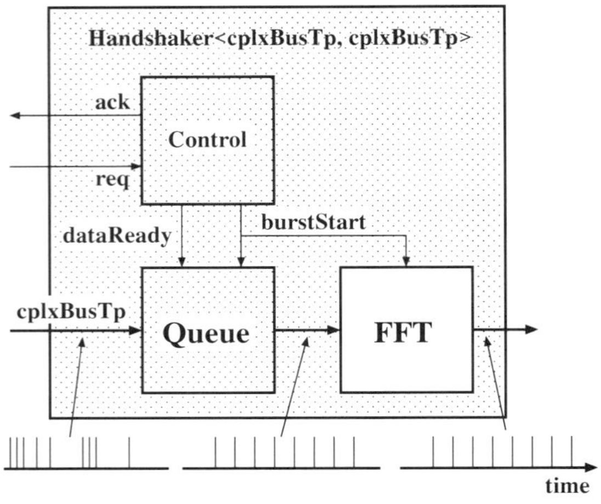

Figure 6: The decorator pattern that implements the handshaking function. The time axis below gives an idea of the appearance of data in the different buses.

Table 1: Code sizes for VHDL respectively C++ implementation of the synchronizer.

Synchronizer	# lines	# tokens
C++	936	3607
VHDL	2100	8200

hardware mapped this is also the the structure of the hardware implementation.

The design was chosen for two reasons. First it is an algorithm that is well suited for implementation with the library because it is data path centric. Second, and most important, an existing VHDL implementation of the algorithm can be used to compare the performances of the C++ and VHDL based designs respectively. The VHDL version has been implemented in hardware. The C++ version has been verified at VHDL level. The same algorithms were used for all sub blocks. For the Rect2Pol and the Rotate blocks, the CORDIC algorithm was chosen.

It is important to stress here that the comparison only compares hard facts like line and token count. Soft facts like reusability, ease of design and robustness cannot be measured objectively by design. However, those are of out most importance for the success of a design paradigm. The relative merits of the soft facts must therefore to the larger part be judged from the arguments given. Only to a minor extent do they appear as measurable hard facts in a design of this comparatively small size.

In table 1 the total number of lines and the token count is given for both implementations. It can be seen that the C++ code is roughly half of the size. It is true for the token count as well which is a more accurate estimate that the line count as it does not depend on coding style to the same extent. We believe that the results in the table are fair for this kind of design.

The smaller code size in the C++ design is mainly due to two factors. First, the number of reusable components was

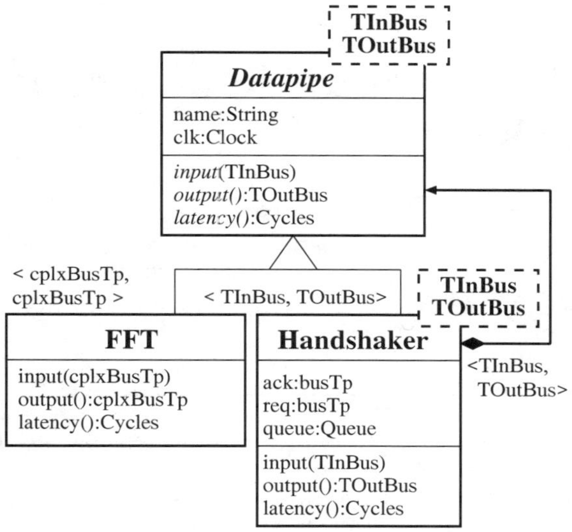

Figure 7: The handshaking decorator.

higher due to the well structured object-oriented library. Second, C++ as language allows for a more compact description compared to VHDL.

7. CONCLUSIONS

It has been shown that several software design patterns with minor modifications, can be applied to the design of a hardware data path library. The usage of design patterns is beneficial as the result is structures that are modular, reusable, robust and require little overhead. As shown only one implementation is required for each of StorageAdaptor and Handshaker to add the desired functionality.

All software patterns cannot be used in hardware design, however they can provide insight into how good structures are designed, and thus, act as inspiration in the design of dedicated hardware patterns.

We have shown by an example applying the described patterns that a C++ design is roughly half in code size compared to a VHDL design. We do not however claim that code size is an adequate measure of the merits of the presented library. Several important properties of a library like usability, reusability, ease of use and structure can not be objectively measured by a rough figure like code size. However, we believe it gives a hint about the performance that can be expected.

8. ACKNOWLEDGMENTS

This work is founded by the Integrated Electronic Systems Program (INTELECT) of the Swedish Foundation for Strategic Research (SSF).

9. REFERENCES

[1] S. Liao, S. Tjiang, and R. Gupta, "An efficient implementation of reactivity for modeling hardware in the scenic design environment," in *Proc. of the 34th Design Automation Conference*, June 1997, pp. 70–75.

[2] SystemC, http://www.systemc.org.

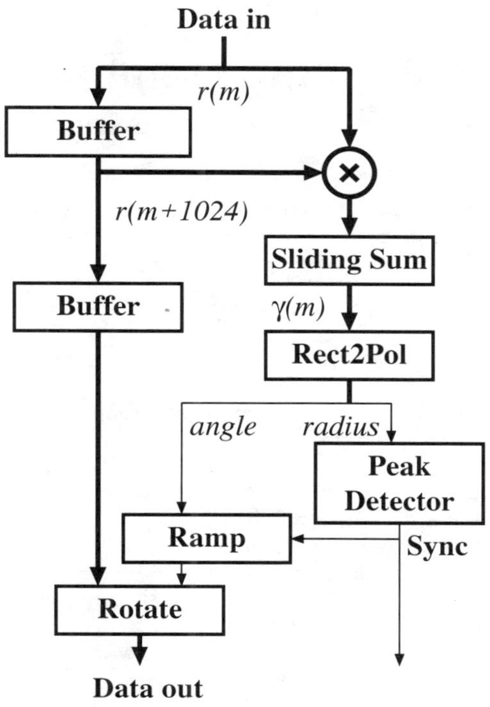

Figure 8: The data flow view of the synchronizer. Bold wires are complex numbers. Thin wires are scalars except form the sync wire which is boolean.

[3] P. Schaumont, S. Vernalde, L. Rijnders, M. Engels, and I. Bolsens, "A programming environment for the design of complex high speed asics," in *Proceedings of 35th Design Automation Conference*, San Fransisco, CA, 1998, pp. 315 – 320.

[4] E. Gamma, R. Helm, R. Johnson, and J. Vlissides, *Design Patterns, Elements of Reusable Object-Oriented Software*, Addison-Wesley, 1994.

[5] J. Coplien and D. Schmidt, *Pattern Languages of Program Design*, Addison-Wesley, 1995.

[6] J. Vlissides, J. Coplien, and N. Kerth, *Pattern Languages of Program Design 2*, Addison-Wesley, 1996.

[7] K. Beck, J. Coplien, R. Crocker, L. Dominick, G. Meszaros, F. Paulish, and J. Vlissides, "Industrial experience with design patterns," in *Proc. of 18th International Conference on Software Engineering*, March 1996, pp. 103 –114.

[8] P. Schaumont, R. Cmar, S. Vernalde, M. Engels, and I. Bolsens, "Hardware reuse at the behavioral level," in *Proceedings of the Design Automation Conference*, 1999, p. 784.

[9] M. Austern, *Generic Programming and the STL*, Addison-Wesley, 1999.

[10] S. Johansson and P. Nilsson, "Hardware implementation of an ofdm syncronization algorithm," in *Proc. of Midwest symposium on Circuits and Systems*, Las Cruces, New Mexico, August 1999.

[11] M. Fowler, *UML Distilled*, Addison-Wesley, 1997.

Accelerating Boolean Satisfiability through Application Specific Processing

Ying Zhao, Sharad Malik,
Department of Electrical Engineering,
Princeton University, NJ

Matthew Moskewicz
Department of Electrical Engineering and Computer Science, University of California at Berkeley, CA

Conor Madigan
Department of Electrical Engineering and Computer Science, MIT, MA

Abstract
This paper presents our work in developing an application specific multiprocessor system for SAT, utilizing the most recent results such as the development of highly efficient sequential SAT algorithms, the emergence of commercial configurable processor cores and the rapid progress in IC manufacturing techniques. Based on an analysis of the basic SAT search algorithm, we propose a new parallel SAT algorithm that utilizes fine grain parallelism. This is then used to design a multiprocessor architecture in which each processing node consists of a processor and a communication assist node that deals with message processing. Each processor is an application specific processor built from a commercial configurable processor core. All the system configurations are determined based on the characteristics of SAT algorithms, and are supported by simulation results. While this hardware accelerator system does not change the inherent intractability of the SAT problems, it achieves a 30-60x speedup over and above the fastest known SAT solver -- Chaff. We believe that this system can be used to expand the practical applicability of SAT in all its application areas.

Keywords
Boolean satisfiability, Application specific, Multiprocessor, Configurable processor core

1. Introduction
SAT serves as the canonical NP-complete problem, and thus has received significant attention in the theoretical computer science community. It is also a practical problem encountered in several application domains, especially in Electronic Design Automation (EDA) and Artificial Intelligence. In the EDA domain, SAT is embedded in many areas of design synthesis and validation [1,2,3] - some of these being test pattern generation, combinatorial and sequential logic verification, logic synthesis, functional timing analysis, and routing. Any acceleration in solutions to this problem will have direct benefit for many applications in these areas.

Since the basic Davis-Putnam search algorithm [4] was proposed forty years ago, significant effort [5,6,7,8] has been spent in determining efficient heuristics that accelerate solutions for problem instances encountered in practice. Recently, we have seen the development of Chaff [8], a highly efficient algorithm that demonstrates 10-100x speedup compared to all previous software solutions. This has enhanced the scope of problem instances for which we can now find solutions in reasonable compute time using SAT software packages running on general-purpose processors.

Recently the development of high-density programmable logic has led to the development of a class of SAT accelerators by several research groups [9,10]. These accelerators exploit the fact that programmable logic enables a hardware accelerator to be synthesized specific to each *instance* of the SAT problem. These works have been able to demonstrate several orders of magnitude speedup for many problem instances. However, the hardwiring of the algorithms greatly compromises the ability to support complex control and dynamic data structures. Thus, these solutions cannot utilize the advanced features in the algorithms, which have been shown to bring orders of magnitude in speedup. In fact, these accelerators cannot tackle the really difficult problem instances that they were expected to deal with. Besides, the circuit compilation cost has in many cases become the dominant component of the solution time. It is exactly these limitations that we hope to overcome by using a programmable solution, but by using specially matched architectures rather than general-purpose processing. Such processors are referred to Application Specific Processors (ASPs) and are seeing increasing use in various application domains. Recently, some commercial offerings [11] of configurable processor cores have cut the development cost for ASPs significantly.

Developing parallel solutions [12,13] to deal with computationally intensive problems like SAT is not a new idea. However, all the current parallel SAT algorithms target general -purpose multiprocessor architectures and their associated operating system support, which have a very high communication overhead. Consequently, they are all based on the partitioning of the search space and utilize the coarse parallelism among searches in different subspaces, to avoid the high communication cost. Until now, the speedup and scalability of these algorithms have not been very encouraging, because they are likely to cause significant load-imbalance due to unpredictable workloads in the separate sub-spaces.

The multiprocessor system presented in this paper is built with specialized processing nodes and communication network. Each processing node consists of an ASP built from a commercial configurable processor core and a communication assist hardware unit for message passing. Through this system, we hope to achieve significant speedup over current general purpose processing.

The rest of this paper is organized as follows. The SAT algorithms are introduced in next section. Section 3 presents the system prototype. The simulation environment is described in Section 4. Details of the performance evaluation of the system are presented in Section 5.

2. SAT Algorithms

Given a Boolean formula that is typically expressed in conjunctive normal form (CNF), the goal of SAT is to either find an assignment to the variables so that the formula evaluates to 1, or determine that no such assignment exists.

Although there are several different types of SAT algorithms, backtrack based complete search algorithms are the most popular. The high-level data flow shown in Figure 1 is applicable to all the algorithms falling into this category. They begin with an empty assignment. **decide()** selects a branching variable and assigns a 0 or 1 value to it. Then, **deduct()** performs BCP (Boolean Constraint Propagation) to determine the direct and transitive implications of this assignment. If no conflict is detected during **deduct()**, **decide()** is called again to pick the next assignment, and the procedure repeats. Otherwise, **diagnose()** is performed to determine the reason of the conflict, find the backtrack point, and generate the conflict clause. Then, **backtrack()** will remove the impact of all the implications becoming invalid and pick a new decision. In addition, **db_compact()** is another subroutine that has become very important while dealing with big problem instances encountered in practical applications. It performs clause deletion, clause database compaction and clause database updates/cleanup after the compaction, to maintain reasonable cache performance.

```
SAT_SOLVER() {
   while (true) {
     if (decide() == FALSE)
      return;                    //problem is satisifiable
     if (deduct() == CONFLICT) {
      if (diagnose() == FALSE)
       return;      //problem is unsatisfiable
      else
       backtrack();
     }
   }
```

Figure 1 Backtrack based SAT algorithm

In addition to the sequential algorithms introduced above, researchers have proposed various parallel SAT algorithms [12,13], trying to utilize the computation power of multiprocessor systems. In these algorithms the search space is partitioned by a control processor into small disjoint subspaces, each of which is assigned to a processor. As shown in Figure 2, the processors search the assigned subspace using a sequential SAT algorithm. All the processor will return SAT if any of them finds a solution, otherwise UNSAT if there is no unexplored search space left. Since the search space is inherently unbalanced, all these algorithms use some type of dynamic load balancing techniques to achieve decent performance.

```
Parallel_SAT_Solver ()
{
  while (there are unexplored spaces) { //control processor
    for (i=1, ..., N-1) {       //N-1 search processors
      if ( Sequential_SAT_Solver () == SAT )
        return SAT;
    }
  }
  return UNSAT;
}
```

Figure 2 Current, typical parallel SAT algorithms

3. System Prototype

There are always two tightly correlated elements involved in the application specific system design: the application and the underlying system architecture. The performance of the system is determined by how well these two elements match each other. Developing an efficient parallel system opens up a broad set of design considerations. Obviously, it is impractical to try all the possible combinations. Therefore, we start with an initial parallel algorithm and system architecture determined via application analysis. Then, the design process is an iterative refining procedure for both these two elements, supported by the simulation results.

3.1 Algorithm Characteristics

Among the most popular complete search algorithms, we have GRASP[5], SATO[6], Satz[7] and most recently Chaff[8]. These algorithms share the same high-level control flow and primitive operations, thus targeting these features is likely to be beneficial to future algorithms that may be developed.

We have done an extensive application analysis based on these algorithms by running them on a general-purpose single processor. The conclusion is that SAT problems are control, computation and data intensive. More specifically, they have the following features:

1. More than 99% of the execution time is spent on four major subroutines: **decide()**, **deduct()**, **backtrack()** and **db_compact()**.
2. There is a large amount of coarse and fine grain parallelism in the application.
3. SAT algorithms are all extremely memory bandwidth intensive, which suggests a distributed memory MIMD multiprocessor architecture.

3.2 A New Parallel Algorithm

Based on the algorithm characteristics, we propose a new parallel algorithm – MP_SAT. In terms of control flow, MP_SAT is similar to a sequential algorithm, with the computational intensive part being distributed. Unlike the existing parallel SAT algorithms, MP_SAT focuses on utilizing the fine grain parallelism in the clause and variable operations. In fact, utilizing fine grain parallelism is the basic idea behind most hardware accelerators. However, it usually implies higher communication cost for programmable solutions, and thus has been limited to software packages containing regular data accesses and operations, like those found in most signal and image processing applications. In our design, we will show how to match the system architecture with the algorithm, so that we can exploit the potential for higher performance improvement and better processor load balancing associated with fine grain parallelism, and avoid the costly communication at the same time. In this section, we introduce the tasking partitioning and communication scheme in MP_SAT.

3.2.1 Task Partitioning

MP_SAT uses a hybrid task partitioning method that combines data based and function based decomposition. Each of the computationally expensive functions in all SAT algorithms repeatedly performs the same operations on a large set of data and there is no strong correlation among the data. This implies a natural data partition: each processor has a subset of the clauses and variables. And the functions running on each processor works on its own data subset in parallel, as shown in Figure 3. Through the data partitioning, not only multiple operations can be performed in parallel, in many cases, the cost of each individual operation is also reduced. These processors are called PPs (Processing Processors).

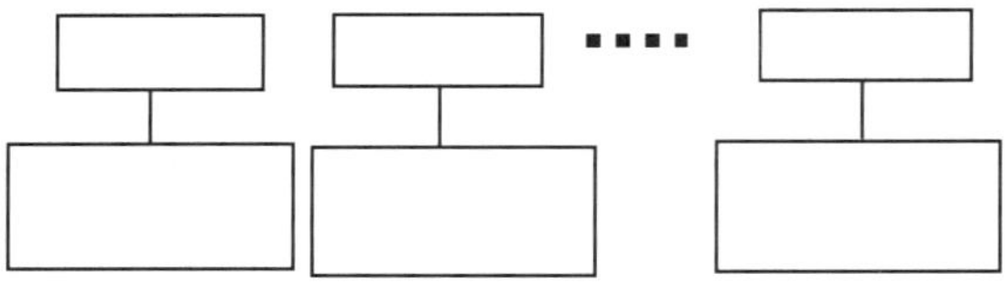

Figure 3 Data partition based parallelization

Other than the PPs, a Master Processor (MP) is needed to monitor the search state, coordinate the operations of all processors and perform global functions like **diagnose()**.

3.2.2 Communication and Synchronization Scheme

In a distributed memory MIMD system, processors exchange data via explicit message passing. Careful design of the communication scheme in both the algorithm and the hardware system is needed to minimize the communication cost.

In MP_SAT, the timely detection of new messages is not critical. For example, while a PP is doing **deduct()**, it need not know that new implications are coming in immediately since it can only start to process the new implications after it finishes the current one. In addition, as will be introduced in Section 3.3, the message buffers provided by the system can prevent the busy status of the message receiver stalling the sender. Thus, polling provides an efficient synchronization method with low overhead in our system, in contrast to interrupt. Each processor checks for new messages whenever it completes processing the current message. By doing this, we avoid wasting machine cycles caused by over polling and prevent the message buffers from being over loaded with unread messages at the same time.

There is one special message that is time sensitive: conflict. Although it does not affect the results of the program if the conflict message uses the same transmission scheme as other messages, it may affect the performance and complicate the control. Basically, all operations that a PP performs from the time MP detects a conflict until the time the PP starts to process the conflict messages are useless operations that will cause extra amount of work during **backtrack()**. Thus, a direct broadcast channel is used specifically for a conflict message. Global synchronization is also performed through the broadcast channel.

3.3 Hardware architecture

3.3.1 High level architecture

MP_SAT has two features: intensive communication based on message passing and message driven operations. Transmitting messages at high speed and with least interference with the computation are important considerations in the system design. We achieve these goals by using separate hardware units for communication, which greatly increases the parallelism between computation and communication. Therefore, each processing node in the system consists of a processor and a communication node. The processors have been designed to be straightforward message generator/consumer, with the corresponding communication nodes performing the message routing and buffering. Figure 4 shows the architecture with these processing nodes connected via a two-dimensional mesh.

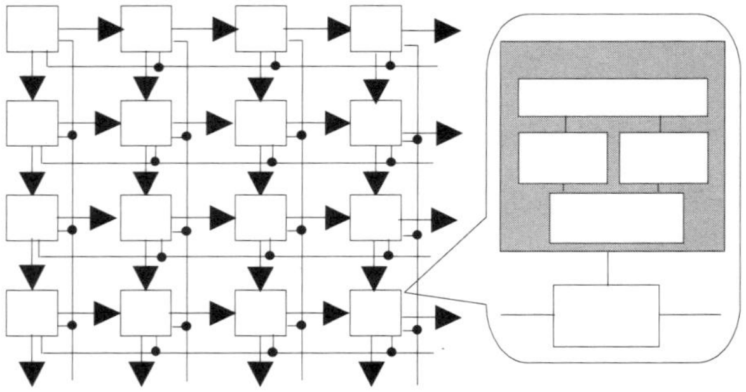

Figure 4 System architecture using embedded DRAM

The global broadcast wire is pipelined to avoid the delay and crosstalk problems associated with deep sub-micron designs. As shown in Figure 4, there is one pipelined broadcast line in each row and each column. A processor sends out the conflict message by setting the global wire to high. The signal is transferred via the vertical wire to each row, then via the horizontal wire to each processor. The maximum delay of this wire is 2n cycles, where n is the dimension of the network.

During our simulation, we have found that the parallel execution of communication and computation can bring more than 50% in overall performance, which shows that using separate hardware for communication is very efficient for communication intensive applications.

3.3.2 Processors

The processors in our system are application specific processors built from a commercial configurable processor core. These processors are customized to match the data access patterns and atomic operations in SAT algorithms. For details about the processor design, please see [14]. Here, we just give a short overview of them. To accommodate the memory bandwidth requirement, the datapath of the processor is chosen to be 128 bits. 11 new instructions are added to the basic configurable processor core, which fit in three categories: bit operation, parallel operations utilizing 128bits datapath and compound instructions for frequently appearing instruction sequences. The new instructions bring about a 2-4X speedup, at a cost of 2400 gates. The final processor has 53.9k gates, and runs at 300MHz. These processors also have direct input/output ports, which allow them to talk to other components directly, without going through the ALU or the standard bus interface.

3.3.3 Communication Node

Each communication node consists of two parts:

- Communication channels. Each of the channels is a FIFO buffer dedicated to a pair of communicating processors, storing the messages between these two processors. The number of channels needed in each communication node is affected by the network topology. Based on simulation results, the size of each channel is determined to be 20 messages.
- Control logic that performs the message routing and channel empty/full detection, which can be modeled as a Finite State Machine. These finite state machines are very small and have been synthesized from a Verilog description to a circuit with approximately 100 gates.

Figure 5 shows the architecture of a communication node in a two-dimensional mesh topology.

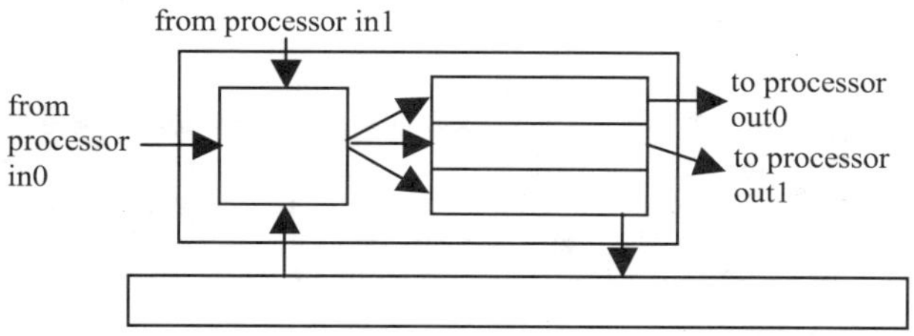

Figure 5 Communication node in a two-dimensional mesh

3.3.4 Communication Protocol

The communication protocol mainly includes the network topology and routing scheme. We chose a two-dimensional mesh topology due to the following reasons:

- Mesh topology gives a balanced bandwidth across all the processors. We have found that 90% of the messages in MP_SAT are broadcast messages. Thus, topologies like tree usually cause some "hot spots" that will become the communication bottleneck.
- Mesh has very good scalability and achieves good trade-off between the diameter and number of connections.
- Planar topologies like two-dimensional mesh make designing single chip multiprocessor system simpler, since all processors are connected with uniformly short connections.

In our system, the combination of message buffering and the parallel execution of computation and communication greatly reduce the possibility of network congestion. In addition, since all the operations in MP_SAT are message driven, transmitting messages fast is crucial in exploiting the parallelism. Therefore, we use deterministic routing. The communication nodes determine the route of a message based on the self-contained address information in its header.

To avoid the deadlock caused by loops in the network topology, a processor stalls whenever there are less than two spaces left in any of the buffers in its communication node. In this way, each communication node can guarantee that there is always empty space in all its local buffers. Thus, the messages can keep moving. Even if all the buffers are very close to full, as long as no new messages are dispatched to the network, the messages can be consumed and finally removed.

4. Simulation Environment

Our simulation environment consists of two simulators that run at different abstraction levels, accuracy and speed.

MP_SIM is a cycle-accurate multiprocessor simulator built based on a commercial cycle-accurate Instruction Set Simulator (ISS). It is designed to be highly flexible, so that can be used to model various communication schemes. It is also very easy to configure by making the network configuration and routing scheme transparent to user applications.

To overcome the speed limitation of cycle accurate simulation, we have implemented a C++ simulator that simulates the multiprocessor system behavior at a high level of abstraction. This simulator is event (message) driven. The cycle count is generated by calculating latencies for each individual operation (cache simulation, network communication, etc.). These latencies are calculated using the same architecture parameters. The purpose of this simulator is to get the overall cycle count, rather than to simulate the real cycle accurate behavior of the parallel algorithm. Since this simulator runs at a much higher level, it achieves approximately 50-80x speedup compared with the cycle accurate simulation, which allows us to simulate bigger problems running on more processors. First, we run the simulator on the examples we have run using MP_SIM, and compare the two sets of results. We find that the cycle counts obtained from the high level simulators are within [-12%, 5%] of the results from MP_SIM, which indicates that the results of the new simulator are reasonably close to the exact results.

5. Design Evaluation

5.1 Parallel Speedup

The speedup is the most basic metric to determine the validity of a parallel system design. Figure 6 shows the speedup of the parallel system while using different numbers of processors, compared with the basic Xtensa processor. The performance is measured using the number of clock cycles needed to solve the problems. The cycle counts of the parallel system are obtained using MP_SIM. The *sequential* results are obtained by running Chaff, a highly efficient sequential program on the single processor Xtensa ISS. Since they run at the same clock frequency, the *speedup* is calculated by dividing the cycle count of the parallel system by the *sequential* results. Generally speaking, the bigger the problem size, the higher speedup. This is understandable since larger problems usually have higher level of parallelism, and thus higher processor utilization rate.

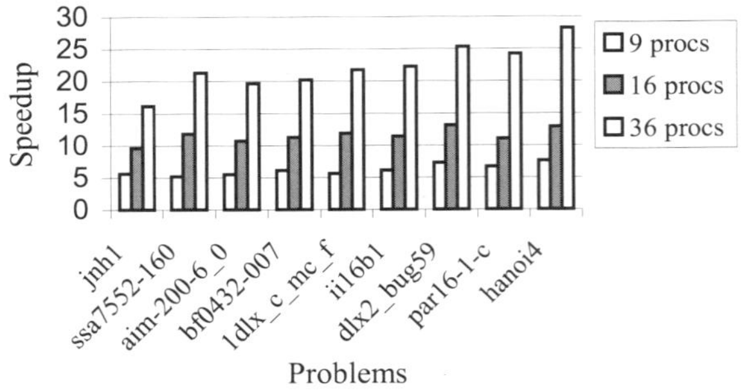

Figure 6 Speedup vs. number of processors

5.2 Scalability/efficiency Analysis

Figure 7 shows the efficiency of the parallel system, which is calculated by dividing speedup by the number of processors. Generally speaking, although speedup may increase, efficiency always decreases as the number of processors increases, due to the higher communication cost and the limited parallelism. This decrease is reflected very well in Figure 7. The figure also shows that the efficiency is generally higher for bigger problems.

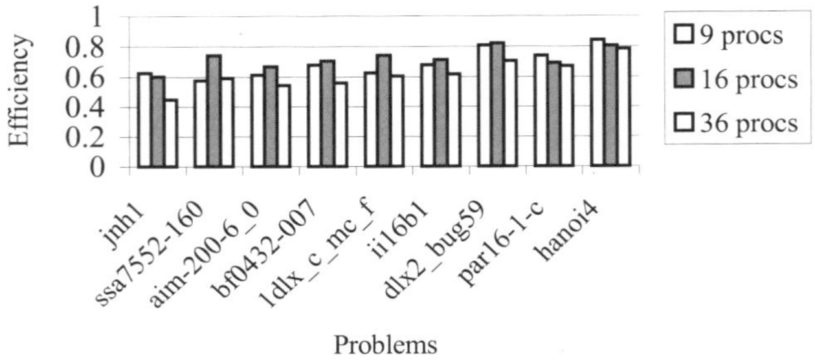

Figure 7 Efficiency vs. number of processors

For any parallel system, there must be a certain point where the efficiency has dropped so much that increasing processors may lead to lower speed. This is called the limitation of the scalability. This limitation is very important, since it also points out the performance limitation of the parallel system. We first perform a theoretical analysis of this limitation by examining how many operations can actually be performed in parallel. The parallelism of our system comes from three sources.

- Inserting variables to a sorted list in parallel in **backtrack()**.
- Compacting the clause database in parallel in **db_compact()**.
- Parallel execution of BCP in **deduct()**.

For almost all the problems we have experimented with, the number of variables to be processed per backtracking is less than or close to 100. Therefore, if we use more than 100 processors, there must be some processors remaining idle during **backtrack()**. Of course, the more processors we use, the smaller each sub-list, thus, the faster each insert operates. We expect that the parallelism limitation of **backtrack()** happens when the communication cost of collecting candidates from the PPs starts to outweigh the advantage of smaller list.

db_compact() has almost perfect parallelism as long as all the processors have approximately the same amount of clauses or literals. In addition, due to the data distribution, the data size on each processor in the multiprocessor system reduces to approximately 1/(number of processors) of the data size on a single processor. Thus, the need for database compact is greatly reduced. Actually, for all the problems we have run, none of them needs to call **db_compact()** when the number of processors is bigger than 16 in the parallel system. Therefore, for this function, more processor always means better performance.

The efficiency of parallel BCP is determined by the number of implications and clauses to evaluate upon one decision. In fact, even for the hardest problems we have seen so far, the number of clauses evaluated at each decision level is less than or close to 2000. We expect to see the parallelism in clause evaluation much smaller than this number since the generation of implications is a *chained* process. Actually, the average number of clauses to be evaluated per implication is only 5-10. Thus, the parallelism in BCP comes mostly from the parallel evaluation of more than one implication. This again confirms that the fast transmission of messages is very important for our algorithm. Since the parallel execution of BCP is the most important source of the performance improvement, it is also the main source of the limited parallelism.

The above analysis clearly demonstrates the limitation of the parallelism in MP_SAT. Figure 8 and Figure 9 show the speedup and efficiency of some big problems [15] running on the multiprocessor system, obtained using the high level simulator. These results show that our system can achieve approximately 80%-90% in efficiency for large size problems.

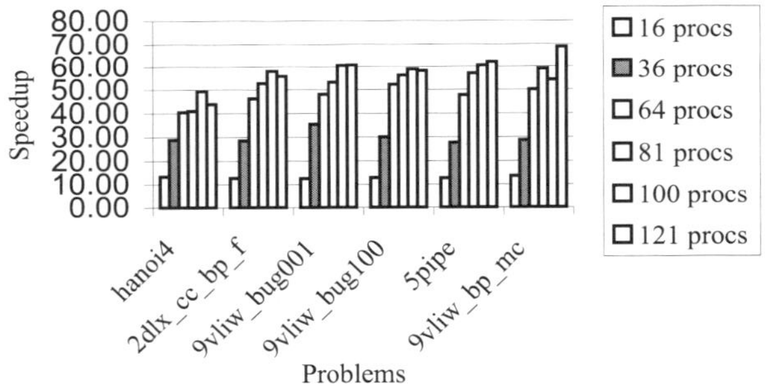

Figure 8 Efficiency vs. number of processors for big problems

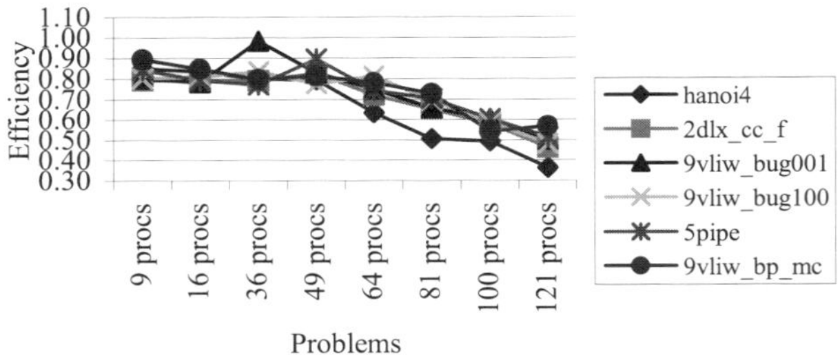

Figure 9 Efficiency vs. number of processors for big problems

From the above analysis and simulation, we can see that the limited degree of parallelism implies that this system is not scalable to very large number of processors. Although the optimum number of processors varies for different problem sizes, even for the biggest problem in our set, a system with more than 81 processors will have significantly lower efficiency than a system with a smaller number of processors. Actually, during our simulation, we find that when the number of processors increases from 81 to 100, the system sees little performance improvement for most of the problems, if any. And we see slow down for most of the problem instances when the number of processors changes from 100 to 121. This is actually consistent with our theoretical analysis of the degree of parallelism available. We also see speed anomaly in some cases, caused by the difference between the search path of sequential and parallel algorithm. In many MIMD systems, the limitation of scalability is the ratio between communication and computation. However, in our system, the communication cost has been lowered significantly because of the usage of a separate communication node, the scalability is mainly limited by the amount of parallelism available.

5.3 Parallelism profile

The parallelism profile can be measured based on the utilization of each processor. The processor utilization is defined as:

utilization = busy_time/(busy_time+idle_time)

where, *busy_time* represents the time spent by the processor doing computation or communication, and *idle time* represents the time during which the processor was not doing anything. This includes the machine cycles while a processor is waiting for messages or is stalling because of the network congestion. Figure 10 shows the utilization of each processor in a 16-processor system. In general, we observe very high utilization of all the processors. Although it is not exact for each individual case, the utilization is generally higher for bigger problems. Besides, the load balancing between processors is very good, only varies by less than 2%.

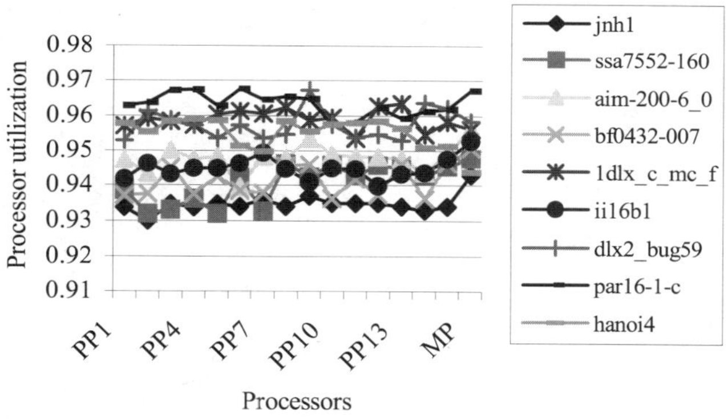

Figure 10 Parallelism profile of a 16-processor system

6. Conclusions

This paper has presented the design of an application specific multiprocessor system for SAT problems, which includes an application specific processor built from a commercial configurable processor core and a separate hardware communication unit on each processing node. The network topology and communication protocol are both determined based on the application characteristics. The system achieves a 30-60X over Chaff, the fastest known single processor SAT solver. We also show that very high efficiency can be achieved in a multiprocessor system, even for communication and control intensive algorithms. In the work introduced here, we utilize the most recent advances in several areas: high performance SAT solvers, commercial configurable processor cores and progress in the IC manufacturing techniques, to accelerate the SAT problems.

7. References

1 P. Stephan, R. Brayton, and A. Sangiovanni-Vincentelli. Combinational Test Generation Using Satisfiability. In *IEEE Transactions on Computer-Aided Design of Integrated Circuits and Systems*, pages 1167-1176, September 1996.

2 W. Kunz and D. Sotoffel. Reasoning in Boolean Networks. Kluwer Academic Publishers, 1997.

3 S. Devadas. Optimal Layout via Boolean Satisfiability. In *Proceedings of IEEE International Conference on Computer-Aided Design*, 1989.

4 M. Davis and H. Putnam. A computing Procedure for Quantification Theory. In *Journal of the ACM*, pages 201-215, 1960.

5 J. Silva and K. Sakallah. GRASP-A New Search Algorithm for Satisfiability. In *IEEE ACM International Conference on CAD-96*, page 220-227, November 1996.

6 H. Zhang. SATO: An efficient propositional prover. In *Proceedings of the International Conference on Automated Deduction*, pages 272-275, July 1997.

7 C min Li. Equivalency Reasoning to solve a class of hard SAT problems. Available from http://www.cs.washington.edu/homes/kautz/challenge/cli.ps.

8 M. Moskewicz, C. Madigan, Y. Zhao, L. Zhang and S. Malik. Engineering a (Super?) Efficient SAT solver. In *Proceedings of Design Automation Conference*, 2001.

9 M. Abramovici and D. Saab. Satisfiability on Reconfigurable Hardware. In *Seventh International Workshop on Field Programmable Logic and Applications*, September 1997.

10 P. Zhong, M. Martonosi, S. Malik and P. Ashar, Solving Boolean Satisfiabiligy with Dynamic Hardware Configuration. In *Proceedings International Workshop on Field Programmable Logic and Applications, FPL'98*, August 1998.

11 Xtensa configurable processor. http://www.tensilica.com

12 Benjamin W. Wah, Guo-Jie Li and Chee Fen Yu. Multiprocessing of combinational search problems. In *IEEE computer*. Pages 93-108, June 1985.

13 C. Powley, C. Ferguson and R. Korf. Parallel heuristic search: Two approaches. In *Vipin Kumar, P.S. Gopalakrishnan, and L.N.Kanal, editors, Parallel Algorithms for Machine Intelligence and Vision.* Springer-Verlag, New York, NY 1990.

14 Y. Zhao, S. Malik, M. Moskewicz and C.Madigan. Matching Architecture to Application via Configurable Processors: A Case Study with Boolean Satisfiability. In *Proceedings of International Conference on Computer Design*, 2001.

15 Velev, M., FVP-UNSAT.1.0, FVP-UNSAT.2.0, VLIW-SAT.1.0, SSS-SAT.1.0, Superscalar Suite 1.0/1.0a, Available from: http://www.ece.cmu.edu/~mvelev.

Considering Power Variations of DVS Processing Elements for Energy Minimisation in Distributed Systems

Marcus T. Schmitz
Dept. of Electronics and Computer Science
University of Southampton
Southampton, SO17 1BJ, United Kingdom
m.schmitz@ecs.soton.ac.uk

Bashir M. Al-Hashimi
Dept. of Electronics and Computer Science
University of Southampton
Southampton, SO17 1BJ, United Kingdom
bmah@ecs.soton.ac.uk

ABSTRACT

Dynamic voltage scaling (DVS) is a powerful technique to reduce power dissipation in embedded systems. Some efficient DVS algorithms have been recently proposed for the energy reduction in distributed system. However, they achieve the energy savings solely by scaling the system task with respect to the timing constraints, while neglecting that power varies among the tasks executed by DVS processing elements (DVS-PEs). In this paper we investigate the problem of considering DVS-PE power variations dependent on the executed tasks, during the synthesis of distributed embedded systems and its impact on the energy savings. Unlike previous approaches, which minimise the energy consumption by exploiting the available slack time without considering the PE power profiles, a new and fast heuristic for the voltage scaling problem is proposed, which improves the voltage selection for each task dependent on the individual power dissipation caused by that task. Experimental results show that energy reductions with up to 80.7% are achieved by integrating the proposed DVS algorithm, which considers the PE power profiles, into the co-synthesis of distributed systems.

1. INTRODUCTION

Power dissipation has become a major issue in embedded system design, due to reliability and battery life time in portable application. One technique to tackle the problem of power consumption is dynamic voltage scaling [19], which reduces the power dissipation P by dynamically scaling the supply voltage V_{dd} and operational frequency f of the embedded processor [3, 10, 14] according to the system requirements. The power dissipation and the operational frequency are expressed by the following equations:

$$P_{dyn} = C_L \cdot N_{0\rightarrow 1} \cdot f \cdot V_{dd}^2 \quad (1)$$

$$f = k \cdot (V_{dd} - V_t)^2 / V_{dd} \quad (2)$$

ISSS'01, October 1-3, 2001, Montréal, Québec, Canada.

where C_L is the switching capacitance, $N_{0\rightarrow 1}$ denotes the switching activity, k is a circuit dependent constant and V_t is the circuit threshold voltage.

There has been extensive research on DVS algorithms with early research focused on single processor systems executing independent tasks [11, 21]. Recently DVS has also been applied to distributed embedded systems. In [9] a task scheduling algorithm based on a list scheduling with dynamic re-calculation of priorities is presented. The algorithm attempts to find optimised and feasible schedules by assigning priorities based on the average energy dissipation. If no feasible schedule is found the priorities of the tasks on the critical path are increased and the tasks are rescheduled. The scheduling algorithm presented in [16] aims at a power-conscious joint scheduling of periodic task graphs and aperiodic tasks, which employs DVS and dynamic power management to achieve energy efficiency. They optimise a pre-ordered schedule by distributing the flexibility in the schedule more evenly. These algorithms show that DVS can be applied to distributed embedded systems.

In all of the reported scaling algorithms for distributed systems [9, 16] the PE power consumption of different tasks is neglected during the voltage selection. However, modern VLSI designs make extensive use of low power techniques like, e.g., gated clocks [5], and the PEs in distributed systems are often of heterogeneous nature [20]. Certainly, this results in a PE power profiles, which show power variations. In [13, 17, 18] it was shown that the consideration of PE power variations of the executed task is important from the energy reduction point of view. They proposed suitable DVS algorithms for single DVS-PE systems. However, the trend of embedded systems implementations is going towards distributed systems [20].

The aim of this paper is to investigate the problem of considering DVS processor power variations dependent on tasks, during the synthesis of distributed embedded systems and its impact on energy savings. A new off-line scaling heuristic is proposed, which is sufficiently fast enough (polynomial time complexity) to permit its use during the design space exploration phase of the co-synthesis process, further reducing the energy dissipation by optimising the scheduling and mapping of the specification tasks towards DVS usability.

The remainder of the paper is organised as follows. Section 2 motivates the consideration of PE power variations among tasks, using an illustrative example. In Section 3 the specification model is given and the variable power DVS problem is formulated. Section 4 presents a constructive

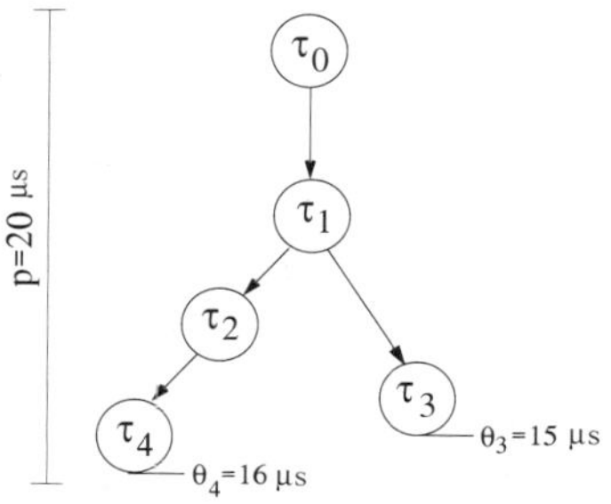

Figure 1: Task graph example

task	*WCET (μs)*	*Power (mW)*	*Mapping*
τ_0	1.5	85	PE0
τ_1	3.0	20	PE1
τ_2	7.5	15	PE1
τ_3	1.5	80	PE1
τ_4	1.5	100	PE0
$\tau_0 \rightarrow \tau_1$	0.5	5	CL0
$\tau_3 \rightarrow \tau_4$	1.0	5	CL0

Table 1: Exaction times, power dissipations, and mapping of tasks and communications

heuristic to solve the variable power DVS problem. In Section 5 experimental results are given, which demonstrate the necessity of considering PE power variations. Section 6 presents some conclusions.

2. MOTIVATIONAL EXAMPLE

This section addresses why PE power variations among tasks in distributed systems need to be considered in order to reduce the system energy consumption. This is illustrated by the following simple example. Fig. 1 gives a system specification using a task graph (TG), with two hard deadlines at $15\mu s$ and $16\mu s$. The period between two invocations of the task graph is $20\mu s$. The worst-case execution times (WCET), the nominal power dissipations and the mapping of each task and communication are shown in Table 1.

Scheduling the given specification on a distributed system consisting of two PEs (PE0 and PE1) connected by a link (CL0), could result in the feasible schedule (executing tasks at nominal supply voltage) given in Fig. 2. Using the execution values in Table 1 the dynamic energy dissipation of the system can be calculated as $577.5nJ$. Obviously, task τ_3 and τ_4 finish execution before their deadlines are exceeded, leaving a slack of $1\mu s$, which can be used to reduce the energy dissipation through supply voltage scaling and hence reducing the power dissipated by the tasks. Lets consider two cases for the identification of scaling voltages: First, when the voltage selection process neglects the individual PE power dissipation and second, when the power profile is taken into account in order to refine the voltage schedule.

One approach to optimise the energy dissipation, which neglects the power profile, is to distribute the slack time evenly among the tasks (similar to [16]), as shown in Fig. 3(a). Each task execution in this example is extended by a factor of $14.5/13.5 = 1.074$, since the total execution times (both path of the TG) account for $13.5\mu s$ and the slack is $1\mu s$. Thereby the new execution times can be calculated as

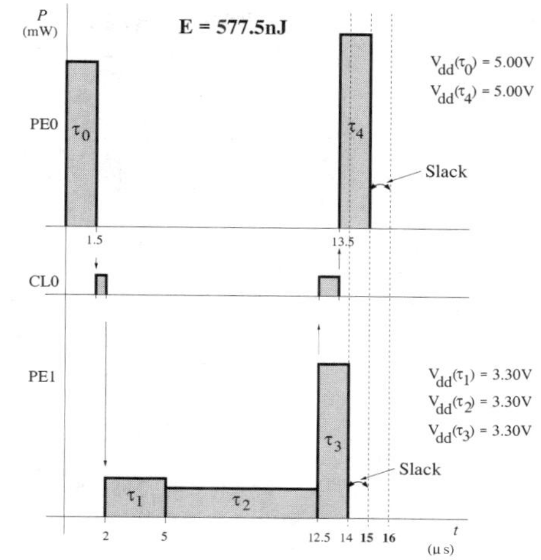

Figure 2: Tasks execution at nominal supply voltage

$t_0 = 1.61\mu s$, $t_1 = 3.22\mu s$, $t_2 = 8.56\mu s$, $t_3 = 1.61\mu s$, and $t_4 = 1.61\mu s$. According to this execution times the supply voltages of PE0 and PE1 can be reduced to $4.79V$ and $3.16V$, respectively, using Equation (2). This values were calculate taking into account the different maximal supply voltages V_{max} and threshold voltages V_t of PE0 ($V_{max} = 5V, V_t = 1.2V$) and PE1 ($V_{max} = 3.3V, V_t = 0.8V$). Using the new execution times, the individual task power dissipations can be reduced to $P_0 = 72.57mW$, $P1 = 17.08mW$, $P_2 = 12.81mW$, $P_3 = 85.42mW$, and $P_4 = 85.38mW$, as calculated by Equation (1). This results in a total energy dissipation $E = 530.3nJ$, a reduction of 8.2%.

Now consider the second case when the PE power dissipation dependent on tasks is considered during the voltage selection. Intuitively, the tasks τ_0,τ_3 and τ_4 will reduces the energy dissipation more than the tasks τ_1 and τ_2, when voltage scaled, due to their high power consumption and therefore should be extended more then the remaining tasks. Fig. 3(b) shows an improved voltage schedule. This schedule was generated using the scaling algorithm introduced later in Section 4. To demonstrate the principle behind the proposed approach it is necessary to give the following definition.

DEFINITION 1. *We define an energy gradient Δt_τ as the difference between the energy dissipation of task τ with the execution time t and the reduced energy dissipation (due to voltage and clock scaling) of the same task, when extended by a time quantum Δt. Formally:*

$$\Delta E_\tau = E_\tau(t) - E_\tau(t + \Delta t) \tag{3}$$

where $E_\tau(t)$ and $E_\tau(t + \Delta t)$ are calculated using Equations (1) and (2). □

For a simple illustration of the proposed method the time quantum Δt is set to $0.1\mu s$. Based on this time quantum an energy gradient ΔE_τ can be calculated for all tasks, using Equation (3). The resulting energy gradients are $\Delta E_0 = 127.5nJ - 117.9nJ = 9.60nJ$, $\Delta E_1 = 2.34nJ$, $\Delta E_2 = 1.56nJ$, $\Delta E_3 = 8.99nJ$, and $\Delta E_4 = 11.3nJ$. Obviously, the task with the highest energy gradient ΔE_τ will improve the total energy dissipation by the highest amount and therefore this task is extended by Δt; in our case task τ_4. Due to the

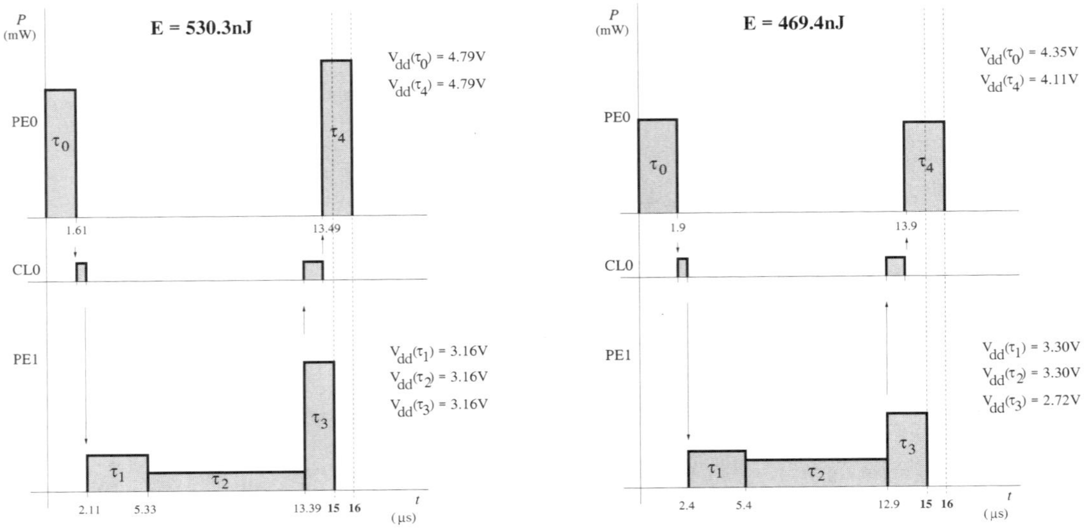

(a) Voltage scheduling assuming constant power of tasks

(b) Voltage scheduling of the proposed approach allowing for power variations

Figure 3: Voltage schedules showing reduced energy consumption

non-linear relationship of execution time and power dissipation, the energy gradient needs to be re-calculate after each extention of a task. This is $\Delta E_4 = 9.65nJ$ for task τ_4 in the first iteration. Based on these observations, tasks with the highest energy gradient are iteratively extended until no further extention is possible due to hard deadline constraints. This results in the schedule shown in Fig. 3(b), which reveals a total energy dissipation of $469.4nJ$, a reduction of 18.7%. Although using a simple example, this clearly indicates the advantage of voltage scaling methods, which take the power profile into account during supply voltage optimisation.

3. MODEL SPECIFICATION AND PROBLEM FORMULATION

Specifications of typical embedded systems are often represented by a task graph model. These are directed acyclic graphs $G_S(\mathcal{T}, \mathcal{C})$ where $\mathcal{T} = \{\tau_0, \tau_1, \ldots, \tau_N\}$ represent tasks, $\mathcal{C} = \{\gamma_{ij} = (\tau_i, \tau_j, \chi_{ij})\}$ represent precedence constraints and data dependencies (also called communications) between two tasks (τ_i, τ_j), and χ_{ij} indicates the data amount to be transfered. Tasks might be associated with a hard deadline θ_i by which its execution must be finished, in order to fulfil feasibility requirements. The target architecture, represented by a directed graph $G_A(\mathcal{P}, \mathcal{L})$, consists of processing elements $\pi \in \mathcal{P}$ (e.g. general purpose processors, ASIPs, DVS-μPs, etc.) and communication links (CL) $\lambda \in \mathcal{L}$ (e.g. point-to-point connections, busses, etc.). For each task/PE and communication/CL combination, properties like execution time and power dissipation are given beforehand. These values are either based on previous design experience or on sophisticated estimation techniques [2, 15].

3.1 Power Variation DVS Problem

Unlike previous approaches, which identify supply voltages for each task execution without the consideration of the dissipated power, our optimisation problem involves a refined voltage selection for each task, dependent on the individual power dissipation caused by task execution. The problem can be stated as followed:

Find for all DVS-PE mapped tasks $\tau \in \mathcal{T}_{\rm DVS}$ of the system specification a single scaling voltage V_{dd} (between the threshold voltage V_t and the nominal supply voltage V_{max}), under consideration of the individual power dissipations $P_{max}(\tau)$ and worst case execution time $t_{min}(\tau)$, such that the dynamic energy dissipation E_Σ is minimised and no deadline and precedence constraints are violated.

Therefore, minimise

$$E_\Sigma = \sum_{\tau \in \mathcal{T}_{DVS}} \frac{P_{max}(\tau) \cdot t_{min}(\tau)}{V_{max}^2(\tau)} \cdot V_{dd}^2(\tau) \tag{4}$$

subject to

$$V_t(\tau) < V_{dd}(\tau) \leq V_{max}(\tau), \forall \tau \in \mathcal{T}_{DVS} \tag{5}$$

limiting the applicable supply voltages range. Further, no hard deadline violation can be tolerated in order to yield feasibility and therefore

$$t_S(\tau) + t_{exe}(\tau) \leq \theta(\tau), \forall \tau \in \mathcal{T}_d \tag{6}$$

where t_S denotes the task start time and $\mathcal{T}_d$ is the set of all hard deadline tasks. The execution time function $t_{exe} : \mathcal{T} \rightarrow \mathbb{R}^+$ follows equation $(t_{min}(\tau) \cdot V_{dd}(\tau) \cdot (V_{max}(\tau) - V_t(\tau)^2))/((V_{dd}(\tau) - V_t(\tau))^2 \cdot V_{max}(\tau))$, which can be derived from Equation (2). Furthermore, the execution order of the tasks and communications must be respected and is expressed as follows:

$$t_S(\gamma) + t_{com}(\gamma) \leq t_S(\tau), \forall \tau \in \mathcal{T}, \gamma \in \mathcal{C}^{in}(\tau) \tag{7}$$

where t_{com} presents the communication time of communication event γ and $\mathcal{C}^{in}$ is the set of all ingoing edges of task τ. In addition, no execution overlap on any resource $\epsilon \in (\mathcal{P} \cup \mathcal{L})$ is permitted and therefore the execution intervals i, formed by the start and end times of events, are not allowed to intersect, as given formally in Equation (8).

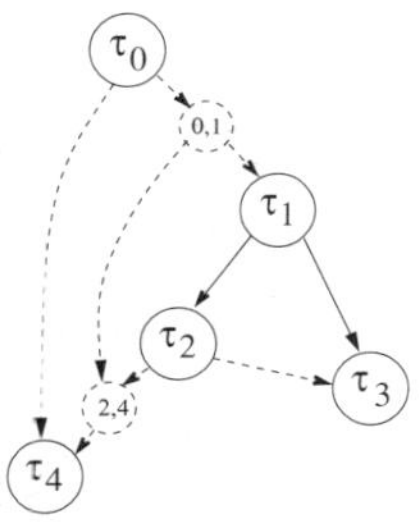

Figure 4: Mapped and scheduled task graph with pseudo communication tasks and edges

$$i(\epsilon_n) \cap i(\epsilon_m) = \varnothing, \forall(\epsilon_n, \epsilon_m) \tag{8}$$

Note that the power dissipation $P_{max}(\tau)$ of each task given in Equation (4) is *not* constant, but might vary from task to task, unlike in previous approaches. A constructive heuristic to solve this optimisation problem is presented in Section 4.

4. PROPOSED POWER VARIATION (PV) DVS ALGORITHM

Allowing the PE power variations among tasks makes it difficult to identify suitable scaling voltages for the tasks such that the energy dissipation is minimised. Recently, a hybrid global/local search strategy [1] has been proposed to find optimised execution voltages for each task. While this formulation of the problem might be applied to consider power variations among tasks, its implementation using a genetic algorithm combined with a local search will lead to prohibitively large computational time (with reported times of 20 minutes of 28 node task graphs) hindering a efficient exploration of the system level design space, when used in the inner most loop of the co-synthesis. The aim of this section is to introduce a new voltage scaling algorithm capable of identifying refined scaling voltages by considering the individual power dissipation based on the executed task. The presented algorithm is sufficiently fast enough to permit its use during the design space exploration phase to allow the optimisation of the scheduling and mapping towards DVS usability. The proposed scaling algorithm has a polynomial time complexity of $\mathcal{O}(m \cdot n(3n + e + n \log n))$, with $n = |\mathcal{T}|$ and $e = |\mathcal{C}|$. The factor m depends on the Δt_{min} and is introduced to capture the fact that tasks mind be extended more than once. However, this time complexity is a worst case estimation, which is unlikely to be reached due to the progressively elimination of extendable tasks during the optimisation run.

Fig. 5 gives the pseudocode of the proposed voltage scaling algorithm. Its input consists of the specification task graph G_S, a mapping of tasks to the architecture, a schedule of tasks and communications, architectural information (e.g. execution time and power dissipation of tasks), and the minimum extention time Δt_{min} (defined to prevent insignificant small extentions, which would slow down the DVS algorithm). Initially (line 01), the specification task graph is transformed into a *mapped and scheduled task graph* (MSTG) to capture the mapping and scheduling information into the task graph. This is carried out in two steps. First, communications between different PEs are converted into pseudo

Algorithm: *PV_DVS_OPTIMISATION*

Input: - task graph $G_S(\mathcal{T}, \mathcal{C})$
- mapping and schedule
- architectural information
- minimum extention time Δt_{min}

Output: - energy optimised voltages $V_{dd}(\tau)$
- dissipated dynamic energy E

01: $G_S \curvearrowright$ MSTG
02: $\mathbb{Q}_E \leftarrow \varnothing$
03: **for** all $(\tau \in \mathcal{T}_d)$ $\{\Delta t_d(\tau) := \theta(\tau) - t_E(\tau)\}$
04: **for** all $(\tau \in \mathcal{T})$ {calculate t_ϵ}
05: **for** all $(\tau \in \mathcal{T})$ {**if** $t_\epsilon \geq \Delta t_{min}$ **then** $\mathbb{Q}_E := \mathbb{Q}_E + \tau$}
06: $\Delta t = \frac{\min t_\epsilon}{|\mathbb{Q}_E|}$, **if** $\Delta t < \Delta t_{min}$ **then** $\Delta t = \Delta t_{min}$
07: **for** all $(\tau \in \mathbb{Q}_E)$ {calculate $\Delta E(\tau)$}
08: reorder $\mathbb{Q}_E$ in decreasing order of ΔE
09: **while** $(\mathbb{Q}_E \neq \varnothing)$ {
10: select task $\tau_{\Delta E max} \in \mathbb{Q}_E$
11: $t(\tau_{\Delta E max}) := t(\tau_{\Delta E max}) + \Delta t$
12: update $E_{\tau_{\Delta E max}}$
13: **for** all $(\tau \in \mathcal{T})$ {update t_S, t_E and t_ϵ}
14: **for** all $(\tau \in \mathbb{Q}_E)$
{**if** $(t_\epsilon(\tau) < \Delta t_{min}) \vee (V_{dd}(\tau) \leq V_t(\tau))$
then $\mathbb{Q}_E := \mathbb{Q}_E - \tau$}
15: $\Delta t = \frac{\min t_\epsilon}{|\mathbb{Q}_E|}$, **if** $\Delta t < \Delta t_{min}$ **then** $\Delta t = \Delta t_{min}$
16: **for** all $(\tau \in \mathbb{Q}_E)$ {update $\Delta E(\tau)$}
17: reorder $\mathbb{Q}_E$ in decreasing order of ΔE
18: }
19: **for** all $(\tau \in \mathcal{T})$ {**return** $V_{dd}(\tau)$}
20: **return** E_Σ
21: MSTG $\curvearrowright G_S$

Figure 5: Pseudocode of the proposed variable power DVS algorithm (PV-DVS)

communication tasks to allow an unification of communications and tasks. Second, for each successive execution of tasks on same resources a pseudo edge is introduced between the these two tasks [4], if it does not already exists. In this way it becomes possible to easily and fast traverse the task graph in the chronological correct order by using a breadth first search algorithm (linear time complexity). An example MSTG is shown in Fig. 4, which is the transformed version of the task graph given in Fig. 1, for the schedule of Fig. 2. The next step (line 02) initialises the extentable task queue $\mathbb{Q}_E$. This is followed (line 03) by the computation of the deadline slacks Δt_d of all deadline tasks $\tau \in \mathcal{T}_d$. Having determined these slacks the algorithm can now proceed (line 04) to identify extendable tasks and calculate their maximal expendability t_ϵ. This is done in a reversed breadth-first search manner. All task extendable by at least Δt_{min} are added to the queue of extendable tasks $\mathbb{Q}_E$ (line 05). Next (line 06), the extention time Δt is computed as the minimal extention time found in $\mathbb{Q}_E$, divided by the number of elements in $\mathbb{Q}_E$. If Δt is smaller then Δt_{min} it is set to Δt_{min} to avoid unnecessary optimisation runs, which would increase m in the complexity function $\mathcal{O}$. In the last two steps of the initialisation phase (line 07–08) the energy gradients ΔE for all extendable tasks are calculated and the extendable task queue $\mathbb{Q}_E$ is reordered in decreasing order of the energy gradients. The energy gradient value reflects the energy gain if a particular task is extended by Δt. Therefore it is this energy gradient that allows the algorithm to identify the

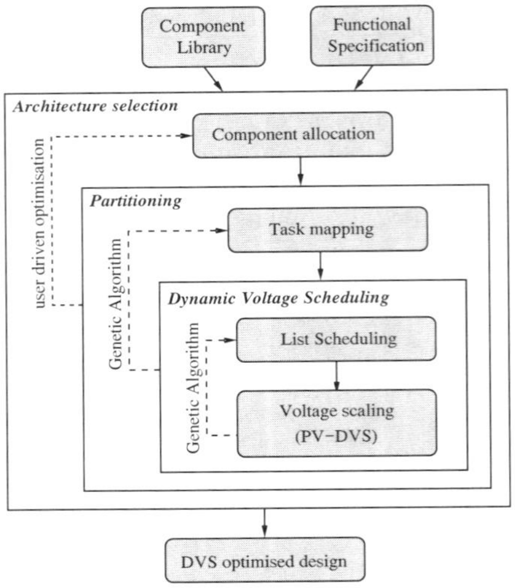

Figure 6: Typical system level co-synthesis including DVS

tasks which will result in the highest energy reduction and therefore an improved voltage selection is possible. The following loop (line 09) is repeated until no extendable tasks are left. In each iteration a single task with the highest energy reduction gradient ΔE (the first task in the queue) is picked out of the the extendable task queue (line 10). This task is then (line 11) extended by Δt and its energy value is updated (line 12). Since the extention of the task might influence successor tasks, the extention needs to be propagated through the task graph (line 13). This is done by traversing all nodes and edges of the MSTG from the extended task to the end tasks, using a breadth-first search algorithm. In the next step (line 14) inextensible tasks are removed from the extendable task queue $\mathbb{Q}_E$ when either, their extendabilty t_ϵ is smaller then Δt_{min}, or now further voltage reduction is possible due to the limited supply voltage range. After this (line 15), the extention time Δt is recalculated and all energy gradients of extendable task are recomputed (line 16). Since the energy gradients might have change the queue $\mathbb{Q}_E$ is reordered (line 17). If no extendable tasks are left the algorithm finishes by returning the scaled voltages (line 19) and the total dissipated energy (line 20). Furthermore, the MSTG is transformed back into a "normal" TG, in order to allow for the next scheduling optimisation step, which leads to a different assignment of pseudo edges.

5. EXPERIMENTAL RESULTS

This section demonstrates through the use of benchmark examples that the consideration of PE power variations leads to energy savings in distributed embedded systems. The design flow outlined in Fig. 6, along with the proposed DVS algorithm, have been implemented using C++ on a Pentium-III/750 PC with 128MB RAM running the Linux operating system. Scheduling and mapping are optimised using techniques based on genetic algorithms similar to the reported approaches in [7] and [8]. However, unlike [8] we do not applied a hole filling technique in the list scheduler, which tries to fill idle times with suitable task, since such idle times are exploited by the DVS technique. Due to the space restriction we can not give a detailed elucidation here. The six benchmarks we use here are partly (*hou*) from literature [12] and partly (*tgff*) generated by TGFF [6]. The allocated components for the *hou* examples are the optimised architectures given in [12] (DVS extended), while for the *tgff* graphs an architecture was chosen randomly, with 2 to 4 PEs, such that feasible schedules and mappings could be generated. All results given here represent average values obtained by 10 optimisation runs.

Table 2 gives the results of three experiments using the above mentioned benchmarks of various complexity (i.e. number of tasks and edges). The first experiment (I) shows a comparison between a DVS approach, which neglectes the power variations (EVEN; similar to [16]) and the proposed approach (PV), which takes the power profile into account during the voltage selection. Both, techniques are applied to identical mappings of the tasks and the schedules are generated by a mobility based list scheduling algorithm. The heading E_{EV}/E_{max} refers to the ratio of the reduced energy dissipation (neglecting power variations) E_{EV} and the energy dissipation at nominal supply voltage E_{max}. It is seen that for all benchmarks the energy dissipation could be reduced. For example, in the case of *tgff1* the energy dissipation is reduced to 53.8%, compared to the system running at nominal voltage. Similar, the heading E_{PV}/E_{max} shows the ratio between the reduced energy dissipation E_{PV} using the proposed DVS algorithm and the energy dissipation at nominal supply voltage E_{max}, reflecting the energy saving achieved by the proposed approach. It can be observed that in all cases the introduced technique was able to further reduce the power consumption of the system. For benchmark *tgff1* the energy dissipation could be reduced to 29.3% of the initial power consumption. This is a further reduction of 24.5%, when compared to the DVS technique which neglects the power profile. Although the introduced DVS technique shows a computational overhead due to its iterative extention of tasks the optimisation was carried out in less $0.2s$ for all examples.

While the employment of the proposed DVS heuristic reduces energy when compared to power neglecting DVS approaches, further savings can be achieved when the heuristic is combined with a scheduling optimisation. This is shown in column of Table 2. This column gives a comparison between the energy dissipations of a GA based scheduling (GS) E_{GS} and a mobility based scheduling (MS) E_{MS}, both using the proposed PV-DVS algorithm. It can be observed that the GA based list scheduling was able to improve the energy dissipation in 5 out of 6 cases when compared to mobility based list scheduling, with reductions of up to 35.7% (*tgff3* on top of the results given in the first experiment (I) of Table 2. The computational times for this experiments varied between $0.14s$ and $32.61s$, for the GA based list scheduling.

The last experiment (III) is concered with the optimised mapping of tasks to PEs such that DVS can be further exploited and hence the energy dissipation is further reduced. Table 2 shows the results of this experiment in the Column Mapping, which gives the ratio between the mapping and scheduling optimised energy dissipation E_{MGSPV} based on the proposed PV-DVS algorithm, and the energy dissipation E_{MGSmax} of the mapping and scheduling optimised implementations running at nominal supply voltage. Overall energy reductions of up to 80.7% (*tgff4*) are achieved. Certainly, the improved results require longer computional times, which are located between $2s$ and $3070s$, compared to 1.58 and $77.24s$ when no DVS is considered.

Benchmark Example	*No. of tasks/edges*	DVS (I)		Scheduling (II)	Mapping (III)
		EVEN E_{EV}/E_{max}	PV E_{PV}/E_{max}	E_{GS}/E_{MS}	E_{MGS}/E_{MGSmax}
tgff1	8/9	0.538	0.293	0.990	0.279
tgff2	26/43	0.962	0.859	0.942	0.718
tgff3	40/77	0.772	0.448	0.643	0.452
tgff4	20/33	0.950	0.871	0.999	0.193
hou	20/29	0.927	0.781	0.776	0.585
hou_clust	8/7	0.794	0.714	1.000	0.622

Table 2: Experimental results of various benchmarks used for DVS, scheduling, and mapping optimisation

6. CONCLUSION

This paper has addressed the problem of energy minimisation in distributed embedded systems including DVS processing elements. It has been shown that it is unnecessary to assume that PE power is constant during the execution of task. Indeed, by considering the power variations of the PEs during the synthesis further energy savings can be achieved. A new heuristic taking into account the PE power variations based on the executed task has been proposed and its capability to identify suitable scaling voltages has been shown. Experimental results demonstrate that combining the proposed scaling heuristic with a genetic algorithm based design space exploration yields to substantially reduced (up to 80.7%) energy dissipations. The energy savings have been achieved in moderate computational time due to the polynominal time complexity of the proposed scaling algorithm.

Acknowledgements

The authors gratefully acknowledge Petru Eles for useful comments and suggestions on this paper. They also wish to acknowledge EPSRC for funding this research project.

7. REFERENCES

[1] N. Bambha, S. Bhattacharyya, J. Teich, and E. Zitzler. Hybrid Global/Local Search Strategies for Dynamic Voltage Scaling in Embedded Multiprocessors. In *Proc. CODES*, pages 243–248, April 2001.

[2] C. Brandolese, W. Fornaciari, F. Salice, and D. Sciuto. Energy Estimation for 32 bit Microprocessors. In *Proc. CODES*, pages 24–28, May 2000.

[3] T. D. Burd, T. A. Pering, A. J. Stratakos, and R. W. Brodersen. A Dynamic Voltage Scaled Microprocessor System. *IEEE Journal of Solid-State Circuits*, 35(11):1571–1580, November 2000.

[4] P. Chretienne, E. G. Coffman, J. K. Lenstra, and Z. Liu. *Scheduling Theory and its Applications*. John Wiley & Sons, 1995.

[5] S. Devadas and S. Malik. A Survey of Optimization Techniques Targeting Low Power VLSI Circuits. In *Proc. DAC*, pages 242–247, 1995.

[6] R. Dick, D. Rhodes, and W. Wolf. TGFF: Task Graphs for free. In *Proc. CODES*, pages 97–101, March 1998.

[7] R. P. Dick and N. K. Jha. MOGAC: A Multiobjective Genetic Algorithm for Hardware-Software Co-Synthesis of Distributed Embedded Systems. *IEEE Trans. on CAD*, 17(10):920–935, Oct 1998.

[8] M. Grajcar. Genetic List Scheduling Algorithm for Scheduling and Allocation on a Loosely Coupled Heterogeneous Multiprocessor System. In *Proc. DAC*, pages 280–285, 1999.

[9] F. Gruian and K. Kuchcinski. LEnS: Task Scheduling for Low-Energy Systems Using Variable Supply Voltage Processors. In *Proc. ASP-DAC*, pages 449–455, Jan 2001.

[10] V. Gutnik and A. Chandrakasan. Embedded Power Supply for Low-Power DSP. *IEEE Trans. on VLSI Systems*, 5(4), 425–435 1997.

[11] I. Hong, D. Kirovski, G. Qu, M. Potkonjak, and M. B. Srivastava. Power Optimization of Variable-Voltage Core-Based Systems. *IEEE Trans. on Computer-Aided Design*, 18(12):1702–1714, Dec 1999.

[12] J. Hou and W. Wolf. Process Partitioning for Distributed Embedded Systems. In *Proc. CODES*, pages 70 – 76, March 1996.

[13] T. Ishihara and H. Yasuura. Voltage Scheduling Problem for Dynamically Variable Voltage Processors. In *Proc. ISLPED*, pages 197–202, 1998.

[14] A. Klaiber. The Technology behind Crusoe Processors, January 2000. http://www.transmeta.com.

[15] Y.-T. S. Li, S. Malik, and A. Wolfe. Performance Estimation of Embedded Software with Instruction Cache Modeling. In *Proc. ICCAD*, pages 380–387, Nov. 1995.

[16] J. Luo and N. K. Jha. Power-conscious Joint Scheduling of Periodic Task Graphs and Aperiodic Tasks in Distributed Real-time Embedded Systems. In *Proc. ICCAD*, pages 357–364, Nov 2000.

[17] A. Manzak and C. Chakrabarti. Variable Voltage Task Scheduling for Minimizing Energy or Minimizing Power. In *Proc. Internation Conference on Acoustics, Speech, and Signal Processing*, pages 3239–3242, 2000.

[18] T. Okuma, T. Ishihara, and H. Yasuura. Real-Time Task Scheduling for a Variable Voltage Processor. In *Proc. ISSS*, pages 24–29, 1999.

[19] M. Weiser, B. Welch, A. Demers, and S. Shenker. Scheduling for reduced CPU energy. In *Proc. USENIX Symposium on Operating Systems Design and Implementation (OSDI)*, pages 13–23, 1994.

[20] W. H. Wolf. Hardware/Software Co-Design of Embedded Systems. In *Proceedings of the IEEE*, pages 967–989, July 1994.

[21] F. Yao, A. Demers, and S. Shenker. A scheduling model for reduced CPU energy. In *IEEE Symposium on Foundations of Comp. Science*, pages 374–382, 1995.

Functional Abstraction driven Design Space Exploration of Heterogeneous Programmable Architectures

Prabhat Mishra
University of California, Irvine
444 Computer Science
Irvine, California, USA
pmishra@cecs.uci.edu

Nikil Dutt
University of California, Irvine
444 Computer Science
Irvine, California, USA
dutt@cecs.uci.edu

Alex Nicolau
University of California, Irvine
444 Computer Science
Irvine, California, USA
nicolau@cecs.uci.edu

ABSTRACT

Rapid Design Space Exploration (DSE) of a programmable architecture is feasible using an automatic toolkit (compiler, simulator, assembler) generation methodology driven by an Architecture Description Language (ADL). While many contemporary ADLs can effectively capture one class of architecture, they are typically unable to capture a wide spectrum of processor and memory features present in DSP, VLIW, EPIC and Superscalar processors. The main bottleneck has been the lack of an abstraction underlying the ADL (covering a diverse set of architectural features) that permits reuse of the abstraction primitives to compose the heterogeneous architectures. We present in this paper the functional abstraction needed to capture such wide variety of programmable architectures. We illustrate the usefulness of this approach by specifying two very different architectures using functional abstraction. Our DSE results demonstrate the power of reuse in composing heterogeneous architectures using functional abstraction primitives allowing for a reduction in the time for specification and exploration by at least an order of magnitude.

Keywords

Functional Abstraction, ADL, Design Space Exploration, DSP, VLIW, Superscalar, Programmable Architecture

1. INTRODUCTION

Contemporary processor architectures vary widely in terms of their architectural features: program address generation and instruction dispatch features are widely used in DSP processors; VLIW processors use strong compiler support to ensure correct execution of long instruction words; superscalar processors on the other hand, use hardware scheduling techniques, register renaming etc; and multimedia processors support SIMD operations. Furthermore, each architecture has a different type of branch prediction mechanism, different execution style (in-order/out-of-order), different way of detecting hazards, different way of handling interrupts/exceptions, and last but not least different memory subsystems[16]. Emerging architectures have combined features of classical architectures (DSP, VLIW and Superscalar). For example, the Intel Itanium combines features of VLIW and superscalar; the TI C6x family combines features of DSP and VLIW. Moreover, during design space exploration using customized IP cores, designers may want to add certain architectural features (e.g., some superscalar features to a VLIW processor core) to see how it impacts area, power, performance and other important design parameters. Similarly, to find the best match between the application characteristics and the memory organization features (caches, stream buffers, access modes, SRAM, DRAM etc.), the designer needs to explore different memory configurations in combination with different processor architectures, and evaluate each such system for a set of metrics (such as cost, power and performance). To enable this, designers need (i) a way of specifying wide variety of processor-memory features and (ii) automatic software toolkit generation to enable rapid design space exploration.

In this paper, we present a functional abstraction based specification technique, which is capable of capturing a wide variety of programmable architectures. The key advantage of this approach is that it allows designers to make fast design decisions by reusing the abstraction primitives while composing heterogeneous architectures. The rest of the paper is organized as follows. Section 2 presents related work addressing functional abstraction as well as ADL-driven DSE approaches. Section 3 outlines our approach and the overall flow of our environment. Section 4 presents the functional abstraction needed to capture the wide variety of architectural features and memory configurations. Section 5 illustrates how contemporary example architectures can be described using this functional abstraction based ADL approach. Section 6 presents the design space exploration results using this approach. Section 7 concludes the paper.

2. RELATED WORK

While code reuse is traditionally widespread in software engineering, the viability of this technique in the field of hardware design has also been demonstrated [10]. In [20] a database oriented reuse management system is presented. There has been work on parameterized [5], as well as functions and objects based [9], system design. In [18] a system design flow for fast design, prototyping and efficient IP reuse

ISSS'01, October 1-3, 2001, Montréal, Québec, Canada.

is presented. In [12] a complete codesign environment for embedded systems which combines automatic partitioning with reuse from a module database is presented. However, previous work has not addressed functional abstraction techniques for diverse processor-memory architectures, with the goal of allowing reuse and composability in the context of architectural design space exploration.

In our approach the viability and advantages of reuse in the context of software toolkit generation is studied. Recent approaches on language-driven design space exploration ([1], [2], [11], [4], [6], [19], [22]), use ADLs to capture the processor architecture, generate automatically a software toolkit for that processor, and provide feedback to the designer on the quality of the architecture.

nML [4] has been used by the retargetable code generation environment CHESS [1] to describe DSP and ASIP processors. In ISDL [2], constraints on parallelism are explicitly specified through illegal operation groupings. This could be tedious for complex architectures like DSPs which permit operation parallelism (e.g. Motorola 56K) and VLIW machines with distributed register files (e.g. TI C6X). MIMOLA [11] descriptions are structure-based, and generally very low-level, and laborious to write. MDes [22] allows only a restricted retargetability of the simulator to the HPL-PD processor family. MDes permits the description of the memory system, but is limited to the traditional cache hierarchy. LISA [3] and RADL [21] capture VLIW DSP processors. The approach of [8] uses LISA and SystemC based framework for fast hardware-software co-simulation. These previous ADL-based approaches have, in general, been targeted towards a specific class of architectures, with limited descriptive facilities for complex memory organizations.

EXPRESSION [6], on the other hand, is an ADL designed to capture a wide range of programmable architectures, including DSP, VLIW, and Superscalar, together with their distinct architectural features. This is possible due to the functional abstractions we have developed to support such an ADL-driven approach. Indeed, an ADL such as EXPRESSION critically needs the power of reuse in composing heterogeneous architectures using functional abstraction primitives; this facilitates rapid generation of software toolkits for a wide range of architectures, thus allowing effective design space exploration of heterogeneous processor-memory architectures.

3. BACKGROUND

In order to understand and characterize the diversity of contemporary architectures, we surveyed each major architectural domain viz., RISC, DSP, VLIW, Superscalar, and EPIC [13]. We studied the similarities and differences of each architectural feature in different architectural domains. Broadly speaking, the structure of a processor consists of functional units, connected using ports, connections and pipeline latches. Similarly, the structure of a memory subsystem consists of SRAM, DRAM, cache hierarchy etc. Although a broad classification makes the architecture look similar, each architecture differs in terms of the algorithm it employs in branch prediction, the way it detect hazards, the way it handle exceptions etc. Moreover, each unit has different parameters for different architectures (e.g., number of fetches per cycle, levels of cache, cache line size etc.). Depending on the architecture a functional unit may perform the same operation at different points in time. For example, read-after-write(RAW) hazard detection followed by operand read occurs in the decode unit for some architectures (e.g., DLX [7]), whereas in some others these operations are performed in the issue unit (e.g., MIPS R10K). Some architectures even allow operand read in the execution unit (e.g., ARM7). On the other hand, some architectures do not issue operations if RAW hazard is detected while others issue the operation in spite of RAW hazard (use snooping to read the data at execution stage using feedback paths). In other words, the same functionality is used at different points in the pipeline for different architectures.

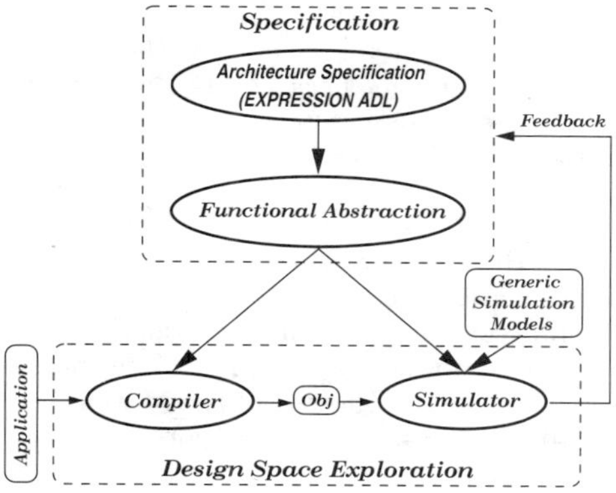

Figure 1: The Flow in our approach

We can observe some fundamental differences from the study above; the architecture may use: (i) the same functional or memory unit with different parameters, (ii) the same functionality in different functional or memory unit, (iii) new architectural features. The first difference can be eliminated by defining generic functions with appropriate parameters. The second difference can be eliminated by defining generic sub-functions, which can be used by different architectures at different points in time. The last one is difficult to alleviate since it is new, unless this new functionality can be composed of existing sub-functions.

Based on our observations we have defined the necessary generic functions, sub-functions and computational environment needed to capture a wide variety of processor and memory features. Section 4 presents the functional abstraction needed to capture the wide variety of programmable architectures. We have developed the associated generic simulation models, which is a one-time activity and independent of the architecture; these can be stored in a library and reused in an ADL to compose and evaluate new architectures.

Figure 1 shows the flow in our approach. In our IP library based design space exploration scenario, the designer starts by specifying the design using functional abstractions using the EXPRESSION ADL. The software toolkit including compiler, simulator, and assembler can be automatically generated from the functional abstraction. The input application program is compiled and simulated and the feedback is used to modify the specification.

4. FUNCTIONAL ABSTRACTION

Functional abstraction allows the system designer to describe a wide variety of architectures in a hierarchical fashion. In this section we present functional abstraction by way of illustrative examples. We first explain the functional abstraction needed to capture the structure and behavior of the processor and memory subsystem, then we discuss the issues related to defining generic controller functionality, and finally we discuss the issues related to handling interrupts and exceptions.

4.1 Structure of a Generic Processor

We capture the structure of each functional unit using parameterized functions. In the following specific example, the fetch unit functionality contains several parameters, such as the number of operations read per cycle, number of operations written per cycle, reservation station size, branch prediction scheme, number of read ports, number of write ports etc. These ports are used to connect different units. The fetch unit is described using sub-functions. Each subfunction is defined using appropriate parameters. For example, *ReadInstMemory* reads n operations from the instruction cache using current PC address (returned by *ReadPC*) and writes them to the reservation station. The fetch unit reads m operations from the reservation station and writes them to the output latch (fetch to decode latch) and uses a BTB based branch prediction mechanism.

```
FetchUnit(# read per cycle, res-Station size, ......)
{
  address = ReadPC()
  Instructions = ReadInstMemory(address, n)
  WriteToReservationStation(Instructions, n)
  outInst = ReadFromReservationStation(m);
  WriteLatch(decode_latch, outInst)

  pred = QueryPredictor(address)
  IF pred
  {
     nextPC = QueryBTB(address)
     SetPC (next_PC)
  } ELSE
     IncrementPC(x)
}
```

We have defined parameterized functions for all functional units present in contemporary programmable architectures, such as the fetch unit, branch prediction unit, decode unit, issue unit, execute unit, completion unit, interrupt handler unit, PC Unit, Latch, Port, Connection etc. We have defined sub-functions for all the common activities e.g., ReadLatch, WriteLatch, ReadOperand, RenameRegister etc. We have also defined a few sub-functions e.g., RenameRegister, GraduateOperation using sub-functions to allow a finer granularity of architectural exploration. The notion of generic sub-function allows the flexibility of specifying the system in finer detail. It also allows reuse of the components. Furthermore, these components can be pre-verified. Thus the task of verification will reduce mainly to performing interface verification at all levels.

4.2 Behavior of a Generic Processor

The behavior of a generic processor is captured through the definition of opcodes. Each opcode is defined as a function, with a generic set of parameters, which performs the intended functionality. The parameter list includes source and destination operands, necessary control and data type information. We have defined a set of common sub-functions e.g., ADD, SUB, SHIFT etc. The opcode functions may use one or more sub-functions. For example, the MAC (multiply and accumulate) uses two sub-functions. These opcode functions are used as a parameter for the generic function of the execution unit.

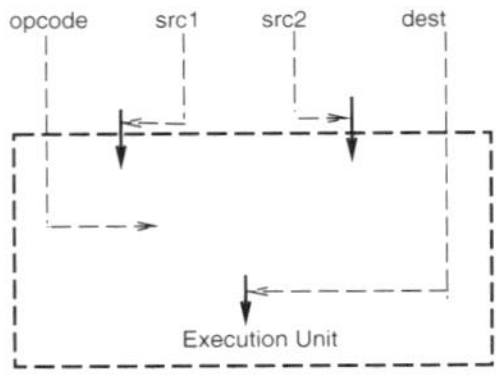

Figure 2: Example of distributed control

4.3 Structure of a Generic Memory Subsystem

The memory represents a major bottleneck in modern embedded systems. Each type of memory module, such as the SRAM, cache, DRAM, SDRAM, stream buffer, victim cache etc., is modeled using a function with appropriate parameters. For example, the cache function has parameters: cache size, line size, associativity, word size, replacement policy, write policy, read/write access times etc. These functions also have parameters for specifying pipelining, parallelism, access modes (e.g., normal read, page mode read, burst read) etc. Again, each function is composed of sub-functions.

4.4 Generic Controller

A major challenge for functional abstraction of programmable architectures, is the modeling of control for a wide range of architectural styles. We define control in both a distributed and centralized manner. The distributed control is transfered through pipeline latches. While an instruction gets decoded the control information needed to select the operation, the source and the destination operands are placed in the output latch as shown in Figure 2. These decoded control signals pass through the latches between two pipeline stages unless they become redundant. For example, when the value for src1 is read that particular control is not needed any more; instead the read value will be in the latch. We have shown here only the control information of the latch. The latch contains data values and predicate registers (if applicable) as well.

The centralized control is maintained by using a generic control table. The number of rows in the table is equal to the number of pipeline stages in the architecture. The number of columns is equal to the maximum number of parallel units present in any pipeline stage. Each entry in the control table corresponds to one particular unit in the architecture. It also contains information specific to that unit e.g., busy bit (BB), stall bit (SB), list of children, list of parents, opcodes supported etc. The control table captures all the necessary details to perform selective or complete stalling of the pipelines. Stalling happens due to three kinds of hazards: structural hazards, data hazards and control hazards.

4.5 Interrupts and Exceptions

Another major challenge for functional abstraction is the modeling of interrupts and exceptions. We now briefly describe the abstraction needed to capture the wide variety of exceptions and interrupts possible in programmable architectures. Each exception is captured using an appropriate sub-function. Opcode related exceptions (e.g., divide by zero) are captured in the opcode functionality. Functional unit related exceptions (e.g., illegal slot exception) are captured in functional units. External interrupts (e.g., reset, debug exceptions) are captured in the control unit functionality.

We model an interrupt handler unit that services these exceptions. It has information regarding the priority of interrupts and which exceptions generate what interrupt. The generic interrupt handler has a parameterized priority table. The interrupt handler unit generates one particular interrupt based on the priority. Before execution of that particular interrupt service routine, context saving and complete/partial flushing occurs. The specific type of flushing is decided by the semantics of that interrupt: complete flushing clears the entire pipeline; partial flushing means flushing only the instructions behind the interrupted instruction and allowing the previous instructions to continue using the program order information available in completion queue. Again, these actions are part of parametric sub-functions that allow a finer grain of microarchitectural exploration.

We have also defined the functional abstraction needed for the DMA, co-processor and external interface. The detailed description of generic abstractions for all of the microarchitectural components are too long to describe in this paper, and can be found in [13].

5. CONTEMPORARY EXAMPLE ARCHITECTURES

Using the functional abstraction approach outlined above, we have been able to describe the DLX [7], TI C6x, MIPS R4000, MIPS R10K, Intel Itanium and PowerPC architectures representing a diverse set of processor-memory styles. In this section, we demonstrate the ability to describe two architectures with radically different processor and memory styles using functional abstraction: MIPS R10K is a superscalar processor with two level of cache; TI C6x is a hybrid processor containing both DSP and VLIW features with a novel memory organization (partitioned register file, cache hierarchy and configurable scratch pad SRAM etc.).

5.1 MIPS R10K Architecture

The MIPS R10000 is a dynamic, superscalar microprocessor that implements the 64-bit Mips-4 instruction set architecture. It fetches and decodes four instructions per cycle and dynamically issues them to five fully-pipelined, low-latency execution units. Instructions can be fetched and executed speculatively beyond branches. Instructions graduate in order upon completion. Although execution is out of order, the processor still provides sequential memory consistency and precise exception handling. With speculative execution, it calculates memory addresses and initiates cache refills early. In this section, we outline how we specify components of the MIPS R10K using the functional abstraction and the generic parameters described in Section 4.

The fetch unit function is invoked with the appropriate parameter values. Both the number of instructions fetched per cycle and the number of instructions sent to decode stage per cycle are set to four. The number of entries in reservation station is set to zero. The number of entries in completion queue (Active List in R10K terminology) is set to 32.

The decode functionality is instantiated with read connection from fetch latch and write connections to MemIssue, IntIssue and FloatIssue units. It uses the register renaming sub-function while decoding instructions. It inserts the decoded instruction in the completion queue (ActiveList) which maintains the program order. The decode logic decides where to dispatch (MemIssue, IntIssue or FloatIssue) a particular instruction based on the supported opcodes information available in the control unit. Table 1 shows the simplified control table for the MIPS R10K architecture, where the rows indicate the pipeline stages and columns represent parallel functional units. For illustration, we do not show all the details, such as the opcodes supported by each unit, list of children, list of parents etc., although we model them.

The IntIssue, FloatIssue and MemIssue functions are instantiated with a reservation station size of 16 entries. Each issue unit performs operand read and RAW hazard detection (using appropriate sub-functions) before performing out-of-order issue.

Execution units are instantiated using appropriate opcode functionalities. The Address Queue (MemIssue unit) reads data and tag using virtual address while the physical address is computed. It checks whether the load is a hit or miss once the physical address is available. This is different than the conventional way of hit or miss detection. In conventional architectures the load request is done using physical address and hit or miss detection is done inside the memory subsystem. This illustrates our ability to reuse the hit or miss detection sub-functions in the processor side (although conventionally it remains on the memory side).

Table 1: Control table for R10K architecture

		Fetch BB:0 SB:0		
		Decode BB:0 SB:0		
MemIssue BB:0 SB:0	IntIssue BB:0 SB:0		FloatIssue BB:0 SB:0	
AddrCalc BB:0 SB:0	ALU1 BB:0 SB:0	ALU2 BB:0 SB:0	FADD1 BB:0 SB:0	FMPY1 BB:0 SB:0
TLB BB:0 SB:0	FADD2 BB:0 SB:0	FMPY2 BB:0 SB:0	SQRT BB:0 SB:0	FDIV BB:0 SB:0
	FADD3 BB:0 SB:0		FMPY3 BB:0 SB:0	

The memory hierarchy consists of two levels of cache. The parameters for the primary cache are: associativity - 2, cache size - 2K double-words, line size - 4 , word size - 64 bits, replacement - LRU, write policy - write back, number of lines - 512, access time - 1 cycle. Similarly secondary cache functionality is instantiated with the appropriate parameters: associativity - 2, cache size - 512K double-words, line size - 16, word size - 64 bits, replacement - LRU, write policy - write back, number of lines - 32K, access time - 2 cycles.

Each functional unit invokes the appropriate sub-functions to capture exception conditions. The interrupt handler function captures the priority table of 19 interrupts. In this manner we are able to concisely capture a state-of-the-art dynamic superscalar architecture using the functional abstraction approach. Furthermore, we now have the ability to quickly change its architectural parameters and view their effects on performance, code size etc.

5.2 TI C6x Architecture

We now demonstrate the ability to capture components of a hybrid VLIW DSP architecture using our functional abstraction technique. TI C6x is an 8-way VLIW DSP processor with a novel memory subsystem (cache hierarchy, configurable SRAM, partitioned register file). TI C6x processor has a deep pipeline, composed of 4 fetch stages (PG, PS, PR, PW), 2 decode stages (DP, DC), followed by the 8 functional units.

The fetch functionality consists of four stages viz., program address generation, address send, wait, and receive. Each of the four stages is modeled using respective sub-functions with appropriate parameters. The architecture fetches one VLIW instruction (eight parallel operations) per cycle.

The decode function decodes the VLIW word and dispatches upto eight operations per cycle to eight execution units. Each execution unit performs operand read and hazard checks (using sub-functions). At the end of computation each execution unit writes back (using sub-function) the result to register file.

The TI C6x architecture has a novel memory organization, comprised of a 2-level cache hierarchy and a programmable SRAM space. The L1 program cache is 4K bytes, direct mapped with line size 64 bytes. The L1 data cache is 4K bytes, associativity 2 and line size 32 (bytes). The L2 cache is 64K bytes and depending on the mode of configuration, the memory space is divided between SRAM and associative cache. Memory modules are instantiated with appropriate parameters for capturing the memory subsystem.

Each functional unit invokes the appropriate sub-functions to capture exception conditions. The interrupt handler function captures the priority table of 14 interrupts. Reset and NMI has higher priority than INT4 to INT15 interrupts. In this manner, we are able to capture a hybrid DSP/VLIW architecture using our functional abstraction. Furthermore, we again have the ability to tweak architectural parameters (and compose new features) using the functional abstraction approach.

6. EXPERIMENTS

We performed extensive architectural design space exploration by varying different architectural features, achieved by reusing the abstraction primitives with appropriate parameters. In this section we illustrate the usefulness of our approach in three architecture exploration dimensions.

6.1 Exploration varying Processor Features

Contemporary superscalar processors use in-order completion/graduation to ensure sequential execution behavior in the presence of out-of-order execution. Here, we explore the MIPS R10K processor in the presence of out-of-order graduation without violating functional correctness. We described the MIPS R10K architecture (with in-order graduation and 8 entry Active List) using the functional abstraction approach and generated the software toolkit. We modified the description to perform out-of-order graduation and generated the software toolkit rapidly. We used a set of benchmarks from the multimedia and DSP domains. Figure 3 presents a subset of the experiments we ran to study the performance improvement due to out-of-order graduation. The light bar presents the number of execution cycles when in-order graduation is used whereas the dark bar presents the number of execution cycles when out-of-order graduation is used. We observe an average performance improvement of 10%. During in-order graduation certain instructions (independent of the instructions above in the Active List) complete execution but are not allowed to graduate since some long latency operations are on top of the Active List and are yet to complete. As a result, the Active List becomes full soon and the decode stalls. This situation becomes more prominent when the top instruction is a load and the load misses. We modified the memory subsystem to study the impact of cache misses along with out-of-order graduation and observed upto 27% performance improvement (in benchmark StateExcerpt when hit ratio is zero). The complete study of the out-of-order graduation for the MIPS R10K processor can be found in [14].

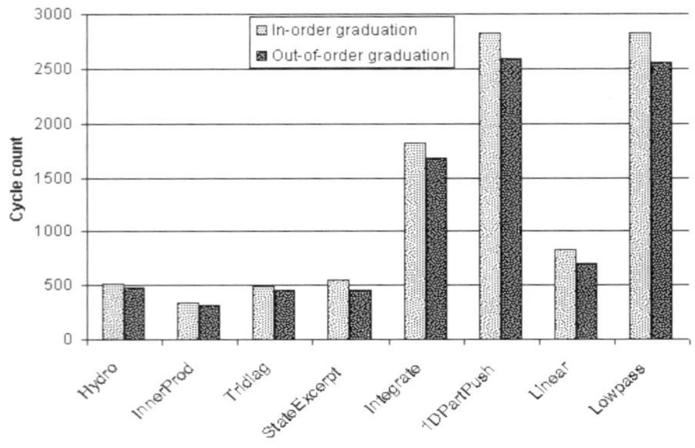

Figure 3: Cycle counts for different graduation styles

Due to the high modeling efficiency of functional abstraction the original description and toolkit generation took less than a week; the graduation style modification and toolkit generation took less than a day; the experiments and analysis took few hours; the complete exploration experiment took approximately one week.

6.2 Co-processor based Exploration

In the context of co-processor codesign for programmable architectures we have explored the performance impact using a co-processor for the TI C62x environment. First, we described the TI C62x architecture in the EXPRESSION ADL (where multiplication is done in the functional unit) using functional abstraction and generated the software toolkit. Next, we modified the description by adding a co-processor (with DMA controller and local memory) that supports multiplication and generated the software toolkit rapidly. This co-processor has its own local memory and uses DMA to transfer data from main memory. We then used a set of DSPStone fixed point benchmarks to explore and evaluate the effects of adding a coprocessor. Figure 4 presents a subset of the experiments we ran to study the performance improvement due to the co-processor. The light bar presents the number of execution cycles when the functional unit is used for the multiplication whereas the dark bar presents the number of execution cycles when the co-processor is used. We observe an average performance improvement of 22%. The performance improvement is due to the fact that the co-processor is able to exploit the vector multiplications available in these benchmarks using its local memory. Moreover, the functional units operate in register-to-register mode whereas the co-processor operates on its memory-memory mode. As a result the register pressure and thereby spilling gets reduced in the presence of the co-processor. However, the functional unit performs better when there are mostly scalar multiplications. The complete study of the co-processor based design space exploration can be found in [17].

6.3 Memory Subsystem Exploration

Another important dimension for architectural exploration is the investigation of different memory configurations for a programmable architecture. We explored different memory

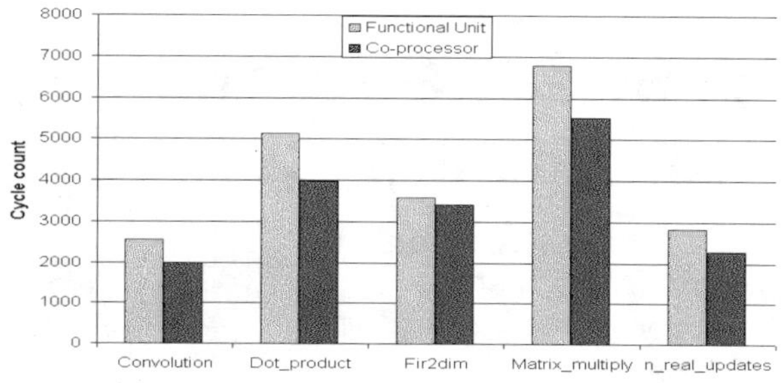

Figure 4: Functional unit vs. Co-processor

configurations for the TI C6x architecture with the goal of studying the trade-off between cost and performance. Detailed experiments can be found in [15].

7. SUMMARY

This paper proposed a functional abstraction based design space exploration methodology which is capable of capturing a wide variety of programmable architectures. A key advantage of the generic function based design space exploration is that it allows designers to rapidly compose new architectures (by reusing the generic abstractions within an ADL such as EXPRESSION), generate automatically a customized software toolkit and quickly perform a compiler-in-the-loop exploration exercise that allows comparative evaluation of different architectural features. The notion of generic subfunctions allows the flexibility of specifying the system in finer detail. Furthermore, since these components can be pre-verified, the task of verification will reduce mainly to performing interface verification at all levels of the design hierarchy.

We demonstrated the power of our approach in the context of three very different architectural exploration scenarios. We are able to rapidly generate a software toolkit for each instance of a configured architecture and perform detailed simulations of the compiled application to evaluate the effects of different processor and memory configurations. It took less than a week to complete the specification and derive an optimized toolkit for each class of explored architectures, and another week to perform detailed exploration experiments by tuning the architecture. Feedback from our industrial sponsors indicate that each such exploration experiment typically takes on the order of 6 months to 1 year for a compiler-in-the-loop exploration even for a fairly "standard" architectural family. Thus we are able to reduce the exploration time by at least an order of magnitude. Therefore, we believe this functional abstraction approach solves a critical bottleneck for rapid architectural exploration; the ability to reuse parameterized functions and sub-functions enables true heterogeneous processor-memory architectural exploration particularly in the context of IP-based System-on-Chip(SOC) design.

Our ongoing work targets the use of this functional abstraction based design space exploration for generating synthesized hardware automatically. Furthermore, we plan to extend this specification technique to generate FSM automatically and perform property checking during rapid design space exploration.

8. ACKNOWLEDGMENTS

This work was partially supported by grants from NSF (MIP-9708067), DARPA (F33615-00-C-1632) and Motorola Corporation. We would like to gratefully acknowledge Jonas Astrom for his contribution to the functional abstraction work.

9. REFERENCES

[1] G. Goosens et al. CHESS: Retargetable code generation for embedded DSP processors. In *Code Generation for Embedded Processors*. Kluwer, 1997.

[2] G. Hadjiyiannis et al. ISDL: An instruction set description language for retargetability. *DAC*, 1997.

[3] V. Zivojnovic et al. LISA - machine description language and generic machine model for HW/SW co-design. In *VLSI Signal Processing*, 1996.

[4] M. Freericks. The nML machine description formalism. TR SM-IMP/DIST/08, TU Berlin, 1993.

[5] T. Givargis and F. Vahid. Parameterized system design. In *CODES Workshop*, 2000.

[6] A. Halambi et al. EXPRESSION: A language for architecture exploration through compiler/simulator retargetability. In *Proc. DATE*, Mar. 1999.

[7] J. Hennessy and D. Patterson. *Computer Architecture: A quantitative approach*. Morgan Kaufmann Publishers Inc, San Mateo, CA, 1990.

[8] A. Hoffmann et al. A framework for fast hardware software co-simulation. *DATE*, 2001.

[9] A. Jantsch and I. Sander. On the roles of functions and objects in system specification. *CODES*, 2000.

[10] M. Koegst et al. A systematic analysis of reuse strategies for design of electronic circuits. *DATE*, 1998.

[11] R. Leupers and P. Marwedel. Retargetable code generation based on structural processor descriptions. *Design Automation for Embedded Systems*, 3(1), 1998.

[12] M. Meerwein et al. Linking codesign and reuse in embedded systems design. In *CODES Workshop*, 2000.

[13] P. Mishra et al. Functional abstraction of programmable embedded systems. TR UCI-ICS 01-04, 2001.

[14] P. Mishra et al. A study of out-of-order completion for the MIPS R10K superscalar processor. TR UCI-ICS 01-06, University of California, Irvine, 2001.

[15] P. Mishra et al. Memory subsystem description in EXPRESSION. TR UCI-ICS 00-31, 2000.

[16] P. Mishra et al. Processor-memory co-exploration driven by an architectural description language. *VLSI Design 2001*.

[17] P. Mishra et al. Coprocessor codesign for programmable architectures. TR UCI-ICS 01-13, 2001.

[18] F. Pogodalla et al. Fast prototyping: a system design flow for fast design, prototyping and efficient ip reuse. *CODES*, 1999.

[19] V. Rajesh et al. Processor modeling for hardware software codesign. In *VLSI Design 1999*

[20] A. Reutter and W. Rosenstiel. An efficient reuse system for digital circuit design. In *Proc. DATE*, 1999.

[21] C. Siska. A processor description language supporting retargetable multi-pipeline dsp program development tools. In *Proc. ISSS*, Dec. 1998.

[22] The MDES User Manual, 1997. *www.trimaran.org*

Modeling and Simulation of Steady State and Transient Behaviors for Emergent SoCs

JoAnn M. Paul, Arne J. Suppé, Donald E. Thomas
Electrical and Computer Engineering Department
Carnegie Mellon University
Pittsburgh, PA 15213 USA
{jpaul, suppe, thomas} @ ece.cmu.edu

Abstract

We introduce a formal basis for viewing computer systems as mixed steady state and non-steady state (transient) behaviors to motivate novel design strategies resulting from simultaneous consideration of function, scheduling and architecture. We relate three design styles: hierarchical decomposition, static mapping and directed platform that have traditionally been separate. By considering them together, we reason that once a steady state system is mapped to an architecture, the unused processing and communication power may be viewed as a platform for a transient system, ultimately resulting in more effective design approaches that ease the static mapping problem while still allowing for effective utilization of resources. Our simulation environment, frequency interleaving, mixes a formal and experimental approach as illustrated in an example.

Keywords

Hardware/Software Codesign, Computer System Modeling and Simulation, System on Chip Design

1. Introduction

Emergent system on chip (SoC) designs are fundamentally different from other computing systems for the combination of three primary reasons. The first is that they contain multiple, heterogeneous *clock domains*. Clock domains are an abstraction of the physical limits of synchronous design — beyond these limits, computation and communication must be partitioned among multiple interacting domains. These domains give rise to custom hardware devices, heterogeneous processor types, and communication links (busses and networks). Secondly, their complexity requires that designers consider system wide effects of anticipated hardware and anticipated software over the lifetime of the product. That is, architectures and software evolve over time. The third reason is that the systems will contain a mix of real-time and untimed behaviors. The notion of the purely reactive, embedded system is disappearing. Increasingly, untimed, desktop-style functionality is being integrated on embedded computers.

Computer systems can be thought of as consisting of two types of behavior — that which is steady state, and that which is transient or non-steady state. The behavior of a *steady state* system is fixed with respect to an external, absolute time reference. For systems with hard real-time deadlines the most significant time reference is typically determined by the response time of the system to sets of inputs. The system must compute a bounded amount of work within a bounded amount of time in reaction to a time-bounded set of inputs. Over a system period, the system can be thought of as having a fixed or steady-state behavior. In contrast, the behavior of a *transient, non-steady state system* is not designed to external time constraints nor finite computation. Rather they adapt their behavior to unknown execution times, aperiodic input arrival times, and internal state via dynamic scheduling techniques. These behaviors are sometimes called untimed because the system timing is internal and not tied to an absolute, external reference. Because these untimed forms of system behavior are being mixed with hard real-time behavior, effective SoC design requires architecture, schedulers, and functionality to be designed together.

Steady state system design has been dominated by formal analysis — these reactive systems are statically analyzed as a task mapping problem ensuring that hard deadlines will be met for tasks with periodic or sporadic arrival times for a given set of resources and task execution times [12]. The givens in such schedulability analysis include the set of tasks to be scheduled, their deadlines, their execution times on the hardware, the scheduling algorithm, and the hardware resources upon which they will execute [13]. Transient system design has been dominated by simulation and benchmarking — analyzing performance under a representative set of operating conditions often with the objective of improving the relative balance of system processing. For this, performance enhancements are proposed and their designs are then explored via simulation-based experimentation.

Systems that are designed to only a steady state reactive paradigm rarely attain a perfect match between processing power and load — leftover processing power will result. However, if the leftover processing power, that in excess of the power needed to execute the steady state functionality, can be utilized for non-steady-state processing, the system resources may be over-designed intelligently without waste. A motivation for designing systems with both steady state and transient behavior is that transient system applications scale more effectively with the processing power of their platforms because they are not limited to the processing of externally time-bounded inputs. Thus they effectively take advantage of Moore's Law.

When designing steady and non-steady state digital systems, three distinct *design styles* dominate: *hierarchical decomposition*, *static mapping*, and *platform*-based. A *hierarchical* style is traditionally associated with hardware design, and implies a self-consistently partitionable and composable specification of resources, where detail is filled in by sub-models without destroying the hierarchy of the higher-level system.

A *static mapping* design style arises from a separation into two distinct design domains. The most pertinent example at this level of design is that of functional tasks and processing resources, or function and architecture. The resultant designs in each domain must be resolved (mapped) to the other for the whole system to be formed. The mapping is static and is motivated by real-time, physical constraints placed on the overall system behavior.

ISSS'01, October 1-3, 2001, Montreal, Quebec, Canada.

A *platform*-based system is constructed by an application layer that directs a service or resource layer. The layering permits resource-layer details to be hidden from the application layer, and for the resource layer to be designed independently of higher-levels of the system model. In computer systems design, the platform layering might consist of a processor providing resources to a scheduler (e.g., an operating system — O/S), which in turn provides resources to the tasks it schedules.

We formalize how a mix of these distinct design styles will be needed to support the design of emergent systems and motivate how design approaches that blend formal analytical and experimentation-based simulation techniques are needed. Further, we will show how effective future SoC design requires that the function, architecture and scheduling of the system be considered concurrently in support of a mix of steady-state and transient processing. This is a step not considered previously in the codesign of reactive systems (e.g. [5]). We show how our modeling environment, frequency interleaving, is a basis for our approach.

2. Function, Architecture, and Scheduling

An architecture, A(t), is a weighted graph of resources with a set of N processing nodes, and J communication arcs.

$$A(t) = (\{P_1(t),\ldots,P_n(t),\ldots,P_N(t)\}, \{B_1(t),\ldots,B_j(t),\ldots B_J(t)\})$$

Each processing node has power $P_n(t)$, and each communication arc has bandwidth $B_j(t)$; all are a function of time (t).

System functionality is a weighted graph F(t) of M computation threads and D sets of information exchanged between them.

$$F(t) = (\{L_1(t),\ldots,L_m(t),\ldots,L_M(t)\}, \{E_1(t),\ldots,E_d(t),\ldots E_D(t)\}$$

Each potentially concurrent thread of execution represents a loading $L_m(t)$ on a computing resource, and a demand $E_d(t)$ on communication resources; all are a function of time (t).

F(t) is the net computation of the system and not the behavior required to construct a system. For instance, schedulers are a set of behavior, U(t), specifying how a set of computational threads is shared by a resource. Together, the functionality, architecture, and schedulers are mapped by Y to form a system S(t) as in

$$(S(t),X(t)) = Y(F(t), A(t), U(t)) \qquad \textbf{Rel 1}$$

Y implicitly requires consideration of system-wide effects while the U(t) schedulers are local to system resources. This is a key difference between a static mapping and a platform-based design style. A platform-based style permits local scheduling decisions to be made in the absence of system-wide detail.

Rel 1 also defines the result of the mapping of the functionality, architecture and schedulers as a tuple, (S(t), X(t)). S(t) is the *net behavior* of the system. X(t) is the *remainder architecture*. When the computation power of the original architecture, A(t), exceeds the computation demand of the functionality mapped to the system, F(t), and the schedulers, U(t), a net amount of processing and communication power X(t) is extra in a system. The original system architecture is transformed by this mapping and scheduling to another (the remainder) architecture which is potentially capable of carrying out additional behavior.

A(t) and F(t) also have an associated amount of storage. Since our focus is the temporal response of systems and not their storage requirements, the memory/state model is omitted for brevity.

2.1 Steady State Systems

A steady state system is designed to respond to its externally time-bounded I/O, conceptually performing a bounded amount of work over a time. Steady state systems result from either a hierarchical hardware decomposition or a static mapping design style. We define a pure *hierarchical hardware decomposition* system as a 1:1 correspondence between tasks and architecture:

$$((L_i \Leftrightarrow P_i), (E_j \Leftrightarrow B_j))\forall(i, j) \quad .$$

In these systems, M=N, J=D and load perfectly matches computation demand. For example, a hardware state machine and datapath provide the exact power needed to implement a task represented by load L. Because of the exact match, X(t)=0.

A *statically mapped system* is one where M>N — the number of tasks in the system exceeds the number of computation nodes. Consider a system for which M=2 and N=1. The two tasks must be mapped to a single processor resource; a scheduler is needed. Given the time-bounded characteristic of the system, there is a finite period, T, over which the system's behavior is conceptually constant. More formally, the mapping of systems with M>N requires a scheduler, U, itself a function of time, that maps the computation loads onto the processors; here scheduler U_1 resolves our two tasks to a processor:

$$U_1(t, L_1(t), L_2(t)) \rightarrow P_1(t)$$

Schedulers are viewed as an entity mapped to the processing resource, while tasks are mapped to the schedulers. In general, schedulers can be null for single tasks mapped to individual resources; the scheduling mechanism for the resource is the task itself. In this way, M>N tasks are resolved to N resources, implying N schedulers as

$$\{L_1(t),\ldots,L_M(t)\} \rightarrow \{P_1(t),\ldots,P_N(t)\} \Rightarrow \{U_1(t),\ldots,U_N(t)\}$$

Rel 2

Over the steady state system period, T, behavior may be considered constant for Q steady-state tasks as shown below.

$$\{L_1,\ldots,L_Q\} \rightarrow \{P_1,\ldots,P_N\} \Rightarrow \{U_1,\ldots,U_N\} \qquad \textbf{Rel 3}$$

The time-bound T effectively acts as a barrier within which sets of computation must be completed, but also to which faster internal processing is wasted. A *purely* steady state system can do no more computation than the processing required in the system period. Thus, for purely steady state systems, when processing power is increased, the system does no more work. More formally for a steady state mapped system

$$(S(T),X(T)) = Y(F(T), A(T), U(T))$$

when A(T) is increased, F(T), U(T), and S(T) remain constant, and leftover processing power X(T) results. The most conservative design of steady state systems is when X(T) is large, while the most efficient system in terms of resource usage is when X(T) is small. Rather than trying to match A(T) and F(T), it can be more productive to understand how to utilize X(T) for transient system processing. We discuss how transient systems achieve this next.

Although we have considered only computation nodes and the computation complexity of tasks without regard to information exchange in the architecture, consideration of a mapping of information exchange to communication channels follows the same line of reasoning.

2.2 Transient Systems

The design goal for transient systems is a *platform* for which a time-independent range of applications, task durations, input sets, and internal state will have acceptable performance. In transient systems, the platform, functional processing, net processing and extra processing power may all be functions of time. Thus, one important goal may be to minimize X(t) over all t. In contrast to steady state systems, net processing, F(t) is not bound to the availability of externally time-bounded inputs. An increase in architectural power, A(t), could result in a corresponding net increase in F(t) since the system can process more information so long as there are inputs or internal state to process — this is architecture-power scalability. Although perfect scalability is limited, at least some scalability results for many applications.

Transient systems are constructed from the *platform design style* as a generalization of the task mapping problem. Schedulers map K non-steady state tasks to processor resources as

$$U_n(t, L_1(t), \ldots, L_K(t)) \rightarrow P_n(t) \qquad \textbf{Rel 4}$$

For some transient systems, K may be dynamic. For example, an unknown number of server threads may be spawned to service separate requests. Or, the system may contain early notions of anticipated functionality, which may not be finalized until well after the system is shipped. The essence of platform design is that the task set is presumed to be larger than may execute over some period of time. The scheduler dynamically composes the system functionality at runtime in processing inputs and internal state.

2.3 Merging Steady and Non-steady State

Emerging SoC computing systems will include both steady and non-steady state behavior. While resources may be shared in both types of systems, the scheduling of the sharing in a steady state system is matched to its external, temporal processing requirements. Resource sharing is based on time periods and functionality is never resource starved over T. In contrast, scheduling of functionality in a transient system is based first on the availability of data, then on the availability of resources — transient functionality may be resource starved.

The response of transient processing is measured as execution time after a data-dependent start time, or latency. The data- and resource-dependent progress of a non-steady state task, k, is in general measured over an interval $\delta_k=[s_k, s_k+i*r_k]$. s_k represents a start time since the start of system execution, or relative to t=0. In general, s_k may be tied to some other data-dependency. r_k is a rate typically drawn from some *internal* system reference, such as a processor frequency or communications bandwidth. The length of the interval is $i*r_k$, constructed as an integer-valued number, i, of execution times of the reference rate.

When a designer is interested only in the relative progress of a set of data-dependent tasks and not latency, s_k can be arbitrary and taken to be zero. δ_k then becomes an *observation window* for task k of the effects of data, resource power, and task scheduling interactions across a number of resources. While T captures an external constraint as a data-independent interval during which a set of steady state tasks is *guaranteed* to execute, δ_k is a *designer's reference*. Indeed, a designer may choose to observe the cumulative progress of one or more tasks over a number of successive δ_k, simplifying the need to consider the complete execution history of the system, since when $s_k=0$ and $i=\infty$, $\delta_k= (0, \infty)$ for the range of t. This also allows the designer to design systems relative to *internal* system performance references. In general, for a system with K non-steady state tasks, K observation windows exist in a set $\Delta=\{\delta_1,...,\delta_K\}$, one for each transient task.

Mixed steady-state and non-steady state systems are constructed when schedulers can allow for a partitioning of the utilization of the system resources. Thus, for mixed digital systems

$$\{F(T), F(\Delta)\} \Rightarrow \{U_1(T, \Delta), \ldots, U_N(T, \Delta)\} \qquad \textbf{Rel 5}$$

The mixed steady state and non-steady state system behaviors F are formed by schedulers local to each resource. These form the guaranteed, steady-state system mapping along with non-steady-state, data-dependent resource sharing. Relation 6 combines relations 2, 3, and 5 for an architecture with constant processing power in a system with M tasks (Q of which are steady state and K of which are non-steady state) scheduled by N schedulers, each of which resolve steady state and transient functionality.

$$\{L_1(t), \ldots, L_K(t), L_{K+1}, \ldots, L_M\} \rightarrow \{P_1, \ldots, P_N\}$$
$$\Rightarrow \{U_1(T, \Delta), \ldots, U_N(T, \Delta)\} \qquad \textbf{Rel 6}$$

Thus, the most effective means of scheduling the individual system resources is first with respect to all of the steady-state processing (i.e., T) and then with respect to a designer's reference which captures the relative execution of all transient tasks in the system on the system resources on which they are executing, using the system-wide set, Δ. Note that while Q=M-K is bounded in relation 6, K may be dynamic and unbounded for dynamic multitasking.

The key design consideration for general concurrent computer systems is captured in relation 6. While resource sharing scheduling decisions are made by schedulers local to resources (the U_n), the most effective resource sharing scheduling decisions for a set of data-eligible tasks minimizes data starvation of the tasks in other parts of the system. Some global system context is required in each local resource. While relation 6 represents a simplification over the transient response of the entire system over all time, t, additional simplification is possible.

The effective set of observation windows required for consideration at each U_n is clearly much smaller. We define τ_n, as a *scheduling scope*, permitting simplification of the system-wide set of observation windows required for effective resource scheduling decisions at resource n. Each τ_n may be a set of intervals in

$$\{L_1(t), \ldots, L_K(t), L_{K+1}, \ldots, L_M\} \rightarrow \{P_1, \ldots, P_N\}$$
$$\Rightarrow \{U_1(T_1, \tau_1), \ldots, U_N(T_N, \tau_N)\} \qquad \textbf{Rel 7}$$

where we also allowed the steady state scheduling considerations of each local scheduler to be designed to a set of local periodic references, T_n.

A scheduling scope must permit at least some degree of knowledge about the flow of data outside of its scope, in addition to having adequate knowledge about the most effective use of heterogeneous resources within its own scope. Clearly, this requires an explicit form of scheduling that simultaneously takes into consideration functional data dependencies for data-dependent task activation along with architectural resource capability for effective resource sharing — thus, the concurrent design of function, architecture, and schedulers.

We are defining the basis of a design environment which will allow the designer to more effectively design the schedulers $U_n(T_n,\tau_n)$ for the way function, architecture and schedulers interact in the formation of a layered platform system. Clearly the complexity of such interactions requires a simulation and design environment that simultaneously captures system functionality, architecture and schedulers, modeling the internal behavior of the system along with its net response.

3. Frequency Interleaved Simulation (FI)

Our design environment [2] uses a textual specification to capture a layered system model composed of software models, software scheduler/protocol models, and resource models. It includes *frequency interleaved simulation* targeting integration of steady-state hardware and mapped design styles with non-steady state platform-based design. It introduces pure software models into a simulation environment, allowing for unrestricted modeling of the software and hardware virtual machines.

All computation in FI [2] is modeled by two fundamental thread types — C and G(F). C and G(F) threads execute in a shared memory modeling environment, from which communications can be explicitly modeled or inferred from the manner in which inputs are read and outputs are generated among individual threads or thread groupings.

C threads are rate-based threads that continuously sample inputs and generate outputs at fixed rates or frequencies (f_i), regardless of any other type of data events such as changes on inputs. Thus their activation is guaranteed. Since each C thread potentially has a different frequency, the activations are interleaved in time.

C threads capture the steady state response of traditional hardware resources, including the cycle accurate models of processors, busses and ASICs. C threads are, however, a more general modeling abstraction than cycle accurate hardware models. They can be used to model finer details of rate-based hardware descriptions [11], thus permitting a basis for partitioning a cycle accurate hardware model.

The most significant difference between C threads and other modeling environments with multi-rate capabilities [16], including HDLs, is that C threads provide the resource basis for a platform style of design. C threads are the foundation of all scheduling in the system, just as real hardware resources provide a foundation for all system execution.

C threads provide this capability by supporting G(F), or *guarded functional* threads. In general, G(F) threads can be activated by any other thread in the system. However, some specific types emerge (discussed later). Used to model software, G(F) threads:

- have *functional dependencies* — they do not have guaranteed, independent, activation properties as C threads do. Rather their activation depends on the state of the functional execution.
- can be eligible to execute, but *resource starved*,
- can be *dynamic in number* — they can be created and destroyed, as needed,
- need not execute atomically — atomicity must be explicitly modeled by the designer, e.g., as a *critical section*,
- have flexible forms of *time resolution* — functional instrumentation of a G(F) thread's source code determines how much computational complexity was represented between successive calls back to a *scheduling domain*.

We also define G(C) threads which are scheduler threads; they are guarded by a C thread and schedule G(F) threads. We also define G(T) threads which are guarded by a real-time constraint. Together, C threads and G threads form the basis of mixing hierarchical decomposition, static mapping, and directed platform design styles for simulation and analysis of steady-state and transient system responses.

3.1 Thread-based Design Abstractions

Consider the simple system of Figure 1 which represents two busses interconnected by a network. Each bus has a single processor, one or two memory mapped hardware devices, and some global (to the bus) memory space. This architecture was selected as it and Figure 2 will be used in a later example. (Thus, this system is meant as an illustration. It can be extended to include an arbitrary number of processors and hardware devices per bus, and an arbitrary number of busses and networks.) Each of the processor resources, hardware devices, and communication channels could be a *conceptual clock domain*. In this view, the system resource model contains eight clock domains. Thus A=({P},{B}) where $P=\{P_1,H_1,H_2,P_2,H_3\}$ and $B=\{B_1, B_2,N_1\}$.

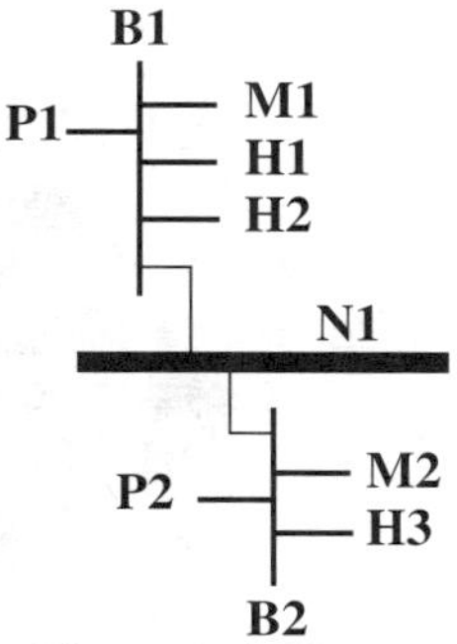

Figure 1 A System Architecture

Each of these clock domains allows independent manipulation of its power P or bandwidth B to translate state from inputs to outputs. Each is modeled as a separate C thread in FI. Not shown on the purely architectural diagram of Figure 1 are the software threads and software schedulers important to the static mapping and platform-based design styles. Figure 2 shows these threads as G(C) threads above the C threads. We draw the set of C threads that models the system resources at the bottom of the figure, labeled P_1, and P_2, associated with clock domains (or frequencies) f_1, and f_6 respectively. These are also scheduling domains because they provide the basis for functionality that executes on the C thread resource, loading its resource power. Note that we have left B_1 and B_2 out of Figure 2; to simplify the example, we assume their execution rates are sufficiently large compared to other rates in the system and thus do not slow the processing.

Scheduling domains, or U_n are labeled in the FI scheduling diagram as $U_1(T_1,\tau_1) = G_{11}(C)$ and $U_6(T_6,\tau_6) = G_{61}(C)$. The first subscript denotes the unique clock domain to which the scheduler is mapped. The second subscript is *1*, implying that the only function which may activate the scheduler is the underlying C thread itself. Thus, $G_{61}(F) == G(C_6)$, where C_6 is clock domain 6.

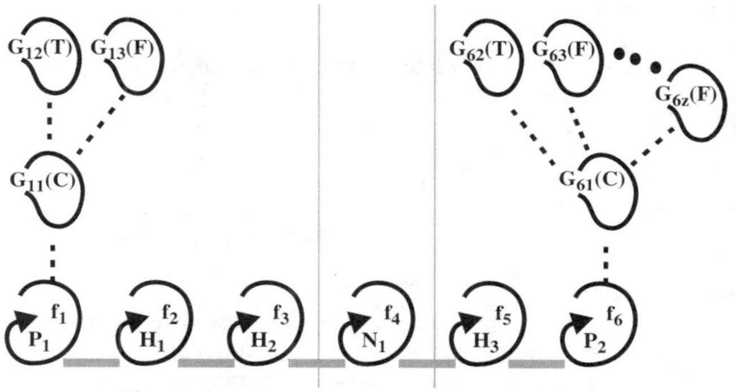

Figure 2 A Frequency Interleaved Schedule

A *platform* is the coupling of a scheduling domain to an underlying C thread, as illustrated in Figure 2 and defined by relation 6. Outside of the schedulers, all other G threads are activated by schedulers. Since the system depicted in Figure 2 is following an example presented later, a G(F) and G(T) thread are bound to clock domain 1 (the processor on Bus 1). An unbounded number of additional threads are bound to clock domain 6, the processor on Bus 2. This can be captured as in relation 6 as

$$\{G_{13}(F), G_{63}(F), \ldots, G_{6z}(F), G_{12}(T), G_{62}(T)\} \rightarrow \{P_1, P_2\}$$
$$\Rightarrow \{G_{11}(C_1) = U_1(T_1, \tau_1), G_{61}(C_6) = U_2(T_2, \tau_2)\}$$

Thus, G(F) threads model transient forms of processing with dynamic functional and data dependencies, G(T) threads represent steady state behaviors scheduled by a statically mapped scheduler [1], and G(C) threads are scheduling domains.

Comparing our approach to others, none allow the designer to reason directly about the resulting interactions and system-level characterizations of independently manipulable models of resource power, resource loading, and resource sharing captured by relation 2 of our model. Further, some current high-level system design methodologies ignore the modeling of the hardware [3], limit software to hardware-like finite models of computation [5], or apply synthesis to a restricted portion of the design space [6][7][8][9]. Others view all system scheduling as being either hardware-like or single processor RTOS-based [10], or they resolve all modeling to either token-based encapsulated computation and communication [4][14], or gate-like discrete event scheduling [15].

3.2 G(F) Thread Time Resolution

All execution in an FI simulation is resolved back to a set of C threads each with its own frequency defined relative to the others. The frequencies are normalized with respect to the smallest and inverted producing time periods. Note that some threads are based on physical timing data, giving the simulation a real time basis.

G(C) threads that schedule other G(F) threads are *scheduling domains*. The underlying resource C thread provides *power* P to the scheduling domain thread, which in turn selects which of the G(F) threads should execute and keeps track of how much load L it put on the resource. If one G(F) thread finishes and there is still power left for others, execution continues with one of them. Finally, the scheduler returns to the C thread which will reactivate later as specified by its calculated period.

Schedulers have a variety of means of resolving functional execution to a time budget. For instance, a collection of G(F) threads can consume a time budget on the basis of thread execution, memory access, or more complex means. Different operations may be instrumented as determined by the designer. Coarse time estimates allow for system designers to utilize intuition and allow software execution to be relatively resource independent for high-level models.

The designer is completely free to select the appropriate scheduling policy and time budgets. This permits a rate for system resources which is far lower than that which would be required if instruction set simulators were being utilized. Since the lower rate represents a more abstract model, it also allows the resource to be viewed as a platform for more complex behavior early in the system design process, thus enabling early system level modeling.

4. Example

In previous research [2], our simulations results were within 5% of an actual measured laboratory setup, giving confidence to the modeling and simulation capabilities of our approach. In this work, we modeled and simulated a streaming MPEG-1 Layer III audio decoder [17] in a client-server model distributed over a network. Our system architecture is that of Figure 1, and FI thread relationships are that of Figure 2. This example contains an illustrative set of interacting steady-state and transient system behaviors. Our goal is to simulate the system to determine the steady state processing requirements for P_1, and then to determine the performance of the transient tasks also being processed by P_1. As before, the busses are not modeled. Bus domain 2 (P_2,H_3) is a thread-on-accept file server, which dynamically loads the CPU and network. A network buffer (NIC), H3, provides a clean interface to the switch. The network C thread, N_1, fills and empties the interface buffers asynchronously. The high-level model of the network utilized only a single C thread.

Bus domain 1 (P_1,H_1,H_2) depicts the thread relationships for the client. It has an additional piece of hardware (H_2) in the form of a buffer for the audio DAC. The client scheduling domain thread, G_{11}(C), schedules two threads, G_{12}(T) and G_{13}(F). G_{12}(T) is the MPEG decoder task. It is computationally complex with a steady state response which can be met when the processing power of the client CPU, P_1, is adequate. Once the power is determined, P_1 is free to execute transient tasks. For this, we modeled G_{13}(F) which simply writes data to the network buffer. Because of space constraints, we focus on the behavior of the client with the assumption that the network and the server are always fast enough to meet the data demands of the CPU. However, the network buffer remains bounded in size and only empties itself periodically.

4.1 Instrumentation

The hardware is instrumented in two places: the output buffer of the DAC, H_2, and the output buffer of the NIC, H_1. We monitor the performance of G_{12}(T) and G_{13}(F). The NIC buffers are fixed in size and are emptied each time they execute, the rate of which is determined by the buffer's frequency. Performance is measured as percentage of occupied buffer slots at each execution.

The frequency of the C thread that models P_1, and so the execution rate of its scheduling domain thread G_{11}(C), is varied in our simulation. Time budgeting of the G(T) and G(F) threads mapped to a scheduling domain is resolved to this underlying power. Each time G_{11}(C) executes it gives priority to the MPEG task, G_{12}(T), allowing it to run until the DAC output buffer is filled or the MPEG task has exceeded the processing power of P_1's C thread. This is measured by assigning a cost to the inverse modified DCT (mDCT) function of the MPEG software. Each time this function is executed, P_1's C thread is charged a fixed amount by the scheduling domain thread mapped to it, G_{11}(C).

When the total time budget of the execution of G(F) and G(T) threads mapped to a G(C) scheduling domain exceeds some maximum value, the computational capacity of the underlying resource has been exceeded. Other C threads in the system simulation are then allowed to execute. Thus, steady state and non-steady state system responses are determined by a mix of processing power (the rate of the C threads), scheduling decisions (modeled in the G(C) threads), computation loads (determined in the G(F) and G(T) threads), and data availability.

4.2 Simulation Results

For this experiment, the audio and NIC buffers have a period of one and the frequency (power) of the client processor P_1 resource is varied. With a 44.1 kilosamples per second per channel output rate of the DAC buffer, each channel 16 bits, and a 64 byte buffer, each flush of the buffer accounts for about 0.36 ms. When we assign a frequency of one to this buffer we also give a meaning to the frequency of the other C threads in the system. For example, if the processor resource has a frequency of 0.5, then each execution of the processor resource C thread accounts for 2*0.36 ms or 0.72 ms. The audio buffer is 64 bytes and the network buffer is 256 bytes. On P_1, each inverse mDCT costs 15 and each network write costs 2, with a total computation cost not to exceed 100.

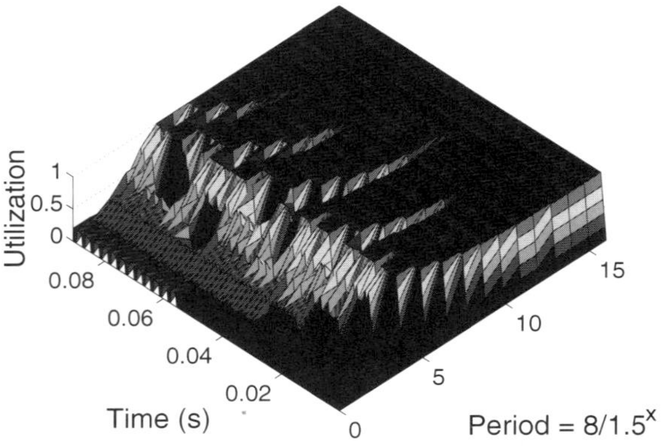

Figure 3 Steady State System Response

Figure 3 is a plot of DAC buffer utilization over time vs. the period of P_1 (inverse-frequency). The graph is semi-logarithmic on period, averaged over 5 time values for clarity. On the x-axis, 8 is the period at which the buffer utilization starts rising appreciably. The denominator is chosen to condense the data for better viewing. The start-up time is strongly dependent on the period of the processor resource. P_1 is unable to meet demand until its period is near $8/1.5^{13} = 0.04$, or about 24 times the speed of the buffer. With a 0.36 ms buffer cycle time, P_1 must cycle every 0.36 ms/24 = 0.015 ms. The maximum amount of computation is 100, and each inverse mDCT costs 15, then we can have at most 6.66 inverse mDCTs per cycle. P_1 must therefore sustain about $4.4*10^5$ inverse mDCT/s in order to meet steady state demand for G(T).

The periodic horizontal streaks result from the way the algorithm reads a frame of data and then proceeds to do all the inverse mDCT operations at once, starving the buffer as P_1 is overloaded. From this, a designer might reduce peak loads by either altering the algorithm or using a buffer design that is better able to handle bursty traffic.

Figure 4 is a plot of the utilization of the NIC, H_2, which is filled by the transient task, $G_{13}(F)$, which $G_{11}(C)$ only executes when $G_{12}(T)$ is I/O bound. When $G_{12}(T)$ is compute bound, $G_{13}(F)$ suffers, as is evident by the streaks which match those in Figure 4. $G_{13}(F)$ eventually plateaus when it also becomes I/O bound.

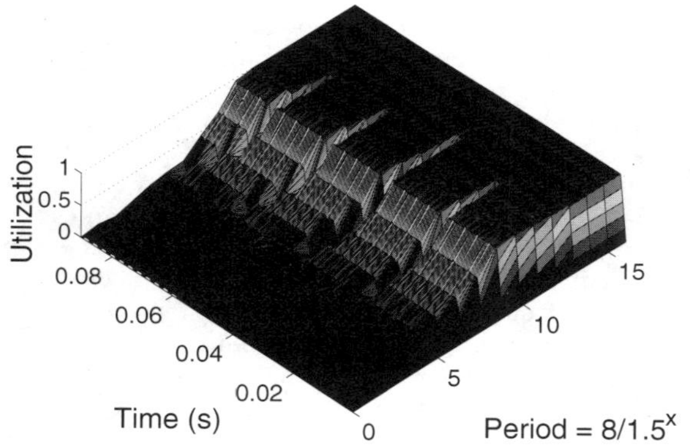

Figure 4 Transient System Response

The key difference in observing the behavior of the steady-state MPEG thread, $G_{12}(T)$, and the transient processing of the background thread, $G_{13}(F)$, is seen by examining each graph on the basis of three regions. Each graph has a sloped region for low processor frequencies, a rilled region in which processing is mostly saturated, and a completely saturated region. But while the steady-state task, $G_{12}(T)$, is only correct in the region in which steady state performance is met all the time, the performance of a transient task may be acceptable over all three regions. While performance of the transient task is clearly better in the completely saturated region, its net performance may also be measured as a cumulative amount of processing over the scheduling scope, i.e. for τ_6=0.10s. That is, the net difference between the processing in the rilled region as compared to the completely saturated region may be negligible. Thus, our modeling and simulation capability allowed us to determine the processing power required in a complex system and then determine the performance of the leftover transient tasks.

5. Conclusion

Current digital system design approaches have been limited by the view that the entire system must be characterized by a single design style, such as reactive, real-time, or general-purpose. By starting with an observation that all system behaviors may be classified as steady-state or transient, and all design styles may be classified as hierarchical decomposition, static mapping or directed platform, we developed a formalism to show how existing design styles may be related. We used this to show how viewing system design as the simultaneous manipulation of function, architecture, and schedulers can result in novel design methodologies that more closely match emergent systems as well as simplify the need to match real-time processing requirements to resources. We introduce how local scheduling decisions for transient behavior can be optimized across broader system scheduling scopes. We presented FI simulation as the basis for unifying design styles through a mix of formalism and simulation-based experimentation. We are continuing to develop our modeling approach.

6. Acknowledgments

We thank our other research team members: Henele Adams, Chris Andrews, Chris Eatedali and Neal Tibrewala. This work was supported in part by the General Motors Collaborative Research Lab at Carnegie Mellon, ST Microelectronics, NSF Award EIA-9812939, and the Pittsburgh Digital Greenhouse.

7. References

[1] J.M. Paul, S.N. Peffers, D.E. Thomas. "A Codesign Virtual Machine for Hierarchical, Balanced Hardware/Software System Modeling," *DAC*, 2000.

[2] N.K. Tibrewala, J.M. Paul, D.E. Thomas. "Modeling and Evaluation of Hardware/Software Designs," *9th international Workshop on Hardware/Software Codesign,* 2001.

[3] B. Selic. "Turning Clockwise: Using UML in the Real-Time Domain," *Comm. of the ACM,* pp. 46-54. Oct. 1999.

[4] J. Davis II, M. Goel, C. Hylands, B. Kienhuis, E. Lee, et. al, "Overview of the Ptolemy Project," ERL Technical Report UCB/ERL No. M99/37, Dept. EECS, Berkeley. July 1999.

[5] F. Balarin, M Chiodo, P. Giusto, H. Hsieh, A. Jurecska, L. Lavagno, C. Passerone, A. Sangiovanni-Vincentelli, et.al, *Hardware-Software Co-design of Embedded Systems. The Polis Approach.* Boston: Kluwer. 1997.

[6] D. Gajski, F. Vahid, S. Narayan, J. Gong. "SpecSyn: An Environment Supporting the Specify-Explore-Refine Paradigm for Hardware/Software System Design," *IEEE Trans. VLSI '98.*

[7] Y. Li, W. Wolf, "Hardware/Software Co-Synthesis with Memory Hierarchies," *Proc. of ICCAD98*, pp. 430-436. 1998.

[8] R. Ortega, G. Borriello. "Communication Synthesis for Distributed Embedded Systems," *ICCAD98.* pp. 437-453. '98.

[9] K. Rompaey, D. Verkest, I. Bolsens, H. De Man. "CoWare - A design environment for heterogeneous hardware/software systems," P*roceedings of EURO-DAC* 1996.

[10] D. Desmet, D. Verkest, H. De Man. "Operating System Based Software Generation for Systems-on-chip," *DAC* 2000.

[11] A. Dasdan, D. Ramanathan, R. Gupta. "Rate derivation and its applications to reactive, real-time embedded systems," *DAC* 1998.

[12] G. Buttazzo. *Hard real-time computing systems: predictable scheduling algorithms and applications.* Boston: Kluwer, '97.

[13] P. Pop, P. Eles, Z. Peng. "Schedulability Analysis for Systems with Data and Control Dependencies," *EURO-DAC 2000.*

[14] http://www.inmet.com/sldl/

[15] http://www.systemc.org/

[16] http://www.mathworks.com/

[17] http://www.iis.fhg.de/

Synthesizing Distributed Real-Time Systems Modeled by a Timed Version of a Subset of LOTOS

Ahmed Khoumsi
Université de Sherbrooke, Dep. GEGI, Sherbrooke, CANADA
E-mail : khoumsi@gel.usherb.ca

ABSTRACT

This paper deal with the synthesis of distributed real time systems (DRTS). More precisely, we propose : (1) a language for modelling synthesized DRTSs and services they provide, and (2) a synthesis procedure which derives a specification of DRTS from a specification of a desired service. The derived DRTS provides the desired service given as input. In addition to order constraints, the synthesized DRTS also guarantees timing constraints specified in the desired service. A clock is used in each site of the DRTS and, contrary to previous methods, we take into account the inaccuracy of clock synchronizations.

Keywords

Synthesis, Distributed real time systems, Timed Simplified Basic Lotos, Clock synchronization.

1. INTRODUCTION

Synthesis uses as input a global specification of distributed desired service, and its aim is to derive automatically a component specification for each site of the distributed system. The synthesis method guarantees that the synthesized components provide the desired service. In the computer network community, such components are called *protocol entities* (PE). The service is described at a high level, where only the interactions with the user are visible (see Fig. 1.a). The synthesized PEs provide the desired service by interacting with the environment (i.e., the user) and by communicating with each other through a communication medium (see Fig. 1.b). The communication inter-PE is not observable by the user and allows the PEs to coordinate among themselves. We will use the basic principle of synthesis which was initially described in [1] as follows : if in the specification of the desired service, an event A is executed by PE^a and is followed by the execution of an event B by PE^b, then : (i) after PE^a executes A, it sends a message to PE^b; and (ii) after PE^b receives the message, it may execute B. Here, each event is either the reception of an input coming from the environment or the sending of an output to the environment. The specifications of the set of PEs will be called *protocol specicification*.

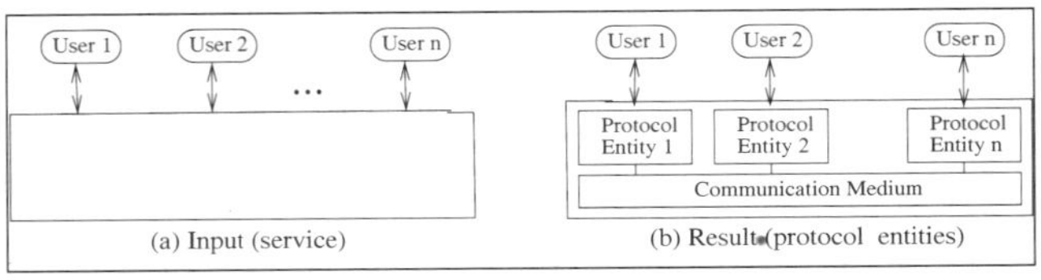

Figure 1: Input and result of synthesis.

A synthesis method was developed in the past [1], and has subsequently been improved in several papers [9, 4, 7, 6, 8, 5, 10]. Temporal aspects are dealt with in [6, 8, 10], but with certain assumptions related to the transit time in the communication medium. In [6] the transit time is assumed negligible, and in [8] it is estimated by a maximum value. As for [10], the author assumed that the network can estimate with a very good accuracy every transit time; this assumption allowed to obtain the same results as if the clocks used in the different sites of the distributed system are perfectly synchronized. In the present article, we improve the method in [10] by *not* assuming that the network can estimate every transit time. Besides, we assume more realistically that each clock is synchronized with a reference clock with a given *nonnull inaccuracy* which can be determined.

The rest of the paper is structured as follows. In Sect. 2, we present the formal language used to describe the synthesized system and the given service it provides. In Sect. 3, we explain our synthesis approach. In Sect. 4, we propose a synthesis algorithm and we illustrate it by an example. Finally in Sect. 5, we conclude.

2. SPECIFICATION LANGUAGE TSBL

Let us consider the Simplified Basic Lotos (SBL) of [9] which is a subset of Basic Lotos [2]. An event (which is assumed instantaneous) is said *logically enabled* when its execution is possible, according to the SBL behaviour expression being executed. The language we propose extends SBL and is denoted TSBL (for Timed SBL). From a specification A written in SBL, we obtain a specification A^t written in TSBL by associating an interval to each event of A. The semantics of an interval U associated to an event x is as follows : *the delay separating the instant when x becomes logically enabled and the instant of its execution must fall within U*. The syntax of TSBL may therefore be defined by the

ISSS'01, October 1-3, 2001, Montréal, Québec, Canada.

production rules of Table 1. "*Spec_Def*", "*Proc_Def*" and "*e*" are non-terminal symbols, and "*EventId*", "*ProcId*", "PROC" and "END" are terminal symbols. Note that "*Spec_Def*" is the *starting* non-terminal symbol. The symbols " ; ", " ||| " and " [] " are the operators of *sequence*, *parallel composition* and *choice*, respectively.

In a service specification (see Example 2.1), *EventId* is in the form $\langle a^i, U \rangle$. It represents the execution of a in Site i with the timing constraint defined by the interval U. In a protocol specification, *EventId* may be in the form $\langle a^i, U \rangle$ or in other forms which represent *sending* and *reception* of coordination messages between the protocol entities. An example of protocol specification will be given in Sect. 4.5.

1.	*Spec_Def*	$\rightarrow$	*Proc_Def*		
2.	*Proc_Def*	$\rightarrow$	PROC	*ProcId* $= e$	END
			Proc_Def$_1$		
3.	*Proc_Def*	$\rightarrow$	PROC	*ProcId* $= e$	END
4.	e	$\rightarrow$	*ProcId*		
5.	e	$\rightarrow$	*EventId*		
6.	e	$\rightarrow$	$e_1 ; e_2$		
7.	e	$\rightarrow$	$e_1 \parallel\!| e_2$		
8.	e	$\rightarrow$	$e_1 [] e_2$		
9.	e	$\rightarrow$	(e_1)		

Table 1: Production rules of TSBL (where $e_1 = e_2 = e$ and $Proc\_Def_1 = Proc\_Def$).

EXAMPLE 2.1. PROC $A = X ; Y ; A$ END,
PROC $X = (\langle a^1, [0,4] \rangle \parallel\!| \langle b^2, [1,5] \rangle)$ END, and
PROC $Y = (\langle c^3, [1,4] \rangle [] \langle d^3, [2,6] \rangle)$ END. This specification means : (1) the infinite sequence $XYXYXY\cdots$ is executed; (2) in X, both a^1 *and* b^2 are executed, independently of each other; (3) in Y, either c^3 *or* d^3 is executed; (4) in the first occurrence of X, the instants of a^1 and b^2 must fall within the intervals $[0,4]$ and $[1,5]$, respectively, relatively to the instant 0 when A begins its execution; (5) If in the ith occurrence of X, ν_a^i and ν_b^i are the instants of a^1 and b^2, then the ith occurrence of Y becomes logically enabled at instant $\max(\nu_a^i, \nu_b^i)$. If c^3 is selected in Y, then it is executed at an instant ν_c^i such that $(\nu_c^i - \max(\nu_a^i, \nu_b^i)) \in [1,4]$. If d^3 is selected in Y, then it is executed at an instant ν_d^i such that $(\nu_d^i - \max(\nu_a^i, \nu_b^i)) \in [2,6]$. Let ν_x^i be the instant of the selected event. (6) In the $(i+1)$th occurrence of X, a^1 is executed at an instant ν_a^{i+1} such that $(\nu_a^{i+1} - \nu_x^i) \in [0,4]$, and b^2 is executed at an instant ν_b^{i+1} such that $(\nu_b^{i+1} - \nu_x^i) \in [1,5]$. The expression $\max(x,y)$ denotes the greatest of x and y.

3. OUR APPROACH OF SYNTHESIS

3.1 Basic principle of synthesis

The inputs of the synthesis procedure are : (1) a specification *SERV* of the desired service, written in TSBL; and (2) a model of the communication medium which specifies that the transit delay *tm* of a message sent by Site i and received by Site j is such that $tm \in M_{i,j} = [\mu_{i,j}, \rho_{i,j}]$ where $\mu_{i,j}$ and $\rho_{i,j}$ are given for each pair (Site i,Site j). The result of synthesis consists of several specifications PS^i $(i = 1, 2, \cdots)$ written in TSBL, where each PS^i describes the protocol entity in Site i (PE^i).

DEFINITION 3.1. *(Starting event, ending event, starting site, ending site)* In an expression A written in TSBL, the set of the first (resp. last) events which become logically enabled is denoted by SE_A (resp. EE_A), and an element of SE_A (resp. EE_A) is called *starting* (resp. *ending*) event of A. The set of sites identifiers where the starting (resp. ending) events are executed is denoted by SS_A (resp. ES_A). An element of SS_A (resp. ES_A) is called a *starting* (resp. *ending*) site of A. The set of starting (resp. ending) events of A which are executed in a given Site i is denoted by SE_A^i (resp. EE_A^i). Note that the semantics of "starting" and "ending" does not depend on timing constraints.

EXAMPLE 3.1. *(Starting event, ending event, starting site, ending site)* For the following specification :
$A = (\langle a^1, I \rangle ; \langle b^2, J \rangle) \parallel\!| (\langle c^3, K \rangle ; \langle d^4, L \rangle ; \langle e^1, M \rangle)$, we obtain : $SE_A = \{a^1, c^3\}$, $EE_A = \{b^2, e^1\}$, $SS_A = \{1, 3\}$ and $ES_A = \{2, 1\}$.

DEFINITION 3.2. *(Starting site-interval, ending site-interval)* If we consider a starting (resp. ending) event a^i and the corresponding interval U, then the pair (i, U) is called starting (resp. ending) site-interval.

The basic idea of synthesis comes from the observation that all order and timing constraints are defined by the use of the operator " ; " as follows. An expression "$e1 ; e2$" means that : (1) the starting events of $e2$ are executed *after* the ending events of $e1$, and (2) the timing constraints of the starting events of $e2$ are defined relatively to the instant when the last ending event of $e1$ has been executed. To guarantee these (order and timing) constraints, the basic principle of synthesis is the following : for every expression "$e1 ; e2$" in *SERV*, messages are sent from the ending sites of $e1$ to the starting sites of $e2$ as follows :

For every ending Site i of $e1$: when the ending events in EE_{e1}^i have been executed, then PE^i sends a message to all the starting sites of $e2$. The message contains the following two informations : (1) the indication that all the events in EE_{e1}^i have occurred, and (2) the instant (measured by the clock of PE^i) when the last event in EE_{e1}^i has occurred.

For every starting Site j of $e2$: when PE^j has received a message from each ending site of $e1$, then it may execute the starting events of SE_{e2}^j at instants which respect their timing constraints.

EXAMPLE 3.2. *(Application of the principle of synthesis in the non-real-time case)* We consider the service "$e1 ; e2$", where $e1 = (\langle a^1, [0, \infty] \rangle \parallel\!| (\langle b^1, [0, \infty] \rangle ; \langle c^2, [0, \infty] \rangle))$ and $e2 = (\langle d^3, [0, \infty] \rangle [] \langle e^3, [0, \infty] \rangle)$. The ending events of $e1$ are a^1 and c^2, and their corresponding ending sites are 1 and 2. The starting events of $e2$ are d^3 and e^3, and their corresponding starting site is 3. Therefore, we expect that after each a^1 and c^2, a message is sent to Site 3. When PE^3 receives the *two* messages, it then may execute d^3 or e^3. If we replace " ||| " by " [] " in "$e1$", then PE^3 must receive a *single* message before to execute d^3 or e^3. Sect. 3.4 and 4.5 illustrate the synthesis principle in the real-time case.

3.2 Clocks and their synchronizations

In order to guarantee timing constraints, each PE^a has a local clock κ^a. There exist several methods for synchronizing clocks. We consider, without loss of generality, that all the clocks used by the PEs are synchronized to the same *reference clock* RC. The accuracy of synchronization of each κ^a can be estimated and depends on the synchronization method. [3] presents two synchronization methods, called Cristian and NTP respectively, and presents also estimations of their accuracies. In the present study, the accuracy of synchronization of each κ^a with RC is assumed known and is denoted $\pm\delta_a$, which means that at any instant after the synchronization, the difference between RC and κ^a falls within $[-\delta_a, \delta_a]$. For simplicity and without loss of generality, instead of considering specifically the δ_a of each κ^a, we will consider an upper bound Δ of all the δ_a. In other terms, we consider that the difference between RC and every κ^a falls within $[-\Delta, \Delta]$. Therefore at any instant after the synchronization of all the clocks with RC, the difference between two any clocks falls within $[-2\Delta, 2\Delta]$.[1]

3.3 Deriving timing constraints of the PEs

DEFINITION 3.3. *(Timing requirement, timing constraint)* Henceforth, the terms "requirement" and "constraint" are associated to services and protocols, respectively. In other terms, timing requirements are defined in the specification of a desired service, and timing constraints are defined in the synthesized specifications of protocol entities.

NOTATION 1. *($\nu_x^{\kappa^i}$)* If x is an event, $\nu_x^{\kappa^i}$ denotes the instant of x. If x is a set of events, $\nu_x^{\kappa^i}$ denotes the instant of the last event of x, i.e., the instant when all the events of x have occurred. This instant is given in the reference of the clock κ^i.

We have explained in Sect. 3.1 that *after* a PE executes its ending events of $e1$, it *sends* a message to all the starting sites of $e2$. Similarly, *before* a PE executes its starting events of $e2$, it must *receive* a message from each ending site of $e1$. The aim of timing constraints derivation is the following. From the timing requirements of the starting events of $e2$, we must derive timing constraints of : (i) the delays which separate the ending events of $e1$ and the subsequent send-operations; and (ii) the delays which separate the receive-operations and the subsequent starting events of $e2$. Note that a derived timing constraint is a constraint on a delay which separates two events executed by the same PE. For any event x, let $U_x = [\gamma_x, \delta_x]$ be the interval which defines the timing requirement of x. In an expression "$e1\,;\,e2$", timing constraints of the PEs are derived as follows :[2]

For every $i \in ES_{e1}$ **and every** $k \in SS_{e2}$, $k \neq i$: the timing requirements of the events $x \in SE_{e2}^k$ can be guaranteed *only if* :

$$\forall x \in SE_{e2}^k : \delta_x \geq \rho_{i,k} \tag{1}$$

Let σ be the last ending event of $e1$ in Site i. Assuming Eq. 1, the timing requirements of the events in SE_{e2}^k can be guaranteed *only if* the delay ts which separates σ and the subsequent send-operation towards Site k satisfies :

$$ts \leq \min_{k \in SS_{e2}}^{x \in SE_{e2}^k} (\delta_x - \rho_{i,k}) \tag{2}$$

The message sent from Site i to Site k contains the instant $\nu_{EE_{e1}^i}^{\kappa^i}$ (measured by κ^i) of σ.

For every $k \in SS_{e2}$ **and every** $x \in SE_{e2}^k$:

- For each $i \in ES_{e1}$, PE^k receives from PE^i a message which contains the instant $\nu_{EE_{e1}^i}^{\kappa^i}$ (measured by κ^i) of the last ending event of $e1$ in Site i.

  Therefore PE^k can estimate the instant $\nu_{EE_{e1}}^{\kappa^k}$ (in the reference of κ^k) of the last event of EE_{e1} (i.e., the instant when $e2$ becomes logically enabled) by :

$$\nu_{EE_{e1}}^{\kappa^k} \in [\max_{i \in ES_{e1}} (\nu_{EE_{e1}^i}^{\kappa^i}) - \Delta,\ \max_{i \in ES_{e1}} (\nu_{EE_{e1}^i}^{\kappa^i}) + \Delta] \tag{3}$$

  Assuming Eq.1 and 2 for every $i \in ES_{e1}$, the timing requirement of x can be guaranteed *if and only if* :

$$(\delta_x - \gamma_x) \geq 2\Delta \tag{4}$$

  Let $\nu_r^{\kappa^k}$ be the instant when all the messages coming from EE_{e1} have been received by PE^k, and let $tr = \nu_x^{\kappa^k} - \nu_r^{\kappa^k}$. Assuming Eq.1 and 2 (for every $i \in ES_{e1}$) and Eq. 4, the timing requirement of x is guaranteed *if* :

$$(tr + \nu_r^{\kappa^k} - \max_{i \in ES_{e1}} (\nu_{EE_{e1}^i}^{\kappa^i})) \in [\gamma_x + \Delta, \delta_x - \Delta] \tag{5}$$

3.4 Example of timing constraint derivation

We consider $(\langle a^1, U\rangle \,|||\, \langle b^2, V\rangle)\,;\,(\langle c^3, Y\rangle)$, where $Y = [\gamma_{c^3}, \delta_{c^3}] = [3, 10]$. The intervals U and V are not relevant for the following explanations where we will show how the timing requirement of c^3 can be guaranteed. The model of the communication medium is defined by $M_{1,3} = [\mu_{1,3}, \rho_{1,3}] = [2, 6]$ and $M_{2,3} = [\mu_{2,3}, \rho_{2,3}] = [2, 5]$. We take $\Delta = 0.1$.

The sequencing of events is represented in Fig. 2. From the synthesis principle, after the execution of a^1, a message containing the information p_a and $\nu_{a^1}^{\kappa^1}$ is sent by PE^1 to Site 3 (written $s_3(p_a, \nu_{a^1}^{\kappa^1})$) and then received by PE^3 (written $r_1(p_a, \nu_{a^1}^{\kappa^1})$). In this message, p_a is a parameter which indicates that a^1 has occurred and $\nu_{a^1}^{\kappa^1}$ is the instant of a^1 measured by κ^1. In the same manner, after the execution of b^2, a message containing the information p_b and $\nu_{b^2}^{\kappa^2}$ is sent by PE^2 to Site 3 (written $s_3(p_b, \nu_{b^2}^{\kappa^2})$) and then received by PE^3 (written $r_2(p_b, \nu_{b^2}^{\kappa^2})$). For clarity, the superscript of ν_x^c has been omitted in Fig. 2. The timing requirement of the service requires that $tt \in [\gamma_{c^3}, \delta_{c^3}] = [3, 10]$, and the communication medium model implies that $tm_{1,3} \in M_{1,3} = [2, 6]$ and $tm_{2,3} = M_{2,3} = [2, 5]$. The synthesis of protocol timing constraints consists of determining constraints $ts_a \leq \phi_a$, $ts_b \leq \phi_b$ and $tr \in [\alpha, \beta]$ such that : $tm_{1,3} \in M_{1,3}$, $tm_{2,3} = M_{2,3}$, $ts_a \leq \phi_a$, $ts_b \leq \phi_b$ and $tr \in [\alpha, \beta]$ imply $tt \in [\gamma_{c^3}, \delta_{c^3}]$.

The timing requirement of c^3 can be guaranteed only if (see Eq. 1) : $\delta_{c^3} \geq \rho_{1,3}$ and $\delta_{c^3} \geq \rho_{2,3}$. These inequations are satisfied because they mean $10 \geq 6$ and $10 \geq 5$, respectively. The timing requirement of c^3 can be guaranteed only if (see Eq. 2) : $ts_a \leq (\delta_{c^3} - \rho_{1,3})$, i.e., $ts_a \leq (10 - 6) = 4$, and $ts_b \leq (\delta_{c^3} - \rho_{2,3})$, i.e., $ts_b \leq (10 - 5) = 5$. When PE^3 has received the two messages, from PE^1 and PE^2 respectively, then from $\nu_{a^1}^{\kappa^1}$ and $\nu_{b^2}^{\kappa^2}$ contained in the two messages respectively,

[1]For lack of space, the proof is omitted.

[2]For lack of space, we have omitted proofs of Eq. 1, 2, 3, 4 and 5.

PE^3 estimates the instant $\nu_{EE_{e1}}^{\kappa^3}$ (in the reference of κ^3) when c^3 becomes logically enabled by (see Eq. 3) : $\nu_{EE_{e1}}^{\kappa^3} \in [\max(\nu_{a^1}^{\kappa^1}; \nu_{b^2}^{\kappa^2}) - 0.1, \max(\nu_{a^1}^{\kappa^1}; \nu_{b^2}^{\kappa^2}) + 0.1]$. Assuming $ts_a \leq 4$ and $ts_b \leq 5$, the timing requirement of c^3 can be guaranteed if and only if (see Eq. 4) : $(\delta_{c^3} - \gamma_{c^3}) \geq 2\Delta$. This inequation is satisfied because it means $(10 - 3) \geq 0.2$. Assuming $ts_a \leq 4$ and $ts_b \leq 5$, the timing requirement of c^3 is satisfied if (see Eq. 5) : $(tr + \nu_r^{\kappa^3} - \max(\nu_{a^1}^{\kappa^1}; \nu_{b^2}^{\kappa^2})) \in [\gamma_{c^3} + \Delta, \delta_{c^3} - \Delta]$, which can be written : $(tr + \nu_r^{\kappa^3} - \max(\nu_{a^1}^{\kappa^1}; \nu_{b^2}^{\kappa^2})) \in [3.1, 9.9]$.

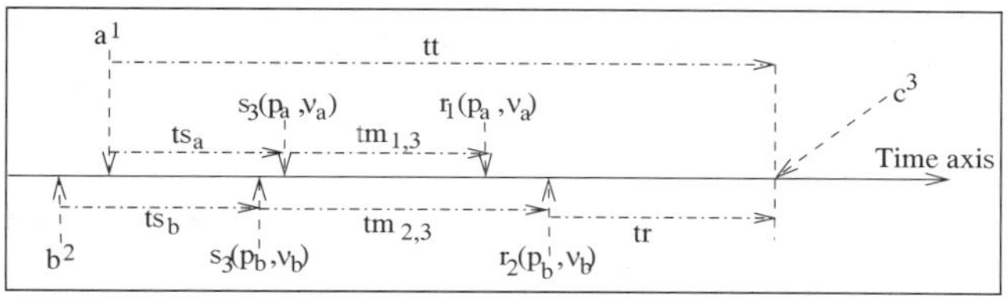

Figure 2: Sequencing of events.

4. SYNTHESIS ALGORITHM

4.1 Attributes

DEFINITION 4.1. *(Preceding, following)* In "e1 ; e2" : (i) an ending site of e1 is called a *preceding* site of e2; (ii) a starting site of e2 is called a *following* site of e1; and (iii) we say that e1 *precedes* e2 and e2 *follows* e1. The same definition holds if we replace "site" by "site-interval".

In order to synthesize a protocol specification from a service specification $SERV$ written in TSBL, a syntax tree is generated by applying consecutively the production rules of TSBL, starting from the non-terminal symbol $SERV$. Each node (resp. leaf) of the syntax tree corresponds to a subexpression (resp. terminal symbol in the form $\langle a^i, U \rangle$) of $SERV$. For this reason, we will not distinguish nodes (resp. leaves) with their corresponding expressions (resp. terminal symbols). For each node n of the syntax tree, we define synthesized attributes which are evaluated from the leaves towards the root, and inherited attributes which are evaluated from the root towards the leaves.

DEFINITION 4.2. *(Synthesized attributes)* SSI_n is the set of **S**tarting **S**ite-**I**ntervals of n, and ES_n is the set of **E**nding **S**ites of n.

DEFINITION 4.3. *(Inherited attributes)* PS_n is the set of **P**receding **S**ites of n, and P_n is equal to NIL or (PS_n, N), where N identifies the node which precedes n. P_n is equal to NIL if it is not preceded by any node, i.e., if $PS_n = \{\}$ and N is not defined. FSI_n is the set of **F**ollowing **S**ite-**I**ntervals of n.

DEFINITION 4.4. *(Preceding attribute, following attribute)* P_n and FSI_n are called preceding attribute and following attribute of n, respectively.

The synthesized attributes are evaluated for all the nodes, and are then used to evaluate the inherited attributes. The latter are used to synthesize the protocol specification. In an expression "e1 ; e2" of the service specification, FSI_{e1} and P_{e2} can be intuitively introduced as follows :

- FSI_{e1} is used (1) to determine the send-operations which follow the ending events of e1, and (2) to compute the timing constraints of these send-operations.
- P_{e2} is used to determine the receive-operations which precede the starting events of e2. These receive-operations correspond to the send-operations determined by FSI_{e1}.

4.2 Evaluations of the attributes

The rules for evaluating the synthesized attributes of a node in the syntax tree depend on the production rule used to define this node (see Table 1). These rules are :

2.	$SSI_{ProcId} := SSI_e$	$ES_{ProcId} := ES_e$
3.	$SSI_{ProcId} := SSI_e$	$ES_{ProcId} := ES_e$
4.	$SSI_e := SSI_{ProcId}$	$ES_e := ES_{ProcId}$
5.	$SSI_e := SSI_{EventId}$	$ES_e := ES_{EventId}$
6.	$SSI_e := SSI_{e_1}$	$ES_e := ES_{e_2}$
7.	$SSI_e := SSI_{e_1} \cup SSI_{e_2}$	$ES_e := ES_{e_1} \cup ES_{e_2}$
8.	$SSI_e := SSI_{e_1} \cup SSI_{e_2}$	$ES_e := ES_{e_1} \cup ES_{e_2}$
9.	$SSI_e := SSI_{e_1}$	$ES_e := ES_{e_1}$

The rules for evaluating the inherited attributes are :

2.	$P_e := NIL$	$FSI_e := \{\}$
3.	$P_e := NIL$	$FSI_e := \{\}$
4.	$P_{ProcId} := NIL$	$FSI_{ProcId} := \{\}$
5.	$P_{EventId} := NIL$	$FSI_{EventId} := \{\}$
6.	$P_{e_1} := NIL$	$FSI_{e_1} := SSI_{e_2}$
	$P_{e_2} := (ES_{e_1}, N(e_1))$	$FSI_{e_2} := \{\}$
7.	$P_{e_1} = P_{e_2} := NIL$	$FSI_{e_1} = FSI_{e_2} := \{\}$
8.	$P_{e_1} = P_{e_2} := NIL$	$FSI_{e_1} = FSI_{e_2} := \{\}$
9.	$P_{e_1} := NIL$	$FSI_{e_1} := \{\}$

Note : the inherited attributes are not defined for the root of the syntax tree.

EXAMPLE 4.1. *(Syntax tree with attributes)* For the specification : PROC $A = (\langle b^2, [0, 10] \rangle \parallel\!\mid \langle a^1, [1, 9] \rangle) ; B$ END PROC $B = (\langle c^3, [6, 12] \rangle \,[]\, \langle d^3, [7, 11] \rangle) ; A$ END, we obtain the two syntax trees represented in Fig. 3.

4.3 Other notations and definitions

NOTATION 2. *(Bold italic characters)* A bold italic character is interpreted litterally. For example, ***Helxo*** represents the string "Hello" if the variable x is set to the character ***l***.

DEFINITION 4.5. *($Send_k(p, \nu, \mathcal{C}, \xi)$)* $Send_k(p, \nu, \mathcal{C}, \xi)$ corresponds to a send-operation towards Site k which follows the execution of one or several events in a Site i. Let a^i be the last of these events. $Send_k(p, \nu, \mathcal{C}, \xi)$ means : (i) a message containing parameters p and ν is sent to Site k, where ν is the instant of a^i measured by κ^i; (ii) the timing requirements of the events in Site k which follow the receive-operation corresponding to the present send-operation, can be guaranteed *only if* : the boolean expression $\mathcal{C}$ is *true* and $ts \leq \xi$, where ts is the delay separating a^i and the send-operation.

DEFINITION 4.6. *($SEND(FSI_e, p, i)$)* Let e be a node identified by p in the syntax tree, and its following attribute be $FSI_e = \{(k_1, [\gamma_{k_1}, \delta_{k_1}]), (k_2, [\gamma_{k_2}, \delta_{k_2}]), \cdots, (k_m, [\gamma_{k_m}, \delta_{k_m}])\}$.

$$SEND(FSI_e, p, i) = (\boldsymbol{Send}_{k_1}(p, \boldsymbol{\nu}_i, \mathcal{C}_{i,k_1}(e), \xi_{i,k_1}(e)) \parallel\!\mid \cdots \parallel\!\mid \boldsymbol{Send}_{k_m}(p, \boldsymbol{\nu}_i, \mathcal{C}_{i,k_m}(e), \xi_{i,k_m}(e)))$$

Where : $\xi_{i,k}(e) = \min_{(k,[\gamma_x,\delta_x]) \in FSI_e}(\delta_x - \rho_{i,k})$ and $\mathcal{C}_{i,k}(e) =$

$(\forall(k,[\gamma_x,\delta_x]) \in FSI_e \ : (\delta_x \geq \max(\rho_{i,k};\gamma_x + 2\Delta)$.
$\mathcal{C}_{i,k}(e)$ is deduced from Eq. 1 and 4, and $ts \leq \xi_{i,k}(e)$ is deduced from Eq. 2.
If $FSI_e = \{\}$ then $SEND(FSI_e, p, i) = \textbf{\textit{empty}}$.

Definition 4.7. *($Rec_i(p,\nu)$)* $Rec_i(p,\nu)$ corresponds to a receive-operation and means : (i) a message coming from Site i and containing parameters p and ν is received; and (ii) there is no timing constraint on this receive-operation.

Definition 4.8. *($REC(P_e,p)$)* Let e be a node identified by p in the syntax tree, and its preceding attribute be $P_e = (\{i_1, i_2, \cdots, i_n\}, N)$.

$$REC(P_e,p) = (\boldsymbol{Rec}_{i_1}(N, \boldsymbol{\nu}_{i_1}) \ ||| \cdots ||| \ \boldsymbol{Rec}_{i_n}(N, \boldsymbol{\nu}_{i_n})) \ ; \ (\boldsymbol{\tau}(p) = \boldsymbol{CurrentTime} - \max(\boldsymbol{\nu}_{i_1}, \cdots, \boldsymbol{\nu}_{i_n}))$$

Intuitively, $REC(P_e,p)$ means that for each preceding Site i_u of the node e, a message coming from i_u and containing N and ν_{i_u} is received by a PE^k. From $\tau(p)$, PE^k can estimate the delay which separates the instant when e has become logically enabled and the instant when all the messages from Sites $i_1, i_2, \cdots, i_n$ have been received. This delay falls within $[\tau(p) - \Delta, \tau(p) + \Delta]$.

Definition 4.9. *($EventId_{t\pm\Delta}$, $ProcId_{t\pm\Delta}$)* Let t and Δ be two positive values. For $EventId = \langle a^i, [\gamma,\delta]\rangle$, $EventId_{t\pm\Delta} = \langle a^i, [\gamma - t + \Delta, \delta - t - \Delta]\rangle$.
$ProcId_{t\pm\Delta}$ identifies a procedure obtained from $ProcId$ by replacing every starting event E of $ProcId$ by $E_{t\pm\Delta}$

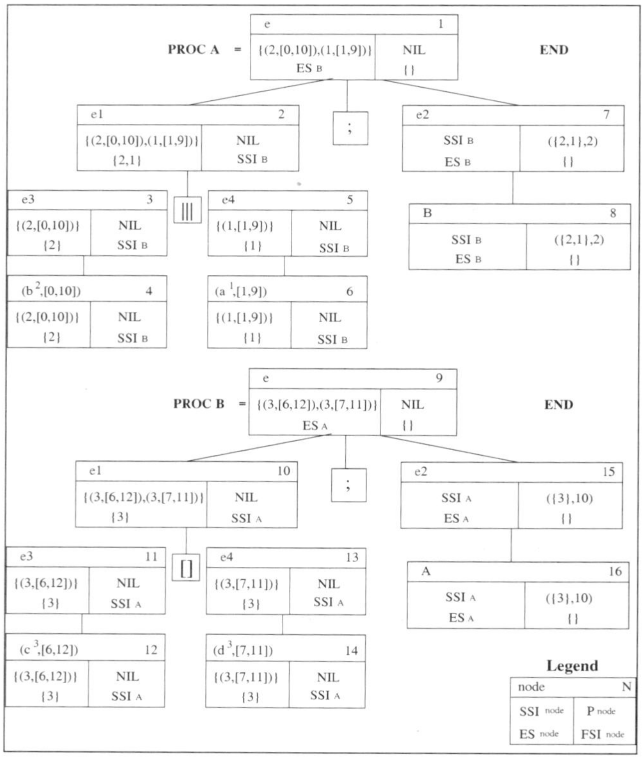

Figure 3: Syntax trees with attributes obtained from Example 4.1

4.4 Synthesis procedure

Once the inherited attributes evaluated, they can be used to derive the real-time PEs as follows. For each Site j, the specification PS^j of PE^j is obtained by applying the following transformation Tr_j to the root of the syntax tree.

1. $Tr_j(Spec\_Def) := Tr_j(Proc\_Def)$
2. $Tr_j(Proc\_Def) :=$ **PROC** $ProcId = Tr_j(e)$ **END** $Tr_j(Proc\_Def_1)$
3. $Tr_j(Proc\_Def) :=$ **PROC** $ProcId = Tr_j(e)$ **END**
4. $Tr_j(e) := ProcId_{\tau(N(e))\pm\Delta}$
5. $Tr_j(e) :=$ <u>if</u> $site(EventId) = j$ <u>then</u> $EventId_{\tau(N(e))\pm\Delta}$ <u>else</u> ***empty***
6. $Tr_j(e) :=$ $Tr_j(e_1)$;
   <u>if</u> $j \in ES_{e_1}$ <u>then</u> $SEND(FSI_{e_1}, N(e_1), j)$
   <u>else</u> ***empty*** ;
   <u>if</u> $j \in SSI_{e_2}$ <u>then</u> $REC(P_{e_2}, N(e_2))$
   <u>else</u> ***empty*** ;
   $Tr_j(e_2)$
7. $Tr_j(e) :=$ $Tr_j(e_1)$ ||| $Tr_j(e_2)$
8. $Tr_j(e) :=$ $Tr_j(e_1)$ [] $Tr_j(e_2)$
9. $Tr_j(e) :=$ ($Tr_j(e_1)$)

After that, the subscript $\tau(N(e))\pm\Delta$ is removed from every $EventId_{\tau(N(e))\pm\Delta}$ or $ProcId_{\tau(N(e))\pm\Delta}$ which is not preceded by a $REC(*,*)$.

4.5 Example of Protocol Derivation

We consider the service specification of Example 4.1. The model of the communication medium is : $M_{1,3} = M_{3,1} = [3,6]$, $M_{2,3} = M_{3,2} = [4,7]$. We take $\Delta = 0.1$. If we apply the synthesis procedure of Sect. 4.4, we obtain the following specifications PS^1, PS^2 and PS^3.

PS^1 : $A := \langle \boldsymbol{a^1}, [\boldsymbol{1}, \boldsymbol{9}]\rangle$; $\boldsymbol{SEND(SSI_B, 2, 1)}$; $\boldsymbol{B}$
$B := \boldsymbol{REC((\{3\}, 10), 15)}$; $\boldsymbol{A_{\tau(15)\pm0.1}}$
which can be written (see Def. 4.6 and 4.8) :
$A := \langle \boldsymbol{a^1}, [\boldsymbol{1}, \boldsymbol{9}]\rangle$; $\boldsymbol{Send_3(2, \nu_1, true, 5)}$; $\boldsymbol{B}$
$B := \boldsymbol{Rec_3(10, \nu_3)}$; $(\boldsymbol{\tau(15) = CurrentTime - \nu_3})$; $\boldsymbol{A_{\tau(15)\pm0.1}}$

In the procedure A, after the execution of a^1, a message with arguments 2 and ν_1 is sent to Site 3. The argument 2 identifies a^1 as being the part of the node 2 which is executed in Site 1. The argument ν_1 is the instant, measured by κ^1, of a^1. The argument *true* is the result of Eq. 1. In order to be able to guarantee the timing requirements of c^3 and d^3, the delay separating a^1 and the send-operation must be smaller than the argument 5 (= min(11–6, 12–6), see Eq. 2). After the send-operation, B is executed.

In the procedure B, PE^1 receives from Site 3 a message with arguments 10 and ν_3. The argument 10 identifies the expression which has been executed by PE^3 before the transmission of this message as being defined by the node 10. Therefore, the reception of the message indicates that c^3 or d^3 has been executed. From ν_3 which indicates the instant of c^3 or d^3, PE^1 computes $\tau(15) = CurrentTime - \nu_3$. From $\tau(15)$, PE^1 can estimate the delay which separates the instant when a^1 has become logically enabled and the instant of the receive-operation. This delay falls within $[\tau(15) - \Delta, \tau(15) + \Delta]$. After the receive operation, $A_{\tau(15)\pm\Delta}$ is executed. The index $\tau(15)\pm\Delta$ allows to transform the initial timing requirement of a^1, which is specified relatively to the instant when c^3 or d^3 has been executed, into a timing constraint relatively to the instant of the receive-operation.

PS^2 : $A := \langle \boldsymbol{b^2}, [\boldsymbol{0}, \boldsymbol{10}]\rangle$; $\boldsymbol{SEND(SSI_B, 2, 2)}$; $\boldsymbol{B}$
$B := \boldsymbol{REC((\{3\}, 10), 15)}$; $\boldsymbol{A_{\tau(15)\pm0.1}}$
which can be written :

$A := \langle b^2, [0, 10]\rangle$; $Send_3(2, \nu_2, true, 4)$; B
$B := Rec_3(10, \nu_3)$; $(\tau(15) = CurrentTime - \nu_3)$; $A_{\tau(15)\pm 0.1}$

The explanations which can be given here are similar to those of PS^1. Note that procedures B of PS^1 and PS^2 are syntactically equivalent, but their semantics are different because their respective $\tau(15)$ are different.

PS^3 : $A := REC((\{2, 1\}, 2), 7)$; $B_{\tau(7)\pm 0.1}$
$B := (\langle c^3, [6, 12]\rangle \; [] \; \langle d^3, [7, 11]\rangle)$;
$SEND(SSI_A, 10, 3)$; A

which can be written :
$A := (Rec_2(2, \nu_2) \; ||| \; Rec_1(2, \nu_1))$;
$\tau(7) = CurrentTime - \max(\nu_2, \nu_1)$; $B_{\tau(7)\pm 0.1}$
$B := (\langle c^3, [6, 12]\rangle \; [] \; \langle d^3, [7, 11]\rangle)$;
$(Send_2(10, \nu_3, true, 3) \; ||| \; Send_1(10, \nu_3, true, 3))$; A

In the procedure A, PE^3 receives from Sites 1, 2 two messages with arguments $(2, \nu_2)$ and $(2, \nu_1)$, respectively. The argument 2 in the message received from Site 1 (resp. Site 2) identifies a^1 (resp. b^2) as being the part of the node 2 which is executed in Site 1 (resp. Site 2). The arguments ν_1 and ν_2 are the instants of a^1 and b^2 measured by κ^1 and κ^2, respectively. From ν_1 and ν_2, PE^3 computes $\tau(7) = CurrentTime - \max(\nu_2, \nu_1)$. From $\tau(7)$, PE^3 can estimate the delay which separates the instant of the last of a^1 and b^2 from the instant of the last of the two receive-operations. This delay falls within $[\tau(7) - \Delta, \tau(7) + \Delta]$. After the receive operations, $B_{\tau(7)\pm\Delta}$ is executed. The index $\tau(7)\pm\Delta$ allows to transform the initial timing requirements of c^3 and d^3, which are specified relatively to the instant when the last of a^1 and b^2 has been executed, into a timing constraint relatively to the instant of the last of the two receive-operations.

In the procedure B, after the execution of c^3 or d^3, a message with arguments 10 and ν_3 is sent to Sites 1, 2. The argument 10 identifies the expression which has been executed as being defined by the node 10. After the send-operation, A is executed.

Remark : Since third arguments of all the *Send* operations are *true*, then the synthesized protocol specification guarantees the timing requirements of the service specification. If, for instance, we take $M_{2,3} = [4, 12]$, then the third argument of $Send_3$ of PS^2 becomes *false*. That means that the modified model of the communication medium does not allow to guarantee the timing requirements of c^3 and d^3, even if the timing constraints of the PEs are satisfied.

5. CONCLUSION

In this paper, we propose a method for synthesizing protocols entities which provide a given real-time service. The desired service and the synthesized protocol entities are specified by a timed version of a subset of Lotos. The proposed synthesis method improves several previous methods which, either consider temporal aspects but with important restrictions, or do not consider temporal aspects at all. We consider the realistic case where the clocks used in the different sites of the distributed system are synchronized with a given *nonnull* inaccuracy. The method has been applied to two concrete examples, namely, a real-time version of a simplified version of the X25 protocol, and a real-time assembly system involving manipulator robots. But for lack of space, these two examples are not presented in the article.

The proposed method assumes that in the service specification, there is a timing requirement on a delay separating two events a and b only if these is the order requirement "b is after a". In other terms, there is no timing requirement between events which are not explicitly constrained by an order constraint with each other. In the near future, we intend to study the removal of this assumption.

6. REFERENCES

[1] G. Bochmann and R. Gotzhein. Deriving protocols specifications from service specifications. In *Proceedings of the ACM SIGCOMM Symposium*, USA, 1986.

[2] T. Bolognesi and E. Brinskma. Introduction to the iso specification language lotos. *Computer Networks and ISDN Systems*, 14(1):25–59, 1987.

[3] G. Coulouris, J. Dollimore, and T. Kindberg. *Distributed Systems: Concepts and Design.* Addison-Wesley (2nd edition), 1998.

[4] R. Gotzhein and G. Bochmann. Deriving protocols specifications from service specifications including parameters. *ACM Transactions on Computer Systems*, 8(4):255–283, 1990.

[5] C. Kant, T. Higashino, and G. Bochmann. Deriving protocol specifications from service specifications written in lotos. *Distributed Computing*, 10(1):29–47, 1996.

[6] M. Kapus-Kolar. Deriving protocol specifications from service specifications with heterogeneous timing requirements. In *Proceedings of IEEE Third Int. Conf. on Soft. Engin. for real-Time Systems*, pages 1093–1096, Cirenchester, UK, 1991.

[7] M. Kapus-Kolar. New results on deriving protocol specifications from service specifications. In *Proceedings of MELECON*, pages 1093–1096, Ljubljana, Yugoslavia, 1991.

[8] M. Kapus-Kolar and J. Rugelj. Deriving protocol specifications from service specifications with simple relative timing requirements. In *Proceedings of ISMM INT. WORKSHOP on PARALLEL COMPUTING*, Italy, 1991.

[9] F. Khendek, G. Bochmann, and C. Kant. New results on deriving protocol specifications from services specifications. In *Proceedings of the ACM SIGCOMM Symposium*, pages 136–145, 1989.

[10] A. Khoumsi. New results for deriving protocol specifications from service specifications for real-time applications. In *Proceedings of The Fifth Maghrebian Conference on Software Engineering and Artificial Intelligence*, Tunis, Tunisia, December 1998.

Control and Communication Performance Analysis of Embedded DSP Systems in the MASIC Methodology

Abhijit K. Deb, Johnny Öberg, Axel Jantsch
Department of Microelectronics and Information Technology
Royal Institute of Technology
Electrum 229, 164 40 Kista, Sweden
Tel: +468 752 1115, +468 752 1305, +468 752 1221
Email: abhijit | johnny | axel @ ele.kth.se

ABSTRACT

The time required by an embedded system to process information does not only depend on the amount of data; it also depends heavily on the synchronization overhead, bus protocol and communication architecture. This paper presents a technique to estimate the performance of the control and communication part of an embedded system modeled using the MASIC methodology. A key concept in MASIC is the strict separation of the computation part from the control and communication. Based on this clear separation of concerns the estimator analyzes the communication delay. Our method targets applications with intense, but regular data flow with a fair amount of complex control. Examples are base stations or mobile terminals. For these applications the method allows a cycle accurate estimation of the delay due to the communication. Hence, different architectures can be evaluated and e.g. the effect of different bus arbitration and different DMA block sizes can be assessed. Thus, the proposed method is an aid for the designer to explore the system with different system level decisions.

Keywords

Performance analysis, Grammar, Embedded DSP systems.

1. INTRODUCTION

As the modeling of an embedded DSP system is refined to an implementation phase, typically a bus-based architecture emerges where the system bus provides the communication between the DSP blocks and accesses the shared memory. Since the bus is a shared communication channel, it requires arbitration. Therefore, an embedded core interested in transmitting data first needs to wait to handshake with the arbiter which results in a synchronization overhead. Hence it is important for the performance analysis technique to consider this overhead [3]. The bus protocol and SoC communication architecture also affects the system performance. Effects of shared memory access and DMA block size on the performance of HW/SW systems, where system operation is dominated by memory accesses, have been reported in [5]. Ignoring these effects caused by control and communication would result in inaccurate performance estimates, which in turn would lead to non-optimal design decisions. Simulation of the RTL models of embedded core with the host environment gives accurate estimates. However, RT level is too detailed to be efficient enough during exploration of the design space. Moreover, detailed RTL hardware models of embedded processors are often not available.

The performance estimation technique presented in this paper considers the delay caused by the control and communication part of the MASIC model of an embedded system. Performance often refers to both the *numbers of clock cycles required for a particular implementation* and the *period of the clock cycle needed to meet the constraints*. Our work deals with the former aspect, while the later is to be dealt with at a lower level of abstraction. The MASIC, *Maths to ASIC*, methodology [8-10] models an embedded system as a set of communicating FSMs. The communication and synchronization among the cores give rise to a complex architecture and control scheme that we refer to as the GLObal Control Configuration and Timing (GLOCCT). The estimator takes the MASIC description of the communicating FSMs, replaces the nodes of the GLOCCT FSM by varying weighted arcs, and builds an internal representation of the system known as the Delay Graph (DG). To analyze the system performance, the DG is simulated with input events at different time instances. Though the data flow rate may vary among different parts of the system, the rate is fixed for each particular path. Hence the arrival of the events, that is, the set of input vectors to the DG can be deduced accurately. The estimator applies the input events on the DG and computes the following information:

- *Bus usage* – shows the amount of time each resource is occupying the bus.
- *Component execution trace* – includes the time a component needs to wait to get access to the shared resources and the time to finish its communication.
- *System performance* – gives the total time that the system needs to consume a certain amount of data using user given system attributes.

Before describing the proposed technique, we present few related works in the next section. Section 3 briefly describes the MASIC methodology of embedded DSP systems design. Next, we

ISSS '01, October 1-3, 2001, Montréal, Québec, Canada.

illustrate the proposed performance estimation technique in section 4. The following section shows the results computed from the LPC speech coding example. Finally, in section 6, we conclude the work presented in this paper.

2. RELATED WORK

A number of system performance analysis techniques were proposed in the early 90s that targeted the behavioral specification containing mutually exclusive paths due to the presence of conditionals. It was assumed that the branches of an if-then-else have an equal probability of execution. Bhattacharya et. al. have proposed a Markov chain based technique that takes care of the fact that, the branch probability may be unequal [1]. They have derived the branch probability and the state transition probability to calculate the expected number of clock cycles needed for a schedule. A Control Flow Graph (CFG) model based on a homogeneous Markov chain has been reported in [2]. They have used a probabilistic finite state machine to model the schedule and evaluate the effectiveness. Since scheduling of the CFG is mainly a path based approach, they have used scheduled paths from the CFG and constructed an FSM corresponding to the resulting schedule.

However, the approaches described above do not take the synchronization overhead into account. In many real life systems like telecommunication, networking applications, embedded control applications, multimedia applications, etc. the system is described as a set of concurrent communicating processes. Though the clock period estimation of a system is not affected whether the system is described and implemented as a single process or as a set of communicating processes, the number of required clock cycle estimation is affected. Hence a synchronization graph based approach is reported where the synchronization overhead is considered using a static performance analysis technique [3]. They begin by constructing a synchronization graph corresponding to a set of communicating processes. Later on, the loops in the graph are divided into different communication layers. Analysis of a single communication layer results in the estimate of a system with multi layer communication. The technique statically calculates the worst case performance of a system of communicating processes.

The Bus and Synchronization Event (BSE) graph was introduced to evaluate the performance of a bus-based SoC architecture [4]. The authors showed the effects of bus architecture and bus protocol on the system performance. They used a dynamic estimation approach, which is split into two phases. Initially, the system specification is partitioned into HW and SW, and a cosimulation is performed where the communication between components is modeled in an abstract manner. Secondly, from the initial cosimulation, they extracted a set of computation and communication traces for each of the components that was known as the BSE graph. Our proposed performance analysis technique does not require an initial cosimulation. The estimator takes the grammar based MASIC notation of the system to evaluate the performance. Before we describe the proposed technique, the following section gives a brief overview of the MASIC methodology.

3. THE MASIC METHODOLOGY

Even if the functionality of a DSP system remains the same, the architecture may need to be amended to be able to deal with

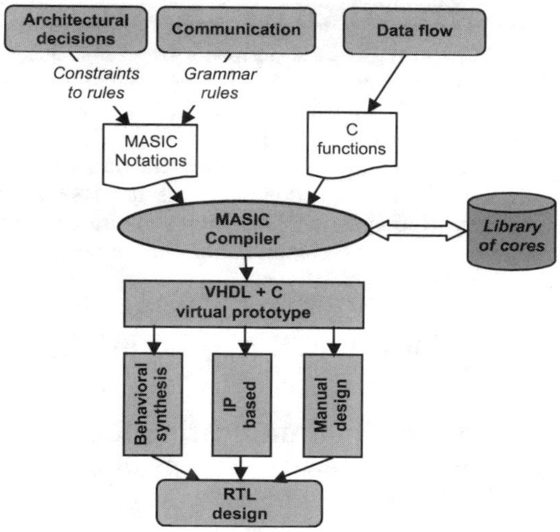

Figure 1: MASIC design flow

different product families or HW/SW combination. Furthermore, it requires being configurable to be able to work with next generations of products. All these requirements suggest that the functionality be kept separated from the architecture and communication. As such, design methodologies have been proposed to separate these two aspects [6,7]. The MASIC methodology uses grammar notations to capture a design at a higher level of abstraction and separates the functionality from the architecture and communication, which represents the GLOCCT of the system [8,9]. The MASIC design flow is shown in Figure 1. Modeling in MASIC begins at the functional level where the algorithm development and verification is concerned with making sure that the specified signal processing figures of merit are met. The output of this phase is a set of DSP functions in C, which represents the data flow part of the system model. The GLOOCT is expressed in the MASIC grammar notations in which the grammar rules describe the communication and synchronization, and the constraints to the rules manifest the architectural decisions. The architectural decisions characterize the chip level architecture that includes processor cores, busses, memories, external interfaces and sharing of resources. The MASIC compiler reads the system model written using the MASIC notations and generates a VHDL description that links to the C functions.

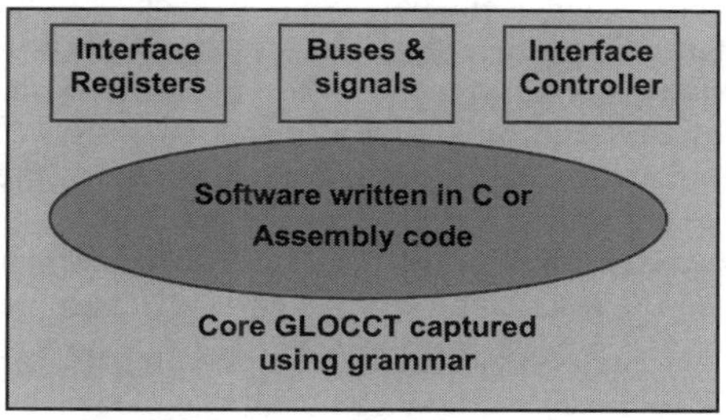

Figure 2: MASIC model of the core

Embedded systems are often modeled using a set of communicating FSMs [10,11]. MASIC uses grammar notations to describe the communicating FSMs and employs a library to manipulate the cores. An embedded core is viewed at two different layers as shown in Figure 2. The primary intention of the model is to focus on the interface between the host and the core. The outer layer provides the interface of the core to the system GLOCCT. This layer includes peripheral registers, buses and the associated control logic, which is referred to as core level GLOCCT. The inner layer contains the software in C, which is a DSP function developed in the functional modeling phase of the design. The GLOCCT provides the mean to transfer data among the cores while the C function performs the DSP computation when the data is transferred [10]. For a future implementation phase, the C-function is compiled for the target processor and elaborated over system clock cycles.

4. PERFORMANCE ANALYSIS TECHNIQUE

4.1 A Pair of Communicating FSMs

Let us consider a core wishing to read a memory using a bus. The system is built using the asynchronous bus protocol described in the Figure 3. The choice of asynchronous protocol stems from the fact that the target system will have a number of cores connected to the system bus and they might run on different clock speeds and have different response times. The operation sequence is initiated with the arrival of an IO read signal, which creates the arc between states *C1* and *C2*. Here, we use the symbol *C1→C2* to represent the arc between nodes *C1* and *C2*. With this arc the core sends `rdReq` signal to the memory. At the same time, it places the memory address on the multiplexed bus. However, the estimator does not account for data assignment statements, like putting address or data on the bus. It only considers the synchronization signals, which generate events and synchronize the system. Hence the estimator does not need to perform any exhaustive computation to find the performance figures.

The memory reacts to the `rdReq` signal by asserting the `Ack` and reads the address from the bus, which is shown in *M1→M2*. The core sees the acknowledgement and drops the `rdReq` and relinquishes the bus, in *C2→C3*. With the remaining steps, the word is read from the memory and the cycle is completed when the core finally drops the `Ack` signal. The MASIC notations are used to describe the control steps of the above model. The total time needed to complete the whole operation can be estimated from the time required in each of these steps.

The total time needed to complete the cycle is the summation of time elapsed in the nodes and time elapsed in the arcs. We target the Mealy type implementation with a clocked output stage. Hence all the arcs of the FSM will take one clock cycle, if not annotated with a memory access time information as discussed below. The time taken by a node depends on a signal from the communicated process. If the desired signal is already present, the machine does not wait in the node and the wait time in the node is zero. Otherwise, it waits in the node until it receives the signal. Depending on the reaction time of the communicated process, we replace a node with a weighted arc, which gives the wait time in the node.

Let us apply these observations on the model of the Figure 3. If we do not consider the initial wait time, the core FSM starts with the *C1→C2*, which requires one cycle. The wait time in the node *C2* depends on *M1→M2*, which is another cycle. After one more cycle it crosses the *C2→C3* and waits in node the *C3* for *M2→M3* be completed. Since this arc is related to memory access we cannot apply the general rule of one cycle for an arc. In this

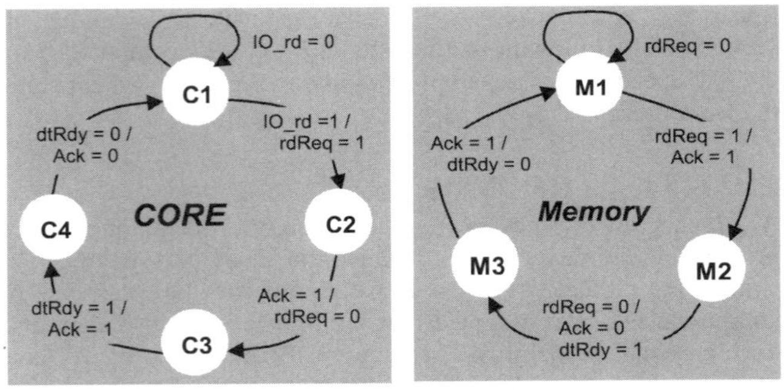

Figure 3: Communicating FSMs in MASIC

sequence of operations, the memory receives the address during *M1→M2*. Therefore, the wait time in the node *C3* can be estimated as: ***max (roof(memory_access_time/clock_period), 2)***. The MASIC description does not contain any information about memory access time. This information is given to the estimator. The rest of the arcs take one cycle each. Thus the core will take seven cycles to perform the operation, if memory access time is less than or equal to two clock cycles.

So far, the wait time in a node corresponds to an arc in the communicated FSM. The scenario changes when several of them communicates with each other. We model such a situation by creating a DG of the system.

4.2 Systems with Multiple FSMs

To be able to connect multiple cores to the system bus we need to introduce a bus arbiter, which ensures that only one core has control over the bus at a particular time. Thus a core wishing to transfer data using the bus needs to wait to handshake with the arbiter. The GLOCCT provides the bus arbitration, which could be of any kind. As an example, let us describe a round robin arbitration scheme where the GLOCCT sequentially reads the request from each core to grant the bus and moves to the next one as shown in the Figure 4. The read operation still works in the same way as described in Figure 3, with the exception that it incorporates a wait state labeled as *C2* to synchronize with the GLOCCT. The time spent in this state shows the wait time in the performance analysis. Along with the read cycle, now the core FSM also includes the memory write cycle. With the arrival of an `IO_wr`, instead of generating a memory `wrReq`, the core generates a request to the GLOCCT and waits in node *C6*. To get an estimate of this system we need to consider the GLOCCT input events associated with a time instance and generate the resulting system response.

Let us consider that the arbiter begins at time `t` to react to the input events shown in Figure 5. At time `t`, there is no request from core-1 though core-2 wishes to write to the memory. Hence, the GLOCCT does not wait in node *G1* and the estimator replaces node *G1* with an arc of weight zero to build the DG. It would, however, need a clock for the *G1→G3*. A request from core-2 has been waiting since time `t` and this request brings the system from *G3* at `t+1` to *G4* at `t+2`. At this time `Grant2` signal also appears. It communicates with two different nodes of the core-2 as shown by the dotted arrows in Figure 4. Since Core-2 was waiting in node *C6* the path *C6→C7* is chosen that in turn communicates with the memory. From this point the core and the memory perform a set of operations, similar to the previously described read cycle. These are shown by the dotted arrows in the Figure 4. The

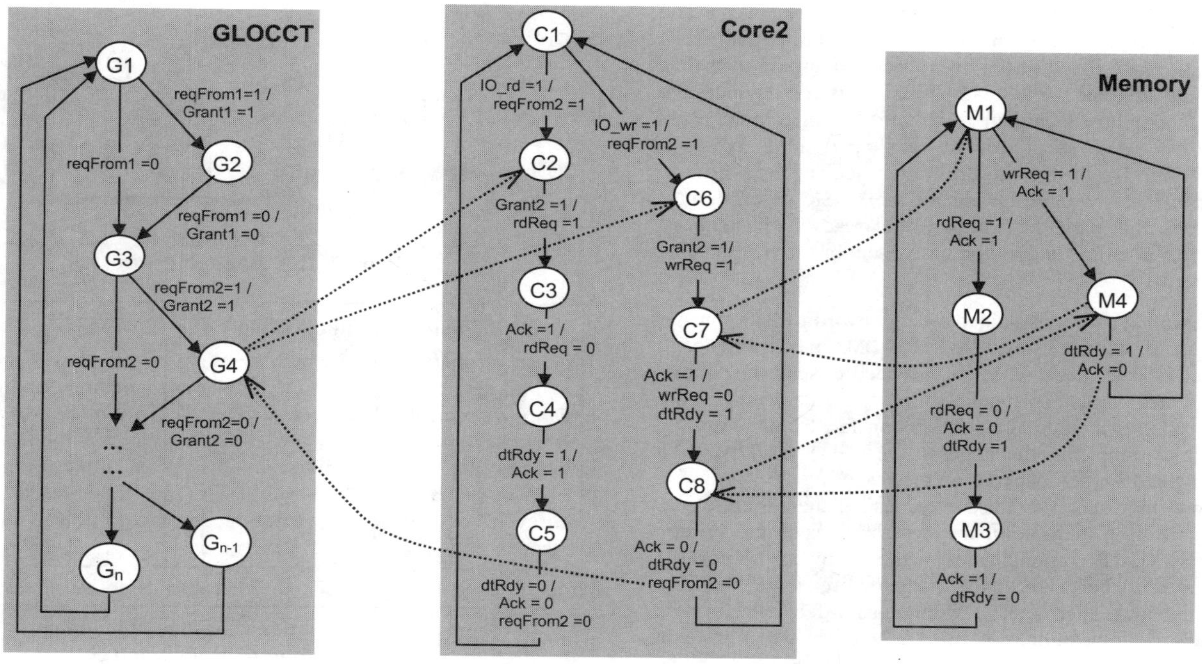

Figure 4: Effect of a set of communicating FSMs

operation finishes when the core2 reaches *C1* after five clock cycles. A read cycle, alternatively, would require seven cycles to traverse from node *C2* to *C1*. Hence, a node might have different wait time depending on the operation. To build the DG, we replace node *G4* with an arc of weight five for write cycle and weight seven for read cycle. On the other hand, a node might have a weight of zero, as was the case with node *G1*. Depending on the input event one of the weighted arcs is chosen, which gives the time elapsed in the node. The arcs of the FSM are not replaced in the DG and they correspond to a time of one clock period, unless annotated with memory access information as explained in the previous sub section. In this way, the effects of all the communicating FSMs are mapped together in the DG. The DG is simulated with the input events at different time instances to get the performance figures.

4.3 Tracing the Resource Execution

The DG of the system is the basis of the estimator. A start up sequence gives the initial state of the system. From that point the estimator simulates the DG of the system with the input events and fills up the rows of the Execution Trace Table (ETT) with the output response as shown in the Figure 5.

Let us assume that the GLOCCT in Figure 4 begins at time `t` with state *G1*. It receives input events `ReqFrom1` and `ReqFrom2` at time `t` as shown in the Figure 5. Since `ReqFrom1` is low, the FSM moves through *G1→G3*. Hence, we put state *G3* at the time `t+1` and keep the input event `ReqFrom2` in input event register. The length of the input event register is one. The sender can rewrite the register. For instance, in the event of a timed out request the sender broadcasts a zero, which changes the content of the input event register.

The `ReqFrom2` is read from the register at time `t+1` that causes the machine to move to G4. Hence, we put core-2 in *G4* at time `t+2`. In addition we also generate the `Grant2,` as it is a synchronizing signal. For a write cycle, we know from the discussion in the previous sub section that the arbiter stays in *G4* for five cycles after the grant is made. Hence we put the GLOCCT in *G4* from time `t+3` to `t+7`, at the end of which we know that the `ReqFrom2` will be dropped low. Therefore, the input event register is made zero at `t+7`, which causes the machine to move to *G5* and drop the `Grant2` signal at time `t+8`. The ETT shows that the event `ReqFrom2` waits for one cycle and takes seven cycles to be processed.

Time	t	t+1	t+2	t+3	t+4	t+5	t+6	t+7	t+8
State of GLOCCT	G1	G3	G4	G4	G4	G4	G4	G4	G5
Grant1		0	0	0	0	0	0	0	0
Grant2		0	1	1	1	1	1	1	0
ReqFrom1	0	0	0	0	0	0	0	0	0
ReqFrom2	1	1	1	1	1	1	1	0	0

Figure 5: Execution trace table

The ETT grows with time as it receives more input events and generates corresponding system responses. If the same pattern of communication and data transfer are repeated over and over then it is enough to simulate the DG with input events corresponding to one frame. Though the technique is explained using a round robin arbiter, it is not restricted to any particular type of implementation. To change the arbitration scheme to a priority arbiter, for instance, we need to change the MASIC description of the system. In that case the arbiter would read all the requests from the cores at a time and assign the system bus to a core using a preset priority.

Until now, we have only explained a single word of data transfer over the bus. It will be efficient to use a DMA mode transfer to shift a block of data, because we do not need to send the address with all the data words. To model a block data transfer the core and memory FSMs include DMA mood transfer. In that case, the DG is built by replacing the nodes of the GLOCCT FSM by a varying weighted arc that depends on the size of the DMA transfer. For a system with multiple clocks we consider the system clock, which is typically a multiple of the slowest clock in the system. When the GLOCCT communicates with a slower process the estimator updates the value of the weighted arcs using the ratio between the clock speeds. Bus width also affects the system performance. If, for example, we use a 16 bit bus to transfer a 32 bit word then we change the core and memory FSM to include the extra steps needed. To show the effect of the architectural change on system performance, the estimator builds a DG from the modified MASIC model and the ETT shows a longer response time for an input event.

5. RESULTS

In this section we apply the described performance analysis technique on the Linear Predictive Coding (LPC) speech processing system. We shall model the system with different system level decisions and investigate their effects on the system performance. A 20 ms frame of speech data is buffered at a sampling rate of 8 kHz. The system takes a frame of 160 samples, which corresponds to a 20 ms frame and performs the Hamming windowing operation on the samples of the speech frame. The result is stored in the memory. Next the autocorrelation block reads the 160 samples stored by the Hamming block and computes 50 autocorrelation lags. Finally, the LPC block takes these values and compute 10 coefficients and a pitch period, which is stored back in the memory. We decided to perform these

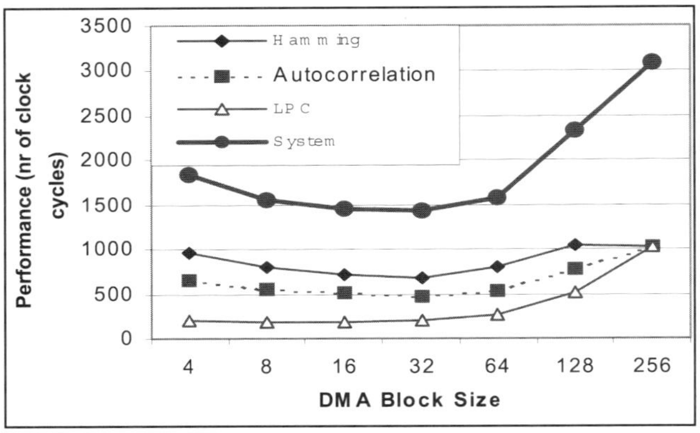

Figure 6: Effect of DMA size on performance

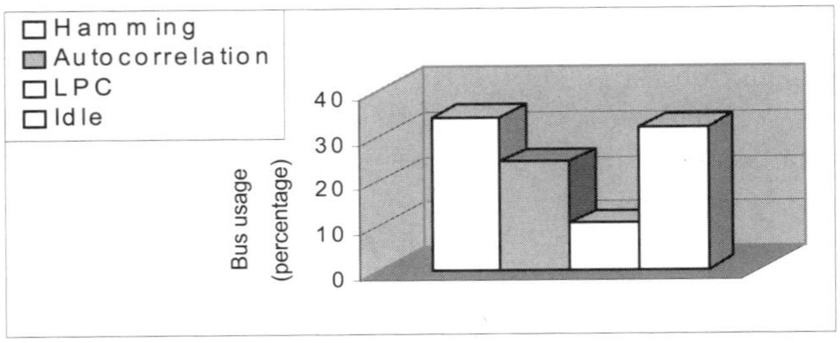

Figure 7: Bus usage statistics

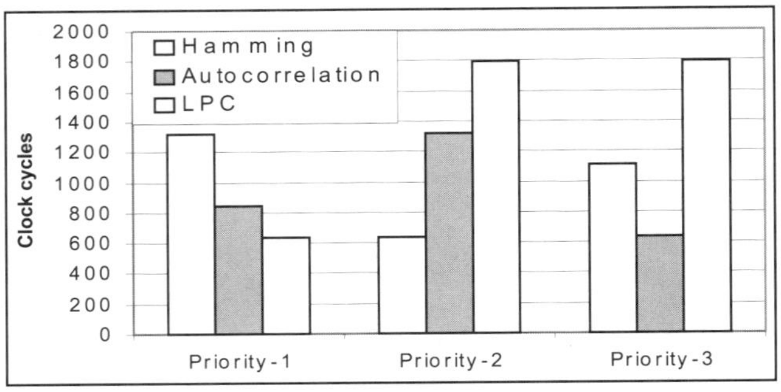

Figure 8 : Computation time available under different priority schemes

operations on three different cores, which are connected to the shared memory by a multiplexed bus. The speech processing system works in a globally pipelined manner where each of the blocks works on the set of data computed by the previous block in the earlier frame. The interface of the core is captured in the MASIC notation and the computation is performed using C function, as described in section 3. The GLOOCT provides the interface of the system, and communication and synchronization between the cores and the memory.

The estimator takes the MASIC description and builds the DG of the system. Since the same pattern of data communication is performed over every 20 ms frame, we simulated the DG with the input events corresponding to a single speech frame. First we studied the effects of different realistic DMA block sizes on the system performance as shown in the Figure 6. We considered different sizes starting from 4 to 256. For each of the cases, same input events are applied on the DG to construct the ETT, which shows total cycles needed to consume the input events. As expected, the performance increases with the increase in block size. However, the performance of the LPC block starts to deteriorate after 16 because it outputs only 11 words. On the other hand, the Hamming block deteriorates after 64, because it operates on 160 words and a bigger block causes some non-meaningful words in the last block. Figure 6 shows that the overall system performance is optimum with a DMA size of 32 words. Since we know the optimum size of the blocks, we use this size to check the bus usage figures. Figure 7 shows the percentage of bus usage by different blocks that include both reading data from the memory and writing the results back to the memory. The idle time shown in the figure is calculated assuming a budget of 2000 cycles.

The bus usage figures show the amount of time required by each of the DSP blocks within each speech frame. These figures help the designer to assign the priority to different blocks. The block with a higher priority receives its data first and gets more time to finish its task. Hence, we experimented with different priority given to different blocks. Figure 8 shows the computation time available to each of the blocks in three different priority schemes assuming a budget of 2000 cycles. These figures help the designer to assign priority to individual blocks so that the computation timing requirements are met.

6. CONCLUSION

This paper presents a performance estimation technique that has been integrated in the MASIC environment. The technique targets applications with predictable data rates. The estimator works on the higher abstraction level of MASIC models. It does not perform any computationally exhaustive method as would have been needed at a lower level. Despite working on the higher level model, it gives an accurate estimate, which considers the synchronization overhead, effects of shared memory access and memory access time. Experimental results have been presented, which show the effects of different system level decisions on system performance. Thus it helps the designer to probe the model from a higher level of design abstraction by assisting the designer to optimize the model with different system level decisions. For instance, making a dedicated link between the two most frequently communicating components would lessen the traffic on system bus. Changing the arbitration scheme or DMA block size might result in less wait time for a component.

7. REFERENCES

[1] S. Bhattacharya, S. Dey, and F. Brglez, "Performance Analysis and Optimization of Schedules for Conditional and Loop-Intensive Specifications". *In 31st Design Automation Conf*, pp. 491-496, June 1994.

[2] M. Rahmouni and A.A. Jerraya, "Formulation and evaluation of scheduling techniques for control flow graphs". *In the Proc. of European Design Automation Conference*, pp. 386-391, Sep. 1995.

[3] S. Dey and S. Bommu, "Performance analysis of a system of communicating processes". *In the IEEE/ACM Int. Conf. on Computer-Aided Design*, pp. 590-597, 1997.

[4] K. Lahiri, A. Raghunathan and S. Dey, "Fast performance analysis of bus-based system-on-chip communication architectures". *In IEEE/ACM Int. Conf. on Computer-Aided Design*, pp. 566-572, 1999.

[5] M. Lajolo, A. Raghunathan, S. Dey, L. Lavagno, A. Sangiovanni-Vincentelli, "A Case Study on Modeling Shared Memory Access Effects during Performance Analysis of HW/SW Systems". *In Proc. of Int. Workshop on Hardware-Software Codesign*, pp. 117-121, Seattle, USA, March 1998.

[6] J.A. Rowson and A. Sangiovanni-Vincentelli, "Interface Based Design". *In the Proc. of Design Automation Conf.*, pp. 178-183, June 1997.

[7] C.K. Lennard, P. Schaumont, G. Jong, A. Haverinen and P. Hardee, "Standards for system-level design: practical reality or solution in search of a question?" *In Proc. Design, Automation and Test in Europe Conf.* pp. 576–583, Paris, France. 2000.

[8] A.Hemani, Abhijit. K. Deb, J.Öberg, A.Postula, D.Lindqvist and B. Fjellborg, "System Level Virtual Prototyping of DSP SoCs Using Grammar Based Approach". *Design Automation for Embedded Systems*, Vol.5, No.3, August 2000, pp.295-311.

[9] Abhijit K. Deb, A. Hemani, and J.Öberg, "A Heterogeneous Modeling Environment of DSP Systems Using Grammar Based Approach". In the Proc. of 3rd Forum on Design Languages, pp. 365-370, Tubingen, Germany, Sep. 2000.

[10] Abhijit K. Deb, A. Hemani, J. Öberg, A. Postula, and D. Lindqvist, "Hardware software codesign of DSP systems using grammar based approach". *In Proc. of the 14th Int. Conf. on VLSI Design*, pp.42-47, Bangalore, India, January 2001.

[11] M. Chiodo, P. Giusto, A. Jurecska, H.C. Hsieh, A. Sangiovanni-Vincentelli, L. Lavagno, "Hardware-software codesign of embedded systems". *IEEE Micro*, vol. 14 4, pp. 26-36, Aug. 1994.

Author Index

NOTES